HANDBOOKS

D1383221

NEW ORLEANS

LAURA MARTONE

Contents

Maps

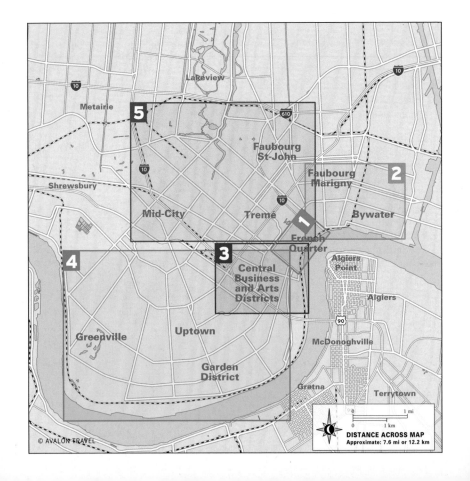

✪ SIGHTS

1	VOODOO SPIRITUAL TEMPLE	88	MADAME JOHN'S LEGACY	138 ◖	JACKSON SQUARE	160 ◖	THE NEW ORLEANS SCHOOL OF COOKING
28	NEW ORLEANS MUSICAL LEGENDS PARK	96	GALLIER HOUSE	139	PONTALBA APARTMENTS AND THE 1850 HOUSE	161	JEAN LAFITTE NATIONAL HISTORICAL PARK AND PRESERVE
33	HERMANN-GRIMA HOUSE	97	LALAURIE MANSION	145	BEAUREGARD-KEYES HOUSE	165	JACKSON BREWERY
68 ◖	THE HISTORIC NEW ORLEANS COLLECTION	122	THE ARSENAL	146	OLD URSULINE CONVENT	176	NEW ORLEANS JAZZ NATIONAL HISTORICAL PARK
		123	THE CABILDO			182	FRENCH MARKET
		128	ST. LOUIS CATHEDRAL			191	OLD U.S. MINT
		131	THE PRESBYTÉRE			192	AUDUBON INSECTARIUM
						197	AUDUBON AQUARIUM OF THE AMERICAS
						199	WOLDENBERG RIVERFRONT PARK

✪ RESTAURANTS

13	BAYONA	48	ACME OYSTER HOUSE	76	OLD COFFEEPOT RESTAURANT	113	NOLA RESTAURANT
18	GW FINS	49	DICKIE BRENNAN'S STEAKHOUSE	79 ◖	YO MAMA'S BAR AND GRILL	121	LA DIVINA GELATERIA
19	ARNAUD'S RESTAURANT	50	MR. B'S BISTRO	91	CAFÉ AMELIE	126	GUMBO SHOP
22	RALPH BRENNAN'S RED FISH GRILL	56	CAFE BEIGNET	92	CC'S COMMUNITY COFFEE HOUSE	133	MURIEL'S JACKSON SQUARE
24	DICKIE BRENNAN'S BOURBON HOUSE SEAFOOD	59	BRENNAN'S	95	CROISSANT D'OR PATISSERIE	137	STANLEY
25 ◖	GALATOIRE'S	62	ANTOINE'S RESTAURANT	98	MONA LISA RESTAURANT	142	IRENE'S CUISINE
26	FELIX'S RESTAURANT & OYSTER BAR	63	THE RIB ROOM	101	DICKIE BRENNAN'S PALACE CAFÉ	143	STELLA!
32	OCEANA GRILL	73	ROYAL BLEND COFFEE & TEA HOUSE	112	K-PAUL'S LOUISIANA KITCHEN	151	SEKISUI SAMURAI SUSHI
47	PORT OF CALL	74	THE COURT OF TWO SISTERS			153	FELIPE'S TAQUERIA
						154	IRIS
						162	JOHNNY'S PO-BOYS
						163	CRESCENT CITY BREWHOUSE
						164 ◖	CAFÉ MASPERO
						169	CAFÉ DU MONDE
						170	TUJAGUE'S
						179	COOP'S PLACE
						181	ANGELI ON DECATUR
						185	EL GATO NEGRO
						187	LOUISIANA PIZZA KITCHEN
						189	CAFE ENVIE & ESPRESSO BAR

✪ NIGHTLIFE

4	RAWHIDE 2010	34	BOURBON STREET BLUES COMPANY	42 ◖	BOURBON PUB & PARADE	77 ◖	PAT O'BRIEN'S
5	DAVENPORT LOUNGE	36	DUNGEON	43	OZ NEW ORLEANS	78 ◖	PRESERVATION HALL
9	THE BOMBAY CLUB	37	MAISON BOURBON JAZZ CLUB	45	CAFE LAFITTE IN EXILE	80	ORLEANS GRAPEVINE WINE BAR & BISTRO
17	GOOD FRIENDS BAR	38	KRAZY KORNER	46 ◖	LAFITTE'S BLACKSMITH SHOP BAR	99	GOLDEN LANTERN BAR
27	JEAN LAFITTE'S OLD ABSINTHE HOUSE	39	CATS MEOW	51	CAROUSEL BAR	107	W LIVING ROOM
29	IRVIN MAYFIELD'S JAZZ PLAYHOUSE	40	FRITZEL'S EUROPEAN JAZZ PUB	70	ONE EYED JACKS	114	NAPOLEON HOUSE
31	THE FAMOUS DOOR					149	HOUSE OF BLUES
						156 ◖	THE KERRY IRISH PUB
						177	MRB
						178	MOLLY'S AT THE MARKET
						180	PRAVDA!
						184	PALM COURT JAZZ CAFE
						190	BALCONY MUSIC CLUB

✪ ARTS AND LEISURE

3	THE AMERICAN BICYCLE RENTAL COMPANY	69	KAKO GALLERY	104	CALLAN FINE ART	120	JAMIE HAYES GALLERY
11	MUSÉE CONTI WAX MUSEUM	83	CRAIG TRACY'S PAINTED ALIVE BODYPAINTING GALLERY	105	A GALLERY FOR FINE PHOTOGRAPHY	124	FRIENDS OF THE CABILDO
20	GERMAINE CAZENAVE WELLS MARDI GRAS MUSEUM	85	NEW ORLEANS HISTORIC VOODOO MUSEUM	106	MICHALOPOULOS GALLERY	129	RODRIGUE STUDIO NEW ORLEANS
60	MARTIN-LAWRENCE GALLERIES	86	TANNER ORIGINAL PAINTINGS AND MURALS	111	WILLIAMS RESEARCH CENTER	140	PHOTO WORKS NEW ORLEANS
				115	NEW ORLEANS PHARMACY MUSEUM	168	ROYAL CARRIAGES
						174	DUTCH ALLEY ARTIST'S CO-OP
						193	SOUTHERN REPERTORY THEATRE
						194	THE THEATRES AT CANAL PLACE
						198	ENTERGY IMAX THEATRE
						200 ◖	STEAMBOAT NATCHEZ

✪ SHOPS

41 ◖	MARIE LAVEAU'S HOUSE OF VOODOO	71	BOUTIQUE DU VAMPYRE	104		116	NEW ORLEANS SILVERSMITHS
53	BEVOLO GAS AND ELECTRIC LIGHTS	72	ROUX ROYALE	105		117	LUCULLUS
54	JOAN GOOD ANTIQUE JEWELRY	75	M.S. RAU ANTIQUES	106		118	HEMLINE
55 ◖	KEIL'S ANTIQUES	82	BOURBON FRENCH PARFUMS	111		119	LOUISIANA LOOM WORKS
57	VINTAGE 329	87	PAPIER PLUME	115		125	FAULKNER HOUSE BOOKS
58	VALOBRA JEWELRY AND ANTIQUES	93	FIFI MAHONY'S			127	FOREVER NEW ORLEANS
61	JAMES H. COHEN & SONS, INC.	100	FLORA SAVAGE			130	MASKARADE
65	RAZZLE DAZZLE	103	CRESCENT CITY BOOKS			134 ◖	TRASHY DIVA BOUTIQUE
66	FLEUR DE PARIS	109	BOTTOM OF THE CUP TEA ROOM			135	VOODOO AUTHENTICA
67	SWORD & PEN	110	A BOUTIQUE FOR THE HOI POLLOI			136	VOLUPTUOUS VIXEN
						141	IDEA FACTORY
						150 ◖	LOUISIANA MUSIC FACTORY
						152	BECKHAM'S BOOKSHOP
						157 ◖	SOUTHERN CANDYMAKERS
						158	PEACHES RECORDS
						159	CIGAR FACTORY NEW ORLEANS
						166	SAVE NOLA
						167	THE SHOPS AT JAX BREWERY
						171	EVANS CREOLE CANDY FACTORY
						172	LITTLE TOY SHOP
						173	JAVA HOUSE IMPORTS
						175	CENTRAL GROCERY
						183 ◖	FRENCH MARKET
						186	ARTIST'S MARKET & BEAD SHOP
						188	RARE FINDS
						195	THE SHOPS AT CANAL PLACE
						196	RHINO CONTEMPORARY CRAFTS CO.

✪ HOTELS

2	MAISON DUPUY HOTEL	15	THE OLIVIER HOUSE HOTEL	35	THE INN ON BOURBON	89	NINE-O-FIVE ROYAL HOTEL
6	THE RITZ-CARLTON NEW ORLEANS	16	HÔTEL ST. MARIE	44	BOURGOYNE GUEST HOUSE	90	THE CORNSTALK HOTEL
7	THE IBERVILLE SUITES	21	ASTOR CROWNE PLAZA – FRENCH QUARTER	52 ◖	HOTEL MONTELEONE	94	HOTEL ROYAL
8	CHATEAU LEMOYNE	23	CHATEAU BOURBON	64 ◖	OMNI ROYAL ORLEANS	102	QUARTER HOUSE RESORT
10	PRINCE CONTI HOTEL	30 ◖	ROYAL SONESTA HOTEL– NEW ORLEANS	81	BOURBON ORLEANS HOTEL	108	W NEW ORLEANS– FRENCH QUARTER
12	DAUPHINE ORLEANS HOTEL			84	BISCUIT PALACE GUEST HOUSE	132	PLACE D'ARMES HOTEL
14	AUDUBON COTTAGES					144	HÔTEL PROVINCIAL
						147	SONIAT HOUSE HOTEL
						148	LE RICHELIEU
						155	BIENVILLE HOUSE HOTEL

Our Lady
of Guadalupe
Church

STORYVILLE

**FRENCH
QUARTER**

SEE MAP 4

CANAL STREET

**New Orleans
Musical Legends
Park**

BOURBON STREET

BIENVILLE AVE

CONTI ST

ST. LOUIS ST

TOULOUSE ST

ST. PETER ST

**Hermann-
Grima
House**

**The Historic
New Orleans
Collection**

EXCHANGE PL

EXCHANGE PL

CHARTRES ST

DORSIERE ST

CABILDO ALY

The Arsenal

**The
Cabildo**

WILKINSON ST

ST. PETER ST

**The New Orleans
School of Cooking**

DECATUR ST

CLINTON ST

N PETERS ST

**Jackson
Brewery**

**Jean Lafitte
National Historical
Park and Preserve**

**Audubon
Insectarium**

N PETERS ST

N PETERS ST

CLAY ST

N FRONT BLVD

SEE MAP 3

**Woldenberg
Riverfront
Park**

CONVENTION CENTER BLVD

**Audubon Aquarium
of the Americas**

N RAMPART ST

N RAMPART ST

Voodoo Spiritual Temple 1

SEE MAP 5

BURGUNDY ST

N 4

DAUPHINE ST

17 N

VIEUX CARRÉ

47 R

ORLEANS ST

40 41 N S 42 N 44 H 45 N 46 N

BOURBON STREET

ST ANN ST 43 84 ST PHILIP ST URSULINES AVE BARRACKS ST

80 N 81 H 85 A

Gallier House **LaLaurie Mansion**

82 S 83 89 90 92 R 96 97 98 R 99 N 100

ROYAL ST ROYAL ST

129 A 86 87 91 R 93 S 94 H 95 R

St. Louis Cathedral 132 **Madame John's Legacy** 88 **Beauregard-Keyes House** SEE MAP 2

128 130 S 135 H 145 147

PERE ANTOINE ALY 131 R **The Presbytère** 134 S

CHARTRES ST 133 CHARTRES ST ESPLANADE AVE

Jackson Square 137 S 136 S 141 142 R 143 144 H R **Old Ursuline Convent** 146 148 N

138 139 A MADISON ST GOV NICHOLLS ST

140 A **Pontalba Apartments and the 1850 House** 177 N

170 S 173 S 175 S 178 N N 179 N 180 N 181 N 188 S 189 N 190 N

DECATUR ST 172 176 DECATUR ST

169 R 171 S 174 **New Orleans Jazz National Historical Park** **French Market** 184 N 191

182 183 185 S 186 187 S

Old U.S. Mint

N PETERS ST FRENCH MARKET PL BARRACKS ST

Mississippi River

0 100 yds
0 100 m

DISTANCE ACROSS MAP
Approximate: 0.9 mi or 1.5 km

© AVALON TRAVEL

To N JOHNSON ST

1 Celebration Distillation

N PRIEUR ST

N ROMAN ST

N DERBIGNY ST

N CLAIBORNE AVE
N CLAIBORNE AVE

N ROBERTSON ST

N ROBERTSON ST

SEE MAP 5

N VILLERE ST

N VILLERE ST

URQUHART ST

URQUHART ST

HENRIETTE DELILLE

MC SHANE PL

MARAIS ST

MARAIS ST

3

ST CLAUDE AVE
ST CLAUDE AVE

4

5

6

13

8 9

14

10

12

11

FAUBOURG
MARIGNY

15

17

18

DAUPHINE ST

21

22

Washington
Square
Park

23

43

44

46 47 48

45

49

KEREREC ST

19

20

24

25

26

27

33

28

34

29 30

31

32

35

39

40

41

42

50

51

52

53

DECATUR ST

36

37

38

DECATUR ST

SEE MAP 1

FRENCH
QUARTER

BARRACKS ST

URSULINES AVE

New Orleans
Mint

N PETERS ST

Mandeville Street
Wharf

Esplanade Avenue
Wharf

Gov. Nicholls Street
Wharf

Mississippi River

0   200 yds

0   200 m

DISTANCE ACROSS MAP
Approximate: 1.8 mi or 2.9 km

© AVALON TRAVEL

⊕ SIGHTS

| 1 | CELEBRATION DISTILLATION | 2 | MUSICIANS' VILLAGE |

⊕ RESTAURANTS

6	FATOUSH	40	ADOLFO'S
11	WASABI SUSHI & ASIAN GRILL	43	THE ORANGE COUCH
21	LA PENICHE	46	SCHIRO'S CAFE
22	SUKHOTHAI	49	FLORA GALLERY & COFFEE SHOP
24	MARIGNY BRASSERIE & BAR	51	NEW ORLEANS CAKE CAFE & BAKERY
30	THE PRALINE CONNECTION	53 ⊕	FEELINGS CAFE
35	MONA'S CAFÉ	55	SATSUMA CAFE
37	MOJITOS RUM BAR & GRILL	56	ELIZABETH'S RESTAURANT
		59	THE JOINT

⊕ NIGHTLIFE

3	SWEET LORRAINE'S JAZZ CLUB	27	D.B.A. NEW ORLEANS
4	HI-HO LOUNGE	31	BLUE NILE
10	JOHN PAUL'S	32	THE MAISON
13	ALLWAYS LOUNGE & THEATRE	39 ⊕	THE SPOTTED CAT MUSIC CLUB
14	PHOENIX & NEW ORLEANS EAGLE	41	APPLE BARREL BAR
17	BUFFA'S BAR & RESTAURANT	48	MIMI'S IN THE MARIGNY
25	SNUG HARBOR JAZZ BISTRO	54	THE COUNTRY CLUB
		60	VAUGHAN'S LOUNGE
		61	BACCHANAL WINE

⊕ ARTS AND LEISURE

| 5 | BARRISTER'S GALLERY | 26 ⊕ | BICYCLE MICHAEL'S |
| 23 | WASHINGTON SQUARE PARK | | |

⊕ SHOPS

7	ISLAND OF SALVATION BOTANICA	42	AMERICAN AQUATIC GARDENS & GIFTS
28	ELECTRIC LADYLAND TATTOO	57	NEW ORLEANS ART SUPPLY
29	FAUBOURG MARIGNY ART BOOKS MUSIC		

⊕ HOTELS

8	MARIGNY MANOR HOUSE	36	FRENCHMEN HOTEL
9	ELYSIAN GUEST HOUSE	38	HOTEL DE LA MONNAIE
12 ⊕	ELYSIAN FIELDS INN	44	OLD HISTORIC CREOLE INN
15	THE BURGUNDY BED AND BREAKFAST	45	ROYAL STREET COURTYARD BED AND BREAKFAST
16	BYWATER BED & BREAKFAST	47	BALCONY GUEST HOUSE
18	MAISON DUBOIS	50	B & W COURTYARDS BED AND BREAKFAST
19	LA MAISON MARIGNY	52	LIONS INN BED & BREAKFAST
20	ROYAL STREET INN & BAR	58	MAISON DE MACARTY
33	LAMOTHE HOUSE HOTEL		
34	THE LANAUX MANSION BED AND BREAKFAST		

Musicians' Village

St. Vincent de Paul Cemetery

BYWATER

Pauline Street Wharf

Poland Avenue

✪ SIGHTS

19	MERCEDES-BENZ SUPERDOME
44	GALLIER HALL
57	ST. PATRICK'S CHURCH
78	LEE CIRCLE
83	**THE NATIONAL WWII MUSEUM**
90	*SCRAP HOUSE*
92	**BLAINE KERN'S MARDI GRAS WORLD**

◉ RESTAURANTS

4	DOMENICA	56	MIKE'S ON THE AVENUE
7	MILA RESTAURANT	65	ERNST CAFE
13	LE FORET	69	TOMMY'S CUISINE
25	HORINOYA RESTAURANT	72	EMERIL'S NEW ORLEANS
28	SINGHA THAI CAFE	74	RIOMAR
30	LÜKE	76	ROCK-N-SAKE BAR & SUSHI
35	BON TON CAFE	84	THE AMERICAN SECTOR
37	MOTHER'S RESTAURANT	85	UGLY DOG SALOON & BBQ
36	**AUGUST**	86	COCHON
38	THE GRILL ROOM	87	NOLA GROCERY AND PO-BOYS
41	BESH STEAK		
47	CAFÉ ADELAIDE		
54	HERBSAINT BAR AND RESTAURANT		

◐ NIGHTLIFE

1	HANDSOME WILLY'S BAR & LOUNGE	62	**VIC'S KANGAROO CAFE**
2	CLUB AMPERSAND	63	LUCY'S RETIRED SURFERS BAR & RESTAURANT
5	THE SAZERAC BAR	75	REPUBLIC NEW ORLEANS
15	LOA BAR	77	MULATE'S
39	**POLO CLUB LOUNGE**	88	THE HOWLIN' WOLF
42	WHISKEY BLUE	89	THE METROPOLITAN
61	W.I.N.O.		

◎ ARTS AND LEISURE

20	ALLSTATE SUGAR BOWL	60	**NEW ORLEANS SCHOOL OF GLASSWORKS & PRINTMAKING STUDIO**
21	NEW ORLEANS SAINTS	67	SOUTHERN FOOD & BEVERAGE MUSEUM
22	TULANE GREEN WAVE	70	LOUISIANA CHILDREN'S MUSEUM
23	NEW ORLEANS HORNETS	71	SØREN CHRISTENSEN GALLERY
32	ELMWOOD FITNESS CENTER DOWNTOWN	73	LEMIEUX GALLERIES
46	LAFAYETTE SQUARE	80	**THE OGDEN MUSEUM OF SOUTHERN ART**
49	PIAZZA D'ITALIA	81	LOUISIANA'S CIVIL WAR MUSEUM AT CONFEDERATE MEMORIAL HALL
50	AMERICAN ITALIAN MUSEUM	82	CONTEMPORARY ARTS CENTER
53	*CREOLE QUEEN*		
57	SPANISH PLAZA		
57	UPTOWN ANGLER		
59	JEAN BRAGG GALLERY OF SOUTHERN ART		

◉ SHOPS

9	ADLER'S	66	AIDAN GILL FOR MEN
10	RUBENSTEINS	68	RIVERWALK MARKETPLACE
11	MEYER THE HATTER		
14	SPA ATLANTIS PROFESSIONAL SPA & SALON		

◐ HOTELS

3	QUALITY INN & SUITES DOWNTOWN	34	COUNTRY INN & SUITES BY CARLSON-NEW ORLEANS FRENCH QUARTER
6	THE ROOSEVELT NEW ORLEANS	40	WINDSOR COURT HOTEL
8	RENAISSANCE NEW ORLEANS PERE MARQUETTE HOTEL	43	W NEW ORLEANS
12	JW MARRIOTT NEW ORLEANS	45	THE WHITNEY WYNDHAM HOTEL
16	**INTERNATIONAL HOUSE HOTEL**	48	**LOEWS NEW ORLEANS HOTEL**
17	OMNI ROYAL CRESCENT HOTEL	51	HARRAH'S NEW ORLEANS HOTEL
18	LOFT 523	55	LAFAYETTE HOTEL
24	HYATT REGENCY NEW ORLEANS	64	RENAISSANCE NEW ORLEANS ARTS HOTEL
26	HOMEWOOD SUITES NEW ORLEANS	79	THE HOTEL MODERN NEW ORLEANS
27	LE PAVILLON HOTEL	91	HAMPTON INN & SUITES NEW ORLEANS-CONVENTION CENTER HOTEL
29	DRURY INN & SUITES-NEW ORLEANS		
31	HILTON NEW ORLEANS/ST. CHARLES AVENUE HOTEL		
33	INTERCONTINENTAL NEW ORLEANS		

Louisiana State University Health Sciences Center

New Orleans City Hall

Mercedes-Benz Superdome
19 ✪ A 20,21,22

New Orleans Arena
A
23

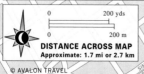

0 200 yds

0 200 m

DISTANCE ACROSS MAP
Approximate: 1.7 mi or 2.7 km

SEE MAP 4

© AVALON TRAVEL

SEE MAP 5

Storyville

SEE MAP 1

French Quarter

Jackson Square

Woldenberg Riverfront Park

Mississippi River

Harrah's

World Trade Center

Central Business District

Gallier Hall

Lafayette Square

Harrah's

Hilton

Riverwalk Marketplace

St. Patrick's Church

Arts District

Lee Circle

The National WWII Museum

Ernest N. Morial Convention Center

Scrap House

90

To Blaine Kern's Mardi Gras World

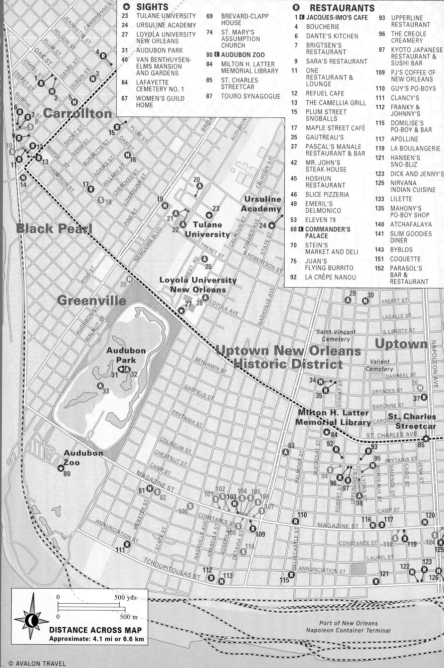

SIGHTS

23	TULANE UNIVERSITY
24	URSULINE ACADEMY
27	LOYOLA UNIVERSITY NEW ORLEANS
31	AUDUBON PARK
40	VAN BENTHUYSEN-ELMS MANSION AND GARDENS
64	LAFAYETTE CEMETERY NO. 1
67	WOMEN'S GUILD HOME
69	BREVARD-CLAPP HOUSE
74	ST. MARY'S ASSUMPTION CHURCH
80	AUDUBON ZOO
84	MILTON H. LATTER MEMORIAL LIBRARY
85	ST. CHARLES STREETCAR
87	TOURO SYNAGOGUE

RESTAURANTS

1	JACQUES-IMO'S CAFE
4	BOUCHERIE
6	DANTE'S KITCHEN
7	BRIGTSEN'S RESTAURANT
9	SARA'S RESTAURANT
11	ONE RESTAURANT & LOUNGE
12	REFUEL CAFE
13	THE CAMELLIA GRILL
15	PLUM STREET SNOBALLS
17	MAPLE STREET CAFÉ
35	GAUTREAU'S
37	PASCAL'S MANALE RESTAURANT & BAR
42	MR. JOHN'S STEAK HOUSE
45	HOSHUN RESTAURANT
46	SLICE PIZZERIA
49	EMERIL'S DELMONICO
53	ELEVEN 79
68	COMMANDER'S PALACE
70	STEIN'S MARKET AND DELI
75	JUAN'S FLYING BURRITO
92	LA CRÊPE NANOU
93	UPPERLINE RESTAURANT
96	THE CREOLE CREAMERY
97	KYOTO JAPANESE RESTAURANT & SUSHI BAR
109	PJ'S COFFEE OF NEW ORLEANS
110	GUY'S PO-BOYS
111	CLANCY'S
112	FRANKY & JOHNNY'S
115	DOMILISE'S PO-BOY & BAR
117	APOLLINE
119	LA BOULANGERIE
121	HANSEN'S SNO-BLIZ
123	DICK AND JENNY'S
125	NIRVANA INDIAN CUISINE
133	LILETTE
135	MAHONY'S PO-BOY SHOP
140	ATCHAFALAYA
141	SLIM GOODIES DINER
143	BYBLOS
151	COQUETTE
152	PARASOL'S BAR & RESTAURANT

Carrollton

Black Pearl

Ursuline Academy

Tulane University

Greenville

Loyola University New Orleans

Audubon Park

Uptown New Orleans Historic District

Saint Vincent Cemetery

Uptown

Valient Cemetery

Milton H. Latter Memorial Library

St. Charles Streetcar

Audubon Zoo

DISTANCE ACROSS MAP
Approximate: 4.1 mi or 6.6 km

0 500 yds
0 500 m

Port of New Orleans
Napoleon Container Terminal

NIGHTLIFE

2	MAPLE LEAF BAR
3	CARROLLTON STATION
5	OAK
14	COOTER BROWN'S TAVERN & OYSTER BAR
16	SNAKE AND JAKE'S CHRISTMAS CLUB LOUNGE
19	THE BOOT BAR & GRILL
30	CURE
34	NEUTRAL GROUND COFFEEHOUSE
76	HALF MOON BAR & RESTAURANT
81	MONKEY HILL BAR
88	THE COLUMNS HOTEL
91	DELACHAISE WINE & FOOD
95	THE KINGPIN
103	ST. JOE'S BAR
113	DOS JEFES UPTOWN CIGAR BAR
116	LE BON TEMPS ROULE
120	IGOR'S BUDDHA BELLY BURGER BAR
122	45 TCHOUP
126 ◖	TIPITINA'S
142	THE BULLDOG

ARTS AND LEISURE

20	NEWCOMB ART GALLERY
21	LUPIN THEATER
22	DIXON HALL
25	WOLFPACK ATHLETICS
28	NUNEMAKER AUDITORIUM
29	LA NUIT COMEDY THEATER
32 ◖	AUDUBON PARK
33	AUDUBON PARK GOLF COURSE
43	GEORGE & LEAH MCKENNA MUSEUM OF AFRICAN AMERICAN ART
44	ZEITGEIST MULTI-DISCIPLINARY ARTS CENTER
58	COLISEUM SQUARE
63	HOUSE OF BROEL'S VICTORIAN MANSION, WEDDING CHAPEL, AND DOLLHOUSE MUSEUM
79	THOMAS MANN GALLERY I/O
83	PRYTANIA THEATRE
98	WILD LOTUS YOGA UPTOWN
132	COLE PRATT GALLERY
134	GALERIE ROYALE

SHOPS

8	BALLIN'S LTD.
10	SYMMETRY JEWELERS AND DESIGNERS
18	MAPLE STREET BOOK SHOP
50	PRIMA DONNA'S CLOSET
65	GARDEN DISTRICT BOOK SHOP
71	BUSH ANTIQUES
72	HOUSE OF LOUNGE
73	DUNN & SONNIER ANTIQUES
77	JIM RUSSELL RECORDS
78	SHOP OF THE TWO SISTERS
82	PERLIS CLOTHING
94	ST. JAMES CHEESE COMPANY
100	RETRO-ACTIVE
101	BLUE FROG CHOCOLATES
102	DIRTY COAST
104	PIED NU
105	HAZELNUT NEW ORLEANS
106	EARTHSAVERS
107	SCRIPTURA
108	MIMI
114	OCTAVIA BOOKS
118	THE BEAD SHOP
124	TOP DRAWER ANTIQUES
127	FEET FIRST
128	AUX BELLES CHOSES NEW ORLEANS
129	ORIENT EXPRESSED
130	SHADYSIDE POTTERY
131 ◖	MIGNON FAGET
136	MAISON DE PROVENCE
137	LILI VINTAGE BOUTIQUE
138	BIG FISHERMAN SEAFOOD
139	NEW ORLEANS MUSIC EXCHANGE
144	FUNKY MONKEY
145	BOOTSY'S FUNROCK'N
146	AS YOU LIKE IT SILVER SHOP
147	SUCRÉ
148 ◖	BELLADONNA DAY SPA
149	PIPPEN LANE
150	DOMBOURIAN ORIENTAL RUGS

SEE MAP 3

Central City Historic District

Garden District

Women's Guild Home

Brevard-Clapp House

Van Benthuysen-Elms Mansion and Gardens

Lafayette Cemetery No. 1

Touro Synagogue

St. Mary's Assumption Church

Lower Garden District

Coliseum Square

Lyons Park

Seventh St. Wharf

Harmony St. Wharf

Mississippi River

HOTELS

26	PARK VIEW GUEST HOUSE
36	DIVE INN GUEST HOUSE
38	SOUTHERN COMFORT BED & BREAKFAST
39	HUBBARD MANSION BED & BREAKFAST
41	THE GRAND VICTORIAN BED & BREAKFAST
47	AVENUE GARDEN HOTEL
48	MAISON ST. CHARLES HOTEL & SUITES NEW ORLEANS
51	CLARION HOTEL GRAND BOUTIQUE
52 ◖	THE GREEN HOUSE INN
54	THE PRYTANIA PARK HOTEL
55	THE QUEEN ANNE
56	FAIRCHILD HOUSE BED & BREAKFAST
57	ST. CHARLES GUEST HOUSE
59 ◖	TERRELL HOUSE BED AND BREAKFAST
60	THE MCKENDRICK-BREAUX HOUSE
61	HENRY HOWARD HOUSE INN
62	MAGNOLIA MANSION
66	SULLY MANSION BED & BREAKFAST
86	AVENUE INN BED AND BREAKFAST
89	MAISON PERRIER
90	HAMPTON INN NEW ORLEANS GARDEN DISTRICT HOTEL
99	THE CHIMES BED & BREAKFAST
153	GARDEN DISTRICT BED & BREAKFAST

610

BASEBALL DR

City Park

Roosevelt Mall Dr

1 2
A

New Orleans
Museum of Art

CATINA ST
MILNE BLVD
ROSEMARY PL
WOODLAWN PL

HAWTHORNE PL

MOUND AVE

PONTALBA ST
MARSHALL FOCH ST
W PARK PL
N PARK PL
MIDDLE PK PL
E PK PL
HIDALGO ST

CANAL BLVD
CANAL BLVD
VICKSBURG ST
GENERAL DIAZ ST
NAVARRE AVE

GREENWOOD DR
WEIBLEN PL

ORLEANS AVE

MARCONI DR

STADIUM DR

New Orleans
Botanical Garden 5

FRIEDERICHS DR

VICTORY AVE

Delgado
Community College

6 R

LELONG AVE

Greenwood
Cemetery

CLAYTON DR

Holt
Cemetery

DREYFOUS AVE

DREYFOUS AVE

4

Metairie
Cemetery

PONTCHARTRAIN BLVD

METAIRIE RD

CITY PARK AVE

CITY PARK AVE

R 8

Pitot House
Museum and
Gardens

12

St. Patrick
Cemetery
No. 2

9

Cypress
Grove
Cemetery

10

TOLEDANO

St. Patrick
Cemetery
No. 1

New Orleans
Country Club

LAST ST

QUINCE ST

HAMILTON ST
HEATON ST

HOLLYGROVE ST
PEAR ST

BEECH ST
EAGLE ST

MONROE ST

ULLOA ST

AIRLINE DR

DIXON ST

PALMETTO ST

PALMETTO ST

JONET ST
PALM ST

EDINBURGH ST

S CARROLLTON AVE
S CARROLLTON AVE
S SHORT ST

DUBLIN ST
DIXON ST

TEACH ST

10

TULANE AVE

OLIVE ST
EDINBURGH ST
FERN ST

DANTE ST

WASHINGTON AVE

Xavier University
of Louisiana

DREXEL DR

PINE ST

DIXON ST

GRAVIER ST

TULANE AVE

S CLARK ST

S PIERCE ST

S SCOTT ST

S CORTEZ ST

S GENOIS ST

S TELEMACHUS ST

S CLARK ST

S DUPRE ST

S WHITE ST

S BROAD ST
S BROAD ST

JEFFERSON DAVIS PKY
S JEFFERSON DAVIS PKY

CALLIOPE ST

HOWARD AVE

10

SEE MAP 4

Mid-City

CANAL ST

H

N 36

Canal St

N BROAD ST

500 yds

500 m

DISTANCE ACROSS MAP
Approximate: 3.4 mi or 5.5 km

© AVALON TRAVEL

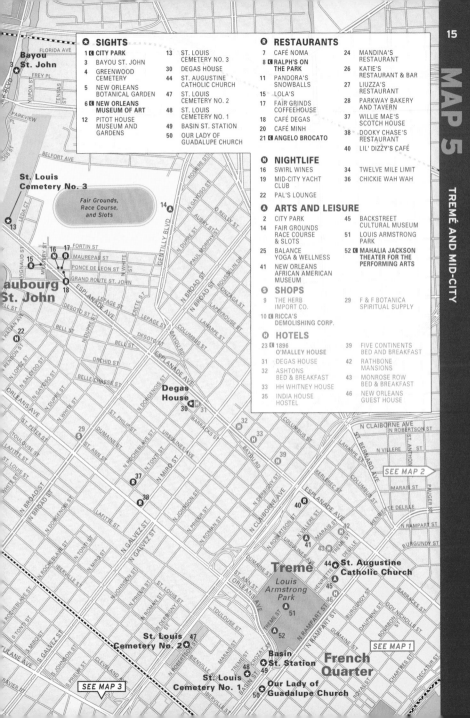

SIGHTS

1	CITY PARK	13	ST. LOUIS CEMETERY NO. 3
3	BAYOU ST. JOHN	30	DEGAS HOUSE
4	GREENWOOD CEMETERY	44	ST. AUGUSTINE CATHOLIC CHURCH
5	NEW ORLEANS BOTANICAL GARDEN	47	ST. LOUIS CEMETERY NO. 2
6	NEW ORLEANS MUSEUM OF ART	48	ST. LOUIS CEMETERY NO. 1
12	PITOT HOUSE MUSEUM AND GARDENS	49	BASIN ST. STATION
		50	OUR LADY OF GUADALUPE CHURCH

RESTAURANTS

7	CAFÉ NOMA	24	MANDINA'S RESTAURANT
8	RALPH'S ON THE PARK	26	KATIE'S RESTAURANT & BAR
11	PANDORA'S SNOWBALLS	27	LIUZZA'S RESTAURANT
15	LOLA'S	28	PARKWAY BAKERY AND TAVERN
17	FAIR GRINDS COFFEEHOUSE	37	WILLIE MAE'S SCOTCH HOUSE
18	CAFÉ DEGAS	38	DOOKY CHASE'S RESTAURANT
20	CAFÉ MINH	40	LIL' DIZZY'S CAFÉ
21	ANGELO BROCATO		

NIGHTLIFE

16	SWIRL WINES	34	TWELVE MILE LIMIT
19	MID-CITY YACHT CLUB	36	CHICKIE WAH WAH
22	PAL'S LOUNGE		

ARTS AND LEISURE

2	CITY PARK	45	BACKSTREET CULTURAL MUSEUM
14	FAIR GROUNDS RACE COURSE & SLOTS	51	LOUIS ARMSTRONG PARK
25	BALANCE YOGA & WELLNESS	52	MAHALIA JACKSON THEATER FOR THE PERFORMING ARTS
41	NEW ORLEANS AFRICAN AMERICAN MUSEUM		

SHOPS

9	THE HERB IMPORT CO.	29	F & F BOTANICA SPIRITUAL SUPPLY
10	RICCA'S DEMOLISHING CORP.		

HOTELS

23	1896 O'MALLEY HOUSE	39	FIVE CONTINENTS BED AND BREAKFAST
31	DEGAS HOUSE	42	RATHBONE MANSIONS
32	ASHTONS BED & BREAKFAST	43	MONROSE ROW BED & BREAKFAST
33	HH WHITNEY HOUSE	46	NEW ORLEANS GUEST HOUSE
35	INDIA HOUSE HOSTEL		

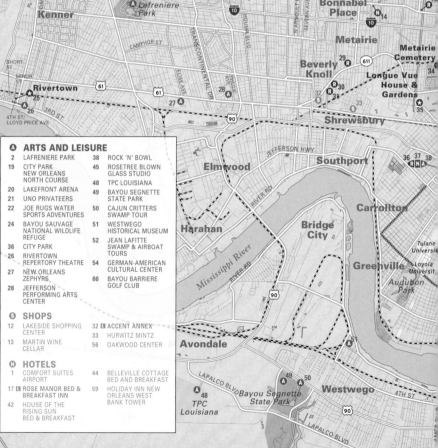

⊙ SIGHTS

23	FORT PIKE STATE HISTORIC SITE	46	OLD ARABI HISTORIC DISTRICT	15	HERITAGE GRILL	39	MIKIMOTO JAPANESE RESTAURANT & SUSHI BAR

23 FORT PIKE STATE HISTORIC SITE
25 RIVERTOWN
34 METAIRIE CEMETERY
35 ◖ LONGUE VUE HOUSE & GARDENS
41 ALGIERS POINT HISTORIC DISTRICT

46 OLD ARABI HISTORIC DISTRICT
47 CHALMETTE BATTLEFIELD AND NATIONAL CEMETERY
53 BARATARIA PRESERVE

15 HERITAGE GRILL
16 DEANIE'S SEAFOOD BUCKTOWN
18 MONDO
29 VEGA TAPAS CAFE
30 THE GALLEY
31 CAFÉ B
36 YE OLDE COLLEGE INN

39 MIKIMOTO JAPANESE RESTAURANT & SUSHI BAR
40 FIVE HAPPINESS
55 NINE ROSES
57 TONY MANDINA'S RESTAURANT
58 KIM SON RESTAURANT

⊙ RESTAURANTS

3 CAFFE! CAFFE!
4 ZEA ROTISSERIE & GRILL
6 CAFE EQUATOR
7 ◖ DRAGO'S SEAFOOD RESTAURANT

8 KOSHER CAJUN NEW YORK DELI & GROCERY
9 MORNING CALL COFFEE STAND
11 ANDREA'S RESTAURANT

⊙ NIGHTLIFE

5 MO'S CHALET
10 4 SEASONS & THE OUT BACK BAR

14 HURRICANES SPORTS BAR
37 ◖ ROCK 'N' BOWL
43 OLD POINT BAR

West End

W ESPLANADE AVE

Westgate

Willowdale

Bucktown

Kenner

DOWNS BLVD

Lafreniere Park

VETERANS MEMORIAL BLVD

Bonnabel Place

Metairie

Beverly Knoll

Longue Vue House & Gardens

Metairie Cemetery

Rivertown

CAMPHOR ST

Shrewsbury

4TH ST
LLOYD PRICE AVE

3RD ST

⊙ ARTS AND LEISURE

2 LAFRENIERE PARK
19 CITY PARK NEW ORLEANS NORTH COURSE
20 LAKEFRONT ARENA
21 UNO PRIVATEERS
22 JOE RUGS WATER SPORTS ADVENTURES
24 BAYOU SAUVAGE NATIONAL WILDLIFE REFUGE
36 CITY PARK
26 RIVERTOWN REPERTORY THEATRE
27 NEW ORLEANS ZEPHYRS
28 JEFFERSON PERFORMING ARTS CENTER

38 ROCK 'N' BOWL
45 ROSETREE BLOWN GLASS STUDIO
48 TPC LOUISIANA
49 BAYOU SEGNETTE STATE PARK
50 CAJUN CRITTERS SWAMP TOUR
51 WESTWEGO HISTORICAL MUSEUM
52 JEAN LAFITTE SWAMP & AIRBOAT TOURS
54 GERMAN-AMERICAN CULTURAL CENTER
60 BAYOU BARRIERE GOLF CLUB

⊙ SHOPS

12 LAKESIDE SHOPPING CENTER
13 MARTIN WINE CELLAR

32 ◖ ACCENT ANNEX
33 HURWITZ MINTZ
56 OAKWOOD CENTER

⊙ HOTELS

1 COMFORT SUITES AIRPORT
17 ◖ ROSE MANOR BED & BREAKFAST INN
42 HOUSE OF THE RISING SUN BED & BREAKFAST

44 BELLEVILLE COTTAGE BED AND BREAKFAST
59 HOLIDAY INN NEW ORLEANS WEST BANK TOWER

Elmwood

Southport

Carrollton

Harahan

Bridge City

Greenville

Tulane University

Loyola University

Audubon Park

Mississippi River

Avondale

Westwego

Bayou Segnette State Park

TPC Louisiana

LAPALCO BLVD

JEFFERSON HWY

RIVER RD

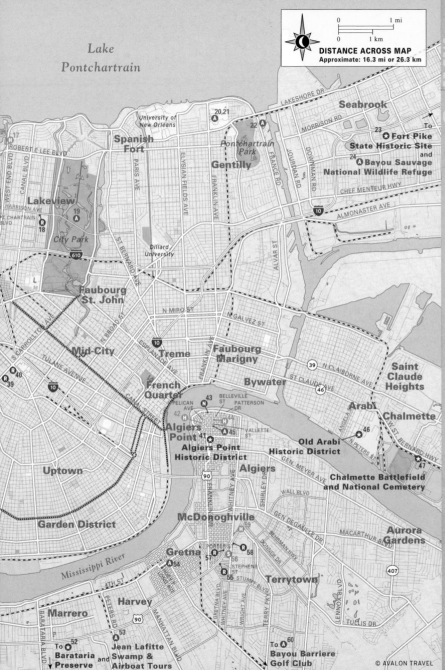

Lake

Pontchartrain

DISTANCE ACROSS MAP
Approximate: 16.3 mi or 26.3 km

0   1 mi
0   1 km

LAKESHORE DR

Seabrook

University of
New Orleans

20,21

MORRISON RD

23   To
Fort Pike
State Historic Site
and
24   Bayou Sauvage
National Wildlife Refuge

Spanish
Fort

22

Pontchartrain
Park

Gentilly

DOWNMAN RD

JOURDAN RD

FRANCE RD

CHEF MENTEUR HWY

ROBERT E LEE BLVD

17

WEST END BLVD

CANAL BLVD

PARIS AVE

ELYSIAN FIELDS AVE

FRANKLIN AVE

ALMONASTER AVE

10

Lakeview

HARRISON AVE

PT. CHARTRAIN
BLVD

19

18

City Park

ST BERNARD AVE

Dillard
University

ALVAR ST

610

L

Faubourg
St. John

N MIRO ST

N GALVEZ ST

N BROAD ST

S CARROLLTON AVE

Mid-City

ESPLANADE AVE

10

Treme

Faubourg
Marigny

FRANKLIN AVE

39

N CLAIBORNE AVE

Saint
Claude
Heights

TULANE AVENUE

R 40
39

10

CANAL STREET

French
Quarter

Bywater

ST CLAUDE AVE

46

Arabi

Chalmette

BELLEVILLE
ST

PATTERSON
DR

PELICAN
AVE

43

Algiers
Point   41

42

N

45

VALLETTE
ST

Algiers Point
Historic District

Old Arabi
Historic District

ANGELA ST

46

N PETERS ST

W. ST. BERNARD HWY

47

Uptown

Algiers

90

WHITNEY AVE

FRANKLIN ST

SHIRLEY DR

GEN. MEYER AVE

Chalmette Battlefield
and National Cemetery

Garden District

Mississippi River

McDonoghville

WALL BLVD

GEN DEGAULLE DR

BERMAN HWY

MACARTHUR BLVD

Aurora
Gardens

Gretna

56
57

PORTERS
R 58

STEPHENS
ST

56 STUMPF BLVD

WRIGHT AVE

GRETNA BLVD

TERRY PKWY

DONNER DR

Terrytown

LENNOX BLVD

407

54

Marrero

Harvey

PETERS RD

90

MANHATTAN BLVD

BARATARIA BLVD

4TH ST

52
Barataria
Preserve   and

Jean Lafitte
Swamp &
Airboat Tours

TULLIS DR

60
To Bayou Barriere
Golf Club

© AVALON TRAVEL

Discover New Orleans

New Orleans is a city that's hard to forget. Nestled between the brackish Lake Pontchartrain and the serpentine Mississippi River, it was once home to pirates, soldiers, voodoo priestesses, and plantation owners – and their legacy is palpable even today in the city's Cajun cuisine and lively jazz, its Southern manners and dark history.

It's my past that connects me to New Orleans. Those born and raised here understand the city's relentless pull. I remember, as a child, munching on a Plum Street sno-ball on a sweltering summer day, visiting the alligators at Audubon Zoo, watching Mardi Gras parades with my friends, crabbing in Lake Pontchartrain with Dad, bicycling through City Park with Mom, and sampling the seafood restaurants of Metairie with my grandfather. Although my childhood homes are gone and relatives have left the city, the memories still come alive – even if the faces have changed.

New Orleans is no stranger to adversity – from great fires to historic battles to yellow fever epidemics – but no matter what befalls this resilient town, it always rises from the ashes. New Orleans will, for me, always be synonymous with home. Once you experience its unique charms, laissez-faire attitude, and enduring spirit, you too are certain to fall under its spell.

Planning Your Trip

▶ WHERE TO GO

French Quarter

The undisputed heart of New Orleans, the French Quarter beckons with its wealth of seafood restaurants, historical museums, and varied street performers. Peruse the art galleries and antiques shops along Royal Street, stroll beside the Mississippi River, enjoy live music on Bourbon Street, or take a carriage ride through the fabled avenues. Iconic images like the St. Louis Cathedral, flickering gas lamps, and wrought-iron balconies make the Vieux Carré the city's most photographed neighborhood.

Faubourg Marigny and Bywater

East of the French Quarter, the residential Faubourg Marigny and Bywater neighborhoods also lure their share of visitors. Sandwiched between Esplanade Avenue, the Mississippi River, and the Industrial Canal, this vast area is especially popular among local music lovers, who nightly flock to the moody jazz clubs and low-key eateries on Frenchmen Street.

Central Business and Arts Districts

West of the French Quarter lies the Central Business District (CBD). Here, you'll encounter some of the city's finest hotels, plus diversions like the prominent Harrah's New Orleans casino. The CBD also boasts the Mercedes-Benz Superdome, home to the New Orleans Saints football team. The adjacent Arts District, also known as the Warehouse District, contains numerous art galleries, the Contemporary Arts Center, the impressive National WWII Museum, and Lee Circle, a roundabout featuring a statue of General Robert E. Lee.

wrought-iron balconies in the French Quarter

Garden District and Uptown

The eclectic Uptown area is filled with as many run-down apartment buildings as well-landscaped estates. Browse antiques shops and vintage clothing boutiques on funky Magazine Street, ride the streetcars on oak-shaded St. Charles Avenue, explore popular bars and eateries in the Riverbend, and stroll amid the magnificent mansions in the Garden District. Uptown is also home to the longstanding Tulane University as well as the famous Audubon Zoo, part of verdant Audubon Park.

Tremé and Mid-City

Two areas flooded by Hurricane Katrina, the Tremé and Mid-City have slowly rebounded since that devastating storm. Situated northwest of Rampart Street, the Tremé has nurtured many local musicians over the years and now entices tourists with places like St. Louis Cemetery No. 1, site of Marie Laveau's celebrated tomb. Farther north, Mid-City features several popular attractions, including City Park, the New Orleans Museum of Art, and the Fair Grounds, home to the annual New Orleans Jazz & Heritage Festival.

Greater New Orleans

Stretching from Lake Pontchartrain to the western bank of the Mississippi River, Greater New Orleans encompasses several unique neighborhoods and attractions. In Lakeview and Gentilly, visitors can attend concerts at the Lakefront Arena, shop and dine on Harrison Avenue, ride bikes along scenic Lakeshore Drive, and play golf in upper City Park. Farther west, Metairie and Kenner offer shopping centers and restaurants, while the West Bank invites hikers, anglers, and canoeists to explore Barataria Preserve.

▶ WHEN TO GO

When and where you go will depend on your interests, but try to allow yourself at least a week (or longer) to appreciate New Orleans. Although the city is a year-round destination, summer is the least crowded time to visit, except during major events like the Essence Music Festival and Southern Decadence. Temperatures are fairly high June–September, when hurricane season is at its peak. While fall is more comfortable, winter and spring constitute the high season here. Annual events, such as Mardi Gras, the French Quarter Festival, and the New Orleans Jazz & Heritage Festival, lure the bulk of out-of-towners during these months. Lodging rates are inflated in high season, as well as during major events and holiday weekends, and advance reservations may be necessary.

a typically vibrant Mardi Gras float

Explore New Orleans

▶ THE THREE-DAY BEST OF NEW ORLEANS

The following three-day tour is an all-too-brief sampling of the best cultural and recreational attractions the city has to offer. If possible, try to visit New Orleans during one of its signature events, such as Mardi Gras, the French Quarter Festival, the New Orleans Jazz & Heritage Festival, Southern Decadence, or Halloween.

Day 1

▶ Start your day in the French Quarter with some warm café au lait and sugar-covered beignets at the world-famous Café Du Monde, part of the historic French Market, a collection of eateries, gift stores, and praline shops.

Musicians play within earshot of noshers at the original Café Du Monde.

the Old U.S. Mint, an engrossing museum at the French Quarter's edge

MARDI GRAS MADNESS

Bourbon Street on Mardi Gras Day

elaborate floats, marching bands, motorcycle squads, dancers and other entertainers, and, sometimes, royal courts. Those walking or riding in the parades will toss cups, bead necklaces, commemorative doubloons, and other trinkets to the spectators lining the route. Each year brings a new theme, often with a historical, mythical, or topical bent. Only one official parade runs through the French Quarter – the irreverent, downright raunchy Krewe du Vieux. Parades elsewhere in the city (including Uptown, Mid-City, and Metairie) are surprisingly family-friendly.

Parade routes are listed in *The Times-Picayune* and on websites such as www.mardigras.com, www.mardigrasday.com, and www.mardigrasneworleans.com. Here are the major parades during Mardi Gras weekend.

Few festivals exemplify the joyous spirit of New Orleans more than Mardi Gras (a French term meaning "Fat Tuesday"). While the season technically starts on January 6, Mardi Gras weekend extends from the Friday before Fat Tuesday through midnight on Fat Tuesday, the day before Lent begins.

Mardi Gras' most famous events are the free public parades sponsored and hosted by krewes (private clubs). Parades feature

BACCHUS

Officially established in 1968, Bacchus (www.kreweofbacchus.org) is one of the Mardi Gras "super-krewes". Signature floats include the Bacchasaurus, Bacchagator, Bacchawhoppa, and Baby Kong.

When: The Bacchus parade begins at 5 P.M. on the Sunday prior to Mardi Gras.

Where: From Napoleon Avenue and Tchoupitoulas Street, it rolls through Uptown on Na-

▶ After breakfast, stroll through picturesque Jackson Square and tour the stunning structures that surround this well-landscaped park. Besides the majestic St. Louis Cathedral, you'll see curious historical exhibits inside the Cabildo and the Presbytère and glimpse period Creole furnishings inside the 1850 House, part of the lovely Pontalba Apartments.

▶ Stroll past the quaint boutiques and verdant balconies of Chartres Street and then walk down gallery-lined Royal Street to the Gallier House. Stop by the Beauregard-Keyes House, then cross the street for a self-guided tour of the Old Ursuline Convent. Nearby, the magnificent Old U.S. Mint is now an engaging museum about the building's history as well as the city's jazz legacy.

▶ At night, don your finest attire for a quintessential French Creole dinner at Galatoire's on Bourbon Street. Afterward, walk to the world-famous Preservation Hall for a short jazz concert.

poleon Avenue, along St. Charles Avenue, and down Canal Street, ending at the Ernest N. Morial Convention Center.

ENDYMION

Founded in 1967, Endymion (www.endymion.org) is the city's largest parade, a "super-krewe" that features enormous floats and magnificent court costumes.

When: Following an annual block party, Endymion typically rolls through Mid-City at 4:30 P.M. on the Saturday prior to Mardi Gras.

Where: The parade starts near City Park and travels down Canal Street and St. Charles Avenue, culminating with "Domecoming" in the Mercedes-Benz Superdome.

ORPHEUS

Founded in 1993 by Harry Connick Jr., Orpheus (www.kreweoforpheus.com) is the largest of the newer parades and is especially popular among music fans, as many of the floats boast live concerts.

When: The parade begins at 6 P.M. on Lundi Gras ("Fat Monday").

Where: From the corner of Napoleon Avenue and Tchoupitoulas Street, it rolls through Uptown on Napoleon Avenue, then along St. Charles Avenue, down Canal Street, and to the convention center and the Orpheuscapade, a black-tie event.

REX

Since 1872, Rex (www.rexorganization.com) has reigned as the king of Mardi Gras. The parade features majestic floats and masked riders. Mardi Gras officially ends with the Rex Ball at the Municipal Auditorium in Louis Armstrong Park.

When: The Rex Parade starts at 10 A.M. on Mardi Gras.

Where: The parade travels down Napoleon Avenue from the intersection with South Claiborne Avenue in Uptown, then along St. Charles Avenue and down Canal Street toward the Mississippi River.

ZULU

Officially begun in 1909, Zulu (www.kreweofzulu.com) is one of the most anticipated parades of the Mardi Gras season. Zulu usually presents a Lundi Gras Festival (a free music event) the day before Fat Tuesday.

When: The parade begins at 8 a.m. on Mardi Gras.

Where: From the corner of Jackson and South Claiborne Avenues in Uptown, it travels along Jackson Avenue, continues north on St. Charles Avenue, crosses Poydras and Canal Streets in the Central Business District, and ends at Orleans Avenue and North Galvez Street in the Faubourg Tremé.

▶ End your evening at the candlelit Lafitte's Blacksmith Shop Bar for a late-night drink.

Day 2

▶ Take a walk along the Mississippi riverfront and explore the varied marine exhibits inside the Audubon Aquarium of the Americas.

▶ Next, enjoy a river cruise aboard the *Creole Queen,* an authentic paddlewheeler. Then stroll to the nearby National WWII Museum, where you can watch an immersive documentary and experience a variety of exhibits pertaining to the Allied victory in the Second World War.

▶ Catch a Canal Street streetcar ride to verdant City Park, a beloved 1,300-acre sanctuary. Rent bikes, ride a classic carousel, or stroll through the New Orleans Botanical Garden and New Orleans Museum of Art. Afterward, enjoy a sumptuous meal of contemporary Creole cuisine at Ralph's on the Park.

HAUNTED NEW ORLEANS

New Orleans is often considered the most haunted town in America. Given the voodoo lore and Catholic traditions of this atmospheric Southern port, the spooky marshes and swamps that surround it, and a checkered past rife with piracy, slavery, and murder, New Orleans is seemingly fertile ground for the spirit world.

- **Antoine's Restaurant:** Some diners claim that this 1840 eatery is still overseen by proprietor Antoine Alciatore, whose tuxedo-clad spirit has been known to appear in various dining rooms.

- **Beauregard-Keyes House:** At General Beauregard's former home, visitors have allegedly heard the screams and moans of dying soldiers from the Battle of Shiloh.

- **The Columns Hotel:** Overnight guests have witnessed the spirits of a well-dressed gentleman in various bedrooms, a "woman in white" in the garden, and a young girl wandering the third floor of this Uptown hotel.

- **Hotel Monteleone:** This historic landmark is supposedly home to more than a dozen entities, not the least of which is a 10-year-old boy who plays hide-and-seek with other young spirits.

- **Hôtel Provincial:** At this French Quarter hotel, guests have occasionally seen and heard the spirits of wounded soldiers, allegedly treated at this site during the Civil War.

- **LaLaurie Mansion:** In 1834, neighbors discovered several tortured, starving slaves chained in the attic of this ornate house. Since then, passersby have claimed to hear moans, screams, and other terrible sounds emanating from the premises. Though closed to the public, it's routinely included on ghost tours in the French Quarter.

- **Muriel's Jackson Square:** This upscale restaurant is supposedly haunted by Pierre Antoine Lepardi Jourdan, the building's former

the supposedly haunted LaLaurie Mansion

owner, who committed suicide upstairs after losing his dream house in a poker game.

- **Oak Alley Plantation:** Visitors have seen ghosts, felt inexplicable caresses, and heard the mysterious clip-clops of an invisible horse-drawn carriage at this famous Vacherie plantation.

- **St. Louis Cathedral:** Some have heard the tenor voice of Père Dagobert, an 18th-century priest who insisted on the proper burial of six French rebel leaders who had been killed by the Spanish and left outside in the heat and rain.

- **St. Louis Cemetery No. 1:** According to local legend, you can request a favor of the spirit of Marie Laveau, the so-called "Voodoo Queen of New Orleans," by visiting this Tremé cemetery, leaving an offering before her supposed resting place, and knocking on her crypt three times.

- At night, have a drink in the courtyard of Pat O'Brien's in the French Quarter, known for its flaming fountain. Listen to live music or watch a burlesque show at One Eyed Jacks.

- If you're still wide awake, head to Bourbon Pub & Parade, a 24-hour gay nightclub that features variety shows, drag queen competitions, comedy showcases, and late-night dancing.

Day 3

- Hop on the St. Charles streetcar to the Garden District, where you can relax in verdant Coliseum Square, visit Lafayette Cemetery No. 1, and stroll amid historic homes, such as the Brevard-Clapp House, where novelist Anne Rice once lived.

Pat O'Brien's, home of the hurricane

- Explore the antiques shops, art galleries, and varied boutiques along funky Magazine Street.

- Hop back on the streetcar and head west to lush Audubon Park to play golf or tennis, go horseback riding, or gaze at the

Tourists will find several historic mansions in the Garden District.

orangutans, elephants, and other playful animals at Audubon Zoo.

▶ Take a cab to Commander's Palace and splurge on dinner at this classic New Orleans–style restaurant.

▶ After dinner, catch some live rock and blues music at well-loved Uptown joints like Tipitina's or the Maple Leaf Bar, or venture to Rock 'n' Bowl for a round of bowling plus live music.

the Audubon Aquarium of the Americas

▶ A ROMANTIC WEEKEND

History, luxury, and revelry converge in this sensual city, a popular place for romantic getaways. Accommodations range from intimate guesthouses in the Faubourg Marigny and Mid-City to elegant B&Bs in the Garden District to historic hotels in the French Quarter, and though all promise a romantic weekend, staying in the Quarter will ensure the most atmospheric experience.

Friday

Check into your hotel and have lunch at Muriel's Jackson Square, a stunning, supposedly haunted Creole restaurant not far

Ghosts supposedly haunt Muriel's Jackson Square, an ideal spot for a romantic dinner.

The Hôtel Provincial houses Stella!, one of the Quarter's most romantic restaurants.

Saturday

Pick up a pastry from the Croissant D'or Patisserie, then take a stroll along the riverside Moon Walk and have a morning picnic at Woldenberg Riverfront Park, a 16-acre greenspace. Afterward, take a breezy riverboat cruise on the Steamboat *Natchez*, a nostalgic paddlewheeler famous for its peppy calliope.

Have a late lunch at Bayona, then walk four blocks to the magnificent Hotel Monteleone, where you and your sweetheart can relish an intimate couples massage at Spa Aria. Have a drink at the hotel's Carousel Bar, where literary legends once mingled.

Mosey back to your hotel then venture down Royal Street, for a romantic dinner in the dimly lit courtyard at Café Amelie. After dinner, take a private carriage ride through the French Quarter via Royal Carriages.

Carriage rides offer a delightful overview of the Quarter.

from the St. Louis Cathedral. Stroll east to Frenchmen Street, where you can rent bikes from Bicycle Michael's, then take a self-guided tour of the Faubourg Marigny and French Quarter.

Either return your bikes when you're done or keep them for the weekend, then head to the Historic New Orleans Collection and tour the historical structures and exhibits that this engaging complex comprises. Afterward, mosey amid the antiques shops, art galleries, bookstores, and clothing boutiques along Royal and Chartres Streets.

Once the sun goes down, have a romantic dinner at the Marigny's Feelings Cafe, which features an intimate courtyard and piano bar, or the Quarter's Stella!, an elegant restaurant serving eclectic cuisine. After dinner, enjoy some live jazz and a midnight burlesque show at Irvin Mayfield's Jazz Playhouse.

The Steamboat *Natchez* paddlewheel rests between trips on the Mississippi River.

Sunday

After checking out of your hotel, stroll to the Court of Two Sisters for a lively jazz brunch. Following brunch, take a jazz tour via Historic New Orleans Tours, which guides participants on a walking tour of sites like Preservation Hall, St. Louis Cemetery No. 1, and Louis Armstrong Park. After the tour, head to La Divina Gelateria for a cup of artisanal gelato, then take one last stroll around the photogenic French Quarter.

SIGHTS

With an engrossing history that involves pirates and prostitutes, soldiers and slave owners, voodoo queens and vampire lore, New Orleans has lured curious outsiders for decades. While fine restaurants and boisterous music clubs lure tourists, other attractions can be equally seductive. Families come for the kid-friendly Audubon Aquarium of the Americas, the fascinating Audubon Insectarium, Blaine Kern's Mardi Gras World, and the monkey-filled Audubon Zoo. Art lovers flock to the Degas House, the New Orleans Museum of Art, and the art-filled French Quarter. Gourmands will enjoy classes at the New Orleans School of Cooking, outdoor enthusiasts will appreciate oases like City Park, the New Orleans Botanical Garden, and Audubon Park. But it's history buffs who will be particularly enamored with the Big Easy.

Besides engrossing exhibits at the National WWII Museum, the city boasts a wide array of historic homes, statues, and structures—many of which can be found in the French Quarter. The city's original neighborhood was laid out in 1722 and suffered various fires and regime shifts before becoming the still-authentic heart of New Orleans that it is today. Most visitors venture to Jackson Square, the bustling, picturesque sanctuary on Decatur Street, bounded by classic wrought-iron fencing and surrounded by several noteworthy buildings: the remarkable St. Louis Cathedral, the adjacent Cabildo and Presbytère, and the gorgeous Pontalba Apartments. Beyond, the charming Hermann-Grima House awaits, as does the magnificent Old U.S. Mint, a particularly imposing courthouse, the assorted structures known as the

HIGHLIGHTS

LOOK FOR 🄲 TO FIND
RECOMMENDED SIGHTS.

🄲 **Best Place to Take the Kids:** Overlooking the Mississippi River, the spectacular **Audubon Aquarium of the Americas** delights youngsters as much as adults. It presents fascinating exhibits about important aquatic habitats around the world, from the Amazonian rainforest to the Gulf of Mexico (page 31).

🄲 **Best Glimpse of History:** Situated on Royal Street, **The Historic New Orleans Collection** encompasses several notable structures, from a Creole cottage to the Greek Revival-style Merieult House, as well as numerous engrossing exhibits pertaining to the state's history (page 37).

🄲 **Most Iconic Landmark:** Considered the historic heart and soul of the French Quarter – and, by extension, New Orleans – verdant **Jackson Square** is fringed by such iconic buildings as the St. Louis Cathedral, the Cabildo, the Arsenal, the Presbytère, and the Pontalba Apartments. Besides being a scenic spot for a picnic, it's the perfect place to get your bearings before exploring the rest of the Big Easy (page 37).

🄲 **Best Place for Culinary Enthusiasts:** If you're interested in learning how to prepare gumbo, jambalaya, shrimp Creole, pralines, bread pudding, and other local staples, watch a demonstration or take a hands-on cooking class at **The New Orleans School of Cooking** in the French Quarter (page 40).

🄲 **Most Colorful Attraction:** Children and adults alike relish a guided tour of **Blaine Kern's Mardi Gras World,** where you can stroll amid kaleidoscopic floats, observe the artists of the world-renowned Blaine Kern Studios at work, and learn about the history of the Carnival season (page 45).

🄲 **Most Patriotic Locale:** No matter your perspective on the necessity of war, you'll find it hard not to be impressed by **The National WWII Museum,** where you can watch an immersive documentary about America's "greatest generation," have an old-fashioned dining experience in the Stage Door Canteen, and peruse a wealth of permanent and traveling exhibits about the Allied victory in the Second World War (page 47).

🄲 **Best Place for Animal Lovers:** After sampling Uptown's convivial restaurants, shopping on Magazine Street, or admiring historic homes along St. Charles Avenue, be sure to visit the **Audubon Zoo,** where you can watch elephant and sea lion shows, observe the antics of primates and jaguars, and experience a Louisiana swamp (page 48).

🄲 **Most Enchanting Stroll:** A 1,300-acre swath of greenery, **City Park** contains one of the Big Easy's top cultural attractions, the New Orleans Museum of Art, as well as the kid-friendly Carousel Gardens Amusement Park and Storyland playground. It's also an excellent place for walking, especially across the picturesque bridges, amid the moss-covered oak trees, and through the park's New Orleans Botanical Garden (page 56).

🄲 **Best Sculpture Collection:** In addition to showcasing a marvelous array of French, American, African, and Japanese artwork, the **New Orleans Museum of Art** features a picturesque five-acre sculpture garden that displays more than 60 important sculptures amid stately trees, winding paths, pedestrian bridges, and scenic lagoons (page 59).

🄲 **Best Attraction Off the Beaten Path:** Not far from the city's border with Metairie lies one of the area's most underrated historic sites, the **Longue Vue House & Gardens,** a lush oasis featuring a Classical Revival-style mansion that once belonged to local community pillars Edgar and Edith Stern (page 66).

Historic New Orleans Collection, and oodles of historical markers.

History buffs will find plenty to love beyond the Quarter, from the distinctive homes of the Faubourg Marigny and Garden District to the crumbling cemeteries in the Tremé and Mid-City neighborhoods to Uptown's well-regarded universities. Even beyond the main tourist areas, you'll find worthwhile sights, such as the Longue Vue House & Gardens near the Jefferson-Orleans parish line. In a city defined—for both good and bad—by water, it's also fun to wander through Woldenberg Riverfront Park alongside the Mississippi River

or venture north to Lake Pontchartrain, just to watch the passing sailboats.

Naturally, you might think about the negative aspects of water at such times—namely, the damage and floods of Hurricane Katrina. While that destruction is still evident in places like Lakeview, Mid-City, the Ninth Ward, and New Orleans East, New Orleans has experienced a renaissance since 2005. This fast-growing city is now brimming with refurbished attractions, brand-new establishments, and newer or younger residents responsible for many of New Orleans's most cutting-edge events and diversions.

French Quarter Map 1

The French Quarter is a pedestrian-friendly neighborhood with a deliciously contradictory nature. At once marked by traditional European architecture and lush Caribbean-style courtyards, high-end art galleries, and Bohemian shops, this eclectic historic district appeals to tourists and residents alike. Simply walking amid the old-fashioned gas lamps constitutes a sight in itself—albeit a tantalizing, multisensory one. Enjoy the street musicians, the clip-clop of bypassing carriages, the *Natchez* calliope, and an air often scented with the mingled perfume of sweet olive trees, chicory-laced coffee, boiled seafood, and, yes, mule manure.

THE ARSENAL

600 St. Peter St., 504/568-6968 or 800/568-6968, www.crt.state.la.us/museum
HOURS: Tues.-Sun. 10 A.M.-4:30 P.M.
COST: $6 adult, $5 senior and student, free under 13

Situated near Jackson Square and adjacent to the historic Cabildo, the Greek Revival–style Arsenal was constructed in 1839 and became part of the Louisiana State Museum complex in 1915. Badly damaged during the Cabildo fire of 1988, this national historic landmark has since been carefully restored. Both permanent and rotating exhibits are installed in the first and second floors of the building; among

the former, *Louisiana and the Mighty Mississippi* explores how flatboats, ferries, steamboats, and keel boats helped New Orleans evolve into one of the world's greatest river ports during the 19th century. The related exhibit *The Coffee Trade and the Port of New Orleans* examines the economic importance of the city's coffee trade.

◖ AUDUBON AQUARIUM OF THE AMERICAS

1 Canal St., 504/581-4629 or 800/774-7394, www.auduboninstitute.org
HOURS: Tues.-Sun. 10 A.M.-5 P.M.
COST: $21 adult, $17 senior and student, $14 child 2-12, free under 2

Established in 1990 by the Audubon Nature Institute—the same folks who operate the historic Audubon Zoo—the Audubon Aquarium of the Americas is one of the most popular tourist destinations in downtown New Orleans. Situated at the southern end of 16-acre Woldenberg Riverfront Park, alongside the Mississippi River, this contemporary glass-and-brick building houses several intriguing exhibits, most notably the 400,000-gallon Gulf of Mexico habitat, which features a variety of sharks, stingrays, sea turtles, and other saltwater creatures amid the barnacled pilings of an offshore oil rig replica. Kids especially favor this family-friendly attraction, where they can

SIGHTS

© LAURA MARTONE

the Audubon Aquarium of the Americas, just steps from the Mississippi River

touch cownose rays, watch penguin feedings, participate in entertaining nature shows, climb above an Amazonian rainforest, and, via an underwater glass tunnel, stroll through the moray eels and tropical fish of a Caribbean coral reef.

Visitors to this exceptional, two-story aquarium will observe a wide array of aquatic and amphibious creatures—not to mention Spots, the unusual white alligator who lives in the Mississippi River gallery. There are also two gift shops on the premises. Adjacent to the aquarium is the **Entergy IMAX Theatre** (Tues.–Sun. 10 A.M.–5 P.M., $10.50 adult, $9.50 senior and student, $7.50 child 2–12, free under 2), which typically showcases vibrant nature documentaries, such as *Hurricane on the Bayou* (2006) and *Under the Sea 3D* (2009). In addition to their regular hours, the aquarium and IMAX theater are also open on most Monday holidays as well as Mondays during the summer months. The last ticket is sold an hour before closing. Discounted self-parking is available whether you have your

ticket validated at the aquarium or the IMAX theater.

AUDUBON INSECTARIUM

423 Canal St., 504/581-4629 or 800/774-7394, www.auduboninstitute.org
HOURS: Tues.-Sun. 10 A.M.-5 P.M.
COST: $16 adult, $13 senior and student, $11 child 2-12, free under 2

On the site of the former Fort St. Louis now stands the U.S. Custom House—a stately, slightly intimidating gray structure that occupies an entire block. Today, part of this 30,000-square-foot building is home to the Audubon Insectarium, which contains the largest free-standing collection of insects in the United States—about 900,000 species in all. Visitors have the opportunity to touch all kinds of creatures, although many others (like the despised cockroaches) are presented through displays from a safe distance. Even the museum's Tiny Termite Café has an insect-themed appearance—and the glass-topped tables are actually terrariums, so you might find yourself, as I once did, eating directly over a live tarantula. The museum's bug-cooking demonstration "café," Bug Appétit, illustrates how people around the world routinely snack on insects as an excellent source of protein. Less harrowing for squeamish visitors is the massive butterfly room set within a Japanese-style garden. Note that, in addition to its regular hours, the insectarium is also open on most Monday holidays.

BEAUREGARD-KEYES HOUSE

1113 Chartres St., 504/523-7257, www.bkhouse.org

HOURS: Mon.-Sat. 10 A.M.-3 P.M.

COST: $10 adult, $9 senior and student, $4 child 6-12, free under 6

Opposite the Old Ursuline Convent stands the Beauregard-Keyes House, one of relatively few raised cottages in the French Quarter; the entrance and main floor are one level above the street. After the Civil War, the handsome mansion, which was finished in 1826, became the home of the Confederate general P. G. T. Beauregard. Over the years that followed, the house had a number of owners, and

by the mid-1920s, it was nearly slated for demolition before a group of women, aware that Beauregard had lived here after the Civil War, began a campaign to save it. In 1944, novelist Frances Parkinson Keyes (pronounced KIZE) took possession of the house, and it was she who hired a firm to carefully restore it. She lived in the house until 1969 and wrote several of her 50-odd books here, including *Dinner at Antoine's, Blue Camellia, The Chess Players,* and *Madame Castel's Lodger.* Today, her extensive collections of antique dolls, fans, and folk costumes are on display, and some of her books are available in the on-site gift shop.

One of the lead attractions here is the formal garden, laid out by the wife of Switzerland's consul to New Orleans, who owned the house in the 1830s. From beyond the outer wall, you can see the parterre garden through brick "windows" fashioned with iron grills. Of course, a stroll through this lovely space is included in any of the guided house tours, which depart every hour on the hour. Roses, daylilies, crape myrtle, azaleas, sweet olive trees,

© DANIEL MARTONE

the Beauregard-Keyes House on Chartres Street

THE PIRATE'S ALLEY FAULKNER SOCIETY

New Orleans has long served as an inspiration and temporary home base for many well-known American writers, including Tennessee Williams, Anne Rice, and William Faulkner – all of whom have left lasting marks on this historic city. In the case of William Faulkner (1897-1962), you'll find several vestiges of his legacy, including the Pirate's Alley Faulkner Society (624 Pirate's Alley, www.wordsandmusic.org). Not to be confused with the William Faulkner Society (www.faulknersociety.com) – a nationwide organization dedicated to the research, scholarship, and criticism of Faulkner's writings – the Pirate's Alley Faulkner Society is a nonprofit arts organization situated in the **Faulkner House** near Jackson Square.

Located behind the Cabildo, opposite the St. Louis Cathedral's rear garden, the Faulkner House was once the home of William Faulkner, the ground floor of which he subleased from artist William Spratling in 1925. It was here that the unsung poet and future Nobel Laureate authored his first novel, *Soldiers' Pay* (1926), wrote a series of poetic essays that would eventually become a collection called *New Orleans Sketches,* and gathered inspiration for some of his later books, including *Mosquitoes* (1927) and *The Wild Palms* (1939). Today, Faulkner's former quarters serve as **Faulkner House Books,** an intimate bookshop owned and operated by attorney Joseph J. DeSalvo Jr. and offering a decent selection of fine Southern literature, including rare editions.

In 1990, DeSalvo and his partner, designer Rosemary James – who together restored the Faulkner House, which is now their residence and can be toured by advance arrangement – founded the Pirate's Alley Faulkner Society along with Faulkner scholar W. Kenneth Holditch. Intended as a tribute to Faulkner himself, the society honors and supports writers through classes, outreach

© DANIEL MARTONE

Pirate's Alley, between The Cabildo and the St. Louis Cathedral

programs, and year-round events, such as the annual **William Faulkner – William Wisdom Creative Writing Competition** and **Words & Music: A Literary Feast in New Orleans,** a weeklong multi-arts festival in November. In conjunction with the Words & Music festival, the organization also produces *The Double Dealer,* an annual literary journal established in 1993, as an homage to the original *Double Dealer,* which existed in the 1920s and featured the early work of William Faulkner, Ernest Hemingway, and Sherwood Anderson. Typically, the Words & Music festival also features writing seminars and workshops, book signings and readings, live concerts and performances, cocktail parties, and, of course, writing competitions.

irises, magnolia trees, and evergreen shrubs blend and bloom in one of the Quarter's loveliest gardens.

THE CABILDO

701 Chartres St., 504/568-6968 or 800/568-6968, www.crt.state.la.us/museum

HOURS: Tues.-Sun. 10 A.M.-4:30 P.M.

COST: $6 adult, $5 senior and student, free under 13

On the upriver side of the St. Louis Cathedral stands the Cabildo, the building in which the formal transfer of Louisiana to the United States took place after the Louisiana Purchase. The Spanish first constructed the Cabildo as their seat of government in the 1770s, but it and its replacement were destroyed during both major city fires. The current structure, made of brick and stucco and built in the Spanish style with Moorish influences, was erected in 1794, serving again as home to the Spanish administrative body, after which it became the Maison de Ville (Town Hall) during the very brief time the French reclaimed New Orleans. It would serve as the Louisiana Supreme Court headquarters for much of the 19th and early 20th centuries, and it was actually the site where the landmark *Plessy v. Ferguson* decision (which legalized segregation) was handed down. Many prominent visitors have been officially received in the Cabildo, from statesmen Henry Clay and the Marquis de Lafayette to such distinguished figures of the arts as Mark Twain and Sarah Bernhardt. The building looks more French than Spanish today, because the original flat-tile roof was replaced with a Second Empire mansard roof in the late 1840s.

Part of the Louisiana State Museum since 1911, the Cabildo contains a comprehensive and fascinating exhibit tracing the history of Louisiana through the past 200 years. The exhibits are grouped into 11 chronological sections, beginning with the region's Native Americans and ending with Reconstruction. Each section uses maps, photographs and drawings, historical documents, and narrative signs to describe the period and theme.

For a truly memorable experience, consider taking one of the morning **Yoga at the Cabildo** classes (Tues. and Thurs. 7:30–8:30 A.M., Sat. 8:30–9:30 A.M., $12). Held in a lovely, light-filled gallery, these classes are ideal for residents and tourists at all levels of practice.

FRENCH MARKET

Decatur St. and N. Peters St. btwn. St. Peter St. and Barracks St., 504/522-2621, www.frenchmarket.org

HOURS: Vary depending on the business

COST: Free, though dining and shopping costs apply

One of the city's most famous attractions, the French Market is a picturesque, multi-block collection of shops, eateries, and stalls. Legend has it that this site stood as a Choctaw trading post long before the Spanish established an early market here in 1791. Parts of the current structure date to 1813. Originally, the stalls contained only a meat market, but subsequent structures were added all along North Peters Street throughout the 19th century, housing markets of fresh produce, flowers, spices, and other goods. Coffee stands were opened at opposite ends of the stalls, and one remains to this day—the delightful **Café Du Monde** (www.cafedumonde.com).

The **Farmers Market,** a covered, open-air market building, is fun for any gourmand. Highlights include bottled hot sauce, pralines and other Louisiana vittles, Cajun and Creole spices and herbs, and fresh seafood, produce, and sandwiches. The lower half of the market building is an open-air bazaar filled with jewelry and dresses, Asian figurines and African masks, and other souvenirs.

Besides a few other eateries, the market also contains retail shops that sell everything from toys, souvenirs, and candies to African oils, Latin American hammocks, and local artwork. A small shaded seating area, **Latrobe Waterworks Park,** is a peaceful spot to munch on the edibles you might have purchased. You might also enjoy visiting during annual events like the New Orleans Roadfood Festival in late March and the Creole Tomato Festival in early June.

© DANIEL MARTONE

Visitors relish a pleasant afternoon in the French Market's Latrobe Waterworks Park.

GALLIER HOUSE

1132 Royal St., 504/525-5661, www.hgghh.org

HOURS: Mon. and Thurs.-Fri. 10 A.M.-3 P.M., Tues. and Wed. by appt., Sat. noon-4 P.M.

COST: $12 adult, $10 senior, student, and child 8-18, free under 8

On the riverside of Royal Street stands the Gallier House, part of a museum that also includes the Hermann-Grima House on St. Louis Street. The former home of famed New Orleans architect James Gallier Jr., who designed the house in 1857, it's filled with exquisite furnishings from the 19th century, plus elaborate faux marble and faux bois (wood painted very carefully to resemble a more precious type of wood). Considered one of the more accurately restored landmarks in New Orleans, the two-story stucco facade is noted for its ornate balustrade balcony and slender, finely crafted columns. The 45-minute guided tour, which is available on the hour, includes a look at the Victorian home, the on-site carriageway, the carefully restored slave quarters, and a finely maintained garden, which sparkles with fountains and slate walks.

HERMANN-GRIMA HOUSE

820 St. Louis St., 504/525-5661, www.hgghh.org

HOURS: Mon.-Tues. and Thurs.-Fri. 10 A.M.-3 P.M., Wed. by appt., Sat. noon-4 P.M.

COST: $12 adult, $10 senior, student, and child 8-18, free under 8

Just off rowdy Bourbon Street, you'll encounter one of the Quarter's best house-museums: the Hermann-Grima House, a steep-roofed Federal-style mansion built in 1831 and resembling the sort you'd more often see in Savannah or other old cities of British origin. One unusual feature is the Quarter's only horse stable, adjacent to the charming courtyard garden. The house, which is run by the same people who operate the Gallier House on Royal Street, offers informative, on-the-hour tours that reveal the customary lifestyle enjoyed by prosperous Creole families between 1830 and 1860.

For an even greater understanding of dining and entertaining traditions in 19th-century

New Orleans, consider taking an intimate **Creole cooking class** (504/274-0741, Oct.–May by appt., $150 pp) in the restored, open-hearth kitchen (the only functional one left in the French Quarter, a holdover from the home's antebellum days). These half-day classes, which are limited to eight participants at a time, entail a hands-on lesson in preparing a seasonal, multicourse Creole breakfast and lunch, plus a formal, wine-paired Creole luncheon in the lovely courtyard. If you have less time to spare, opt for the two-hour **hearth demonstration lunch** (Thurs. 11 A.M.–2 P.M., $45 pp), which can accommodate up to 15 guests at once. Whichever class you choose, you'll be treated to a guided tour of the property and will be able to take home any recipes of the food you've tasted.

◖ THE HISTORIC NEW ORLEANS COLLECTION

533 Royal St., 504/523-4662, www.hnoc.org
HOURS: Tues.-Sat. 9:30 A.M.-4:30 P.M., Sun. 10:30 A.M.-4:30 P.M.
COST: Free, though tours cost $5 pp

Amid the art galleries of Royal Street lies one of the city's most underrated attractions. Established in 1966 by avid collectors General L. Kemper Williams and his wife, Leila, this complex includes the Greek Revival–style **Merieult House.** Built in 1792, the house now contains the **Williams Gallery,** featuring rotating history exhibits, and the **Louisiana History Galleries,** 11 chambers that each explore a specific period of the state's history (from the French Colonial years to the 20th century) using authentic maps, books, furniture, and artwork.

From the courtyard (which, though lovely, can be a bit stifling on a warm day), you'll notice a few other buildings, such as the Spanish Colonial–style **Counting House** and the three-story Maisonette, which now contain administrative offices. One exception is the **Williams Residence,** an 1880s Italianate townhouse that the museum founders occupied until 1963. Docent-led tours (Tues.–Sat. 10 A.M., 11 A.M., 2 P.M., and 3 P.M., Sun. 11 A.M., 2 P.M., and 3 P.M.) enable you to view this room-by-room

survey of how an upscale early 20th-century home would have been furnished, including several antiques, various watercolors, and vintage maps of New Orleans.

This impressive complex of interconnected buildings also includes three structures on Toulouse Street: a former banking house, a Creole cottage, and the two-story **Louis Adam House,** where Tennessee Williams once boarded. While here, you should also make time for the impressive museum shop, where you'll find everything from local novels and history books to vintage maps and iconic jewelry.

JACKSON BREWERY

600 Decatur St., 504/566-7245,
www.jacksonbrewery.com
HOURS: Daily 10 A.M.-7 P.M.
COST: Free, though dining and shopping costs apply

On the riverside of Decatur, not far from Jackson Square, stands the regal Jackson Brewery building, once the largest independent brewery in the South. German architect Dietrich Einsiedel designed the fanciful structure, with its imposing central tower, in 1891. The brewery closed in the 1970s, and the four-story building, with expansive views of the river, has since been restored as the **Shops at Jax Brewery,** a collection of varied bars, restaurants, and shops, mainly selling clothing, jewelry, artwork, and other gifts.

◖ JACKSON SQUARE

Decatur St. btwn. St. Peter St. and St. Ann St.,
504/658-3200, www.jackson-square.com
HOURS: Daily sunrise-sunset
COST: Free

Originally known as the Place d'Armes, Jackson Square was renamed in honor of the seventh U.S. president, Andrew Jackson, who led the United States to victory during the Battle of New Orleans. A 14-foot-tall bronze statue of Jackson serves as the square's centerpiece and ranks among the city's favorite photo ops.

Filled with flowers, trees, benches, and grassy areas, Jackson Square is a wonderful place to sit and read a newspaper, eat a muffuletta from one of the nearby cafés, and absorb the oldest section of New Orleans. (Note that no dogs or bikes are permitted; littering, soliciting, and feeding the birds are also illegal.) More often than not, you'll spy mimes, artists, fortune tellers, musicians, and other entertainers along the sidewalks that fringe Jackson Square, sometimes even after the park has closed at night. Horse-drawn carriages usually line Decatur Street, awaiting tourists for guided excursions through the Quarter.

This picturesque greenspace is surrounded by several historic buildings, including the gorgeous **St. Louis Cathedral,** as well as the **Cabildo, Arsenal,** and **Presbytère.** Along the northeastern and southwestern sides of the square lie the **Pontalba Apartments,** the oldest apartment buildings in the country. Here, you'll find the historic **1850 House** and, on the lower levels, several eateries and worthwhile shops, including food lovers' emporiums like Creole Delicacies and an outpost of the Tabasco Country Store.

JEAN LAFITTE NATIONAL HISTORICAL PARK AND PRESERVE

419 Decatur St., 504/589-3882 or 504/589-2636, www.nps.gov/jela

HOURS: Daily 9 A.M.–5 P.M.

COST: Free, though donations are accepted

A couple of blocks upriver from Jackson Square, you'll reach the main office of Jean Lafitte National Historical Park and Preserve, which was established in 1978 to preserve a variety of natural and historical resources and properties throughout the Mississippi River Valley. The park actually has six distinct units, this one and two others in metro New Orleans (Chalmette Battlefield just east of the city and Barataria Preserve on the West Bank) and three in Cajun Country that deal with the history and culture of Cajun immigration; these latter sites are in Thibodaux, Lafayette, and Eunice. The center's best feature is its one-hour walking tour along the riverfront, given at 9:30 each morning and led by a knowledgeable ranger. These free tours are limited to just

25 people and fill up quickly at busy times; availability is on a first-come, first-served basis. Other special programs and lectures are held at different times of the year, and rotating exhibits in the visitors center focus on various historical and cultural aspects of New Orleans and Louisiana.

On a small grassy island along Decatur Street, across from the park's visitors center, note the dignified statue of the man who first plotted New Orleans at the site of the present-day French Quarter, Jean Baptiste Le Moyne, Sieur de Bienville, brother of the explorer Pierre Le Moyne, Sieur d'Iberville. Jean Baptiste's decision in 1699 to establish a fortification on this miserable swampy spot raised the skepticism of many, but of course, New Orleans has flourished to become one of the world's most charming (yet still swampiest and at times miserably hottest) cities.

LALAURIE MANSION

1140 Royal St.

HOURS: Closed to the public

This curious gray house is worth mentioning if only because of its dark history. Routinely included on the walking ghost tours offered in the French Quarter, this notoriously haunted mansion was once owned by the twice-widowed Madame Delphine Macarty de Lopez Blanque and her third husband, Dr. Louis LaLaurie. After moving into this home in 1832, the couple soon became the toast of the town, dazzling their peers with lavish parties. When a fire broke out in the mansion in 1834, the neighbors made a horrifying discovery: several tortured, starving slaves chained in the attic. The neighbors were further enraged to learn that some of Delphine's slaves had died under mysterious circumstances. To evade punishment, Delphine and her family fled to Europe, where she died several years later. Over the ensuing decades, the building has served as headquarters of the Union Army, a gambling house, and the home of Nicolas Cage. Through all of its incarnations, however, the LaLaurie Mansion has often been the source of ghostly tales.

the LaLaurie Mansion at Royal and Gov. Nicholls Streets

MADAME JOHN'S LEGACY

632 Dumaine St., 504/568-6968 or 800/568-6968, www.crt.state.la.us/museum

HOURS: Currently closed to the public

Madame John's Legacy is a fine example of a Louisiana French Colonial–style (or Creole) home from the late 18th century. The house was built to replace a home lost in the great fire of 1788. It survived the next, smaller fire of 1794 and is today one of just a few remaining pre-1800s buildings in the Quarter. The historic complex, which fronts Dumaine Street, comprises three buildings: a main house, a two-story *garçonniere,* and a kitchen with a cook's living quarters. Now part of the Louisiana State Museum, the home is currently closed to the public, but once it reopens, tours of the main house—the only building typically open to the public—will be self-guided.

NEW ORLEANS JAZZ NATIONAL HISTORICAL PARK

916 N. Peters St., 504/589-4841, www.nps.gov/jazz

HOURS: Tues.-Sun. 9 A.M.-5 P.M.

COST: Free

While the official headquarters of New Orleans Jazz National Historical Park are technically located at 419 Decatur Street—the same address as those of Jean Lafitte National Historical Park and Preserve—the visitors center is actually situated in the French Market. Here, you can participate in weekly ranger-led programs, from lectures to musical demonstrations that explore the origin, development, and evolution of New Orleans–style jazz. In addition, you can pick up brochures featuring an 11-stop tour of historic jazz sites in the Crescent City as well as the **Jazz Walk of Fame** in Algiers Point, a line of old-fashioned lampposts that highlight several jazz greats, from Louis Armstrong to Louis Prima. Self-guided audio tours are also available through the website or by phoning 504/613-4062.

Moreover, the park oversees jazz-related exhibits at the **Old U.S. Mint** (400 Esplanade Ave., Tues.–Sun. 10 A.M.–4:30 P.M.) as well as jazz exhibits, concerts, and workshops at **Perseverance Hall** (Sat. 9 A.M.–5 P.M.), a historic building in Louis Armstrong Park that was once a Masonic Lodge, the oldest in Louisiana, and later a multiuse event venue where African American jazz musicians would perform for black and white audiences. Today, Perseverance Hall is home to the national historical park's *Music for All Ages* program (Sat. 11 A.M.–noon), during which kids can bring their own instruments, perform with a professional brass band, and learn the skills and etiquette required for such an endeavor.

NEW ORLEANS MUSICAL LEGENDS PARK

311 Bourbon St., 504/888-7608, www.neworleansmusicallegends.com

HOURS: Sun.-Thurs. 8 A.M.-10 P.M., Fri.-Sat. 8 A.M.-midnight

COST: Free

While strolling down Bourbon, note the small New Orleans Musical Legends Park, which was established in 1999 and now contains several bronze statues honoring some of the city's most legendary performers, including jazz

© DANIEL MARTONE

clarinetist Pete Fountain, trumpet greats Al Hirt and Louis Prima, pianists Fats Domino and Ronnie Kole, and nightclub singer Chris Owens. Additional statues, busts, and plaques will be added through the years as notable jazz musicians are inducted. Besides the statues, the park includes a lovely fountain, several tables and chairs, and a few food stalls, selling surprisingly tasty fare, from gumbo to beignets. So, grab some food, find a seat, and listen to live jazz music (daily 10 A.M.–close), courtesy of Steamboat Willie.

◖ THE NEW ORLEANS SCHOOL OF COOKING

524 St. Louis St., 504/525-2665 or 800/237-4841, www.neworleansschoolofcooking.com

HOURS: Daily 9 A.M.–6 P.M., though class times vary

COST: Varies depending on the class

While most visit New Orleans to taste its one-of-a-kind food, it's also possible to learn how to make such wonderful cuisine. Since 1980, the New Orleans School of Cooking, situated in a renovated, 19th-century molasses warehouse, has invited local Cajun and Creole chefs to teach residents and visitors alike the basics of Louisiana-style cooking, sharing history and tall tales along the way. The popular demonstration lunch classes (Mon.–Sat. 10 A.M.–12:30 P.M. and 2–4 P.M., Sun. 10 A.M.–12:30 P.M. $24–29) include generous samplings of the demonstrated menu items, plus recipes and refreshments.

Private three-hour cooking classes ($125 pp) are also available, provided there are at least eight students in attendance. Besides the meal itself, beverages, recipes, and a souvenir apron are all included. Dishes may include gumbo, jambalaya, shrimp Creole, pralines, bread pudding, or other local staples. Of course, non-chefs can still peruse the on-site **Louisiana General Store,** which offers a plethora of Cajun and Creole products, from cookbooks and cookware to spices and gift baskets.

OLD URSULINE CONVENT

1100 Chartres St., 504/529-3040, www.stlouiscathedral.org/convent.html

the Old Ursuline Convent, opposite the Beauregard-Keyes House

© DANIEL MARTONE

HOURS: Mon.-Sat. 10 A.M.-4 P.M.

COST: $5 adult, $4 senior, $3 student, free under 6

The lovely Old Ursuline Convent is believed to be the oldest extant building in the Mississippi River Valley. King Louis XV of France established the Old Ursuline Convent in 1745 to house the Ursuline nuns who first came to New Orleans in the late 1720s, making them the first nuns to establish a permanent foothold in what is now the United States. This convent was their second home, completed in 1753; they moved to a new space at 4580 Dauphine Street in 1824, and then to their present Uptown home, at 2635 State Street, in 1912. In those early decades, the convent housed everyone from French orphans and wounded British soldiers to exiled Acadians and the city's destitute masses. During the early 1800s, the nuns conducted a school for the education of daughters of wealthy Louisiana plantation owners.

The convent is part of a large ecclesiastic complex called the Archbishop Antoine Blanc Memorial, owned by the Catholic Archdiocese of New Orleans. The entire complex—which includes the adjacent gardens, the attached **St. Mary's Church,** and several related outbuildings—is named for the first archbishop of New Orleans, Antoine Blanc, who held this post from 1850 to his death in 1860. Today, a museum is open for self-guided tours. Incidentally, the Ursuline Academy still functions at the convent's State Street locale and is the oldest continuously operated school for women in the United States.

OLD U.S. MINT

400 Esplanade Ave., 504/568-6993 or 800/568-6968, www.crt.state.la.us/museum

HOURS: Tues.-Sun. 10 A.M.-4:30 P.M.

COST: $6 adult, $5 senior and student, free under 13

Fashioned with a granite facade and made of stucco and Mississippi River mud brick, the Old U.S. Mint was constructed in 1835 at the behest of the U.S. president Andrew Jackson. This is the only building in the country to have functioned as both a U.S. and a Confederate mint. It also housed Confederate troops for a time during the Civil War. With the Union occupation, the mint was shut down until Reconstruction, at which time it resumed service.

In 1909, the mint was decommissioned, and in 1981, it was added to the state museum system. Today, it contains a fascinating variety of exhibits, including a chronicle of the building's history as a mint, an exploration of the city's jazz legacy, a display of Newcomb pottery, and a state historical center and archive. There's also a large tribute to Louis Armstrong, as well as three colorful murals depicting New Orleans's fabled Storyville red-light district, one of the city's cultivators of jazz. In addition, a small display is dedicated to the building's architect, William Strickland, who trained under famous Greek Revival architect Benjamin Latrobe and who also designed the Tennessee State Capitol, as well as the mints in Charlotte and Philadelphia.

PONTALBA APARTMENTS AND THE 1850 HOUSE

523 St. Ann St., 504/568-6968 or 800/568-6968, www.crt.state.la.us/museum

HOURS: Tues.-Sun. 10 A.M.-4:30 P.M.

COST: $3 adult, $2 senior and student, free under 13

The Pontalba Apartments were commissioned by Baroness Micaela Almonester de Pontalba in 1849 (the lower building, on St. Ann) and 1851 (the upper building, on St. Peter). She had inherited the land from her father, Don Andres Almonester, the man who had financed the Cabildo, Presbytère, and St. Louis Cathedral after the devastating fire of 1788.

Each row of buildings, when it first opened, contained 16 separate houses on the upper levels and a series of shops on the lower levels. After the Civil War, Jackson Square and its environs began to deteriorate and the Pontalba Apartments functioned as rather unfashionable tenements. In 1921, William Ratcliffe Irby bought the Lower Pontalba Building and willed the property to the Louisiana State Museum. The grand old townhouses were subdivided into smaller apartments.

The 1850 House was restored in 1955 by the museum to serve as an example of a fine New Orleans townhouse of the 1850s. Most of the interior furnishings were donated to the museum but are authentic to the exact period. Today, the 1850 House is a small but popular museum, which also has an excellent book and gift shop. The actual apartment occupies the two floors above the shop. Visitors can stand at edges of the doorways and peer into the rooms, gaining a sense of an 1850s row house owned by a family of somewhat considerable means. Plaques on the third floor detail the lives of the home's inhabitants from 1850 to 1861.

THE PRESBYTÈRE
751 Chartres St., 504/568-6968 or 800/568-6968, www.crt.state.la.us/museum
HOURS: Tues.-Sun. 10 A.M.-4:30 P.M.
COST: $6 adult, $5 senior and student, free under 13

Built in 1797 as a home for the priests of St. Louis Cathedral, and standing just on the downriver side of it, the two-story Presbytère on Jackson Square bears a structural resemblance to the Cabildo. It was never used for its intended purpose, as its financier, Don Andres Almonester (a Spaniard of considerable means who also funded the Cabildo and St. Louis Cathedral), died before it was completed. The new U.S. government eventually completed it and used it to house the Louisiana state courts during the 19th century.

Like the Cabildo, it became part of the Louisiana State Museum in 1911. It houses a colorful permanent exhibit on the history of Mardi Gras both in the city and the state. Videos and audiotapes and a wide array of artifacts detail how Louisianians have celebrated Carnival through the years and how this event has grown to become one of the most popular festivals in the world. You'll also encounter *Living with Hurricanes: Katrina and Beyond,* a heartbreaking yet inspiring exhibit that utilizes photographs, eyewitness accounts, artifacts, and multimedia displays to explore the history and science of hurricanes. In particular, you'll learn more about the loss and destruction caused by Hurricanes Katrina and Rita in 2005, as well as the service, solidarity, and resilience demonstrated by residents and others in their aftermath.

ST. LOUIS CATHEDRAL
615 Père Antoine Alley, 504/525-9585, www.stlouiscathedral.org
HOURS: Vary daily
COST: Free, though donations are accepted

The lakeside end of Jackson Square is dominated by the St. Louis Cathedral, one of the most magnificent cathedrals in the United States. The current building was constructed in 1794 in the Spanish style, with two round spires rising from the facade, and then virtually rebuilt and remodeled in 1849. Simpler churches have stood on this site since the 1720s, not longer after the arrival of the French explorer Jean Baptiste Le Moyne, Sieur de Bienville, who established New Orleans as a permanent settlement in 1718. During the 1849 remodel, huge steeples were added to the two symmetrical round towers, and the building has received additional restorations over the years. The cathedral was designated a minor basilica in 1964 by Pope Paul VI. Mass is held every day, and the gift shop is open 9 A.M.–6 P.M. daily. Visitors are welcome to take a guided tour of the property; as an alternative, simply wander inside and explore the gorgeous architecture, including kaleidoscopic stained-glass windows, on your own. Just keep in mind that this is an actual church, so be respectful of those who have come for prayer and quiet reflection. Also, if you're in town during December, consider attending one of the free jazz concerts on offer here.

VOODOO SPIRITUAL TEMPLE
828 N. Rampart St., 504/522-9627, www.voodoospiritualtemple.org
HOURS: Mon.-Sat. 10:30 A.M.-6 P.M., Sun. 11 A.M.-2 P.M.
COST: Free, though donations are accepted

Operated by Priestess Miriam, this center of voodoo worship and healing offers voodoo services, consultations, rituals, lectures, and workshops, as well as city tours. An on-site gift shop, meanwhile, sells handcrafted voodoo dolls, talismans, gris-gris and mojo bags, blessed candles, aroma oils, herbs and incense, art and jewelry, and books and CDs related to voodoo. The Voodoo Spiritual Temple is a

© DANIEL MARTONE

the Voodoo Spiritual Temple on N. Rampart Street

frequent stop on other city tours, like the walking tour hosted by the New Orleans Historic Voodoo Museum; while on such tours, you'll typically be able to experience the temple's impressive altar room, filled with spiritual altars of all kinds. Be respectful; these altars constitute a strictly "look but don't touch" attraction. Be aware, too, that the hours of the temple are flexible, so don't be surprised to find the front door locked at random times.

WOLDENBERG RIVERFRONT PARK
Mississippi River btwn. Canal St. and St. Peter St.
HOURS: Daily 24 hours
COST: Free

Named for philanthropist Malcolm Woldenberg (1896–1982), lovely Woldenberg Riverfront Park is a 16-acre greenspace and redbrick promenade that extends along the riverfront from the aquarium to Jackson Brewery. It's actually along this stretch that Jean Baptiste Le Moyne, Sieur de Bienville, established the site of New Orleans in 1718. Crape myrtle and magnolia trees provide shade over the numerous park benches, affording romantic views of the Mississippi River, the docked paddlewheelers, and Algiers Point on the West Bank. One of the original quays, **Toulouse Street Wharf,** is home to the palatial excursion riverboat, the **Steamboat Natchez.** Fringing the park is the **Moon Walk,** a wooden boardwalk that stretches along the riverfront, between St. Philip and St. Peter Streets. It was named for the New Orleans mayor who had it constructed in the 1970s, Moon Landrieu (father of U.S. Senator Mary Landrieu). Musicians, tourists, and homeless individuals are all drawn to this scenic spot; just be aware that it's often a little sketchy at night.

Within Woldenberg Park (which incidentally serves as one of the main sites for the annual French Quarter Festival) you'll also spot several significant sculptures. The stunning, 20-foot-tall **Monument to the Immigrant** statue, for instance, was created by noted New Orleans artist Franco Alessandrini, who fashioned it from white Carrara marble; it commemorates

New Orleans's role as one of the nation's most prolific immigrant ports throughout the 19th century. Other sculptures of distinction include Robert Schoen's bizarre *Old Man River,* an 18-foot tribute to the Mississippi River carved from 17 tons of Carrara marble, and John Scott's *Ocean Song,* a series of eight 10-foot-tall, stainless-steel pyramids. My favorite, however, is the mesmerizing *New Orleans Holocaust Memorial* (www.holocaustmemorial.us), created by Israeli artist Yaacov Agam, dedicated in 2003, and featuring nine colorful panels, which meld to form different images depending on where you're standing.

Faubourg Marigny and Bywater   Map 2

CELEBRATION DISTILLATION
2815 Frenchmen St., 504/945-9400, www.neworleansrum.com
HOURS: Mon.-Fri. 9 A.M.-5 P.M., Sat. 1:30-5:30 P.M.
COST: $10 pp

Considered the oldest premium rum distillery in the country, Celebration Distillation is home to Old New Orleans Rum, a spirit made with Louisiana's own blackstrap molasses. If you're curious about the entire distillation process, consider taking a guided tour (Mon.–Fri. noon, 2 P.M., and 4 P.M., Sat. 2 P.M. and 4 P.M.), which usually lasts about 45 minutes and concludes with a visit to the on-site tasting room, where you'll sometimes have the chance to sample rum varieties that have yet to be put on the market. The distillery doesn't lie within walking distance of the French Quarter; you'll have to drive, take a cab, or hop aboard the shuttle, which departs from the French Market at 11:45 A.M., 1:45 P.M., and 3:45 P.M. Monday–Friday. Reservations are required for the pickup service, though not for the actual tour; still, you should always phone ahead just to make sure that tour times haven't been canceled due to private events.

MUSICIANS' VILLAGE
Alvar St. and N. Johnson St., 617/354-2736, www.nola-musiciansvillage.org
HOURS: Daily 24 hours
COST: Free

Although it feels strange to promote a private residential neighborhood as an attraction, I'd be remiss if I didn't acknowledge the hard work and tireless dedication of the New Orleans Area Habitat for Humanity in creating the Musicians' Village. Roughly bordered by Alvar, North Derbigny, Mazant, and North Johnson Streets in the Upper Ninth Ward, this post-Katrina rebuilding effort has helped to reconstruct a community stricken by that terrible hurricane and preserve part of the city's musical culture. Conceived by Harry Connick Jr. and Branford Marsalis—and supported by such celebrities as Sting and Clint Eastwood—the Musicians' Village now consists of 72 colorful single-family homes and the **Ellis Marsalis Center for Music,** named in honor of the New Orleans native, legendary jazz pianist, and patriarch of the Marsalis clan. The recently completed center features musical programs and performances. If you choose to drive through this area and see, as the website says, "how a meaningful vision and focused efforts can provide immediate relief as well as long-term hope for the survival of a great city and many of its most essential citizens," just remember that this is a residential neighborhood, and should be respected as such.

Central Business and Arts Districts Map 3

◖ BLAINE KERN'S MARDI GRAS WORLD

1380 Port of New Orleans Pl., 504/361-7821 or 866/307-7026, www.mardigrasworld.com

HOURS: Daily 9:30 A.M.–4:30 P.M.

COST: $19.95 adult, $15.95 senior, $12.95 child 2-11, free under 2

The top reason that families venture to the Port of New Orleans is to visit Blaine Kern's Mardi Gras World, the public face of world-renowned Blaine Kern Studios—which, since 1947, has been the largest builder of Carnival sculptures and parade floats in the country. Formerly situated in Algiers, Mardi Gras World is now across the river on the East Bank, where visitors can take a guided tour of the facility. The tour includes a stroll amid kaleidoscopic floats, the observation of working artists and artisans, and a video about the history of the city's Mardi Gras celebration. Though Mardi Gras may take place over a relatively short period late each winter, this place hums with activity every day of the year—with the exception of Easter Day, Thanksgiving Day, Christmas Day, and, somewhat ironically, Mardi Gras Day.

GALLIER HALL

545 St. Charles Ave., www.nola.gov

HOURS: Mon.-Fri. 9 A.M.–5 P.M.

COST: Free

Gallier Hall, a hulking white Greek Revival–style building, was named for its architect, James Gallier Sr., who designed and erected the structure between 1845 and 1853. Boasting massive Ionic columns, the stunning, three-story marble structure served as the New Orleans City Hall from the mid-19th through mid-20th centuries. Today, it's used as a special-events facility and reception hall; it's also the spot where the city mayor greets the royal courts of Mardi Gras krewes like Zulu and Rex. Several important people have been laid in state here, including Confederate President Jefferson Davis, Confederate General P. G. T. Beauregard, and R&B musician Ernie K-Doe. Guided tours are available by appointment.

LEE CIRCLE

St. Charles Ave. and Howard Ave.

HOURS: Daily 24 hours

COST: Free

Formerly known as Tivoli Place, Lee Circle is now the hub for a small arts and museum district that has evolved on the streets just downriver from here since the mid-1990s. This is the one regal traffic circle in downtown New Orleans, and it imparts a slightly formal, urban air—a hint of Paris or London. Rising high over the traffic circle, which is a stop on the St. Charles streetcar line, stands a magnificent bronze statue of Robert E. Lee, the Confederate Civil War general; it sits atop a graceful marble column, the entire memorial rising 60 feet over the circle. Depending on which direction you're coming from, it serves as a gateway to the Garden District or the CBD.

MERCEDES-BENZ SUPERDOME

1500 Sugar Bowl Dr., 504/587-3822 or 800/756-7074, www.superdome.com

HOURS: Vary depending on the event

COST: Varies depending on the event

Known until recently as the Louisiana Superdome, this massive, 52-acre structure is home to NFL's New Orleans Saints, Tulane Green Wave football, college football's Allstate Sugar Bowl, as well as major concerts and some of the city's most popular annual events. The city commissioned construction of the dome in 1966; however, construction didn't begin until 1971, finishing four years later. The gargantuan arena is the largest domed stadium in the world, holding more than 76,000 fans for football. The roof alone covers about 13 acres and rises to a height of about 273 feet (nearly as tall as a 30-story building).

In the immediate wake of Hurricane Katrina, the Superdome was more infamous for its role as an evacuation center during the aftermath of the storm. The roof and interior were completely refurbished in 2006, in time

THE MAGIC OF BLAINE KERN

© LAURA MARTONE

the original Mardi Gras World buildings in Algiers

For many years, families have flocked to **Blaine Kern's Mardi Gras World** (www.mardigrasworld.com). This vibrant attraction offers visitors a behind-the-scenes glimpse at the magic of Mardi Gras, one of the city's oldest traditions. Here, you'll see a variety of colorful floats and get the chance to watch the artists and artisans of **Blaine Kern Studios** (www.kernstudios.com) hard at work.

As the name indicates, the heart and soul behind Blaine Kern's Mardi Gras World and Blaine Kern Studios is Blaine Kern himself – the man known as Mister Mardi Gras. Born in 1927, Blaine grew up on the West Bank of the Mississippi River. His early interest in the arts was inspired by his proximity to New Orleans as well as the vocation of his father, Roy, a sign painter who survived the Depression by painting names on the bows of freighters.

When Blaine's mother was hospitalized, he offset the family's medical bills by painting a mural in the hospital – a mural that captured the attention of a surgeon who was also the captain of a Mardi Gras krewe. Blaine began designing floats soon afterward and was eventually hired to fashion a complete parade. In 1947, he established Blaine Kern Studios in Algiers and, over time, became the Big Easy's leading parade creator, working with Rex, Zulu, Bacchus, and all the legendary krewes.

Following his travels to Italy, where he was impressed by the extravagant animation and prop concepts that distinguished the European style of float building, Blaine began to embrace the monumental scale and lavish ornamentation that mark contemporary Mardi Gras parades. Today, Blaine Kern Studios produces floats and props for more than 40 New Orleans parades, including Endymion and Orpheus, as well as pageants around the world. In addition, Kern props and sculptures enhance themed environments in Walt Disney World, Universal Studios, Japan's Toho Park, and many other entertainment centers around the world.

Indeed, Blaine Kern is largely responsible for the extravaganza that the city's Carnival season has become. No wonder he's universally recognized as Mister Mardi Gras!

for the Superdome to host the Saints' 2006–2007 season opener—which the Saints won handily over the Atlanta Falcons, with a crowd of more than 70,000 "Who Dats" cheering. In 2011, the Superdome underwent an $85 million renovation that completely modernized the facility, adding three elevators, more than 3,000 new seats, extra restrooms, and other amenities.

THE NATIONAL WWII MUSEUM

945 Magazine St., 504/528-1944,
www.nationalww2museum.org
HOURS: Daily 9 A.M.–5 P.M.
COST: $19 adult, $15 senior, $9 student and child 5-12, free under 5

One of the nation's most exalted historians, the late Stephen Ambrose, founded the National WWII Museum here in the early 1990s. Ambrose, a professor at the University of New Orleans, lived in New Orleans until his death in 2002. He is best known for such riveting World War II histories as *Band of Brothers,*

© LAURA MARTONE

The National WWII Museum, perhaps the CBD's most impressive attraction

The Wild Blue, D-Day, Citizen Soldiers and *The Victors.*

The museum opened to the public on June 6, 2000, the 56th anniversary of the amphibious World War II invasion. This is the only museum in the United States dedicated to this event, which involved more than a million Americans. It may seem a random location for such a museum, but the Andrew Higgins factory, which now houses the museum, built ships during World War II, including some of the very vehicles that transported infantrymen to Normandy.

A museum visit can be an all-day (or multi-day) affair; after all, it might take that long to absorb the enormous collection of exhibits documenting the Allied victory in World War II, not to mention watching the immersive 4-D, Tom Hanks–narrated documentary *Beyond All Boundaries* (Sun.–Thurs. 10 A.M.–4 P.M., Fri.–Sat. 10 A.M.–5 P.M., $11 adult, $9 senior, $8 student and child 5–12, $5 child under 5) in the new 250-seat **Solomon Victory Theater.** If you have time, consider having a meal at the on-site, John Besh–helmed restaurant, the **American Sector,** or an old-fashioned dinner theater experience in the **Stage Door Canteen.**

SCRAP HOUSE

Convention Center Blvd. and John Churchill Chase St., www.sallyheller.com
HOURS: Daily 24 hours
COST: Free

As you drive past the enormous Ernest N. Morial Convention Center, keep an eye out for the colorful sculpture that's simply known as *Scrap House.* Completed by artist Sally Heller in 2008 and fashioned from ordinary materials and recycled elements (wood, wallpaper, oil drums, and solar lights), this outdoor installation resembles a denuded tree that's cradling a ramshackle house. Not surprisingly, this powerful yet whimsical piece is meant to serve as a monument to Mother Nature's unpredictable powers, inspired as Heller was by the remnants of houses and other cultural debris left in the wake of Hurricane Katrina in 2005.

ST. PATRICK'S CHURCH

724 Camp St., 504/525-4413, www.oldstpatricks.org
HOURS: Vary daily
COST: Free, though donations are accepted

Not far from Lafayette Square and Gallier Hall, St. Patrick's Church was the first place of worship built in the city's American Sector. The sector was so named because it's where 19th-century Americans built their homes and businesses in order to distinguish their lifestyles from those of the Creoles residing in the French Quarter, New Orleans's original settlement. Blessed by Bishop Antoine Blanc in 1838 and completed by 1840, St. Patrick's Church is one of the few structures left in a district once filled with magnificent mansions and high-end mercantile stores. When the parish was first established in 1833, the area was known as the Faubourg St. Mary; the church itself developed from a need for the Americans, many of whom were Irish, to worship in a structure as noteworthy as the French Quarter's St. Louis Cathedral. In the early 1850s, it was this stunning church where Bishop Antoine Blanc received the pallium as the first Archbishop of New Orleans. Though severely damaged by a hurricane in 1915, the church has since been renovated several times. Today, this national historic landmark is celebrated not only for its historic significance but also for its lavishly ornate interior, high vaulted ceilings, majestic paintings, and fine stained-glass windows.

Garden District and Uptown   Map 4

AUDUBON PARK

St. Charles Ave. and Walnut St., 504/861-2537,
www.auduboninstitute.org
HOURS: Daily 5 A.M.-10 P.M.
COST: Free

Leafy Audubon Park (bounded by East Drive, St. Charles Avenue, Walnut Street, and River Drive) occupies the former estate of Etienne De Boré, New Orleans's first mayor. During the Civil War, the land alternately hosted a Confederate camp and a Union hospital. Afterwards, it became an activation site for the now-lauded Buffalo Soldiers who helped defend America's western frontier. In 1871, the city bought the swampy land, which became famous after hosting the World's Industrial and Cotton Centennial Exposition in 1884, Louisiana's first world's fair and a 100th-anniversary celebration of the first shipment of Louisiana cotton to a foreign port. At the festival, the park's grounds and buildings were lighted with electricity, just six years after Thomas Edison first began experimenting with electric light bulbs.

In 1886, city planners changed the property's name from Upper City Park to Audubon Park in honor of artist and ornithologist John James Audubon, who temporarily lived in both New Orleans and St. Francisville and painted many of his famous *Birds of America* illustrations while staying in Louisiana. By the turn of the 20th century, the city had commissioned landscape architect John Charles Olmsted—whose family firm had earned fame for its design of New York's Central Park—to redevelop the property into a world-class urban sanctuary. Today, this 340-acre spread features moss-covered oak trees, well-manicured lawns, a lovely lagoon containing an important bird rookery, and several recreational diversions, from a golf course to a paved 1.8-mile exercise trail. Audubon Park is a delightful spot for picnicking, strolling, and admiring the assortment of impressive statues, many of them depicting animals and set within the park's zoo, and many created by WPA artists during the 1930s.

AUDUBON ZOO

6500 Magazine St., 504/581-4629 or 800/774-7394,
www.auduboninstitute.org
HOURS: Tues.-Fri. 10 A.M.-4 P.M., Sat.-Sun. 10 A.M.-5 P.M.
COST: $16 adult, $13 senior and student, $11 child 2-12, free under 2

Below Magazine Street, toward the river, lies 58-acre Audubon Zoo, a significant part of the larger Audubon Park. Established in 1914, it

© DANIEL MARTONE

an Asian elephant at the Audubon Zoo

now contains historic buildings, notable sculptures, and nearly 2,000 animals from around the world. This relatively small zoo is a wonderful place to stroll with friends and family, watch the animals' antics (especially when the weather is mild), and explore verdant, overgrown gardens rife with just about every species of flora known to Louisiana.

Perhaps my favorite attraction is the award-winning **Louisiana Swamp** exhibit, the next best thing to taking a swamp tour and even better in one respect: You're guaranteed to see marsh wildlife up close and personal. The swamp exhibit is an actual re-creation of a Depression-era Cajun swamp settlement, complete with old bayou shacks and a trapper's cottage. In addition to learning about alligators, black bears, red foxes, raccoons, and other critters, you'll also see Spanish moss, cypress knees, and other flora common in the swamp. I always find it hard to leave this part of the zoo—the albino alligators never cease to amaze and the ever-frisky, endlessly entertaining river otters are delightful.

Another highlight of the zoo is the **Jaguar Jungle** exhibit, which re-creates a Mayan rainforest and includes two dignified yet powerful jaguars, along with toucans, anteaters, spider monkeys, and sloths. The display also features realistic reproductions of the stone carvings at famous Chichén Itzá and Copán archaeological sites.

Other crowd-pleasers include the giraffes in the African Savanna exhibit, a pair of nearly 400-pound white tigers in the Asian Domain, a huge Indonesian komodo dragon and other curious reptiles, several rather extroverted gorillas and orangutans, a variety of monkeys, entertaining elephant and sea lion presentations, plus the giant reptilian replicas at the relatively new **Dinosaur Adventure** ($4 pp). Kids especially love to run up and down the well-landscaped Monkey Hill, touch turtles and other animals along the Discovery Walk, experience interactive games inside the EarthLab, pet free-roaming goats and sheep in the Embraceable Zoo, and ride the **carousel** ($2 pp), which features 60 figures of endangered species. **Animal feedings** are also a big draw—especially involving the giraffes and gators—and these are scheduled throughout the day. You'll also find a free-flight aviary here, as well as a colorful flamingo exhibit, a South American exhibit, a wildlife theater, a narrated train excursion ($5), a seasonal splash park ($7 pp), and several gift shops, concession stands, cafés, and sno-ball carts.

If you're taking the St. Charles streetcar, disembark at the Audubon Park stop for both the park and the zoo. If you're coming by car, the zoo has plenty of free parking, though the lot and nearby grassy areas can fill up quickly during annual events like Boo at the Zoo and the Louisiana Swamp Fest, both of which are in the fall.

BREVARD-CLAPP HOUSE
1239 1st St.
HOURS: Closed to the public

Long celebrated as a haven for writers, New Orleans has inspired several famous American authors, not the least of which is Anne Rice, whose best-selling novel *Interview with a Vampire* (1976) put her on the literary map. Born in New Orleans on October 4, 1941, she lived in the Big Easy for the first 16 years of her life. Returning with her husband, Stan Rice, in 1978, she eventually moved into the Brevard-Clapp House, a stately Greek Revival and Italianate mansion in the Garden District. Built in 1857 by James Calrow and Charles Pride, this stunning structure was first home to a wealthy merchant named Albert Hamilton Brevard. In 1869, years after Brevard had passed away, the house was acquired by Reverend Emory Clapp, whose wife lived here until 1934.

The Rices called the Brevard-Clapp House home from 1989 to 2004 (though Stan passed away in 2002). During that time, it served as the inspiration for Mayfair Manor, the fictional home of Rice's Mayfair Witches. Rice, who became a fixture in the neighborhood, also bought and restored St. Elizabeth's Orphanage at 1314 Napoleon Avenue, a massive former boarding house and girls' orphanage built in 1865. Though Rice has since sold the orphanage and relocated to California, she will always be considered one of the city's finest literary assets.

LAFAYETTE CEMETERY NO. 1
1400 Washington Ave.
HOURS: Mon.-Fri. 7 A.M.-2:30 P.M., Sat. 7 A.M.-noon
COST: Free

Established in 1833, Lafayette Cemetery No. 1 is one of only a few "cities of the dead" in New Orleans that are relatively safe to explore, at least during the day. Bordered by Prytania Street, Washington Avenue, Coliseum Street, and 6th Street in the Garden District, the cemetery is especially popular with fans of Anne Rice's *The Vampire Chronicles* trilogy; it was featured in the movie *Interview with the Vampire.* Also featured in the film *Double Jeopardy,* the Lafayette Cemetery was once part of a plantation owned by the Livaudais family. As a cemetery, it has always been nonsegregated and nondenominational; you'll see the tombs of American merchants, African families, and German, Irish, Italian, English, Scottish, and Dutch immigrants, not to mention several Union and Confederate soldiers.

If visiting alone, be advised that the office is at 1427 6th Street. Honestly, though, taking a guided tour is preferable, especially for history buffs. Tours are offered by various companies, including **Save Our Cemeteries** (504/525-3377 or 888/721-7493, www.saveourcemeteries.org, $20 adult, free under 12), a nonprofit organization that preserves the city's burial grounds. The one-hour walks are held at 10:30 A.M. Monday through Saturday. Whether you come alone or with a group, please be respectful at all times; it is, after all, an active cemetery that still welcomes mourners nearly every day.

LOYOLA UNIVERSITY NEW ORLEANS
6363 St. Charles Ave., 504/865-3240 or 800/456-9652, www.loyno.edu
HOURS: Vary daily
COST: Free

Tulane University's most prominent neighbor, Loyola University faces St. Charles Avenue just opposite verdant Audubon Park; it's impossible to miss as you drive along St. Charles, whether via bike, vehicle, or streetcar. Established by the Jesuit order in 1904 as Loyola College, the school had been a long time in coming. The Jesuits were among the earliest settlers of New Orleans; a Jesuit chaplain even accompanied Pierre Le Moyne, Sieur d'Iberville, on his second expedition here. Credited with introducing the sugarcane crop to Louisiana, the Jesuits were sadly banned from the French colonies in 1763. After the Jesuit order was restored, however, the Bishop of New Orleans beseeched the French Jesuits to establish a Jesuit college here.

In 1849, despite concerns about New Orleans's yellow fever epidemic, Jesuit priests opened the College of the Immaculate Conception at Baronne and Common Streets in what is now the CBD. Though the college became a beloved institution, local Catholic leaders still longed for a school in a less-congested area. Following the 1884 World's Industrial and Cotton Centennial Exposition in Audubon Park, it became clear that the nearby Foucher Plantation—which was owned by Paul Foucher, the son-in-law of Etienne De Boré, New Orleans's first mayor—would make for an ideal location for a school. By 1904, Loyola College had opened, along with a Catholic college-prep academy; in 1911, the Jesuit schools in New Orleans were reorganized, and all college-prep students were sent to the College of the Immaculate Conception, paving the way for Loyola to become a full-fledged, private university in 1912. Over the years, it grew and expanded, eventually becoming one of the most well-respected universities in the South, open to all faiths and currently nurturing more than 4,900 students annually. Today, visitors are free to wander amid the school's stately redbrick buildings, built in the Tudor Gothic style; it's also not a bad place to catch concerts and sporting events.

MILTON H. LATTER MEMORIAL LIBRARY

5120 St. Charles Ave., 504/596-2625, www.nutrias.org
HOURS: Mon. and Wed. 9 A.M.-8 P.M., Tues. and Thurs. 9 A.M.-6 P.M., Sat. 10 A.M.-5 P.M., Sun. noon-5 P.M.
COST: Free

Besides being a delightful place to relax for a while, the art-filled Milton H. Latter Memorial Library is also a much-loved architectural landmark. Built in 1907, this enormous, Italianate–Beaux Arts mansion was home to a variety of curious residents, including Marguerite Clark, an American stage and silent film star. Born in Avondale, Ohio, in 1883, and known for such films as *The Prince and the Pauper* and *Uncle Tom's Cabin,* the diminutive, age-defying actress married Harry Palmerston Williams, a New Orleans–based businessman and plantation owner, in 1918. Their marriage lasted until Williams's death in a plane crash in 1936. Clark died only four years later of pneumonia, and both husband and wife are buried in the city's Metairie Cemetery. Following Clark's death, the gorgeous Uptown mansion was purchased by the Latter family, who bequeathed it to the city in 1948. Intended to commemorate the Latters' son, who had died in World War II, the stunning structure became a branch of the New Orleans Public Library and has beckoned both bibliophiles and architectural aficionados ever since.

ST. CHARLES STREETCAR

S. Carrollton Ave. and S. Claiborne Ave. to Canal St. and Carondelet St., 504/248-3900, www.norta.com
HOURS: Vary daily
COST: $1.25 one-way

No one should leave New Orleans without taking a ride on one of the city's famous, oft-photographed streetcars. While there are presently three separate lines—the St. Charles, the Canal Street, and the Riverfront—the most famous by far and most beloved by residents and tourists alike is the St. Charles line, which dates back to 1835 and has been featured in numerous films over the years, including *Runaway Jury* and *The Skeleton Key.* Because of the line's presence on the National Register of Historic Places, the olive-green Perley Thomas streetcars currently in use must be preserved as they looked in 1923, which makes for a historical riding experience. Complete with old-fashioned wooden seats, the St. Charles streetcar takes passengers from Canal Street, between the CBD and the French Quarter; past the historic homes, hotels, restaurants, and attractions

A historic streetcar rolls along St. Charles Avenue.

of oak-shaded St. Charles Avenue, including the Garden District, Loyola and Tulane Universities, and Audubon Park; to the restaurants, boutiques, and residential areas of South Carrollton Avenue. The line terminates at South Claiborne Avenue, a transfer point for the city's bus lines. A one-way ride on the St. Charles line, which runs 24 hours daily, lasts about 45 minutes and, in my opinion, is well worth the time.

ST. MARY'S ASSUMPTION CHURCH

2030 Constance St., 504/522-6748,
www.stalphonsusneworleans.com
HOURS: Vary daily
COST: Free, though donations are accepted

Roughly six blocks from lovely Coliseum Square stands the regal St. Mary's Assumption Church, one of several architectural landmarks in the Garden District. Despite suffering some damage during Hurricane Katrina, the church is still absolutely gorgeous—inside and out. Constructed between 1858 and 1866, this massive, German Baroque Revival–style

structure boasts an incredibly intricate facade, with several stunning, arched stained-glass windows. The interior is equally impressive, with a high, vaulted ceiling, ornate columns, and a hand-carved altar that was reportedly imported from Munich.

The history of this church is equally interesting. Prior to the American Civil War, the Garden District and the Irish Channel composed a separate town called Lafayette. In the early 1840s, when numerous German and Irish immigrants, many of whom were Catholic, arrived in this French-speaking area, Bishop Antoine Blanc asked a German-speaking Redemptorist priest, Father Peter Czackert, to minister to them. Initially, he rented a dance hall for services; eventually, though, a frame church, the first St. Mary's Assumption, was constructed on Josephine Street, becoming the state's first Catholic Church for Germans. By the late 1850s, the Redemptorists had built three permanent churches: St. Alphonsus, which served the Irish parishioners; St. Mary's Assumption, which replaced the frame church and served the German parishioners; and the Romanesque Notre Dame de Bon Secours, which was intended for the French-speaking Catholics but was ultimately damaged by a hurricane in 1918 and demolished seven years later.

Today, you can attend Mass at St. Mary's or simply come to hear the wonderful bells. At nearby **St. Alphonsus Church** (2025 Constance St., 504/524-8116, www.stalphonsusneworleans.org, Tues., Thurs., and Sat. 10 A.M.–2 P.M.) you can appreciate the historical art and ornate architecture, not to mention a permanent display about the history of Irish Catholic life in New Orleans. Just around the corner, you'll encounter the **National Shrine of Francis Xavier Seelos and Seelos Welcome Center** (919 Josephine St., 504/525-2495, www.seelos.org, Mon.–Fri. 9 A.M.–3 P.M., Sat. 10 A.M.–3:30 P.M.), a small museum dedicated to the heroic, ever-cheerful Redemptorist priest who came to New Orleans during the dreaded yellow fever epidemic and ministered tirelessly at St. Mary's, ultimately succumbing to the fever in 1867 at the age of 48.

TOURO SYNAGOGUE

4238 St. Charles Ave., 504/895-4843, www.tourosynagogue.com

HOURS: Vary daily

COST: Free, though donations are accepted

I paid my first visit to Touro Synagogue as a teenager, and despite all of the impressive religious institutions I'd seen before then, I remember being particularly moved by this magnificent edifice. The interior of the domed sanctuary is particularly stunning, with its beautiful stained-glass windows, stately altar, and tremendous organ.

The synagogue's history stretches back to 1828, when the Congregation Gates of Mercy was founded on North Rampart Street, becoming the first synagogue outside of America's original 13 colonies. In 1846, part of the congregation seceded to form the Congregation Dispersed of Judah. Following the yellow fever epidemic of the late 1870s, the two congregations reunited in 1881 and moved into a building on Carondelet Street. Eventually, the newly merged congregation took the name Touro Synagogue in honor of their benefactor, a Jewish merchant-philanthropist named Judah Touro. Touro, though born in Rhode Island, had spent much of his life in New Orleans. Besides being a benefactor of many Jewish, Catholic, and Protestant charities, he also served in the War of 1812 and founded Touro Infirmary, which still exists today.

Touro Synagogue joined the Reform movement in 1891, and the current sanctuary, designed by local architect Emile Weil, was dedicated on New Year's Day of 1909. Today, visitors are welcome to venture inside, particularly for events like the Jazz Fest Shabbat—a worship service that, for more than two decades, has combined Judaism and jazz. Free and open to the public, this popular Friday evening Sabbath service during the New Orleans Jazz & Heritage Festival has featured some of the city's most famous jazz musicians, including Allen Toussaint, Irma Thomas, Marcia Ball, and Kermit Ruffins.

TULANE UNIVERSITY

6823 St. Charles Ave., 504/865-5000, www.tulane.edu

HOURS: Vary daily

COST: Free

Whether you drive along St. Charles Avenue or hop aboard the historic streetcar, you're sure to spot the magnificent Tulane University on the northern side of the road, right next door to the city's Loyola University. This private nonsectarian research university began as the Medical College of Louisiana in 1834, the South's second-oldest medical school; the need for it was brought about in part by the city's constant struggles to contain deadly yellow fever epidemics. In 1847, it became the University of Louisiana, a public institution, but an enormous bequest by wealthy New Orleanian Paul Tulane allowed the university to be reorganized as a private university in 1884 and ultimately expand into a much more comprehensive facility; it was renamed Tulane in honor of this financial gift, which totaled more than $1 million in land, cash, and securities. In 1886, the women-only H. Sophie Newcomb Memorial College was established as part of the university; eight years later, the entire school moved to its present campus on St. Charles Avenue.

Over the ensuing decades, Tulane became one of the top schools in the South. In 2005, Hurricane Katrina resulted in the closure of the Newcomb College—or, rather, a merging of the two schools. Today, Tulane has more than 13,350 students, and the 110-acre Uptown campus includes more than 80 buildings. The older Tulane buildings are set along or near St. Charles and include several Romanesque structures of considerable architectural acclaim. It's a pretty campus in which to stroll, and it's also popular for its yearly schedule of affordable concerts and plays, including those offered during the summertime **New Orleans Shakespeare Festival.** Another worthy onsite stop is the **Newcomb Art Gallery,** a free art gallery that features some of the artwork

SIGHTS

produced at Newcomb College from the late 19th through the early 20th centuries.

URSULINE ACADEMY

2635 State St., 504/861-9150,
www.ursulineneworleans.org
HOURS: Vary daily
COST: Free

Established in 1727 by a dozen Ursuline nuns from France and part of the Sisters of the Order of Saint Ursula, the Ursuline Academy is distinctive for two reasons: It's the country's oldest continuously operating school for girls *and* the oldest Catholic school in the United States. Although the academy's first permanent location was the Old Ursuline Convent in the French Quarter, it relocated, without interruption, to Dauphine Street in 1824, before finally settling at its current spot near Loyola University in 1912. In 1924, a gilded statue was erected in the chapel here; the **National Shrine of Our Lady of Prompt Succor** (2701 State St.) commemorates the miraculous military victory of the Battle of New Orleans that took place during the War of 1812. In 1976, the shrine was declared a national historic landmark. Every year on January 8, Our Lady and her infant are honored by the Archbishop of New Orleans during a splendid High Mass.

VAN BENTHUYSEN-ELMS MANSION AND GARDENS

3029 St. Charles Ave., 504/895-9200,
www.elmsmansion.com
HOURS: By appt.
COST: Free

Amid the many elegant buildings along St. Charles Avenue stands this grand, Italianate-style mansion, which was built in 1869 for Watson Van Benthuysen II, a New Yorker who moved to New Orleans in the 1840s. During the American Civil War, Van Benthuysen (who was a relative of President Jefferson Davis by marriage), became an officer in the Confederate Army. Nicknamed the "Yankee in Gray," he earned prominence in New Orleans as both a wine and tobacco merchant as well as president of a streetcar company. Van

the Garden District's Van Benthuysen-Elms Mansion

© DANIEL MARTONE

Benthuysen died in his home in 1901; three decades later the mansion served as the German Consulate until the commencement of World War II. In 1852, the home was purchased by John Elms Sr., who at the time was the owner of the largest coin-operated amusement company in the South. Following his death in 1968, his relatives began hosting private functions here—a practice continued today by the third generation of the Elms family. The picturesque home is filled with antique furnishings, gold sconces, and ornamental cornices and is the site of weddings, corporate parties, and such; it's also available for private group tours.

WOMEN'S GUILD HOME

2504 Prytania St., 504/899-1945,

www.neworleansopera.org

HOURS: By appt.

COST: Free

Built in 1865 and formerly known as the Davis-Seebold Residence, this eye-catching, Greek Revival–style mansion became the home of the Women's Guild of the New Orleans Opera Association. It's particularly noted for its small octagonal tower, though the color scheme—all white with dark-green shutters—plus the manicured lawn and wrought-iron fencing all make for a lovely photograph. Furnished in 18th- and 19th-century European and American furniture, artwork, antiques, and collectibles, this well-appointed Garden District home is the frequent site of wedding ceremonies and receptions, though group tours are possible by appointment.

Tremé and Mid-City   Map 5

BASIN ST. STATION

501 Basin St., 504/293-2600, www.basinststation.com

HOURS: Daily 9 A.M.–5 P.M.

COST: Free

The massive building situated at Basin and St. Louis Streets looks as though two buildings have merged into one—the first made of red brick and the second a more modern canary yellow. Despite its incongruous appearance, Basin St. Station serves as a pseudo-gateway to the historic Faubourg Tremé neighborhood. Situated next to St. Louis Cemetery No. 1, which is famous as Marie Laveau's final resting place, the former New Orleans Terminal Company/Southern Railway Freight Office Building has been newly renovated and ultimately transformed into a cultural center. Built in 1904 in the Neoclassic style, the original building has been retained as the facade of the now partially new structure. The second and third floors are reserved for a variety of offices, including the headquarters of the nonprofit Save Our Cemeteries, and the fourth level and rooftop terrace essentially serve as a private function venue. The first level is the one intended for visitors. Here, you'll find a

staffed visitors center, a walking tour kiosk, educational exhibits, a coffee shop, and a gift shop—not a bad place to start before beginning your neighborhood wanderings.

BAYOU ST. JOHN

Wisner Blvd., btwn. Orleans Ave.

and Lake Pontchartrain

Bayou St. John runs along the eastern side of Wisner Boulevard, from Orleans Avenue to Lake Pontchartrain. At one time it was a lot longer than it is today. In fact, a portage once linked this bayou to the Mississippi River, making it particularly attractive to early French explorers, traders, and trappers. In 1701, the French established a small fort at the lake end of the bayou to protect this important route. Originally called Fort St. Jean, it would eventually be known as Old Spanish Fort by many native New Orleanians. Despite the bayou's smaller stature, it was partially the reason that the French established New Orleans where they did—at the river end of the portage route, where the French Quarter sits today. Dredged to accommodate larger vessels, Bayou St. John supposedly became the site of Marie

Laveau's voodoo rituals in the 19th century; by the early 20th century, commercial use of this once-important waterway had declined. Until the 1930s, houseboats were allowed on the bayou. Today it's simply a picturesque, slow-moving body of water, lined by greenery and frequented by sunbathers, picnickers, and privacy-seeking residents of Mid-City. It's also the site of various annual events, such as the Greek Festival in late May.

◖ CITY PARK

1 Palm Dr., 504/482-4888, www.neworleanscitypark.com
HOURS: Vary seasonally
COST: Free, though activity fees apply

City Park is bordered by Robert E. Lee Boulevard, Marconi Drive, City Park Avenue, and Wisner Boulevard near the Lakeview and Mid-City neighborhoods. Considerably larger than New York City's Central Park, this 1,300-acre park sits on what had once been a swampy oak forest. It still contains the nation's largest collection of mature live oaks, some believed to date to the 1400s or earlier. Stop by

the **Timken Center,** housed in a 1913 Spanish Mission–style building, for sandwiches, ice cream, and other refreshments before exploring the park.

City Park encompasses several worthwhile attractions. The **New Orleans Botanical Garden** is filled with a variety of thematic gardens; it's a wonderful place for a relaxing stroll. Another tranquil locale is the **Sydney and Walda Besthoff Sculpture Garden,** a free outdoor extension of the New Orleans Museum of Art. It's pleasant just to meander through the rest of the park, where you'll find various old-fashioned stone bridges and oodles of moss-covered oak trees.

Children are especially fond of the **Carousel Gardens Amusement Park** (mid-Mar.–May and mid-Aug.–mid-Nov. Sat.–Sun. 11 A.M.–6 P.M., June–Aug. Thurs. 10 A.M.–6 P.M., Fri. 10 A.M.–10 P.M., Sat. 11 A.M.–10 P.M., Sun. 11 A.M.–6 P.M., $3 pp entry, $3 per ride, or $20 for unlimited rides), which features numerous children's rides and a miniature train that tours the park. The historic

City Park's Storyland

STORYVILLE

One block west of the French Quarter along Basin Street, which parallels Rampart, lies a still-dicey neighborhood that has been infamous for well over a century. Once known as Storyville, it was, from 1897 until 1917, the only officially sanctioned and legal red-light district in the country. For nearly 200 years, prostitution thrived along streets all over New Orleans, a city that had more than its share of sailors, traders, laborers, and others seeking company during long spells away from home.

For years, city politicos debated the best way to deal with this social fact of life, figuring that if they couldn't root out prostitutes and bordellos, they might as well sanction them – and tax them. It was city alderman Sidney Story who, in 1897, came up with the bright idea to create a legal red-light district, a neighborhood that was obviously named after him.

By all accounts, the system worked wonderfully well. Potential customers could peruse a directory, the *Blue Book*, containing names of brothels and prostitutes, along with prices, the various services available, and photos of many of the women. The city's illegitimate music movement, jazz, flourished in the city's legitimate sex district, as many bordellos hired jazz musicians (including Jelly Roll Morton and King Oliver) to entertain the patrons. At its peak, the neighborhood licensed 750 ladies of the evening, and prostitution continued to be a successful business in Storyville well into the 1960s, more than four decades after the red-light district was made illegal again.

For a sense of the neighborhood's history, watch the Louis Malle-directed movie *Pretty Baby*, released in 1978 and starring a young Brooke Shields. For more information, read *Storyville, New Orleans: Being an Authentic, Illustrated Account of the Notorious Red Light District*, by Al Rose, also released in 1978.

---

carousel was established here in 1906 and eventually became listed on the National Register of Historic Places; it's now considered the last antique wooden carousel in Louisiana. Admission prices for the amusement park only apply to those 36 inches in height or taller; children shorter than that are entitled to free entry as well as free rides, if accompanied by a paid adult. The $20 admission option includes entry plus unlimited rides, just in case you plan to be here a while.

Another kid-friendly spot is the year-round **Storyland** (Mon.–Fri. 10 A.M.–5 P.M., Sat.–Sun. 10 A.M.–6 P.M.), one of my favorite sanctuaries as a child. The property features 26 larger-than-life sculptures, each based on a different fairy tale.

DEGAS HOUSE

2306 Esplanade Ave., 504/821-5009, www.degashouse.com
HOURS: Tours by appt.
COST: $15 pp donation suggested

Constructed in 1852, the expertly restored Degas House is the only former residence of famed French Impressionist Edgar Degas that's open to the public. The artist, whose mother and grandmother were born in New Orleans, lived here briefly from 1872 to 1873 while visiting his maternal relatives. During his stay, he painted at least 22 works of art, including *A Cotton Office in New Orleans* (1873), which became the first Impressionist painting ever purchased by a museum. The one-hour tours require reservations and are usually conducted by Degas' great-grandniece; enjoy a narrated walk through the house, also a well-regarded B&B, and view the documentary *Degas in New Orleans: A Creole Sojourn.*

If you have any artistic inclination, consider joining the **Bottles and Brushes with Degas** event (various days at 5:30 P.M.). Typically featuring a Degas-inspired creation or an iconic New Orleans image, these sessions usually include an hour of socializing, followed by a painting lesson. Reservations ($40 pp) are required and include paint, brushes, canvases, and an adult beverage. Wear comfortable clothes—anything that paint and/or wine won't ruin. There's a dedicated parking lot nearby, though if it fills up, street parking may still be available.

GREENWOOD CEMETERY

5200 Canal Blvd., 504/482-8983,
www.greenwoodnola.com

HOURS: Daily 8 A.M.–4:30 P.M.

COST: Free

At the convergence of Canal Street, City Park Avenue, and Canal Boulevard, along the western fringes of Mid-City, you'll encounter several old cemeteries. Surrounded by sturdy walls and filled with curious statuary, these aboveground graveyards are worth a look. If you only have time for one, venture inside Greenwood Cemetery, the 150-acre "city of the dead" on the north side of City Park Avenue, just east of I-10. Established by the Firemen's Charitable & Benevolent Association in 1852, Greenwood helped relieve the overcrowding at nearby Cypress Grove Cemetery. (The city faced a major yellow fever epidemic in the early 1850s, and there was an unfortunate need for additional graves.) **Cypress Grove Cemetery,** situated on the south side of City Park Avenue, was established in 1838 as the first cemetery to honor New Orleans's volunteer firemen and their families.

Today, Greenwood is notable for several reasons. It's the site of New Orleans's first Civil War memorial, dedicated in April 1874. The **Confederate Monument** is a masonry mausoleum topped with a marble pedestal, on which stands the statue of a Confederate infantrymen resting on his rifle. Designed by architect Benjamin M. Harrod, the statue was carved in Italy and made of Carrara marble; at the pedestal base are integral busts of Robert E. Lee, Stonewall Jackson, and other Confederate generals. The memorial marks the mass grave of 600 Confederate soldiers, whose remains were gathered by the Ladies Benevolent Association of Louisiana.

Other impressive landmarks here include the six-foot-high **Firemen's Monument,** an Italian marble statue erected in 1887 in honor of the 50th anniversary of the Firemen's Charitable & Benevolent Association. The tomb of **Lodge No. 30 of the Benevolent and Protective**

Order of Elks is a marble chamber erected in 1912 by Albert Weiblen (one of the South's most successful builders of tombs and cemetery monuments) and seemingly guarded by a majestic bronze elk. Several tombs are dedicated to fraternal organizations, such as the Police Mutual Benevolent Association, and to key New Orleanians, such as Abial Daily Crossman and John Fitzpatrick, two 19th-century mayors of New Orleans. **John Kennedy Toole,** the Pulitzer Prize–winning author of the posthumously published novel *A Confederacy of Dunces,* also rests here.

NEW ORLEANS BOTANICAL GARDEN

1 Palm Dr., City Park, 504/483-9386,
http://garden.neworleanscitypark.com

HOURS: Tues.–Sun. 10 A.M.–4:30 P.M.

COST: $6 adult, $3 child 5–12, free under 5

The 12-acre New Orleans Botanical Garden opened in 1936 as the City Park Rose Garden, the Big Easy's first public classical garden. A project of the Works Progress Administration (WPA), it brought together the unique visions of landscape designer William Wiedorn, building architect Richard Koch, and artist Enrique Alférez. Dozens of grand statues set throughout City Park are largely the work of Alférez, a local artist of immense talent who died in 1999. Many of his designs are garden benches and reliefs of the female figure, and most are surrounded by the park's lush landscaping.

Rechristened the New Orleans Botanical Garden in the early 1980s, this lovingly tended sanctuary now contains more than 2,000 types of plants, including azaleas, camellias, roses, tropical and aromatic plants, palm trees, and other ornamental trees and shrubs all set within thematic gardens. Unfortunately, Hurricane Katrina dealt a serious blow to this beloved garden, damaging some of the trees, flooding the outer gardens, and destroying electricity-dependent greenhouse plants like the orchids and bromeliads. Thanks to donors and dedicated volunteers, the botanical garden reopened in March of 2006 and has flourished since.

Special attractions here include the colorful **Butterfly Walk** and **Hummingbird Garden,** both of which are chiefly maintained by volunteers; the tranquil **Yakumo Nihon Teien Japanese Garden,** an ideal setting for traditional tea ceremonies; the **Historic New Orleans Train Garden,** a fascinating, Paul Busse–designed layout that represents the city of New Orleans, complete with miniature streetcars; and the **Conservatory of the Two Sisters,** a gorgeous, glass-domed building erected in the 1930s. Just outside the conservatory is a lovely lily pond, flanked by gorgeous rose bushes. Amateur botanists may also appreciate the **demonstration garden,** while history buffs should stroll through the **original WPA formal garden.** The **Stove House** was the garden's original greenhouse; it now nurtures a cactus collection. The **Garden Study Center** is a historic, English-style building built by the late Richard Koch and originally known as the old Potting Shed.

The garden's entrance is located at the **Pavilion of the Two Sisters** on Victory Avenue, behind the New Orleans Museum of Art. While the Historic New Orleans Train

Garden is open during regular hours, the train only operates on the weekends (Sat.–Sun. 10 A.M.–4:30 P.M.) and during special events. Free parking is available in the nearby parking lot, but the wheelchair-accessible garden does not permit pets, bikes, skates, or skateboards.

◖ NEW ORLEANS MUSEUM OF ART

1 Collins C. Diboll Circle, City Park, 504/658-4100, www.noma.org

HOURS: Tues.-Sun. 10 A.M.-5 P.M.

COST: $10 adult, $8 senior and student, $6 child 7-17, free under 7

The vast holdings of the fabulous New Orleans Museum of Art (NOMA) total about 40,000 objects that span a variety of cultures and eras—from pre-Columbian, Native American, and Mayan artwork to French Impressionist paintings. The city's oldest fine arts institution is justly known for its excellent rotating exhibits, including everything from creative bookmarks to the 19th-century mass production of British decorative arts. The museum is also an architectural marvel, an imposing Beaux Arts–style building

© DANIEL MARTONE

the New Orleans Museum of Art

that dates to 1911 when the museum was initially known as the Isaac Delgado Museum of Art. A cleverly appended modern addition was completed in 1971 and renovated in the 1990s.

The permanent collection is as eclectic as it is extensive. A few rooms are decorated with period 18th- and 19th-century American furnishings and decorative arts, as well as a survey of European and American artists. Included are several paintings by Degas; priceless Easter eggs and other decorative items created by Peter Carl Fabergé; photographs by Ansel Adams, Diane Arbus, and Walker Evans; and works by Monet, Renoir, Gauguin, Picasso, Braque, Chagall, Sargent, Cassatt, and O'Keeffe. One wing contains the impressive Decorative Arts Department, a fascinating array of glasswork and ceramics, mostly of the 19th and 20th centuries. You'll also find African and Asiatic works in a network of smaller galleries.

My favorite part is the **Sydney and Walda Besthoff Sculpture Garden** (Sat.–Thurs. 10 A.M.–4:45 P.M., Fri. 10 A.M.–8:45 P.M., closed major holidays), a relatively new outdoor attraction that's free to visit. Peppered with magnolias, pines, and ancient, Spanish moss–draped live oaks, this peaceful, five-acre spread encompasses gardens, lagoons, footpaths, pedestrian bridges, and more than 60 impressive sculptures. Noted works include sculptures by Henry Moore, Jacques Lipchitz, Pierre Auguste Renoir, Rene Magritte, Ida Kohlmeyer, and Claes Oldenburg. A free cell-phone tour is available. NOMA offers ample free parking, but you can also reach the museum by bike, bus, or the Canal streetcar line. The museum is free on Wednesdays.

OUR LADY OF GUADALUPE CHURCH

411 N. Rampart St., 504/525-1551, www.judeshrine.com
HOURS: Vary daily
COST: Free, though donations are accepted

Situated along the southeastern edge of the historic Tremé neighborhood, this stunning church has been serving local Catholics since 1826. In fact, it's the oldest surviving church building in New Orleans. Originally known as the Mortuary Chapel, it was erected as a burial church for victims of yellow fever. Over the decades, it's served Confederate veterans, Italian immigrants, and Spanish-speaking citizens. Although it's been temporarily abandoned on three occasions—during the Civil War, in the early 1870s, and again in 1915, likely due to its proximity to the infamous Storyville district—it's been returned to service each and every time. Today, Our Lady of Guadalupe Church is the official chapel of the New Orleans Police and Fire Departments. The church is just a short stroll from Louis Armstrong Park and St. Louis Cemetery No. 1, and is often a stop on the lengthy voodoo tour offered by the New Orleans Historic Voodoo Museum.

PITOT HOUSE MUSEUM AND GARDENS

1440 Moss St., 504/482-0312, www.pitothouse.org
HOURS: Wed.-Sat. 10 A.M.-3 P.M.
COST: $7 adult, $5 senior, student, and child, free under 6

Alongside the eastern bank of Mid-City's peaceful Bayou St. John is one of the few surviving Creole colonial plantations in the South. The Pitot House Museum, which overlooks the lazy, slow-moving bayou, is named for an early occupant, James Pitot, the first mayor of New Orleans after it was incorporated. Though Pitot lived in the house from 1810 to 1819, he didn't actually own it the entire time. Curiously, his import-export business was ruined by the British blockade during the War of 1812, forcing him to sell the property and become a tenant instead. At one time or another, lawyers, nuns, and other interesting New Orleanians have dwelled in this lovely, two-story country home.

In the 1960s, the Louisiana Landmarks Society carefully restored the Pitot House to its appearance in the early 1800s, filling it with American antiques that date from the first half of the 19th century. Because it had been moved 300 feet down Moss Street, it was impossible to research the original gardens surrounding the home. The current gardens are interpretive in nature, including plants commonly used from the late 1700s to the early 1840s—such as roses, violets, herbs, and okra, as well as grapefruit, sweet olive, and magnolia trees. Besides serving as the headquarters for the Louisiana Landmarks Society, the museum helps to shed some light on the lifestyle of those who once lived alongside the bayou. The Pitot House Museum is fairly close to St. Louis Cemetery No. 3, City Park, and the New Orleans Museum of Art. To reach it, take the Canal streetcar; if you choose to drive, you'll have to rely on street parking.

ST. AUGUSTINE CATHOLIC CHURCH

1210 Gov. Nicholls St., 504/525-5934,
www.staugustinecatholicchurch-neworleans.org
HOURS: Vary daily
COST: Free, though donations are accepted

Built on a former plantation estate and dedicated in 1842, the St. Augustine Catholic Church is the country's oldest African American Catholic parish. This is not surprising, perhaps, given its location in the Faubourg Tremé, the oldest African American neighborhood in the United States. Prior to the American Civil War, the church welcomed both free black citizens and enslaved individuals as worshippers. Even today, the congregation promotes and celebrates freedom from sin and oppression. Curiously, one of the church's former parishioners was Homer Plessy, the American plaintiff in the landmark U.S. Supreme Court case of *Plessy v. Ferguson,* which ultimately confirmed the "separate but equal" rule (that segregation was legal as long as both blacks and whites had equal facilities).

Tours of the historic church are arranged through the rectory and include its vibrant stained-glass windows as well as an impactful Tomb of the Unknown Slave. You can also visit during the Sunday morning Mass (10 A.M.), which can be an inspirational experience for believers and nonbelievers alike. Note that St. Augustine's is situated two blocks from Louis Armstrong Park in a rather sketchy area, so it's best not to come alone.

ST. LOUIS CEMETERY NO. 1

Basin St. and St. Louis St., 504/482-5065
HOURS: Mon.-Sat. 9 A.M.-3 P.M., Sun. 9 A.M.-noon
COST: Free

Arguably the oldest, most famous, and most

the entrance to St. Louis Cemetery No. 1

© DANIEL MARTONE

intriguing of all of New Orleans's so-called "cities of the dead," St. Louis Cemetery No. 1 has been the final resting place for New Orleanians since the late 18th century. The burial ground was established in 1789, following the Great Fire of 1788, and set outside what was then the city border, above Rampart Street. (Since New Orleans sits below sea level and has a high water table, bodies were buried aboveground. Earlier attempts to bury the dead underground had failed during floods, as the caskets simply floated to the surface.)

Bordered by Basin, Conti, Tremé, and St. Louis Streets, the cemetery currently contains more than 700 tombs and inters thousands. Most of these aboveground structures are owned by families and are designed to hold more than one set of remains. Though constructed of brick, the elaborate tombs are covered in concrete or stucco; some of the oldest ones are little more than crumbled ruins and piles of brick dust. One curious element is the segregated Protestant section near the rear of the predominantly Catholic cemetery.

MARIE LAVEAU: VOODOO QUEEN

Voodoo experienced its heyday in New Orleans in the 19th century. While most voodoo books and paraphernalia available in the French Quarter today are bought by curious tourists, there's no question that some people still take the practice very seriously.

Misconceptions about voodoo abound and are often encouraged by its depiction in popular culture. Voodoo is based on the worship of spirits, called Loa, and a belief system that emphasizes spirituality, compassion, and treating others well. While there's nothing inherently negative about voodoo, its practice does allow its followers to perform rites intended to bring calamity upon their enemies. These traditions, such as piercing miniature effigies with sharp pins or burning black candles, are the most familiar among outsiders.

The origins of voodoo as a religious practice are indistinct. Voodoo rituals are based on a variety of African religious traditions, which were brought to the United States by West African slaves. In 18th-century New Orleans, where slaves were kept by French and Spanish residents, voodoo began to incorporate some of the beliefs and rituals of Catholicism as well.

Marie Laveau (circa 1794–1881) is the historical figure most connected with southern Louisiana's rich voodoo tradition. A beautiful woman of French, African, and Native American extraction, she was New Orleans's high priestess of voodoo from roughly 1830 onward. She had numerous children, and at least one daughter continued to practice for many years after her mother's death, fueling rumors that the original Marie Laveau lived into the early 20th century. Her grave in the **St. Louis Cemetery No. 1,** on Basin Street, is still a site of pilgrimage for voodoo practitioners.

Laveau combined the understanding ear of a psychologist with the showmanship of a preacher to become one of the city's most vaunted spiritual figures. As a young woman, Laveau practiced as a hair stylist in New Orleans, a position that afforded her the opportunity to work inside some of the city's most prominent homes and to earn the confidence of its most prominent women. As she soaked up the gossip of the day, she also dispensed both practical and spiritual advice to her clients, no doubt sprinkling her words with healthy doses of voodoo mysticism and lore. Word of Laveau's talents as a voodoo priestess spread rapidly, and soon she was staging ceremonies in the small yard of her St. Ann Street home. Her most notorious ceremony, held annually in a swamp cabin along Bayou St. John on June 23 (St. John's Eve, the night before the Feast Day of St. John the Baptist), became the stuff of legend.

Laveau was the most famous priestess to captivate New Orleans's residents, but she wasn't the last. Throughout the centuries, a number of women and even some men have carried on the tradition of the voodoo priestess. According to legend, believers can invoke her powers by marking her tomb with three X's (a gris-gris, or charm), scratching the ground three times with their feet, knocking three times on the grave, and leaving a small offering before making a wish. Many people in New Orleans continue to celebrate St. John's Eve and believe that, on this night, the spirit of the Voodoo Queen makes herself known.

© LAURA MARTONE

Marie Laveau's tomb in St. Louis Cemetery No. 1

Famous residents here include Homer Plessy (of *Plessy v. Ferguson* fame) and the much-loved voodoo priestess **Marie Laveau,** whose tomb is a frequent stop on daily voodoo and cemetery tours. Movie star Nicolas Cage (former owner of the historic LaLaurie Mansion in the French Quarter) has managed to stake his own perpetual claim in this crowded cemetery; just look for the incongruous white pyramid that many New Orleanians consider an utter eyesore in this historic place.

It's not advisable to wander through the cemetery on your own, even during the day. Instead, take one of the guided tours offered by several different organizations. **Save Our Cemeteries** (504/525-3377 or 888/721-7493, www.saveourcemeteries.org, Sun.–Thurs. 10 A.M., Fri.–Sat. 10 A.M. and 1 P.M., $20 adult, free under 12) leads hour-long excursions through St. Louis Cemetery No. 1. Tours are available on a first-come, first-served basis and depart from the lobby of the nearby Basin Street Station.

ST. LOUIS CEMETERY NO. 2

N. Robertson St. and St. Louis St., 504/482-5065
HOURS: Mon.-Sat. 9 A.M.-3 P.M., Sun. 9 A.M.-noon
COST: Free

Driving through New Orleans via I-10, you'll notice several aboveground cemeteries. One such site is St. Louis Cemetery No. 2, situated directly below the interstate in the historic Tremé neighborhood. Bordered by North Robertson Street, Iberville Street, North Claiborne Avenue, and St. Louis Street, this curious "city of the dead" was established in 1823 as the fourth cemetery in New Orleans. Encompassing three city blocks, it's actually three times the size of the more famous St. Louis Cemetery No. 1. At the time that it was established, the city was being ravaged by numerous fatal diseases, including cholera, typhoid, smallpox, malaria, diphtheria, yellow fever, even the bubonic plague. Although the need for a cemetery was great, residents wanted it to be placed as far from the French Quarter as possible, if only to keep away the evil spirits that were supposedly being spread by the diseased.

City planners obliged, and eventually, St. Louis Cemetery No. 2 became the permanent resting place of several significant people, including Dominique You, a lieutenant in the Gulf's largest pirate operation; Jacques Phillipe Villere, Louisiana's first native-born governor; Nicholas Girod, the first mayor of New Orleans's American Sector; and Jacques Nicholas Bussiere de Pouilly, a local architect who helped to design several of the city's cemeteries, such as St. Louis No. 1, St. Louis No. 2, Greenwood, and Cypress Grove. In 1974, the nonprofit Save Our Cemeteries organization was established to protect St. Louis Cemetery No. 2 from being demolished. Despite the historical significance of this graveyard, no official tours come here, so if you choose to visit, be sure to come with a group, as it's not located in the safest area.

ST. LOUIS CEMETERY NO. 3

3421 Esplanade Ave., 504/482-5065
HOURS: Daily 8:30 A.M.-4 P.M.
COST: Free

Following the huge yellow fever outbreak of 1853, New Orleans required yet another cemetery. Established in 1854 as Bayou Cemetery, this graveyard was built on an old leper colony, a governor-sanctioned place of exile nicknamed "Leper's Land." Located on Esplanade Avenue between Lada Court and Moss Street, the now-named St. Louis Cemetery No. 3 is actually one of the city's safer cemeteries for daytime exploration—even without an official tour. Just stop by the small office near the entrance gate to pick up a map before meandering through this narrow "city of the dead," which abuts the Fair Grounds Race Course in places and lies only a short stroll away from Bayou St. John and City Park. Here, you'll see several society tombs, such as those of the Dante Lodge of Masons, the Young Men's Benevolent Association, the United Slavonian Benevolent Association, and the Hellenic Orthodox community. As is true for all cemeteries and even most parks in New Orleans, you should not enter after dark; it's also wise to explore with a friend or two.

Greater New Orleans Map 6

ALGIERS POINT HISTORIC DISTRICT

Newton St. and Atlantic Ave. to Mississippi River,
Algiers, www.algierspoint.org

As a child, I used to love sitting on the Moon Walk and gazing across the Mississippi River at the community on the other side. Known as Algiers Point, this residential West Bank neighborhood is filled with a vast cache of notable, if generally modest, residences from the early 18th to the mid-20th centuries, including French Colonial–style plantation houses, Creole cottages, Haitian shotguns, Greek Revival–style mansions, Victorian structures, and British Craftsman–style homes. New Orleans's second-oldest neighborhood, Algiers Point features a handful of pleasant parks, a few B&Bs, several pubs and eateries, and a smattering of shops. Although it's easy to reach, this neighborhood has always felt and continues to feel distinct from the rest of the city, owing to that mile-wide boundary line, also known as the Mississippi River, that separates it from the French Quarter and CBD. From the foot of Canal Street, catch the **passenger and auto ferry** (504/250-9110, www.friendsoftheferry. org), which has been sending people back and forth across the river since 1827. Service is offered 6 A.M.–midnight daily, and there's no charge for pedestrians; if you have a car, you'll pay just $1 for round-trip passage.

BARATARIA PRESERVE

6588 Barataria Blvd., Marrero, 504/689-3690,
www.nps.gov/jela
HOURS: Daily 9 A.M.–5 P.M.
COST: Free

To experience the wetlands of southeastern Louisiana, spend a day at Barataria Preserve, a division of Jean Lafitte National Historical Park and Preserve. Named for notorious pirate Jean Lafitte, who declared himself the King of Barataria, this large West Bank preserve is bounded by Lakes Cataouatche and Salvador, Highway 301, Highway 45, and the Cataouatche Canal. At the preserve, you can explore and learn about one of the world's most substantial delta ecosystems—a series of bayous, marshes, swamps, and woodlands that appear to be almost virginal.

Barataria Preserve is a haven for an amazing variety of plantlife, which thrives in this subtropical climate. Along the natural ridges and levees, there's dense hardwood forest, along with towering live oaks; the habitat changes to palmetto groves on the lower back slopes of the levees. Water covers most of the lower regions of the levees throughout much of the year, so, beyond the swamps, you'll encounter bald cypress trees and treeless marshes.

The preserve's 23,000 acres, including more than 30 miles of waterways, make an ideal trip for canoeing and fishing (fishing requires a license). Separate launches are available for canoes and motorized craft. In addition, several different hiking trails and boardwalks provide a close look at the swamp ecosystem, where you're likely to spy herons, ibises, egrets, turtles, frogs, snakes, and, as in any Louisiana swamp, alligators, which enjoy sunning themselves along dry levees and riverbanks during warmer times of the year.

The visitors center, located near Crown Point, is open daily. Here, you can survey exhibits that highlight how the Mississippi River created Louisiana's wetlands, the national significance of this region, and the relationship between the land and its people. Be sure to stop by the bookstore, where you'll find music, field guides, children's books, and the like. Free guided nature walks are available at 10 A.M. Friday–Monday. The preserve also presents annual events like the wintertime bird walk and the Spring in the Swamp weekend.

CHALMETTE BATTLEFIELD AND NATIONAL CEMETERY

8606 W. St. Bernard Hwy., Chalmette, 504/281-0510,
www.nps.gov/jela
HOURS: Daily 9 A.M.–4:30 P.M.
COST: Free

The Chalmette Battlefield and National Cemetery commemorates the important victory by Andrew Jackson and his American troops during the Battle of New Orleans in 1815—a victory that represented the triumph of American democracy over European aristocracy. Sandwiched between St. Bernard Highway and the Mississippi River, the battlefield lies just six miles southeast of downtown New Orleans; it's the only one of the six sites within Jean Lafitte National Historical Park and Preserve that touches on Louisiana's military history.

Your first stop should be the new visitors center, which replaced one was destroyed by Hurricane Katrina. Opened on January 8, 2011, the 196th anniversary of the battle, the 3,500-square-foot space features maps, displays, period weapons, interactive exhibits, and short films about the War of 1812, the New Orleans campaign, the Battle of New Orleans, and the effect that the American victory had on the state, the country, and the world. Take a minute to peruse the books, period music, and authentic reproductions in the center's bookstore.

Afterward, venture outside and follow the 1.5-mile tour road through the scene of the action. Along the way, you'll encounter interpretive placards at six pull-offs, plus the **1833 Malus-Beauregard House** and the Chalmette National Cemetery, which was actually commissioned as a graveyard for Union soldiers felled during the Civil War. You can visit the graves of four men who fought in the War of 1812, one of whom actually participated in the Battle of New Orleans. Near the visitors center, you'll notice an obelisk standing high over the battlefield; known as the **Chalmette Monument,** it was commissioned in 1840 shortly after former president Jackson returned to the scene of the battle to mark its 25th anniversary.

Free talks are given daily at 2:45 P.M., and the park hosts an annual Battle of New Orleans celebration every January. Although many visitors arrive here by private vehicle, you can also board the **Creole Queen** (1 Poydras St.,

504/529-4567 or 800/445-4109, www.creole-queen.com, daily 2–4:30 P.M., $22 adult, $11 child 6–12, free under 6), which makes a daily trip from the French Quarter to the battlefield. Just be advised that the visitors center is closed on Christmas Day and Mardi Gras Day.

FORT PIKE STATE HISTORIC SITE
27100 Chef Menteur Hwy., 504/255-9171 or 888/662-5703, www.crt.state.la.us/parks
HOURS: Tues.-Sat. 9 A.M.-5 P.M.
COST: $4 adult, free over 62 and under 13

Technically closer to Slidell than to New Orleans, Fort Pike State Historic Site is accessible from both shores of Lake Pontchartrain. Situated roughly 23 miles east of downtown New Orleans via U.S. 90, Fort Pike was constructed between 1819 and 1826, and named for General Zebulon Montgomery Pike, the explorer and soldier whose moniker is also associated with Pike's Peak in the Rocky Mountains. The fort's erection was due, in large part, to the War of 1812. While the United States survived the war, the British army's destruction of the country's capital and the attack on New Orleans underscored the weakness of America's defenses. In response, President James Monroe ordered the construction of an extensive coastal defense system, which included Fort Pike, a masonry fortification that was designed to withstand an attack from land or sea.

Fort Pike was an active place. During the Seminole Wars of the 1830s, it served as a staging area for troops headed to Florida as well as a collection point for hundreds of Seminole prisoners and their black slaves. Fort Pike was also a pit stop for soldiers during the Mexican War of the 1840s. Its peak came in the 1860s, when the fort was captured by the state's Confederate-leaning militia prior to the Civil War, vacated when Union forces took over New Orleans in 1862, and subsequently used by the Union as a base for raids along the Gulf Coast. It was a protective outpost for New Orleans, and a training center where former slaves were instructed to use heavy artillery and eventually became part of the influential United States Colored Troops. Ironically, no cannonballs were ever fired from Fort Pike, and it was officially abandoned in 1890. Eight decades later, it was listed on the National Register of Historic Places. Visitors can enjoy daily tours of the historic fort, have a picnic on the scenic grounds, and make use of the on-site boat launch, which offers anglers terrific access to the bountiful waters of Lake Pontchartrain.

◖ LONGUE VUE HOUSE & GARDENS

7 Bamboo Rd., 504/488-5488, www.longuevue.com
HOURS: Tues.-Sat. 10 A.M.-5 P.M., Sun. 1-5 P.M.
COST: $10 adult, $9 senior, $5 child, free under 3

One of the city's most impressive attractions is often overlooked by visitors, simply because it's slightly off the beaten path. Situated near the border between New Orleans and Old Metairie, the Longue Vue House & Gardens is a lush, exotic eight-acre estate that once belonged to local community pillars Edgar and Edith Stern and their three children. Designed and constructed between 1939 and 1942 by architects William and Geoffrey Platt and landscape architect Ellen Biddle Shipman, the tranquil property was intended to be one organic whole, uniting the house and gardens seamlessly. Ultimately, the designers did just that.

Today, this serene place represents one of the last Country Place Era homes built in America. It comprises a period-furnished Classical Revival–style manor house, several outbuildings, 15 spectacularly landscaped garden areas, and 22 ponds and fountains. Such large residential properties had their heyday between 1880 and 1940, when designers worked closely with their clients to create extravagant, European-influenced gardens. Guided house tours are offered every hour on the hour (the last one at 4 P.M.). On such tours, you'll not only see well-appointed chambers like the dining room, library, ladies' reception room, and master bedroom, but also modern art exhibits and displays about the creation of Longue Vue. For a slightly lower fee ($7 adult, $4 student and child, free under 3), you can opt to skip the house tour and simply explore the gardens, but I wouldn't recommend missing the

opportunity to see as much as you can. Just bear in mind that Longue Vue is closed on several major holidays.

METAIRIE CEMETERY

5100 Pontchartrain Blvd., 504/486-6331, www.lakelawnmetairie.com
HOURS: Daily 8 A.M.-5 P.M.
COST: Free

Where I-10 passes over City Park Avenue, just east of the suburb of Metairie, you'll spot several historic cemeteries, including the confusingly named Metairie Cemetery. After all, it's actually located in New Orleans, not far from the now-infamous 17th Street Canal, which busted open in the aftermath of Hurricane Katrina. Bordered by Fairway Drive, Metairie Road, and I-10, this property once contained a popular racetrack, which was originally built in 1838. Unfortunately, the Civil War and Reconstruction era took their toll, and in May of 1872, the faltering racetrack was converted into a cemetery. Listed on the National Register of Historic Places in 1991, this scenic, aboveground cemetery—part of the Lake Lawn Metairie Funeral Home and Cemeteries, where my own grandparents are interred—is filled with a variety of magnificent family tombs, private mausoleums, and elaborate memorials. Some of these serve as the final resting places of several notable individuals, including nine Louisiana governors, seven New Orleans mayors, General P. G. T. Beauregard and two other Confederate generals, jazz singer Louis Prima, and silent movie star Marguerite Clark. Unlike other cemeteries in New Orleans, this one is relatively safe to visit, though you should always be respectful of the mourners around you.

OLD ARABI HISTORIC DISTRICT

St. Claude Ave. and Angela Ave., Arabi
HOURS: Vary depending on building

In all honesty, most out-of-towners never make it past the city's main tourist areas, but history buffs curious about less-traversed places might appreciate the Old Arabi Historic District. Part of the **San Bernardo Scenic Byway,** a lengthy route along LA-46, from Arabi to Delacroix and Yscloskey, this small historic district actually lies in St. Bernard Parish, just northwest of the Chalmette Battlefield. Roughly bounded by Angela Avenue, St. Claude Avenue, Weinberger Road, and North Peters Street alongside the river, the area features several historic structures, including a 19th-century newspaper office, the parish's first prison, the admittedly rundown LeBeau Plantation, the parish's first high school (now a community center), and the E. Cavaroc House and Domino Sugar Refinery. The area was subdivided in the 1860s and flourished through 1900. Though the plantation and refinery are private, the newspaper office and community center are open to the public. Given the sketchiness of the surrounding neighborhood, however, it's probably best just to take a drive through this historic district en route to the battlefield.

RIVERTOWN

2020 4th St., Kenner, 504/468-7231, www.kenner.la.us
HOURS: Sat. 11 A.M.–4 P.M.
COST: Varies

Though it's not open often, Rivertown will definitely appeal to families with kids. Situated beside the Mississippi River, this expansive education complex comprises several different attractions, including the **Freeport McMoRan Science Complex** (415 Williams Blvd., Kenner), an interactive museum dedicated to the exploration of space and the development of scientific technology. Visitors can explore touch-friendly exhibits on meteorology, electricity, world geography, the human body, and the solar system. Here, you'll also find the **Kenner Planetarium & MegaDome Cinema,** which usually features a handful of engaging light-and-sound shows ($6 adult, $5 senior and child). The **Kenner Space Station,** also a crowd-pleaser, features a robot, a four-billion-year-old meteorite, and a full-size NASA International Space Station prototype. In addition to a replicated historical village known as **Kenner Heritage Park,** Rivertown is also home to the **Rivertown Repertory Theatre** (www.rivertownrepertorytheatre.org), which typically presents five professional musicals and plays from September through May. Recent highlights have included *Chicago* and Neil Simon's *Plaza Suite.*

RESTAURANTS

New Orleans may be known for its beautiful architecture and seemingly never-ending nightlife, but it's the food that beckons. The city's world-renowned reputation for culinary excellence is well-deserved. This is the place that shaped such famous chefs as Paul Prudhomme, Emeril Lagasse, and John Besh—all of whom have embraced the Big Easy's Cajun and Creole roots, not to mention its abundance of fresh seafood.

While New Orleans certainly has its share of upscale, dinner-only restaurants celebrated for their impeccable service, creative fusion cuisine, ever-changing menus, and reliance on fresh, local, seasonal ingredients, it also boasts a wide array of old-time neighborhood haunts. Historic joints, like the Camellia Grill in Uptown and Mandina's Restaurant in

Mid-City, are known for good burgers, shrimp po-boys, overstuffed muffulettas, and classic, must-have local dishes like gumbo, jambalaya, raw oysters, crawfish étouffée, red beans and rice, and bread pudding. Thus New Orleans caters as much to gourmands as it does to budget-conscious travelers just looking for a good meal in between stops.

As in other cities known for good food, New Orleans's restaurants can fill up quickly, especially on the weekends, around holidays like Christmas and Mardi Gras, and during special events, such as Jazz Fest. At such times, reservations are highly recommended; for places where reservations aren't accepted, such as Mona Lisa Restaurant in the Quarter, it's best to dine on the weekdays when it's generally less crowded. Depending on the restaurant—and

© LAURA MARTONE

HIGHLIGHTS

LOOK FOR  TO FIND RECOMMENDED RESTAURANTS.

◖ Best Late-Night Burgers: Though locals disagree over the city's best burger joint, many revelers head to **Yo Mama's Bar and Grill** to satisfy their late-night burger cravings; while the bread can be a bit crumbly, the burgers are always well-prepared, with toppings that range from blue cheese to peanut butter (page 72).

◖ Best Classic Creole Cuisine: One of the few restaurants in Louisiana where men are expected to wear jackets, **Galatoire's** is the quintessential old-school New Orleans tradition, serving superb Creole fare from time-tested recipes (page 74).

◖ Heftiest Sandwiches: There's considerable debate about this category in New Orleans, but many folks concur that the super-casual **Cafe Maspero** produces heavenly, if slightly unorthodox, muffuletta sandwiches (page 82).

◖ Most Romantic Courtyard: Established in 1979, the **Feelings Cafe** now occupies much of the D'Aunoy Plantation in the Faubourg Marigny, where lovers can enjoy an intimate, eclectic dinner in the lush brick courtyard (page 87).

◖ Best See-and-Be-Seen Restaurant: The domain of talented and much-adored chef John Besh, **August** pulls in a stylish crowd of New Orleans's movers-and-shakers, who delight in the restaurant's superbly crafted contemporary cuisine (page 93).

◖ Best Special-Occasion Restaurant: Whether you're celebrating a wedding anniversary, treating your mom on Mother's Day, or simply hoping to enjoy one of the best meals that New Orleans has to offer, book a table at **Commander's Palace,** a legendary restaurant in the Garden District (page 99).

◖ Quirkiest Place for Great Cooking: Long waits are not uncommon at funky **Jacques-Imo's Cafe,** a wonderful neighborhood restaurant in the Riverbend area of Uptown, known for innovative Creole and Cajun food, huge portions, and sassy service (page 100).

Cafe Maspero in the French Quarter

© LAURA MARTONE

◖ Best Desserts: For more than a century, **Angelo Brocato** has doled out delicious homemade ice cream and Italian pastries from its quaint Mid-City storefront space, which was virtually rebuilt in 2006 following heavy flooding from Hurricane Katrina (page 108).

◖ Best Brunch Venue: Part of the fun of brunching at **Ralph's on the Park** is sampling the creative and beautifully presented nouvelle Creole cuisine, but the other benefit is that, after you eat, you can explore adjacent City Park, with its botanical garden, verdant paths, and scenic bridges (page 110).

◖ Best Place to Eat in the Burbs: Situated in a nondescript section of Metairie, a suburb of New Orleans, **Drago's Seafood Restaurant** has earned a cult following for its incredibly delicious charbroiled oysters and other fresh Cajun and Creole seafood dishes (page 116).

neighborhood—you'll often avoid crowds and save money by visiting at lunchtime. And despite New Orleans's laid-back vibe, not all the city's restaurants are suitable for children. In the French Quarter, Faubourg Marigny, Garden District, and Riverbend, for instance, several eateries are more appropriate for couples in the mood for romance.

PRICE KEY

$ Entrées less than $15

$$ Entrées $15-30

$$$ Entrées more than $30

French Quarter   Map 1

AMERICAN
DICKIE BRENNAN'S STEAKHOUSE $$$
716 Iberville St., 504/522-2467,
www.dickiebrennanssteakhouse.com
HOURS: Sat.-Thurs. 5:30-10 P.M., Fri. 11:30 A.M.-2:30 P.M. and 5:30-10 P.M.

Red-meat lovers swear by the hefty cuts served at Dickie Brennan's Steakhouse, which is known for its oyster-topped filet served with creamed spinach and roasted potatoes. Garlic-crusted redfish, blackened prime rib, and the grilled ribeye enhanced with Abita beer–flavored barbecue shrimp are also big draws, not to mention classic desserts like pecan pie, Creole cheesecake, praline chocolate mousse, and bananas Foster bread pudding. Though a clubby, upscale space, the restaurant has a relaxed mood, and presentable casual attire is customary.

JOHNNY'S PO-BOYS $
511 St. Louis St., 504/524-8129,
www.johnnyspoboys.com
HOURS: Daily 8 A.M.-4:30 P.M.

Johnny's Po-Boys opened in 1950 as an unprepossessing, family-owned eatery with tables sheathed in red-checkered cloths and surrounded by bentwood chairs. Though it's only open until the afternoon, Johnny's fills up daily for breakfast and lunch. Not surprisingly, it's best known for its namesake sandwiches, but you can also order omelets, gumbo, seafood platters, and ice cream treats. Classic po-boys include boudin, roast beef, tuna salad, country-fried steak, shrimp, oyster, and the Judge

Bosetta (stuffed with ground beef, Italian and hot sausage, and Swiss cheese).

PORT OF CALL $$
838 Esplanade Ave., 504/523-0120 or 504/522-8450, www.portofcallnola.com
HOURS: Sun.-Thurs. 11 A.M.-midnight, Fri.-Sat. 11 A.M.-1 A.M.

This dark and divey corner tavern is so popular for its hefty burgers—made with freshly ground beef and piled high with mushrooms or melted cheddar—that there's often a line outside the door. Besides burgers, the simple menu also features traditional comfort foods like steaks, salads, and loaded baked potatoes, which either come with the entrées or can be ordered separately. Though not everyone (including me) considers this the city's best burger joint, the nautical decor and strong cocktails make Port of Call a worthy stop.

THE RIB ROOM $$$
Omni Royal Orleans, 621 St. Louis St., 504/529-7046, www.ribroomneworleans.com
HOURS: Mon.-Thurs. 6:30-10:30 A.M., 11:30 A.M.-2 P.M., and 6-9:30 P.M.; Fri. 6:30-10:30 A.M., 11:30 A.M.-2:30 P.M., and 6-10 P.M.; Sat. 6:30-10:30 A.M., 11:30 A.M.-2 P.M., and 6-10 P.M.; Sun. 6:30-10:30 A.M., 11:30 A.M.-2:30 P.M., and 6-9:30 P.M.

Situated in the elegant Omni Royal Orleans, the historic Rib Room is one of the city's best steakhouses. The dining room is unabashedly retro, with its soaring ceilings, comfortable leather chairs, and huge arched windows overlooking Royal Street. The staff is both deft and fun-loving—many employees have

DUNCES AND LUCKY DOGS

RESTAURANTS

© LAURA MARTONE

French Quarter revelers can satisfy their late-night cravings at various Lucky Dogs vending carts.

As a child of New Orleans, I found it hard to avoid reading John Kennedy Toole's Pulitzer Prize-winning novel, *A Confederacy of Dunces* (1980). Posthumously published by LSU Press more than a decade after the author's tragic suicide, this zany depiction of life in the Big Easy during the early 1960s (not to mention a skillful exploration of the city's unique dialects) has since become a cult classic – and a canonical work of modern Southern literature. This picaresque novel centers on Ignatius J. Reilly – a lazy, overweight, quixotic, yet well-educated 30-year-old man who, while living with his mother and searching for gainful employment, meets a host of colorful French Quarter denizens, from kind-hearted strippers to belligerent lesbians.

Though some of the New Orleans landmarks referenced in this madcap novel, such as the old D. H. Holmes department store on Canal Street, no longer exist, some, like the Prytania Theatre, still do. Perhaps the most famous references, though, are the "Paradise Hot Dogs" vending carts that figure prominently into Reilly's angst-filled search for a permanent job. Clearly, Toole was influenced by the ubiquitous red-and-yellow, wiener-shaped **Lucky Dogs** (www.luckydogs.us) vending carts that have prowled the streets of New Orleans, particularly the French Quarter, for more than five decades. Especially popular among late-night partygoers, these street-corner hot dogs may just be mouthwatering to some, but for me, they'll always be a reminder of the first time I read – and fell in love with – *A Confederacy of Dunces*, a book that, as many writers and scholars believe, aptly captures the indomitable spirit of New Orleans.

been here for three or four decades. Though nouvelle foodies may scoff, frequent patrons favor this hip dining venue for its delicious, sometimes innovative, dishes, ranging from well-prepared prime rib and seared tuna medallions to local favorites like crab cakes, Creole gumbo, and turtle soup. Like several other fine-dining establishments in the Quarter, the Rib Room also offers a delectable Sunday jazz brunch.

STANLEY $$

547 St. Ann St., 504/587-0093,
www.stanleyrestaurant.com
HOURS: Daily 7 A.M.-10 P.M.

Prior to Hurricane Katrina, a pleasant branch of the regional chain La Madeleine occupied this corner eatery on the first floor of the Lower Pontalba Apartments. Following the storm, I missed the French-style country café, my favorite lunch spot while interning at a local television station. But I have to admit that Stanley is a worthy successor. Run by chef Scott Boswell, owner and executive chef of the well-regarded Stella!, this friendly, provincial eatery offers delightful views of Jackson Square and creative American comfort food, such as poached eggs with fried oysters, Korean barbecue beef "poor boys," and varied ice cream treats.

YO MAMA'S BAR AND GRILL $$

727 St. Peter St., 504/522-1125,
www.yo-mamas-bar-and-grill.com
HOURS: Daily 11 A.M.-3 A.M.

Not far from Bourbon Street, this late-night hole-in-the-wall lures plenty of repeat customers. While some locals dispute this fact, Yo Mama's is one of the city's best burger joints, offering a variety of toppings, from peanut butter to blue cheese. Unfortunately, the place is often understaffed, and the three booths and curving bar don't accommodate many patrons. But you'll typically find a spot during the off-hours—and if not, the well-stocked jukebox and 89 tequila varieties will keep you busy while you wait.

ASIAN
SEKISUI SAMURAI SUSHI $$

239 Decatur St., 504/525-9595, www.sekisuiusa.com
HOURS: Sun.-Thurs. 11:30 A.M.-10 P.M., Fri.-Sat. 11:30 A.M.-10:30 P.M.

Though New Orleans isn't generally known for sushi, Sekisui Samurai isn't a bad option if you're craving edamame, sashimi, and miso soup. My husband and I have always been able to satisfy our sushi fix here. Situated between the House of Blues and the Kerry Irish Pub, this cozy, often tranquil eatery offers a slew of freshly prepared *nigiri* and sushi rolls, plus tuna *tataki,* seafood udon, shrimp tempura, and other tasty Asian dishes.

CAJUN AND CREOLE
ANTOINE'S RESTAURANT $$$

713 St. Louis St., 504/581-4422, www.antoines.com
HOURS: Mon.-Sat. 11:30 A.M.-2 P.M. and 5:30-9 P.M., Sun. 11 A.M.-2 P.M.

One of the true granddaddies of old-fashioned French-Creole cooking, Antoine's opened in

© DANIEL MARTONE

Opened in 1840, Antoine's Restaurant is one of the oldest eateries in New Orleans.

1840 and, over the years, has served everyone from President Coolidge to Judy Garland. Several well-known dishes, such as oysters Rockefeller and eggs Sardou, were invented at this elegant restaurant. The solicitous waitstaff will happily explain the endless list of culinary options, with cheeses, sauces, salads, and sides all available à la carte, not to mention an extensive wine list. Deciding what to eat, though, is only half the challenge—figuring out *where* to dine can also test your decision-making skills. Choose from one of 14 dining rooms—including the Rex Room, a colorful space filled with Mardi Gras photos, and the Japanese Room, a study in Japanese decorative arts. Before dinner, be sure to stop by the on-site **Hermes Bar** for a cocktail. During the day, enjoy a treat at **Antoine's Annex** (513 Royal St., 504/525-8045), a small coffeehouse offering gelato, pastries, and other light bites.

ARNAUD'S RESTAURANT $$$

813 Bienville Ave., 504/523-5433,
www.arnaudsrestaurant.com
HOURS: Sun.-Thurs. 6-10 P.M., Fri.-Sat. 6-10:30 P.M.

The active corner of Bourbon and Bienville might seem an unlikely place for a fine-dining establishment, but nevertheless, Arnaud's is a terrific spot to sample traditional Creole cuisine. It was established by Arnaud Cazenave, a French wine salesman, in 1918. Favorite dishes include the seafood gumbo, crab cakes, speckled trout amandine, and oven-roasted rock Cornish game hen with Véronique sauce, wild rice, and water chestnut dressing. Sides like smothered okra and soufflé potatoes are equally delectable, as is my favorite appetizer, the oysters Arnaud, which comprises all five of the restaurant's baked oysters, from Bienville to Rockefeller. You can dine in either the elegant main dining room or the smaller jazz bistro, which features live jazz music. Either way, the service is usually friendly and attentive. Before or after dinner, have a cocktail in **French 75,** the on-site bar that was once a gentlemen-only area, and check out the stunning costumes at the **Germaine Cazenave Wells Mardi Gras Museum.** For a more casual meal, head next-door to Arnaud's other eatery, **Remoulade** (309 Bourbon St., 504/523-0377, www.remoulade.com).

BRENNAN'S $$$

417 Royal St., 504/525-9711,
www.brennansneworleans.com
HOURS: Mon.-Fri. 9 A.M.-1 P.M. and 6-9 P.M., Sat.-Sun. 8 A.M.-2:30 P.M. and 6-9 P.M.

It's hard to bypass Brennan's, the legendary pink eatery that initiated the Brennan clan's rise as the Crescent City's first family of the restaurant business. Opened in 1946 by Owen Edward Brennan, the restaurant encompasses several dining areas, plus a lush courtyard. While it's not my favorite option in the Quarter—the atmosphere here can be loud at times, and visiting celebrities tend to get better service than regular folks—the food is definitely worth sampling. Some of the dishes invented on-site include eggs Hussarde, which combines poached eggs with Canadian bacon, hollandaise, and Marchand de Vin sauce; redfish with lump crabmeat Jaime in a mushroom–red wine sauce; and bananas Foster, bananas sautéed in butter, brown sugar, cinnamon, and banana liqueur, then flamed in rum and served over vanilla ice cream. The wine selection is also impressive.

COOP'S PLACE $$

1109 Decatur St., 504/525-9053, www.coopsplace.net
HOURS: Daily 11 A.M.-close

The owner of Coop's sought to create a space that's equally bar and restaurant, and indeed this underrated hangout on raffish Decatur Street succeeds on both counts. Since 1983, this popular local joint has offered the convivial spirit of a neighborhood pub, complete with a pool table in the rear, as well as New Orleans–style cuisine that's consistently high caliber. Dark wooden tables and exposed brick walls give the place a warm feel, as does the welcoming staff. Reservations are not accepted, and, thanks to the presence of video poker machines, guests must be 21 and older.

THE COURT OF TWO SISTERS $$$

613 Royal St., 504/522-7261,
www.courtoftwosisters.com

HOURS: Daily 9 A.M.–3 P.M. and 5:30–10 P.M.

The French Quarter boasts several historic restaurants, including the Court of Two Sisters, established in 1880 by two Creole sisters, Emma and Bertha Camors; it is now run by the Fein brothers. Though the old-fashioned interior can be an elegant yet casual spot for a romantic dinner, the real appeal is the lush, spacious courtyard, particularly during the daily jazz brunch buffet, which features a live jazz trio and an array of hot and cold dishes, from made-to-order omelets, grillades, and turtle soup to shrimp rémoulade, ceviche, and pecan pie.

DICKIE BRENNAN'S PALACE CAFÉ $$$

605 Canal St., 504/523-1661, www.palacecafe.com

HOURS: Mon.–Sat. 11:30 A.M.–2:30 P.M. and 5:30 P.M.–close, Sun. 10:30 A.M.–2:30 P.M. and 5:30 P.M.–close

The Palace Café ranks among the most cosmopolitan of the several outstanding Brennan family restaurants in New Orleans. True, it can seem touristy at times, but don't let that dissuade you—the kitchen consistently prepares some of the city's best and most exciting local fare, and the staff is highly personable and efficient. Signature dishes include andouille-crusted fish, an oyster pan roast, and a crabmeat cheesecake baked in a pecan crust. Every dish is tasty and presented with great flourish. Housed within the historic Werlein's building, this classy restaurant also serves a particularly enjoyable Sunday jazz brunch.

◖ GALATOIRE'S $$$

209 Bourbon St., 504/525-2021, www.galatoires.com

HOURS: Tues.–Sat. 11:30 A.M.–10 P.M., Sun. noon–10 P.M.

Among those few remaining New Orleans restaurants where men must wear a jacket in the evening—and no patron may stroll in wearing shorts—is Galatoire's, which opened in 1905 and has been run by the Galatoire family ever since. While rowdy Bourbon Street might seem an unlikely place for such an elegant restaurant, Galatoire's actually lures many loyal patrons, and true regulars have been coming here for generations, often taking their seat at the same table. Almost as much fun as dining here is watching the local politicos hobnob and broker deals, especially on Friday afternoons. The enormous French-Creole menu includes everything from lavish high-end dishes, such as filet béarnaise, to affordable chicken and seafood entrées. Sweet potato cheesecake and banana bread pudding stand out among the rich desserts. Though the lower dining room maintains a "no reservations" policy, you can reserve a seat in the recently remodeled upstairs area.

GUMBO SHOP $$

630 St. Peter St., 504/525-1486,
www.gumboshop.com

HOURS: Sun.–Thurs. 11 A.M.–10:30 P.M., Fri.–Sat. 11 A.M.–11 P.M.

Given its location near Jackson Square, the Gumbo Shop can be a fairly touristy place, which, unfortunately, doesn't always live up to the hype. Granted, many of the dishes here are worth sampling, from shrimp Creole over rice to crawfish étouffée to a nicely prepared filet mignon with sautéed mushrooms. The seafood okra and chicken andouille gumbos, however, could be better: Though the thick broths are tasty, the gumbos are often skimpy with the ingredients, such as shrimp. Still, the complete Creole dinners are a steal, offering you the choice of an appetizer, vegetable, entrée, and dessert for around $25; the Creole creamed spinach and bread pudding are particularly good options.

K-PAUL'S LOUISIANA KITCHEN $$$

416 Chartres St., 504/596-2530 or 877/553-3401, www.chefpaul.com/kpaul

HOURS: Mon. 5:30–10 P.M., Tues.–Sat. 11 A.M.–2 P.M. and 5:30–10 P.M.

It's probably not fair to describe K-Paul's Louisiana Kitchen as traditional, since much of the food at Paul Prudhomme's famous restaurant is quite innovative. The celebrity chef—who was a household name long before Emeril Lagasse—was largely responsible for

the Gumbo Shop, not far from Jackson Square

popularizing Cajun cooking outside Louisiana, and this is still an excellent, although rather pricey, place to sample such fare. Situated within an 1834 building, the once-intimate dining room took no reservations for many years, but a 1996 expansion added more seating, and nowadays, you can reserve a table. Featuring an intimate courtyard, K-Paul's (which was named after Paul and his late wife, K) also has an open kitchen on both the first and second floors, allowing diners the chance to watch their dishes being prepared.

MR. B'S BISTRO $$$

201 Royal St., 504/523-2078, www.mrbsbistro.com
HOURS: Mon.-Sat. 11:30 A.M.-9 P.M., Sun. 10:30 A.M.-9 P.M.

Opposite the imposing Hotel Monteleone, Mr. B's Bistro is a popular place for business lunches, and given its fashionable bar, attentive service, classy decor, and smoke-free policy, it's easy to understand why. It also doesn't hurt that this bustling eatery—operated by Cindy Brennan, of the famous Brennan clan—serves some truly delicious Creole cuisine. Though

the menu depends on seasonal ingredients and therefore changes often, you can usually expect classic dishes like the bourbon-glazed shrimp salad, gumbo ya ya, barbecue shrimp, pasta jambalaya, shrimp and grits, fried soft-shell crab amandine, and bread pudding with an Irish whiskey sauce. Save a little money by opting for weekday cocktail specials and two-course luncheons. Besides lunch and dinner throughout the week, Mr. B's also offers a wonderful jazz brunch on Sunday. In addition, there's usually live piano music during dinner, 7–10 P.M. Though reservations aren't required here, they are accepted, and the dress code is upscale casual.

MURIEL'S JACKSON SQUARE $$$

801 Chartres St., 504/568-1885, www.muriels.com
HOURS: Mon.-Fri. 11:30 A.M.-2:30 P.M. and 5:30-10 P.M., Sat. 11:30 A.M.-2:30 P.M. and 5-10 P.M., Sun. 11 A.M.-2 P.M. and 5-10 P.M.

Despite the name, Muriel's isn't actually on Jackson Square, but given its corner location at St. Ann and Chartres Streets, it definitely offers a picturesque view of this historic plaza. One of the more elegant restaurants in the Quarter, Muriel's appeals to a wide array of diners, from couples celebrating anniversaries to friends out on the town. No matter why you've come, though, you'll be treated to delicious contemporary Creole cuisine, such as mirlitons (chayote) filled with shrimp and andouille stuffing; a Gulf seafood stew that consists of shrimp, fish, and crabmeat sautéed with fennel, tomatoes, oyster mushrooms, and leeks and simmered in a tarragon-enhanced velouté sauce; and desserts like vanilla bean crème brûlée. In addition to offering two-course lunch specials and three-course prix fixe dinners, Muriel's also features a pre-theater menu available on the evening of any local theater performance. Curiously, Muriel's is one of the few supposedly haunted establishments that seems to relish its past residents.

OLD COFFEEPOT RESTAURANT $\bm{\mathbb{S}}\bm{\mathbb{S}}$

714 St. Peter St., 504/524-3500,
www.theoldcoffeepot.com

HOURS: Sun.-Mon. and Thurs. 8 A.M.-10:30 P.M., Tues.-Wed. 8 A.M.-2:30 P.M. and 5:30-10:30 P.M., Fri.-Sat. 8 A.M.-11:30 P.M.

If you don't mind sassy service that borders on rude at times, make a beeline for the Old Coffeepot, which was established in 1894 and now features one of the best breakfasts in the Quarter. Some of my favorite morning dishes here include Callas cakes, essentially spiced, deep-fried rice balls dusted with powdered sugar and served with creamy grits and maple syrup; eggs Sardou, which consists of poached eggs, creamed spinach, artichoke bottoms, hollandaise, and an English muffin; and the Rockefeller omelet, combining creamed spinach, oysters, cheese, and a cream sauce. Lunch and dinner, featuring Cajun and Creole dishes, are also available.

TUJAGUE'S $\bm{\mathbb{S}}\bm{\mathbb{S}}\bm{\mathbb{S}}$

823 Decatur St., 504/525-8676,
www.tujaguesrestaurant.com

HOURS: Mon.-Fri. 5-10 P.M., Sat.-Sun. 11 A.M.-3 P.M. and 5-10 P.M.

Tujague's is an atmospheric corner tavern that's

been around since 1856, making it the second-oldest continuously operated restaurant in New Orleans. It sits opposite the French Market and serves much of the local Louisiana produce and seafood sold there. The six-course Creole menu varies little from what diners might have eaten more than a century ago: beef brisket in Creole sauce, shrimp rémoulade, soup du jour, and a choice of entrée, dessert, and beverage. In addition to the usual cocktails and wines, Tujague's serves its own microbrewed beer. Drinking here has quite a legacy—the cypress-wood bar is original, shipped here from France the year that the restaurant opened, and it's played host to everyone from President Truman to Harrison Ford.

COFFEE AND DESSERTS

CAFE BEIGNET $\bm{\mathbb{S}}$

334-B Royal St., 504/524-5530, www.cafebeignet.com

HOURS: Daily 7 A.M.-5 P.M.

Nestled beside the French Quarter's stately police station, Cafe Beignet is a cozy, European-style eatery that offers both indoor and outdoor seating. While café au lait and sugar-covered beignets are the popular options here, you'll also find an array of delicious breakfasts, Cajun specialties, and fresh sandwiches, such as crawfish omelets, muffulettas, and turkey and bacon croissants. The chicken and sausage gumbo is particularly delicious. There's also a smaller location of Cafe Beignet in the New Orleans Musical Legends Park (311 Bourbon St.).

CAFÉ DU MONDE $\bm{\mathbb{S}}$

800 Decatur St., 504/525-4544 or 800/772-2927, www.cafedumonde.com

HOURS: Daily 24 hours

Beginning as a humble coffee stand to serve the customers and employees of the produce stalls in the French Market in 1862, Café Du Monde has grown into one of the most legendary food operations in the country. Part of its mystique and popularity is that the place is open around the clock (except for Christmas) and that it serves a small menu, which is conveniently plastered on the napkin dispensers. The mainstays are beignets and dark-roasted coffee

ROUND-THE-CLOCK EATS

For night owls like me, the Big Easy really delivers. In addition to bars, pubs, and live music venues that stay open until the wee hours, you'll find a slew of 24-hour eateries, ideal for late-night or early-morning cravings.

Perhaps the most well known of these round-the-clock joints is **Café Du Monde** (800 Decatur St.), which, except for a brief time around Christmas (6 P.M. on Dec. 24 to 6 A.M. on Dec. 26), is open 24 hours daily. The spacious, open-air patio, with its green-and-white striped awning, old-fashioned ceiling fans, and bustling uniformed servers, has been depicted in countless magazines, television shows, and movies, including 2003's *Runaway Jury*. A simple menu, pasted on each table's napkin dispenser, features a limited selection of items (such as beignets, milk, coffee, and hot chocolate) that have changed little over the years. This charming place lures a wide assortment of patrons, from local families and Midwest tourists to post-prom couples and on-duty police officers (who, admittedly, must order the normally messy beignets without the traditional powdered sugar topping, lest they risk staining their dark uniforms). Despite healthy intentions, I admit to numerous fond memories of Café Du Monde. It's here, after all, that I ventured after many a high school dance and now come with my husband for a late-night sugar fix.

Of course, Café Du Monde isn't the only round-the-clock option in the French Quarter. If you have a yen for more than dessert, head to the **Clover Grill** (900 Bourbon St., 504/598-1010, www.clovergrill.com), a cozy diner where seating is often hard to snag and sassy waiters serve up hamburgers, sandwiches, waffles, omelets, and other greasy-spoon favorites. A couple blocks down Bourbon, the **Quartermaster** (1100 Bourbon St., 504/529-1416, www.quartermasterdeli.net) offers only a few seats alongside the front window, but plenty of culinary options at the deli counter in the rear of this often crowded, albeit dingy, store. After a night of tireless bar-hopping, the Quartermaster is a popular place to stock up on junk food in addition to jambalaya, stuffed potatoes, roast beef po-boys, and a cornucopia of other deli selections. Be aware, though, that as at the Clover Grill, the employees here are rife with attitude.

Patrons 21 years old and over might prefer the **Déjà Vu Bar & Grill** (400 Dauphine St., 504/523-1931, www.dejavunola.com), where you'll find a wide selection of beers, cocktails, and tasty vittles – from burgers and po-boys to seafood platters and breakfast specialties. If you're staying in the French Quarter and would rather not leave your apartment or hotel room, note that the Quartermaster and Déjà Vu offer free delivery for all phone-in food orders.

For even more round-the-clock eateries throughout the city, check out **NOLA 24/7** (www.nola247.com), an online guide to 24-hour restaurants in the Big Easy. Just be advised that the information isn't comprehensive or up-to-date, so be sure to contact the establishments directly.

laced with chicory and traditionally served *au lait*. The mostly open-air café has dozens of small marble tables beneath the green-and-white awning, the sides of which can be unfurled on chilly days. You can also grab one of the few tables in the small, fully enclosed dining area. Servers clad in white shirts with black bow ties and white-paper hats whisk about gracefully, delivering plates of beignets at almost breakneck speed. While no visit to New Orleans is complete without experiencing this original location, you might also notice other branches throughout the city, including one in the Lakeside Shopping Center.

CAFE ENVIE & ESPRESSO BAR ❸

1241 Decatur St., 504/524-3689,
www.cafeenvienola.com
HOURS: Sun.-Thurs. 7 A.M.-midnight, Fri.-Sat.
7 A.M.-1 A.M.

A wonderful place to while away an afternoon, hang out with friends, and watch curious

© DANIEL MARTONE

Breakfasts are divine at Cafe Envie & Espresso Bar.

passersby, Cafe Envie brews a strong coffee and serves plenty of interesting teas and pastries. In addition, this local favorite prepares decent salads and sandwiches, not to mention excellent breakfasts, including a prosciutto and asparagus omelet that I particularly enjoy. Patrons will also find lots of seating, free wireless Internet access, and open French doors that make this corner café even airier.

CC'S COMMUNITY COFFEE HOUSE $

941 Royal St., 504/581-6996,
www.communitycoffee.com
HOURS: Daily 7 A.M.–9 P.M.

The Quarter has a branch of one of the city's most famous coffeehouse chains, CC's, at the corner of Royal and Dumaine Streets, just opposite the neighborhood's only elementary school. It's a cozy spot, meaning that seating is a bit limited, but it's also warmly lit and charmingly furnished, with several cushy armchairs. Besides tasty coffee drinks and delectable cookies, muffins, and scones, this café—a frequent stop on my daily walks—also provides

free wireless Internet access. Numerous other CC's coffeehouses can be found throughout New Orleans and southern Louisiana, from Metairie to Lafayette.

CROISSANT D'OR PATISSERIE $

617 Ursulines Ave., 504/524-4663
HOURS: Wed.–Mon. 6:30 A.M.–3 P.M.

A source of delightful pastries, from napoleons to dark chocolate mousse, the Croissant D'or is a classic French bakery that also serves delicious sandwiches, homemade soups, fresh salads, and yummy breakfasts. Situated in the Lower Quarter, not far from the Old Ursuline Convent, this spacious café—with plenty of tables, local artwork, and a simply furnished courtyard—makes a nice break from exploring the neighborhood's rich architecture. Just be prepared for long lines, especially in the morning.

LA DIVINA GELATERIA $

621 St. Peter St., 504/302-2692,
www.ladivinagelateria.com

HOURS: Mon.-Wed. 11 A.M.-10 P.M., Thurs. 8:30 A.M.-10 P.M., Fri.-Sat. 8:30 A.M.-11 P.M., Sun. 8:30 A.M.-10 P.M.

In the alley behind the Cabildo sits a delightful café with limited outdoor seating, heavenly paninis, varied coffee drinks, and, as the name indicates, plenty of artisanal gelato, available in five different sizes. Though the gelato flavors change daily and seasonally, standards include dark chocolate and pineapple mint sorbetto. My favorites, though, tend to be those that take advantage of local ingredients, such as bourbon pecan, sweet potato, bananas Foster, king cake, and Creole cream cheese, so keep a lookout for them. My favorite sandwich here, the Muffalino, is a reinvented New Orleans classic, a panini featuring salami, mortadella, Italian ham, provolone cheese, and homemade olive salad. You'll find two other locations of La Divina Gelateria Uptown—in the Garden District (3005 Magazine St., 504/342-2634) and at Loyola University (6363 St. Charles Ave., 504/258-2115).

ROYAL BLEND COFFEE & TEA HOUSE $

621 Royal St., 504/523-2716, www.royalblendcoffee.com
HOURS: Daily 8 A.M.-6 P.M.

Amid the art galleries and antiques shops of Royal Street lies my favorite coffeehouse in the Quarter. While you might find better deli sandwiches, soups, salads, muffins, and other pastries elsewhere, the Royal Blend is still a wonderful place to devour such treats. After all, in addition to cozy indoor seating, there's a lovely courtyard here—a quiet place to read a book, get some work done, chat with friends, and sip your preferred coffee, tea, or other beverage. There's also a Royal Blend in Metairie (204 Metairie Rd., 504/835-7779).

ECLECTIC
BAYONA $$$

430 Dauphine St., 504/525-4455, www.bayona.com
HOURS: Mon.-Tues. 6 P.M.-close, Wed.-Sat. 11:30 A.M.-close

A highly regarded restaurant on a quiet stretch of Dauphine, Bayona fuses traditions, recipes, and ingredients from a handful of cultures all known for delicious food—namely, American, French, Italian, Mediterranean, Asian, and North African. Chef Susan Spicer, who was named best chef in the Southeast in 1993 by the prestigious James Beard Foundation, dreams up such imaginative combos as peppered lamb loin with goat cheese–zinfandel sauce. Desserts are no mere afterthought here, and there's a commendable wine list. The setting—an 18th-century Creole cottage filled with trompe l'oeil murals of the Mediterranean countryside, plus a lush courtyard—is the quintessence of romance.

CAFÉ AMELIE $$

912 Royal St., 504/412-8965, www.cafeamelie.com
HOURS: Wed.-Sun. 11 A.M.-9 P.M.

Opposite the oft-photographed Cornstalk Hotel, you'll encounter the enticing Café Amelie, a cute, warmly furnished spot that sits beyond a lush, intimate courtyard, which is, not surprisingly, favored for anniversaries and other romantic occasions. Locals and tourists alike often pause before the simple, ever-changing menu that's posted daily by the wrought-iron gates. The menu, while eclectic, definitely embraces Louisiana-style cuisine, including such classics as chicken and andouille gumbo, satsuma-glazed shrimp, muffulettas, cochon de lait (Cajun roast pig) sandwiches, oven-roasted pork chops, citrus-drizzled crab cakes, and jumbo shrimp and grits with corn macque choux (a side dish of sautéed corn, tomatoes, bell peppers, onions, and various spices).

CRESCENT CITY BREWHOUSE $$

527 Decatur St., 504/522-0571 or 888/819-9330, www.crescentcitybrewhouse.com
HOURS: Mon.-Thurs. noon-10 P.M., Fri.-Sat. 11:30 A.M.-11 P.M., Sun. 11:30 A.M.-10 P.M.

Though some locals consider the Crescent City Brewhouse—which occupies the first two floors of a white-brick building on Decatur—a bit of a tourist magnet, I actually find that, as brewpubs go, it serves surprisingly decent and varied food. Offerings from the menu include baked brie, shucked oysters, seafood cheesecake, redfish Pontchartrain, pork ribs, and a grilled ribeye with asiago cheese and fresh asparagus. Many diners come to sample the various microbrews, which are prepared Bavarian-style, with simple, natural ingredients—the light Weiss beer is a house favorite. This inviting space also lures passersby with its exposed brick walls, shiny brewing equipment, and live music. If possible, opt for balcony or courtyard dining.

IRIS $$$

Bienville House Hotel, 321 N. Peters St.,
504/299-3944, www.irisneworleans.com
HOURS: Mon., Wed., and Sat. 5 P.M.-close, Thurs.-Fri. 11:30 A.M.-2 P.M. and 5 P.M.-close

Located within the elegant Bienville House Hotel, this intimate, relatively quiet restaurant is known for its excellent service, innovative cocktails, and contemporary American cuisine. While the menu at Iris changes often, you might encounter such dishes as foie gras with brioche, sunflower shoots, and truffle vinaigrette; oxtail ravioli with eggplant, olives, and tomatoes; duck leg and pork belly with stone fruits, house-pickled vegetables, and blueberry jus; and flounder with kale, edamame, grilled sweet onion, cherry tomatoes, and corn broth. Though the bar opens at 5 P.M. in the evening, the dining room doesn't open until 6 P.M.

NOLA RESTAURANT $$$

534 St. Louis St., 504/522-6652, www.emerils.com
HOURS: Mon.-Wed. 6-10 P.M., Thurs.-Sun. 11:30 A.M.-2 P.M. and 6-10 P.M.

Though most people have heard about NOLA—Emeril Lagasse's restaurant in the French Quarter—not everyone loves it. When all is said and done, however, NOLA delivers great cooking and a lively dining experience that very nearly lives up to the hype. The menu changes often, but some favorites include garlic-crusted drum, a stuffed chicken wings appetizer with homemade hoisin dipping sauce, and fried green tomatoes with shrimp rémoulade. There's also a selection of excellent desserts, such as king cake bread pudding with Creole cream cheese ice cream, strawberry

compote, and pecan streusel. Keep in mind that it can be hard to get a table here, so book ahead, and expect a wait even when you show up on time for your reservation.

STELLA! $$$

1032 Chartres St., 504/587-0091,
www.restaurantstella.com
HOURS: Daily 5:30-10:30 P.M.

Stella! is a Quarter favorite, in spite of—or perhaps because of—its discreet, slightly out-of-the-way location. Set inside the Hôtel Provincial, Stella! is in the quieter Lower Quarter, halfway between Jackson Square and Esplanade Avenue. Though not everyone loves the silly name, the tribute to Stanley Kowalski can be forgiven, as the food is anything but silly. Once inside this dapper, intimate dining room, you'll be treated to truly creative fare, such as seared Hudson Valley foie gras with toasted brioche and huckleberry jam. While some of the dishes may sound overwrought, the ingredients complement each other nicely—and the presentation is often stunning. The amicable staff and impressive wine selection also help to make this a winning choice for a fine-dining experience.

ITALIAN

ANGELI ON DECATUR $

1141 Decatur St., 504/566-0077,
http://angelirestaurant.webs.com
HOURS: Sun.-Thurs. 11 A.M.-2 A.M., Fri.-Sat. 11 A.M.-4 A.M.

While the French Quarter offers several places to scarf down a big meal after a night of drinking and dancing, Angeli is one of the best. Open into the wee hours, this funky eatery with its walls covered in vibrant local artwork provides a wide range of munchies and light bites, including salads, burgers, sandwiches, pasta dishes, calzones, and appetizers, such as the addictive flatbread with pesto and parmesan cheese. Pizzas are the specialty here—my favorite is the Virtuous Angel, topped with garlic herb sauce, mozzarella cheese, artichokes, spinach, mushrooms, and tomatoes. Angeli draws an eclectic crowd of artists, yuppies, and ravers, especially late at night, and the busy street-corner location allows for optimum people-watching, though if you'd rather not venture out, the restaurant also delivers.

IRENE'S CUISINE $$$

539 St. Philip St., 504/529-8811

HOURS: Mon.-Sat. 5:30-10 P.M.

In the quieter Lower Quarter, at the corner of Chartres and St. Philip Streets, stands a nondescript building that looks more like a warehouse than a fine-dining establishment. Nevertheless, the well-favored Irene's Cuisine is popular among gourmands, especially for romantic dinners and special occasions. The service here is normally attentive, and the Italian and French cuisine is often quite tasty, with highlights like bruschetta, escargot, soft-shell crab pasta, and crème brûlée. Given the restaurant's popularity, reservations are definitely recommended; just be prepared for a couple of drawbacks, such as the crowded nature of the restaurant and surprise charges for soda refills.

LOUISIANA PIZZA KITCHEN $

95 French Market Pl., 504/522-9500,
www.louisianapizzakitchen.com

HOURS: Daily 11 A.M.-10 P.M.

Back in my teenaged years, the Louisiana Pizza Kitchen was one of my favorite eateries in the Quarter, and luckily, it's just as good today. The corner pizzeria sits right on the edge of the French Market, facing the Old U.S. Mint. Vaguely art deco in nature, the gray-brick room features black-and-white–checked floors and local artwork, which, as at Angeli on Decatur, is for sale. Pizzas are of the thin-crust variety, baked with little grease and topped with everything from grilled eggplant and shiitake mushrooms to crawfish and applewood-smoked bacon. Pita wraps, calzones, pasta dishes, hefty salads, and tasty appetizers round out the menu. Try the calamari, which is lightly battered and served with olive salad and homemade marinara, and be sure to check out the Uptown location (615 S. Carrollton Ave., 504/866-5900, www.louisianapizzakitchenuptown.com) if you're in the neighborhood.

MONA LISA RESTAURANT $$

1212 Royal St., 504/522-6746

HOURS: Mon.-Thurs. 5-10 P.M., Fri.-Sun. 11 A.M.-10 P.M.

If you appreciate well-prepared Italian cuisine—and would rather avoid the crazier end of the French Quarter—head to the more residential part of Royal Street, where sits a local favorite, the Mona Lisa Restaurant. As ideal for romantic dinners as family outings, this cozy eatery has at least three things going for it: the friendly service, affordable yet delicious food, and warm, homey decor, including ceiling fans, red-and-white checkered tablecloths, and walls that are literally covered with assorted *Mona Lisa* renditions, from copies of the classic da Vinci painting to a Picasso-style version. While I've never had a bad appetizer, salad, pizza, or pasta dish here, my favorite items include the Mediterranean pizza, spinach lasagna, chicken parmesan, and Mardi Gras pasta, which features shrimp and sausage with linguini and a creamy red sauce. In addition, you can save some money by bringing your own wine—the corkage fee here is quite reasonable.

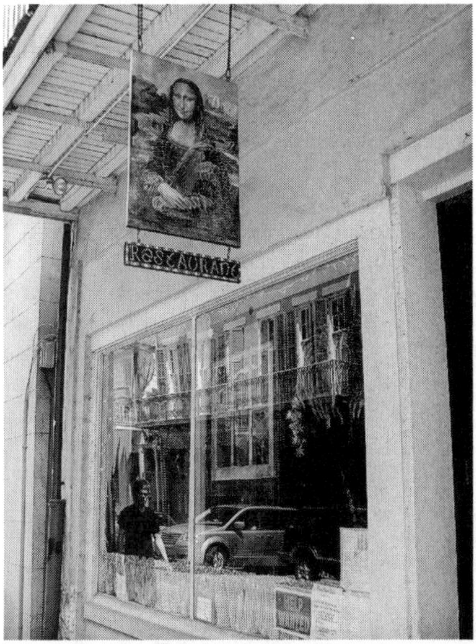

© DANIEL MARTONE

Variations of the famous da Vinci painting cover the walls of the Mona Lisa Restaurant.

MEXICAN

EL GATO NEGRO $$

81 French Market Pl., 504/525-9752,
www.elgatonegronola.com

HOURS: Mon.-Fri. 11 A.M.-10 P.M., Sat.-Sun. 9 A.M.-10 P.M.

Opposite the French Market, El Gato Negro is a delicious, if pricey, spot for fans of authentic Mexican cuisine. Highlights include the tableside guacamole and yellowfin tuna ceviche, chicken and steak fajitas, pulled pork tacos, and pan-seared wild salmon with sautéed shrimp, salsa, squash, poblano peppers, Vidalia onions, and mushrooms. Rare beers, varied tequilas, and hand-squeezed margaritas and mojitos are also on offer. Casual indoor dining and outdoor seating are both available. If you're exploring the neighborhoods of Greater New Orleans, be sure to stop by the Lakeview location (300 Harrison Ave., 504/488-0107).

FELIPE'S TAQUERIA $

301 N. Peters St., 504/267-4406,
www.felipestaqueria.com

HOURS: Sun.-Tues. 11 A.M.-11 P.M., Wed. 11 A.M.-1 A.M., Thurs. 11 A.M.-11 P.M., Fri.-Sat. 11 A.M.-2 A.M.

One of my favorite late-night haunts for inexpensive grub is Felipe's Taqueria, just around the corner from one of my other favorite spots, the Kerry Irish Pub. In fact, my husband and I have been known to scarf down some tasty tacos, burritos, and tamales between live music sets at the Kerry. Opened in 2004, the space itself is attractive and inviting, with high ceilings, solid wooden tables, and a separate bar area, where the television is always tuned to sporting events. The menu is fairly simple, and all dishes are made to order, right in front of you, which explains why everything, from the super burrito to the chicken flautas, tastes so fresh. If you have room, be sure to order the Felipe's Special, an appetizer that consists of corn chips, freshly made salsa and guacamole, and queso dip. There's also an Uptown location (86215 S. Miro St., 504/309-2776).

SEAFOOD

ACME OYSTER HOUSE $$

724 Iberville St., 504/522-5973, www.acmeoyster.com

HOURS: Sun.-Thurs. 11 A.M.-10 P.M., Fri.-Sat. 11 A.M.-11 P.M.

Since 1910, the Acme Oyster House—which also has locations in Metairie (3000 Veterans Memorial Blvd., 504/309-4056) as well as Covington and Baton Rouge—has been a reliable option for fresh bivalves. Decked out with red-checkered tablecloths and packed with tourists, this casual place can be crazy at times, but for some, it's worth braving the frenzy for tasty soft-shell crab po-boys, shrimp platters, seafood gumbo, and jambalaya, plus a first-rate oyster Rockefeller bisque. While it might not be oyster nirvana, as some people claim, Acme's rich history and convenient location make it a decent choice. Be advised, though, that the prices here are slightly higher than those of comparable joints.

☾ CAFE MASPERO $

601 Decatur St., 504/523-6250,
www.cafemaspero.com

HOURS: Sun.-Thurs. 11 A.M.-10 P.M., Fri.-Sat. 11 A.M.-11 P.M.

For more than four decades, Cafe Maspero has been one of the Quarter's most popular

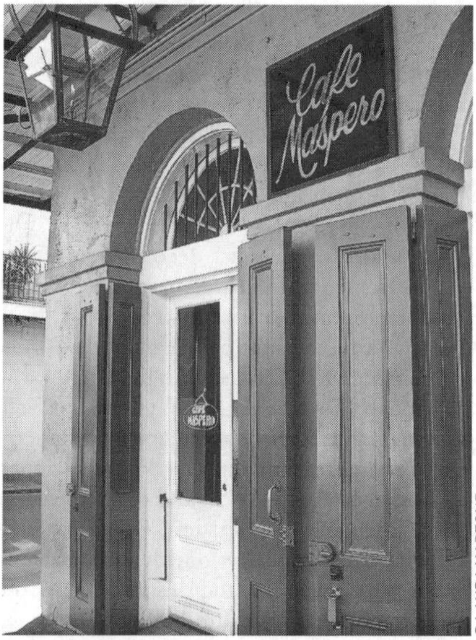

© LAURA MARTONE

Cafe Maspero offers some of the cheapest seafood in the French Quarter.

eateries. Ideal for budget-conscious travelers, it features several local staples, including fried seafood platters, jambalaya, and muffulettas. In fact, if gumbo and raw oysters were on the menu, my husband and I would probably never eat anywhere else. Despite the low prices, portions are usually gigantic, and while there are occasional lulls, this spacious, admittedly dingy joint is typically hopping—with full wooden tables, bustling servers, and long lines of tourists and locals. Though the oft-open French doors invite refreshing breezes from the Mississippi River, they also welcome native inhabitants like hungry mice.

DICKIE BRENNAN'S
BOURBON HOUSE SEAFOOD $$$

144 Bourbon St., 504/522-0111,
www.bourbonhouse.com
HOURS: Sun.-Thurs. 6:30 A.M.-10 P.M., Fri.-Sat.
6:30 A.M.-11 P.M.

Across the street from Ralph Brennan's Red Fish Grill, you'll encounter Dickie Brennan's Bourbon House Seafood. As the latter name indicates, this often crowded seafood eatery may not share the same owner as its neighbor, but it does offer a similar caliber of seasonal seafood. Besides the enormous raw oysters, other favorite dishes include the grilled alligator, seafood gumbo, and shrimp po-boy. My favorite dish is *le grand plateaux de fruits de mer,* which features freshly shucked raw oysters, local Cajun caviar, boiled Gulf shrimp, mussels, marinated crab fingers, and seasonal seafood salads. In keeping with its name, this popular restaurant also houses an incredible assortment of bourbon, from Crown Royal to Jack Daniel's. With its large, glass windows, it offers entertaining views of the madness along Bourbon Street, but be advised that service here can be slow, and the wait for a table can be long.

FELIX'S RESTAURANT
& OYSTER BAR $$

739 Iberville St., 504/522-4440, www.felixs.com
HOURS: Mon.-Thurs. 10 A.M.-11 P.M., Fri.-Sun. 10 A.M.-1 A.M.

While there's usually a line outside the Acme Oyster House, I actually prefer the less expensive seafood eatery across the road. Just off crazy Bourbon Street, Felix's Restaurant & Oyster Bar has been serving local seafood fanatics since the early 1900s. Though known for its oysters on the half shell, this super-casual joint prepares all of New Orleans's seafood favorites well, including the shrimp rémoulade, seafood gumbo, blackened alligator, grilled catch of the day, oysters Rockefeller, oysters Bienville, and fried seafood platter. Unfortunately, though, the service can be spotty here.

GW FINS $$$

808 Bienville Ave., 504/581-3467, www.gwfins.com
HOURS: Daily 5-10 P.M.

GW Fins is a bit of a departure from most seafood-based New Orleans restaurants: Although many local dishes are offered here, the kitchen serves fresh fish from all over the world, ranging from Canadian salmon to New Zealand John Dory. The setting, a converted warehouse with lofty ceilings, warm woods, and cushy booths, is contemporary and upbeat—seemingly more suitable for the CBD than the French Quarter. Worthy specialties include wood-grilled pompano with pineapple basil glaze, sweet potato hash, and crispy plantains; New Bedford sea scallops with mushroom risotto; and parmesan-crusted lemon sole with jumbo lump crab, asparagus, and crispy capers. There's nothing overly convoluted or cutesy about the cooking—just fresh fish with modern ingredients, presented with flair—and the wine list is equally impressive. Reservations are recommended, and the dress code is business casual.

OCEANA GRILL $$

739 Conti St., 504/525-6002, www.oceanagrill.com
HOURS: Daily 8 A.M.-1 A.M.

Having expanded into the space formerly occupied by the Olde N'awlins Cookery, the multilevel Oceana Grill encompasses numerous, colorfully decorated rooms, plus a courtyard. It's not far from bustling Bourbon Street. While some locals dismiss this late-night, family-owned joint as a pricey tourist trap, my husband and I actually appreciate Oceana's friendly service and specialty cocktails, not to mention dishes like seafood gumbo, crabmeat cakes, Cajun jambalaya pasta, and chocolate Kahlua mousse. My favorite item here is the platter of raw oysters, which are usually large, clean, and perfectly chilled.

RALPH BRENNAN'S
RED FISH GRILL $$$

115 Bourbon St., 504/598-1200, www.redfishgrill.com
HOURS: Sun.-Thurs. 11 A.M.-10 P.M., Fri.-Sat. 11 A.M.-3 P.M. and 5-11 P.M.

There aren't many restaurants on exuberant Bourbon Street worth seeking out, but Ralph Brennan's Red Fish Grill is an exception. Opened in 1996, the restaurant—set inside a former department store just a block from Canal—helped to revive a block that was once dominated by department stores and, consequently, felt a bit dark and ominous at night. The cavernous main dining room reverberates with piped-in rock music, and huge redfish mobiles dangle overhead—this is no wallflower of a restaurant, but the noisy, festive ambience makes it fun for singles, friends dining together, and anybody heading out afterward for a tour of Bourbon's nightlife. To one side lies a spacious oyster bar with huge oyster half-shell sculptures; you can order from the main menu in here, too. The barbecued oysters are a great starter, served with a tangy blue-cheese dipping sauce, and the kitchen also turns out an amazingly decadent chocolate bread pudding. Few dishes, though, beat the hickory-grilled redfish served with wild mushroom potatoes and topped with jumbo lump crabmeat and a lemon-butter sauce.

Faubourg Marigny and Bywater   Map 2

AMERICAN
THE JOINT $

701 Mazant St., 504/949-3232,
www.alwayssmokin.com
HOURS: Mon.-Sat. 11:30 A.M.-9 P.M.

New Orleans might not be known for its barbecue, but that doesn't stop local meat lovers from heading to the Joint, a super-casual dive on the eastern end of the Bywater celebrated throughout the city for its "carnivore cuisine." Featured on Guy Fieri's popular Food Network show *Diners, Drive-ins, and Dives,* this downhome, often crowded place offers delicious pork spareribs, pulled pork sandwiches, beef brisket plates, barbecued chicken, and Cajun sausage. Even the sides here are stellar, so be sure to save room for the macaroni and cheese, baked beans, and cole slaw. If you're really hungry, you won't go wrong with the desserts either, particularly the peanut butter pie.

LA PENICHE $$

1940 Dauphine St., 504/943-1460
HOURS: Thurs.-Tues. 24 hours

During normal dining hours, La Peniche is nothing fancy, just a friendly, reasonably priced neighborhood café serving satisfying breakfast, lunch, and dinner fare. Offerings include grits, country-fried steak, pecan waffles smothered with peanut butter, good burgers and po-boys, coffee, and desserts. At 3 in the morning, however, La Peniche feels like paradise, especially after you've just stumbled out of a bar or caught a case of the late-night munchies—the place is open 24 hours except for one 42-hour span from Tuesday at 2 P.M. till Thursday at 8 A.M. Even if you're not able to dine here all night, the dishy staff and colorful local following make it a fun place to eavesdrop or make new friends.

SATSUMA CAFE $

3218 Dauphine St., 504/304-5962,
www.satsumacafe.com
HOURS: Sun.-Tues. 7 A.M.-5 P.M., Wed.-Sat. 7 A.M.-5 P.M. and 6:30-10 P.M.

Though Satsuma Cafe has its critics—particularly because of its slow service and hipster crowd—plenty of locals swear by this spacious, art-filled Bywater eatery. In addition to standard coffeehouse fare, such as espresso drinks and lemon-blueberry muffins, you'll find a wide array of delectable, often healthy breakfast, lunch, and dinner options, such as the tofu and black bean scramble, toasted pear and brie melt, shrimp ceviche, and seared mahi-mahi with spinach, herb salad, and blood orange gastrique. The freshly squeezed juices are also worth sampling; my favorite is the Popeye, which consists of spinach, lemon, kale, and apple. Satsuma's is also a decent place for vegans; some of the soups, sandwiches, and muffins are made with them in mind.

ASIAN
SUKHOTHAI $\textcircled{\$}\textcircled{\$}$
1913 Royal St., 504/948-9309,
www.sukhothai-nola.com

HOURS: Tues.-Sun. 11:30 A.M.-2:30 P.M. and 5:30-10 P.M.

For some of the best Thai food in the city, drop by cozy SukhoThai, a relatively quiet eatery nestled in the Faubourg Marigny. Here, the friendly service and local artwork help to create a hip yet informal vibe, and the menu is quite extensive, offering tasty soups, noodles, curry, vegetarian dishes, and seafood specialties, including the glass noodle shrimp bake—my personal favorite. In case you get hungry while antiques shopping, there's also a SukhoThai in Uptown (4519 Magazine St., 504/373-6471).

WASABI SUSHI & ASIAN GRILL $\textcircled{\$}\textcircled{\$}$
900 Frenchmen St., 504/943-9433,
www.wasabinola.com

HOURS: Mon.-Thurs. 11:30 A.M.-2:30 P.M. and 5-10 P.M., Fri.-Sat. 11:30 A.M.-2:30 P.M. and 5-11 P.M., Sun. 5-10 P.M.

Near the edge of the Faubourg Marigny, just a few blocks up Frenchmen Street from the main cluster of bars and restaurants, sits this dark, cozy space—at once a mellow neighborhood bar and a stellar Japanese restaurant. Besides excellent sushi and sashimi, Wasabi also serves delightful dishes like crab asparagus soup, squid salad, and wasabi honey shrimp, plus various, ever-changing daily specials. If you're in Lakeview, be sure to stop by Wasabi's West End location (8550 Pontchartrain Blvd., 504/267-3263).

© DANIEL MARTONE

Thai lovers head to SukhoThai in the Marigny.

CAJUN AND CREOLE

ELIZABETH'S RESTAURANT $ $

601 Gallier St., 504/944-9272,
www.elizabeths-restaurant.com
HOURS: Tues.-Sat. 8 A.M.-2:30 P.M. and 6-10 P.M., Sun.
8 A.M.-2:30 P.M.

Situated within a modest white-frame house by the levee, along the southern edge of the Bywater, easygoing Elizabeth's serves exceptional breakfast and lunch, though it does require a lengthy journey from the Quarter. Originally owned by chef Heidi Trull—who coined the slogan "real food done real good"— Elizabeth's is now operated by chef Bryon Peck, who's maintained the beloved eatery's commitment to imaginative meals and friendly service. One popular choice is the salmon and brie grilled cheese on rye, topped with fried eggs and hash or grits. Order a side of praline-flavored bacon to go with it. Lunch favorites include smoked turkey sandwiches, fried shrimp po-boys, and fried green tomatoes with shrimp rémoulade.

THE PRALINE CONNECTION $ $

542 Frenchmen St., 504/943-3934,
www.pralineconnection.com
HOURS: Mon.-Sat. 11 A.M.-10 P.M., Sun. 11 A.M.-9 P.M.

For a sublime blend of soul and Creole cooking, drop by the Praline Connection. Since it opened in 1990, it's been famous for both its crawfish étouffée and its bread pudding with praline sauce. In two simple dining rooms, the staff, clad in natty white shirts, black bow ties, and black fedoras, moves about efficiently with hot platters of jambalaya, red beans and rice, collard greens, fried okra, stuffed bell peppers, and other hearty, often spicy renderings of both soul and Creole cooking. Local beers and wines are sold, and you can pick up the ingredients and seasonings here to prepare your own versions of these foods back home.

COFFEE AND DESSERTS

FLORA GALLERY & COFFEE SHOP $

2600 Royal St., 504/947-8358
HOURS: Daily 6:30 A.M.-midnight

Occupying a busy corner about four blocks east of Washington Square Park, the Flora Gallery & Coffee Shop is a funky little place with sidewalk seating, worn-in furnishings, big portions of coffee elixirs, and home-style cooking. While it's not a bad place to read a book, peruse groovy art, or chat with eccentric locals, it's admittedly not for everyone—particularly at night. After all, it's not far from the somewhat sketchy border between the Marigny and Bywater.

NEW ORLEANS CAKE CAFE & BAKERY $

2440 Chartres St., 504/943-0010,
www.nolacakes.com
HOURS: Daily 7 A.M.-3 P.M.

To satisfy your sweet tooth, venture to this homey café in the Faubourg Marigny, which prepares to-die-for treats, such as red velvet cake with cream cheese frosting, plus specialty cupcakes flavored with champagne, mimosa, and chocolate mousse. Despite the name, this well-regarded neighborhood eatery also serves delicious breakfast and lunch items, including spinach and goat cheese omelets, shrimp and grits, roasted vegetable sandwiches, and grilled tuna salads. The service here is friendly and easygoing, and the crowd is a comfortable mix of students, retirees, gay artists, and hipsters, indicating that everyone is welcome here. Just be prepared for long lines, especially during the weekend brunch.

THE ORANGE COUCH $

2339 Royal St., 504/267-7327,
www.theorangecouchcoffee.com
HOURS: Daily 7 A.M.-10 P.M.

Only two blocks from the loud music clubs of Frenchmen Street lies this tranquil, smoke-free coffeehouse, an airy, light-filled space with modern furniture, contemporary artwork, and, yes, a bright orange couch. Given the trendy interior design and obvious departure from the cozy coffee shop typical of New Orleans, this sleek café might seem better suited for Los Angeles enclaves like Santa Monica or Beverly Hills, but many locals flock here to unwind with friends, listen to live music, and relish a wide array of delicious beverages and treats, such as Vietnamese iced coffee, Thai iced tea, curious milkshakes, decadent sweets, delicious quiches and tomato cheese tartlets, and gourmet Japanese ice cream.

ECLECTIC
€ FEELINGS CAFE 💲💲

2600 Chartres St., 504/945-2222,
www.feelingscafe.com

HOURS: Thurs.-Sat. 6 P.M.-close, Sun. 11 A.M.-2 P.M. and 6 P.M.-close

One of the city's definitive gay restaurants, Feelings Cafe is set on a quiet street in a charmingly decrepit-looking old building several blocks past Frenchmen Street, roughly a 10-minute walk from the Quarter's edge. Though known best for its Sunday brunch, it serves first-rate Creole and continental fare at every meal. Specialties include blue cheese steak, Gulf fish Florentine, and seafood-baked eggplant—essentially, a slice of fried eggplant, topped with a combination of dirty rice,

shrimp, crabmeat, and crawfish and covered with a rich hollandaise. Peanut-butter pie is the trademark dessert. The setting is a shabby-chic dining room with local artwork for sale, along with a shady courtyard and a piano bar. It's a real locals' favorite, worth venturing a bit off the beaten path, especially if you're looking for a little privacy.

MARIGNY BRASSERIE & BAR 💲💲

640 Frenchmen St., 504/945-4472,
www.marignybrasserie.com

HOURS: Sun.-Thurs. 11:30 A.M.-10 P.M., Fri.-Sat. 11:30 A.M.-11 P.M.

Located in the same block as Frenchmen Street's most famous music clubs, the Marigny Brasserie is a slick, modern space whose kitchen puts a unique spin on Louisiana, Southern, Italian, and French ingredients and recipes. The grilled salmon with a bourbon barbecue glaze and creamy scallion-mushroom risotto reflects the kitchen's simple approach to fine, contemporary food. Besides sandwiches, ribs,

RESTAURANTS

© DANIEL MARTONE

Music lovers often head to the Marigny Brasserie & Bar before hitting the concerts along Frenchmen Street.

chicken, gumbo, and pasta dishes, several savory salads are available, including a delicious fried oyster and spinach salad with strawberry vinaigrette and candied pecans. The stylish bar is a relaxing place to sip cocktails before heading to one of the nearby clubs.

MOJITOS RUM BAR & GRILL $$

437 Esplanade Ave., 504/252-4800,
www.mojitosnola.com
HOURS: Mon.-Thurs. 4 P.M.-1 A.M., Fri. 4 P.M.-2 A.M., Sat.-Sun. 11 A.M.-close

While technically situated in the Marigny, Mojitos actually lies along the border that this funky residential neighborhood shares with the French Quarter. Despite its rather obvious location, this delightful eatery hasn't been on my culinary radar for long, but I'm so grateful for the discovery. Besides its relaxing ambience, spacious courtyard, live jazz music, and stupendous rum selection, Mojitos also offers some of the best food in the city. Primarily Caribbean-influenced and Creole-inspired, the menu includes such winning entrées and tapas plates as crawfish pasta, Jamaican pork chops, seared Aruba scallops with white chocolate–chipotle sauce, and black paella, a delectable dish of scallops, shrimp, and calamari served with squid ink rice that temporarily turned my husband's teeth black. In addition to the creative cuisine, many patrons come for the weekday happy hour specials, rum tastings, and weekend jazz brunch.

SCHIRO'S CAFE $

2483 Royal St., 504/944-6666, www.schiroscafe.com
HOURS: Mon.-Fri. 11 A.M.-9:30 P.M., Sat. 9 A.M.-9:30 P.M., Sun. 9 A.M.-3 P.M.

Set inside a strikingly restored historic building in the heart of the Faubourg Marigny, Schiro's Cafe serves multiple needs of its devoted locals—it's not only a full-service restaurant offering New Orleans–style and Indian fare, but it's also a small grocery store and laundry, with a B&B upstairs. The fried catfish platter, which is served on Fridays, is a definite specialty, but on any day, Schiro's is an inexpensive, albeit busy spot for salads, po-boys,

burgers, and other munchies, such as gumbo, lentil soup, chicken curry, and white chocolate mango cheesecake.

ITALIAN
ADOLFO'S $$

611 Frenchmen St., 504/948-3800
HOURS: Daily 5:30-10:30 P.M.

Large portions of traditional Italian and Creole fare are heaped onto the plates at Adolfo's, a longtime neighborhood standby that's especially strong on seafood dishes, such as oysters Pernod and the "ocean sauce," which features shrimp, crawfish, and crab. Granted, it's a small, dingy hole-in-the-wall, where the service can be slow, reservations are typically not accepted, and no credit cards are allowed, but it's not a bad spot to dine before heading to one of Frenchmen's nearby music clubs. Downstairs, the Apple Barrel Bar is a dark and cozy spot to nurse a cocktail before or after dinner.

MEDITERRANEAN
FATOUSH $

2372 St. Claude Ave., 504/371-5074,
www.fatoushrestaurantnola.com
HOURS: Daily 8 A.M.-10 P.M.

For inexpensive Mediterranean cuisine, you can't go wrong with Fatoush—at once a coffeehouse, herbal teahouse, natural juice bar, and organic restaurant offering an eclectic array of breakfast, lunch, and dinner options. Favorites here include the prosciutto and asparagus omelet, grilled eggplant sandwich, and Mediterranean classics like tabouli, stuffed grape leaves, gyros, falafel sandwiches, beef moussaka, and lamb shish kebabs. Though I'm fond of the easygoing atmosphere and friendly staff, the biggest drawback for me is the location; unfortunately, this winning spot is situated on sketchy St. Claude Avenue along the edge of the Faubourg Marigny.

MONA'S CAFÉ $$

504 Frenchmen St., 504/949-4115
HOURS: Mon.-Thurs. 11 A.M.-10 P.M., Fri.-Sat. 11 A.M.-11 P.M., Sun. noon-9 P.M.

In addition to offering a richly stocked

Lebanese and Greek grocery, Mona's Café serves inexpensive Middle Eastern food, including appetizers like falafel, hummus, tabouli, imported olives, and spinach pie. The extensive menu also boasts savory entrées, such as chicken kabobs, gyros, lamb chops, and grape-leaf platters. The only drawback here is the easily distracted waitstaff, but if that doesn't dissuade you, be sure to stop by Mona's other locations in Uptown (1120 S. Carrollton Ave., 504/861-8175) and Mid-City (3901 Banks St., 504/482-7743).

Central Business and Arts Districts — Map 3

AMERICAN

AMERICAN SECTOR $$

The National WWII Museum, 945 Magazine St., 504/528-1940,
www.nationalww2museum.org/american-sector
HOURS: Sun.-Thurs. 11 A.M.-9 P.M., Fri.-Sat. 11 A.M.-11 P.M.

Perhaps the most casual of chef John Besh's downtown restaurants, the American Sector—which is named in honor of the CBD's former moniker—is a wonderful addition to the National WWII Museum. With decor that resembles an old-fashioned airport, this delightful eatery features creative versions of American staples, such as mini-cheeseburgers with bacon-onion marmalade, heirloom tomato soup with grilled ham and cheese, chicken fried steak with mushroom gravy, and bananas Foster shakes. Though the prices are slightly higher than those of the average café, the portions are generous. While you're here, try a vintage cocktail, such as the Last Waltz, which blends vodka, strawberries, mint, ginger, and champagne. Note that parking is free for patrons after 3 P.M.

BESH STEAK $$$

Harrah's New Orleans, 8 Canal St., 504/533-6111,
www.harrahsneworleans.com
HOURS: Daily 5 P.M.-close

The popular local chef John Besh struck gold with Besh Steak at Harrah's, a lavish restaurant that keeps gamers happy and gives the big spenders something to blow their cash on. Opened in 2003, this is a loud, fancy place, with brown leather seats, bold canvases of George Rodrigue's iconic "Blue Dog," and other contemporary touches. A Louisiana spin on a traditional steakhouse, Besh Steak offers large portions and tasty entrées, such as the New York strip steak (aged 30 days) with blue-cheese butter and Abita Amber–battered onion rings.

UGLY DOG SALOON & BBQ $

401 Andrew Higgins Dr., 504/569-8459,
www.uglydogsaloon.net
HOURS: Daily 11 A.M.-close

An easygoing, down-home hangout in the Arts District, the Ugly Dog Saloon can be counted on for cheap drinks, daily lunch

Chef John Besh has several restaurants in the CBD, including the American Sector, part of The National WWII Museum.

© LAURA MARTONE

RESTAURANTS

and dinner specials, and a decent range of slow-cooked, barbecued favorites, such as pulled-pork sandwiches, beef brisket, smoked sausage, and pork spare ribs. Not far from the Ernest N. Morial Convention Center, this no-frills sports bar is ideal for visiting business folks, especially given its daily happy hour and free wireless Internet access. The friendly staff doesn't hurt either. Just note that, while the bar is open late, the kitchen closes at 9 P.M. each night.

ASIAN

HORINOYA RESTAURANT $$

920 Poydras St., 504/561-8914

HOURS: Mon.-Fri. 11 A.M.-2:30 P.M. and 5-9:30 P.M., Sat. 5-10 P.M.

About halfway between the Mercedes-Benz Superdome and the Harrah's casino lies Horinoya, one of the city's most popular sushi restaurants. Though the parking situation here leaves much to be desired, this pleasant, family-owned eatery excels with its attentive waitstaff, wonderful sake selection, and spacious sushi bar. Favorite items include the ponzu-sweetened oysters, udon soup, yellowtail sashimi, tuna *tataki,* and New Orleans sushi roll. Besides the main dining room, which is on the small side, Horinoya offers several semi-private rooms for more traditional Japanese-style dining.

ROCK-N-SAKE BAR & SUSHI $$

823 Fulton St., 504/581-7253, www.rocknsake.com

HOURS: Tues.-Wed. 5-10 P.M., Thurs. 5-11 P.M., Fri. 11 A.M.-2:30 P.M. and 5:30 P.M.-midnight, Sat. 5 P.M.-midnight, Sun. 5-10 P.M.

By many accounts, Rock-n-Sake serves some of the freshest, most interesting sushi in the South, including spicy crawfish rolls, BBQ eel rolls, and wasabi-enhanced *tobiko.* Tofu teriyaki "steak," sashimi appetizers, snow crab salad, pan-seared salmon, udon noodles with thinly sliced beef and onions, and "killer" scallops round out the tasty menu. The dining room is noisy and vibrant, with Mardi Gras masks on the walls, large contemporary paintings, loud rock and pop music blasting in the background, and a young, hip crowd. No wonder plenty of regulars come here to sip sake martinis, melon balls, and other pretty cocktails. There's also a Rock-n-Sake in Baton Rouge.

SINGHA THAI CAFE $$

413 Carondelet St., 504/581-2205

HOURS: Mon.-Fri. 11 A.M.-3 P.M. and 5-9 P.M.

While the Singha Thai Cafe might not be my favorite Thai restaurant in New Orleans, it's certainly not a bad choice if you find yourself in the CBD. Casual, spacious, and known for its usually excellent service, Singha Thai lures regulars with its delectable spring rolls, fried calamari, chicken curry, pad thai, and *pad woon sen.* Just be advised that, as with many downtown restaurants, street parking can be a challenge here.

CAJUN AND CREOLE

BON TON CAFE $$$

401 Magazine St., 504/524-3386, www.thebontoncafe.com

HOURS: Mon.-Fri. 11 A.M.-2 P.M. and 5-9 P.M.

Housed within a historic building erected in the 1840s and featuring brick walls, wrought-iron chandeliers, and red-checkered tablecloths, the nostalgic, amiable Bon Ton Cafe has been serving well-favored Cajun cuisine since 1953. Among the local regulars, popular dishes include the turtle soup, seafood gumbo, crawfish étouffée, and bread pudding with whiskey sauce. Unfortunately, though, this old-fashioned eatery is only open to the public on weekdays, and given the challenging street-parking situation, arriving by foot, cab, or streetcar is recommended.

CAFÉ ADELAIDE $$$

Loews New Orleans Hotel, 300 Poydras St., 504/595-3305, www.cafeadelaide.com

HOURS: Mon.-Thurs. 7-10 A.M., 11:30 A.M.-2 P.M., and 6-9 P.M.; Fri. 7-10 A.M., 11:30 A.M.-2:30 P.M., and 6-9:30 P.M.; Sat. 7 A.M.-12:30 P.M. and 6-9:30 P.M.; Sun. 7 A.M.-12:30 P.M. and 6-9 P.M.

Set inside the glamorous Loews New Orleans Hotel, Café Adelaide is a highly touted, relative newcomer from the Brennan family, offering delicious food for breakfast, lunch, and dinner. Start the day with honeycomb waffles, and try a corn-fried oyster salad for lunch. At dinner, you might begin with the shrimp and tasso corn dogs, then consider notable main dishes like shrimp courtbouillon, jumbo seared sea scallops with beluga lentils, and filet mignon with garlic-roasted artichokes. Lighter fare, as well as a long list of colorful cocktails, is available in the trendy Swizzle Stick Bar.

COCHON ❸❸

930 Tchoupitoulas St., 504/588-2123,
www.cochonrestaurant.com
HOURS: Mon.-Thurs. 11 A.M.-10 P.M., Fri.-Sat. 11 A.M.-11 P.M.

Noted chef Donald Link, of Herbsaint, runs Cochon—a rustic, renovated warehouse space that opened in April 2006 in the Arts District. It serves a stellar blend of Cajun and contemporary American victuals, specializing in small, tapas-style portions, such as baked oyster and kale dressing, fried alligator with chili garlic aioli, and fried boudin with pickled peppers. Highlighted entrées include rabbit and dumplings, smoked ham hocks with bitter greens, and smoked beef brisket with horseradish potato salad. Save room for the hummingbird cake, made with pecans, pineapples, bananas, and a cream cheese frosting. If you're in a hurry, opt for a delectable sandwich from the on-site **Cochon Butcher** (504/588-7675).

ERNST CAFE ❸❸

600 S. Peters St., 504/525-8544, www.ernstcafe.net
HOURS: Daily 11 A.M.-6 A.M.

Not far from Harrah's New Orleans and the Riverwalk Marketplace, the Ernst Cafe has been serving New Orleanians since 1902, when it was founded by John, William, and Charles Ernst. Erected in 1852, this historic structure was, at times, a storage facility, a grocery, and a private residence. Today, this cozy, low-key, and friendly watering hole lures regulars with New Orleans–style dishes like crab

cakes, chicken andouille gumbo, fried oyster po-boys, shrimp Creole, red beans and rice, and crawfish étouffée, plus a slew of beers, including several Abita brews. During your visit, note the café's unique architectural elements, such as the original pressed tin ceiling and the mosaic tile floor, installed in 1902 and featuring an unusual peace symbol that resembles an inverted swastika.

MOTHER'S RESTAURANT ❸❸

401 Poydras St., 504/523-9656,
www.mothersrestaurant.net
HOURS: Daily 7 A.M.-10 P.M.

The celeb photos lining the walls of Mother's attest to its longstanding popularity. Opened in 1938, this glorified cafeteria with brash lighting, Formica tables, and chatty servers still draws a mix of downtown office workers, hungry tourists, and local politicos. The most famous dishes here are the roast beef and baked ham po-boys, but you'll also find delicious jambalaya, seafood gumbo, crawfish étouffée, and other humble Creole and Cajun fare. It opens earlier than most CBD restaurants, which is handy to know if you happen to be returning to your hotel with hunger pangs after a long night of barhopping.

NOLA GROCERY AND PO-BOYS ❸

351 Andrew Higgins Dr., 504/302-9928,
www.nolagrocery.com
HOURS: Daily 7 A.M.-5 P.M.

Within walking distance of the National WWII Museum and the city's convention center, the NOLA Grocery is an inexpensive sandwich shop that's ideal for both tourists and business travelers. While fried seafood plates, varied salads, crawfish pies, and gumbo are offered here, the main focus is, obviously, the vast array of po-boys, with options like fried soft-shell crab, barbecue shrimp, alligator filet, and smoked green onion sausage. If you dare, try specialties like the Surf N Turf, which combines roast beef with fried shrimp or oysters, and if you have room, order a side of sweet potato fries, fried okra, or potato salad.

ECLECTIC

EMERIL'S NEW ORLEANS $$$

800 Tchoupitoulas St., 504/528-9393,
www.emerils.com

HOURS: Mon.-Fri. 11:30 A.M.-2 P.M. and 6-10 P.M., Sat.-Sun. 6-10 P.M.

The bigger and louder of Emeril Lagasse's acclaimed restaurants, Emeril's takes its hits from critics who complain about haughty service and high prices, but this is the domain of one of the world's most famous chefs, and it's always packed. All in all, if you can reserve a table here, go for it—Emeril didn't become famous for no reason. He's an excellent cook with a great kitchen staff, and the food here is more complex and imaginative than at NOLA, his French Quarter restaurant. I've dined here several times over the years, usually for special occasions, and I've always left with fond memories—it's the first place, after all, that I ever tasted escargot. The menu changes often, though you might be lucky enough to sample dishes like the innovative "mac n' cheese"—essentially, sautéed Gulf shrimp with *trofie* pasta, vermouth cream, *guanciale,* and brioche crumbs. Depending on the day, desserts might include classics like Black Forest doberge with cherry compote or Dutch apple tart with maple ice cream. The space is airy, high-ceilinged, and dramatic, the quintessence of Arts District chic.

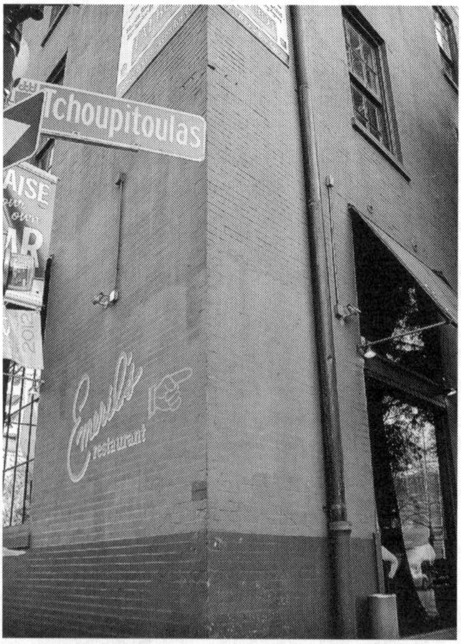

© LAURA MARTONE

Emeril's New Orleans, the famous chef's first restaurant in the Big Easy

THE GRILL ROOM $$$

Windsor Court Hotel, 300 Gravier St., 504/522-1994,
www.grillroomneworleans.com

HOURS: Mon.-Fri. 7-10:30 A.M., 11:30 A.M.-1:30 P.M., and 5:30-10 P.M.; Sat. 7-10:30 A.M., 11:30 A.M.-2:30 P.M., and 5:30-10 P.M.; Sun. 7-10:30 A.M., 11 A.M.-2:30 P.M., and 5:30-10 P.M.

For a classic fine-dining experience—with outstanding service and excellent, albeit pricey, cuisine—book a table at the Grill Room, an award-winning restaurant situated inside the posh Windsor Court Hotel. In addition to an extensive wine selection, the Grill Room features modern American cuisine with seasonal ingredients. While the menu is constantly evolving, dishes can range from well-prepared grouper, with Gulf shrimp, risotto, and garlic spinach, to slow-cooked rack of lamb with Israeli couscous, baby heirloom tomatoes, and parmesan *brodo* (broth). For a unique experience, try chef Drew Dzejak's tasting menu ($85 pp), which usually features 5–6 creative courses. Not surprisingly, most diners are well dressed, and reservations are recommended. Luckily, valet parking is available for those who'd prefer not to struggle for a spot on the street. If you have time, consider having an after-dinner cocktail in the adjacent Polo Club Lounge.

LE FORET $$$

129 Camp St., 504/553-6738,
www.leforetneworleans.com

HOURS: Sun.-Thurs. 5:30-10 P.M., Fri.-Sat. 5:30-10:30 P.M.

Situated near the border between the CBD and the French Quarter, Le Foret is an ideal dining option for those seeking innovative cuisine, impeccable service, and an elegant atmosphere—at any price. Suitable for romantic dinners, this classy yet intimate restaurant offers an ever-changing menu that takes advantage of seasonal ingredients. Past dishes have included seared Hudson Valley foie gras with toasted brioche, pear compote, and watercress; seared diver sea scallops with cauliflower purée, carrots, and warm pancetta vinaigrette; and duck breast with spiced duck confit pasta terrine, radishes, baby beets, duck cracklings, and buttered duck jus. Delectable desserts might range from sacher torte to coconut cream pie. Even the artfully presented, on-the-house appetizers are usually a treat. Unfortunately, though, street parking can be a challenge here.

MILA RESTAURANT 🟡💲💲

Renaissance New Orleans Pere Marquette Hotel, 817 Common St., 504/412-2580, www.milaneworleans.com
HOURS: Mon.-Fri. 11:30 A.M.-2:30 P.M. and 5:30-10 P.M., Sat. 5:30-10 P.M.

As hotel restaurants go, the Pere Marquette's stylish MiLa is exceptional—celebrated for its delicious food, attentive service, creative lighting, and intimate atmosphere. As with many upscale eateries in New Orleans, the food is fresh, seasonal, and innovative. While here, try the deconstructed oysters Rockefeller with spinach, bacon chips, and licorice root; barbecue lobster with lemon confit, fresh thyme, and toasted baguette; pan-seared scallops with heirloom squash, charred spring onion, and curry emulsion; and creamy rice pudding with vanilla bean and glazed strawberries. A seasonal tasting menu and three-course lunch are also available, as are garage, street, and valet parking.

FRENCH

🇨 AUGUST 💲💲💲

301 Tchoupitoulas St., 504/299-9777, www.restaurantaugust.com
HOURS: Mon.-Fri. 11 A.M.-2 P.M. and 5:30-10 P.M., Sat.-Sun. 5:30-10 P.M.

August is presided over by talented and charismatic chef John Besh, the Louisiana born-and-bred kitchen wizard who helms several acclaimed eateries in New Orleans. He opened this Arts District restaurant in 2001, inside a handsome 19th-century French-Creole building, and it's been tough to get a table here ever since. Besh presents uncomplicated yet richly nuanced contemporary American fare, with healthy doses of both local and Mediterranean ingredients. As with Emeril's CBD locale, the menu here is ever-evolving, though you'll often find appetizers like foie gras and gnocchi. Main courses might include a prime filet of beef with porcini and oxtail marmalade or fried soft-shell crab amandine with a warm crab and haricots verts salad. Though it might prove difficult, try to save room for the goat-milk cheesecake with almonds, honey ice cream, and balsamic caramel.

HERBSAINT BAR AND RESTAURANT 🟡💲💲

701 St. Charles Ave., 504/524-4114, www.herbsaint.com
HOURS: Mon.-Fri. 11:30 A.M.-10 P.M., Sat. 5:30-10 P.M.

A boisterous power-lunch bistro that's also a hit with the dinner crowd, trendy Herbsaint sits along a nondescript stretch of St. Charles, its setting brightened by tall windows, soft-yellow walls, and a youthful, good-looking staff. The menu, which blends Southern, French, and Italian influences, includes starters like mussels, beef short ribs, and shrimp and grits with tasso and okra. Main courses, meanwhile, can range from the fish du jour to grilled organic chicken with turnip mashed potatoes and roasted mushrooms. The wine selection is terrific, though you can also try a variety of cool cocktails, such as the Sazerac or the plum gin fizz, not to mention wine-tasting flights of three vintages.

LÜKE 💲💲

Hilton New Orleans/St. Charles Avenue Hotel, 333 St. Charles Ave., 504/378-2840, www.lukeneworleans.com
HOURS: Daily 7 A.M.-11 P.M.

Regional celebrity chef John Besh has several winning restaurants in the CBD, not the least of which is Lüke, an homage to classic

FAMOUS BIG EASY CHEFS

The most well-known dynasty on the Crescent City's restaurant scene is undoubtedly the Brennan clan, members of which own and operate several restaurants throughout New Orleans. In the French Quarter, you can sample a scrumptious breakfast of eggs Hussarde and finish with bananas Foster at **Brennan's** (417 Royal St.), established in 1946. Opt for dinner at **Dickie Brennan's Steakhouse** (716 Iberville St.), known for its well-prepared steaks and exceptional desserts. For fresh seafood, dine at **Ralph Brennan's Red Fish Grill** (115 Bourbon St.) or **Dickie Brennan's Bourbon House Seafood** (144 Bourbon St.), situated opposite each other. While in the Quarter, you can also savor New Orleans–style cuisine at **Dickie Brennan's Palace Café** (605 Canal St.) and a Sunday jazz brunch at **Mr. B's Bistro** (201 Royal St.).

Beyond the Quarter, you'll encounter creative Creole cuisine at Brennan-owned restaurants like **Café Adelaide** (300 Poydras St.) in the CBD, **Commander's Palace** (1403 Washington Ave.) in the Garden District, and **Ralph's on the Park** (900 City Park Ave.) in Mid-City. You'll even find evidence of the Brennan family in the suburb of Metairie, where **Café B** (2700 Metairie Rd.) specializes in New American cuisine and **Heritage Grill** (111 Veterans Memorial Blvd.) features creative Cajun and Southern-style dishes.

Of course, Brennan isn't the only big name in New Orleans. Given the city's longtime reputation for marvelous cuisine, it seems only natural that the Big Easy would boast several famous chefs. For a taste of such culinary expertise, consider visiting one of their well-respected restaurants.

JOHN BESH

Raised in southern Louisiana, chef John Besh (www.chefjohnbesh.com) is dedicated to the culinary bounty and traditions of his native homeland. Today, he celebrates his roots in seven acclaimed restaurants, five of which lie within walking distance of one another in the CBD. These include **Besh Steak** (8 Canal St.), a modern steakhouse in the Harrah's New Orleans; **August** (301 Tchoupitoulas St.), a contemporary French restaurant; **Lüke** (333 St. Charles Ave.), an homage to Franco-German brasseries of old; and **Domenica** (123 Baronne St.), an inviting Italian eatery in the Roosevelt Hotel. In the nearby Arts District, you'll also find the **American Sector** (945 Magazine St.), located in the National WWII Museum and serving American cuisine with a gourmet twist. Besh even has a restaurant outside the city on the bucolic Northshore. Nestled amid verdant grounds, **La Provence** (25020 U.S. 190, Lacombe) is a country-style French restaurant offering dinner and Sunday brunch.

EMERIL LAGASSE

While chef Emeril Lagasse (www.emerils.com) grew up in Massachusetts, polished his culinary skills in France, and worked in fine restaurants throughout New York, Boston, and Philadelphia, he definitely has an affinity for

Franco-German brasseries. Opened in 2007 and adjacent to the Hilton Hotel on St. Charles Avenue, this nostalgic eatery features such winning dishes as the crab omelet with fromage blanc, peppers, mushrooms, and gaufrettes; pâté of rabbit and chicken livers with truffles and country bread croutons; jumbo shrimp with creamy white corn grits; smoked pork shank with bratwurst and homemade sauerkraut; and vanilla cake with crème fraiche and satsuma marmalade. As at other Besh restaurants, the service here is usually attentive, the wine and beer selection is adequate, and the prices are a bit on the high side.

ITALIAN
DOMENICA $$

The Roosevelt New Orleans, 123 Baronne St., 504/648-6020, www.domenicarestaurant.com
HOURS: Daily 11 A.M.–11 P.M.

Located, since 2009, inside the longstanding, extensively renovated Roosevelt Hotel, chef John Besh's Domenica is a warm yet contemporary space that features rustic Italian fare

New Orleans. Lured to the Big Easy by Dick and Ella Brennan, Lagasse became a celebrity at the legendary Commander's Palace, where he served as the executive chef for more than seven years. In 1990, he established **Emeril's New Orleans** (800 Tchoupitoulas St.), a fine Louisiana-style restaurant in the Arts District. In 1992, he opened **NOLA Restaurant** (534 St. Louis St.), a French Quarter eatery that offers creative seafood dishes and other innovative cuisine. Six years later, he established **Emeril's Delmonico** (1300 St. Charles Ave.), an eclectic steakhouse in the historic Garden District. Though Lagasse is also the chef-proprietor of eateries in Las Vegas, Orlando, and Bethlehem, Pennsylvania, his passion for Louisiana's cuisine makes it impossible to avoid at least one of his New Orleans-based restaurants during your visit.

DONALD LINK

Inspired by his grandparents' cooking styles, Louisiana native chef Donald Link (www.donaldlink.com) infuses his local restaurants with his Cajun and Southern roots. Such winners include the **Herbsaint Bar and Restaurant** (701 St. Charles Ave.), which features French-inspired Southern cuisine; **Cochon** (930 Tchoupitoulas St.), a rustic eatery serving traditional Cajun dishes; and **Cochon Butcher** (930 Tchoupitoulas St.), where popular sandwiches include the muffuletta and the classic Cuban. All three are located in the Arts District.

PAUL PRUDHOMME

Born and raised in Louisiana, chef Paul Prudhomme (www.chefpaul.com), the youngest of 13 children, developed a passion for cooking at his mother's side and, as an adult, learned how to blend his native cuisine with other cultural influences. The results of such innovation are evident at his distinctive restaurant, **K-Paul's Louisiana Kitchen** (416 Chartres St.), which Prudhomme and his late wife, K, opened in a historic French Quarter building in 1979. Today, the ever-changing menu includes such classic dishes as crawfish étouffée and blackened Louisiana drum.

SUSAN SPICER

In 1979, chef Susan Spicer began her cooking career in New Orleans as an apprentice to chef Daniel Bonnot at the award-winning Louis XVI Restaurant. Following extensive travels and several stints in local hotel eateries, Spicer eventually established her own restaurant in 1990. Housed in a 200-year-old cottage in the French Quarter, **Bayona** (430 Dauphine St.) presents an eclectic, ever-evolving menu that embraces a variety of cuisines, including American, French, Italian, Mediterranean, Asian, and North African. In 2000, she and three partners opened Herbsaint, which she's since sold to Donald Link. Most recently, Spicer opened **Mondo** (900 Harrison Ave.), a casual, family-style restaurant in Lakeview, where she's lived for the past two decades.

(*domenica* means "Sunday" in Italian). Popular dishes include the wild mushroom soup with truffle bruschetta; fried eggplant panini with tomato pesto, goat cheese, and arugula; prosciutto pizza with tomatoes, arugula, and fresh mozzarella; redfish with celery root purée and warm olive vinaigrette; and the spiced apple cake with buttermilk gelato. If possible, come for happy hour (daily 3–6 P.M.), when all pizzas, beers, well cocktails, and wines by the glass are offered at half price. In addition to the excellent cuisine, Domenica boasts an amiable, knowledgeable staff and a classy ambience, punctuated by the high ceilings, unusual chandeliers, earth-tone walls, and dark wooden tables.

TOMMY'S CUISINE $$$

746 Tchoupitoulas St., 504/581-1103, www.tommysneworleans.com

HOURS: Sun.-Thurs. 5:30-10 P.M., Fri.-Sat. 5:30-11 P.M.

Like Eleven 79, Tommy's Cuisine is a reliable pick for creative Creole-inspired Italian fare. Housed within a charming space in the

Arts District, close to the many art galleries of Julia Street, the warmly lighted dining room—with its paneled walls, mirrors, and old-fashioned sconces—creates an appealing scene. Menu items include mussels marinara, oysters Tommy (baked in the shell with romano cheese, pancetta, and roasted red pepper), seafood-stuffed eggplant, soft-shell crabs with linguini and a reggiano-crawfish sauce, or chicken roasted with white wine, olive oil, and rosemary-garlic jus. If you have room, try the pecan praline bread pudding with a bananas Foster sauce and vanilla ice cream—a glorious combination of the city's greatest desserts.

SEAFOOD

MIKE'S ON THE AVENUE $$$

628 St. Charles Ave., 504/523-7600,
www.mikesontheavenue.com

HOURS: Mon.-Fri. 11:30 A.M.-10 P.M., Sat. 5:30-10:30 P.M.

With modern wooden furnishings, colorful if rudimentary artwork, and large windows that allow unobstructed views of bustling St. Charles Avenue and lovely Lafayette Square, Mike's on the Avenue is a delightful (although pricey) choice for lunch or dinner, especially for seafood lovers. Highlights include barbecue oysters, fish tacos, sake-seared tuna, crab cake pasta, and Creole sushi rolls. If you find yourself waiting for a table, pass the time with a drink at the adjacent bar, Twist. The only drawback at Mike's is that the staff isn't as knowledgeable about the food and wine as one might like.

RIOMAR $$

800 S. Peters St., 504/525-3474,
www.riomarseafood.com

HOURS: Mon.-Fri. 11:30 A.M.-2 P.M. and 6-10 P.M., Sat. 6-10 P.M.

Only two blocks from the convention center, bustling RioMar often fills up with business travelers, though it maintains a warm and personal ambience, owing largely to the well-trained staff and welcoming dining room, set inside a vintage industrial building with a slate floor and barrel-vaulted archways. The specialty here is seafood inspired by Spanish and Latin American cuisine. In all honesty, you could make a small meal of the ceviche sampler, with four types of raw seafood each cured in a different Latin tradition: Aji Amarillo (with yellow pepper sauce and *leche de tigre*), Panamanian (with fish, habanero peppers, and lime), Ecuadorian (with shrimp, tomato, and citrus juice), and Mixto (with shrimp, squid, fish, and charred peppers). Entrée highlights include pan-roasted black drum, five-hour roast pork, littleneck clams steamed with parsley and chorizo, and yellowfin tuna served rare and wrapped in Serrano ham with a chickpea purée and *romesco* sauce.

Garden District and Uptown

Map 4

AMERICAN

BOUCHERIE $$

8115 Jeannette St., 504/862-5514,
www.boucherie-nola.com

HOURS: Tues.-Sat. 11 A.M.-3 P.M. and 5:30-9:30 P.M.

Uptown's Riverbend area boasts several unique restaurants, including Boucherie, a quaint, romantic eatery that offers friendly service, a classy ambience, and upscale, Southern-style cuisine at affordable prices. Both tapas and large plates are available, featuring items like steamed mussels with collard greens and crispy grit crackers; blackened shrimp and grit cakes with bacon vinaigrette; duck confit po-boys with roasted garlic, bread-and-butter pickles, arugula, and Creole tomatoes; and smoked beef brisket with garlicky parmesan fries. Unfortunately, the small size of the restaurant means that it can get a bit claustrophobic at times.

THE CAMELLIA GRILL $

626 S. Carrollton Ave., 504/309-2679,
www.camelliagrill.net

HOURS: Sun.-Thurs. 8 A.M.-midnight, Fri.-Sat. 8 A.M.-2 A.M.

A longtime stalwart for delicious comfort food,

the famous Camellia Grill is a down-home restaurant that specializes in burgers, onion rings, and other greasy-spoon favorites. Breakfast is also an enjoyable meal in this funky old white house in the Riverbend section of Uptown. In addition, there's a long list of pies, cakes, and ice-cream treats. The low prices are ideal, though you might be understandably turned off by the limited seating, long waits, and surly waitstaff. In recent years, a second location has opened in the French Quarter (540 Chartres St., 504/522-1800), an ideal spot for late-night munchies.

DOMILISE'S PO-BOY & BAR $$

5240 Annunciation St., 504/899-9126
HOURS: Mon.-Wed. and Fri.-Sat. 10:30 A.M.-7 P.M.

About 10 blocks west of the intersection of Napoleon Avenue and Tchoupitoulas Street—the starting point for Mardi Gras parades like Bacchus and Orpheus—lies a weathered building that belies the yummy eatery inside. A popular, oft-crowded stop for local foodies, the no-frills Domilise's Po-Boy & Bar offers an assortment of po-boys, with fillings like ham, roast beef and swiss, hot smoked sausage, and fried shrimp. Just be advised that these po-boys are on the expensive side, though their enormous size makes them worth every penny. Given its location, this isn't a bad lunchtime or early dinner option for Tulane students, Magazine Street shoppers, and those exploring nearby Audubon Park.

GUY'S PO-BOYS $

5259 Magazine St., 504/891-5025
HOURS: Mon.-Sat. 11 A.M.-4 P.M.

A lovable dive on a quiet Uptown street corner, Guy's Po-Boys offers daily-changing sandwich specials, to-die-for po-boys (with fillings like shrimp, roast beef, and alligator sausage), red beans and rice, and other comfort chow. The bare-bones decor and friendly staff add to the down-home experience. It doesn't hurt either that the prices are low; the only trouble is that it's a cash-only joint, and the service sometimes crawls, perhaps because of the limited hours.

MR. JOHN'S STEAK HOUSE $$$

2111 St. Charles Ave., 504/679-7697,
www.mrjohnssteakhouse.com
HOURS: Tues.-Thurs. 5:30-9:30 P.M., Fri. 11:30 A.M.-2 P.M. and 5:30-9:30 P.M., Sat. 5:30-9:30 P.M.

If you're looking for an upscale shrine to carnivores, head to Mr. John's Steak House. Conveniently located on the St. Charles streetcar line, this classy restaurant is in fact one of the most highly recommended steakhouses in the city. Besides showcasing simply seasoned steaks, from filet mignon to a porterhouse for two, the menu also features lobster tails with roasted new potatoes and haricots verts, crabmeat ravioli with aged Asiago cheese cream sauce, and baby veal sautéed in white wine, capers, lemon, and butter and served with fettuccine Alfredo. Even the salads, sides, and appetizers are delicious here; try the sizzling crab cake, seared yellowfin tuna, escargot in puff pastry, eggplant parmesan, or fried green tomatoes with jumbo lump crabmeat. Just be prepared to pay a premium for such quality.

PARASOL'S BAR & RESTAURANT $

2533 Constance St., 504/302-1543,
www.parasolsbarandrestaurant.com
HOURS: Sun.-Thurs. 11 A.M.-9 P.M., Fri.-Sat. 11 A.M.-10 P.M.

For inexpensive, overstuffed sandwiches, head to the Irish Channel, where Parasol's Bar & Restaurant has been serving residents of the Garden District and beyond since 1952. A magnet for both locals and tourists—especially around St. Patrick's Day—this friendly neighborhood hangout offers a wide array of delicious po-boys, with classic fillings like roast beef, fried shrimp and oysters, meatballs, and french fries and gravy. Parasol's also serves gumbo, fried seafood baskets, and specialty sandwiches, like the smoked sausage deluxe, which includes cheddar, onions, and Creole mustard.

REFUEL CAFE $$

8124 Hampson St., 504/872-0187, www.refuelcafe.com
HOURS: Tues.-Fri. 7 A.M.-2 P.M., Sat.-Sun. 8:30 A.M.-2 P.M.

A hip spot in the Riverbend area of Uptown, Refuel serves a rich array of coffee and tea drinks plus top-notch breakfast, brunch, and lunch fare. Try the Belgian waffles with fresh strawberries or a three-egg California omelet to start off the day, and for lunch, opt for the Asian seared salmon, chunky Cuban sandwich, or chicken quesadilla. The daily specials are also worth a look.

SLIM GOODIES DINER $

3322 Magazine St., 504/891-3447
HOURS: Daily 6 A.M.–3 P.M.

If you love a good, no-nonsense diner, Slim Goodies is worth seeking out. This colorful hole-in-the-wall serves some of the best breakfasts in the neighborhood, such as the hearty sweet-potato pancakes and egg scrambles, along with giant salads and sandwiches. Try the soulful Robert Johnson burger (with bacon and blue cheese), the veggie-favored STALT (smoked tempeh with avocado spread, lettuce, and tomato), or a Horned Devil salad of mixed greens, swiss and provolone cheeses, tomatoes, ham, and deviled eggs. For dessert, there's the Cloud, a chocolate brownie topped with ice cream and whipped cream. Some diners complain, though, that the menu needs an update, the service can be a bit slow, and the staff is sometimes temperamental.

ASIAN
HOSHUN RESTAURANT $$

1601 St. Charles Ave., 504/302-9716,
www.hoshunrestaurant.com
HOURS: Daily 11:30 A.M.–2 A.M.

Located along the St. Charles streetcar line in the Lower Garden District, the Hoshun Restaurant is a decent dinner option after exploring the Ogden or National WWII Museum in the nearby Arts District—if, that is, you're a fan of Asian cuisine. In fact, the eclectic menu features a wide assortment of Asian dishes, including Vietnamese pho and summer rolls, pad Thai noodles and sweet Thai chili chicken, Japanese sushi and tempura, and Chinese favorites, such as kung pao chicken, Szechuan shrimp, and pumpkin seed–sprinkled plum duck. Decorated with casual elegance in mind, Hoshun is also open late,

which is good news for night owls. The only trouble is that the servers seem harried at times, and though the food is good overall, you'll probably find better examples of each cuisine in other, more focused restaurants.

KYOTO JAPANESE RESTAURANT & SUSHI BAR $$

4920 Prytania St., 504/891-3644, www.kyotonola.com
HOURS: Mon.-Thurs. 11:30 A.M.–2:30 P.M. and 5–10 P.M., Fri. 11:30 A.M.–2:30 P.M. and 5–10:30 P.M., Sat. noon–3 P.M. and 5–10:30 P.M.

If you're in the mood for a movie and headed to Uptown's Prytania Theatre, consider having lunch or dinner at Kyoto, a friendly, low-key sushi joint about four blocks down the street. Though you can order delicious Japanese dishes, such as shrimp tempura, seafood udon, and chicken teriyaki, along with classic sides like edamame and miso soup, the focus here is definitely sushi. In addition to sushi and sashimi combination plates and standard rolls like California, tuna, and rainbow, you'll find special rolls, such as the Stella roll, which features spicy snow crab and scallop inside, with tuna *tataki* on top, in the style of a rainbow roll. For faster service, try eating at the sushi bar. While street parking can be difficult in this residential neighborhood, Kyoto's location is serendipitous—after all, the Creole Creamery, a delightful ice cream shop, is right next door.

CAJUN AND CREOLE
ATCHAFALAYA $$

901 Louisiana Ave., 504/891-9626,
www.atchafalayarestaurant.com
HOURS: Mon. 5:30–10 P.M., Tues.-Sat. 11 A.M.–2:30 P.M. and 5:30–10 P.M., Sun. 10 A.M.–2:30 P.M. and 5:30–9 P.M.

Down in the Irish Channel, off the beaten tourist path, lies this hidden gem, a neighborhood bistro with a very loyal following. The aptly named Atchafalaya, a lengthy, multihued building occupying the corner of Laurel Street and Louisiana Avenue, features high ceilings, natural lighting, stylish furnishings, excellent service, and contemporary Creole cuisine. Highlights on the menu include affordable classics like eggs Atchafalaya, which combines poached eggs with fried green tomatoes, jumbo lump crabmeat, and hollandaise; Gulf shrimp with bacon, smoked tomatoes, and a crispy grit cake; and a Louisiana crab salad that features mixed greens, hearts of palm, cilantro, peanuts, and green curry vinaigrette. The veggie-packed Bloody Marys are also popular here. Unless you stop by during lunchtime on a weekday, though, expect this place to be packed with locals.

BRIGTSEN'S RESTAURANT $$$

723 Dante St., 504/861-7610, www.brigtsens.com
HOURS: Tues.-Sat. 5:30-10 P.M.

One of the first eateries to lure tourists out of the French Quarter and up to the Riverbend area, Brigtsen's occupies a lovely Victorian cottage with a warm, homey dining room, enhanced by soft lighting and lovely wallpaper. The restaurant is perhaps most famous for its amazingly delicious and ever-changing seafood platter, which on a typical night might include grilled drum fish with crawfish and pistachio

lime sauce, shrimp cornbread, baked oyster Bienville, baked oyster LeRuth with shrimp and crabmeat, jalapeño shrimp cole slaw, and a panéed sea scallop with asparagus coulis—all for around $32. Other commendable dishes include a starter of oyster-artichoke gratin with lemon-parmesan sauce, an entrée of roast duck with cornbread dressing and tart dried cherry sauce, and a sinful dessert of pecan pie with caramel sauce.

◖ COMMANDER'S PALACE $$$

1403 Washington Ave., 504/899-8221, www.commanderspalace.com
HOURS: Mon.-Fri. 11:30 A.M.-2 P.M. and 6:30-10 P.M., Sat. 11:30 A.M.-1 P.M. and 6:30-10 P.M., Sun. 10:30 A.M.-1:30 P.M. and 6:30-10 P.M.

There are only so many of New Orleans's most vaunted, fine-dining institutions that you can possibly try during any one visit; even if you have the time, you may not have the appetite. If you must put one place at the top of your list, make it Commander's Palace, which was established in 1880 and became part of the

RESTAURANTS

© DANIEL MARTONE

a typical traffic jam in front of the Garden District's famous Commander's Palace

famed Brennan family empire in 1974. Nestled within a blue-and-white Victorian mansion in the Garden District, this local landmark is a terrific place to try turtle soup, griddle-seared Gulf fish, and bread pudding soufflé—especially if you're uninitiated to such famous New Orleans dishes. Lunch isn't too expensive, especially if you opt for the wonderful three-course Creole luncheon for about $30. At dinner, consider the pecan-crusted Gulf fish, truffled Creole cream cheese gnocchi, and grilled filet mignon served with Yukon gold potato purée, caramelized onions, roasted mushrooms, and tasso *marchands de vin*. The weekend jazz brunches are the stuff of legend, and advance reservations are usually a must for any meal.

DICK AND JENNY'S $$$

4501 Tchoupitoulas St., 504/894-9880,
www.dickandjennys.com
HOURS: Mon. 5:30-10 P.M., Tues.-Thurs. 11 A.M.-2 P.M. and 5:30-10 P.M., Fri. 11 A.M.-2 P.M. and 5:30-10:30 P.M., Sat. 5:30-10:30 P.M.

Dick and Jenny's keeps regulars happy with its neighborhood feel, outgoing staff, and reasonably priced contemporary city fare. Abita Amber–braised lamb belly grillades with thyme–goat cheese grits is a dazzling main dish, and don't miss the shrimp ravigote served atop fried green tomatoes. The only kicker is one you might expect of such a popular place: There's often a pretty long wait for a table, though reservations are now accepted.

EMERIL'S DELMONICO $$$

1300 St. Charles Ave., 504/525-4937,
www.emerils.com
HOURS: Sun.-Thurs. 6-9 P.M., Fri.-Sat. 6-10 P.M.

Situated along the St. Charles streetcar line in the Lower Garden District, not far from Lee Circle and the National WWII Museum, Emeril's Delmonico is a worthy nighttime spot for fans of steak, seafood, Cajun dishes, and Creole cuisine. Originally established in 1895, this legendary restaurant was reopened in 1998 by chef Emeril Lagasse. Today, with its stylish, upscale interior, Delmonico offers such classics as gumbo, barbecue shrimp with a baked grit cake, dry-aged New York strip steaks and ribeyes, pan-fried drum with fingerling potato Lyonnaise and bacon-stewed green beans, and rabbit crêpes with caramelized root vegetables, pancetta, mascarpone, and sage. Besides the weekday happy hour (5–7 P.M.) in the on-site cocktail bar, the complimentary valet parking is another big plus, as is the live music on offer Thursday–Saturday.

🍴 JACQUES-IMO'S CAFE $$

8324 Oak St., 504/861-0886,
www.jacquesimoscafe.com
HOURS: Mon.-Thurs. 5:30-10 P.M., Fri.-Sat. 5:30-10:30 P.M.

Situated on bustling Oak Street, funky Jacques-Imo's Cafe presents a mix of eclectic contemporary dishes and New Orleans standbys. Loyal fans, including me, can't rave enough about the charismatic staff and the ever-changing list of specials, which has, at times, featured smothered rabbit with

Jacques-Imo's Cafe lures hordes of foodies to Uptown's Riverbend neighborhood, especially on the weekend.

© DANIEL MARTONE

roasted-pepper grits and country-fried venison chop with wild mushrooms. The fried mirlitons with oysters and rich oyster-tasso hollandaise are also commendable, as is the shrimp and alligator sausage cheesecake. Every meal comes with delicious butter-topped cornbread muffins, a house salad, and two sides, such as mashed sweet potatoes and smothered cabbage. Finish off your meal with energy-pumping coffee-bean crème brûlée. Reservations are available only for large groups, and the place fills up quickly, so expect quite a wait on most nights. You can always pass the time at the charming bar. To reach the loud, rambling dining room, you actually have to walk through the oft-crowded bar and bustling kitchen; don't be afraid to take a peek at the dishes being prepared—you'll surely see something you like.

MAHONY'S PO-BOY SHOP $$

3454 Magazine St., 504/899-3374,
www.mahonyspoboys.com
HOURS: Mon.-Sat. 11 A.M.-10 P.M.

While browsing the art galleries along Magazine Street, do yourself a favor and head to Mahony's Po-Boy Shop for one of its signature sandwiches. Favorites include the Angus pot roast beef, root beer–glazed ham and cheese, cochon with Creole slaw, jumbo grilled shrimp with fried green tomatoes and rémoulade sauce, and the Peacemaker, which consists of fried oysters, bacon, and cheddar. You'll also find classics like overstuffed fried shrimp po-boys and muffulettas, plus salads, tasty sides, scrumptious desserts, and a full bar. No wonder Guy Fieri included Mahony's on his cross-country tour of America's "diners, drive-ins, and dives" for his popular Food Network show.

ONE RESTAURANT & LOUNGE $$$

8132 Hampson St., 504/301-9061, www.one-sl.com
HOURS: Mon. 5-10 P.M., Tues.-Fri. 11 A.M.-2 P.M. and
5-10 P.M., Sat. 5-10 P.M.

In Uptown's Riverbend area, the ONE Restaurant is the quintessential neighborhood bistro with contemporary cooking that could hold its own anywhere in the city. A specialty is the chargrilled oysters topped with roquefort cheese and red wine vinaigrette, but also consider the liver and mushroom pâté with preserved fennel and roasted pine nuts. Among the entrées, don't miss the braised country pork ribs with collard greens and white-truffle potato croquettes. Founded in 2005, the restaurant sits within a Victorian cottage, and inside, diners can watch chefs at work in the open kitchen.

UPPERLINE RESTAURANT $$$

1413 Upperline St., 504/891-9822, www.upperline.com
HOURS: Wed.-Sun. 5:30 P.M.-close

One of the most convivial restaurants in the city, Upperline is run by colorful owner JoAnn Clevenger, who loves to mingle with patrons and talk about her wonderful art and photography collection, which fills the restaurant's eclectically furnished dining rooms. Executive chef Ken Smith prepares Creole food with plenty of inventive twists and global spins: Slow-roasted duckling with garlic port or ginger peach sauce is one exceptional entrée, and spicy shrimp with jalapeño cornbread and aioli also scores high marks. A fine way to enjoy a meal here is to order the three-course dinner ($40), which might include fried green tomatoes with shrimp rémoulade (a true Big Easy classic that originated here), Louisiana grillades with cheese grits, and warm honey-pecan bread pudding with toffee sauce. It's hard to say who will be angrier at you for indulging in such a meal: your doctor or your dentist.

COFFEE AND DESSERTS
THE CREOLE CREAMERY $

4924 Prytania St., 504/894-8680,
www.creolecreamery.com
HOURS: Sun.-Thurs. noon-10 P.M., Fri.-Sat. noon-11 P.M.

For traditional ice cream, sherbet, or sorbet, check out The Creole Creamery, a handsome retro-hip Uptown ice cream parlor that's served such tantalizing flavors as lavender-pecan chocolate, red-velvet cake, bananas Foster, mint julep, key lime pie, lemon poppyseed, and strawberry margarita. Fortunately, these guys are constantly dreaming up new and often deliciously bizarre flavors—there are so many, in

RESTAURANTS

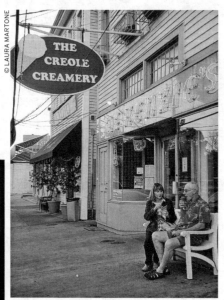

© LAURA MARTONE

THE CREOLE CREAMERY

Expect unique ice cream flavors at The Creole Creamery.

fact, that they rotate often, enabling you to try something new each time you visit. There's a second Creole Creamery in Lakeview (6260 Vicksburg St., 504/482-2924).

HANSEN'S SNO-BLIZ $

4801 Tchoupitoulas St., 504/891-9788,
www.snobliz.com

HOURS: May-Aug. Tues.-Sun. 1-10 P.M.

Conceived on a hot summer day during the Great Depression and opened in 1939 by Ernest and Mary Hansen, this popular, seasonal sno-ball stand still makes its super-saturated creations from Ernest's original ice-shaving machine (the first ever invented) and Mary's secret syrup recipes. Flavors here range from basics like spearmint and coconut to special ones, such as chocolate mint, cream of almond, and tart limeade. Although I prefer simple sno-balls—with just ice and syrup—some patrons swear by toppings like crushed pineapple, condensed milk, and whipped cream, so don't be afraid to experiment.

LA BOULANGERIE $

4600 Magazine St., 504/269-3777

HOURS: Mon.-Sat. 6:30 A.M.-5 P.M., Sun. 7 A.M.-1 P.M.

As the name implies, La Boulangerie is a delightful storefront French bakery that offers some tasty vittles. Here, you can sample some of the lightest, flakiest croissants in town, along with delicious sandwiches, hearty muffins, and delectable pastries, such as the flavorful napoleon. Unfortunately, though, the coffee isn't quite as good as what you'd taste at PJ's or CC's, and the service here can be rather slow.

PJ'S COFFEE OF NEW ORLEANS $

5432 Magazine St., 504/895-2202,
www.pjscoffee.com

HOURS: Mon.-Fri. 6 A.M.-9 P.M., Sat.-Sun. 7 A.M.-9 P.M.

Though you'll find numerous branches of this popular local coffeehouse chain throughout New Orleans and southeastern Louisiana, perhaps my favorite spot is this Uptown location. It's an ideal pit stop during a shopping trip along Magazine Street. Founded in 1984, this is the original shop, where, in addition to enjoying locally roasted coffee and freshly baked pastries, you may appreciate the colorful patrons, relaxing courtyard, and free wireless Internet access. The operating hours are slightly shorter during the summer months.

PLUM STREET SNOBALLS $

1300 Burdette St., 504/866-7996 or 504/256-3298,
www.plumstreetsnoball.com

HOURS: Mid-Mar.-Oct. Sun.-Fri. 2-8 P.M., Sat. noon-8 P.M.

Though Hansen's Sno-Bliz might be a few years older, Plum Street Snoballs has nevertheless been a Crescent City tradition since 1945. Typically served in cardboard containers (the kind you might store leftover fried rice in), these somewhat pricey but oh-so-tasty snoballs boast such flavors as cherry, ice coffee cream, and sugar-free pink lemonade. Besides the seasonal stand on Burdette, Plum Street also sells sno-balls at annual events, such as the French Quarter Festival and Jazz Fest.

ECLECTIC

APOLLINE $$$

4729 Magazine St., 504/894-8869, www.apollinerestaurant.com

HOURS: Tues.-Sat. 5:30-10:30 P.M.

Gourmands often trek to quaint Apolline, an elegant yet laid-back dinnertime spot situated a few blocks west of Napoleon Avenue and known for its attentive service, quiet atmosphere, and diverse cuisine. Favorite appetizers include the homemade boudin with Dijon mustard, baked Louisiana oysters with leek confit, and sautéed sweetbreads with stone-ground grits, while main dishes range from grilled diver scallops, accompanied by corn and fava bean succotash, bacon plank, and corn purée, to the grilled pork porterhouse, served with braised kale, mashed sweet potatoes, and a cane syrup demi-glace. Try to save room for the goat cheese mousse, which includes honey pâté de fruit, lavender crème anglaise, and pistachio powder. Like many Uptown eateries, Apolline is located in a former bungalow; the simple decor, which includes pale walls, white linen tablecloths, flickering candles, as well as mirrors and ceiling recesses that seemingly enlarge the space, makes this quaint restaurant ideal for a romantic dinner. Outdoor seating is also available.

COQUETTE $$$

2800 Magazine St., 504/265-0421, www.coquette-nola.com

HOURS: Sun.-Tues. 5:30-10 P.M., Wed.-Sat. 11:30 A.M.-3 P.M. and 5:30-10 P.M.

On the corner of Magazine Street and Washington Avenue in the Garden District, a lovely, two-story structure houses Coquette, an intimate space that resembles a romantic French bistro and presents eclectic, contemporary American cuisine. Although the simple menu changes daily, dependent on seasonal ingredients and the chef's whim, past highlights have included the roasted Gulf oysters with bacon, Swiss chard, and Herbsaint liqueur; collard green ravioli with duck confit, orange, and bacon; and the pork loin with foie gras, cabbage, and apple marmalade. As with many New Orleans restaurants, lunchtime is the most affordable time to sample the kitchen's delectable creations; the three-course lunch ($20), for instance, is an inexpensive way to try such favorites as fried oysters with cherry tomatoes, arugula, and rémoulade sauce; black drum with local vegetables and lemon butter; and a sweet potato tart with bourbon Chantilly.

DANTE'S KITCHEN $$$

736 Dante St., 504/861-3121, www.danteskitchen.com

HOURS: Mon. and Wed.-Fri. 6 P.M.-close, Sat.-Sun. 10:30 A.M.-2 P.M. and 6 P.M.-close

On a quiet street in Uptown's Riverbend area, not far from the Mississippi River, stands an adorable, canary-yellow bungalow, which houses one of the neighborhood's most popular restaurants. Featuring multiple rooms, each of which is uniquely decorated with colorful walls and abstract artwork, Dante's Kitchen can accommodate numerous diners while providing an intimate dining experience. Dinnertime options here range from small plates, such as the slow-smoked pork belly with cannellini beans, parsley sauce, arugula, and a pork cracklin' salad, to entrées like the pan-roasted Gulf fish with red grape and oxtail marmalade, herb coconut rice, and smoked salt. The weekend brunch, meanwhile, might include such favorites as bread pudding French toast, accompanied by powdered sugar and a seasonal fruit sauce, and grilled shrimp, served with grits and an andouille red-eye gravy. Though reservations are recommended for dinner, they're not accepted for brunch.

GAUTREAU'S $$$

1728 Soniat St., 504/899-7397, www.gautreausrestaurant.com

HOURS: Mon.-Sat. 6-10 P.M.

After exploring Tulane University, Audubon Zoo, and other Uptown haunts, indulge in a fancy meal at Gautreau's, a uniquely elegant restaurant only a few blocks north of the St. Charles streetcar line. Situated in what appears to be an old house, this small, extremely popular restaurant features high ceilings, drape-like walls, and a knowledgeable, accommodating staff. Given the noise level at times, though, Gautreau's is probably more suitable for small groups of friends than, for instance, romantic dinners. The menu is constantly evolving, and while most of the dishes here are creative and worth remembering, favorites have included the duck confit with German potato salad and mustard crème fraiche, sautéed halibut with preserved lemon yogurt and fried artichokes, and the caramelized banana split with vanilla ice cream, warm banana bread, butterscotch, chocolate sauce, and toasted walnuts. Reservations are highly recommended here.

FRENCH
LA CRÊPE NANOU $$

1410 Robert St., 504/899-2670

HOURS: Sun.-Thurs. 6-10 P.M., Fri. 11 A.M.-3 P.M. and 6-11 P.M., Sat. 6-11 P.M.

For a hint of Europe, head two blocks south of the St. Charles streetcar line, where you'll find La Crêpe Nanou, a cute little red, 1950s-style

© LAURA MARTONE

La Crêpe Nanou offers a classic French bistro experience, complete with alfresco dining.

French bistro known for its intimate ambience, gracious service, and unpretentious wine list, all of which make it ideal for romantic dinners and special occasions. The old-fashioned cuisine is equally winning. Dinnertime highlights include the French onion soup, mussel appetizer, seafood au gratin, filet mignon with béarnaise sauce, and, of course, the crêpes, with fillings like shrimp, smoked salmon, ratatouille, and crawfish with lobster sauce. If you have room, the salads and dessert crêpes are also worth sampling. Also, depending on the weather, you should consider sitting outside.

LILETTE $$$

3637 Magazine St., 504/895-1636, www.liletterestaurant.com

HOURS: Tues.-Thurs. 11:30 A.M.-2 P.M. and 5:30-9:30 P.M., Fri.-Sat. 11:30 A.M.-2 P.M. and 5:30-10:30 P.M.

A high-ceilinged storefront restaurant along a lively stretch of Magazine, Lilette is one of the neighborhood's more idiosyncratic and enjoyable eateries, a setting equally suitable for a special occasion or a meal before or after shopping—given that both lunch and dinner are served. Unlike those of many of the city's upscale contemporary dining establishments, Lilette's kitchen—run by chef-owner John Harris—rarely attempts to improve upon Creole or Cajun cooking and instead borrows heavily from France and Northern Italy for inspiration. The grilled hanger steak with thinly cut fries and marrowed bordelaise tastes fresh from a Paris bistro. More complex, however, is the entrée of roasted Muscovy duck breast with Tuscan kale, butternut squash, sage, and satsuma-coriander jus. Creative soups, salads, and seafood dishes round out the eclectic menu.

INDIAN
NIRVANA INDIAN CUISINE $$

4308 Magazine St., 504/894-9797, www.insidenirvana.com

HOURS: Tues.-Sun. 11:30 A.M.-2:30 P.M. and 5:30-10:30 P.M.

New Orleans doesn't have a wealth of Indian restaurants, but Nirvana has deftly served the needs of curry and naan fans since 1982. The extensive menu includes such traditional fare as tandoori chicken; shrimp biryani; *seenkh* kebab, which features ground lamb sausage; chicken vindaloo, a spicy dish with potatoes; and lamb *saag,* which includes creamed spinach. At lunch (and for dinner on Thursday and Sunday), there's a phenomenal $9.95 buffet that has a justifiably fanatical following. No matter when you come, though, you can eat inside the vibrant dining room or, depending on the weather, opt for the leafy patio.

SARA'S RESTAURANT ⓈⓈⓈ

724 Dublin St., 504/861-0565,
www.sarasrestaurant.com

HOURS: Tues.-Sat. 5 P.M.-close

A lovely pale-blue Riverbend café with marvelous cooking and amiable service, Sara's occupies one of the neighborhood's many delightful little cottages, on a row with several cheery shops. In addition to boasting an extensive wine list, it's a source of delicious, offbeat cuisine that fuses Indian, Mediterranean, Thai, French, and Creole flavors. Sesame-crusted salmon with jasmine rice, coconut shrimp simmered in red and green curries, and *saag paneer* (homemade Indian farmer's cheese with baby spinach and spices) reflect the kitchen's deft handling of these varied cuisines. The salads and desserts are equally divine; try the spinach and smoked gouda, and be sure to save room for the Chocolate Sin cake.

ITALIAN
ELEVEN 79 ⓈⓈⓈ

1179 Annunciation St., 504/299-1179,
www.eleven79.com

HOURS: Mon.-Wed. 5-10 P.M., Thurs.-Fri.
11:30 A.M.-2:30 P.M. and 5-10 P.M., Sat. 5-11 P.M.

Quirky Eleven 79 has a strong local following for its Creole-inspired Italian fare. The fried calamari, roasted artichoke, and barbecued shrimp are heavenly appetizers, and you won't go wrong with the oysters *pannare* served with caviar. Veal parmesan and lemon chicken are popular entrées, though the dinner and dessert menus change often. This diminutive, charming restaurant occupies a restored

bungalow in the shadows of the Pontchartrain Expressway bridge, just on the border between the Warehouse and Lower Garden Districts.

PASCAL'S MANALE RESTAURANT & BAR ⓈⓈ

1838 Napoleon Ave., 504/895-4877,
www.neworleansrestaurants.com/pascalsmanale

HOURS: Mon.-Fri. 11:30 A.M.-2 P.M. and 5 P.M.-close, Sat. 5 P.M.-close

While my husband and I appreciate upscale, creative cuisine, we're equally fond of casual neighborhood restaurants that capture the New Orleans of old. Like Mandina's in Mid-City, Pascal's Manale Restaurant & Bar is one such place. Founded in 1913 and usually filled with colorful locals, this friendly, family-run eatery offers both classic Italian and Creole cuisine, plus a lively, cash-only oyster bar. Popular dishes here include the turtle soup, seafood gumbo, barbecue shrimp, freshly shucked oysters, pasta with crabmeat and scallops in a light cream sauce, and, naturally, bread pudding. The trouble is that, as with Mandina's, the service can be inconsistent. The food, which also seems to vary in quality, can be a bit on the pricey side. Be prepared, too, for a long wait—even if you've reserved a table.

SLICE PIZZERIA Ⓢ

1513 St. Charles Ave., 504/525-7437,
www.slicepizzeria.com

HOURS: Mon.-Sat. 11 A.M.-11 P.M., Sun. 11 A.M.-10 P.M.

If you get the munchies while exploring the Garden District, make a beeline for Slice Pizzeria, a bustling pizza joint along the St. Charles streetcar line. While it might not offer the best pizza in the city, this modern-looking eatery is indeed a popular spot, and many locals swear by the thin, hand-tossed crust. In fact, I'm especially fond of the white pie, the crust of which is brushed with olive oil and topped with mozzarella, ricotta, romano, and fresh minced garlic. The toppings here are numerous, such as eggplant, spinach, capers, kalamata olives, sun-dried tomatoes, artichoke hearts, basil pesto, roasted red peppers, gorgonzola, goat cheese, pepperoni, prosciutto, shrimp, andouille sausage, and many more. Other dishes, like the steamed mussels, varied salads, massive calzones, four cheese ravioli, and grilled salmon panini, are also worth tasting. There's a second Uptown location of Slice (5538 Magazine St., 504/897-4800).

STEIN'S MARKET AND DELI $

2207 Magazine St., 504/527-0771, www.steinsdeli.net

HOURS: Tues.-Fri. 7 A.M.-7 P.M., Sat.-Sun. 9 A.M.-5 P.M.

Amid the quaint stores and antiques shops along offbeat Magazine Street, you'll encounter Stein's Market and Deli, a casual, often crowded joint featuring communal tables, deli-style sandwiches, a terrific beer selection, and a slew of specialty goods, from balsamic vinegars to loose-leaf teas. Try the smoked salmon and cream cheese bagel for breakfast, the classic reuben for lunch, and the homemade cookies and brownies anytime. Luckily, there's quite a variety of breads, meats, cheeses, and sides available. The deli's spacious parking lot is also a big plus, as are the picnic tables out front—a great spot for people-watching.

MEDITERRANEAN

BYBLOS $$

3218 Magazine St., 504/894-1233, www.byblosrestaurants.com

HOURS: Sun.-Thurs. 11 A.M.-10 P.M., Fri.-Sat. 11 A.M.-11 P.M.

Some folks swear that the original Byblos, an excellent Mediterranean restaurant in Old Metairie (1501 Metairie Rd., 504/834-9773), is better than the location on Magazine Street. Both, however, are delightful eateries, though the Uptown locale is indeed larger and a bit more atmospheric, boasting a casual yet lively ambience. The extensive menu features everything from hummus, falafel, and stuffed grape leaves to salade niçoise, chicken *shawarma,* and rack of lamb. You'll also find Byblos fare in the food courts at Tulane University and Lakeside Shopping Center.

MAPLE STREET CAFÉ $$

7623 Maple St., 504/314-9003, www.maplestreetcafenola.com

HOURS: Mon.-Thurs. 11 A.M.-2:30 P.M. and 5-9:30 P.M.,

Fri.-Sat. 11 A.M.-10 P.M., Sun. noon-9 P.M.

Make the trek way Uptown to the Maple Street Café, a dapper neighborhood restaurant opened in 1995 and now serving first-rate contemporary versions of continental and Mediterranean cooking. A bountiful Greek salad or oyster amandine makes a delightful starter, while a pepper-crusted duck breast drizzled with a fig sauce is typical of the main dishes, which change often. Housed within a small cottage amid quaint boutiques and other eateries, the narrow two-tier dining room has a tile floor and cream-colored walls. Seating is also available in a small courtyard.

MEXICAN

JUAN'S FLYING BURRITO $

2018 Magazine St., 504/569-0000, www.juansflyingburrito.com

HOURS: Sun.-Thurs. 11 A.M.-10 P.M., Fri.-Sat. 11 A.M.-11 P.M.

Youthful and raffish Juan's Flying Burrito has wooden booths, brick walls, an artsy, alternative staff, and an eclectic crowd. Art covers the

Magazine Street shoppers can enjoy a quick bite at Juan's Flying Burrito.

walls, and loud music fills this joint, one of the best quick bites along the lower stretch of Magazine, close to antiques shops and other boutiques. The fare is a mod take on Tex-Mex, with such filling fare as pork 'n' slaw tacos, bacon and blue cheese quesadillas, and the Veggie Punk burrito, stuffed with potatoes, jalapeños, pinto beans, jack and cheddar cheese, lettuce, and salsa. You'll also find a nice range of beers and margaritas—not to mention a second location in Mid-City (4724 S. Carrollton Ave., 504/486-9950) at the bustling intersection of South Carrollton Avenue and Canal Street. Though the Mid-City spot is a little less funky, the dedicated parking lot is a definite plus.

SEAFOOD

CLANCY'S $$$

6100 Annunciation St., 504/895-1111, www.clancysneworleans.com

HOURS: Mon.-Wed. 5:30-10:30 P.M., Thurs.-Fri. 11:30 A.M.-2 P.M. and 5:30-10:30 P.M., Sat. 5:30-10:30 P.M.

Uptown has become such a great dining destination that Clancy's, which had been a discreet locals' hangout for many years, has almost come to feel a tad touristy. No matter the increasing crowds, the staff works hard to accommodate everyone and make both regulars and newcomers feel right at home. The loosely Creole-meets-Italian menu changes often but usually has a few reliable standbys, such as shrimp rémoulade, fried oysters with brie, smoked soft-shell crab with crabmeat, seared sea scallops in a basil-walnut pesto sauce, and filet mignon with stilton and a red-wine demi-glace. There are several dining areas in this rambling building—the quietest and most romantic is upstairs, the more convivial and social is in the front room adjacent to the bar.

FRANKY & JOHNNY'S $$

321 Arabella St., 504/899-9146, www.frankyandjohnnys.com

HOURS: Sun.-Thurs. 11 A.M.-9 P.M., Fri.-Sat. 11 A.M.-10 P.M.

Since I was a kid, Franky & Johnny's has been one of my favorite neighborhood eateries. Situated in a residential area, not far from Tchoupitoulas, this easygoing, no-frills dive offers several New Orleans–style dishes, such as red beans and rice, boudin balls, and muffulettas. Seafood, though, is the joint's specialty. Beyond fried shrimp, oyster, and catfish platters and po-boys, many patrons come for whatever boiled seafood is in season. Just don't be surprised to see celebrities while you're here; I once witnessed John Goodman happily munching on boiled crawfish with his family, and as is common in laid-back New Orleans, no one bugged him while he ate—not even me.

Tremé and Mid-City

Map 5

AMERICAN

PARKWAY BAKERY AND TAVERN $

538 Hagan Ave., 504/482-3047, www.parkwaypoorboys.com

HOURS: Wed.-Mon. 11 A.M.-10 P.M.

Founded in 1911 near Bayou St. John and closed for nearly four months following Hurricane Katrina, the Parkway Bakery and Tavern is a terrific place to dine after exploring City Park and the historic cemeteries of Mid-City. Despite the name, this popular eatery is mainly known for its delicious, well-stuffed po-boys, with fillings like tomatoes and mozzarella, pastrami, grilled ham, fried catfish, Italian meatballs, and alligator sausage. Many patrons also rave about the potato salad, sweet potato fries, and "surf & turf" po-boy, a winning combination of hot roast beef, fried shrimp, and gravy. Beyond the food, though, patrons also favor the Parkway for its friendly staff and nostalgic atmosphere—the walls, after all, are filled with old photographs and local memorabilia.

WILLIE MAE'S SCOTCH HOUSE $

2401 St. Ann St., 504/822-9503

HOURS: Mon.-Sat. 11 A.M.-5 P.M.

Between the historic Tremé and Esplanade

Ridge neighborhoods—incidentally, not the best areas to explore alone at night—you'll encounter Willie Mae's Scotch House, a legendary, old-school joint primarily known for its fried chicken, which, by most accounts, is both crispy and juicy. The flavorful red beans and rice, cornbread, and lemonade are also well regarded, but no matter what you order, you can bet that it won't break the bank. The staff is friendly and attentive, though given the sketchy neighborhood, I'd highly recommend arriving here by car or cab.

ASIAN
CAFÉ MINH $$

4139 Canal St., 504/482-6266, www.cafeminh.com
HOURS: Mon.-Thurs. 11:30 A.M.-2:30 P.M. and 5-9 P.M., Fri. 11:30 A.M.-2:30 P.M. and 5-10 P.M., Sat. 5-10 P.M.

Like many Mid-City restaurants, Café Minh occupies an old-fashioned house on a residential block, only a few steps from the Canal Street streetcar line and roughly a block from the busy intersection of Canal and Carrollton. Though the name reveals its Asian roots, the restaurant actually boasts a fusion of Vietnamese, French, and Creole cuisines. Favorite dishes include the spring rolls, Asian pear salad, crabmeat and watermelon salsa, bouillabaisse, Creole tomato and crabmeat napoleon with wasabi vinaigrette, and colorful peach and blueberry cobbler, but be advised that the menu changes often. The interior is elegant, more so than the homey exterior might indicate; the seating, however, is limited, so try to dine here during off-hours.

CAJUN AND CREOLE
DOOKY CHASE'S RESTAURANT $$

2301 Orleans Ave., 504/821-0535
HOURS: Tues.-Thurs. 11 A.M.-3 P.M., Fri. 11 A.M.-3 P.M. and 5-9 P.M.

Established in 1941, Dooky Chase's is one of New Orleans's most famous restaurants. While the city might boast more consistent eateries, this unassuming place is definitely worth a stop, if only for the classy ambience and rich history. Indeed, many locals swear by the Creole and Southern dishes served here,

especially the okra gumbo, fried chicken, red beans and rice, collard greens, and peach cobbler—all of which are part of the lunchtime buffet. Walk-ins and reservations are both welcome. Unfortunately, the food is a bit pricey, and the servers, while friendly, seem harried much of the time. Also, be prepared for sketchy surroundings—this is the Tremé, after all.

LIL' DIZZY'S CAFÉ $$

1500 Esplanade Ave., 504/569-8997
HOURS: Mon.-Sat. 7 A.M.-2 P.M., Sun. 8 A.M.-2 P.M.

Situated in the Faubourg Tremé, about five blocks from the French Quarter, Lil' Dizzy's Café is admittedly not much to look at, but nevertheless, this nondescript corner restaurant has long been a favorite among locals. The friendly staff and down-home surroundings make you feel as though you're dining in someone's house, and the homestyle Creole and Southern cuisine is well worth the price. Highlights on the lunch buffet include fried chicken, fried catfish, macaroni and cheese, red beans and rice, seafood gumbo, biscuits, and bread pudding. While the original is a must-see, there's also a Lil' Dizzy's in the CBD (610 Poydras St., 504/212-5656), which is open for both lunch and dinner.

COFFEE AND DESSERTS
☕ ANGELO BROCATO $

214 N. Carrollton Ave., 504/486-1465,
www.angelobrocatoicecream.com
HOURS: Tues.-Thurs. 10 A.M.-10 P.M., Fri.-Sat. 10 A.M.-10:30 P.M., Sun. 10 A.M.-9 P.M.

After a day of exploring City Park, head southwest on Carrollton, toward Canal Street, and take a snack-break detour at Angelo Brocato's, an old-world bakery and ice cream parlor that's famous not only for its superb Italian pastries, such as the classic cannoli, but for tantalizing house-made ice cream, Italian ice, and gelato in all kinds of tempting flavors, such as spumoni, chestnut, and amaretto. The most popular treat—and my life-long favorite—is the lemon ice, a simple yet expertly blended concoction of water, granulated sugar, and fresh lemons. This beloved Mid-City eatery celebrated its 100th anniversary in 2005,

© LAURA MARTONE

For more than 100 years, Angelo Brocato has served an array of Italian pastries and gelato.

only to be smacked hard by the wrath of Katrina. The storm caused the place to close for nearly a year, but the virtually rebuilt Angelo Brocato reopened in July 2006, much to the relief of sweet-toothed devotees throughout the city.

FAIR GRINDS COFFEEHOUSE $

3133 Ponce de Leon St., 504/913-9072, www.fairgrinds.com

HOURS: Daily 6:30 A.M.-10 P.M.

A cheerful neighborhood coffeehouse just off Esplanade Avenue and only two blocks from the historic Fair Grounds Race Course, the amusingly named Fair Grinds serves all the usual hot and iced coffee drinks, plus fresh-squeezed juices and a variety of muffins, quiches, empanadas, and other light snacks. Filled with racetrack collectibles and framed photographs, the homey space is well suited for reading or working on your laptop.

PANDORA'S SNOWBALLS $

901 N. Carrollton Ave.

HOURS: Daily 12:30-7:30 P.M.

If you've never before had a sno-ball—perhaps the city's most popular summertime treat, essentially a cup of finely shaved ice doused with flavored syrup—you might wonder how best to eat one. On a hot summer's day, just do as the locals do: simply wait for some of the ice to melt, slurp up the syrup with a straw, then use a spoon to eat the ice on top. You can practice this technique at Pandora's, a humble, cash-only take-out window serving up sno-balls in dozens of flavors—such as kiwi, almond, strawberry cheesecake, watermelon, piña colada, praline cream, and sugar-free grape—plus soft-serve ice cream, frozen yogurt, burgers, hot dogs, and the like.

ECLECTIC

CAFÉ NOMA $

New Orleans Museum of Art, 1 Collins Diboll Circle, 504/482-1264, www.cafenoma.com

HOURS: Tues.-Thurs. 10 A.M.-5 P.M., Fri. 10 A.M.-9 P.M., Sat.-Sun. 10 A.M.-5 P.M.

While not as fancy as Ralph Brennan's other Mid-City eatery, Ralph's on the Park, Café NOMA is still a worthy lunchtime spot, especially for art lovers. After all, it's situated inside the New Orleans Museum of Art (NOMA), which sits along the southern edge of City Park. Here, you'll find delectable pastries, a limited wine and beer selection, and fresh, creative fare, such as salmon bruschetta, potato-leek soup enhanced with bacon, blueberry and arugula salad, a prosciutto and Gruyère panini, and a chipotle-marinated portobello mushroom slider with spinach, sun-dried tomatoes, red onions, and Vermont cheddar.

ⓒ RALPH'S ON THE PARK $$$

900 City Park Ave., 504/488-1000,
www.ralphsonthepark.com

HOURS: Mon. 5:30-9 P.M., Tues.-Thurs. 11:30 A.M.-2 P.M. and 5:30-9 P.M., Fri. 11:30 A.M.-2 P.M. and 5:30-9:30 P.M., Sat. 5:30-9:30 P.M., Sun. 11 A.M.-2 P.M. and 5:30-9 P.M.

Located within steps of leafy City Park, the aptly named Ralph's on the Park is one of only two Brennan family–helmed dining operations in Mid-City, and it's absolutely worth the trip. First off, it's far from the madding crowds of the Quarter and CBD, making for a more relaxed, convivial dining experience. It's

also set inside a lovely historic building that was constructed in 1860 as a coffeehouse and concession stand for the nearby park. Then there's the elegant, innovative food, such as flaky mushroom tarts, blue crab beignets, and ribeye-wrapped scallops with foie gras, cauliflower purée, roasted red new potatoes, and port wine beef sauce. It's also one of the best brunch options in town.

FRENCH
CAFÉ DEGAS $$

3127 Esplanade Ave., 504/945-5635,
www.cafedegas.com

HOURS: Wed.-Sat. 11 A.M.-3 P.M. and 6-10 P.M., Sun. 10:30 A.M.-3 P.M. and 6-9:30 P.M.

Nestled amid foliage on tree-lined Esplanade Avenue, the cozy Café Degas serves such superb French cuisine as escargot, French onion soup, salade niçoise, and Dijon-crusted rack of Australian lamb with ratatouille, haricots verts, fingerling potatoes, and smoked Vidalia onions. There's nothing overly trendy or complicated about Degas. The cooking is authentic

Ralph's on the Park, one of two Brennan family eateries near City Park

© DANIEL MARTONE

and reminiscent of true French bistro fare. The ambience is winning, too—it's the ideal spot for a romantic dinner. In warm weather, you can enjoy a meal on the lush garden patio, which is the perfect place to end an afternoon of exploring Mid-City.

ITALIAN

LIUZZA'S RESTAURANT $

3636 Bienville Ave., 504/482-9120, www.liuzzas.com

HOURS: Mon.-Sat. 11 A.M.-10 P.M.

Like most New Orleans families, we have several favorite dining haunts, and Liuzza's is one of them. Situated about two blocks from the Canal Street streetcar line, this down-home bar and restaurant has been a Mid-City landmark since 1947. As with many of its neighbors, the menu here features classic Cajun, Creole, and seafood dishes, though it excels with Italian items like garlic bread, stuffed artichokes, lasagna, and the Frenchuletta, essentially a muffuletta on French bread. Two of my favorite pasta dishes are the crawfish Telemachus, which features a crawfish cream sauce, and eggplant St. John, which includes eggplant medallions in a shrimp and artichoke sauce. After a visit to the Fair Grounds Race Course, consider stopping by **Liuzza's by the Track** (1518 N. Lopez St., 504/218-7888), an equally popular joint among Mid-City denizens.

MEDITERRANEAN

LOLA'S $$

3312 Esplanade Ave., 504/488-6946, www.lolasneworleans.com

HOURS: Sun.-Thurs. 5:30-9:30 P.M., Fri.-Sat. 5:30-10 P.M.

Part of the bumper crop of fine restaurants along the historic Esplanade Ridge, Lola's is a casual, small-scale operation whose owners have focused, since its opening in 1994, on food above all else. Indeed, the Spanish- and Mediterranean-inspired cooking stands up to any in the city: Consider the fresh ceviche, spicy grilled calamari, refreshingly chilled gazpacho, and fragrantly seasoned paella heaped with shrimp, fish, calamari, scallops, mussels, and vegetables. Just be advised that reservations aren't accepted here. Also, while there's a limited selection of beer, wine, and homemade sangria, you're welcome to bring your own alcohol for a $5-per-bottle corkage fee.

SEAFOOD

KATIE'S RESTAURANT & BAR $$

3701 Iberville St., 504/488-6582, www.katiesinmidcity.com

HOURS: Mon. 11 A.M.-3 P.M., Tues.-Thurs. 11 A.M.-9 P.M., Fri.-Sat. 11 A.M.-10 P.M., Sun. 9 A.M.-3 P.M.

Just around the corner from longstanding Liuzza's, and only a block from the Canal Street streetcar line, lies this well-loved neighborhood eatery, known for its friendly staff, easygoing atmosphere, and delicious food. Though the menu features both Italian and New Orleans–style cuisine, the specialty here is seafood, such as crawfish beignets, overstuffed crab cakes, catfish meunière, shrimp and artichoke pizza, and my favorite—the fried green tomato and shrimp rémoulade po-boy. Multiple diners may choose to share the Barge, an entire French bread loaf stuffed with fried shrimp, oysters, and/or catfish, which can serve up to four people. Opened in 1984, the family-owned Katie's Restaurant enjoyed many years of success, until Hurricane Katrina's devastation forced its closure. After a 4.5-year renovation, however, Katie's is once again a favorite spot for Mid-City denizens and other New Orleanian foodies—it was even the recent focus of Guy Fieri's Food Network show *Diners, Drive-ins, and Dives.*

MANDINA'S RESTAURANT $$

3800 Canal St., 504/482-9179, www.mandinasrestaurant.com

HOURS: Mon.-Thurs. 11 A.M.-9:30 P.M., Fri.-Sat. 11 A.M.-10 P.M., Sun. noon-9 P.M.

If you're seeking a classic New Orleans–style restaurant—where the dress code is casual and the menu features local Creole and Italian staples like turtle soup, fried seafood, soft-shell crab amandine, veal parmesan, red beans and rice, stuffed bell peppers, crawfish étouffée, and bread pudding—look no farther than Mandina's. Originally established as an Italian grocery store in 1898, the family-owned Mandina's eventually became a full-service restaurant in 1932. Since then, this capacious, multi-room restaurant has been a popular local hangout, particularly for cops, attorneys, and politicians at lunchtime. It's one of my family's favorite spots, too; for years, I've enjoyed the ample portions of eggplant sticks, shrimp rémoulade, Italian salad, and oyster-artichoke soup. Reservations aren't accepted here, but it's rarely difficult to find a table, and while the parking lot is rather small, there's usually ample street parking—not to mention the fact that it's conveniently located on the Canal Street streetcar line. The only drawback is that the servers, many of whom have been here awhile, aren't as friendly and attentive as one might like.

Greater New Orleans   Map 6

ASIAN
CAFE EQUATOR $$
2920 Severn Ave., Metairie, 504/888-4772,
www.cafeequator.com
HOURS: Mon.-Thurs. 11A.M.-9P.M., Fri.-Sat. 11A.M.-10P.M.,
Sun. noon-9P.M.

After spending a few hours at the Lakeside Shopping Center, I usually skip the food court and hop across Severn, where sits one of my favorite Thai restaurants. While not everyone walks away with fond memories—often citing less-than-attentive service, less-than-flavorful food, and limited parking—I've always enjoyed my dining experiences here. For one thing, the vibe is intimate and, for the most part, peaceful—unlike many New Orleans–area restaurants, this one is actually ideal for quiet conversation. For another thing, the food has always been exactly what I craved. Besides obvious choices like the summer rolls, pan-fried chicken dumplings, and pad thai, other favorites include the coconut soup, glass noodle soup, and *pad woon zen*—a dish of clear noodles sautéed with chicken, shrimp, bean sprouts, shiitake mushrooms, onions, and yellow squash.

FIVE HAPPINESS $$
3605 S. Carrollton Ave., 504/482-3935,
www.fivehappiness.com
HOURS: Sun.-Thurs. 11A.M.-10P.M., Fri.-Sat. 11A.M.-11P.M.

Close to the campus of Xavier University and not far from I-10, Five Happiness serves commendable Mandarin and Szechuan fare in a sleek, Asian-inspired dining room that was completely renovated after Hurricane Katrina. House favorites include honey-roasted pecan shrimp and crispy whole fish with a choice of garlic brown, black bean, or Kung Pao sauce. The bird's nest of minced shrimp, dried black mushrooms, and water chestnuts within iceberg lettuce wraps is as tasty as it is artful. Don't be dissuaded by the neighboring fast-food restaurants and auto-repair shops—this is the real deal.

KIM SON RESTAURANT $$
349 Whitney Ave., Gretna, 504/366-2489,
www.kimsonnola.com
HOURS: Mon.-Sat. 11A.M.-2:45P.M. and 5-8:45P.M.

Though the exterior might be less than inspiring, Kim Son is indeed one of the best Asian restaurants on the West Bank—if not in the entire Greater New Orleans area. Serving a wide assortment of Chinese and Vietnamese cuisine, this casual eatery is a favorite among locals, including vegetarians—and it doesn't hurt that the lunch and dinner specials are ideal for budget-conscious diners. Popular dishes here include the crab rangoon, hot and sour shrimp soup, charcoal-broiled beef, salted baked shrimp, and crawfish with lobster sauce. Unfortunately, though, the servers aren't always as attentive as you might like, especially during the lunchtime rush.

MIKIMOTO JAPANESE RESTAURANT & SUSHI BAR $$
3301 S. Carrollton Ave., 504/488-1881,
www.mikimotosushi.com
HOURS: Sun.-Thurs. 11A.M.-10:30P.M., Fri. 11A.M.-11P.M.,
Sat. 4-11P.M.

Just a few blocks northeast of the Rock

'n' Bowl, you'll encounter the Mikimoto Japanese Restaurant & Sushi Bar, a decent, fairly inexpensive Mid-City option for fans of sashimi and tempura. Highlights here include the udon soup, pan-fried gyoza, chicken tempura, baked scallops, wasabi mussels, and creative sushi rolls, such as the Nola roll—which consists of fresh salmon and avocado, wrapped in seaweed and rice and topped with mussels and crabmeat. The service is typically amiable and efficient; the only trouble is that it's often pretty crowded here, meaning that parking in the convoluted lot can be a challenge at times.

NINE ROSES ❸❸
1100 Stephens St., Gretna, 504/366-7665
HOURS: Sun.-Tues. and Thurs. 10:30 A.M.-9:30 P.M., Fri.-Sat. 10:30 A.M.-10 P.M.

Gretna, a community on the West Bank of the Mississippi River, has several well-loved Asian restaurants, including Nine Roses—a Vietnamese eatery also known as Hoa Hong 9. This casual, inexpensive joint boasts a truly enormous, rather intimidating menu, filled with delectable, authentic dishes like spring rolls, jellyfish salad, imitation shark fin soup, goat curry, and whole steamed fish with scallions, ginger, and a tangy soy sauce.

CAJUN AND CREOLE
KOSHER CAJUN
NEW YORK DELI & GROCERY ❸❸
3519 Severn Ave., Metairie, 504/888-2010,
www.koshercajun.com
HOURS: Mon.-Thurs. 10 A.M.-7 P.M., Fri. and Sun. 10 A.M.-3 P.M.

Whenever you're craving chopped liver, pastrami, corned beef, knishes, matzoh ball soup, and other Jewish deli favorites, the Kosher Cajun New York Deli fits the bill. Situated near the always-busy intersection of West Esplanade Avenue and North Causeway Boulevard—not far from the Lakeside Shopping Center and my paternal grandparents' former home—this family-friendly lunchroom and delicatessen is a popular place for a lunchtime sandwich or an early supper of falafel, lamb chops, and the

like. You'll also find a nice selection of gourmet prepared foods and groceries—supposedly, one of the state's largest selections of kosher products.

COFFEE AND DESSERTS
CAFFE! CAFFE! ❸
4301 Clearview Pkwy., Metairie, 504/885-4845,
www.caffecaffe.com
HOURS: Mon.-Fri. 7 A.M.-9 P.M., Sat. 8 A.M.-9 P.M., Sun. 8 A.M.-1 P.M.

If you find yourself in Metairie and in need of a light bite, head to Caffe! Caffe!, a friendly coffeehouse that offers affordable salads, sandwiches, wraps, and desserts. Naturally, you'll also find a wide array of coffee drinks and fruity teas, including a red velvet cake–flavored iced coffee. If you're really hungry, you can always order one of the bakery's amazing cakes and pies, from pumpkin cheesecake to key lime pie. There's another location in Metairie (3547 N. Hullen, 504/267-9190), not far from the Lakeside Shopping Center.

MORNING CALL COFFEE STAND ❸
3325 Severn Ave., Metairie, 504/885-4068,
www.morningcallcoffeestand.com
HOURS: Daily 24 hours

Similar in concept to the French Quarter's Café Du Monde, Morning Call is open around the clock and serves a short menu that includes specialties like beignets and piping-hot café au lait. Originally established on Decatur Street in 1870, Morning Call moved to its present Metairie location in 1974, so unlike Café Du Monde, it's never overrun with tourists. By the same token, though, it doesn't have nearly as interesting a location—it's in a small strip mall across from Lakeside Shopping Center. Still, the interior is quite elegant. Long mirrored marble counters line one side of the room; the other contains small wooden tables. Servers in white paper caps skirt about the room, delivering coffee and doughnuts. Next door is Lakeside News, a good place to pick up all manner of newspapers and magazines; it's usually open daily from 4:30 A.M. to 10 P.M.

RESTAURANTS

© LAURA MARTONE

Metairie's Morning Call Coffee Stand serves hot coffee and beignets 24 hours daily.

ECLECTIC

CAFÉ B ❸❸❸

2700 Metairie Rd., Metairie, 504/934-4700,
www.cafeb.com
HOURS: Mon.-Thurs. 11:30 A.M.-2 P.M. and 5-9 P.M.,
Fri. 11:30 A.M.-2 P.M. and 5-10 P.M., Sat. 5-10 P.M., Sun.
10 A.M.-2 P.M.

Local restaurateur Ralph Brennan—the man behind such well-regarded eateries as Ralph Brennan's Red Fish Grill and Ralph's on the Park—has expanded his empire to Metairie, New Orleans's most active suburb. Situated on Metairie Road, a winding thoroughfare punctuated by curious shops and restaurants, the Café B is a casual bistro, with simple decor and a cheery ambience. Helmed by chef Chris Montero, the menu features New Orleans–style dishes and gourmet twists on old American favorites, ideal for lunch, dinner, or Sunday brunch. Highlights include shrimp beignets, oyster-artichoke soup, shrimp and lobster ravioli, macaroni and cheese, hanger steak and garlic *frites,* and chicken pot pie.

HERITAGE GRILL ❸❸

111 Veterans Memorial Blvd., Metairie, 504/934-4900,
www.heritagegrillmetairie.com
HOURS: Mon.-Fri. 11 A.M.-7 P.M.

Although the Heritage Grill, another of Ralph Brennan's New Orleans–area restaurants, is technically located in Jefferson Parish, you'll actually find it just beside the border between New Orleans and Metairie. Ideal for business lunches or an early weekday dinner, this tastefully decorated eatery offers friendly service and delicious New American–Creole cuisine. Try the crawfish bruschetta, turkey club, crawfish grilled cheese, homemade ginger ale, and lemon ice box pie. Just be advised that dishes here tend to be on the salty side.

MONDO ❸❸

900 Harrison Ave., 504/224-2633,
www.mondoneworleans.com
HOURS: Mon.-Thurs. 11:30 A.M.-2:30 P.M. and
5:30-10 P.M., Fri. 11:30 A.M.-2:30 P.M. and 5:30-10:30 P.M.,
Sat. 5:30-10:30 P.M., Sun. 11 A.M.-2 P.M.

In June 2010, Susan Spicer, the well-regarded

chef behind the French Quarter's romantic Bayona, opened an easygoing, unpretentious neighborhood place in Lakeview, one of the areas hit hardest by Hurricane Katrina and, since then, experiencing a rebirth. Though relatively new, this delightful spot has already become a favorite among Mid-City and Lakeview residents who appreciate the easily accessible parking and creative cuisine. Aptly named Mondo, this bright, modern-looking eatery features flavors from around the world. Though the menu changes often, you'll typically find eclectic dishes like Thai shrimp and pork meatballs, broiled fish tacos, steamed mussels in chorizo–white wine broth, Chinese braised duck leg, veggie muffulettas, pear and gorgonzola pizza, and cinnamon beignets. The Sunday brunch is equally varied. Reservations are only available for large groups.

VEGA TAPAS CAFE $$

2051 Metairie Rd., Metairie, 504/836-2007, www.vegatapascafe.com

HOURS: Mon.-Sat. 5:30 P.M.-close

One of a handful of Southshore suburban restaurants that actually merit making a special trip from downtown, the Vega Tapas Cafe is the classiest of several eateries in a small strip mall in Old Metairie. Peach walls and high ceilings create an elegant but informal ambience for sampling tapas, most with a vaguely Mediterranean but always innovative spin. Favorite dishes have included the jumbo lump crabmeat and baby arugula salad with crumbled feta, red onion, crispy shallots, and a blood orange vinaigrette; an eggplant napoleon layered with arugula, sun-dried tomatoes, fresh mozzarella, and basil pesto; and pan-roasted veal sweetbreads and mushrooms with crispy serrano and sherry butter.

ZEA ROTISSERIE & GRILL $$

Clearview Mall, 4450 Veterans Memorial Blvd., Metairie, 504/780-9090, www.zearestaurants.com

HOURS: Sun.-Thurs. 11 A.M.-10 P.M., Fri.-Sat. 11 A.M.-11 P.M.

Given New Orleans's unique culinary offerings, I tend to avoid chain restaurants here, but I have to admit that the Zea Rotisserie & Grill is one regional chain that's worth patronizing. With branches that stretch from Lafayette to Uptown New Orleans to Birmingham, Zea specializes in well-prepared meaty fare, such as roasted chicken with a sweet-and-spicy chili glaze, St. Louis–style spare ribs with Thai sauce, twice-cooked crispy duck with honey-soy sauce, and filet mignon medallions with a marsala wine reduction and roasted garlic-herb butter. But the menu is really quite eclectic, offering a wide range of foods from all over the world, such as Mediterranean hummus, duck empanadas, chicken florentine soup, Southern-fried catfish, and wood-grilled rainbow trout. It's a cavernous place, usually echoing with chatter and lively conversation.

ITALIAN

ANDREA'S RESTAURANT $$$

3100 19th St., Metairie, 504/834-8583, www.andreasrestaurant.com

HOURS: Sun.-Thurs. 11 A.M.-9 P.M., Fri.-Sat. 11 A.M.-10 P.M.

I've never quite understood the extremely negative reviews for Andrea's. While it's true that the decor could use some updating and that cheaper Italian food can be found elsewhere, I've always enjoyed the seafood, northern Italian, and continental dishes served here, such as the charbroiled oysters, fried calamari, *caprese* salad, turtle soup, porcini ravioli, shrimp scampi, baked red snapper, and white chocolate mousse. Not far from the Lakeside Shopping Center, this spacious, relatively quiet restaurant is ideal for both romantic dinners and family gatherings, though the crowd here tends to be older than that of most downtown restaurants. Like many establishments in Metairie, though, Andrea's offers convenient parking, and the service is usually attentive—chef Andrea Apuzzo often roams through the dining room, checking on his guests. If you have time before or after your meal, consider having a cocktail in the adjacent **Capri Blu Bar,** a piano bar that's open every day but Sunday, from 11 A.M. to close.

TONY MANDINA'S RESTAURANT $$

1915 Pratt St., Gretna, 504/362-2010,
www.tonymandinas.com

HOURS: Tues.-Thurs. 11 A.M.-2 P.M., Fri. 11 A.M.-2 P.M. and 5-9 P.M., Sat. 5-9 P.M.

The West Bank, especially Gretna, is a good bet for Italian cooking, and the family-owned Tony Mandina's definitely does this genre justice. Specializing in southern Italian cuisine, the menu strays from the traditional with a handful of exceptional, locally influenced seafood dishes. Come for the classic lasagna, chicken parmesan, and eggplant Dominic Jude, which features battered eggplant medallions layered with shrimp and crabmeat and topped with a creamy shrimp Alfredo sauce. On the weekend, you'll be treated to live piano music while you dine.

SEAFOOD

DEANIE'S SEAFOOD BUCKTOWN $$

1713 Lake Ave., Metairie, 504/831-4141,
www.deanies.com

HOURS: Tues.-Sun. 11 A.M.-10 P.M.

Since I was a child, my family has ventured often to Deanie's Seafood, a small, casual eatery in Metairie's Bucktown—a former fishing village on the western side of the 17th Street Canal, which so famously flooded Lakeview after Hurricane Katrina. Established in 1961 as the neighborhood's first seafood market, Deanie's is often crowded with locals, who come here for seafood and okra gumbo, barbecue shrimp, fried artichoke hearts, boiled crabs, shrimp po-boys, the crabmeat au gratin, the enormous seafood platter, and, for mudbug lovers, the crawfish quartet, which features crawfish balls, fried crawfish tails, crawfish au gratin, and crawfish étouffée. Even the complimentary spicy red potatoes that precede the meal are worth tasting. Although I prefer this comfortable, family-friendly spot in Bucktown, there's also a more modern-looking Deanie's in the French Quarter (841 Iberville St., 504/581-1316).

◖ DRAGO'S SEAFOOD RESTAURANT $$$

3232 N. Arnoult Rd., Metairie, 504/888-9254,
www.dragosrestaurant.com

HOURS: Mon.-Sat. 11 A.M.-9 P.M.

Try to make a reservation a few days in advance for Drago's, a riotously popular restaurant with limited seating and parking. As the name indicates, the emphasis here is on seafood, much of it prepared with a Louisiana slant. The lobster dishes are particularly noteworthy; try the lobster Marco, a whole lobster stuffed with fresh sautéed shrimp and mushrooms in a light cream sauce over angel hair pasta. Apart from the usual local seafood options, such as raw oysters and fried shrimp platters, you'll also find delicious choices like the blackened duck breast over linguini with oysters and cream sauce. You can either sit at the bar, which affords a clear view of the grill cooks charbroiling oysters, or dine in one of the noisy but festive dining rooms. The high volume of business has just one drawback: The waitstaff often seems harried and understandably frazzled. If you'd rather not trek out to Metairie, there's also a Drago's inside the CBD's Hilton New Orleans Riverside (2 Poydras St., 504/584-3911).

THE GALLEY $$

2535 Metairie Rd., Metairie, 504/832-0955

HOURS: Tues.-Sat. 11 A.M.-9 P.M.

When I was younger, my paternal grandparents would often take me to the Galley, a fun, casual seafood shack on winding Metairie Road that's as good today as it was back then. Though many diners swear by the veggie-filled Bloody Mary, it's the boiled seafood that lures most people. Besides spicy boiled crabs, crawfish, and shrimp, top picks here include crawfish-stuffed hush puppies with crawfish sauce, soft-shell crab po-boys, grilled crab cakes, and shrimp and crabmeat au gratin. Several tasty sides and appetizers are also available, such as sweet potato fries, macaroni and cheese, and gumbo. Not surprisingly, given its longstanding reputation among locals, the Galley can get a wee bit crowded at times.

YE OLDE COLLEGE INN $$

3000 S. Carrollton Ave., 504/866-3683,
www.collegeinn1933.com

HOURS: Tues.-Sat. 4-11 P.M.

Part of a complex that, as of recently, includes

Dine at Ye Olde College Inn, then head to the adjacent Rock 'n' Bowl for some live music.

the Rock 'n' Bowl—a wonderful place to spend an evening bowling with the family and listening to live music—Ye Olde College Inn has been a New Orleans landmark since 1933. Expect friendly service, a nostalgic vibe, an eclectic crowd of families and sports fans, and well-prepared classics like turkey and andouille gumbo, shrimp and grits, fried green tomato and shrimp rémoulade po-boys, fresh Gulf fish with lump crabmeat, and, for dessert, a fried bread pudding po-boy. Keep a lookout for the daily specials, too.

NIGHTLIFE

New Orleans is deservedly famous for its active nightlife. The entire city boasts a cornucopia of funky watering holes, festive gay bars, stylish hotel lounges, and legendary tourist magnets—like Pat O'Brien's, famous for its knock-me-under-the-table hurricanes. New Orleans can also be a wonderful place for night owls, especially given the prevalence of 24-hour bars and restaurants.

The Big Easy's reputation as a party town is well deserved, and the pulse of that party is often found on Bourbon Street in the French Quarter. Unabashed strip clubs, karaoke bars, daiquiri shops, pulsating dance spaces, and a few well-respected jazz venues line the colorful strip. But it can also be a loud, sometimes obnoxious, often smelly thoroughfare that can become frighteningly crowded at certain times

of the year (Mardi Gras, Halloween). Truly a drunken scene most nights, Bourbon is not for everyone, but it's worth a look—at least once— if only to experience the fervor with which this city indulges in music, alcohol, and socializing.

Thankfully, relishing a night out can involve a wide array of activities, and it is the boisterous music scene that truly distinguishes New Orleans. This is one of the world's premier destinations for jazz, blues, rock, soul, zydeco, and Cajun music. The city's live music venues are equally varied, ranging from friendly neighborhood bars like the Kerry Irish Pub to capacious music halls like Tipitina's. Locals tend to favor Frenchmen Street in the Faubourg Marigny, home to several longstanding joints that mainly cater to jazz, blues, and rock fans. You'll also find several decent jazz bars in the

HIGHLIGHTS

LOOK FOR ◖ TO FIND
RECOMMENDED NIGHTLIFE.

◖ **Most Historic Bar:** Locals, tourists, and celebrities alike converge at **Lafitte's Blacksmith Shop Bar,** a small, moody, often noisy tavern housed within one of the oldest buildings in the French Quarter, along the more residential stretch of Bourbon Street (page 123).

◖ **Best Courtyard Cocktails:** Though some locals consider **Pat O'Brien's** one of the city's more crowded tourist traps, the bar's spacious courtyard – with a flaming fountain as its unique centerpiece – is a wonderful place to enjoy classic hurricanes and other cocktails in the humid night air (page 127).

◖ **Most Refined Hotel Bar:** If you're looking for an elegant watering hole, where patrons prefer cognac, caviar, and upscale apparel, consider donning your finest duds and heading to the **Polo Club Lounge,** a longtime fixture inside the glamorous Windsor Court Hotel (page 127).

◖ **Best Wine Bar:** Though New Orleans offers several worthwhile wine bars, the CBD's **W.I.N.O.** distinguishes itself – for both its varied wine selection and its informative wine-tasting classes (page 130).

◖ **Best All-Around Music Club:** If you have the chance to watch live music at just one club, venture away from the French Quarter and stop by **Tipitina's,** a long-running locals' favorite that draws some of the top zydeco, jazz, blues, and Cajun talents from around the city and beyond (page 133).

◖ **Most Unusual Spot for Zydeco:** Recently relocated from Mid-City, Uptown's ever-popular **Rock 'n' Bowl** allows couples, families, and music lovers the chance to knock down some pins amid live zydeco, blues, jazz, swing, and other musical performances (page 134).

◖ **Best Neighborhood Haunt:** Locals especially favor the **Kerry Irish Pub,** a relatively small yet comfortable French Quarter bar known for its laid-back bartenders, assortment of imported beers, and nightly live music, ranging from Irish to country to classic rock (page 134).

◖ **Most Historic Jazz Venue:** Opened in 1961, the intimate, world-renowned **Preservation Hall** presents wonderful, if brief, old-time jazz concerts within its inviting vintage confines. Just be advised that patrons line up early for these nightly performances (page 137).

◖ **Best Jazz in the Marigny:** Though the Faubourg Marigny is a hotbed of live music venues, the **Spotted Cat Music Club** – a dark, smoky joint on Frenchmen Street – is your best bet for an assortment of jazz, from old-time tunes to modern improvisation. Often cramped inside, the bar still provides limited space for dancing (page 137).

◖ **Best Gay Bar:** Situated on a busy Bourbon Street corner, the **Bourbon Pub & Parade** is the top game in town for the gay and lesbian crowd, featuring cocktails and mingling on the ground floor and dancing upstairs (page 141).

© LAURA MARTONE

NIGHTLIFE

Lafitte's Blacksmith Shop Bar, one of the oldest structures in the Quarter

Quarter; if, like me, you prefer old-fashioned jazz, then you might appreciate the late-night burlesque shows that take place at joints like One Eyed Jacks.

Safety in the Big Easy

The city's unabashed revelry can be deceptively disarming. This is a town with drive-through daiquiri shops, where you can walk down Bourbon with enormous "go-cups" of beer, and where residents tend to be a very friendly bunch. Unfortunately, though, this is still a relatively dangerous city, where inebriated tourists have been known to wander off the beaten path, misplace their hotel, and encounter aggressive muggers instead. The best advice that I can offer is to travel in groups, have fun in moderation, and make sure that someone is sober enough to find a safe path back to the hotel.

If partying on Bourbon Street, note that while it is closed to automobile traffic at night, you should still be careful at each intersection where cars are allowed to cross. Bear in mind that many bars are cash-only, and restrooms are typically reserved for paying customers; in fact, on busy nights like New Year's Eve, many no-cover music venues will charge a nominal fee.

Bars and Lounges

THE BOMBAY CLUB

830 Conti St., 504/586-0972 or 800/699-7711, www.thebombayclub.com

HOURS: Sun.-Thurs. 5-10 P.M., Fri.-Sat. 5 P.M.-midnight

Map 1

While this elegant restaurant—decorated in the style of an exclusive British gentlemen's club—offers sumptuous contemporary Creole cuisine, many patrons come for its reputation as a fashionable martini bar. Indeed, it's well known for its leather-bound, velvet-lined cocktail menu, featuring designer martinis, such as the James Bond–influenced Vesper or the Sweet Heat Margarita. On most weekends, you'll also be treated to live jazz. As with many upscale establishments in New Orleans, casual attire is permitted, though jackets are preferred for men.

THE BOOT BAR & GRILL

1039 Broadway St., 504/866-9008, www.thebootneworleans.com

HOURS: Daily 11 A.M.-6 A.M.

Map 4

For college students in need of a study break, you can't beat the Boot's convenient location. It's literally across the street from Tulane University and not much farther from Loyola's campus. As fun-lovin' and no-frills as a bar can get, this popular hangout is especially ideal for those on a budget; drink specials, after all, are rampant, from 50-cent shots and one-dollar domestic beers on Tuesday (10 P.M.–1 A.M.) to $6.50 Abita beer pitchers on Saturday during the college football season.

THE BULLDOG

3236 Magazine St., 504/891-1516, http://bulldog.draftfreak.com

HOURS: Mon.-Tues. 2 P.M.-close, Wed.-Sun. noon-close

Map 4

Like many bars in the Uptown area, the Bulldog is often a late-night haven for college students, especially those from the relatively nearby campuses of Tulane and Loyola. Of course, older, well-past-college-age locals like me favor this casual, dog-friendly watering hole, too. Both the tasty burgers and eclectic beer selection, which includes 50 draft varieties and 100 more in bottles, are definite lures. The courtyard though often crowded, provides excellent people-watching opportunities along Magazine Street.

CAROUSEL BAR

Hotel Monteleone, 214 Royal St., 504/523-3341, www.hotelmonteleone.com

HOURS: Daily 11 A.M.-1 A.M.

Map 1

Even if you're not staying at the legendary

Hotel Monteleone, you can still enjoy a libation in the colorful Carousel Bar on the first floor. The prime attraction—the rather kitschy, 1940s-style, 24-seat bar—is festooned with bright lights and garish decorations, but the real treat is that, as its name implies, the bar almost imperceptibly revolves around the center of the room. Stop by to savor the old-world ambience, watch passersby on Royal Street, listen to live music, and drink in the literary company of Tennessee Williams and Truman Capote.

CARROLLTON STATION
8140 Willow St., 504/865-9190,
www.carrolltonstation.com
HOURS: Mon.-Sat. 3 P.M.-close, Sun. noon-close
`Map 4`

Located in the Riverbend area of Uptown and named after a nearby streetcar barn, the rustic Carrollton Station is a classic neighborhood bar. Supposedly once the site of a brothel, it's now a well-favored locals' hangout, where you can sample more than 50 reasonably priced beers, relax with friends in the backyard patio, watch your favorite spectator sport, and listen to live local music on the weekend. Video poker machines, darts and ping pong, wireless Internet access, and weekly events, such as stand-up comedy on Wednesday (9 P.M.) and pub trivia on Thursday (6:30 P.M.), are also big draws.

COOTER BROWN'S
TAVERN & OYSTER BAR
509 S. Carrollton Ave., 504/866-9104,
www.cooterbrowns.com
HOURS: Mon.-Sat. 11 A.M.-2 A.M., Sun. 11 A.M.-1 A.M.
`Map 4`

Situated in Uptown's Riverbend neighborhood, not far from the Mississippi River, this casual sports bar is a favorite among nearby residents and college students alike. Established in 1977 and filled with caricatures of dead, beer-drinking celebrities, this lovable watering hole features pool tables and video poker machines, numerous televisions for diehard sports fans, more than 400 bottled brands of domestic

BIG SPENDERS IN THE BIG EASY

While it's not exactly Las Vegas – and the Louisiana cities of Shreveport and Lake Charles are considerably more popular as gambling hubs – the Greater New Orleans area does boast three major gaming facilities.

The mother ship for gamblers here, **Harrah's New Orleans** (8 Canal St., 504/533-6000 or 800/847-5299, www.harrahsneworleans.com), opened in the late 1990s under a cloud of controversy. It's one of the largest gaming facilities in the South, a massive property with more than 2,100 slot machines and 100 gaming tables, plus a full-service hotel. It has several excellent restaurants, including the vaunted Besh Steak and the trendy Bambu, as well as the Gordon Biersch brewpub and a pretty good buffet.

The metro area's second big gaming hall is the **Treasure Chest Casino** (5050 Williams Blvd., Kenner, 504/443-8000 or 800/298-0711, www.treasurechest.com), which is actually an ornate floating casino docked on Lake Pontchartrain, not far from the Louis Armstrong New Orleans International Airport. Here, you'll find live nightly entertainment, a poker room, and a buffet restaurant.

If that's not enough, head across the Mississippi River to the West Bank, where the **Boomtown Casino** (4132 Peters Rd., Harvey, 504/366-7711 or 800/366-7711, www.boomtownneworleans.com) offers more than 30 table games and 1,500 slot machines. In addition, you can choose from five dining venues: a casual oyster bar, a scrumptious buffet, an express café, the intimate Pier 4, and the aptly named Asia, featuring Chinese and Vietnamese specialties.

NIGHTLIFE

and imported beers (not to mention roughly 40 draft selections), plus to-die-for raw oysters, boiled seafood, and enormous po-boys. As a bonus, Cooter Brown's lies within walking

NIGHTLIFE

distance of the St. Charles streetcar line, so there's no excuse to drink and drive.

CURE

4905 Freret St., 504/302-2357, www.curenola.com

HOURS: Sun.-Thurs. 5 P.M.-midnight, Fri.-Sat. 5 P.M.-2 A.M.

Map 4

With its weathered brick interior walls, funky chandeliers, and stylishly lit liquor display, Cure simultaneously evokes the vibe of a quint-essential New Orleans bar and a swanky, Los Angeles cocktail lounge. Besides signature con-coctions like the Generation Adrift—which combines tequila, orange and lemon juice, peach liqueur, and old-fashioned bitters—this stylish Uptown hot spot also offers delecta-ble tapas dishes, such as pear salad and spicy Jamaican meat pie.

45 TCHOUP

4529 Tchoupitoulas St., 504/891-9066

HOURS: Mon.-Wed. 2 P.M.-2 A.M., Thurs. 2 P.M.-4 A.M., Fri.-Sat. 2 P.M.-6 A.M., Sun. 11 A.M.-2 A.M.

Map 4

Not far from the Mississippi River and formerly known as the Shiloh Lounge, this extremely smoky, loud, but well-loved dive bar features pool and darts, affordable yet strong drinks, amiable bartenders, and a well-stocked jukebox. Dimly lit and admittedly grungy, it's a great lounge for hanging out with pals, soaking up the tunes, or just hiding from the world for a while.

HALF MOON BAR & RESTAURANT

1125 St. Mary St., 504/593-0011, www.halfmoonnola.com

HOURS: Daily noon-2 A.M.

Map 4

Memorably featured in films as diverse as *Ray* (2004) and *The Skeleton Key* (2005), Half Moon has been a fixture in New Orleans for more than seven decades. In general, you'll find a gaggle of locals at this friendly joint, which isn't far from Coliseum Square in the funky Lower Garden District. A decent place to hang out with friends, unwind after antiques shopping, watch a Saints or Hornets game,

or shoot a game of pool, darts, air hockey, or Skee-Ball, Half Moon also serves up half-pound burgers, chicken sandwiches, and other delectables, starting at 5 P.M. and lasting until the wee hours.

HANDSOME WILLY'S BAR & LOUNGE

218 S. Robertson St., 504/525-0377, www.handsomewillys.com

HOURS: Mon.-Thurs. 2 P.M.-midnight, Fri. noon-4 P.M., Sat. 6 P.M.-close

Map 3

You have to admire the perseverance of the folks who run Handsome Willy's—a rockin' music club and bar that opened on the site of a for-mer brothel in 2005, was virtually destroyed by Hurricane Katrina the same year, and yet man-aged to reopen again only a few months later. It helps that the club has developed a loyal follow-ing for booking great bands, from house music to funk to hip-hop. Its proximity to the Superdome and New Orleans Arena also makes it popular among sports fans. Besides offering weekday happy hours (2–6 P.M.), Willy's serves free food on Friday (5–9 P.M.) and opens its doors on Sunday during the Saints' home games.

HURRICANES SPORTS BAR

1414 Veterans Memorial Blvd., Metairie, 504/833-0050

HOURS: Daily 11 A.M.-4 A.M.

Map 6

While not as unique as other New Orleans–area bars, Hurricanes is popular among local sports fans and, given its Metairie location, handy for those with time to kill before a flight. In addition, this often crowded joint offers drink specials, trivia games, and an ex-tensive menu of burgers, pizzas, and other ca-sual fare. You'll also hear live music on many evenings, which means that, not surprisingly, it's a popular place for late-night dancing on the weekend.

IGOR'S BUDDHA BELLY BURGER BAR

4437 Magazine St., 504/891-6105

HOURS: Daily 11 A.M.-3 A.M.

Map 4

Similar in feel and concept to Igor's Check

Point Charlie, its sibling in the Marigny, this funky dive bar lures a variety of slackers, artists, and students, particularly from Tulane and Loyola. One of the better late-night options on Magazine, it occupies an odd space that includes both a dining area and a self-service laundry. The half-pound burgers are seriously good, and on Monday, Igor's has been known to serve free red beans and rice until it runs out of the stuff.

JEAN LAFITTE'S OLD ABSINTHE HOUSE

240 Bourbon St., 504/523-3181,
www.oldabsinthehouse.com
HOURS: Sun.-Thurs. 9 A.M.-2 A.M., Fri.-Sat. 9 A.M.-4 A.M.
Map 1

Contained within a building that dates back to the early 1800s and once served as a corner grocery, the Old Absinthe House is especially popular among lawyers and other professionals. Furnished with antique chandeliers, a copper-topped bar, and the paraphernalia of famous football legends, this cozy tavern is an ideal spot to sip malt scotches and fancy concoctions like the Ramos Gin Fizz or Absinthe House Frappe. With friendly, well-trained bartenders, it can definitely get crowded at night, but this historic place is well worth a stop—even if it's only a quick one.

THE KINGPIN

1307 Lyons St., 504/891-2373, www.kingpinbar.com
HOURS: Daily 3:30 P.M.-close
Map 4

Situated just two blocks south of elegant St. Charles Avenue, this classic, ever-friendly dive bar features one of the city's longest happy hours (daily 3:30–9 P.M.). Besides offering a decent beer selection, the Kingpin often hosts live bands, and the jukebox is always on standby. It's also worth noting that, during football season, this well-loved (though often crowded and smoke-filled) watering hole opens its doors at 11:30 A.M. on the weekend.

LAFITTE'S BLACKSMITH SHOP BAR

941 Bourbon St., 504/593-9761,

www.lafittesblacksmithshop.com
HOURS: Daily 11 A.M.-close
Map 1

According to legend, pirate Jean Lafitte operated this spot as a blacksmith shop—to serve as a front for other, less legitimate enterprises. Built before the city's devastating 18th-century fires, Lafitte's is one of the few original French-style buildings left in the Quarter. A bar since the 1940s, when Tennessee Williams frequented it, this cozy, candlelit place is now one of the city's most popular hangouts. Tourists, locals, and celebrities alike flock here to listen to live piano music, commune with the on-site ghost, and watch the eccentric passersby.

LE BON TEMPS ROULE

4801 Magazine St., 504/895-8117
HOURS: Daily 11 A.M.-3 A.M.
Map 4

One of Uptown's many cool spots for mingling and hoisting a frosty mug of beer, Le Bon Temps Roule draws a full range of Uptowners, from college students to hipsters to music fans. On some nights, you can dance to live rock and blues bands, and a stellar jukebox is always available; just be advised that the floor is uneven in places, so take care while dancing. This smoky, often loud dive bar also turns out decent pub grub, such as quesadillas, chili cheeseburgers, and barbecue wings.

LOA BAR

International House Hotel, 221 Camp St.,
504/553-9550, www.ihhotel.com
HOURS: Daily 4 P.M.-close
Map 3

Located inside the fabulous International House Hotel, the Loa Bar feels both hip and vaguely spiritual. After all, "Loa" refers to benevolent deities or divine spirits in the voodoo tradition. Its tall Gothic church mirrors and hundreds of glowing candles certainly enhance that vibe, but where some modern bars feel over-designed and uncomfortable, Loa offers plenty of sumptuous sofas and cushioned seating. As a bonus, the staff is surprisingly relaxed and hospitable.

NIGHTLIFE

JEAN LAFITTE: PIRATE OR PRIVATEER?

Piracy and its slightly more acceptable cousin, privateering, have been part of southern Louisiana lore since the time of the region's settlement. This infamous and often ruthless practice developed in the Gulf of Mexico in the 16th century, when high-seas thieves began targeting Spanish galleons loaded with silver and gold and headed for Spain's colonies in the New World. During times of war, European nations legitimized piracy, authorizing the crews of these renegade vessels to stop and seize the ships of opposing nations.

Louisiana evolved into a hotbed of piracy because of its geography and topography: The state's irregular, marshy shoreline was punctuated with hundreds of hidden, protected coves, which made perfect havens for pirates. They could elude authorities, smuggle and hide their spoils, and build and repair ships in secret. During the 19th century, the most infamous of these spots was Barataria Bay, a massive body of water just east of present-day Grand Isle; its northern edge lies about 40 miles due south of New Orleans as the crow flies. The bay sits at the north-central tip of the Gulf of Mexico, about 500 miles north of

Mexico's Yucatán Peninsula, 650 miles northwest of Cuba, 450 miles west of Florida's Gulf Coast, and 450 miles east of Texas's Gulf Coast. Strategically, no location offered better access to so many lucrative colonial shipping routes.

In this bay, the infamous Baratarians established a colony for illicit deeds that included warehouses and docks. Pirate ships returned here with their bounties and then auctioned them to visitors from New Orleans. Sometimes, they hauled their goods directly to New Orleans, where they found a vast and eager market. Everything was sold by the Baratarians, including precious metals, foods, spices, rum, and African slaves. They were led during the height of their success by the Lafitte brothers, Jean and Pierre.

Unofficially, and even officially for a time, authorities in New Orleans turned a blind eye to Jean Lafitte and his operations, unwilling to shut off the constant stream of valuable and heavily discounted goods into the city. In fact, it wasn't until Lafitte's disregard for the law became too flagrant that Governor William Claiborne finally ordered his arrest, offering a $500 reward for his capture.

LUCY'S RETIRED SURFERS BAR & RESTAURANT

701 Tchoupitoulas St., 504/523-8995,
www.lucysretiredsurfers.com
HOURS: Mon.-Fri. 11 A.M.-close, Sat.-Sun. 10 A.M.-close
Map 3

Nestled within the Arts District, Lucy's Retired Surfers Bar feels like a frat-sorority party on most evenings, especially weekends. It's known as one of the city's more popular meat markets, and it's also a great place to slurp down a few margaritas. In addition, you can enjoy a delicious brunch on Saturday and Sunday mornings—the perfect cure for a hangover. Interestingly, there's also a Lucy's up the river in Baton Rouge, not to mention one in Austin, Texas.

MID-CITY YACHT CLUB

440 S. St. Patrick St., 504/483-2517,
www.midcityyachtclub.com
HOURS: Mon.-Thurs. noon-2 A.M., Fri. noon-4 A.M., Sat. 11 A.M.-4 A.M., Sun. 11 A.M.-2 A.M.
Map 5

Housed within a two-story building in a Mid-City residential neighborhood, this casual, super-friendly watering hole isn't a bad place to relax after exploring nearby City Park or the area's historic cemeteries. Definitely a favorite among local football, baseball, and other sports fans, the Yacht Club has eight high-definition televisions and an enormous projection screen, so you'll be able to watch several games at once. Other amenities include a well-stocked jukebox, a decent beer and flavored vodka selection, free wireless Internet access,

In 1814, a fleet of American military ships descended upon the Baratarians' headquarters, seizing eight schooners, about 40 houses, nearly 100 men, and countless spoils. Jean Lafitte and other group leaders heard of the impending attack before its onset and successfully hid from authorities before making their escape.

The War of 1812 was in full swing at this point, and late in 1814, the British launched plans to ascend the Mississippi River and attack New Orleans. At this point, Lafitte's exploits were legendary across the high seas, and the British decided to approach him with an offer, figuring that he'd happily jump at the opportunity to exact his revenge against U.S. authorities. Lafitte was offered $30,000 and a captainship in the British Navy if he would join in their attack on the Americans.

Lafitte declined. Whether due to some deep-seated loyalty to the United States or, more likely, because he believed he stood to gain more by aligning himself with the U.S. government, he tipped off Governor Claiborne about the impending British attack. He then volunteered his own considerable militia and fleet to defend New Orleans against the British –

if Claiborne would agree to drop all charges against Jean and Pierre Lafitte and their fellow Baratarians.

Claiborne relayed the offer to General Andrew Jackson, who had arrived to lead the defense of New Orleans against the British, and Jackson accepted without hesitation. In January 1815, during the Battle of New Orleans, Jean Lafitte and his cohorts performed admirably, greatly assisting American forces in turning back the British attack. Claiborne and Jackson kept their word, and U.S. authorities left the Baratarians alone from that point forward.

The final fate of the Lafitte brothers is unrecorded. All that's known is that several years later, they moved their operations to Galveston Bay in Texas, but few additional details can be confirmed. In 1819, the U.S. Congress passed a law declaring piracy a crime punishable by death, and the government finally began pursuing and prosecuting pirates more vigorously. Such circumstances may have helped to curtail the Lafittes' operations, but no matter what became of the dashing buccaneer, his legacy and tales concerning his exploits live on.

NIGHTLIFE

air-conditioning that's especially welcome during baseball season, and free hot dogs, meatballs, and other vittles on game days.

MOLLY'S AT THE MARKET

1107 Decatur St., 504/525-5169,
www.mollysatthemarket.net
HOURS: Daily 10 A.M.–6 A.M.
`Map 1`

If you find yourself wandering down Decatur in the wee hours, you'll discover relatively deserted sidewalks and many closed-up establishments, save for places like the 24-hour Café Du Monde and, of course, Molly's—a boisterous dive bar that's often the savior of night owls. Founded in 1973, this always loud, often smoky hangout definitely has a loyal local following. Patrons appreciate the fun-loving

ambience, embrace the ongoing food and drink specials, such as $1 tacos on Tuesday and Thursday, and flock here for special events like the annual Halloween and St. Patrick's Day parades.

MONKEY HILL BAR

6100 Magazine St., 504/899-4800,
www.monkeyhillbar.com
HOURS: Mon.–Thurs. 3 P.M.–2 A.M., Fri.–Sat. 3 P.M.–3 A.M., Sun. 6 P.M.–2 A.M.
`Map 4`

Located three blocks east of Audubon Zoo, this inviting yet stylish bar was no doubt named after Monkey Hill, a slope in the zoo's African Savanna section that many a local child—including me—has gleefully rolled down. In the fun-filled spirit of its namesake, this watering hole has become an adult's playground, offering a sizable drink selection, relaxing couches, pool and shuffleboard tables, and a 120-inch, high-definition screen, ideal for watching sports. Like many other New Orleans–area bars, Monkey Hill opens earlier on Sunday during football season.

MRB

515 St. Philip St., 504/222-5672
HOURS: Sun.-Mon. and Wed.-Thurs. 11 A.M.-10 P.M., Fri.-Sat. 11 A.M.-midnight
Map 1

Just a block off Decatur Street, MRB—short for Mississippi River Bottom—is a low-key, dimly lit tavern, featuring pool tables, a leafy rear patio, and, when in season, all-you-can-eat boiled crabs and crawfish. Once considered a gay bar, MRB seems to lure a variety of patrons these days, including sports lovers during the Saints' regular season. Be sure to greet the owner's friendly, three-legged dog, who's nearly always on-site.

NAPOLEON HOUSE

500 Chartres St., 504/524-9752,
www.napoleonhouse.com
HOURS: Mon. 11 A.M.-5:30 P.M., Tues.-Sat. 11 A.M.-close
Map 1

After strolling around Jackson Square, head a couple blocks down Chartres to yet another fabled locale, the Napoleon House, which Mayor Nicholas Girod once proffered as a refuge for Napoleon during his exile. Built in 1797 and owned by the Impastato family since 1914, this world-famous landmark is a terrific place to park your feet for a while, especially if you favor classical music and a casual atmosphere. Even the food is worth a stop; the menu features Italian and New Orleans–style cuisine, from bruschetta and spumoni to boudin and jambalaya. Food is typically served until 5:30 P.M. on Monday, 10 P.M. Tuesday–Thursday, and 11 P.M. Friday–Saturday.

PAL'S LOUNGE

949 N. Rendon St., 504/488-7257
HOURS: Daily 3 P.M.-3 A.M.
Map 5

Within easy driving distance of City Park and the Fair Grounds Race Course, this well-loved dive bar has many locals' seal of

the courtyard at Pat O'Brien's

© LAURA MARTONE

NIGHTLIFE

approval. Though it's often loud and smoky, it's hard not to appreciate the amiable regulars, efficient bartenders, and creative drinks. Besides sporting events, many patrons come for group viewings of *Treme, True Blood,* and other popular shows. Like many neighborhood bars throughout the city, Pal's opens earlier on Sunday whenever the beloved Saints are playing, making it a popular haven for Mid-City football fans. Be advised, too, that the joint is open until 4 or 5 A.M. on Friday and Saturday nights.

◀ PAT O'BRIEN'S

718 St. Peter St., 504/525-4823 or 800/597-4823, www.patobriens.com

HOURS: Mon.-Thurs. noon-close, Fri.-Sun. 10 A.M.-close

Map 1

Even if you shy away from pricey tourist traps, you should experience the world-famous Pat O'Brien's at least once. Here, you'll find several unique spaces, including the crowded main bar, the lively piano bar, the courtyard restaurant, the intimate Bourbon Bar, and the spacious patio, which features a rather cool flaming fountain. As I've discovered the hard way, though, the hurricanes and mint juleps can be particularly strong here, so take my advice and sip slowly.

◀ POLO CLUB LOUNGE

Windsor Court Hotel, 300 Gravier St., 504/522-1994 or 504/523-6000, www.grillroomneworleans.com or www.windsorcourthotel.com

HOURS: Mon.-Thurs. 11:30 A.M.-midnight, Fri.-Sat. 11:30 A.M.-1 A.M., Sun. 11 A.M.-midnight

Map 3

The elegant Windsor Court Hotel is home to the Polo Club Lounge, a classy space furnished with equestrian oil paintings, historical memorabilia, and leather furniture, all of which recall the ambience of a private British club. Adjacent to the Grill Room, this second-floor lounge presents live nightly jazz in addition to hard-to-find wines, champagnes, and specialty liquors—and a menu that includes caviar and truffle fries. It's also one of the few smoke-free lounges in town.

NIGHTLIFE

HOW TO MAKE A HURRICANE

In the Big Easy, not all hurricanes have a negative connotation. When not in reference to a destructive tropical storm, the term "hurricane" denotes the vibrant red cocktail that was created during World War II — when rum was more plentiful than other liquor varieties — at **Pat O'Brien's** (718 St. Peter St.), a popular bar in the French Quarter. Named for the tall, curvaceous, hurricane lamp-shaped glasses in which they're usually served, hurricanes are sweet, refreshing, and, like the eye of a Category 5 storm, deceptively smooth, so be sure to exercise caution while drinking them. As my friends and I have discovered the hard way, alcoholic hurricanes can certainly pack a wallop.

While the courtyard of Pat O's is probably the perfect place to enjoy a hurricane (in a much-coveted souvenir glass), you can always make your own, using this simple recipe.

Ingredients

2 oz. light rum
2 oz. dark rum
2 oz. passionfruit juice
1 oz. orange juice
½ oz. lime juice
1 tbsp. simple syrup
1 tbsp. grenadine
cherry
orange slice

Instructions

Shake all liquid ingredients in a cocktail shaker with ice.

Strain into an ice-filled hurricane glass.

Garnish with a cherry and an orange slice.

Enjoy!

PRAVDA!

1113 Decatur St., 504/581-1112, www.pravdaofnola.com
HOURS: Mon.-Wed. 7 P.M.-close, Thurs.-Sun. 2 P.M.-close
Map 1

Just steps from the French Market lies this sexy, Gothic–style lounge—furnished with red velvet, antique lamps and chandeliers, and bizarre paintings—which always reminds me of the manor house in *The Rocky Horror Picture Show*. Given that the bar's name means "truth" in Russian, it's probably no surprise that there are more than 50 vodka varieties available, plus coffee, tea, wine, and supposedly the state's largest selection of absinthe. I'm a big fan, too, of Pravda's chocolate martinis, not to mention the romantic courtyard and the small plates of Russian cuisine that are available Thursday–Sunday 5–10 P.M.

THE SAZERAC BAR

The Roosevelt New Orleans, 123 Baronne St., 504/648-1200, www.therooseveltneworleans.com
HOURS: Daily 11 A.M.-2 A.M.
Map 3

The Sazerac Bar, located at the CBD's grand Roosevelt New Orleans, is perhaps the most famous hotel lounge in the city. Named for the noted cocktail—a concoction of rye whiskey, Pernod, sugar, lemon oil, and the local Peychaud's bitters—the bar was once a favored haunt of Governor Huey P. Long, the infamous "Kingfish" of Louisiana. This legendary bar also inspired the nearby Sazerac Restaurant, a first-rate hotel eatery that serves creative New Orleans fare.

SNAKE AND JAKE'S CHRISTMAS CLUB LOUNGE

7612 Oak St., 504/861-2802, www.snakeandjakes.com
HOURS: Daily 7 P.M.-close
Map 4

Open every day of the year—including, you guessed it, Christmas—Snake and Jake's is indeed one of the Crescent City's most legendary dive bars. Routinely voted a favorite among locals, this neighborhood joint is cozy, friendly, and open into the wee hours. Happy-hour specials are offered 7–10 P.M. nightly. While here, be sure to keep a lookout for Jake, the bar's cute feline mascot; just be aware of the occasional mood swing.

ST. JOE'S BAR

5535 Magazine St., 504/899-3744
HOURS: Mon.-Fri. 5 P.M.-close, Sat. 3 P.M.-close, Sun. 6 P.M.-close
Map 4

A nice place to blend your appreciation of a good drink with your admiration for religious iconography, St. Joe's is a quintessential Uptown neighborhood bar with a twist. The place, after all, is filled with ancient wooden crosses, recovered church pews, votive candles, and other vestiges of Christianity. The vibe is funky and slightly irreverent, and there's a cool jukebox, plus a cheery patio out back. Depending on the crowd, St. Joe's usually stays open until 1 or 2 A.M.

TWELVE MILE LIMIT

500 S. Telemachus St., 504/488-8114
HOURS: Sun.-Thurs. 5 P.M.-midnight, Fri.-Sat. 5 P.M.-2 A.M.
Map 5

Mid-City residents flock to this friendly neighborhood bar, where, in addition to affordable drinks and occasional doberge cupcakes (a local delicacy), you can expect free food on Monday, beginning at 7 P.M., and delicious barbecue on every other night (Sun. and Tues.–Thurs. 5–10 P.M., Fri.–Sat. 5 P.M.–midnight). During the NFL football season, this low-key joint typically opens at noon, just in time for diehard Saints fans.

VIC'S KANGAROO CAFE

636 Tchoupitoulas St., 504/524-4329, www.satchmo.com/vics
HOURS: Mon.-Fri. 5 P.M.-close, Sat.-Sun. 6 P.M.-close
Map 3

A festive Aussie-inspired bar in the Arts District, Vic's Kangaroo Cafe features live music throughout the week, plus a "hoppy" hour 5–7 P.M. on weekdays. In addition to offering Australian wines, Vic's serves fairly traditional "Down Under" and New Orleans–style pub fare, from shepherd's pie to crab cakes. Don't be fooled by its seemingly sedate location, a haggard old building on a quiet stretch of Tchoupitoulas; it's actually quite spirited inside, with a crowd that's typically young and raucous.

WHISKEY BLUE

W New Orleans, 333 Poydras St., 504/207-5016 or 504/525-9444, www.whotelsneworleans.com
HOURS: Mon.-Thurs. 5 P.M.-2 A.M., Fri.-Sat. 5 P.M.-4 A.M.
Map 3

Nestled amid other high-end hotels in the CBD, the W New Orleans attracts a cool clientele to its Whiskey Blue cocktail lounge, a frequent spot for see-and-be-seen soirees. It's no surprise, given the slick contemporary decor—including leather club chairs, banquette seating, and intimate lighting. Noted nightlife celeb Rande Gerber, husband of Cindy Crawford, runs this and similarly stylish operations in Los Angeles, Chicago, New York, Atlanta, and Fort Lauderdale.

W LIVING ROOM

W New Orleans–French Quarter, 316 Chartres St., 504/581-1200, www.whotelsneworleans.com
HOURS: Daily 24 hours
Map 1

Recline in a plush sofa at the W Living Room, a supremely inviting yet stylish lounge at the W New Orleans—French Quarter, only a few blocks from Jackson Square. In addition to a lavish outdoor courtyard, this intimate lounge, designed by the Gerber Group, features book-lined shelves, specially designed game tables, and free wireless, high-speed Internet access. No wonder hotel guests tend to stay awhile.

Wine Bars

BACCHANAL WINE

600 Poland Ave., 504/948-9111,
www.bacchanalwine.com
HOURS: Mon.-Thurs. noon-11 P.M., Fri.-Sun. noon-midnight
Map 2

Often spotted in HBO's acclaimed show *Treme,* Bacchanal is at once a wine bar and retail shop, a New York–style deli, an international bistro, and, when weather allows it in the exposed courtyard, a live music venue. As most patrons attest, this local favorite offers an ever-changing, culinary experience that you must embrace first-hand to understand. "Get your wine and cheese up front, get your food and music out back," explains one patron. "Help yourself, have fun, get funky, this ain't no Galatoire's!"

DELACHAISE WINE & FOOD

3442 St. Charles Ave., 504/895-0858,
www.thedelachaise.com
HOURS: Daily 5 P.M.-close
Map 4

In addition to daily wine and cocktail specials, this highly recommended spot presents an extensive list of bottled beers and wines by the glass. Gourmands will also appreciate the tasty culinary delights on offer each evening until midnight. Past items have included eggplant cannoli, spicy frog legs, *manchego* cheese gnocchi, grilled Jamaican jerk pork chops, foie gras with caramelized apples and oyster mushrooms, and bourbon-vanilla crème brûlée. Typically, the bar closes around 2 or 3 A.M., depending on the crowd.

OAK

8118 Oak St., 504/302-1485, www.oaknola.com
HOURS: Tues.-Sat. 5 P.M.-close
Map 4

Nestled within Uptown's Riverbend area, near the happenin' corner of Oak Street and Carrollton Avenue, this cosmopolitan yet comfortable wine bar features hundreds of hand-selected wines, as well as numerous beers and signature cocktails. While sampling the varietals, you can also partake of various small plates, such as duck confit and Gulf shrimp tacos. Food is typically served until 11 P.M. on weekdays and midnight on weekends. In addition, you'll be treated to live jazz, folk, or R&B music Wednesday–Saturday.

ORLEANS GRAPEVINE WINE BAR & BISTRO

720 Orleans St., 504/523-1930,
www.orleansgrapevine.com
HOURS: Daily 4 P.M.-close
`Map 1`

An occasional complaint about the French Quarter is that there aren't enough reasonably priced yet sophisticated bars. The intimate Orleans Grapevine, however, fits the bill perfectly. Set inside a restored 1809 building, it's a classy yet casual bistro located in the oft-overlooked block between the peaceful rear garden of the St. Louis Cathedral and the craziness of Bourbon Street. Besides featuring an extensive list of 450 bottled wines and 75 varietals by the glass, the Grapevine turns out an elegant and tasty menu, including such revolving delicacies as baked brie and stuffed flounder. You can expect meal service 5–10:30 P.M. Sunday–Thursday and 5–11:30 P.M. Friday–Saturday.

SWIRL WINES

3143 Ponce de Leon St., 504/304-0635,
www.swirlinthecity.com or
http://swirlandsavor.blogspot.com
HOURS: Mon. noon–7 P.M., Tues.-Thurs. and Sat. 11 A.M.-8 P.M., Fri. 11 A.M.-9 P.M.
`Map 5`

Just two streets away from the Fair Grounds Race Course—home to the world-famous New Orleans Jazz & Heritage Festival—lies this sensational wine bar and retail market. Besides offering sumptuous wines (some of which are pretty affordable) and well-paired cheeses, Swirl also presents wine tastings on Friday as well as other wine-related events. Of

Wine lovers enjoy a tasting class at the CBD's W.I.N.O.

© DANIEL MARTONE

course, the real asset is Swirl's amiable, well-informed staff.

W.I.N.O.

610 Tchoupitoulas St., 504/324-8000,
www.winoschool.com
HOURS: Mon.-Thurs. 11 A.M.-10 P.M., Fri. 11 A.M.-1 A.M., Sat. noon-1 A.M., Sun. 2-10 P.M.
`Map 3`

Situated in the CBD, the cleverly abbreviated Wine Institute of New Orleans is more than just a wine bar and retail shop. In addition to sampling a variety of wines in the front area of this modern-looking emporium, wine connoisseurs can take informative classes in the rear, from an introduction to wine class ($35 pp), which my husband and I thoroughly enjoyed, to food and wine pairings ($40 pp). Reservations are usually necessary, though walk-ins are welcome.

Live Music

BLUES AND ROCK
APPLE BARREL BAR
609 Frenchmen St., 504/949-9399
HOURS: Daily 1 P.M.-close
COST: No cover, though a one-drink minimum applies
Map 2

Just steps from the Spotted Cat Music Club, in the heart of the Marigny's lively music scene, this intimate, somewhat dingy bar lures an ever-revolving crowd of blues and jazz lovers nightly. Hip yet happily low-keyed, this is an ideal spot for sipping cocktails before heading out to the noisier music clubs along Frenchmen—though, be advised, it can still get pretty loud in here, depending on who's playing at the moment. Closing time can vary between 3 and 5 A.M.

BLUE NILE
532 Frenchmen St., 504/948-2583,
www.bluenilelive.com
HOURS: Sun.-Thurs. 7 P.M.-2 A.M., Fri.-Sat. 6 P.M.-4 A.M.
COST: Cover varies
Map 2

A Faubourg Marigny mainstay and a regular sight on HBO's *Treme,* the spacious Blue Nile presents a broad mix of cool music, from blues and jazz to reggae and garage rock. Frequent acts include the Honey Island Swamp Band and local fave Kermit Ruffins and the BBQ Swingers; typically, there are two shows each night, with the first starting around 7 or 8 P.M. and the second kicking off at 10 or 11 P.M. With its plush lounge seating and tile floors, it's a funky yet elegant place to socialize with friends early in the evening; just be prepared for a long bathroom wait, especially on crowded nights.

D.B.A. NEW ORLEANS
618 Frenchmen St., 504/942-3731,
www.drinkgoodstuff.com
HOURS: Mon.-Thurs. 5 P.M.-close, Fri.-Sun. 4 P.M.-close
COST: Cover varies
Map 2

Located in a building from the late 19th century, this dimly lit, hipster-infested hangout in the Faubourg Marigny is a good place to meet locals, hear live rock and blues bands, and, on occasion, catch performances from the likes of Jimmy Buffett and Stevie Wonder. The drink selection encompasses about a zillion beers (including plenty of my favorite imported options), plus many types of whiskey and tequila. Typically, the crowd is young and laid-back but with a touch of style.

HOUSE OF BLUES
225 Decatur St., 504/310-4999,
www.hob.com/neworleans
HOURS: Daily 11:30 A.M.-close
COST: Cover varies
Map 1

Part of the famous chain, this predictably popular tourist haunt has been enticing legions of music fans since its 1994 opening. Home to a large folk art collection, the funky, colorful concert venue features two music halls, which can accommodate about 370 and 840 guests, respectively. Various performers play here, from major rock bands to local jazz and blues musicians, and the on-site restaurant serves New Orleans favorites like shrimp po-boys and key lime pie. Especially popular is Sunday's Gospel Brunch, which combines world-class performances with a Southern-style buffet.

THE HOWLIN' WOLF
907 S. Peters St., 504/522-9653,
www.howlin-wolf.com
HOURS: Daily 5 P.M.-2 A.M.
COST: Cover varies
Map 3

For the most part, you'll catch top blues and funk acts at the Howlin' Wolf, a cavernous nightclub in the Arts District, not far from the city's convention center. This is indeed one of the Big Easy's largest and most prominent live music venues, which has been known to host rock, alternative, pop, and R&B bands, too. Over the

NIGHTLIFE

years, some of the more famous performers have included Jimmy Page, Allison Krauss, Dr. John, Harry Connick Jr., and the Foo Fighters. If you happen to find yourself on the Northshore, be sure to check out the Mandeville location at 1623 Montgomery Street.

MAPLE LEAF BAR

8316 Oak St., 504/866-9359, www.mapleleafbar.com
HOURS: Daily 3 P.M.-3 A.M.
COST: Cover varies
Map 4

One of Uptown's most popular live music venues, the Maple Leaf Bar serves up some of the best blues, jazz, funk, rock, and zydeco in the city. Established in 1974 and now one of the Big Easy's longest-running music clubs, the Maple Leaf has played host to music students from Tulane, local legends like the Radiators, and surprise headliners such as Bonnie Raitt. Fashion shows, poetry readings, and other non-musical events aren't uncommon either.

OLD POINT BAR

545 Patterson St., Algiers, 504/364-0950, www.oldpointbar.com
HOURS: Daily 11 A.M.-close
COST: No cover
Map 6

In historic Algiers Point, situated across the

A COLLEGE TOWN

While it might be common knowledge that Louisiana State University (LSU) in Baton Rouge has more of a "party school" reputation than the collegiate institutions of New Orleans, from an undergraduate's perspective, the Big Easy isn't a bad place to spend your college years. Besides the fact that New Orleans is known for such annual bacchanals as Southern Decadence, Mardi Gras, and the New Orleans Jazz & Heritage Festival, it's also a pretty cheap town to enjoy late-night libations. Bourbon Street alone has its share of bargains, including inexpensive beers at the **Rat's Hole** (410 Bourbon St., 504/568-9338) and **Huge Ass Beers** at the Steak Pit (609 Bourbon St., 504/525-3406), where you can purchase enormous, relatively cheap souvenir cups filled with your beer of choice. Depending on the time of day, hawkers carrying signs for happy-hour drink specials are also a common sight.

Though you'll find plenty of college-aged youths in live music venues throughout the city, from the Marigny's **Spotted Cat Music Club** (623 Frenchmen St.) to Uptown's **Maple Leaf Bar** (8316 Oak St.) to various meat-market dance spaces in the French Quarter, you're most likely to spot them in local hangouts close to the adjacent campuses of Tulane University and Loyola University New Orleans on St. Charles Avenue. Popular spots include the **Boot Bar & Grill** (1039 Broadway St.), which sits next to Tulane and offers all manner of drink specials, and **Cooter Brown's Tavern & Oyster Bar** (509 S. Carrollton Ave.), a Riverbend sports bar that features numerous televisions, more than 400 brands of domestic and imported beers, plus to-die-for raw oysters and boiled seafood. Though a bit of a hike from the universities on St. Charles, the stretch of Magazine Street between Jefferson and Jackson Avenues also has its share of student-friendly joints, including the **Bulldog** (3236 Magazine St.), a late-night watering hole with decent grub and a diverse beer selection; **Igor's Buddha Belly Burger Bar** (4437 Magazine St.), another late-night spot where you can enjoy delicious burgers while doing your laundry; and **Le Bon Temps Roule** (4801 Magazine St.), which, as the name's meaning ("the good time rolls") implies, is a loud dive bar with live music, a decent jukebox, and room for dancing.

Of course, there's one thing to remember if you're a student in New Orleans: While the drinking age is officially 21 and over, some establishments welcome patrons 18 and over, which means, even if you can't drink, you'll still be able to listen to live music and mingle with your friends. Though I hesitate to admit this, it's also true that many bars card their patrons far less often than they should– at least according to the law.

river from the French Quarter and the CBD, lies the weathered Old Point Bar. Housed within a century-old building that once served as a dry goods store, this oft-filmed, pet-friendly tavern is a popular spot for cocktails, conversation, and canines. On almost every evening, expect live blues, jazz, Cajun, country, and rock music—not to mention karaoke and open-mic nights. Depending on the crowd, the bar can close anytime between 2 and 6 A.M.

REPUBLIC NEW ORLEANS

828 S. Peters St., 504/528-8282, www.republicnola.com
HOURS: Vary depending on the show
COST: Cover varies
Map 3

Situated in the downtown Arts District, Republic New Orleans occupies a cavernous, historic space that was once a coffee warehouse, a set for Oliver Stone's film *JFK,* and the original location of the Howlin' Wolf. Now, this upscale music club and special-events facility is often the site of concerts, parties, fashion shows, and other gatherings, such as the vampire ball that my husband and I once attended on Halloween weekend.

(TIPITINA'S

501 Napoleon Ave., 504/895-8477, www.tipitinas.com
HOURS: Vary depending on the show
COST: Cover varies
Map 4

For catching rock (both hard-edged and down-home), jazz, zydeco, Cajun, and blues, there may be no club in the city more acclaimed or more festive than Tipitina's, a longstanding venue in the heart of Uptown. Purists may tell you that Tip's has lost its edge and no longer presents the best—or at least most distinctive—local acts, but anybody looking for an introduction to the city's eclectic music scene should head here. Entertainment varies greatly, but no matter what's playing, you can probably dance to it.

NIGHTLIFE

© DANIEL MARTONE

the Balcony Music Club at Decatur and Esplanade

CAJUN AND ZYDECO
MULATE'S
201 Julia St., 504/522-1492 or 800/854-9149,
www.mulates.com
HOURS: Sun.-Thurs. 11 A.M.-10 P.M., Fri.-Sat. 11 A.M.-11 P.M.
COST: No cover
Map 3

Similar to the former Mulate's in Breaux Bridge, this down-home Cajun restaurant and dance hall features live bands, plenty of dancing space, and a menu filled with Louisiana favorites. Located in the Arts District, the New Orleans–based Mulate's occupies a much larger building than the one in Cajun Country did, but in both cases, the music is far superior to the food. In fact, you can expect live entertainment here nightly (Sun.–Thurs. 7–10 P.M., Fri.–Sat. 7–10:30 P.M.).

◆ ROCK 'N' BOWL
3000 S. Carrollton Ave., 504/861-1700,
www.rocknbowl.com
HOURS: Mon.-Fri. 4 P.M.-close, Sat. 2 P.M.-close
COST: Cover varies
Map 6

Although some residents still prefer the old Mid-City location, the new-and-improved Rock 'n' Bowl is still a music (and bowling) institution, luring couples and families alike. An offbeat place to catch live bands of all types, it's especially known for zydeco, jazz, blues, and swing, but anything is possible here, including performances by regional favorites like Tab Benoit and Amanda Shaw. Savvy locals often show up early for a few rounds of bowling, which, if you time it right, could enable you to catch the concert without paying a cover charge.

COUNTRY AND FOLK
HI-HO LOUNGE
2239 St. Claude Ave., 504/945-4446,
www.hiholounge.net
HOURS: Daily 5 P.M.-2 A.M.
COST: Cover varies
Map 2

While the Hi-Ho might not be in the safest part of town, it's nevertheless a wonderful spot for music lovers and those itchin' to dance. On at least three, if not five, nights a week, you might hear folk, bluegrass, country, funk, punk, even hip-hop. Besides offering food at times—such as $2 red beans and rice on Monday, Korean cuisine on Tuesday, and barbecue on Thursday—this low-key, cash-only dive bar also hosts special events, such as semi-regular *Treme* screenings, which patrons tend to take pretty seriously.

◆ THE KERRY IRISH PUB
331 Decatur St., 504/527-5954, www.kerryirishpub.com
HOURS: Mon.-Fri. 1 P.M.-close, Sat.-Sun. noon-close
COST: No cover, though a one-drink minimum applies
Map 1

Diehard regulars and curious out-of-towners converge at this cozy neighborhood hangout—admittedly, my favorite—for imported beers, friendly conversation, and live music nightly. In addition to Irish, most of the performers play country, folk, and classic rock selections. Situated beside a firehouse in a rather touristy part of the Quarter, the Kerry features, besides the small stage, a projection set-up and two televisions ideal for Saints' game-viewing, several tables and chairs, mounted photographs of past musicians, and a small space that, despite the brick floors, allows for dancing. Some patrons may also appreciate the pool table, laid-back but efficient bartenders, and entertaining graffiti in the ladies' restroom. The hours here are pretty flexible; Saints' games and special events might inspire an earlier opening, while a well-attended concert can keep the doors open until well past 2 A.M.

NEUTRAL GROUND COFFEEHOUSE
5110 Danneel St., 504/891-3381,
www.neutralgroundcoffeehouse.com
HOURS: Sun.-Thurs. 7 P.M.-midnight, Fri.-Sat. 7 P.M.-1 A.M.
COST: No cover
Map 4

Originally opened in 1974 as the Penny Post and moved in the late 1970s to its current residential location, this funky coffeehouse and live music venue was a favorite haunt for me and my mother when I was a child. So, I'm delighted that, despite a name change and several reluctant closures, it's still the same cozy, quirky joint that it always was. Although coffee, tea, and pastries are typically available, refreshments aren't the specialty here. In fact, the real draw is the live entertainment, which, depending on the night, might entail a poetry slam, a folk concert, or something else altogether. Quiet reading, conversation, and board games are popular diversions, too.

JAZZ
BALCONY MUSIC CLUB
1331 Decatur St., 504/522-2940
HOURS: Daily 6 P.M.-1:30 A.M.
COST: Cover varies
Map 1

No matter the evening, it's difficult to cross the corner of Decatur Street and Esplanade Avenue without catching some of the fantastic tunes coming from the usually open doors of the funky Balcony Music Club. Though you're most likely to hear brass, jazz, or funk, anything is possible here. If you're still in the mood for fun after this place closes, just hop across Esplanade to **Igor's Check Point Charlie** (501 Esplanade Ave., 504/281-4847), a lively 24-hour bar, grill, music club, game room, and self-service laundromat.

BUFFA'S BAR & RESTAURANT
1001 Esplanade Ave., 504/949-0038,
www.buffasbar.com
HOURS: Daily 24 hours
COST: No cover
Map 2

Situated between the French Quarter and the Faubourg Marigny since 1939, Buffa's feels like a well-kept secret, despite its obvious location on Esplanade. A popular neighborhood hangout for those who venture inside, Buffa's offers a variety of vittles and libations all day and night. The real treat is the smoke-free back room, where patrons can listen to traditional jazz musicians. One of my favorite regular bands is the Royal Rounders, whose eclectic,

often chuckle-worthy shows might feature, in addition to jazz, everything from blues to pop to R&B.

CHICKIE WAH WAH
2828 Canal St., 504/304-4714,
www.chickiewahwah.com
HOURS: Mon.-Thurs. 11 A.M.-10 P.M., Fri.-Sat. 11 A.M.-11 P.M.
COST: Cover varies
Map 5

One of the Crescent City's most offbeat live music venues is the aptly named Chickie Wah Wah, a cozy joint just northwest of Broad Avenue. On most evenings, you'll be treated to some of the city's best musicians, including some of my own favorites, like the Pfister Sisters, old-time singer Meschiya Lake, and stellar piano player Tom McDermott. While you're listening, you can enjoy fried green tomatoes, crawfish pasta, spinach and artichoke pizza, and several other delectable items, including vegan dishes, from the on-site **Garage Pizza** (504/214-5177), open Tuesday–Saturday. In addition, this smoke-free club offers a convenient rear parking lot, an on-site ATM, free wireless Internet access, and a weekday happy hour (4–7 P.M.).

THE COLUMNS HOTEL
3811 St. Charles Ave., 504/899-9308 or
800/445-9308, www.thecolumns.com
HOURS: Sun.-Thurs. 10:30 A.M.-midnight, Fri.-Sat. 10:30 A.M.-2 A.M.
COST: No cover
Map 4

This stately plantation-style mansion, erected in 1883, is typically hard to miss while gazing out the window of a St. Charles Avenue streetcar. On every night save for Sunday, the hotel presents exceptional New Orleans jazz, Brazilian samba, and other live entertainment in its romantic Victorian Lounge. Offering an extensive menu of beer, wine, mint juleps, tapas dishes, and other cocktails and bistro fare, the nonsmoking space has hosted an array of celebrities over the years, from John Goodman to Clint Eastwood.

NIGHTLIFE

DAVENPORT LOUNGE

The Ritz-Carlton New Orleans, 921 Canal St., 504/670-2828 or 504/524-1331, www.ritzcarlton.com

HOURS: Sun.-Thurs. 11 A.M.-midnight, Fri.-Sat. 11 A.M.-1 A.M.

COST: No cover

Map 1

Named in honor of the Ritz-Carlton's headline entertainer, Jeremy Davenport, the Davenport Lounge presents live jazz on certain evenings (Thurs. 5:30-9 P.M., Fri.-Sat. 9 P.M.-1 A.M.), in addition to serving a range of New Orleans–style appetizers and an array of tempting cocktails. In this regal, third-floor lobby lounge, adjacent to the hotel's M bistro, you can also listen to live music during afternoon tea (Sat.-Sun. 1-3 P.M.) and Sunday brunch (9 A.M.-1 P.M.).

DOS JEFES UPTOWN CIGAR BAR

5535 Tchoupitoulas St., 504/891-8500, www.dosjefescigarbar.com

HOURS: Daily 5 P.M.-close

COST: No cover

Map 4

Not far from the river, the laid-back Dos Jefes Uptown Cigar Bar draws locals and college students alike for live jazz and folk music. As the name implies, patrons can also take advantage of the on-site humidor, which is filled with an assortment of premium cigars. In addition, the bar offers a daily happy hour (5-7 P.M.), which features everything from $2 long necks to $3 wines to $4 mojitos and martinis.

FRITZEL'S EUROPEAN JAZZ PUB

733 Bourbon St., 504/586-4800, www.fritzelsjazz.net

HOURS: Daily 10 A.M.-2 A.M.

COST: No cover, though a one-drink minimum applies

Map 1

One of the city's oldest operating jazz clubs, Fritzel's books some of the better jazz musicians along raucous Bourbon Street. This is a decent place to catch very traditional jazz, which seems to overpower the blues usually coming from the nearby Funky Pirate bar. On the downside, the drink prices are pretty hefty and the hostess and servers can be rather intrusive.

IRVIN MAYFIELD'S JAZZ PLAYHOUSE

Royal Sonesta Hotel–New Orleans, 300 Bourbon St., 504/553-2299 or 504/586-0300, www.irvinmayfield.com

HOURS: Mon.-Tues. and Sat. 8 P.M.-close, Wed.-Fri. 5 P.M.-close, Sun. 7 P.M.-close

COST: No cover

Map 1

Situated on the ground floor of the elegant Royal Sonesta Hotel, in the heart of Bourbon Street's revelry, this stylish club welcomes jazz aficionados and curious tourists every night of the week. Although the musicians rotate nightly, you're always guaranteed to hear some stellar performers. On Friday night, be sure to stick around until midnight, when you'll be able to experience a classy burlesque show. Just bear in mind that, given the cozy space, zero cover charge, and no-reservation policy, the room fills up quickly, so get here early.

MAISON BOURBON JAZZ CLUB

641 Bourbon St., 504/522-8818, www.vieuxcarrevenues.com/maisonbourbon

HOURS: Daily 11 A.M.-2 A.M.

COST: No cover, though a one-drink minimum applies

Map 1

Near the ever-bustling corner of St. Peter and Bourbon Streets lies one of the more reputable music venues in the Quarter. One of only a few jazz clubs left on Bourbon, the longstanding Maison Bourbon is where many of the city's most famous jazz musicians, including Harry Connick Jr., cut their musical teeth, and today's house band is just as entertaining. Be aware, though, that, to make up for the lack of a cover charge, the drink prices here tend to be rather steep.

MO'S CHALET

3201 Houma Blvd., Metairie, 504/780-2961, www.moschalet.com

HOURS: Daily 11 A.M.-2 A.M.

COST: No cover

Map 6

Far from the city's main tourist areas, Mo's Chalet is a favored place among middle-aged music lovers. Situated near the Clearview Mall, it's also not a bad spot to unwind after a long day of shopping. On most evenings, you'll encounter live jazz, blues, and R&B performers, especially local favorites like the Bucktown All-Stars, and many patrons stick around for the late-night jam sessions. Although most out-of-towners won't find themselves here, it's ideal for those craving more of an old-school crowd.

PALM COURT JAZZ CAFE

1204 Decatur St., 504/525-0200,
www.palmcourtjazzcafe.com
HOURS: Wed.-Sun. 7 P.M.-close
COST: No cover
Map 1

One of the Big Easy's most famous and delightful live jazz venues is the Palm Court Jazz Cafe, situated in a handsome, 19th-century building near the historic French Market. Besides Southern-style ceiling fans and an elegant mahogany bar, the restaurant features exposed-brick walls lined with photos of jazz greats, plus a kitchen producing tasty Creole fare. Because seating is arranged at tables over dinner, reservations are a must.

◖ PRESERVATION HALL

726 St. Peter St., 504/522-2841,
www.preservationhall.com
HOURS: Daily 8-11 P.M.
COST: $12 pp
Map 1

Since 1961, Preservation Hall has been one of the city's top places to hear true New Orleans jazz. The band and the venue were formed expressly to keep the legacy of the city's distinctive style of jazz music alive for generations to come, and top musicians continue to perform in the surprisingly intimate concert hall. Housed within a weathered, 1750s-era house, which once contained a cobbler shop and a grocery, it's a charming, laid-back place, with vintage wooden benches, folding chairs, and a good bit of standing room. After the all-too-brief concert, feel free to stroll along the carriageway, to the landscaped courtyard for a breath of fresh air. Just be sure to get here early, as the line forms quickly for these nightly concerts.

SNUG HARBOR JAZZ BISTRO

626 Frenchmen St., 504/949-0696,
www.snugjazz.com
HOURS: Sun.-Thurs. 5 P.M.-midnight, Fri.-Sat. 5 P.M.-1 A.M.
COST: $15-35 pp
Map 2

At the aptly named Snug Harbor Jazz Bistro, a cozy, classy, contemporary spot in the Faubourg Marigny, you can sip cocktails in the downstairs bar or relish tasty regional cuisine in the adjacent dining room, before heading upstairs to catch some of the city's top jazz acts. Occupying a renovated, 19th-century storefront on Frenchmen, Snug Harbor has been showcasing top musicians, from Ellis Marsalis to Charmaine Neville, as well as nurturing young talent for more than three decades.

◖ THE SPOTTED CAT MUSIC CLUB

623 Frenchmen St., www.spottedcatmusicclub.com
HOURS: Daily 4 P.M.-2 A.M.
COST: No cover, though a one-drink minimum applies
Map 2

Practically across the street from Snug Harbor

© DANIEL MARTONE

NIGHTLIFE

The Spotted Cat Music Club is a favorite among local jazz aficionados.

lies the Spotted Cat, a less famous, cash-only jazz club that qualifies as one of the coolest little music finds in the city—if also one of the smokiest. Often featured on HBO's *Treme* series, this happily cramped, dark, and sweaty dance hall offers a long happy hour, a nice selection of designer martinis, and terrific live bands. Although you'll occasionally hear rock, blues, bluegrass, salsa, and other dance-worthy musical styles, modern and traditional jazz are definitely the mainstays here. Local favorite Meschiya Lake and the Little Big Horns, known for their old-time jazz performances, often pack in the crowds—and inspire old-fashioned dancing among the regulars. (In fact, they're the reason that my husband and I often find ourselves here.)

SWEET LORRAINE'S JAZZ CLUB

1931 St. Claude Ave., 504/945-9654,
www.sweetlorrainesjazzclub.com
HOURS: Tues.-Sat. 5 P.M.-close, Sun. 7 P.M.-close
COST: Cover varies
Map 2

On a quiet, historic street along the sketchy edge of the Faubourg Marigny, you'll find Sweet Lorraine's, a definite local favorite for live jazz. While you listen to the ever-changing performers, be sure to sample Southern-style dishes like blackened catfish, cornbread-stuffed chicken breasts, and pecan pie with praline sauce. The club also features a selective wine and martini menu.

VAUGHAN'S LOUNGE

800 Lesseps St., 504/947-5562
HOURS: Daily noon-2 A.M.
COST: Cover varies
Map 2

Granted, most tourists will never find themselves in the far corner of the Bywater, near the convergence of the Mississippi River and the Industrial Canal, but if you decide to make the trip, be sure to stop by this ultra-casual, somewhat dingy neighborhood bar. Jazz trumpeter Kermit Ruffins frequently plays here on Thursday night, when the crowd is admittedly at its peak. Unfortunately, the well-loved but ramshackle joint has no ATM, and the drinks are rather pricey, but the camaraderie of the eclectic crowd and friendly staff usually ensures a memorable experience.

Dance Clubs

BOURBON STREET BLUES COMPANY

441 Bourbon St., 504/566-1507
HOURS: Vary daily
COST: No cover, save for special events
Map 1

Amid the T-shirt shops and strip clubs of Bourbon Street, you'll find a couple of clubs devoted to the blues, though I'm afraid this isn't one of them. Despite the name, the Bourbon Street Blues Company is essentially a dance club, where twentysomething revelers groove to a cover band or DJ. Expect a three-for-one happy hour every day, from opening until 9 P.M., and feel free to venture upstairs, where the balcony is ideal for people-watching. The hours here are never constant; sometimes, the doors won't open until 2 P.M., while at other times, the place is hoppin' for 24 hours straight.

CATS MEOW

701 Bourbon St., 504/523-2788,
www.catskaraoke.com
HOURS: Mon.-Thurs. 4 P.M.-4 A.M.,
Fri.-Sun. 2 P.M.-4 A.M.
COST: No cover, save for special events
Map 1

Situated at a rather busy corner on Bourbon Street, this ever-popular, two-story karaoke bar can be somewhat cheesy for some, but the place nevertheless has a loyal following. Even celebrities like "Weird Al" Yankovic and Tori Spelling have stopped by to entertain the masses. While here, visitors can also dance to live and DJ-mixed swing, classic rock, disco, dance, pop, and hip-hop music, or opt for a bit of people-watching on the upper balcony.

CLUB AMPERSAND

1100 Tulane Ave., 504/587-3737,
www.clubampersand.com
HOURS: Vary depending on the event
COST: Cover varies
Map 3

Occupying a former Whitney Bank in the city's CBD, sexy Ampersand is a favorite spot for students and other young stylish partygoers. Depending on the night, you'll encounter hip-hop, reggae, Latin, international, R&B, and other tunes that make it easy to dance. The spacious, two-story club features a large dance floor, intimate sitting rooms, a VIP suite, and a courtyard.

DUNGEON

738 Toulouse St., 504/523-5530
HOURS: Tues.-Sun. 10:30 P.M.-close
COST: No cover, save for special events
Map 1

Among the Quarter's more energetic haunts, Dungeon, whose ownership recently changed hands, is a preferred place for dancing into the wee hours. Accessible via a pseudo-creepy outer gate and a narrow alleyway, the club features a typically crowded dance floor, plus three unique bar areas, decorated with fake skulls and human-sized cages. House drinks include the Witch's Brew, the Dungeon's answer to Pat O'Brien's traditional hurricane. Adjacent to the gateway is a front bar that the staff jokingly refers to as the "daycare dungeon"—mainly because it's open earlier (daily 6 P.M.–close).

THE FAMOUS DOOR

339 Bourbon St., 504/598-4334
HOURS: Mon.-Thurs. 3 P.M.-close, Fri.-Sun. noon-close
COST: No cover, save for special events
Map 1

One of several lively dance clubs along Bourbon Street, the Famous Door is a super-casual, unpretentious space, where there's usually a live cover band, playing everything from Journey to Jimmy Buffett, and plenty of room for dancing. Admittedly, it's a bit smoky, and the crowd usually has a heavy drunk tourist quotient. It's not exactly known for great New Orleans–style music, but if you're in the right frame of mind, you'll probably have a good deal of fun. As with other clubs along Bourbon, closing times can vary here; on a busy weekday, the place might not pack it in before 3 or 4 A.M., while weekend crowds could stay as late as 5 A.M.

NIGHTLIFE

© DANIEL MARTONE

The Maison, a roomy dance club on Frenchmen Street

NIGHTLIFE

KRAZY KORNER

640 Bourbon St., 504/524-3157, www.krazykorner.com
HOURS: Mon.-Fri. 5 P.M.-close, Sat.-Sun. 2 P.M.-close
COST: No cover, save for special events
Map 1

Situated at one of the busiest intersections in the Quarter, the Krazy Korner might not be as quintessential New Orleans as its neighbor, the Maison Bourbon Jazz Club, but it can still be a lively place to hear live and DJ-helmed jazz and R&B. If you appreciate loud, smoky, super-casual clubs with a full bar and plenty of dancing space, then you'll fit right in here.

THE MAISON

508 Frenchmen St., 504/371-5543,
www.maisonfrenchmen.com
HOURS: Daily 5 P.M.-close
COST: No cover, save for special events
Map 2

One of the more spacious venues in the Marigny, this multilevel bar, restaurant, and live music venue consists of three separate areas: a front dining and music room, a rear lounge and stage, and the upper Penthouse bar, which comprises a separate stage, a comfortable lounge, and plenty of room for dancing. Although the Maison is a preferred spot for private events, from film screenings to wedding receptions, it's mainly home to concerts and DJ-helmed dance parties, featuring jazz, funk, soul, Latin dance music, even swing dance lessons.

THE METROPOLITAN

310 Andrew Higgins Dr., 504/568-1702,
www.themetropolitannightclub.com
HOURS: Vary depending on the event
COST: Cover varies
Map 3

Just a block from the Ernest N. Morial Convention Center, you'll encounter this massive, two-story, Los Angeles–style nightclub, which, at more than 36,000 square feet in size, is often the premier choice for major events, from tailgate parties to fashion shows. This enormous warehouse-turned-club contains two main rooms, equipped with smoke machines, strobe lights, and video screens and featuring DJ-spun hip-hop, rock, house, techno, and other popular formats. In addition to a slew of bartender stations and VIP sections, the Metropolitan also offers valet parking and VIP table service. Given this upscale vibe, you should expect pricey drinks and high cover charges.

MIMI'S IN THE MARIGNY

2601 Royal St., 504/872-9868,
www.mimisinthemarigny.net
HOURS: Sun.-Thurs. 4 P.M.-5 A.M., Fri.-Sat. 4 P.M.-6 A.M.
COST: No cover
Map 2

Nestled within a quiet residential part of the Faubourg Marigny, Mimi's has long been a popular hot spot, particularly among locals. Downstairs, you'll find a neighborhood bar with couches, stools, and a pool table, while the upstairs space is a live music venue, with a decent amount of room for dancing. You can expect concerts and DJ-helmed dance parties every night of the week, not to mention dance lessons on occasion. In addition, you should try the tasty tapas on offer, from almond-stuffed dates to beef empanadas; the kitchen is typically open Sunday–Thursday 6 P.M.–2 A.M. and Friday–Saturday 6 P.M.–4 A.M.

ONE EYED JACKS

615 Toulouse St., 504/569-8361,
www.oneeyedjacks.net
HOURS: Vary depending on the event
COST: Cover varies
Map 1

Perhaps my favorite place to dance in the Quarter, One Eyed Jacks is a spacious, bordello-style venue, with red walls, curious paintings, and moody lighting. Although there's an upstairs lounge, most revelers will only see the two rooms on the first floor: the intimate front bar and the larger showroom, which features a horseshoe-shaped bar, limited seating, a large stage, and oodles of room for dancing. While live concerts are common here, regulars also come for thematic events, like '80s-style dance parties, burlesque shows, and vaudeville nights, which often include comedy sketches, old-fashioned jazz performances, acrobatics, and sexy dance routines.

Gay and Lesbian Venues

ALLWAYS LOUNGE & THEATRE

2240 St. Claude Ave., 504/218-5778,
www.theallwayslounge.com
HOURS: Tues.-Thurs. and Sun. 6 P.M.-midnight, Fri.-Sat.
6 P.M.-2 A.M.
COST: Cover varies
`Map 2`

Definitely not for the faint-hearted, the rowdy AllWays Lounge & Theatre welcomes everybody, though it has a predominantly gay and lesbian following. Nudity, wacky sexual acts, and strange musical performances are common in the lounge. The theater features ever-changing productions, including bizarre concerts and counterculture musicals like *The Rocky Horror Show*. Generally speaking, shows start at 10 P.M.

BOURBON PUB & PARADE

801 Bourbon St., 504/529-2107, www.bourbonpub.com
HOURS: Daily 24 hours
COST: Cover varies
`Map 1`

One of the most popular gay dance clubs sits at the often rowdy corner of Bourbon and St. Ann. The Bourbon Pub & Parade has a typically packed video bar on the ground level, a slick dance floor upstairs, and a long wraparound balcony on the second floor—a favorite perch from which to gaze at the throngs of revelers on Bourbon Street, which are particularly colorful during Mardi Gras, June's gay pride season, Southern Decadence, Halloween, and New Year's Eve. Music lovers can expect to see plenty of retro music videos downstairs, while everything from drag shows to hot guy contests to karaoke nights is happening upstairs.

CAFE LAFITTE IN EXILE

901 Bourbon St., 504/522-8397, www.lafittes.com
HOURS: Mon.-Tues. 1 P.M.-5 A.M., Wed.-Sun. 24 hours
COST: No cover
`Map 1`

A block away from Lafitte's Blacksmith Shop Bar, Cafe Lafitte in Exile has been serving the local gay community for roughly as long as any bar in town. It draws more of a thirty- to fiftysomething crowd, a bit more mature than those of the Oz New Orleans and Bourbon Pub & Parade. As with Bourbon, though, you can watch music videos in the downstairs bar and observe curious passersby from the upstairs balcony, which can be particularly eye-opening during uninhibited, skin-baring events like Mardi Gras and Southern Decadence.

THE COUNTRY CLUB

634 Louisa St., 504/945-0742,
www.thecountryclubneworleans.com
HOURS: Daily 10 A.M.-1 A.M.
COST: No cover
`Map 2`

Although this magnificent Bywater mansion—complete with palm trees, a manicured lawn, a Southern-style porch, and classic columns—isn't technically a gay bar, it definitely embraces an "anything goes" vibe. There is, after all, a clothing-optional saltwater pool, not to mention a sauna, a Jacuzzi, and on-site massage and spa services. You can also sip cocktails in the indoor or outdoor bars, enjoy creative cuisine in the restaurant, or watch movies, music videos, and sporting events on the 25-foot screen. If the crowd's really hoppin', the joint might not close until 2 A.M. or later, and while there's no cover charge at the door, you should expect, depending on the time of day, to pay $5–15 to access the rear private area, where you'll find the pool.

4 SEASONS & THE OUT BACK BAR

3229 N. Causeway Blvd., Metairie, 504/832-0659
HOURS: Sun.-Thurs. 4 P.M.-2 A.M., Fri.-Sat. 4 P.M.-4 A.M.
COST: No cover
`Map 6`

If you happen to be in Metairie and need a lively place to unwind, drop by the 4 Seasons, the main gay and lesbian dance club in the suburbs. This casual place has been gay-owned and -operated for more than 15 years, though

NIGHTLIFE

it definitely welcomes any and all respectful patrons. If you're a shameless public singer like me, then you'll definitely appreciate Thursday, when karaoke starts at 9 P.M.

GOLDEN LANTERN BAR

1239 Royal St., 504/529-2860
HOURS: Daily 8 A.M.–2 A.M.
COST: No cover
Map 1

The Quarter boasts several gay-friendly hangouts, including raunchier places like the Corner Pocket on St. Louis Street, where you'll likely see sexy, young gay men shaking their goods. If, however, you prefer a more sedate, off-Bourbon watering hole that's inviting to gay and heterosexual patrons alike, then head to the Golden Lantern, a small, dark locals' bar on a quiet, residential stretch of Royal that serves, as I can attest, one of the best Bloody Marys in the city. One night, in fact, I was feeling so comfortable at the Lantern that I had not one, but three, Bloody Marys while gabbing

Whether gay or straight, most patrons feel comfortable in the laid-back Golden Lantern Bar.

© DANIEL MARTONE

with the various waiters and tour guides who frequent the joint; I didn't realize how strong the drinks were until I attempted to wobble my way back home.

GOOD FRIENDS BAR

740 Dauphine St., 504/566-7191,
www.goodfriendsbar.com
HOURS: Sun.–Thurs. 1 P.M.–2 A.M., Fri.–Sat. 1 P.M.–5 A.M.
COST: No cover
Map 1

Unlike most gay-friendly hangouts in the Quarter, the mellow, longstanding Good Friends Bar isn't too loud or flashy. It's just a casual, pet-friendly neighborhood watering hole, where you'll find a pool table, affordable beer and cocktails, a slightly fancier upstairs area, and attentive bartenders who don't sport the requisite attitude of most gay bars. Saints fans come here, as do low-key locals, and no matter your sexual orientation, you're welcome to join in the karaoke fun every Tuesday night (9 P.M.–midnight).

JOHN PAUL'S

940 Elysian Fields Ave., 504/948-1888,
www.johnpaulsbar.com
HOURS: Mon.–Fri. 9 A.M.–close, Sat.–Sun. 10 A.M.–close
COST: Cover varies
Map 2

Opened in 2005, the former Moulin Rouge Bar has evolved into the perennially popular John Paul's, a friendly neighborhood bar that's now the city's premier venue for drag cabaret. Although you can typically expect no cover charge here, there's often a fee (or at least a requested donation) for certain drag shows, pageants, and other special events. Every Tuesday, patrons can take country-western dance lessons beginning at 8 P.M. and, afterward, show off their newly acquired moves until about 10:30 P.M.

OZ NEW ORLEANS

800 Bourbon St., 504/593-9491,
www.ozneworleans.com
HOURS: Daily 24 hours
COST: Cover varies
Map 1

No matter when I pass by Oz—whether day or

night—it never seems to be as crowded as other venues in the Quarter. Nevertheless, many locals consider it one of the city's top gay dance clubs, especially during special events like Mardi Gras and New Year's Eve. Situated opposite the seemingly more popular Bourbon Pub, Oz provides plenty of room for dancing on the ground floor and more lounge-like spaces upstairs.

PHOENIX & NEW ORLEANS EAGLE

941 Elysian Fields Ave., 504/945-9264,
www.neworleansphoenix.com
HOURS: Daily 24 hours
COST: No cover
Map 2

Marigny residents in search of an alternative bar may appreciate the Phoenix & New Orleans Eagle, a dark and hormone-filled place established in 1983 and now favored by leather-and-Levis types. Hospitable bartenders, amiable regulars, and affordable drinks help to lure folks from the nearby Quarter. It doesn't hurt that there's no cover charge and plenty of free parking, and while the upstairs bar is typically open daily 9 A.M.–close, the downstairs portion never shuts its doors. Not surprisingly, this bar is especially popular during gay-centric events like Southern Decadence.

RAWHIDE 2010

740 Burgundy St., 504/525-8106,
www.rawhide2010.com
HOURS: Mon.-Thurs. 1 P.M.-5 A.M., Fri.-Sun. 24 hours
COST: No cover
Map 1

As the name more than implies, Rawhide 2010 is a gay leather bar, where you'll encounter a mostly male crowd and a decidedly masculine, lusty ambience. Here, you can shoot some pool, mingle with fellow cruisers, and take advantage of various drink specials, such as $0.50 oyster shooters on Friday (starting at 5 P.M.) and $1 well drinks on Sunday (6–8 P.M.). Besides obvious events like Mardi Gras and New Year's Eve, this popular spot also hosts barbecue gatherings on Wednesday (7–9 P.M.), known as "bring your own meat night," as well as an infamous, DJ-fueled "blackout" party on the second Thursday of each month (starting at 9 P.M.).

NIGHTLIFE

ARTS AND LEISURE

A longtime haven for artists, writers, and musicians, New Orleans has an especially rich, multicultural tradition in the arts. The city is home to several impressive museums as well as numerous outstanding galleries, with particularly strong concentrations along Royal and Chartres Streets in the French Quarter, around Julia Street in the CBD's Arts District, and along funky Magazine Street in Uptown. While the performing arts aren't as pervasive as in other cities—and granted, the recent closure of the longstanding Le Petit Theatre du Vieux Carré hasn't helped—there are still several worthy venues, such as the refurbished Mahalia Jackson Theater in Louis Armstrong Park. In addition, the annual New Orleans Fringe Festival showcases a wide array of experimental theater in venues throughout the city.

When it comes to festivals and special events, New Orleans offers a slew of tripworthy options, especially in the fall, winter, and spring. In a town where locals need little reason to celebrate, Mardi Gras and the New Orleans Jazz & Heritage Festival are just the tip of the iceberg. Not surprisingly, most events revolve around food, music, and art (such as my favorite, the French Quarter Festival), but there are plenty of other celebrations that honor the city's multiethnic culture and observe traditional holidays with a Big Easy slant. Summer events, such as the rowdy Southern Decadence bash around Labor Day, are held when tourism slows and often appeal more to locals. During popular events—especially Mardi Gras and Jazz Fest—the city can fill up quickly, so it's wise to book your

HIGHLIGHTS

LOOK FOR ◖ TO FIND RECOMMENDED ARTS AND ACTIVITIES.

◖ **Best Downtown Spot for Art Lovers:** A block from the National WWII Museum in the downtown Arts District, you can experience one of the country's largest collections of Southern artwork at **The Ogden Museum of Southern Art,** which even features the paintings of celebrated Louisiana folk artist Clementine Hunter (page 149).

◖ **Most Interactive Art Gallery:** Although many visitors come to the **New Orleans School of GlassWorks & Printmaking Studio** to watch skilled artisans at work, another main draw is the chance to take one of several engaging classes, from a paper marbling course to a stained-glass-making workshop (page 153).

◖ **Best Live Performance Venue:** Named for a beloved New Orleans–born gospel singer, the restored **Mahalia Jackson Theater for the Performing Arts** lures plenty of cultural enthusiasts to Louis Armstrong Park for an assortment of live concerts, dance performances, and Broadway shows (page 156).

◖ **Best Free Music Event:** In keeping with its original mission to support local musicians, the annual **French Quarter Festival,** now considered Louisiana's largest free music event, brings together an array of regional jazz, gospel, funk, zydeco, classical, bluegrass, folk, and blues acts (page 159).

◖ **Best Chance to Tour Private Homes:** For more than 75 years, the **New Orleans Spring Fiesta** has highlighted the city's unique history and charm by presenting such events as a parade of horse-drawn carriages, plus a once-in-a-lifetime chance to explore nearly two dozen private homes, gardens, and courtyards in the French Quarter, Garden District, and Uptown neighborhoods (page 160).

◖ **Best All-Around Park:** Extending from St. Charles Avenue to the Mississippi River, historic **Audubon Park** offers a slew of recreational opportunities, including a swimming pool, a golf course, a 1.8-mile jogging path, three playgrounds, several tennis courts, scenic bird-watching spots, and horseback-riding lessons (page 168).

◖ **Best Way to Explore the City:** To experience New Orleans at your own pace, rent a bicycle from **Bicycle Michael's,** a full-service store in the Faubourg Marigny. Take your time exploring the French Quarter, City Park, the Lake Pontchartrain shoreline, and other key areas in this relatively compact city (page 173).

◖ **Most Romantic Tour of the French Quarter:** From Jackson Square, couples can embark upon a mule-drawn carriage excursion of the Vieux Carré through **Royal Carriages,** an ideal way to relish the historic architecture, curious characters, and romantic vibe of one of the country's most atmospheric neighborhoods (page 179).

◖ **Best Way to Experience the Mighty Mississippi:** Whether you opt for a breezy daytime or evening cruise aboard the authentic **Steamboat *Natchez,*** you'll be treated to live jazz, calliope concerts, well-informed guides, Creole refreshments, and marvelous views of the Mississippi River (page 180).

© LAURA MARTONE

the New Orleans School of GlassWorks & Printmaking Studio in the Arts District

trip well ahead. (Or avoid the city altogether if you're not a fan of crowds.)

Beyond arts and festivals, some visitors actually come to New Orleans for year-round recreational pursuits, such as fishing and golfing. Many outdoors-lovers are surprised by the number of lovely parks, as well as the prevalence of bike shops. For sports lovers, New Orleans offers two major teams—the New Orleans Saints and the New Orleans Hornets—plus a historic horse-racing track. But perhaps the most popular way to explore this vibrant city is via guided tour. Luckily, you'll find an assortment of memorable options, including citywide biking excursions, voodoo-focused walking tours, romantic carriage rides, swamp boat trips, and paddlewheel jaunts down the Mississippi River.

The Arts

MUSEUMS

AMERICAN ITALIAN MUSEUM
537 S. Peters St., 504/522-7294,
www.americanitalianmuseum.com
HOURS: Tues.-Fri. 10 A.M.-4 P.M.
COST: $8 adult, $5 senior, free under 12
Map 3

Just steps from the Harrah's casino in downtown New Orleans, you'll find the American Italian Cultural Center, home to the aptly named American Italian Museum. Through the use of family histories, vintage photographs, and other memorabilia, the museum chronicles the history and cultural influence of American Italians in southeastern Louisiana. Visitors who more often associate New Orleans with the French, Spanish, and Caribbean cultures may find the Italian contributions to the city's cuisine, music, festivals, and demographics (including my own heritage) especially curious. In addition to the museum, the center also houses a research library (Thurs.–Fri. 10 A.M.–4 P.M.) that offers Italian language classes and hosts periodic events.

BACKSTREET CULTURAL MUSEUM
1116 Henriette Delille St., 504/522-4806,
www.backstreetmuseum.org
HOURS: Tues.-Sat. 10 A.M.-5 P.M.
COST: $8 pp
Map 5

If you're a fan of HBO's acclaimed show *Treme* or simply curious about the Big Easy's vibrant African American culture, you're in for a treat. Not far from Louis Armstrong Park—the original site of Congo Square—lies the fascinating Backstreet Cultural Museum. The museum contains the world's most comprehensive collection of costumes, films, and photographs from jazz funerals and pleasure clubs, plus Carnival-related groups like the Mardi Gras Indians, Baby Dolls, and Skull and Bone Gang. Beyond the permanent exhibits, the museum also presents public performances of traditional music and dance.

GEORGE & LEAH MCKENNA MUSEUM OF AFRICAN AMERICAN ART
2003 Carondelet St., 504/586-7432,
www.themckennamuseum.com
HOURS: Tues.-Wed. by appt., Thurs.-Sat. 11 A.M.-4 P.M.
COST: $5 adult, $3 senior and student, $2 child 6-12, free under 6
Map 4

Named after the parents of museum founder Dr. Dwight McKenna, this African American art museum endeavors to collect, interpret, and preserve African Diasporan fine art, whether fashioned by emerging artists or renowned masters like Henry Ossawa Tanner and Clementine Hunter. The museum also features temporary exhibits, and group tours are available with advance notice. Similar art is available for purchase at the unrelated **Stella Jones Gallery** (201 St. Charles Ave., 504/568-9050, www.stellajonesgallery.com) in the CBD.

GERMAINE CAZENAVE WELLS MARDI GRAS MUSEUM
813 Bienville Ave., 504/523-5433,

www.arnaudsrestaurant.com/mardi-gras-museum
HOURS: Mon.-Sat. 6 P.M.-close, Sun. 10 A.M.-2:30 P.M.
and 6 P.M.-close
COST: Free
Map 1

Those curious about the glamour of Carnival should head to the Germaine Cazenave Wells Mardi Gras Museum at the fabled Arnaud's Restaurant. The museum, named for the daughter of restaurant founder Count Arnaud, opened in 1983 as a tribute to Ms. Wells—the former queen of more than 22 Mardi Gras balls (1937–1968). On hand are several of Wells's elaborate ball costumes, other courtly Mardi Gras attire, intricate masks, lavish jewelry, and vintage photographs.

GERMAN-AMERICAN CULTURAL CENTER
519 Huey P. Long Ave., Gretna, 504/363-4202,
www.gacc-nola.org
HOURS: Wed.-Sat. 10 A.M.-3 P.M.
COST: Free
Map 6

As a port city, New Orleans has long been a melting pot of ethnicities, including French, Spanish, Italian, African, Caribbean, and, yes, German. On the West Bank, the town of Gretna was actually settled by German immigrants in the mid-1880s—a fact that's celebrated through lectures, programs, events, and exhibits at the German-American Cultural Center in Gretna's historical district. The small museum portion of the center includes black-and-white photographs, vintage signs, and plenty of colorful beer steins.

HOUSE OF BROEL'S VICTORIAN MANSION, WEDDING CHAPEL, AND DOLLHOUSE MUSEUM
2220 St. Charles Ave., 504/522-2220,
www.houseofbroel.com
HOURS: Mon.-Fri. 11 A.M.-3 P.M.
COST: $10 adult, $5 child
Map 4

Near the corner of St. Charles and Jackson Avenues, you'll come to one small but noteworthy attraction, especially if you favor

miniatures. Originally built in 1850, the House of Broel's Victorian Mansion, Wedding Chapel, and Dollhouse Museum was converted, three decades later, into the immense three-story mansion that exists today. The tour, which is available by appointment, not only highlights the living quarters and furnishings of an exceptional Garden District residence, but also offers a look at the hundreds of dolls, miniatures, dollhouses, and other collectibles that fill the rooms.

LOUISIANA CHILDREN'S MUSEUM
420 Julia St., 504/523-1357, www.lcm.org
HOURS: Mon.-Sat. 9:30 A.M.-5 P.M., Sun. noon-5 P.M.
COST: $8 pp, free under 1
Map 3

Besides art galleries and loft offices, the Arts District is also home to the Louisiana Children's Museum, an enormous touch-friendly cache of interactive exhibits, many of which re-create grown-up activities or everyday errands on a small scale. Here, kids can shop in a grocery store, pilot a tugboat on the Mississippi River, and play house inside a Cajun cottage, not to mention learn about the city's architectural history. While most of these exhibits target toddlers and adolescents, older children will appreciate scientific displays like the electrifying plasma balls. Visitors under 16 years old must be accompanied by an adult. The museum is closed on major holidays and on Mondays in the fall, winter, and spring.

LOUISIANA'S CIVIL WAR MUSEUM AT CONFEDERATE MEMORIAL HALL
929 Camp St., 504/523-4522,
www.confederatemuseum.com
HOURS: Tues.-Sat. 10 A.M.-4 P.M.
COST: $7 adult, $5 senior and student, $2 child under 13
Map 3

Situated inside the elegant Confederate Memorial Hall near Lee Circle, the Civil War Museum holds the country's second-largest collection of Confederate memorabilia, including uniforms, weapons, 125 battle flags, and more than 500 tintypes, daguerreotypes, and other vintage photographic images, as well as

Louisiana's Civil War Museum at Confederate Memorial Hall

the personal items of General Robert E. Lee, General P. G. T. Beauregard, and other important Confederate war figures. Designed by Thomas O. Sully, one of the city's most distinguished architects, and opened in 1891, this Romanesque structure is the state's oldest continuously operating museum.

MUSÉE CONTI WAX MUSEUM

917 Conti St., 504/525-2605,
www.neworleanswaxmuseum.com
HOURS: Mon. and Fri.-Sat. 10 A.M.-4 P.M.
COST: $7 adult, $6.25 senior, $6 child 4-17
Map 1

As a child, I was fascinated by this small wax museum. The detailed tableaux utilize costumed wax figures to represent important moments in the history of New Orleans, from its discovery to its indelible influence on the 20th century. Here, you'll spy Napoleon Bonaparte as he decides to sell Louisiana, Andrew Jackson in the midst of the Battle of New Orleans, plus the pirate Jean Lafitte, the sinister Madame LaLaurie, voodoo queen

Marie Laveau, Governor Huey P. Long, and famous musicians like Louis Armstrong and Pete Fountain. Admittedly, the musty museum—which opened in 1964—is showing its age, but it still provides an interesting history lesson, and children will especially enjoy the Chamber of Horrors, with gruesome scenes involving Dracula, Frankenstein's monster, and the Phantom of the Opera. Tours are self-guided, though helpful programs are available in French, German, Spanish, Italian, and Japanese.

NEW ORLEANS AFRICAN AMERICAN MUSEUM

1418 Gov. Nicholls St., 504/566-1136, www.noaam.org
HOURS: Sun.-Tues. by appt., Wed.-Sat. 11 A.M.-4 P.M.
COST: $7 adult, $5 senior and student, $3 child 2-12
Map 5

Within easy walking distance of Louis Armstrong Park lies this curious museum, which, as the name indicates, strives to preserve and promote the African American heritage of New Orleans. Housed within a lovely Creole villa, exhibits focus on the art, culture, music, and history of the Faubourg Tremé, the oldest African American neighborhood in the country. Permanent exhibits include kaleidoscopic quilts made by local artists as well as smaller versions of the colorful murals that currently adorn the pillars of the I-10 overpass along Claiborne Avenue, between Orleans and St. Bernard Avenues.

NEW ORLEANS HISTORIC VOODOO MUSEUM

724 Dumaine St., 504/680-0128,
www.voodoomuseum.com
HOURS: Daily 10 A.M.-6 P.M.
COST: $7 adult, $5.50 senior, $4.50 student, $3.50 child under 12
Map 1

Established in 1972, this small, somewhat cramped museum offers a decent, respectful overview of a practice still shrouded in mystery yet taken very seriously by its practitioners. Displays include a variety of masks, ritual art, and artifacts from Africa and Haiti, where

© LAURA MARTONE

ARTS AND LEISURE

the city's distinctive brand of voodoo practice originated. The exhibits, though ominous, aren't gory in nature, so kids often find them appealing. The focus here is on Marie Laveau, the anointed voodoo priestess who lived in New Orleans from the 1790s until her death in 1881. Though you can arrange private consultations and healing seminars with museum staff, the true highlight is the historian-led walking tour ($19 adult, $10 child under 12), which includes a visit to Congo Square, a stroll through the St. Louis Cemetery No. 1 (site of Marie Laveau's tomb), an encounter with a contemporary voodoo priestess, and plenty of engrossing stories about voodoo, zombies, jazz funerals, Mardi Gras Indians, and other curious aspects of the city's colorful history.

NEW ORLEANS PHARMACY MUSEUM

514 Chartres St., 504/565-8027,
www.pharmacymuseum.org
HOURS: Tues.-Fri. 10 A.M.-2 P.M., Sat. 10 A.M.-5 P.M.
COST: $5 adult, $4 senior and student, free under 6
Map 1

This museum occupies a genuine apothecary shop from the 1820s. Original shop owner Louis J. Dufilho Jr. was the first licensed pharmacist in the nation, having earned his certification in 1816. Displays show what a period pharmacy looked like, including rows of 1850s-style hand-carved mahogany cabinets filled with everything from established drugs to gris-gris voodoo potions; exhibits also tell the story of Louisiana's development in medicine and health care. Other interesting features include an assortment of bloodletting equipment, a medicinal herb garden in the courtyard, and an 1855 Italian marble soda fountain.

◖ THE OGDEN MUSEUM OF SOUTHERN ART

925 Camp St., 504/539-9600,
www.ogdenmuseum.org
HOURS: Wed.-Mon. 10 A.M.-5 P.M.
COST: $10 adult, $8 senior and student, $5 child 5-17, free under 5
Map 3

Literally steps from Lee Circle, you'll find it hard to miss the Ogden Museum of Southern

The Ogden Museum of Southern Art

© LAURA MARTONE

ARTS AND LEISURE

Art, which contains one of the country's largest collections of artwork related to the American South. This impressive complex comprises the contemporary, five-story Stephen Goldring Hall, the restored Howard Memorial Library (which was designed by Louisiana architect H. H. Richardson and rechristened the Patrick F. Taylor Library), and the Clementine Hunter Education Wing, named for the famous Louisiana folk artist who grew up on a cotton plantation in Cloutierville and produced about 4,000 works during her storied career. The artwork here includes all mediums and spans the 18th–21st centuries, representing artists from 15 Southern states as well as Washington, D.C. On Thursday evenings, the museum usually presents live music 6–8 P.M.

SOUTHERN FOOD & BEVERAGE MUSEUM

Riverwalk Marketplace, 500 Port of New Orleans Pl., Ste. 169, 504/569-0405, www.southernfood.org
HOURS: Mon.-Sat. 10 A.M.-7 P.M., Sun. noon-6 P.M.
COST: $10 adult, $5 senior and student
Map 3

In a city that's celebrated around the world for its cuisine, it's surprising that the Southern Food & Beverage Museum has only been open since 2008. Dedicated to the discovery and appreciation of the food, drinks, and related culture of the American South, the museum's temporary and permanent exhibits explore an assortment of tasty topics, including Acadian culture, Southern barbecue and liquor, Gulf Coast seafood, Louisiana's multiethnic cuisine, Galatoire's history, cooking stoves, and praline vendors. Trust me—a visit here will surely stimulate your appetite for the Big Easy's varied culinary offerings.

WESTWEGO HISTORICAL MUSEUM

275 Sala Ave., Westwego, 504/341-3161, www.westwegohistoricalsociety.com/museum.html
HOURS: Mon.-Fri. 9 A.M.-4 P.M.
COST: $3 adult, $2 senior and child under 12
Map 6

If you find yourself on the West Bank, consider making a quick stop at the Westwego

Historical Museum. Housed within the old Fisherman's Exchange/L. J. Bernard Hardware Store Building in Westwego's Salaville Historic District, this small museum explores the town's history with thousands of artifacts and memorabilia in its main exhibit area. In addition, the museum features a restored, turn-of-the-20th-century general store as well as furnished period living quarters upstairs.

WILLIAMS RESEARCH CENTER

410 Chartres St., 504/598-7171, www.hnoc.org
HOURS: Tues.-Sat. 9:30 A.M.-4:30 P.M.
COST: Free
Map 1

Not far from the main campus of the Historic New Orleans Collection, the Williams Research Center (WRC) is an additional facility that contains an extensive library of roughly 35,000 documents and manuscripts, plus more than 300,000 photographs, drawings, prints, and paintings about the history of New Orleans. Housed within a 1915 Beaux Arts structure that once served as a police station and municipal courthouse, this is truly a treasure trove for history buffs. Just remember that this isn't a lending library, but a quiet environment for research. Though it's open to the public, patrons must first consult with the reading room staff before gaining access to this vast wealth of information.

GALLERIES
BARRISTER'S GALLERY

2331 St. Claude Ave., 504/710-4506, www.barristersgallery.com
HOURS: Tues.-Sat. 11 A.M.-5 P.M.
Map 2

Originally located in the French Quarter, this curious gallery eventually shifted to the edge of the Faubourg Marigny—a funky neighborhood that seems to suit the variety of Asian, African, Haitian, and Oceanic folk and outsider art available at Barrister's. Its primary focus is on monthly contemporary exhibits that have an eclectic, unorthodox bent. Just be aware that the gallery's location isn't the safest place in the city.

CALLAN FINE ART

240 Chartres St., 504/524-0025,
www.callanfineart.com
HOURS: Daily 11 A.M.–6 P.M.
Map 1

Fine art lovers should head to the aptly named Callan Fine Art, which focuses on European paintings from 1830 to 1950. You'll find representative works from the Academic, Pastoral, Neoclassic, Impressionist, and Post-Impressionist movements, with the artwork of French Barbizon painters a particular specialty. Curiously, local musician Tony Green displays quite a few of his own drawings and paintings here—most of which capture the vibrancy of jazz musicians, Mardi Gras, and the French Quarter.

COLE PRATT GALLERY

3800 Magazine St., 504/891-6789,
www.coleprattgallery.com
HOURS: Tues.–Sat. 10 A.M.–5 P.M.
Map 4

While browsing the galleries and boutiques of the Magazine Arts District, you should pay a visit to the Cole Pratt Gallery, which features the paintings of more than 40 contemporary Southern artists. Founded in 1993 by the late Cole Pratt, the gallery is now operated by owner and longtime director Erika Olinger, who continues Pratt's legacy of supporting imaginative artists like Phil Sandusky, Robert Lansden, and Karen Stastny.

CRAIG TRACY'S PAINTED ALIVE BODYPAINTING GALLERY

827 Royal St., 504/592-9886, www.paintedalive.com
HOURS: Daily 10 A.M.–6 P.M.
Map 1

Admittedly one of my favorite art galleries along Royal Street, this eye-catching space presents the innovative creations of Craig Tracy, an internationally known artist who paints landscapes, storms, animal prints, and other patterns on naked human bodies, then photographs his living creations. At once gorgeous and mesmerizing, his artwork typically requires intense concentration to discern the

© DANIEL MARTONE

Vivid displays inside Craig Tracy's Painted Alive Bodypainting Gallery often lure curious passersby.

human form. At the gallery, you can often speak to the artist himself and watch videos that document his fascinating process.

DUTCH ALLEY ARTIST'S CO-OP

912 N. Peters, 504/412-9220,
www.dutchalleyartistsco-op.com
HOURS: Daily 10 A.M.-6 P.M.
Map 1

As you stroll through the historic French Market, be sure to visit the Dutch Alley Artist's Co-op, founded in 2003 by artist Ric Rolston. Operated by the two dozen artists whose work is on display, the gallery features a wide array of creations, from John Fitzgerald's prints to Kimberly Parker's seafood collages. Even my former landlord, Linda Sampson, sells her beaded accessories and mourning jewelry here.

GALERIE ROYALE

3648 Magazine St., 504/894-1588,
www.galerieroyale.net
HOURS: Tues. and Thurs.-Fri. 11 A.M.-3 P.M., Wed. by appt., Sat. 11 A.M.-6 P.M.
Map 4

Originally established in the French Quarter in 1988, this elegant fine art gallery now sits in the heart of Uptown's Magazine Arts District. Here, you'll find the contemporary artwork of local painters and sculptors: Adrian Wong Shue's pensive portraits; Mike Klung's otherworldly landscapes; and Phillip Sage's nostalgic New Orleans scenes, which capture iconic images like the St. Charles streetcar, French Market fruit stands, Café Du Monde, kinetic flambeau dancers, and old jazz musicians.

A GALLERY FOR FINE PHOTOGRAPHY

241 Chartres St., 504/568-1313, www.agallery.com
HOURS: Tues.-Wed. by appt., Thurs.-Mon. 10:30 A.M.-5:30 P.M.
Map 1

Although New Orleans boasts several art galleries that focus exclusively on photography, you'll probably find the largest assortment at the aptly named Gallery for Fine Photography. Established in 1973, this prestigious emporium features the work of such titans as Ansel Adams, Edward Curtis, Henri-Cartier Bresson, Walker Evans, Diane Arbus, and Eadweard Muybridge, plus the visionary creations of newer artists. Be prepared for hefty price tags.

JAMIE HAYES GALLERY

617-621 Chartres St., 504/592-4080 or
504/596-2344, www.jamiehayes.com
HOURS: Daily 9 A.M.-7 P.M.
Map 1

In the shadow of the St. Louis Cathedral, these side-by-side gallery spaces feature the whimsical, multicolored paintings, dolls, and jewelry of color-blind artist Jamie Hayes, who, though born in Indiana and raised in Austria, has long considered New Orleans his true home. Many New Orleanians favor his unique perspective of the city, which celebrates—in a wacky, childlike way—the unique music, traditions, and festive spirit of this one-of-a-kind place.

JEAN BRAGG GALLERY OF SOUTHERN ART

600 Julia St., 504/895-7375, www.jeanbragg.com
HOURS: Mon.-Sat. 10 A.M.-5 P.M.
Map 3

A longtime fixture on the New Orleans arts scene, Jean Bragg opened her first antiques shop here in 1979. At the time, she specialized in historic Newcomb College pottery and Louisiana paintings. Since 2005, the Jean Bragg Gallery of Southern Art has been located in the Arts District, where Bragg presents a fine collection of late 19th- and 20th-century crafts and paintings from Louisiana artists, including Gulf Coast Shearwater pottery.

KAKO GALLERY

536 Royal St., 504/565-5445, www.kakogallery.com
HOURS: Daily 10 A.M.-6 P.M.
Map 1

If you favor offbeat contemporary art from local artists and artisans, then the Kako Gallery might be right up your alley. Here, you'll find unique sculptures, paintings, and jewelry from artists like Don Picou, who frequently paints muted scenes of bayous and swamps, and Stan

Fontaine and Diane Millsap, two visionaries whose kaleidoscopic paintings feature the city's most famous landmarks and neighborhoods, from the St. Louis Cathedral to Pirate's Alley to Lafitte's Blacksmith Shop Bar.

LEMIEUX GALLERIES

332 Julia St., 504/522-5988,
www.lemieuxgalleries.com
HOURS: Mon.-Sat. 10 A.M.-6 P.M.
Map 3

In the city's Arts District, posh New York–style galleries seem to prevail, so LeMieux offers an intriguing change of pace. LeMieux presents a wide assortment of visionary, contemporary artwork, including Bobby Wozniak's infrared photographs, Nathan Durfee's bizarre portraits, Theresa Honeywell's tatted tattoos, and Thomas Mann's metallic jewelry. While exploring the greater New Orleans area, consider stopping by the gallery's second space in Metairie (200 Metairie Rd., 504/837-4044).

MARTIN-LAWRENCE GALLERIES

433 Royal St., 504/299-9055,
www.martinlawrence.com
HOURS: Daily 10 A.M.-6 P.M.
Map 1

World-famous Martin-Lawrence Galleries has locations throughout the United States, from San Francisco to Dallas to New York. It's no surprise then that New Orleans, a city favored among art lovers, would boast its own branch on venerable Royal Street. Founded in 1975, Martin-Lawrence Galleries specializes in sculptures, original paintings, and limited edition graphics by such astounding artists as Pablo Picasso, Marc Chagall, Andy Warhol, and Rembrandt van Rijn.

MICHALOPOULOS GALLERY

617 Bienville Ave., 504/558-0505,
www.michalopoulos.com
HOURS: Mon.-Sat. 10 A.M.-6 P.M., Sun. 11 A.M.-6 P.M.
Map 1

Owned by one of the most respected artists in Louisiana, the eponymous Michalopoulos Gallery carries dozens of James Michalopoulos's vibrant, architectural renderings, with their trademark skewed angles and impressionistic brushwork. Many of his works feature Creole houses or classic French Quarter townhouses. Sharon Stone, Bruce Willis, and Bonnie Raitt are among his most notable collectors, and on at least five separate occasions, the New Orleans Jazz & Heritage Festival and Foundation has commissioned him to create the official Jazz Fest poster.

NEWCOMB ART GALLERY

Tulane University, Woldenberg Art Center, near Newcomb Pl. and Drill Field Rd., 504/865-5328,
www.newcombartgallery.tulane.edu
HOURS: Tues.-Fri. 10 A.M.-5 P.M., Sat.-Sun. 10 A.M.-4 P.M.
Map 4

Opened in 1887, the Newcomb College Art School was once at the forefront of the American Arts and Crafts Movement, earning international fame for its unique pottery and for producing such talented graduates as modernist Ida Kohlmeyer and fine jewelry creator Mignon Faget. Unfortunately, Hurricane Katrina forced the school's closure, but you can still see some amazing creations by visiting the Newcomb Art Gallery, which contains more than 400 examples of pottery, metalwork, embroidery, and bound books produced at Newcomb College from the late 19th through the early 20th centuries. Though situated on Tulane University's campus, the gallery's exhibits and programs are free to the public.

◖ NEW ORLEANS SCHOOL OF GLASSWORKS & PRINTMAKING STUDIO

727 Magazine St., 504/529-7279,
www.neworleansglassworks.com
HOURS: Mon.-Sat. 10 A.M.-5 P.M.
Map 3

At the 25,000-square-foot New Orleans School of GlassWorks & Printmaking Studio, you can observe highly skilled glassblowing, torchworking, printmaking, metalworking, and stained-glass artisans in action. Besides browsing their wares, you can also learn how to create your own glasswork, jewelry, and paper arts by taking one of the studio's exceptional classes, which range from two-hour courses on paper marbling to six-week workshops about Venetian glassblowing.

PHOTO WORKS NEW ORLEANS

521 St. Ann St., 504/593-9090 or 877/593-4130, www.photoworksneworleans.com
HOURS: Thurs.-Tues. 10 A.M.-5:30 P.M., Wed. by appt.
Map 1

Acclaimed artist Louis Sahuc sells his fine black-and-white images at Photo Works New Orleans, a small gallery located on historic, oft-photographed Jackson Square. Here, you'll find beautiful, romantic shots of the Crescent City as well as other places to which Sahuc has traveled. Though most people come for the black-and-white photographs, atmospheric color images of New Orleans's unique architecture, events, and musicians are also available.

RODRIGUE STUDIO NEW ORLEANS

730 Royal St., 504/581-4244, www.georgerodrigue.com
HOURS: Daily 10 A.M.-6 P.M.
Map 1

The famous Cajun "Blue Dog" artist George Rodrigue operates his Rodrigue Studio, which relocated from one side of Royal Street to the other, in a warmly lighted space not far from the St. Louis Cathedral. Here, you can buy everything from inexpensive gifts to original oil paintings, depicting the "Blue Dog" amid swamps, cemeteries, and other picturesque places. The inspiration for these works was twofold: a Cajun legend about the *loup-garou* (werewolf) and the owner's terrier, Tiffany, who had died several years before.

ROSETREE BLOWN GLASS STUDIO

446 Vallette St., Algiers, 888/767-3873, www.rosetreeglass.com
HOURS: Mon.-Fri. 9 A.M.-5 P.M.
Map 6

The brainchild of artist Mark Rosenbaum, the Rosetree Blown Glass Studio is in fact the first privately owned glassblowing studio in Louisiana. The first recipient of a Master of Fine Arts in glassblowing from Tulane

© DANIEL MARTONE

Royal Street is rife with intriguing artwork, including the atmospheric silhouettes at Tanner Original Paintings and Murals.

University, Rosenbaum creates iridescent glasses, bowls, vases, candlesticks, holiday ornaments, oil candles, paperweights, perfume bottles, lighting fixtures, and other distinctive glasswork, all of which you can browse in his gallery. If you're staying in New Orleans, you can reach Rosetree, which is located in historic Algiers Point on the West Bank, by ferry or bridge. In preparation for the holiday season, the studio has extended hours in November and December (Sat. 10 A.M.–4 P.M.).

SØREN CHRISTENSEN GALLERY

400 Julia St., 504/569-9501, www.sorengallery.com
HOURS: Tues.-Fri. 10 A.M.-5:30 P.M., Sat. 11 A.M.-5 P.M.
Map 3

With its high ceilings, lofty windows, white brick walls, and uncluttered displays, the spacious Søren Christensen Gallery resembles the kind of place you might find in New York City. Though I typically prefer smaller, more intimate spaces, I've often relished a stroll through this elegant gallery, where art lovers will find contemporary paintings, sculptures, and photography by nationally and internationally recognized artists.

TANNER ORIGINAL PAINTINGS AND MURALS

830 Royal St., 504/524-8266, www.hauntingart.com
HOURS: Thurs.-Mon. 10 A.M.-7 P.M.
Map 1

Situated across the street from Craig Tracy's riveting bodypainting gallery is perhaps my favorite art gallery in the French Quarter. Enticing to many a passerby, Tanner's storefront features his spellbinding, often eerie paintings of stark forests shrouded in fog, illumined by sunshine or starlight, or enhanced by otherworldly hues. The scenes resembling photo negatives are especially haunting. You can purchase canvas and paper reproductions or, if you're lucky, the original paintings, but as with many Royal Street–based art galleries, the prices here aren't cheap.

THOMAS MANN GALLERY I/O

1812 Magazine St., 504/581-2111 or 800/875-2113, www.thomasmann.com
HOURS: Mon.-Sat. 11 A.M.-5 P.M.
Map 4

Thomas Mann, a nationally recognized artist who specializes in jewelry and home accessories, sells his work in galleries throughout the country. His flagship store, the Thomas Mann Gallery I/O, has been in New Orleans since 1988. Here, you'll find the largest collection of Mann's techno-romantic and one-of-a-kind jewelry in addition to whimsical contemporary art, glassware, stemware, jewelry, and gifts, made by Mann and other designers.

PERFORMING ARTS
CONTEMPORARY ARTS CENTER

900 Camp St., 504/528-3800 or 504/528-3805, www.cacno.org
HOURS: art gallery Thurs.-Sun. 11 A.M.-4 P.M.; event times vary
COST: $5 adult, $3 senior and student, varies for shows and events
Map 3

Within walking distance of Lee Circle, the Ogden Museum of Southern Art, and the National WWII Museum, the Contemporary Arts Center (CAC) is a multipurpose venue that houses an innovative art gallery as well as performing arts spaces. In addition to staging lectures, performances, and concerts, the CAC often serves as a main location for the New Orleans Film Festival and other annual events.

JEFFERSON PERFORMING ARTS CENTER

EJHS Auditorium, 400 Phlox Ave., Metairie, 504/885-2000, www.jpas.org
HOURS: Vary depending on the show
COST: Varies
Map 6

Operated by the Jefferson Performing Arts Society (JPAS), the Jefferson Performing Arts Center hosts major Broadway-style shows and a variety of musical performances throughout the year. Recent shows have included comic gems like *Nunset Boulevard, Hairspray,* and *Flanagan's Wake.* If you find yourself on the West Bank, consider checking the performance schedules for the **Teatro Wego! Theatre** (177 Sala Ave., Westwego) and the **Westwego Performing Arts Theatre** (177 Sala Ave., Westwego), both also operated by the JPAS.

LA NUIT COMEDY THEATER

5039 Freret St., 504/231-7011, www.lanuittheater.com
HOURS: Vary depending on the show
COST: Varies
Map 4

While local theaters host their share of comedic plays and musicals, New Orleans certainly doesn't nurture as many live comedy venues as Chicago and Los Angeles. Perhaps that's why the La Nuit Comedy Theater is so well loved. Nestled within an Uptown residential neighborhood, this delightful, smoke-free club presents several different shows, including *God's Been Drinking* (Fri. 8:30 P.M.), the city's longest-running improv comedy show; the ever-evolving *Fear and Loathing* sketch comedy show (Fri. 9:30 P.M.); free, open-mic, stand-up routines (Fri. 11 P.M.); and

ComedySportz matches (Sat. 7 P.M.). Besides offering improv comedy and sketch comedy–writing classes, La Nuit is also home to the annual New Orleans Comedy Arts Festival (NOCAF), which usually takes place during the Mardi Gras season.

LUPIN THEATER

Tulane University, Dixon Performing Arts Center, near Newcomb Pl. and Freret St., 504/865-5106, www.tulane.edu
HOURS: Vary depending on the show
COST: Varies
Map 4

Situated on Tulane University's Uptown campus, the Lupin Theater hosts most of the theatrical productions and dance performances presented by Tulane's Department of Theatre and Dance. Although the lineup changes with each school year, shows typically range from Greek comedies and Shakespearean plays to ballet and modern dance performances by the Newcomb Dance Company. Lupin is also home to the annual **New Orleans Shakespeare Festival at Tulane** (504/865-5105), which usually features three of Shakespeare's seminal works during the summer months.

MAHALIA JACKSON THEATER FOR THE PERFORMING ARTS

1419 Basin St., 504/287-0351, www.mahaliajacksontheater.com
HOURS: Vary depending on the show
COST: Varies
Map 5

Located within Louis Armstrong Park, the Mahalia Jackson Theater is a popular venue for live concerts, dance performances, Broadway shows, and festival events, especially since its complete restoration following Hurricane Katrina. Named for New Orleans–born gospel singer Mahalia Jackson, the theater also hosts regular performances by the **New Orleans Opera Association** (504/529-2278 or 800/881-4459, www.neworleansopera. org), the **Louisiana Philharmonic Orchestra** (504/523-6530, www.lpomusic.com), and the

New Orleans Ballet Association (504/522-0996, www.nobadance.com), which books some of the world's most important ballet companies. Parking is located inside the gated park, accessible via the Orleans Avenue entrance. Just be advised that this can be an unsafe part of town, especially at night, so avoid coming to the theater alone, and be aware of your environs at all times.

RIVERTOWN REPERTORY THEATRE

325 Minor St., Kenner, 504/468-7221, www.rivertownrepertorytheatre.org
HOURS: Vary depending on the show
COST: Varies
Map 6

Although most tourists tend not to venture into the suburbs while visiting New Orleans, communities like Metairie and Kenner are not without their diversions. Not far from the city's airport, you'll find the Rivertown Repertory Theatre, which has been hosting live theater for more than 24 years. Part of the Rivertown Museum complex near the Mississippi River, this long-running venue presents dramas, comedies, and Broadway musicals from September through May. Recent shows have included the Tony Award–winning musical *Chicago* and Neil Simon–penned comedies like *Rumors* and *Plaza Suite.*

SOUTHERN REPERTORY THEATRE

504/522-6545, www.southernrep.com
HOURS: Vary depending on the show
COST: Varies

Founded in 1986, Southern Repertory Theatre stages about a half dozen plays each year by New Orleans–based writers as well as noted Southern playwrights, such as Tennessee Williams, Lillian Hellman, and Lorraine Hasberry. The 2012 season includes standards such as *A Streetcar Named Desire,* as well as the local "City Series" and "Louisiana Cycle." Performances are held at rotating venues throughout the city; tickets are available online or by calling the box office (One Canal Place, 4th Floor, 504/523-9857, Wed.–Fri. 3–6 P.M., Sat. 1–5 P.M.).

CONCERT VENUES
DIXON HALL

Tulane University, near Newcomb Pl. and Freret St.,
504/862-3214 or 504/865-5269, www.tulane.edu

HOURS: Vary depending on the show

COST: Varies

`Map 4`

For a change of pace from the city's ubiquitous live rock, blues, and Cajun concerts, head to Dixon Hall at Tulane University. Erected in 1929 and named after the first and only president of Newcomb College, this Italian Renaissance–style building houses music classrooms, practice and listening rooms, and an auditorium that usually features jazz and classical music concerts, plus musical theater performances—most of which are free.

LAKEFRONT ARENA

6801 Franklin Ave., 504/280-7222 or 504/280-7171,
www.arena.uno.edu

HOURS: Vary depending on the show

COST: Varies

`Map 6`

Built in 1983, the 10,000-seat Lakefront Arena is a multipurpose venue near Lake Pontchartrain. Home to the University of New Orleans Privateers basketball team, it's also hosted a wide array of musical acts over the years. As a teenager, I saw everyone from Rush to Tom Petty and the Heartbreakers here. Today, you're just as likely to catch a Death Cab for Cutie concert as you are a Chris Tucker comedy act or a Disney show.

NUNEMAKER AUDITORIUM

Loyola University, Monroe Science Complex, Calhoun St. and Marquette Pl., 3rd Fl., 504/865-2074, www.loyno.edu

HOURS: Vary depending on the show

COST: Varies

`Map 4`

At Loyola University, something interesting is often happening at the Nunemaker Auditorium, a 400-seat lecture and concert hall where students of the school's College of Music and Fine Arts often present recitals, solo and ensemble performances, and live opera. Next to the Monroe building, the Communications/Music Complex also houses the 600-seat **Louis J. Roussel Performance Hall** on the second floor. Here, you can enjoy free concerts of the university's chamber orchestra, symphony orchestra, jazz band, and concert band.

CINEMA
ENTERGY IMAX THEATRE

1 Canal St., 504/581-4629 or 800/774-7394,
www.auduboninstitute.org/visit/imax

HOURS: Tues.-Sun. 10 A.M.-5 P.M.

COST: $10.50 adult, $9.50 senior and student, $7.50 child 2-12, child under 2 free

`Map 1`

Adjacent to the Audubon Aquarium of the Americas, alongside the Mississippi River, the family-friendly Entergy IMAX Theatre usually presents a handful of vibrant films at any given time. Recent selections have included *Under the Sea 3D* and *Hurricane on the Bayou*, a fascinating documentary that explores the

© LAURA MARTONE

ARTS AND LEISURE

Uptown's Prytania Theatre presents blockbusters, independent flicks, and film festivals.

detrimental impact of Hurricane Katrina and Louisiana's vanishing wetlands, as shown through the eyes of local residents (including two of my favorite musicians, Tab Benoit and Amanda Shaw). Although show times vary for each film, one typically starts every hour.

PRYTANIA THEATRE

5339 Prytania St., 504/891-2787, www.theprytania.com
HOURS: Vary daily depending on the show
COST: $8.50 adult, $6.50 senior and child
Map 4

Uptown's Prytania Theatre is an old-fashioned movie house that shows Hollywood blockbusters, classic films, and midnight movies on its massive single screen. It's also a principal venue for the annual **New Orleans Film Festival** in the fall, not to mention home to the **Film-O-Rama** event in May and the **French Film Fest** in July. Parking is sometimes hard to find in the residential neighborhood that surrounds the theater.

THE THEATRES AT CANAL PLACE

The Shops at Canal Place, 333 Canal St., 3rd Fl.,
504/581-5400, www.thetheatres.com
HOURS: Vary daily depending on the show
COST: $12 pp
Map 1

This movie theater—the only one in the French Quarter—is fancier than even Hollywood audiences might expect. With reserved seating and high-end digital projection, the retro-style cinema presents blockbusters, independent films, and film festivals. In addition, the theater features a full-service café and a premium cocktail bar. Still, while many patrons appreciate the in-theater table service, some complain that the house lights are never dim enough. Bear in mind, too, that no one under 18 is allowed.

ZEITGEIST MULTI-DISCIPLINARY ARTS CENTER

1618 Oretha Castle Haley Blvd., 504/352-1150,
www.zeitgeistinc.net
HOURS: Vary daily depending on the show
COST: $8 adult, $7 senior and student
Map 4

Traditional moviegoers will encounter several multiplex cinemas in the suburbs surrounding New Orleans, from Metairie to Harahan and beyond. Those seeking a more countercultural vibe, however, will appreciate the longstanding Zeitgeist, which has presented everything from acclaimed Canadian documentaries to the films of Andy Warhol and Atom Egoyan. Founded in 1986 by Rene Broussard—a BFA student at the University of New Orleans at the time—this no-frills venue has hosted a variety of plays, concerts, visual and performance art shows, and literary events over the years. It's also home to the annual **New Orleans Middle East Film Festival.** The only drawback is its location in the Lower Garden District, which can be a sketchy area day or night.

Festivals and Events

SPRING

CRESCENT CITY CLASSIC

Jackson Square to City Park, 504/861-8686,
www.ccc10k.com
COST: Free to watch, $25-35 to enter race

Since 1979, the Crescent City Classic, one of the nation's largest 10K road races (in part, due to the city's flat terrain), has been held in New Orleans every April, usually on the Saturday of Easter weekend. Roughly 20,000 runners, walkers, and athletes from around the globe participate in the annual race. From its start at Jackson Square, the course runs along Decatur, Poydras, and Basin Streets, then heads up Esplanade Avenue to culminate in City Park. Participants, their friends and families, and even the public can attend the rollicking post-race festival, a celebration of local music and cuisine. Though the festival is free for participants, all other attendees must pay a nominal fee ($5 pp, free under 12); however, the pre-race health and fitness expo is free.

◧ FRENCH QUARTER FESTIVAL

Various locations, 504/522-5730 or 800/673-5725, www.fqfi.org/frenchquarterfest

COST: Free, though food costs apply

Map 1

Begun in 1984 to support local musicians, the four-day French Quarter Fest, which typically occurs in early or mid-April, has since evolved into Louisiana's largest free music event. The nearly 20 outdoor stages—from Jackson Square to Woldenberg Riverfront Park—host local jazz, gospel, funk, zydeco, classical, bluegrass, folk, and blues acts, so you won't see Bob Dylan here (unless he's one of the attendees). Besides live music, you'll also find plenty of food for sale, including jambalaya, boiled crawfish, stuffed artichokes, sno-balls, and other regional treats.

GREEK FESTIVAL NEW ORLEANS

Holy Trinity Greek Orthodox Cathedral, 1200 Robert E. Lee Blvd., 504/282-0259, www.greekfestnola.com

COST: $5 pp, free under 12

Map 6

Alongside Bayou St. John, and within a quick drive of both Lake Pontchartrain and City Park, stands the impressive Holy Trinity Cathedral. I fondly remember passing by the Greek Orthodox church, supposedly the oldest congregation in the Americas, nearly every morning during my high school years. I have equally fond memories of the lively, well-attended festival that they hosted every Memorial Day weekend since the mid-1970s. Like any self-respecting Hellenic bash, this one presents live Greek music, Greek-style dancing, and, naturally, traditional Greek cuisine, from souvlaki to baklava. The festival also features a playground, a 5K race, and tours of the cathedral.

LOUISIANA CRAWFISH FESTIVAL

Sigur Center, 8245 W. Judge Perez Dr., Chalmette, 504/278-1506, www.louisianacrawfishfestival.com

COST: Varies

Map 6

If you're a "mudbug" lover, do yourself a favor and head to Chalmette in late March for the Louisiana Crawfish Festival. Since 1975, this popular, family-friendly event has celebrated crawfish season with live music, arts and crafts, amusement games and rides, and, of course, regional cuisine. Besides shrimp and alligator

During the annual French Quarter Festival, music lovers flock to free concerts on the grounds of the Old U.S. Mint.

© LAURA MARTONE

ARTS AND LEISURE

dishes, sno-balls and king cakes, and classic all-American options, the samplings here encompasses almost every crawfish-related meal imaginable: crawfish pies, boiled crawfish, crawfish fried rice, crawfish quesadillas, and, my personal favorite, crawfish étouffée over fried green tomatoes.

NEW ORLEANS JAZZ & HERITAGE FESTIVAL (JAZZ FEST)

Fair Grounds Race Course & Slots, 1751 Gentilly Blvd., 504/410-4100 or 504/558-6100, www.nojazzfest.com
COST: $45–65 adult, $5 child 2–10, child under 2 free
Map 5

Established in 1970 in Beauregard Square, this musical extravaganza, which has since moved to Mid-City's Fair Grounds, has grown to be nearly as popular as Mardi Gras. Held on two weekends in late April and early May, this event, also known as Jazz Fest, features music workshops, artisanal and culinary demonstrations, Native American powwow performances, arts-and-crafts vendors, an unbelievable array of food stalls, and numerous stages that buzz with jazz, blues, zydeco, rock, gospel, and folk musicians. Among the top acts who have performed at Jazz Fest are Fats Domino, Jimmy Buffett, Dave Matthews, Paul Simon, Bob Dylan, Tom Petty, Etta James, Allen Toussaint, Pete Fountain, Buckwheat Zydeco, Dr. John, and various members of the Marsalis and Neville clans. The foundation behind this popular festival also sponsors smaller food-and-music events like the **Tremé Creole Gumbo Festival** in mid-December.

◖ NEW ORLEANS SPRING FIESTA

Various locations, 504/581-1367 or 800/550-8450, www.springfiesta.com
COST: $25–30 pp for home tours, $13–15 pp for walking tours

Typically held in late March, the Spring Fiesta grants you the unique opportunity to step inside nearly two dozen private homes, gardens, and courtyards in the French Quarter, Garden District, and Uptown neighborhoods—an unparalleled experience that, as I can attest, is completely worth the seemingly steep cost. For more than 75 years, this one-of-a-kind event has honored the city's unique history and charm by offering such eye-opening tours, plus a delightful parade of horse-drawn carriages and the presentation of the Spring Fiesta Queen and her court at Jackson Square.

NEW ORLEANS WINE AND FOOD EXPERIENCE

Various locations, 504/529-9463, www.nowfe.com
COST: Varies
Map 3

Late May is the perfect time for foodies and wine connoisseurs to visit the Big Easy, as that's typically when you'll encounter the five-day New Orleans Wine and Food Experience (NOWFE). For more than two decades, this mouthwatering event has benefited local non-profit organizations while, at the same time, showcasing hundreds of national and international wines from more than 100 wineries, including the Northshore's Pontchartrain Vineyards, along with food from about 75 of the city's top restaurants, from Antoine's to the Oceana Grill. Featuring various dinners, tastings, and seminars, the NOWFE also celebrates local celebrity chefs like John Besh, Donald Link, and Susan Spicer.

TENNESSEE WILLIAMS/NEW ORLEANS LITERARY FESTIVAL

Various locations, 504/581-1144 or 800/990-3378, www.tennesseewilliams.net
COST: Varies
Map 1

Devotees of the city's most famous literary luminary rush to the Big Easy in late March to attend the Tennessee Williams/New Orleans Literary Festival. For more than a quarter century, this event has celebrated the playwright who gave us such iconographic works as *A Streetcar Named Desire* and *The Glass Menagerie*. The five-day gathering is replete with writing classes helmed by experts and notables, celebrity interviews, panel discussions, stagings of Williams's plays, fiction and poetry readings, and the always fun Stanley and Stella Shouting Contest. Attendees in recent years have included George Plimpton, Dorothy Allison, Laura Lippman, and Piper Laurie.

SUMMER
GO 4TH ON THE RIVER

Various locations, www.go4thontheriver.com
COST: Free, though some fees apply
`Map 1`

In early July, visitors typically descend upon New Orleans for the annual **Essence Music Festival,** a celebration of African American music and culture. At about the same time, Go 4th on the River beckons locals and tourists alike to celebrate not only America's independence but also the New Orleans riverfront. Besides promoting attractions alongside the Mississippi River, such as the Jax Brewery and Audubon Aquarium of the Americas, this all-day extravaganza features live music at Washington Artillery Park and Spanish Plaza, cruises on two vintage paddlewheel riverboats, and one of the largest fireworks displays in the country.

NEW ORLEANS BURLESQUE FESTIVAL

Various locations, 504/975-7425,
www.neworleansburlesquefest.com
COST: Varies

In a city known as the birthplace of jazz, where a legal red-light district once thrived, and which once had the largest concentration of burlesque clubs in the country, it's no surprise that burlesque shows are once again a popular form of entertainment. My husband and I have often attended titillating performances in One Eyed Jacks and Irvin Mayfield's Jazz Playhouse. But in mid-September, an entire three-day event dedicated to this sexy, glamorous, and comedic art descends on the city. Founded in 2009, the annual New Orleans Burlesque Festival features parties and performances in various locations, plus the main event—a competition in which the world's finest burlesque dancers vie for the Queen of Burlesque title. Indeed, a sight worth seeing.

SATCHMO SUMMERFEST

Old U.S. Mint, 400 Esplanade Ave., 504/522-5730 or 800/673-5725, www.fqfi.org/satchmosummerfest
COST: Free, though food and seminar costs apply

New Orleans celebrates the legacy of one of its most famous sons in early August with Satchmo SummerFest, a popular, four-day event that's organized by the same folks behind the equally popular French Quarter Festival. This mostly free festival, which mainly takes place on the well-manicured grounds of the Old U.S. Mint, includes live music by brass, swing, and early jazz bands, plus free dance lessons and an assortment of local cuisine. At other locations throughout the Quarter, you can experience seminars and exhibits about Louis "Satchmo" Armstrong and his era. During the festival, make time for the special jazz Mass at the St. Augustine Church, followed by a traditional second-line parade.

SOUTHERN DECADENCE

Various locations, www.southerndecadence.com
COST: Varies

Every Labor Day weekend, the French Quarter and the Faubourg Marigny are flooded with eager participants and onlookers of Southern Decadence, an annual Mardi Gras–like festival that's been celebrating the city's gay lifestyle, music, and culture since 1972. Held at various gay-friendly venues, from Rawhide 2010 to Bourbon Pub & Parade, the six-day event includes dance and pool parties, beefcake contests, singles' mixers, drag shows, and a leather-gear block party. It's one of the wildest and most popular gay-and-lesbian celebrations in the country.

TALES OF THE COCKTAIL

Various locations, 504/948-0511,
www.talesofthecocktail.com
COST: Varies

Given that the Big Easy is known as a late-night party town, where imbibing spirits is seemingly a way of life, it's only apt that it would be home to the annual Tales of the Cocktail. Started in 2003 and usually occurring in late July, this five-day event lures a slew of mixologists, authors, bartenders, chefs, and cocktail enthusiasts with its impressive lineup

ARTS AND LEISURE

of seminars, dinners, competitions, and tasting rooms. Activities take place in a variety of locations, from the French Quarter's historic Hotel Monteleone to the Harrah's casino in the CBD.

VIEUX TO DO

French Market and Old U.S. Mint

COST: Free, though food costs apply

On the second weekend of June, residents and visitors typically honor the culture of southern Louisiana with three free festivals that collectively make up the Vieux To Do. The historic French Market is home to the **Creole Tomato Festival** (504/522-2621, www.frenchmarket.org); for more than two decades, the festival has celebrated one of the state's most popular fruits with a farmer's market, a parade, food booths, and cooking demonstrations. At the Old U.S. Mint, you can enjoy live regional music at the **Louisiana Cajun-Zydeco Festival** (504/558-6100, www.jazzandheritage.org/cajun-zydeco) and taste an array of local delicacies at the **Louisiana Seafood Festival** (504/957-7241, www.louisianaseafoodfestival.org), which also features cooking demonstrations, book signings, and an arts-and-crafts market.

FALL

CRESCENT CITY BLUES AND BBQ FESTIVAL

Lafayette Square, 540 St. Charles Ave., 504/558-6100, www.jazzandheritage.org/blues-fest

COST: Free, though food costs apply

Map 3

The New Orleans Jazz & Heritage Festival and Foundation might be known for its signature springtime event at the Fair Grounds, but that's certainly not all it does. Since 2006, the aptly named Crescent City Blues and BBQ Festival brings together two of my favorite things: Southern-style soul and blues music and delicious, finger-lickin' barbecue. You'll often find me in the CBD's picturesque Lafayette Square for this three-day, mid-October event, where I've been known to scarf down a pulled-pork sandwich while grooving to the

likes of Tab Benoit, Marcia Ball, and Kenny Wayne Shepherd. This often crowded event features two stages, roughly a dozen food vendors, a regional crafts fair, an Abita-sponsored sports bar, secured bike parking, and, in nearby Gallier Hall, an oral history stage that presents live, free-to-attend interviews of participating musicians.

GRETNA HERITAGE FESTIVAL

Downtown Gretna, 504/361-7748 or 888/447-3862, www.gretnafest.com

COST: $15 pp, free under 13

Map 6

In early October, thousands of revelers cross the Mississippi for Gretna's Heritage Festival, a three-day event presenting live performances by local and international jazz, country, rock, blues, soul, Latino, and Cajun musicians on eight different stages. Previous performers have included Cowboy Mouth, Dash Rip Rock, Tracy Lawrence, Sara Evans, the Iguanas, and Amanda Shaw & the Cute Guys. In addition to events at the downtown German Heritage Center, this family-friendly festival features a German beer garden, an Italian village, carnival-style rides and games, an arts-and-crafts show, and a multiethnic food court. Tickets are usually cheaper online; if you plan to stay the whole weekend, consider purchasing the $40 weekend pass.

LOUISIANA SWAMP FESTIVAL

Audubon Zoo, 6500 Magazine St., 504/581-4629 or 800/774-7394, www.auduboninstitute.org

COST: $16 adult, $13 senior and student, $11 child 2-12, child under 2 free

Map 4

In early November, shortly after the annual Boo at the Zoo has ended for the season, the Audubon Zoo hosts the family-friendly Louisiana Swamp Festival, a great excuse to visit this historic zoological park (especially since the weather is usually pleasant and more appealing to the animals). Even better, the two-day festival is included with the zoo's general admission cost, so you won't pay any extra for the event. Swamp Fest celebrates the state's Cajun culture and heritage with handmade arts

HALLOWEEN IN THE CRESCENT CITY

October has always been my favorite month in New Orleans – it's usually cool, crisp, inviting, and just a little bit eerie. Historians and travel experts regularly cite the French Quarter as one of the most haunted places in America – and whether or not you believe in the spirit world, a sense of this city's infamous past is palpable as you stroll along the lamp-lit streets at night. Of course, the Quarter isn't the only spooky aspect of New Orleans. The surrounding moss-covered swamps have a decidedly creepy vibe, while Garden District mansions and River Road plantations offer their own ghostly encounters.

Not surprisingly, New Orleans is a wildly popular place for All Hallows' Eve. People venture here to visit the many voodoo shops, experience aboveground cemeteries, take a haunted walking tour of the French Quarter, and mingle with hordes of costumed revelers along Bourbon and Frenchmen Streets. In addition, locals and visitors alike flock to seasonal haunted houses like the **Mortuary Haunted House** (www.themortuary.net), set inside a supposedly haunted former mortuary, and the **House of Shock Horror Show** (www. houseofshock.com), which features pyrotechnics and bizarre human stunts.

Of course, many horror aficionados also appreciate the city's longtime vampire connection. The principal setting for Anne Rice's famous novel *Interview with the Vampire*, New Orleans is also home to two annual vampire balls: the **New Orleans Vampire Ball,** sponsored by Anne Rice's Vampire Lestat Fan Club (www.arvlfc.com), and the **Endless Night Vampire Ball** (www.endlessnight.com). Vampire tours, which are available through **Haunted History Tours** (www.hauntedhisto-

rytours.com) and **Spirit Tours New Orleans** (www.neworleanstours.net), are also a popular way to spend Halloween here.

In a town known for gay-friendly bashes like Mardi Gras and Southern Decadence, it surely comes as no surprise that there's also a gay-friendly Halloween celebration. Simply known as **Halloween in New Orleans** (www.gayhalloween.com), this weekend-long bash has evolved from a small gathering in 1984 into one of the biggest gay-and-lesbian parties in the country. If you're looking for well-dressed drag queens this is definitely the time to visit the Big Easy.

For those with kids, New Orleans also hosts family-friendly events like Audubon Zoo's **Boo at the Zoo** (www.auduboninstitute.org/boo-zoo), which usually occurs during the last two weekends of October and features trick-or-treat fun, games and entertainment, a ghost train, and a haunted house. On Halloween itself, Molly's at the Market always presents **Molly's Halloween Parade** (www.mollysatthemarket.net/halloween), a spirited procession through the French Quarter. New Orleans is predominantly a Catholic city, which means that **All Saints' Day** (Nov. 1) and **All Souls' Day** (Nov. 2) are fairly important holidays – a time when many residents make a point of visiting their loved ones at cemeteries throughout the city. Simultaneously, lots of locals celebrate the Mexican holiday of **Día de los Muertos** by dressing all in black, painting skulls on their faces, and congregating in front of the St. Louis Cathedral – truly a sight to behold.

No matter how you choose to celebrate Halloween, it's sure to be memorable in the Crescent City.

and crafts, not to mention special feedings and hands-on encounters with Louisiana swamp animals. In addition, you can listen to live Cajun and zydeco music, take a Cajun dance lesson, and nosh on the food of Louisiana's Cajun Country, from grilled alligator sausage to cochon du lait po-boys.

NEW ORLEANS FILM FESTIVAL

Various locations, 504/309-6633,
www.neworleansfilmsociety.org
COST: Varies

Established in 1989, the nonprofit New Orleans Film Society (NOFS) presents several annual events favored by local cinephiles. At Uptown's Prytania Theatre, NOFS presents **Film-O-Rama,** a weeklong, mid-May showcase of foreign and independent films—including recent flicks like *13 Assassins* and *Hobo with a Shotgun*—as well as the **French Film Festival** in mid-July. At the Contemporary Arts Center (CAC), NOFS hosts the free **New Orleans International Children's Film Festival** in mid-September. The pinnacle of NOFS programming is the New Orleans Film Festival (NOFF), a relatively popular mid-October event that has honored independent cinema for more than two decades. In fact, one of NOFF's earliest winners was *Hated* (1994), a well-received documentary by first-time director Todd Phillips, who has since directed such comedic hits as *Old School* (2003) and *The Hangover* (2009). The weeklong event usually takes place in multiple venues throughout the city, including the Prytania and the CAC.

OAK STREET PO-BOY FESTIVAL

Oak St. and S. Carrollton Ave., www.poboyfest.com
COST: Free, though food costs apply
Map 4

Though relatively new on the Big Easy's foodie scene, the Oak Street Po-Boy Festival (formerly the New Orleans Po-Boy Preservation Festival) has quickly become a much-anticipated event every fall. For one day in late November, residents and out-of-towners alike converge at the intersection of Oak Street and South Carrollton Avenue in Uptown's Riverbend area for this mouthwatering event. Besides listening to a slew of live music, attendees can peruse arts and crafts, learn about the history of the po-boy, and, of course, sample a variety of local cuisine from more than 40 restaurants. While here, you'll have the chance to sample an assortment of po-boys, including my personal favorite, a shrimp rémoulade po-boy, which is especially tasty if served with fried green tomatoes.

VOODOO MUSIC EXPERIENCE

City Park, 1 Palm Dr., www.thevoodooexperience.com
COST: $175-600 pp for weekend, child under 11 free
Map 5

Halloween weekend is usually a busy time of year in New Orleans. Besides vampire balls, impromptu parades, and haunted walking tours, the city has long been host to the three-day Voodoo Music Experience, a boisterous City Park event that features both art installations as well as live musical performances. Past performers have dramatically ranged from Soundgarden and Snoop Dogg to Beausoleil and Dr. John. Advance tickets cost $60 per day or $150 for the weekend; for $500, you can opt for the ultimate experience, which includes a three-day parking pass, food and drink specials, full bar services, and access to upgraded restrooms and a reserved viewing area, among other amenities. Though tickets might be available on-site, be prepared for sold-out crowds. For ticketing questions, contact **Elevate** (877/569-7767, www.elevate.com).

WINTER

ALLSTATE SUGAR BOWL

Mercedes-Benz Superdome, 1500 Sugar Bowl Dr.,
504/828-2440, www.allstatesugarbowl.com
COST: Varies
Map 3

Besides being home to the New Orleans Saints, the Louisiana Superdome is also the site of one of the most beloved college football games, the Allstate Sugar Bowl. Typically, it's played in early January between two of the nation's top

CHRISTMAS NEW ORLEANS STYLE

Christmastime is simply huge in New Orleans, celebrated with great fanfare as befits a city that loves to have fun and clings dearly to long-held traditions. Known as "Christmas New Orleans Style" (www.christmasneworleans.com), our celebration entails a variety of events and activities throughout the month of December. Besides City Park's dazzling **Celebration in the Oaks,** there are jazz, gospel, and choral concerts held at **St. Louis Cathedral** and a variety of clubs, including **Preservation Hall. Jackson Square** plays host to public Christmas caroling, usually a free event that occurs on the Sunday prior to Christmas. Historic buildings throughout the French Quarter and Garden District, not to mention plantations along the Great River Road, are gussied up with Christmas lights and decorations. Revelers can also enjoy a variety of seasonal walking tours, including the **Candlelight Tour of Historic Homes and Landmarks,** held in mid-December and often including such attractions as the Old Ursuline Convent, the 1850 House, the Gallier House, and the Historic New Orleans Collection.

Of course, beyond the moderate weather, various Hanukkah celebrations, and New Year's Eve fireworks extravaganza, December is also an excellent time for foodies. After all, this is the season of *réveillon,* an ancient Creole and Catholic celebratory feast dating to the 1830s. Although it was originally held on Christmas and New Year's Eve, *réveillon* now happens throughout the month of December and is celebrated by everyone, regardless of religious affiliation.

Still, for many people, the most special *réveillon* dinners are held on Christmas or New Year's Eve. The Christmas meal, typically the more restrained of the two eves, was traditionally held after midnight Mass at St. Louis Cathedral. Families would return home and spend time together sharing a fairly austere meal of egg dishes, sweetbreads, and a rum cake. The New Year's Eve feast consists of elaborate desserts, plenty of whiskey and wine, and lots of laughing, singing, and dancing.

Dozens of restaurants in New Orleans offer special *réveillon* menus in December. These are prix-fixe menus, usually four or five courses, and many establishments offer *réveillon* on Christmas Eve, Christmas Day, New Year's Eve, and New Year's Day, although you should reserve well ahead for these dates. Favorite venues for this celebration include **Galatoire's, Antoine's Restaurant, Commander's Palace, Tujague's, the Rib Room, Muriel's Jackson Square,** and the **Gumbo Shop.**

At traditional Tujague's, the choices are limited and the menu straightforward: shrimp rémoulade, a soup of the day, beef brisket with Creole sauce, braised lamb shanks in a Creole stew, bread pudding, and chicory-laced coffee. More cutting-edge places around town have fancier and more unusual offerings.

collegiate teams. Until recent format changes, the Sugar Bowl also occasionally hosted college football's BCS National Championship Game—including, in 2004, when the LSU Tigers defeated the Oklahoma Sooners. In addition to the Sugar Bowl, there's usually an Allstate Fan Fest, a free music event that takes place in the parking lot beside Jax Brewery; past performers have included Blues Traveler, the Gin Blossoms, the Neville Brothers, and Trombone Shorty. It's nearly impossible to find a hotel room in New Orleans when this event comes to town, so plan well ahead if you wish to attend.

CELEBRATION IN THE OAKS

City Park, 1 Palm Dr., www.celebrationintheoaks.com
COST: $7 pp, free under 3
Map 5

From late November through the end of December, City Park comes alive for the Celebration in the Oaks, a fabulous holiday light show that draws more than a 120,000 visitors annually. Sights include a life-size Nativity scene, a Dripping Snow Tree, a lighted tableau inspired by the beloved children's tale *Cajun Night Before Christmas,* a 20-foot-tall poinsettia Christmas tree in the botanical

ARTS AND LEISURE

THE HISTORY OF FAT TUESDAY

It's appropriate that New Orleans should have the most famous Mardi Gras – or Carnival – celebration in the United States. After all, it was on Mardi Gras (French for "Fat Tuesday") of 1699 that explorer Pierre Le Moyne, Sieur d'Iberville, first encamped here along the Mississippi River. Well, to be exact, Le Moyne chose a spot about 60 miles downriver from today's New Orleans, but his visit marked the city's beginning.

Records suggest that the city's early French inhabitants began holding parties and dances coinciding with Fat Tuesday as early as the 1720s; such pre-Lenten festivities continued until the late 1700s, when New Orleans fell under Spanish rule. Even after New Orleans became part of the United States, street masking wasn't legalized again until 1827. In fact, the first documented Mardi Gras parade was held in 1837, though the krewes (private clubs that sponsor parades and gala balls) were not formed until 1857, when the krewe of **Comus** illuminated the city with its fiery torches. Comus started the traditions of having secret Carnival societies named after mythological characters, presenting thematic pageant-style parades – with dancers and entertainers frolicking alongside the floats and marchers – and holding post-parade balls.

Amid the kaleidoscopic costumes and floats, you'll see three principal colors while experiencing Mardi Gras: purple, green, and gold. These hues represent justice, faith, and power, respectively, and were introduced to Mardi Gras in 1872 by the first parade of **Rex,** which also gave the event an official anthem, "If Ever I Cease to Love," from a burlesque play of that period.

Lafayette crowned its first king in 1897 and has been throwing the state's biggest Mardi Gras parades and balls outside New Orleans ever since. Mobile, Alabama – about a three-hour drive east of New Orleans – holds arguably the best Mardi Gras celebration in the country outside Louisiana. This genial city is recognized as the first in the nation to hold a Mardi Gras celebration, back in 1703. The Mobile event is, like many Mardi Gras celebrations held outside New Orleans, decidedly family-oriented.

One of the most notable 20th-century developments for New Orleans's Mardi Gras was the formation of the **Zulu** krewe in 1909. Its African American members joined together to make fun of the exclusive Rex krewe; its king, for instance, "ruled" with a scepter made of a banana stalk and a crown fashioned from a can of lard. Zulu continues to be one of the most-watched parades of Mardi Gras.

The celebration has seen both low and high points throughout the past century. It was canceled for a couple of years during World War I and again for four years during World War II. It enjoyed somewhat limited success during the Depression. By the 1950s, however, Mardi Gras was back in full swing, beginning to enjoy international acclaim, expanding to the suburbs beyond New Orleans, and utilizing tractors in lieu of mules to pull the floats. It was in the late 1960s that the krewe of **Bacchus** altered tradition by using gigantic floats in its parade, inviting a Hollywood celebrity to serve as its king (Danny Kaye was the first, in 1969), and replacing its private ball with a dinner dance to which both members and outsiders were invited via ticket purchase.

Since that time, Mardi Gras has grown tremendously. Many new krewes and parades have come (and quite a few have gone) since the 1970s, and many more events and parties have opened to the public. In 1991, the New Orleans City Council passed an antidiscrimination ordinance that made it illegal for parading krewes to maintain a private membership. A few of the long-running krewes protested by canceling their parades, but Rex complied and, for the first time, opened its membership to persons of all colors. The number of visitors, foreign and domestic, who descend upon New Orleans during Mardi Gras has skyrocketed, and although attendance was down in 2006, the first Mardi Gras following Hurricane Katrina, the event has since become hugely popular and highly successful once again. Indeed, there's no reason to think that this vibrant, festive event won't continue to delight thousands of locals and visitors for years to come.

garden, the fancifully illumined Storyland and Carousel Gardens, and a gallery of trees decorated by local schools and community groups. You can drive through the park, walk the two-mile route, or see it via a quaint train ride. This magical trip through the largest live-oak forest in the world is not to be missed during the holidays. Be sure to take advantage of the live music, inexpensive refreshments, and synthetic ice-skating rink ($5 pp).

MARDI GRAS

Various locations, www.mardigrasday.com
COST: Free

If you're a fan of colorful, exciting festivals, there is no better time to visit New Orleans than during Mardi Gras season, which usually falls in February and lasts the two to three weeks prior to Lent (from Epiphany to Ash Wednesday). Festivities include everything from colorful street masks and costumes to pageant-style parades with street dancers and marchers, to gala balls and events. In New Orleans, some of the most worthwhile parades include the krewes of Endymion, Bacchus, Orpheus, Zulu, and Rex; dog lovers might appreciate the Mystic Krewe of Barkus in the French Quarter.

Unfortunately, Mardi Gras can also include public nudity and drunkenness, horrendous crowds, and crime. The wild goings-on during Mardi Gras in the French Quarter have given the overall event a reputation for debauchery; if you're seeking that kind of experience, the Quarter on Fat Tuesday will not let you down. However, Mardi Gras elsewhere in the city—notably in Uptown along the St. Charles Avenue parade route or in Metairie along Veterans Memorial Boulevard—is much more family-oriented and tends to be dominated by locals, or at least by Louisianians. Just about every community in the state throws memorable Mardi Gras parades, parties, and other events leading up to the big day, and these are equally wholesome, catering to locals and families.

Masked riders toss beads from a colorful Mardi Gras float.

ARTS AND LEISURE

ST. JOSEPH'S DAY

Various locations,
www.mardigrasneworleans.com/supersunday.html
COST: Free

Introduced to New Orleans during the 19th century by its many Sicilian immigrants, St. Joseph's Day is still celebrated with great ardor in the city's Italian American community. The observance of this feast on March 19 traces back to the Middle Ages, when people built altars to St. Joseph, who they believed had answered their prayers and delivered them from famine. Modern participants continue to celebrate by constructing elaborate and riotously colorful altars in their homes and churches. Besides a public parade in the French Quarter, smaller celebrations take place in private homes; signs welcome friends and strangers alike to view family altars and enjoy cakes, breads, and other foods. Oddly enough, the Italian holiday has also become significant for the city's Mardi Gras Indians, an African American troupe of Carnival revelers who usually host a vibrant parade on Super Sunday, the Sunday following St. Joseph's Day.

ST. PATRICK'S DAY PARADE

Various locations
COST: Free

Beyond the city's obvious connection to Creole and Cajun cultures, New Orleans also has a large contingent of Irish Americans. St. Patrick's Day is a significant holiday here, and Irish establishments throughout the city—including my favorite, Kerry Irish Pub in the French Quarter—hold lively parties on St. Paddy's Day (traditionally March 17). Molly's at the Market hosts its own music-filled St. Patrick's Day Parade within a week of the actual holiday, but the city's biggest annual parade by far usually rolls down Magazine Street and St. Charles Avenue, with large Mardi Gras–style floats, oodles of marchers, and plenty of green beads and doubloons. No matter which parade you choose to attend, wear something green or else you'll risk many a stranger's pinch!

Recreation

PARKS AND PLAZAS

◖ AUDUBON PARK

St. Charles Ave. and Walnut St., 504/861-2537,
www.auduboninstitute.org
HOURS: Daily 5 A.M.–10 P.M.
COST: Free
Map 4

One of New Orleanians' favorite places for strolling is verdant Audubon Park, a 340-acre property that extends from St. Charles Avenue to the Mississippi River. Besides encompassing Audubon Zoo, this beloved park features a pleasant lagoon, moss-draped live oak trees, and lush lawns with picnic areas. Named after ornithologist John James Audubon, who once lived in southern Louisiana, Audubon Park also offers a slew of athletic facilities, including several tennis courts and soccer fields, three playgrounds, a golf course, a swimming pool, and a paved 1.8-mile path ideal for walking,

jogging, and in-line skating. In addition, you can take horseback-riding lessons at **Cascade Stables** or view a variety of egrets, herons, and cormorants on **Ochsner Island,** which sits within the park's lagoon and is more commonly known as Bird Island.

BARATARIA PRESERVE

6588 Barataria Blvd., Marrero, 504/689-3690,
www.nps.gov/jela
HOURS: Daily 9 A.M.–5 P.M.
COST: Free
Map 6

The 23,000-acre Barataria Preserve, a unit of Jean Lafitte National Historical Park and Preserve, is a popular bird-watching spot among both locals and visitors. Situated just south of the city, on the West Bank of the Mississippi River, this enormous preserve comprises bayous, swamps, marshes, forests, and roughly nine miles of hiking trails. Don't miss the **Bayou Coquille Trail,** a half-mile, pavement-and-boardwalk path that's known for myriad sightings of snakes, alligators, nutrias, and some of the more than 300 bird species that dwell here. (Just be advised that pets, even leashed ones, are not allowed on the trails.) The park, which is closed on Christmas Day and Mardi Gras, is also favored among canoeists and kayakers.

BAYOU SAUVAGE NATIONAL WILDLIFE REFUGE

East of New Orleans via I-10, 985/882-2000, www.fws.gov/bayousauvage
HOURS: Daily sunrise–sunset
COST: Free
Map 6

Of the eight national wildlife refuges in southeastern Louisiana, Bayou Sauvage is by far the closest to New Orleans. Established in 1990 and situated between Lake Pontchartrain and Lake Borgne, this 24,000-acre preserve is actually America's largest urban national wildlife refuge. Hikers, anglers, canoeists, and photographers appreciate the varied habitats

here, which include freshwater and brackish marshes, canals, lagoons, bayous, and coastal hardwood forests. Bird-watchers and wildlife enthusiasts also favor this region, as it's home to more than 340 bird species, plus turtles, alligators, otters, nutrias, feral hogs, raccoons, and white-tailed deer. While there's no on-site visitors center, you'll find interpretive boardwalks and kiosks as well as restrooms and trailheads along U.S. 90. From New Orleans, take I-10 east to I-510, head south on I-510 for two miles, turn left on U.S. 90, and continue for four miles to the refuge.

BAYOU SEGNETTE STATE PARK

7777 Westbank Expwy., Westwego, 504/736-7140 or 888/677-2296, www.crt.state.la.us
HOURS: Sun.-Thurs. 7 A.M.-9 P.M., Fri.-Sat. 7 A.M.-10 P.M.
COST: $1 pp, free over 62 and under 4
Map 6

Though you won't find any state parks within New Orleans's city limits, Bayou Segnette is only a 20-minute drive from the French Quarter. Situated near the West Bank community of Westwego, this large, family-friendly

© DANIEL MARTONE

Joggers enjoy the exercise path that snakes through City Park.

ARTS AND LEISURE

park features playgrounds, picnic areas, a seasonal wave pool ($10 adult, $8 child), and a boat launch that makes it easy for boaters and anglers to explore the area's peaceful waterways, which are brimming with trout, redfish, bass, perch, and catfish. Other popular activities here include hiking, canoeing, and camping (877/226-7652 for reservations, $18–26 nightly).

CITY PARK

1 Palm Dr., 504/482-4888,
www.neworleanscitypark.com
HOURS: 24 hours daily, though facility hours vary seasonally
COST: Free, though activity fees apply
Map 5

Encompassing 1,300 acres of lawns, lagoons, and moss-covered oak trees, City Park has long been a preferred spot for rest and recreation, especially for the nearby communities of Mid-City, Lakeview, and Gentilly. No matter where I lived as a child (even the year I called Slidell home), City Park was always one of my favorite places in New Orleans. My mother and I spent numerous afternoons here, feeding the ducks, strolling across picturesque bridges, and riding our bikes along the winding roads. Outdoor enthusiasts can take advantage of the on-site golf course; eight miles of lagoons ideal for fishing, canoeing, and pedal-boating; boat rentals ($12 per half hour) and bike rentals ($8–10 hourly, $25–30 daily); a tennis center (504/483-9383, $10–13 hourly); a dog park; and the 13-acre **Equest Farm** (504/483-9398, www.equestfarm.com), which offers horseback-riding lessons. The park also features two stadiums: the **Pan American Stadium,** home to the New Orleans Jesters soccer team (www.nolajesters.com), and the **Tad Gormley Stadium,** often a concert venue.

COLISEUM SQUARE

Coliseum St. and Race St., www.coliseumsquare.org
HOURS: Daily 24 hours
COST: Free
Map 4

Bordered by Coliseum, Race, and Camp Streets, this oddly shaped park offers residents in the Lower Garden District a lush, peaceful place to read, relax, picnic, or walk a dog or two. Filled with shady oak trees, inviting benches, and well-manicured lawns, the park is punctuated by a lovely fountain, an ideal, if popular, spot to hang out with friends and neighbors. Unfortunately, there are no public bathrooms here.

LAFAYETTE SQUARE

St. Charles Ave. and Lafayette St.,
www.lafayette-square.org
HOURS: Daily 24 hours
COST: Free
Map 3

South of Poydras Street lies the attractive Lafayette Square, which was laid out in the late 18th century as the American Quarter's version of the Place d'Armes (now Jackson Square). Bound by St. Charles Avenue, Camp Street, and North and South Maestri Places, it was originally called Place Gravier but was rechristened in honor of the Marquis de Lafayette, who visited the city in 1825. With its ample park-bench seating, the shaded, landscaped park—one of the CBD's few patches of greenery—continues to be a pleasant place to relax, read a newspaper, or listen to live music. In fact, you can catch free concerts by some of the city's top bands and musicians every Wednesday at 5 P.M., from late March to mid-June. Known as the **YLC Wednesday at the Square** (504/585-1500, www.wednesdayatthesquare.com), this 12-week concert series has featured the likes of Tab Benoit, Marcia Ball, Kermit Ruffins, and the Iguanas. Local bars and restaurants sell food and drinks to benefit the Young Leadership Council. You can also purchase the work of local artisans in the Artist Village.

LAFRENIERE PARK

3000 Downs Blvd., Metairie, 504/838-4389,
www.lafrenierepark.org
HOURS: Daily 5 A.M.–9:45 P.M.
COST: Free
Map 6

Need to kill a little time before heading to the airport? Pay a quick visit to Lafreniere Park, a lush, 155-acre green space accessible via I-10. Encompassing various lawns, fountains,

CONGO SQUARE

Between the aftermath of Hurricane Katrina and the popularity of HBO's acclaimed series *Treme*, a national spotlight has been cast on the Faubourg Tremé, the country's oldest African American neighborhood and an area celebrated for its musical contributions to New Orleans. Within the Tremé lies Louis Armstrong Park, named after one of the city's most famous musicians and featuring an open space historically known as Congo Square. It was here during the French and Spanish colonial era of the 1700s that slaves gathered on Sunday to sing, dance, and play music together.

Following the Louisiana Purchase, these weekly gatherings grew in size and influence, luring visitors from around the country as well as African and Creole slaves. Residents gathered to observe African-style dancing, marveling at the hundreds of costumed women and half-dressed men that moved to the rhythms of varied musical instruments, from African drums to European violins to American-style banjos.

As harsh American slavery practices usurped the more lenient French colonial style, the gatherings declined, stopping well before the American Civil War. By the late 1800s, the square once again became a famous musical venue, featuring a series of Creole brass band concerts, and was renamed Beauregard Square in honor of Confederate General P. G. T. Beauregard. In the 1920s, part of the Tremé community behind Beauregard Square was displaced to make way for the New Orleans Municipal Auditorium. In the 1960s, a controversial urban renewal project commandeered even more land, which eventually became Louis Armstrong Park.

In 1970, the city held the first New Orleans Jazz & Heritage Festival at Beauregard Square. Attendees witnessed performances by luminaries like Mahalia Jackson, Duke Ellington, Pete Fountain, Al Hirt, Clifton Chenier, Fats Domino, the Meters, and the Preservation Hall Band. The annual festival's growth ultimately forced a move to its present location in Mid-City, but Beauregard Square continues to be a significant gathering place in the community, playing host to music festivals, brass band parades, drum circles, and protest marches. The legacy of this historic space has influenced numerous generations of New Orleans musicians, including Johnny Wiggs, Donald Harrison, and Wynton Marsalis, all of whom have written African-themed jazz music inspired by the former slave gatherings at Congo Square. Fittingly, the New Orleans City Council officially voted in 2011 to restore the traditional Congo Square moniker to this legendary part of the Tremé.

gardens, marshes, picnic areas, and a lovely lagoon, Metairie's largest park also offers soccer and softball fields, a two-mile jogging and walking path, a carousel, a dog park, and a Frisbee golf course. Boating and fishing are popular diversions here, too. In addition, Lafreniere Park is often the site of tournaments, parish celebrations, and fireworks displays.

LOUIS ARMSTRONG PARK

835 N. Rampart St., 504/658-3200
HOURS: Daily sunrise–sunset
COST: Free
`Map 5`

Though created by two controversial "land grabs" of the Faubourg Tremé (one in the 1920s and another in the 1960s), Louis Armstrong Park is currently one of the lovelier urban parks in New Orleans. Unfortunately, it's also one of the more dangerous ones, so it's best not to wander through this gated park alone. Named after the famous New Orleans–born jazz trumpeter and singer, Louis Armstrong Park now comprises pleasant lagoons and grassy areas, historic **Congo Square**, which is designated by a historical marker, and the recently renovated **Mahalia Jackson Theater for the Performing Arts.**

PIAZZA D'ITALIA
Lafayette and Commerce Sts.
HOURS: Daily 24 hours
COST: Free
Map 3

Not far from the American Italian Cultural Center, you'll encounter the picturesque Piazza d'Italia, which is dedicated to the city's Italian American community and its indelible influence on New Orleans. Designed in 1978 by the renowned, postmodernist architect Charles Moore and partially restored in 2004, the plaza now serves as a gathering place for residents, a relaxing spot for a lunch break, and site of St. Joseph's Day celebrations.

SPANISH PLAZA
1 Poydras St.
HOURS: Daily 24 hours
COST: Free
Map 3

Between the Audubon Aquarium of the Americas and the Riverwalk Marketplace is this pleasant square, an ideal spot to gaze at the bustling Mississippi. Originally known as Eads Plaza—in honor of the engineer who enhanced the navigability of the river's mouth—the square was rededicated by Spain in 1976 to commemorate its influence on the Crescent City's history and to serve as an ongoing promise of fraternity. As a symbolic reminder, the seals of Spanish provinces encircle the central fountain. Today, Spanish Plaza is a common gathering place for residents and tourists alike, as well as the site of free public concerts throughout the year.

ST. BERNARD STATE PARK
501 St. Bernard Pkwy., Braithwaite, 504/682-2101, www.crt.state.la.us
HOURS: Sun.-Thurs. 7 A.M.-9 P.M., Fri.-Sat. 7 A.M.-10 P.M.
COST: Free
Map 6

If you have a sudden urge to leave the city for a while, head south on the St. Bernard Highway (LA-46) through the towns of Arabi, Chalmette, Meraux, Violet, and Poydras to this recreational oasis beside the Mississippi River. The woodlands, wetlands, and artificial lagoons at this family-friendly park also offer picnic tables, barbecue grills, public restrooms, a seasonal swimming pool ($4 pp daily), and a nearby boat launch. In addition, St. Bernard State Park serves as an affordable home base for families hoping to explore New Orleans without spending a fortune on accommodations; after all, the park offers 51 inexpensive campsites (877/226-7652 for reservations, $16–20 nightly) with partial hookups.

WASHINGTON SQUARE PARK
700 Elysian Fields Ave., 504/658-3200
HOURS: Daily sunrise-sunset
COST: Free
Map 2

Just a few steps from the Marigny's world-famous blues and jazz clubs lies this small recreational area, sandwiched between Royal Street, Elysian Fields Avenue, Dauphine Street, and Frenchmen Street. Originally known as Founders Park, it was eventually renamed to commemorate the Washington 141st Artillery regiment, one of the country's oldest military units. Featuring benches, grassy areas, and a playground, it's popular among local musicians, nearby residents, and, yes, homeless individuals. While it's generally a safe place to sunbathe, have a picnic, play Frisbee, or relax under an oak tree during the day, the surrounding area can be a little sketchy at night, so perhaps it's a good thing that the park is closed after dark. Technically, alcohol, pets, and bikes aren't allowed in Washington Square Park, but not surprisingly, many visitors pay these rules little mind.

BIKING
THE AMERICAN BICYCLE RENTAL COMPANY
317 Burgundy St., 866/293-4037, www.amebrc.com
HOURS: Mon.-Fri. 10 A.M.-5 P.M., Sat.-Sun. 10 A.M.-6 P.M.
COST: $10-15 hourly, $35-55 daily
Map 1

With narrow streets, a relatively high amount of traffic, and concerns about theft, New Orleans is not an ideal city for biking, but you'll still spy quite a few cyclists in places like the Marigny and City Park. (It helps that most of southern Louisiana comprises flat, scenic biking terrain.) If you'd like to tour the city at your own pace, head to this helpful French Quarter shop, which rents cruisers and city tandem bikes by the hour, half day, and full day. Those in town a bit longer can even keep them for three days ($80–150) or a five-day period ($125–205). All rentals include free locks, helmets, and maps, plus baskets for female riders and rear racks for male cyclists.

◖ BICYCLE MICHAEL'S

622 Frenchmen St., 504/945-9505,
www.bicyclemichaels.com
HOURS: Mon.-Tues. and Thurs.-Sat. 10 A.M.-7 P.M., Sun. 10 A.M.-5 P.M.
COST: $35-110 daily, $140-320 weekly
`Map 2`

Amid the live music clubs of Frenchmen Street stands this laid-back, full-service bike store, which handles sales, provides rentals, and even offers repair services. Choose among city hybrids, mountain bikes, off-road bikes, and tandems. Then, depending on how long you keep the rental (from a half day to a full, seven-day week), you can explore the Faubourg Marigny, the nearby French Quarter, City Park, the Lake Pontchartrain shoreline, and other key areas in this relatively compact city. Although locks, biking advice, and local tips are free, there are nominal costs for helmets ($5 daily), baskets ($5), and maps ($6–8).

BIG EASY BIKE TOURS

504/377-0973, www.bigeasybiketours.com
HOURS: Daily 8-11 A.M., 1:30-4:30 P.M., and 5-8 P.M.
COST: $49 pp

While biking can be a great way to explore New Orleans, not everyone is eager to do it alone. If you'd prefer a guided excursion, consider a company like Big Easy Bike Tours, which offers three separate routes. Although all of these narrated, customizable tours begin in the historic French Quarter, passing such landmarks as Jackson Square and the French Market, they each head in a different direction:

into the American Sector and Garden District, up the Creole-influenced Esplanade Avenue, or on a 20-mile course that includes places like the Tremé, City Park, and Lake Pontchartrain.

CONFEDERACY OF CRUISERS

504/400-5468, www.confederacyofcruisers.com
HOURS: Varies daily
COST: $45 pp

More intimate than a bus excursion yet faster than a walking tour, guided bike trips can be an excellent way to experience this laid-back city, and if you'd prefer to see less-traveled neighborhoods, then Confederacy of Cruisers is the ideal operator. Using comfortable, easy-to-ride cruising bikes, these slow-paced, three-hour, customizable tours cover areas like the Faubourg Marigny, Faubourg Tremé, and Bywater—places not seen by most tourists. Along the way, you'll learn about the unique history, architecture, and culture of New Orleans.

CRESCENT CITY CYCLISTS

888/901-9581, www.crescentcitycyclists.org
HOURS: Vary

Whether you're a resident or a frequent visitor, you might appreciate the chance to bike around the city in a safe group atmosphere. If so, consider joining the Crescent City Cyclists, the oldest bike club in the greater New Orleans area. Besides annual events, this dedicated club hosts leader-led rides nearly every weekend, exploring rural and urban areas on both shores of Lake Pontchartrain. Guest riders are welcome on any club ride, though membership is required for subsequent rides. Every participant should have a helmet, a road-worthy bike, and the ability to perform minor repairs in a pinch.

JOY RIDE BIKE RENTALS

504/982-1617, www.joyridebikerentals.com
HOURS: Vary
COST: $30 daily, $130 weekly

Perhaps the most convenient way to procure a bike is through the aptly named Joy Ride Bike Rentals, a delivery rental service that caters to both residents and out-of-towners who either have

ARTS AND LEISURE

no car or would prefer not to drive. No matter where you're staying, the Joy Ride staff will bring a bike to you and pick it up the following day (obviously, reservations are required). All rentals are one-speed, cruiser-style bikes, though various sizes are available. Every rider must have a valid ID or credit card, wear a helmet at all times, and lock up the bike whenever it's not in use.

BOWLING
ROCK 'N' BOWL
3000 S. Carrollton Ave., 504/861-1700,
www.rocknbowl.com
HOURS: Mon.-Fri. 4 P.M.-close, Sat. 2 P.M.-close, Sun.
hours vary
COST: $24 hourly per lane, $1 for shoe rental
Map 6

While the Rock 'n' Bowl is one of the city's most popular live music venues—and certainly one of my favorite places to catch local acts like Kermit Ruffins, Amanda Shaw, and Tab Benoit—it's still primarily a family-friendly bowling alley. There's a maximum capacity of six bowlers per lane and, given how busy this joint can get, it's advisable to call ahead for lane availability. Besides live music, you'll also find a limited menu, with basic vittles like cheeseburgers, hot dogs, and chicken wings.

KAYAKING AND FISHING
JOE RUGS WATER SPORTS ADVENTURES
6001 France Rd., 504/621-3858,
www.joerugswateradventures.com
HOURS: Daily 8 A.M.-6 P.M.
COST: $10 hourly, $50 daily
Map 6

Located at **Pontchartrain Landing** (504/286-8157 or 877/376-7850, www.pontchartrain-landing.com), a waterfront RV park not far from Lake Pontchartrain and the Lakefront Arena, this year-round, water-sports outfitter is an ideal choice for kayakers. Joe Rugs rents out Jet Skis and Waverunners, offers parasailing and sunset cruises, and organizes charter fishing trips (daily 8 A.M.–noon and 6–10 P.M., $75 pp). There's also a convenient boat launch, a marina with full hookups, and a boat storage area.

REEL HAPPY FISHING CHARTERS
504/737-2039 or 504/812-9487,
www.neworleanscharters.com
HOURS: Vary
COST: $350-425 per trip

Admittedly, New Orleans doesn't offer much in the way of fishing charters. So, if you've come to experience the bountiful waters of southeastern Louisiana, you're more likely to find fishing guides on the Northshore and in Cajun Country. Luckily, though, Captain Mike Garey offers trips through the brackish waters that lie within a half-hour's drive from the French Quarter. This knowledgeable veteran has been fishing our "sportsman's paradise" for more than three decades, so he knows how to find the best spots for reeling in redfish and speckled trout—both of which I've been lucky enough to catch many times on my dad's fishing boat.

UPTOWN ANGLER
601 Julia St., 504/529-3597, www.uptownangler.com
HOURS: Mon.-Fri. 10 A.M.-6 P.M., Sat. 10 A.M.-4 P.M.
COST: Varies
Map 3

Based, of all places, in the city's trendy Arts District, the Uptown Angler stocks an assortment of fishing essentials, including rods, reels, boots, waders, vests, waterproof bags, even kayaks. In addition, the helpful store offers fly-fishing classes, usually held at Metairie's Lafreniere Park, and guided redfishing charters, typically in the marshes between Venice and Hopedale. Trip rates ($450 per half day, $575 daily) include rods, reels, flies, ice, water, and transportation from the Uptown Angler.

GOLF
AUDUBON PARK GOLF COURSE
Magazine St. and Golf Club Dr., 504/212-5290,
www.auduboninstitute.org
HOURS: Mon. 10 A.M.-sunset, Tues.-Sun. 7 A.M.-sunset
COST: $30-40 pp w/golf cart
Map 4

Part of Louisiana's Audubon Golf Trail, the Audubon Park Golf Course has technically existed since 1898. After languishing over the years, it was completely overhauled in 2001, and now the Denis Griffiths–designed course is looking better than ever. Voted one of the state's top public courses by *Golf Digest,* the 18-hole, par-62 executive course features contoured fairways, well-manicured greens, four lagoons, and century-old oak trees. Here, you'll find a dozen par-3 holes, four par-4s, and two par-5s.

BAYOU BARRIERE GOLF CLUB

7427 Hwy. 23, Belle Chasse, 504/394-9500,
www.bayoubarriere.com
HOURS: Daily sunrise–sunset
COST: $19-26 pp w/golf cart
Map 6

The West Bank of the Mississippi River is home to several well-favored golf courses, including this well-landscaped, 27-hole option nestled alongside the Intracoastal Canal in Belle Chasse. In addition to this popular course, the Bayou Barriere Golf Club features a spacious clubhouse where you'll find the Bayou Grill offering a limited menu of breakfast items, salads, sandwiches, and libations.

CITY PARK NEW ORLEANS NORTH COURSE

1051 Filmore Ave., 504/483-9410,
www.cityparkgolf.com
HOURS: Daily sunrise–sunset
COST: $27-40 pp w/golf cart
Map 6

When itching for a round, many local golfers, including both my husband and my father, head to City Park, home to the North Course, an 18-hole course that offers four sets of tees, making it ideal for golfers of varying skill levels. The course also features a practice center (daily 7 A.M.–8 P.M.) with 74 driving-range stalls and two grassy hitting areas; private lessons are also available. Few municipalities in this country have better public golf within the city limits.

TPC LOUISIANA

11001 Lapalco Blvd., Avondale, 504/436-8721,
www.tpc.com
HOURS: Daily sunrise–sunset
COST: $110 pp
Map 6

The PGA tour's Zurich Classic, which once took place at the famous English Turn Golf and Country Club, now occurs annually at the Tournament Players Club of Louisiana, a $20 million course created for professional tournament play. Opened in 2004, the course closed shortly afterward due to damage from Hurricane Katrina, but has since reopened. Famed golfing architect Pete Dye, with assistance from PGA touring professionals Steve Elkington and Kelly Gibson, designed the fabulous layout. A 20-minute drive from downtown New Orleans, the 18-hole course is part of the Audubon Golf Trail and stretches across a 250-acre tract of wetlands. There are five sets of tees, an exceptional pro golf shop, and the TPC Grill. Professional golf instruction is also available.

HEALTH CLUBS AND YOGA STUDIOS

BALANCE YOGA & WELLNESS

120 S. Cortez St., 504/309-9618,
www.balanceyogawellness.com
HOURS: Vary
COST: Varies
Map 5

Though many might not associate the Big Easy with the practice of yoga, there are actually quite a few studios here, which is good news for yoga-obsessed residents like me. One of the most well-favored studios is Balance Yoga & Wellness, an airy space in Mid-City not far from the busy intersection of Canal Street and South Carrollton Avenue. Besides breathing instruction and wellness consultations, the studio offers a variety of classes that embrace several different yoga styles, including ashtanga, anusara, hatha, prenatal, and therapeutic yoga. The best thing about Balance Yoga is its knowledgeable instructors, who make participants feel comfortable, no matter their skill level.

ELMWOOD FITNESS CENTER DOWNTOWN

1 Shell Square, 701 Poydras St., Ste. 1300,
504/588-1600, www.elmwoodfitness.com
HOURS: Mon.-Fri. 5 A.M.–9 P.M., Sat. 8 A.M.-2 P.M.
COST: Varies
Map 3

Despite New Orleans's reputation for

ARTS AND LEISURE

debauchery, where overindulgence is a way of life, there are numerous ways for fitness-minded folks to keep up with their exercise routines. One such option is the expansive Elmwood Fitness Center Downtown, a 16,000-square-foot facility in the CBD—the perfect location for business travelers, conventioneers, and vacationers staying in the nearby French Quarter. Besides weight and cardiovascular rooms, Elmwood Fitness offers a whirlpool and sauna, three racquetball courts, massage services, a juice bar, and a variety of classes, from yoga to spinning to kickboxing. Elmwood also has locations in Metairie (Heritage Plaza, 111 Veterans Memorial Blvd., Ste. 475, Metairie, 504/832-1600) and Harahan (Elmwood Plaza Shopping Center, 1200 S. Clearview Pkwy., Ste. 1200, Harahan, 504/733-1600).

WILD LOTUS YOGA UPTOWN
4842 Perrier St., 504/899-0047,
www.wildlotusyoga.com
HOURS: Vary daily
COST: Varies
Map 4

If you're staying in the Uptown area and looking for a place to unwind, make a trip to Wild Lotus Yoga Uptown, a well-respected yoga studio in the residential neighborhood near St. Charles and Napoleon Avenues. Any given week, you can take one of 40 different classes, ranging from gentle restorative yoga to spicy shakti flow. Wild Lotus also offers a separate location (2372 St. Claude Ave.) along the edge of the Faubourg Marigny.

SPECTATOR SPORTS
Baseball
NEW ORLEANS ZEPHYRS
Zephyr Field, 6000 Airline Dr., Metairie, 504/734-5155,
www.zephyrsbaseball.com
COST: $8-12 adult, $7-11 senior and child 2-12, free under 2
Map 6

New Orleans might not have a Major League Baseball team, but that doesn't keep local baseball fans from heading to the 10,000-seat Zephyr Field to watch the Minor League New Orleans Zephyrs, the Triple-A affiliate of the MLB's Miami Marlins. With a swimming pool, two hot tubs, 16 luxury suites, a party shack, and games starring players just one level away from big-league baseball, the Zephyrs enjoy some of the highest attendance of any Triple-A team—more than 320,000 fans every season. Opened in 1997, Zephyr Field has also hosted numerous college baseball games and tournaments; it's even starred in a couple films, including *Mr. 3000.*

UNO PRIVATEERS
University of New Orleans, Maestri Field, 6801 Franklin Ave., 504/280-4263, www.unoprivateers.com
COST: Varies
Map 6

Some of the city's colleges boast fairly decent sports programs, including the University of New Orleans (UNO), which at times has had an excellent men's baseball team. Home games typically occur at Maestri Field, located on UNO's East Campus alongside Lake Pontchartrain. Parking is available beside the field. Depending on the season, spectators can also enjoy men's football and basketball, plus women's volleyball and basketball.

Basketball
NEW ORLEANS HORNETS
New Orleans Arena, 1501 Girod St., 504/525-4667 or 504/593-4700, www.nba.com/hornets
COST: Varies
Map 3

Adjacent to the Mercedes-Benz Superdome, the **New Orleans Arena** (504/587-3822 or 504/587-3663, www.neworleansarena.com) is the official home of the New Orleans Hornets, the NBA basketball team that moved from Charlotte to New Orleans in 2002. Before that, New Orleans had gone many years without an NBA team. Open since 1999, the 18,000-seat New Orleans Arena is also a popular concert and performing arts venue, which has hosted the likes of Katy Perry, Def Leppard, and Cirque de Soleil.

WOLFPACK ATHLETICS

Loyola University New Orleans Recreational Sports Complex, Freret St. and Engineering Rd., 5th Fl., 504/864-7225, www.wolfpack.loyno.edu

COST: $6 adult, $3 senior and child

`Map 4`

Adjacent to Tulane's campus along verdant St. Charles Avenue, Loyola University offers a variety of spectator sports, including a men's basketball team that dates back to 1945 and a much newer women's basketball team. Both teams hold their home games at the Den, a facility on the fifth floor of the university's massive sports complex, which stands in the 6300 block of Freret Street.

Football

NEW ORLEANS SAINTS

Mercedes-Benz Superdome, 1500 Sugar Bowl Dr., 504/731-1700, www.neworleanssaints.com

COST: Varies

`Map 3`

With its huge tourism base and wealth of hotel rooms, New Orleans has become a favorite host for major professional sporting events, including the NFL's Super Bowl, which has been held in the **Mercedes-Benz Superdome** (504/587-3822 or 504/587-3663, www.superdome.com) several times since 1978. Built in 1975, the iconic 73,000-seat Superdome is the home stadium of the National Football League's New Orleans Saints, the seemingly jinxed team that—in case you haven't heard—finally won its first Super Bowl in 2010, a win that the Katrina-ravaged city and faithful natives like me desperately needed. Perhaps one of the more curiously named NFL football teams, the Saints are so called for two reasons: in reference to both the popular jazz anthem "When the Saints Go Marching In" and the fact that this predominantly Catholic city was awarded the NFL franchise on November 1, 1966 (All Saints' Day). The Superdome is also a popular event and performance venue, having hosted everything from state fairs to Rolling Stones' concerts.

TULANE GREEN WAVE

Mercedes-Benz Superdome, 1500 Sugar Bowl Dr.,

504/861-9283, www.tulanegreenwave.com

COST: Varies

`Map 3`

Besides serving as the official home of the New Orleans Saints, the **Mercedes-Benz Superdome** (504/587-3822 or 504/587-3663, www.superdome.com) also hosts home games of the Tulane Green Wave, Tulane University's football team, which was established in 1893. Eventually, however, the team will move to an on-campus, 30,000-seat stadium that's expected to be completed by the fall of 2014. Though especially known for its football team, Tulane is also a major force in men's baseball and women's basketball. In addition, students compete in everything from tennis to volleyball to track and field.

HORSE RACING

FAIR GROUNDS RACE COURSE & SLOTS

1751 Gentilly Blvd., 504/944-5515 or 504/948-1111, www.fairgroundsracecourse.com

HOURS: Daily 9 A.M.-midnight

COST: $7 pp for clubhouse, free for grandstand

`Map 5`

Mid-City's Fair Grounds Race Course & Slots is the third-oldest thoroughbred-racing course in the nation, offering live racing from Thanksgiving through March. An off-track-betting parlor is open year-round, so you can always wager on events elsewhere in the country. Key events at the track include the Louisiana Derby and the Fair Grounds Oaks; it's also been the longtime home of the annual New Orleans Jazz & Heritage Festival. Besides concession stands and two "grab-and-go" eateries, the Fair Grounds offers a fancy Clubhouse dining room, which has a strict dress code and is only open on live racing days.

GUIDED AND WALKING TOURS

BLOODY MARY'S NEW ORLEANS TOURS

504/915-7774, www.bloodymarystours.com

HOURS: Vary

COST: Varies

In addition to ghost hunts, voodoo rituals, and psychic readings, the woman known as Bloody

Mary also offers a variety of walking tours. The Tour of the Undead focuses on the city's famous hauntings, vampire lore, and voodoo culture, while the adults-only Haunted Pub Crawl covers several historic watering holes, including the supposedly haunted Lafitte's Blacksmith Shop Bar on Bourbon Street. Besides an evening graveyard walking tour, you can also opt for one of three different van excursions to the city's varied cemeteries. Reservations are required for all of Bloody Mary's tours.

FRIENDS OF THE CABILDO

701 Chartres St., 504/523-3939,
www.friendsofthecabildo.org
HOURS: Mon.-Fri. 9:30 A.M.-4:30 P.M.
COST: $15 adult, $10 student 13-20, free under 12
Map 1

For an intimate tour of the French Quarter, consider taking one of the two-hour, narrated strolls led by the nonprofit Friends of the Cabildo. Conducted by licensed guides, these well-respected tours highlight the history, folklore, and architecture of one of the country's oldest neighborhoods. Tours depart from the **1850 House Museum Store** (523 St. Ann St., 504/524-9118, Tues.–Sun. 9:30 A.M.–4:30 P.M.) and are offered at 10 A.M. and 1:30 P.M. Tuesday–Sunday. All proceeds ultimately benefit the Friends of the Cabildo, a volunteer group that supports the Louisiana State Museum, which oversees such historic properties as the Cabildo and the Presbytère.

HAUNTED HISTORY TOURS

97 Fontainebleau Dr., 504/861-2727 or 888/644-6787,
www.hauntedhistorytours.com
HOURS: Vary
COST: $20 adult, $17 senior and student

If, like many visitors to New Orleans, you're hoping to hear a few ghost stories during your trip, consider one of the entertaining excursions offered by Haunted History Tours, one of the city's oldest walking-tour companies. Tour options include the St. Louis Cemetery No. 1, a ghost tour through the French Quarter, and a voodoo tour, all of which depart from Reverend Zombie's House of Voodoo (725 St.

Peter St.). You can also take a ghost tour or a historical tour in the Garden District, both of which begin in the Lafayette Cemetery No. 1 (1400 Washington Ave.), as well as a vampire tour that departs from the St. Louis Cathedral. Reservations are typically required for all tours.

HISTORIC NEW ORLEANS TOURS

504/947-2120, www.tourneworleans.com
HOURS: Vary
COST: $20 adult, $15 senior and student, $7 child 6-12, free under 6

As you might have guessed, photogenic New Orleans boasts a slew of guided tour companies. One of the most authentic is Historic New Orleans Tours; walking tours focus on French Quarter history, voodoo culture, the city's jazz scene, the Garden District, and legendary hauntings. On the two-hour Garden District Tour, guides explain the history of the city's American Sector, point out notable buildings (including the former homes of Anne Rice and Peyton Manning), and discuss their colorful heritage; you'll also get the chance to explore the aboveground tombs within Lafayette Cemetery No. 1, which has made notable appearances in such films as *Interview with the Vampire* and *Double Jeopardy*. In addition, this well-respected company offers swamp and plantation tours, plus van excursions through the city's varied neighborhoods. Tickets can be purchased through **Zerve** (800/979-3370, www.zerve.com).

LE MONDE CRÉOLE TOURS

624 Royal St., 504/568-1801, www.mondecreole.com
HOURS: Daily 10:30 A.M.
COST: $22 adult, $16 student and child 10-18, free under 10

If you're curious about the Creole culture that helped to shape New Orleans, then don't hesitate to take one of the guided strolls offered by Le Monde Créole Tours. The tours are inspired by the memoirs of Laura Locul (1861–1963), a Creole woman and plantation mistress, whose Vacherie plantation is one of my favorite attractions outside the city. These excursions offer glimpses into private courtyards and

the Steamboat *Natchez*, docked at the end of Toulouse Street

cruises ($24.50 adult, $12.25 child 6–12, free under 6) at 11:30 A.M. and 2:30 P.M. daily, departing from the foot of Toulouse Street, just behind the Jax Brewery. While on board, you can visit the steam engine room, listen to live narration about the history of the port, enjoy a concert of the onboard, 32-note steam calliope, and opt for a Creole lunch ($11 adult, $8 child under 13). Alternatively, you can board a dinner jazz cruise ($67.50 adult, $33.75 child 6–12, and $13.25 child under 6), which leaves at 7 P.M. nightly and features decent buffet-style dining, live jazz by the Dukes of Dixieland, and gorgeous views of the city. Tickets for the jazz cruise are slightly cheaper without dinner. Although sightseeing on the deck is a highlight of any *Natchez* excursion, climate-controlled indoor seating is always available (and especially welcome on hot or rainy days). Be sure to make reservations, especially for the dinner cruise, and arrive a half hour before boarding time.

ARTS AND LEISURE

SHOPS

In New Orleans, shopping opportunities tend to embrace the most popular aspects of the city's heritage—specifically, its cuisine, music, art, literature, and historical preservation. The French Quarter is rife with praline shops, and visitors rarely leave without strolling through the varied food stalls of the historic French Market. Music and book lovers will find numerous stores that offer the best in everything from local jazz to Faulkner novels. Art and antiques hounds can browse the emporiums along Royal and Chartres Streets, which carry some of the most lavish—and expensive—furnishings in the South, while the Garden District's Magazine Street is considered a less pricey yet still ample source of art, antiques, jewelry, and vintage clothing.

On any given day, shopping in the Big Easy can involve perusing rare first editions, pricking voodoo dolls, decking yourself out in artisan jewelry or Mardi Gras masks, spicing up your wardrobe with vintage corsets and feather boas, or bringing a little bit of the city's culture back home in the form of handblown glass, antique ironwork, or Cajun and Creole seasonings. Though you'll find plenty of national chain stores here—from Hustler Hollywood to Urban Outfitters—much of what you see is unique to this region. While the most interesting shops and boutiques lie in the French Quarter, Arts District, and Uptown neighborhoods, the Greater New Orleans area also has its share of quaint, pedestrian-friendly shopping districts, such as Lakeview's Harrison Avenue, not to mention a handful of decent shopping malls.

© DANIEL MARTONE

HIGHLIGHTS

LOOK FOR (TO FIND RECOMMENDED SHOPS.

(**Finest Antiques Shop:** If you've ever longed to decorate your home in the fashion of those regal mansions that line the streets of the Garden District, then you need to browse the elegant pieces at **Keil's Antiques,** a Royal Street shop that's especially known for its shimmering chandeliers (page 185).

(**Best Music Source:** You'll find a wide array of local and regional blues, jazz, zydeco, and Cajun tunes at the **Louisiana Music Factory,** which also stocks an assortment of relevant books, DVDs, and T-shirts (page 191).

(**Best Place for a Nostalgic Makeover:** On a quaint stretch of Chartres, not far from the historic St. Louis Cathedral, you'll encounter the **Trashy Diva Boutique,** which, along with its two sister shops, offers vintage dresses, corsets, shoes, and accessories (page 194).

(**Best Architectural Treasure Trove:** When old New Orleans homes are torn down, **Ricca's Demolishing Corp.** salvages many of the beautiful architectural remnants and sells them to the public – it's a wonderful place to find mahogany doors, wrought-iron gates, and vintage hardware (page 196).

(**Best Source for Mardi Gras Memorabilia:** The enormous **Accent Annex** is your one-stop shop for all Mardi Gras paraphernalia, including elaborate masks, festive apparel, specialty beads, and other holiday souvenirs (page 197).

(**Sweetest Emporium:** With two stores in the French Quarter, **Southern Candymakers** lures many a passerby with its wide assortment of pralines, toffees, nut clusters, chocolate alligators, and other local confections (page 201).

(**Best Haven for Retail Therapy:** If you need to unwind after a long day of shopping, sightseeing, and indulging in the city's cuisine, head to the **Belladonna Day Spa,** a favorite among locals for its array of massages, facials, manicures, pedicures, and other body treatments (page 204).

(**Best Jewelry Shop:** An esteemed local chain, **Mignon Faget** carries stunning jewelry, much of it designed with traditional Louisiana icons, such as fleur-de-lis cufflinks, oyster earrings, redfish pins, and sno-ball pendants (page 206).

(**Best Place to Lift a Curse:** For spell kits, voodoo dolls, tarot cards, tribal masks, and other spiritual items, head to **Marie Laveau's House of Voodoo,** an often crowded Bourbon Street shop that also features curious religious altars and private readings (page 211).

(**Best Shopping Stroll:** Encompassing several historic blocks from Jackson Square to Barracks Street, the architecturally pleasing **French Market** houses a variety of emporiums, including a flea market, a renovated farmers market, praline shops, art galleries, and a crafts bazaar (page 211).

Locals and tourists alike head to Southern Candymakers for pralines and other tasty treats.

© DANIEL MARTONE

New Orleans is an easygoing town, where a flexible sense of time seems to be the norm. When it comes to shopping, that means that posted hours aren't always strictly enforced. Hours can also change from season to season; in the summer, when the weather is fairly unbearable and tourism slows, shops tend to close a bit earlier. On the positive side, though, window-shopping in this eclectic city can be a wonderful way to pass the afternoon.

SHOPPING DISTRICTS
French Quarter

Known for upscale antiques and first-rate art galleries, **Royal Street** is the most exclusive address for shopping in the French Quarter, though parallel **Chartres Street** has similarly high-end emporiums. In the **Lower Quarter,** from Jackson Square to Esplanade Avenue, you'll find funkier, more youthful boutiques, such as mod clothiers and edgy galleries. **Decatur Street,** meanwhile, is a good place to find cheesy T-shirts, Tabasco sauce, crawfish-embroidered items, souvenir "go-cups," as well as gifts, toys, cards, and novelties that emphasize the off-color humor and irreverent aspects of this festive town. Decatur is also sandwiched by two shopping malls: the **French Market,** which contains retail shops, food stalls, and a flea market, and the more upscale **Shops at Canal Place** alongside Canal Street.

Central Business and Arts Districts

Dominated by high-rise hotels and office towers, most of the CBD has few shops of note, though you'll find a couple of stylish places that cater to men. In addition, the riverside **Arts District** contains several fine-art galleries and other boutiques, particularly along **Julia Street.** You'll also encounter a large shopping mall, the **Riverwalk Marketplace,** alongside the Mississippi River.

Garden District and Uptown

Magazine Street, which follows the curve of the Mississippi River for about six miles from the CBD to Audubon Park, offers an astonishing variety of shops and boutiques. Sassy secondhand clothiers, colorful oyster bars, jamming music clubs, convivial java joints, and historic homes line the way, but it's the lower stretch of Magazine—from about **Canal Street to Jackson Avenue**—that possesses the city's most fascinating antiques district. While you'll spot a few chain stores, the neighborhood still maintains its independent, offbeat vibe. Uptown also boasts the **Riverbend** area, which features several curious shops around the intersection of **St. Charles and Carrollton Avenues.**

Antiques and Vintage

BUSH ANTIQUES
2109 Magazine St., 504/581-3518,
www.bushantiques.com
HOURS: Mon.-Sat. 11 A.M.-5 P.M.
Map 4

Bush Antiques may just tempt you to sleep on your purchase—before you've even purchased it. The dozens of beds sold here are quite spectacular, hailing from all over Europe and North America and ranging from 19th-century iron-and-brass four-posters to whimsical cast-iron sleigh beds. Other specialties include religious items, such as altars, and decorative French ironwork reminiscent of the intricate

balustrades found on so many New Orleans homes. Be sure to check out the rear patio, where you can browse an extensive collection of folk art.

DUNN & SONNIER ANTIQUES
2138 Magazine St., 504/524-3235,
www.dunnandsonnierantiques.com
HOURS: Mon.-Sat. 9 A.M.-5 P.M.
Map 4

Situated in the Lower Garden District, Dunn & Sonnier specializes in flower bulbs, iron garden furniture, and eclectic European antiques, from buffets to barometers. Owned and operated by Roy Dunn and Stephen Sonnier—both of whom have been collectors for more than 25 years—this pleasant, old-world shop is ideal for those hoping to stumble upon a rare find, such as Venetian mirrors, painted Toleware, and other decorative objets d'art.

FUNKY MONKEY

3127 Magazine St., 504/899-5587
HOURS: Mon.-Wed. 11 A.M.-6 P.M., Thurs.-Sat. 11 A.M.-7 P.M., Sun. noon-6 P.M.
Map 4

Favored by local fashionistas for more than 15 years, the offbeat Funky Monkey boutique offers new, used, and vintage clothing for men and women alike. Here, you'll find trendy cocktail dresses, sexy silk robes, handmade costumes, and colorful accessories, much of which is affordably priced. Needless to say, it's a popular stop prior to Halloween and Mardi Gras, so if you don't favor crowds, be sure to plan ahead.

JAMES H. COHEN & SONS, INC.

437 Royal St., 504/522-3305 or 800/535-1853,
http://shop.cohenantiques.com
HOURS: Mon.-Sat. 9:30 A.M.-5:15 P.M.
Map 1

Established in 1898, James H. Cohen & Sons is the oldest—and largest—coin store in the city. Known for its vast, rather expensive, selection of ancient coins, historical currency, military swords, Western-style rifles and revolvers, and other authentic artifacts, from poker chips to iron shackles, it's understandably a popular place for men to browse. In fact, it's one of my husband's favorite places in the Quarter—which, naturally, makes it my first stop come every anniversary.

€ KEIL'S ANTIQUES

325 Royal St., 504/522-4552, www.keilsantiques.com
HOURS: Mon.-Sat. 9 A.M.-5 P.M.
Map 1

Since 1899, when it was established by Hermina Keil, Keil's Antiques has been specializing in 18th- and 19th-century antiques from France and England. The inventory

© DANIEL MARTONE

Gun and coin collectors flock to James H. Cohen & Sons, Inc.

includes everything from marble mantels to magnificent crystal chandeliers to garnet chokers. The Keil family operates two other well-respected stores in the Quarter, Moss Antiques and Royal Antiques, but Keil's has perhaps the most enticing window displays, especially at Christmastime.

LILI VINTAGE BOUTIQUE

3329 Magazine St., 504/931-6848 or 504/891-9311,
www.lilivintage.com
HOURS: Mon.-Sat. 11:30 A.M.-5:30 P.M.
Map 4

As the name indicates, the lovely Lili Vintage Boutique invites shoppers to peruse an enviable, ever-changing collection of vintage jewelry and cocktail dresses, plus unique hats, shoes, purses, and belts. Casual tops, dresses, and jackets are also available. Unlike ordinary thrift stores, the boutique cleans, repairs, and restores all items before displaying them in the shop. If you'd rather not have a lot of new stuff to lug back home, bear in mind that the store also ships items around the world.

LUCULLUS

610 Chartres St., 504/528-9620,
www.lucullusantiques.com

HOURS: Mon.-Fri. 9 A.M.-5 P.M., Sat. 9:30 A.M.-5 P.M.

Map 1

Occupying a 19th-century building near Jackson Square, this charming shop appeals to gourmet cooks, wine connoisseurs, and avid entertainers—not surprising given that it's run by Patrick Dunne, author of *The Epicurean Collector: Exploring the World of Culinary Antiques.* You'll find a wide assortment of culinary treasures, including bronze mortars, crystal champagne flutes, Victorian wine coasters, English basaltware teapots, Italian lace tablecloths, and 19th-century farm tables. The store also offers decorative items like candlesticks, chandeliers, and framed still lifes. Dunne owns a similar shop in Breaux Bridge.

MAISON DE PROVENCE

3434 Magazine St., 504/895-2301,
www.maisondeprovence.com

HOURS: Tues.-Sat. 10:30 A.M.-4:30 P.M.

Map 4

Owned and operated by self-described treasure hunter Terri Goldsmith, this inviting store specializes in French, Italian, and Swedish antiques from the 18th and 19th centuries. Everything you see here, from the Tuscan lanterns and consoles to the French *trumeaux* and birdcages, has been handpicked by Terri herself—and she only chooses items that she wouldn't mind having in her own home. In fact, she's often sad to see them go.

M.S. RAU ANTIQUES

630 Royal St., 504/521-7568 or 888/814-7006,
www.rauantiques.com

HOURS: Mon.-Sat. 9 A.M.-5 P.M.

Map 1

A family-owned, French Quarter landmark since Max Rau opened its doors in 1912, M.S. Rau Antiques is indeed one of the oldest antiques shops in New Orleans. Today, the 30,000-square-foot showroom houses a stupendous collection of 19th-century paintings and sculptures, exquisite clocks and music boxes, striking bedroom and dining sets, antique globes, unusual canes, and so much more. In fact, if you're looking for a special piece of jewelry, you might find it here as well; precious items range from Colombian emerald rings to Cartier diamond necklaces to bangle bracelets courtesy of Tiffany & Co.

RARE FINDS

1231 Decatur St., 504/568-1004,
www.rarefindsneworleans.com

HOURS: Wed.-Mon. noon-6 P.M.

Map 1

Not far from the French Market and the Old U.S. Mint, you'll encounter this incredibly eclectic shop, which has a particular affinity for small, easy-to-carry antiques—the kind that make ideal souvenirs of your trip to New Orleans. The displays here brim with flasks and teacups, costume jewelry and sparkling tiaras, paintings and sculptures, old books and photographs, quaint lamps and glassware, vintage games and dolls, even New Orleans–style collectibles. Rare Finds also handles appraisals and will ship purchases anywhere in the United States.

RETRO ACTIVE

5924 Magazine St., 504/895-5054,
www.retroactivevintage.com

HOURS: Mon.-Sat. 11 A.M.-6 P.M., Sun. 1-5 P.M.

Map 4

Whether you're looking for a Mardi Gras costume or simply hoping to take a walk down memory lane, you'll do well to browse the vintage apparel and accessories at this friendly store. Opened in 1982, Retro Active offers both ladies' and men's fashions—from skirts, dresses, and evening gowns to ties, suits, and uniforms. The shop also boasts coats, shoes, hats, jewelry, vintage toys and games, and home furnishings.

TOP DRAWER ANTIQUES

4310 Magazine St., 504/897-1004,
www.topdrawerantiques.net

HOURS: Thurs.-Sat. 11 A.M.-6 P.M.

Map 4

With more than 7,000 square feet of showroom space, Top Drawer is one of the largest antiques

© DANIEL MARTONE

Vintage 329 lures music, cinema, sports, and literature fans with its array of signed memorabilia.

shops in the Uptown area. Here, you can peruse American and French antique furniture, from beds and bookcases to cabinets and card tables, plus chandeliers, paintings, pottery, and collectibles. Most items have been procured from Garden District homes, area plantations, local country estates, and houses in rural France.

VINTAGE 329

329 Royal St., 504/525-2262, www.vintage329.com
HOURS: Daily 10 A.M.–6 P.M.
`Map 1`

As a writer, music lover, and movie fan, this is my favorite antiques shop in the city. It's here that you might find signed Hemingway novels, an autographed Aerosmith guitar, or an oversized golf ball bearing the signatures of Rodney Dangerfield, Bill Murray, Chevy Chase, Ted Knight, and Michael O'Keefe—the principal cast members of *Caddyshack*. In addition to signed first editions, music memorabilia, and vintage movie posters, you'll also spy old maps, guns, swords, presidential photos, and sports-related items, including football helmets signed by entire NFL teams. Vintage 329 is truly an oasis for history buffs, especially those with deep pockets.

Arts and Crafts

ARTIST'S MARKET & BEAD SHOP

85 French Market Pl., 504/561-0046,
www.artistsmarketnola.com
HOURS: Mon.-Fri. 10 A.M.-5 P.M., Sat.-Sun. 10 A.M.-6 P.M.
Map 1

Literally across the street from the historic French Market, this somewhat cluttered store is filled with paintings, photographs, pottery, textiles, woodwork, hand-blown glass, and other artwork from more than 75 local and regional artists and artisans, plus curious gifts and decorative items, such as snow globes and red velvet Carnival masks. Beading enthusiasts will find a large selection of glass and sterling silver beads, semiprecious stones, beading tools, stringing supplies, and glass rods. Newbies can even take a jewelry-making classes. The shop has two entrances; the second one is at 1228 Decatur Street.

THE BEAD SHOP

4612 Magazine St., 504/895-6161,
www.beadshopneworleans.com
HOURS: Mon.-Sat. 10 A.M.-6 P.M.
Map 4

Occupying a quirky little Creole cottage along Uptown's funky Magazine Street, the Bead Shop is the perfect crafts boutique for a city that celebrates Mardi Gras with such enthusiasm. Beginning beaders and skilled artisans alike will appreciate the shop's extensive selection of beading supplies as well as beads from around the world. If you're not sure how to start making your own jewelry, you can take one of several classes on offer ($20–35); such training sessions cover the basics of crafting everything from woven bead bracelets to stamped pendants.

LOUISIANA LOOM WORKS

616 Chartres St., 504/566-7788,
www.customragrugs.com
HOURS: Daily 11 A.M.-6 P.M.
Map 1

Ronda and Walt Rose have been the owners of Louisiana Loom Works since it opened in 1997. They hand-weave all of the store's colorful rag rugs on the three looms at this shop, where you can examine the wares and observe the production process. Though rag rugs are traditionally made of old clothes, worn-out sheets, and other reusable materials, these are made from new fabrics and cotton thread. You'll find durable, machine-washable rugs of varying sizes and colors, but if you don't see anything you like, the Roses also take custom orders and will ship your rug within about three months.

MASKARADE

630 St. Ann St., 504/568-1018,
www.frenchquartermaskstore.com
HOURS: Daily 10 A.M.-5 P.M.
Map 1

Just a half block from Jackson Square, this charming shop presents a wide assortment of masks, crafted by artists from New Orleans and elsewhere around the country. You'll spy feathery Carnival masks, golden Venetian-style masks, and black leather masks, as well as creations that resemble ladybugs, butterflies, rabbits, leopards, panthers, gazelles, dragons, horned devils, and kitty cats. If, despite such a selection, you don't spot what you like, an artist can customize a mask for you—just in time for Mardi Gras, Halloween, or any other special occasion.

NEW ORLEANS ART SUPPLY

3620 Royal St., 504/949-1525,
www.art-restoration.com
HOURS: Mon.-Fri. 10 A.M.-5 P.M.
Map 2

Though most visitors to New Orleans will never see the Bywater, artists in need of supplies will surely find what they're looking for at this well-regarded store, part of the New Orleans Conservation Guild. In addition to art books and magazines, you'll find a sizable selection of high-quality supplies for glassblowers, printmakers, painters, ceramic artisans, sketch artists, and other creative types.

RHINO CONTEMPORARY CRAFTS CO.
The Shops at Canal Place, 333 Canal St., 2nd Fl., 504/523-7945, www.rhinocrafts.com
HOURS: Mon.-Sat. 10 A.M.-7 P.M., Sun. noon-6 P.M.
Map 1

The mission of RHINO Contemporary Crafts Co. is to promote and sell the handcrafted ceramics, jewelry, furniture, accessories, and decorative arts of local talents. RHINO stands for Right Here in New Orleans, and, indeed, that's where all the goods here were created. So, be sure to stop by before attending a show at the nearby cinema, also located on the third floor of Canal Place.

SHADYSIDE POTTERY
3823 Magazine St., 504/897-1710, www.shadysidepottery.com
HOURS: Mon.-Sat. 10 A.M.-5 P.M.
Map 4

Established in 1988 by Charlie Bohn, a former ceramics student at both Tulane and Loyola Universities, Shadyside Pottery features a veritable cornucopia of practical pottery. Pieces here include textured lamps, microwaveable stoneware platters and mixing bowls, colorful fleur-de-lis trays and coasters, and traditional Raku vases, bowls, and urns—the latter of which were influenced by Bohn's apprenticeship in Japan. You'll even find carved, ceramic, and bronze sinks in the shop.

Books and Music

BECKHAM'S BOOKSHOP
228 Decatur St., 504/522-9845
HOURS: Daily 10 A.M.-5 P.M.
Map 1

Given the French Quarter's knack for inspiring authors, it's no surprise that you'll find several musty-smelling, well-respected used bookstores in the vicinity. Although many locals swear by such places as Arcadian Books, Dauphine Street Books, and the Librairie Bookshop, I'm a fan of the multistory Beckham's, a good source of rare and hard-to-find antiquarian titles. Here, you can relax in an armchair while perusing the secondhand tomes, including a decent collection of first editions.

CRESCENT CITY BOOKS
230 Chartres St., 504/524-4997 or 800/546-4013, www.crescentcitybooks.com
HOURS: Mon.-Sat. 10 A.M.-8 P.M., Sun. 10 A.M.-5 P.M.
Map 1

Now in its new location, this French Quarter bookstore contains two floors of out-of-print and antiquarian titles, plus antique maps and prints. Open since 1992, it's always been an exceptional source for local history and literature, scholarly books, and hard-to-find titles on philosophy, ancient history, and literary criticism—a real book lover's bookstore.

FAUBOURG MARIGNY ART BOOKS MUSIC
600 Frenchmen St., 504/947-3700, www.fabonfrenchmen.com
HOURS: Daily noon-10 P.M.
Map 2

Located at the corner of Chartres and Frenchmen Streets in the heart of the Marigny's famous music scene, this cramped, no-frills secondhand bookshop is often still open when the bands are starting to play. So, en route to one of the nearby jazz, rock, and blues clubs, be sure to make a quick stop here. Somehow fitting with its authentic environs, this eclectic store is rife with curious choices, including New Orleans cookbooks, local short-story collections, art and history titles, old posters and postcards, lesbian literature, and, yes, vintage gay porn.

FAULKNER HOUSE BOOKS
624 Pirate's Alley, 504/524-2940, www.faulknerhouse.net
HOURS: Daily 10 A.M.-5 P.M.
Map 1

Hidden in the alley between the Cabildo and the St. Louis Cathedral, this small bookstore occupies the same space that novelist William

Music lovers often stop by Faubourg Marigny Art Books Music before heading to Frenchmen Street's nearby clubs.

Faulkner inhabited in 1925, when he first arrived in New Orleans as a young poet. It was here, in fact, that he wrote *Soldiers' Pay*. Operated by a knowledgeable staff, frequented by writers and collectors alike, and only closed on Mardi Gras Day, this charming place sells both new and used books, including rare first editions, titles about Southern Americana, epistolary collections, contemporary fiction, and literature by Faulkner, Tennessee Williams, Walker Percy, and other writers inspired by New Orleans.

GARDEN DISTRICT BOOK SHOP

2727 Prytania St., 504/895-2266, www.gardendistrictbookshop.com

HOURS: Mon.-Sat. 10 A.M.-6 P.M., Sun. 10 A.M.-4 P.M.

Map 4

Nestled in the residential Garden District, just a block south of St. Charles Avenue, this popular bookshop features both new and used titles. In addition to regional books, the selection here includes literature, art and design books, options for kids, signed first editions,

and limited editions by well-respected authors from around the country. You can also attend book signings and readings here, and new members are always welcome to join the store's book group, which meets at 6 P.M. on the second Wednesday of every month; the website typically lists the books to be discussed.

JIM RUSSELL RECORDS

1837 Magazine St., 504/522-2602, www.jimrussellrecords.com

HOURS: Mon.-Sat. 11 A.M.-5 P.M.

Map 4

Founded in 1969, this spacious local institution is known for its more than half million LPs, 45s, and 78s in all musical genres. Jim Russell Records is in fact where ardent record collectors go to find the rarest and most obscure vinyl—not just because they'll usually find it, but if what you're seeking isn't here, the knowledgeable staff will try to track it down for you. Though records are the shop's mainstay, cassettes and CDs are also available.

◖ LOUISIANA MUSIC FACTORY

210 Decatur St., 504/586-1094,
www.louisianamusicfactory.com
HOURS: Mon.-Sat. 10 A.M.-7 P.M., Sun. noon-6 P.M.
`Map 1`

Opposite the famous House of Blues concert venue, the Louisiana Music Factory is a noted music shop with a great selection of local and regional blues, jazz, funk, R&B, gospel, Cajun and zydeco, reggae, swamp pop, rock, and hip-hop. This is an especially great place if you're looking for Mardi Gras music, performers of which range from brass bands to Mardi Gras Indians to the Neville Brothers. You'll find both used and new CDs here, plus vinyl records, books, DVDs, videos, and T-shirts. This popular store also does a brisk mail-order business.

MAPLE STREET BOOK SHOP

7529 Maple St., 504/866-4916 or 504/861-2105,
www.maplestreetbookshop.com
HOURS: Mon.-Sat. 9 A.M.-7 P.M., Sun. 11 A.M.-5 P.M.
`Map 4`

Not far from Tulane's campus, you'll find this quaint bookstore, which two sisters, Mary Kellogg and Rhoda Norman, opened back in 1965. Once a hotbed of avant-garde thinkers and book lovers, this independent shop now offers a wide array of new books, many by regional authors like Stephen Ambrose and James Lee Burke. If you're looking for used and rare books, just head to the adjacent Maple Street bookstore (7523 Maple St., 504/866-7059, Mon.–Sat. 10 A.M.–6 P.M., Sun. 11 A.M.–5 P.M.).

OCTAVIA BOOKS

513 Octavia St., 504/899-7323,
www.octaviabooks.com
HOURS: Mon.-Sat. 10 A.M.-6 P.M., Sun. noon-5 P.M.
`Map 4`

Within easy driving distance of Audubon Park and Tulane University, and only a couple blocks south of Magazine Street, Octavia Books is especially popular among local residents and college students. Besides offering biographies, memoirs, fiction, history books, and other standard fare, the store features plenty of local travel guides, cookbooks, and literature, as well as books about New Orleans's unique history, art, architecture, and celebrations. If you have time, be sure to stop by for regular in-store events like readings, signings, and book club meetings; there's a regular book club as well as one for science-fiction fans.

PEACHES RECORDS

408 N. Peters St., 504/282-3322,
www.peachesrecordsneworleans.com
HOURS: Mon.-Thurs. 8 A.M.-9 P.M., Fri.-Sat. 8 A.M.-10 P.M., Sun. 9 A.M.-9 P.M.
`Map 1`

Just a few doors down from the local Hard Rock Cafe, you'll encounter this spacious music store, which features a slew of local tunes, from traditional jazz standards by Louis Armstrong and Jelly Roll Morton to modern funk by the Meters and the Neville Brothers—plus blues, rap, and zydeco. Ernie K-Doe, Fats Domino, Dr. John, Wynton Marsalis, Rockin' Dopsie, Walter "Wolfman" Washington, and the Dukes of Dixieland are just some of the local performers represented here. Beyond music, there's also a small selection of local books, such as travel guides, historical nonfiction, and Cajun children's tales.

Clothing and Shoes

BALLIN'S LTD.
721 Dante St., 504/866-4367,
www.ballinsltd.com
HOURS: Mon.-Sat. 10 A.M.-6 P.M.
Map 4

Fashion-forward shoppers venture here to pick up the latest sportswear, evening attire, boots, shoes, and handbags from Eileen Fisher, Kate Spade, Stuart Weitzman, and other top designers. Established in 1981, this Riverbend shop is in fact the original Ballin's; there are now four other branches in southern Louisiana, including one on Magazine Street that specializes in knitwear as well as locations in Covington, Baton Rouge, and Lafayette.

A BOUTIQUE FOR THE HOI POLLOI
600 Conti St., 504/561-7585,
www.hoipolloiboutique.com
HOURS: Daily 10 A.M.-6 P.M.
Map 1

I often pass the corner of Chartres and Conti Streets on my daily walks through the French Quarter, and whenever I do, I find my gaze always wanders beyond the open doors of this small yet fashionable boutique. As the name indicates, Hoi Polloi truly appeals to the masses, offering everything from affordable hats and comfy pajamas to sassy blouses and eye-catching jewelry. Depending on the day, you might even stumble across artistic glassware, fleur-de-lis souvenirs, or other unique gifts.

DIRTY COAST
5631 Magazine St., 504/324-3745,
www.dirtycoast.com
HOURS: Mon.-Sat. 11 A.M.-6 P.M., Sun. 11 A.M.-4 P.M.
Map 4

Appealing to New Orleanians with fierce local pride—as well as curious tourists—the lovingly named Dirty Coast T-shirt shop offers options for kids and adults alike. Designs honor such iconic images as jazz musicians, aboveground cemeteries, boiled crawfish, bead-covered trees, Audubon Zoo's Monkey Hill, and other unique aspects of the Big Easy, including historic moments like the Louisiana Purchase. You can also pick up po-boy posters, Saints' hoodies and side-view mirror covers, as well as coasters, mouse pads, and doormats emblazoned with the Crescent City's unique water-meter covers—a popular image in jewelry shops throughout New Orleans.

FEET FIRST
4119 Magazine St., 504/899-6800,
www.feetfirststores.com
HOURS: Mon.-Sat. 10 A.M.-6 P.M., Sun. 12:30-5 P.M.
Map 4

Opened in 1977, this popular, family-owned shop has become the city's largest independent retailer of brand-name women's shoes, from Sam Edelman sandals to Keds sneakers. You can also pick up athletic apparel, assorted handbags, hats, necklaces, and silk ties imprinted with local icons, from boiled crabs to LSU Tigers to Mardi Gras floats. There's a second location in the French Quarter (526 Royal St., 504/569-0005).

FLEUR DE PARIS
523 Royal St., 504/525-1899 or 800/229-1899,
www.fleurdeparis.net
HOURS: Daily 10 A.M.-6 P.M.
Map 1

No matter where I happen to be headed along Royal Street, the striking window displays of this elegant boutique always tempt me to linger for just a moment. Beyond the lovely, Parisian-style facade, this classic, well-renowned millinery, which opened in 1980, specializes in customized hats for various occasions, whether an afternoon tea or a Mardi Gras gala. Additionally, you'll find elegant evening gowns, antique jewelry, glimmering brooches, stylish purses, silk shawls, bridal veils, and, not surprisingly, classy lingerie.

HEMLINE

609 Chartres St., 504/592-0242,
www.shophemline.com

HOURS: Mon.-Thurs. 10 A.M.-6 P.M., Fri.-Sun. 10 A.M.-7 P.M.

Map 1

With locations throughout the South, from Dallas to Nashville, this well-favored women's clothing boutique lures visitors and residents alike with its diverse collection, including Diesel, BCBG, Nicole Miller, and other trendy labels. Established in 1994, just a block from Jackson Square, the inviting Chartres Street location is actually the first of this regional chain. While exploring the city, be sure to check out other Hemline stores in the New Orleans area, including one in the Uptown area (3308 Magazine St., 504/269-4005) and another in Old Metairie (605 Metairie Rd., 504/309-8778).

HOUSE OF LOUNGE

2044 Magazine St., 504/671-8300,
www.houseoflounge.com

HOURS: Mon.-Sat. 11 A.M.-6 P.M.

Map 4

As the name suggests, House of Lounge sells sultry dresses and custom corsets—a fabulous collection of pieces that would make for quite an entrance. If you're trying to spice up your love life, you'll also find a cornucopia of camisoles and chemises, teddies and robes, sexy underwear, garter belts, catsuits, masks and blindfolds, bondage accessories, and, of course, feather pasties.

MIMI

5500 Magazine St., 504/269-6464 or 866/255-6464,
www.miminola.com

HOURS: Mon.-Sat. 10 A.M.-5 P.M.

Map 4

Encompassing 5,000 square feet in Uptown New Orleans, this high-end clothing boutique houses a remarkable collection of some of the world's best designers, including Donna Karan, Michael Kors, Devi Kroll, Simon Tu, and Blumarine's. In addition to impeccable clothes, you'll find a slew of complimentary accessories here. With its exclusive in-store salon,

Mimi is also the Gulf South's largest retailer of Vera Wang bridal fashions.

PERLIS CLOTHING

6070 Magazine St., 504/895-8661 or 800/725-6070,
www.perlis.com

HOURS: Mon.-Sat. 9 A.M.-6 P.M.

Map 4

For more than seven decades, Perlis has stood on the corner of Webster and Magazine Streets. At this local institution, you can shop for men's, women's, and boys' clothing, from fancy styles to sportswear, plus gifts and accessories. At the branch inside the Quarter's Jackson Brewery (504/523-6681), browsers can peruse Perlis's signature Cajun clothing, including polo shirts with the store's iconic crawfish logo—extremely popular souvenirs for tourists.

PRIMA DONNA'S CLOSET

1206 St. Charles Ave., 504/525-3327,
www.primadonnascloset.com

HOURS: Mon.-Sat. 10 A.M.-6 P.M.

Map 4

If you're looking for designer clothes at bargain prices, head to Prima Donna's Closet, a consignment shop in the Lower Garden District that offers gently worn, top-of-the-line designer apparel. Labels here include everything from Prada and Chanel to Ralph Lauren and Calvin Klein. There are also branches of Prima Donna's in the French Quarter (927 Royal St., 504/875-4437) and in Metairie (3213 17th St., 504/835-1120).

RUBENSTEINS

102 St. Charles Ave., 504/581-6666 or 800/725-7823,
www.rubensteinsneworleans.com

HOURS: Mon.-Thurs. 10 A.M.-5:45 P.M., Fri.-Sat. 10 A.M.-6 P.M.

Map 3

If you need a men's jacket for your dinner at Galatoire's, consider Rubensteins, a classic, family-owned outfitter carrying such exclusive lines as Hugo Boss, Ralph Lauren, Jack Victor, and Brioni. Situated in the CBD since 1924, this well-respected emporium is actually considered one of the finest men's specialty

© DANIEL MARTONE

Between its three shops on Chartres, the Trashy Diva Boutique offers a variety of retro dresses, corsets, shoes, and accessories.

stores in the country, featuring suits, sweaters, jeans, and fine footwear. Special services include complimentary valet parking, expert alterations, tailored apparel, personal shoppers, and free delivery.

TRASHY DIVA BOUTIQUE

829 Chartres St., 504/581-4555 or 888/818-3482, www.trashydiva.com

HOURS: Sun.-Fri. noon-6 P.M., Sat. 11 A.M.-6 P.M.

Map 1

Not far from the historic St. Louis Cathedral on a relatively quiet stretch of Chartres, you'll encounter my favorite clothing shop in the French Quarter, if not the entire city. Admittedly not the cheapest place to shop, the Trashy Diva Boutique specializes in vintage-style dresses that suit a wide array of female shapes and sizes. Be sure to stop by the sister stores, which offer old-fashioned corsets and lingerie (831 Chartres St., 504/522-8861) as well as retro shoes (839 Chartres St., 504/522-8200)—all of which can make for a killer retro look.

VOLUPTUOUS VIXEN

818 Chartres St., 504/529-3588, www.thevoluptuousvixen.com

HOURS: Sun.-Thurs. 10 A.M.-6 P.M., Fri.-Sat. 10 A.M.-7 P.M.

Map 1

Curvaceous ladies often head to this contemporary boutique, which specializes in ready-to-wear fashions for sizes 12 and up. Located just a few steps from the Trashy Diva stores, the Voluptuous Vixen offers colorful tops, glittery jeans, flirty dresses, and intimate apparel. As a bonus, if you're stumped for what to wear, the friendly staff members will help you choose an outfit that best accentuates your figure.

Furniture and Home Decor

AMERICAN AQUATIC GARDENS & GIFTS

621 Elysian Fields Ave., 504/944-0410,
www.americanaquaticgardens.com
HOURS: Daily 9 A.M.-4 P.M.
`Map 2`

You might wonder why some visitors consider this exotic nursery and gift shop a worthwhile stop in the Faubourg Marigny. Well, besides being a terrific place to purchase curious fountains, outdoor sculptures, creative benches, classic waterlilies, and unusual gifts from around the world, American Aquatic Gardens & Gifts also features a peaceful aquatic garden that offers some solace from the craziness of the French Quarter, only a few blocks away.

AS YOU LIKE IT SILVER SHOP

3033 Magazine St., 800/828-2311,
www.asyoulikeitsilvershop.com
HOURS: Mon.-Fri. 11 A.M.-5 P.M., Sat. 10 A.M.-5 P.M.
`Map 4`

At this well-regarded shop, you can choose from a large selection of silver holloware, flatware, jewelry, and collectibles. On any given day, you might see a striking silver necklace fashioned with garnets and pearls, a pair of heavy sterling candlesticks adorned with chrysanthemums, a souvenir spoon from the 1890s, an engraved baby cup dating from around 1850, and a small sauce ladle fashioned by silversmith and American revolutionary Paul Revere around 1770. As with any shop that features antique items, be prepared for steep prices.

AUX BELLES CHOSES NEW ORLEANS

3912 Magazine St., 504/891-1009,
www.abcneworleans.com
HOURS: Tues.-Sat. 10 A.M.-5 P.M.
`Map 4`

Established in 1991 by two sisters, Bettye Barrios and Anne Barrios Gauthier, this popular shop contains exactly what its name indicates: *belles choses*, which means "beautiful things" in French. After years of traveling and shopping around Europe, Bettye and Anne decided to share their love of European furnishings by selling handpicked home and garden items from the French and English countryside. Browse among lavender soaps and sachet bags, pastel kitchen towels, festive tablecloths, vintage jugs and canisters, and old garden sprinklers.

BEVOLO GAS AND ELECTRIC LIGHTS

318 Royal St., 504/522-9485, www.bevolo.com
HOURS: Mon.-Fri. 8 A.M.-5 P.M., Sat. 9 A.M.-4 P.M.
`Map 1`

While strolling through the French Quarter, especially at night, it's hard to miss the old-fashioned gas and electric lights posted along the sidewalks, hanging beneath the galleries, and mounted beside many doorways. If you're eager to take that atmospheric aspect of New Orleans home with you, then be sure to pay Bevolo a visit. Open since 1945, this spacious showroom features an eye-pleasing variety of copper light fixtures. Bevolo also has an extensive collection of antiques and reproduction pieces, including alabaster mirrors, olive jars and sugar kettles (often used as outdoor decorations), and iron chandeliers, benches, and tables. Handmade Christmas ornaments and copper office accessories are also available. Bevolo has a second location, albeit a bit smaller, at 521 Conti Street.

DOMBOURIAN ORIENTAL RUGS

2841 Magazine St., 504/891-6601, www.domrugs.com
HOURS: Mon.-Fri. 9 A.M.-5 P.M., Sat. 10 A.M.-5 P.M.
`Map 4`

Though this family-owned Oriental rug store—one of the oldest in the Crescent City—has moved several times since opening in 1910, Dombourian Oriental Rugs is still going strong today. If you're looking to redecorate your home, stop by to browse the impressive collection, which includes Persian rugs from the 1890s as well as Turkish reproductions made of Angora wool. The shop also provides expert repairs and cleaning services for both antique and new Oriental rugs that you may already own.

HAZELNUT NEW ORLEANS
5515 Magazine St., 504/891-2424,
www.hazelnutneworleans.com
HOURS: Mon.-Sat. 10 A.M.-6 P.M., Sun. noon-5 P.M.
Map 4

Whether you're a full-time resident or a first-time visitor, you're sure to spot something you like at Hazelnut, an elegant, eclectic Uptown shop that presents exquisite gifts and home accessories, such as napkins, towels, linens, and trays emblazoned with the St. Louis Cathedral, Steamboat *Natchez,* and other iconic local images. Other items here include, but are certainly not limited to, fragrance bottles, oddly shaped salad bowls and serving dishes, clever salt-and-pepper shakers, Italian ceramic dishware, eye-catching barware, black-and-white photographs, bejeweled frames, delicate chandeliers, unusual lamps, and sunburst mirrors—truly, something for almost everyone.

HURWITZ MINTZ
1751 Airline Dr., Metairie, 504/378-1000 or
888/957-9555, www.hurwitzmintz.com
HOURS: Mon.-Sat. 10 A.M.-9 P.M., Sun. noon-7 P.M.
Map 6

The sleek showrooms of Hurwitz Mintz, which has been a fixture in New Orleans since 1923, are something to behold. Owned and operated by the Mintz family for three generations, this impressive store contains more than 126,000 square feet of traditional and contemporary furniture, all cleverly arranged. Though Hurwitz Mintz isn't an antiques shop, it's a terrific place to find reproduction antiques, as well as striking postmodern sofas, beds, barstools, tables, and entertainment consoles that just might complement the antiques you already own. Boasting one of the South's largest selections of bedroom, dining room, living room, and office furniture, Hurwitz Mintz is truly a sight to see, and depending on the items in question, prices can be surprisingly reasonable.

JAVA HOUSE IMPORTS
913 Decatur St., 504/581-1288,
www.javahouseimports.com
HOURS: Daily 10 A.M.-9 P.M.
Map 1

When I lived in the building adjacent to this small, ever-fascinating store, I would often wander inside and peruse its collection of intriguing imported wares. Even though I've long since moved, I still make my way here often. The walls are covered with elongated African masks, the shelves are teeming with misshapen wooden bowls and jovial Buddha figurines (one of which I now own), and you'll even see a wide array of colorful tunics from foreign lands. If you're looking for statues of Hindu deities, bizarre mirrors, kites shaped as dragons, and intricately carved faces that might frighten small children at night, then this is definitely the place for you.

PIED NU
5521 Magazine St., 504/899-4118,
www.piednuneworleans.com
HOURS: Mon.-Sat. 10 A.M.-5 P.M.
Map 4

While Pied Nu features a delightful array of delicate jewelry, cozy furniture, quilted bedding, one-of-a-kind dresses, aromatic lotions, and candles curiously scented like oranges, jasmine, and fig trees, it's the store itself that's the real treasure. Inside this tidy, well-lit boutique, which opened in 1995 and caters to an upscale clientele, everything here is so artfully and yet comfortably arranged that you might just want to move in for a while.

◖ RICCA'S DEMOLISHING CORP.
511 N. Solomon St., 504/488-5524 or 504/482-7337,
www.riccasarchitectural.com
HOURS: Tues.-Fri. 9 A.M.-5 P.M., Sat. 9 A.M.-4 P.M.
Map 5

Just south of City Park, Ricca's Demolishing Corp. is one of several wrecking companies in New Orleans that have seen a huge, if unfortunate, boom in business as a result of Hurricane Katrina. Since Peter A. Ricca opened it in 1956, this 50,000-square-foot emporium has been an amazing source of new and used building materials, including mahogany doors, wrought-iron gates, stained-glass windows, antique chandeliers, brass door knockers, fountains and hitching posts, mailboxes and statuary, all sorts of vintage brackets and hardware, and plenty of other materials—some of which have been salvaged from historic New Orleans homes. In addition, Ricca's provides custom woodwork fashioned from reclaimed cypress and pine.

SHOP OF THE TWO SISTERS
1800 Magazine St., 504/525-2747,
www.shopofthetwosisters.com
HOURS: Mon.-Sat. 10 A.M.-5 P.M.
`Map 4`

The first and second floors of this large corner shop are packed to the rafters with eclectic home furnishings. Set inside a handsome three-story, Greek Revival–style townhouse and run by sisters Lee and Rose, this unique shop features tailored sofas, period chairs, odd lighting fixtures, throw pillows, area rugs, original sculptures, and striking objets d'art—many of them from faraway lands. The third floor houses an interior design studio, where Lee, a licensed interior designer, can help

Magazine Street's Shop of the Two Sisters houses an incredible cornucopia of eclectic home furnishings.

residents and seasonal visitors spruce up their homes and offices. Lee's award-winning work has appeared in places from New Orleans to Manhattan to London.

Gifts and Souvenirs

◖ ACCENT ANNEX
100 N. Labarre Rd., Metairie, 504/834-2003,
www.accentannex.com
HOURS: Mon.-Tues. 9 A.M.-6 P.M., Wed.-Sat. 9 A.M.-7 P.M.
`Map 6`

Not far from the Mississippi River is the Accent Annex, which has long been a one-stop shop for all Mardi Gras paraphernalia, including elaborate masks, festive apparel, specialty beads, and other holiday souvenirs. Although you'll be hard-pressed to leave without a souvenir or two, you can always visit the warehouse on the West Bank (651 Terry Pkwy., Gretna, 504/733-4700), just in case you're looking to stock a parade of your own.

BOOTSY'S FUNROCK'N
3109 Magazine St., 504/895-4102,
www.bootsysfunrockn.com
HOURS: Sun.-Thurs. 11 A.M.-6 P.M., Fri.-Sat. 11 A.M.-7 P.M.
`Map 4`

Perhaps the best, or at least the silliest, of the quirky gift and novelty shops throughout the city, Funrock'n carries bizarre and tacky knickknacks you probably never knew you needed: LSU Tiger capes, funny ice trays, animal hats, dashboard Jesus figurines, Beatles' yellow submarine lunchboxes, inflatable turkeys, fart machines, face paint, and other peculiarities. There's also a branch in the French Quarter (1125 Decatur St., 504/524-1122).

IT'S KING CAKE SEASON!

© DANIEL MARTONE

During Mardi Gras season, king cakes are available at Rouses in the French Quarter.

For a New Orleanian, one of the most anticipated times of the year is Mardi Gras season. Even if you're not a fan of the parades, the marching bands, and the drunken tourist hordes, you probably still have a taste for king cake, the season's most famous treat. My dad, for instance, has recently vowed that his parade-going days are over, but that doesn't mean he'll pass up the chance to enjoy a slice of this iced, sprinkled, or filled delicacy.

If you've never had one before, a king cake is essentially a large cinnamon roll-style cake, shaped like a ring or an oval, often covered with white icing, and almost always decorated with purple, green, and gold sprinkles. Nowadays, you'll also find filled king cakes, with flavors like cream cheese, apple, lemon, blueberry, pecan praline, and the like. Typically, there's a small plastic baby – supposedly meant to represent the baby Jesus – embedded somewhere in each cake (or, for safety's sake, left outside the cake). Per tradition, if you accept a piece containing the baby, you must bring a king cake to the next gathering – this is especially true in schools and office settings.

Although Christmas-style versions often appear in local grocery stores after Thanksgiving, traditional king cakes (which take their name from the three famed kings of the Bible) usually emerge by early January, in celebration of the pre-Lenten period between the Feast of Epiphany and Ash Wednesday. You'll find such delicacies in groceries throughout the region, including **Rouses Supermarket** (701 Royal St., 504/523-1353, http://shop. rouses.com, daily 6 A.M.-1 A.M.) at the corner of St. Peter and Royal Streets, the main grocery store for French Quarter denizens like me. Besides Rouses' skilled bakery, there are several local institutions known for their delicious king cakes, including **Gambino's Bakery and Cafe** (4821 Veterans Memorial Blvd., Metairie, 504/885-7500, www.gambinos. com, Mon.-Sat. 9 A.M.-7 P.M., Sun. 9 A.M.-5 P.M.), **Haydel's Bakery** (4037 Jefferson Hwy., Jefferson Heights, 800/442-1342, www.haydel-bakery.com, Tues.-Fri. 7:30 A.M.-5 P.M., Sat. 8:30 A.M.-4 P.M.), and the seasonal **Manny Randazzo King Cakes** (3515 N. Hullen St., Metairie, 504/456-1476 or 866/456-1476, www. randazzokingcake.com), all of which provide overnight delivery anywhere in the country. However you snag a king cake, though, I wouldn't advise eating too much in one sitting. A little bit of this sweet tradition goes a long way – especially when you're on a diet.

F & F BOTANICA SPIRITUAL SUPPLY

801 N. Broad St., 504/482-9142,
www.orleanscandleco.com
HOURS: Mon.-Tues. and Thurs.-Sat. 7:30 A.M.-5 P.M.
Map 5

Curiously situated across from the Zulu Social Aid & Pleasure Club—the folks behind the Mardi Gras krewe of Zulu—this small shop has been selling spiritual candles and supplies for more than three decades. Owned by Felix Figueroa, F & F Botanica was expanded several times over the years—and was completely remodeled after incurring damage from Hurricane Katrina. Today, you'll find an incredible selection of herbs, incense, candles, charms, soaps, essential oils, artisan jewelry, Mardi Gras beads, spiritual books, Santeria tools, and gift baskets.

FLORA SAVAGE

1301 Royal St., 504/581-4728, www.florasavage.net
HOURS: Mon.-Wed. 11 A.M.-6 P.M., Thurs.-Sat.
10 A.M.-6 P.M.
Map 1

My professional florist of choice, Flora Savage provides striking, exceedingly fresh bouquets and floral designs for birthdays, anniversaries, holidays, weddings, funerals, and all other special occasions. Even better, the staff is friendly, knowledgeable, and patient—and willing to keep your budget in mind. While phone and online orders are perfectly acceptable (delivery service is available throughout the Greater New Orleans area), I highly recommend stopping by this lovely little shop, where you can also purchase balloon bouquets, home decorations, and exotic flowers—including my husband's favorite, stunning stargazer lilies. If you're in town for a special reason and in need of last-minute flowers, don't go anywhere else.

FOREVER NEW ORLEANS

700 Royal St., 504/586-3536
HOURS: Daily 9 A.M.-10 P.M.
Map 1

Located on the first floor of one of the most photographed buildings in the entire French Quarter, this gift shop understandably gets quite a lot of foot traffic. It doesn't hurt that it's halfway between Jackson Square and Bourbon Street. Even I've been in here a few times, lured inside by the plethora of fleur-de-lis souvenirs, from jewelry sets to stationery to glassware. The inventory seems to change often, so it's easy to find some new trinket or must-have item that you never noticed before. Not surprisingly, Forever New Orleans is especially popular with tourists.

ISLAND OF SALVATION BOTANICA

2372 St. Claude Ave., Ste. 100, 504/948-9961,
www.feyvodou.com
HOURS: Tues.-Sat. 10 A.M.-5 P.M.
Map 2

Run by longtime voodoo practitioner Sallie Ann Glassman, this spiritual supply shop is a good place to find herbs, oils, incense, bath salts, specialty candles, Haitian artwork, decorated spirit boxes, spirit-calling sticks, dashboard statues, and voodoo-related books. You can even purchase custom-made gris-gris bags, made with various herbs, stones, oils, and other materials—including a clipping of your own hair or nails. Housed within a ramshackle building along the edge of the Faubourg Marigny (admittedly, not the best part of town), the Island of Salvation Botanica also provides readings, healings, and other spiritual services.

RAZZLE DAZZLE

524 Royal St., 504/568-0001, www.razzledazzle.com
HOURS: Daily 10 A.M.-6 P.M.
Map 1

With eye-catching, holiday-inspired window displays that befit its name, Razzle Dazzle lures many a curious tourist into its magical confines. Brimming with thousands of ever-changing gifts and souvenirs, this somewhat dizzying store features holiday ornaments, lights, and garlands, plus elaborate Mardi Gras masks, fleur-de-lis china and dinnerware, colorful purses, and so much more. In addition, several local artisans display their sketches, watercolors, sculptures, jewelry, and Ju-Ju dolls—all of which are for sale.

ROUX ROYALE

600 Royal St., 504/565-5272
HOURS: Daily 9 A.M.–10 P.M.
Map 1

Directly opposite its sister gift shop, Toulouse Royale—which is itself a decent spot for souvenirs—Roux Royale is a great find for foodies. Unlike most tourist-focused shops, this beautifully arranged space has a definitive purpose: to celebrate the unique cuisine of New Orleans. From colorful aprons and fleur-de-lis glassware to fabulous local cookbooks and Tabasco products, you'll find almost everything you need to bring the taste of the Big Easy home with you—even boxed pralines. If you can't find the right cookbook here, head around the corner to the **Kitchen Witch** (631 Toulouse St.), a bookstore that specializes in rare, hard-to-find, and secondhand cookbooks, including those that pertain to Cajun, Creole, and Louisiana cuisine.

SAVE NOLA

The Shops at Jax Brewery, 600 Decatur St., 1st Fl., 504/558-1951, www.onenola.com
HOURS: Sun.–Thurs. 10 A.M.–7 P.M., Fri.–Sat. 10 A.M.–8 P.M.
Map 1

One of the most curious shops in the former Jackson Brewery was created in the wake of Hurricane Katrina, with the mission of raising funds to rebuild homes in the city's most ravaged neighborhoods. To that end, the store offers affordable hats, mugs, pendants, coaster sets, wooden signs, night-lights, and T-shirts—almost all of which are emblazoned with iconic local images or significant sayings, such as "Save our coast" and "Hell or High Water." If you're shopping for souvenirs, consider this shop where your purchase will end up helping one of Save NOLA's nonprofit partners, such as Habitat for Humanity, Make It Right, and the New Orleans Musicians' Relief Fund.

Gourmet Treats

BIG FISHERMAN SEAFOOD

3301 Magazine St., 504/897-9907,
www.bigfishermanseafood.com
HOURS: Thurs.–Mon. 10 A.M.–6 P.M.
Map 4

The name says it all. For a taste of the Big Easy's famous seafood, head to Big Fisherman Seafood, where, depending on the season, you'll be able to pick up fresh fish, shrimp, oysters, mussels, and crabs, plus live crawfish by the sack—ideal for springtime boils. Alligator, turtle, and crab meat, plus hot boiled crawfish, are also available. Even better, the store will pack your seafood for traveling.

BLUE FROG CHOCOLATES

5707 Magazine St., 504/269-5707,
www.bluefrogchocolates.com
HOURS: Mon.–Fri. 10 A.M.–6 P.M., Sat. 10 A.M.–5 P.M., Sun. noon–5 P.M.
Map 4

Situated in a dainty, blue, wood-frame house in Uptown's Magazine Street shopping district, Blue Frog Chocolates specializes in sinful European candies and truffles. Frequent shoppers especially favor the whimsical, vibrant floral candy that's imported from Sulmona, Italy; typically filled with dark chocolate, nuts, or licorice, this graceful wedding tradition apparently dates to the 15th century.

CENTRAL GROCERY

923 Decatur St., 504/523-1620,
www.centralgroceryneworleans.com
HOURS: Tues.–Sat. 9 A.M.–5 P.M.
Map 1

Like most French Quarter denizens, I do most of my grocery shopping at the Rouses' store at the corner of Royal and St. Peter Streets, but for specialty items, there's no place quite like the Central Grocery on bustling Decatur. Famous for its oversized muffulettas—and the orderly, strictly enforced line that's required to purchase them—this often-crowded grocery stocks all manner of gourmet goodies and seasonings, from olive salad to Italian cookies to Zatarain's crawfish boil. Locals and celebrities alike swear by this shop; once, my husband even spotted

Meryl Streep in the small, rear dining area, noshing on a muffuletta of her own.

EVANS CREOLE CANDY FACTORY

848 Decatur St., 504/522-7111 or 800/637-6675, www.evanscreolecandy.com

HOURS: Mon.-Thurs. 10 A.M.-6 P.M., Fri.-Sun. 10 A.M.-7 P.M.

`Map 1`

Not surprisingly, the French Market boasts more than one praline vendor. Just a few doors down from Aunt Sally's Praline Shop, you'll encounter one of the city's oldest such stores. For more than a century, Evans Creole Candy Factory has been crafting delicious pralines. Still today, you can watch the candy-makers working on a fresh batch of pralines through the big windows of this shop in the French Market, which is also an excellent source for hand-dipped chocolates, dark-chocolate turtles (Creole pecans topped with caramel and dipped in chocolate), chocolate-covered maraschino cherries, and other tempting sweets.

MARTIN WINE CELLAR

714 Elmeer Ave., Metairie, 504/896-7300 or 888/407-7496, www.martinwine.com

HOURS: Mon.-Fri. 9 A.M.-8 P.M., Sat. 9 A.M.-7 P.M., Sun. 10 A.M.-4 P.M.

`Map 6`

If, while in the French Quarter, you have a sudden desire for your own bottle of wine, you can certainly try your luck at Vieux Carré Wine and Spirits, where the clerks are notoriously surly. But, for those with access to a car, I highly recommend a trip to Martin Wine Cellar. Although it deserves ample praise for being the city's best wine and liquor shop and one of its top gourmet grocery stores, it also does one thing as well as any restaurant in the city: massive deli sandwiches. The food at the on-site bistro and deli (504/896-7350, Mon.–Fri. 9 A.M.–8 P.M., Sat. 9 A.M.–5 P.M., Sun. 10 A.M.–4 P.M.) is more typical of Sonoma's wine country than New Orleans. There are no crawfish or oysters on the menu, but you can get such toothsome sandwiches as the Steamboat (corned beef, ham, hickory-smoked bacon, Swiss cheese, onions, and

Creole mustard served hot on an onion roll). After ordering your meal at the counter, take a seat in the plant-filled, glass-brick dining room amid legions of yuppies and epicureans. There's a second locale in the Uptown area (3500 Magazine St., 504/899-7411).

◖ SOUTHERN CANDYMAKERS

334 Decatur St., 504/523-5544 or 800/344-9773, www.southerncandymakers.com

HOURS: Daily 10 A.M.-7 P.M.

`Map 1`

The French Quarter is rife with longstanding praline shops, from Laura's Candies to Leah's Pralines, but Southern Candymakers is my personal favorite. Just a couple blocks from Canal Street, this is a full retail shop with pralines, toffees, nut clusters, chocolate alligators, marzipan, peanut brittle, fudge, and lots of other locally made sweets that will do terrible things to your teeth but will surely make the rest of you quite happy. If you find yourself closer to Esplanade, stop by the Quarter's other location in the historic French Market (1010 Decatur St., 504/525-6170).

Southern Candymakers is a favorite in the Quarter for pralines.

LOUISIANA FOOD FINDS

Some of your most memorable – and distinctive – purchases may be products that you can nosh. From New Orleans to Cajun Country, dozens of businesses specialize in manufacturing notable foods and drinks. Here's a roundup of the best Louisiana-made products, most of which you'll find in local grocery stores and other emporiums:

- **Abita Beer:** Located on the Northshore about an hour from New Orleans, Abita Springs first became famous for its crystalline artesian wells. It's this perfectly pure water that's used by the **Abita Brewing Company** (166 Barbee Rd., Abita Springs, 985/893-3143 or 800/737-2311, www.abita.com) to craft such classic Louisiana elixirs as Abita Amber, Turbodog, Purple Haze, and the seasonally popular Mardi Gras Bock. Tours of the brewery are available at 2 P.M. Wednesday–Friday and at 11 A.M., noon, 1 P.M., and 2 P.M. on Saturday; no reservations are required.

- **Blue Plate Mayonnaise:** Produced by Luzianne (www.luzianne.com), which is based on Magazine Street in the CBD, Blue Plate mayo is made with local cottonseed oil and has been a favorite condiment in these parts since the late 1920s. Luzianne is also one of the largest independent coffee and tea manufacturers in the United States.

- **Camellia Beans:** Since 1923, Harahan-based Camellia Brand (www.camelliabrand.com) has been manufacturing dried kidney beans, the magic ingredient in New Or-

leans's famous red beans and rice. Although red kidney beans are the big seller throughout the state, Camellia also sells black, navy, pinto, garbanzo, split pea, lima, lentil, field pea, black-eyed pea, and crowder pea varieties.

- **Community Coffee and Tea:** Better known nowadays for its string of festive coffeehouses, Community Coffee and Tea (www.communitycoffee.com) is, first and foremost, a coffee and tea producer. Its packaged ground coffee and bagged teas have a deeply loyal following. You can purchase these products at any Community Coffee (a.k.a. "CC's") café or at most specialty food and gift shops.

- **Crystal Hot Sauce:** Tabasco isn't the only game in town when it comes to pepper sauces. The slightly milder Crystal brand hot sauce certainly has its diehard fans. It's made right in New Orleans by Baumer Foods (www.baumerfoods.com), which also produces sauces for steak, chicken wings, and other foods.

- **Dixie Beer:** Formerly made inside a rambling brewery building on New Orleans's Tulane Avenue – which was damaged during Hurricane Katrina and has yet to be restored – this rich, tasty beer is one of the most popular beers of the Deep South. Currently produced by other breweries, Dixie's most popular brews include Jazz Amber Light and Blackened Voodoo Lager. Sip-

ST. JAMES CHEESE COMPANY

5004 Prytania St., 504/899-4737,
www.stjamescheese.com
HOURS: Mon.-Thurs. 11 A.M.-6 P.M., Fri.-Sat. 11 A.M.-8 P.M., Sun. 11 A.M.-4 P.M.
Map 4

When you have a craving for cheese, New Orleans might not be the first place that comes to mind, but this well-loved Uptown store is definitely worth a stop—whether you're a dairy novice or a cheese aficionado. Established in 2006 shortly after the owners returned to their hurricane-ravaged city, the family-run St. James Cheese Company stocks a wide and carefully selected assortment of artisanal cheeses and other gourmet foods, from Oregon blue cheese to Italian salami to Dijon mustard. This delightful shop even offers a range of well-attended classes focusing on chocolate, cheese, and wine pairings.

ping a Dixie Beer while slurping down raw oysters is a classic Louisiana tradition.

- **French Market Coffee:** Chicory, a faintly bitter herb root grown mostly in northern Europe, is dried, ground-roasted, and then blended with French Market coffee beans to create the inimitable flavor that so many java drinkers cherish. Founded in 1890, French Market Coffee (www.frenchmarketcoffee.com) is sold in shops and restaurants all around town.

- **Pralines:** These exquisite melt-in-your-mouth candies are made with cream, butter, caramelized brown sugar, and pecans. They're sold at virtually every food-related gift shop in southern Louisiana, but one of the best sources of authentic pralines is **Aunt Sally's Praline Shops** (810 Decatur St., 800/642-7257, www.auntsallys.com, Sun.-Mon. 9 A.M.-7 P.M., Tues.-Thurs. 9 A.M.-6 P.M., Fri.-Sat. 9 A.M.-8 P.M.) in the French Quarter.

- **Steen's Syrup:** The Steen's Syrup Mill (www.steensyrup.com), a sugarcane syrup-processing plant in the small town of Abbeville, has been going strong since 1910. Buy a bottle of this thick sweetener to pour over pancakes or bake into cakes and cookies.

- **Tabasco Sauce:** The mother of all U.S. hot sauces, Tabasco hardly needs a description here. Louisiana families are known to go through a decent-sized bottle of the stuff every month, and the Tabasco company –

based on Avery Island in the heart of the Cajun wetlands – also makes a number of related sauces, mustards, and snacks. Free tours of the **Tabasco Factory** (337/365-8173, www.tabasco.com, daily 9 A.M.-4 P.M.) are also available.

- **Tony Chachere's:** One of the leading Cajun and Creole prepared-foods companies in Louisiana, Tony Chachere's (www.tonychachere.com) is based in the Cajun town of Opelousas and is known for a vast array of sauces and boxed products. While the blended food mixes, such as Creole jambalaya, are especially good, also check out the tasty seasoning blends.

- **Zapp's Potato Chips:** There's nothing that complements a muffuletta sandwich and a can of Barq's root beer better than a bag of Zapp's Potato Chips (www.zapps.com). Made in Gramercy, these super-crunchy chips truly zip with flavor. Popular selections include Spicy Cajun Crawtators, Hotter 'n Hot Jalapeño, Cajun Dill, Sour Cream and Creole Onion, and Sweet Potato.

- **Zatarain's:** A notable spice producer based in the West Bank suburb of Gretna, Zatarain's (www.zatarains.com) has been turning out tasty food mixes and spices since 1889. The dirty rice mix is particularly good, as are the crab and crawfish boils, but don't overlook such notable delicacies as the root beer extract, frozen sausage and chicken gumbo, and crab cake mix.

SUCRÉ

3025 Magazine St., 504/520-8311,
www.shopsucre.com
HOURS: Sun.-Thurs. 8 A.M.-10 P.M., Fri.-Sat. 8 A.M.-midnight
`Map 4`

While shopping along Magazine Street, treat yourself to something yummy from this sinful store. Brimming with candied pecans, handmade marshmallows, dark chocolate bark, salted caramel chocolate, and signature macaroons, Sucré is sure to satisfy any sweet tooth. During Mardi Gras season, the shop even offers its own unique king cakes, enhanced by a Creole cream-cheese filling. Those in the suburbs are in luck, too; there's a branch of Sucré at the Lakeside Shopping Center (504/834-2277).

Health and Beauty

AIDAN GILL FOR MEN
550 Fulton St., 504/566-4903,
www.aidangillformen.com
HOURS: Mon.-Wed. 10 A.M.-6 P.M., Thurs. 10 A.M.-7 P.M.,
Fri.-Sat. 10 A.M.-6 P.M., Sun. noon-6 P.M.
Map 3

Quirky Aidan Gill entices its loyal male customers—as well as tentative first-timers—with
old-fashioned shaving instruments, upscale
bath products, well-made neckties and cuff
links, even wristwatches. Many come to experience "The Shave at the End of the Galaxy,"
a luxurious, hot-towel shave in the back room.
There's also a location in the Uptown area
(2026 Magazine St., 504/587-9090).

◖ BELLADONNA DAY SPA
2900 Magazine St., 504/891-4393,
www.belladonnadayspa.com
HOURS: Mon.-Tues. 9 A.M.-6 P.M., Wed.-Thurs.
9 A.M.-8 P.M., Fri.-Sat. 9 A.M.-6 P.M.
Map 4

Hip celebs often call at Belladonna Day Spa, an
airy, modern bath-and-body shop that's also a top-
notch unisex spa. Set inside a Victorian house, the
interior treatment rooms are soothing and minimalist, with a Japanese ambience. Detoxifying
seaweed body treatments, mud body rituals,
therapeutic massages, and replenishing facials are
among the most popular services, though you'll
also have the option of various manicures, pedicures, and body buffs. Ideal for both residents and
tourists who have spent a long day of shopping
and sightseeing, this tranquil spa also offers an
assortment of spa products and fine linens. And
don't forget about the **Belladoggie Resort Spa**
(815 Washington Ave., 504/309-9510), where
your beloved pets can be pampered, too.

BOURBON FRENCH PARFUMS
805 Royal St., 504/522-4480 or 800/476-0303,
www.neworleansperfume.com
HOURS: Daily 10 A.M.-5 P.M.
Map 1

For more than 160 years, this aromatic

perfumery has been creating custom-blended
fragrances for its eager clientele. If you're game,
schedule a one-hour private sitting; a special-
ist will analyze your body chemistry, assess
your personality, and record your preferred
scents. Then once your "secret" formula is created, you'll be able to order an entire set of
toiletries, including perfume, cologne, eau de
toilette, powder, lotion, body shampoo, and
foaming bath gel. If you lack the time or patience, you can just as easily choose from the
perfumes, musk oils, voodoo potions, and
other fragrances available on-site. Also on display are elegant perfume bottles, decorated
with everything from flowers to frogs to, yes,
fleurs-de-lis.

EARTHSAVERS
5501 Magazine St., 504/899-8555,
www.earthsaversonline.com
HOURS: Mon.-Sat. 9 A.M.-6 P.M., Sun. 11 A.M.-5 P.M.
Map 4

The environmentally sensitive Earthsavers has
earned a loyal following for its essential oils,
all-natural exfoliants, skin moisturizers, body
scrubs, and other skin-care products. The shop
also offers a wide array of spa services, including Dead Sea mud treatments, aromatherapy
massages, organic facials, and anti-aging foot
and hand peels. If you find yourself in the suburbs, you'll happily find a second branch in
the Lakeside Shopping Center (504/835-0225).

THE HERB IMPORT CO.
5055 Canal St., 504/488-4889 or 877/433-4372,
www.herbimport.com
HOURS: Mon.-Sat. 9 A.M.-8 P.M., Sun. 11 A.M.-6 P.M.
Map 5

Despite its odd location at the convergence of
several Mid-City cemeteries, the Herb Import
Co. is a good place to pick up health-enhanc-
ing products like vitamins, herbal supplements,
detox products, electronic cigarettes, and herbal
smoking blends. You'll also find a wide array
of bath and body products, such as botanical

soaps, massage creams, organic lotions, essential oils, and biotin shampoo. There are also locations in the French Quarter (711 St. Peter St., 504/525-4372) and Uptown (712 Adams St., 504/861-4644).

SPA ATLANTIS
PROFESSIONAL SPA & SALON
740 Gravier St., 504/566-8088, www.spaatlantis.net
HOURS: Mon.-Sat. 10 A.M.-7 P.M., Sun. 10 A.M.-3 P.M.
Map 3

While in the CBD, many spa enthusiasts head to the Balance Spa & Fitness in the Loews New Orleans Hotel, but non-hotel guests will appreciate Spa Atlantis, a professional spa and salon just a half block west of St. Charles Avenue. Owned by a licensed massage therapist, this tranquil place offers a full menu of massage, body, facial, and nail treatments, including warm stone massages, black currant mineral body scrubs, acne-fighting facials, and deluxe spa pedicures. In case you have a sexy night planned, full-body waxing services are also available.

Hobbies and Recreation

CIGAR FACTORY NEW ORLEANS
415 Decatur St., 504/568-1003 or 800/550-0775,
www.cigarfactoryneworleans.com
HOURS: Sun.-Thurs. 10 A.M.-10 P.M., Fri.-Sat. 10 A.M.-11 P.M.
Map 1

If you need a late-night cigarette fix, you can always stop by Mary Jane's Emporium in the 1200 block of Decatur, but for something more distinctive, venture to the Cigar Factory, where you can actually watch cigars being rolled. Besides various tables for enjoying a smoking break, cigar lovers will appreciate the wide selection, walk-in humidor, and knowledgeable staff. You'll find a much smaller branch (504/568-0168) at 206 Bourbon Street.

NEW ORLEANS MUSIC EXCHANGE
3342 Magazine St., 504/891-7670,
www.neworleansmusicexchange.net
HOURS: Mon.-Sat. 10:30 A.M.-6 P.M., Sun. 1-5 P.M.
Map 4

Local bands, DJs, club owners, and others flock to the New Orleans Music Exchange (NOME) for audio equipment, video cameras, and musical instruments—from Fender guitars to Yamaha keyboards to Jupiter trumpets and trombones. Here, you have the choice of buying, selling, renting, or trading equipment and instruments, and the shop's experienced technicians can handle installations as well as repairs. If you're interested in playing the guitar, bass, piano, mandolin, trumpet, or drums, musical lessons are also available through NOME.

PAPIER PLUME
842 Royal St., 504/988-7265, www.papierplume.com
HOURS: Daily 10 A.M.-6 P.M.
Map 1

As a writer, I adore this small, elegant corner shop, which, as the name indicates, offers a plethora of high-end writing supplies and utensils, neatly arranged throughout this well-lit space. Amid the stylish pens, dipping feather quills, old-fashioned inkwell sets, bottled inks, brass seals and wax sticks, leather-bound journals, fancy pen cases, odd desk accessories, and fleur-de-lis stationery, you might find something to appeal to that special writer in your life.

SCRIPTURA
5423 Magazine St., 504/897-1555, www.scriptura.com
HOURS: Mon.-Sat. 10 A.M.-5 P.M.
Map 4

Those who prefer the old-fashioned art of letter-writing will love this well-organized Uptown store, with lovely writing instruments, handmade stationery, custom wax seals, fancy desk accessories, New Orleans–style holiday cards, and Italian, leather-bound albums and journals. You can even order customized invitations for weddings, parties, and other special occasions. There's also a branch in the Lakeside Shopping Center (504/219-1113).

Jewelry and Accessories

ADLER'S

722 Canal St., 504/523-5292 or 800/925-7912,
www.adlersjewelry.com
HOURS: Mon.-Sat. 10 A.M.-5:30 P.M.
Map 3

Among New Orleans's many enticing jewelry
shops, Adler's has the most loyal following—
it's been serving the Crescent City since 1898.
Fine watches and bracelets, engagement rings
and wedding bands, crystal stemware, exquisite china, and ornate flatware are among the
offerings. Another branch is located in the
Lakeside Shopping Center (504/523-1952),
and Adler's is also affiliated with the longstanding Waldhorn & Adler antiques shop
(343 Royal St., 504/581-6379).

ELECTRIC LADYLAND TATTOO

610 Frenchmen St., 504/947-8286,
www.electricladyland.net
HOURS: Mon.-Sat. noon-midnight, Sun. 1-10 P.M.
Map 2

A top pick among locals, this popular tattoo
parlor is nestled among some of the city's best
live music joints in the Marigny. Besides state-
certified tattoo artists, who are capable of ink-
ing everything from vampires to Celtic crosses
to New Orleans–style fleurs-de-lis, you'll find
a resident piercer on-site. Just bear in mind that
this is a cash-only shop. Uptown denizens can
also visit the branch at 8108 Earhart Boulevard
(504/866-6000).

FIFI MAHONY'S

934 Royal St., 504/525-4343, www.fifimahonys.com
HOURS: Mon.-Fri. noon-6 P.M., Sat. 11 A.M.-7 P.M., Sun.
noon-6 P.M.
Map 1

Whether you have a Halloween parade, Mardi
Gras party, or special occasion in your future,
outrageous Fifi Mahony's is your one-stop
salon and makeup counter if you're hoping to
make a bold statement. Pop in and browse the
wigs that come in every color of the rainbow
and then some, plus body glitter, Tony and

Tina cosmetics, wild hair-care products, and
offbeat handbags.

JOAN GOOD ANTIQUE JEWELRY

322 Royal St., 504/525-1705, www.joangood.com
HOURS: Daily 9 A.M.-6 P.M.
Map 1

For special occasions—such as Mother's
Day—I've been known to purchase jewelry
fashioned from garnets, my mom's favorite
stone. On such occasions, there are only two
shops I'll visit: New Orleans Silversmiths and
Joan Good Antique Jewelry. The latter specializes in garnet rings, pendants, brooches,
crosses, and earrings. For more than three decades, Joan has also purveyed antique cameos,
fleur-de-lis lockets, poison rings, chandelier
earrings, Asian figurines, pearl necklaces, and
various precious stones. Sometimes, it's a treat
just to browse the enormous collection; you
never know when you might spot something
unusual, like a beetle-encased pendant.

MEYER THE HATTER

120 St. Charles Ave., 504/525-1048 or 800/882-4287,
www.meyerthehatter.com
HOURS: Mon.-Sat. 10 A.M.-5:45 P.M.
Map 3

While the CBD doesn't boast many notable
clothing and accessory shops, Meyer the Hatter
is indeed worth a look. Established by Sam H.
Meyer in 1894 as Meyer's Hat Box, this family-run business has since moved into a much
bigger space. It now boasts the South's largest
collection of headwear, from stylish Stetsons
and satin top hats to jazz band caps and black-
and-gold Saints visors.

◖ MIGNON FAGET

3801 Magazine St., 504/891-2005 or 800/375-7557,
www.mignonfaget.com
HOURS: Mon.-Sat. 10 A.M.-6 P.M.
Map 4

Mignon Faget has an almost cult following among New Orleans's devotees of fine

© DANIEL MARTONE

New Orleans Silversmiths, a well-respected jewelry shop close to Jackson Square

jewelry. Not surprisingly, Faget has won countless awards for her creations, many of which incorporate icons and images familiar to Louisianians, such as oyster earrings, redfish pins, red-bean charm necklaces, sno-ball pendants, and fleur-de-lis cuff links. You'll find other locations inside the Shops at Canal Place (504/524-2973) and the Lakeside Shopping Center (504/835-2244).

NEW ORLEANS SILVERSMITHS

600 Chartres St., 504/522-8333 or 800/219-8333, www.neworleanssilversmiths.com

HOURS: Mon.-Sat. 10 A.M.-5 P.M., Sun. 11 A.M.-4 P.M.

Map 1

A French Quarter fixture since 1938, New Orleans Silversmiths specializes in modern gold jewelry, estate jewelry, and antique silver holloware. In addition, you'll find corkscrews, decanters, cocktail shakers, candlesticks and candelabra, Victorian napkin rings, garnet pendants, and handcrafted, sterling silver animal figurines. For a taste of New Orleans, the shop even offers café au lait sets as well as fleur-de-lis jewelry and cuff links.

SYMMETRY JEWELERS AND DESIGNERS

8138 Hampson St., 504/861-9925 or 800/628-3711, www.symmetry-jewelers.com

HOURS: Tues.-Sat. 10 A.M.-5 P.M.

Map 4

Situated in Uptown's hip Riverbend area, just a half block from Carrollton Avenue, Symmetry Jewelers has been serving local jewelry lovers since 1975. A variety of artists, including an in-house designer, are responsible for the lovely items you'll see here, from Tom Mathis's gorgeous engagement rings to Nina Nguyen's whimsical necklaces. Interested in taking home a unique souvenir? Choose from the wide array of fleur-de-lis pins, pendants, rings, cuff links, earrings, and belt buckles. In addition, this full-service jewelry store and graphic-design studio handles repairs, restorations, and custom creations.

VALOBRA JEWELRY AND ANTIQUES
333 Royal St., 504/525-6363, www.valobra.net
HOURS: Mon.-Sat. 10 A.M.-6 P.M.
Map 1

Established in 1905, Valobra presents a cornucopia of paintings, distinctive Venetian chandeliers, and antique furnishings, including Italian consoles, American commodes, and French parlor sets. The shop's true specialty, however, is its vast jewelry collection, which encompasses contemporary, antique, and estate pieces and boasts everything from yellow diamond rings to pearl chokers to ruby-studded bracelets. New, preowned, and antique watches are also available.

Kids' Stuff

IDEA FACTORY
838 Chartres St., 800/524-4332,
www.ideafactoryneworleans.com
HOURS: Daily 10 A.M.-6 P.M.
Map 1

Owned by a sometimes surly local named Ken Ford, the Idea Factory is my favorite kid-friendly shop in New Orleans. Just opposite the Trashy Diva boutique, this corner store contains a treasure-trove of handcrafted wooden objects, including clocks, wine corks, cooking utensils, back massagers, thumb pianos, office accessories, mechanical toys, kaleidoscopes, chessboards, and figurines, including an entire Noah's Ark set. On several special occasions, this fascinating place has provided some wonderful gifts for my family, from gorgeous clipboards to curious puzzle boxes.

LITTLE TOY SHOP
900 Decatur St., 504/522-6588
HOURS: Daily 10 A.M.-6 P.M.
Map 1

Located in the historic French Market, this wonderful store is filled with a slew of cool items, including precious miniatures, collectibles, toy

Both kids and adults adore the wooden creations inside the Idea Factory.

© DANIEL MARTONE

soldiers, and imported European toys. You'll also spy plenty of games and gifts that aren't so exquisite and breakable—in other words, toys that you could actually entrust to the hands of playful kids. A second location, **Little Toy Shop Too** (513 St. Ann St., 504/523-1770), is situated in Jackson Square.

ORIENT EXPRESSED

3905 Magazine St., 504/899-3060 or 888/856-3948, www.orientexpressed.com

HOURS: Mon.-Sat. 10 A.M.-5 P.M.

`Map 4`

Started by two art teachers, Bee Fitzpatrick and Dabney Jacob, this quaint gift shop features an eclectic collection of antiques, jewelry, home accessories, amusing tchotchkes, carved santos, and fine porcelain. Most notably, Orient Expressed offers high-quality, hand-smocked children's clothing, which Bee and Dabney started selling in the early 1980s, around the time that their children were born. Ranging from traditional to modern, these clothes are crafted in family-run sewing factories, utilizing fabrics from all around the world, from Vietnam to France to Peru.

PIPPEN LANE

2929 Magazine St., 504/269-0106 or 800/445-3918, www.pippenlane.com

HOURS: Mon.-Sat. 10 A.M.-5 P.M.

`Map 4`

Among the trendy boutiques and emporiums along Magazine Street is this whimsical shop, which, for more than a decade, has specialized in all sorts of cute, imaginative kids' apparel. Besides pajamas, outfits, jackets, and bathing suits for babies, girls, and boys, Pippen Lane also offers shoes, linens, blankets, lunchboxes, and backpacks. Kids may also appreciate the decent selection of books, dolls, stuffed animals, and classic toys, such as jumbo jacks, yo-yos, jump-ropes, and puzzles.

SWORD & PEN

528 Royal St., 504/523-7741, www.swordandpenorleans.com

HOURS: Sun.-Wed. 10 A.M.-4 P.M., Thurs.-Sat. 10 A.M.-5 P.M.

`Map 1`

Formerly known as Le Petit Soldier Shop, Sword & Pen is popular among local history buffs, especially those with a penchant for military history. A wide array of miniature soldier figurines, including those representing both sides of the American Civil War as well as the Revolutionary War, World War I, and World War II, continue battle amid the confines of this shop. Collectors come for intricate model ships as well as figurines that represent Halloween, Mardi Gras, and the New Orleans jazz scene. Though not appropriate for all children, Sword & Pen can appeal to young girls and boys interested in collecting—and displaying—bits of history.

Occult and Voodoo

BOTTOM OF THE CUP TEA ROOM

327 Chartres St., 800/729-7148, www.bottomofthecup.com

HOURS: Daily 10 A.M.-6 P.M.

`Map 1`

Besides offering more than 100 varieties of fine tea, this cozy shop has been giving authentic psychic readings since 1929. In fact, the name of the store is derived from its early days, when the resident psychic would read the tea leaves left at the bottom of a customer's cup. This is also a good spot for tarot cards and metaphysical gifts like crystals, amulets, pendants, wands, and crystal balls.

BOUTIQUE DU VAMPYRE

633 Toulouse St., 504/561-8267, www.feelthebite.com

HOURS: Daily 11 A.M.-7 P.M.

`Map 1`

In a city obsessed with vampire lore and Anne Rice's legacy, it's hard to believe that there aren't more vampire shops here. In fact, the only one that comes to mind is Boutique du Vampyre, one of my favorite browsing haunts.

VOODOO VS. HOODOO

Given the Big Easy's historical ties to the voodoo religion, it surely comes as no surprise that the city is still home to several voodoo practitioners. Whether you're seriously interested in the faith or just curious about this often misunderstood aspect of New Orleans's culture, you'll find several voodoo-related shops in town, most of which provide everything from gris-gris bags to potion oils to handmade African crafts, not to mention rituals and readings. In the French Quarter, such emporiums include **Voodoo Authentica** (612 Dumaine St.), **Reverend Zombie's House of Voodoo** (725 St. Peter St.), **Marie Laveau's House of Voodoo** (739 Bourbon St.), and the **Voodoo Spiritual Temple** (828 N. Rampart St.).

If you've seen *The Skeleton Key* (2005), you might also be aware that some southern Louisianians also practice hoodoo. So, what, you might wonder, is the difference between voodoo and hoodoo? Well, depending on who you ask, that can be a rather complicated question.

The voodoo of New Orleans is similar to that of Haiti, Cuba, and other Caribbean islands, where the ancient West African religion of Vodoun has been influenced by Catholicism. Hoodoo, by contrast, is not a religion, but a folk magic that blends the practices of various cultures, from African and Native American traditions to European grimoires. Often referring to magic spells, potions, and charms that include conjuration, witchcraft, rootwork, and Biblical recitation, hoodoo supposedly enables people to access supernatural forces in order to improve aspects of their daily lives, including love, luck, health, money, and employment. Naturally, some people also use hoodoo for more nefarious reasons, such as revenge on those who have "crossed" them. No matter

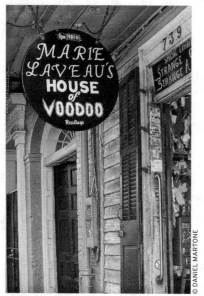

© DANIEL MARTONE

Marie Laveau's House of Voodoo features an array of voodoo dolls, tarot cards, and other curiosities.

what your intentions, though, as with other magico-religious traditions, hoodoo often involves the utilization of herbs, roots, minerals, animal bones and other parts, candles, bodily fluids, and an individual's possessions.

In truth, many modern-day voodoo followers integrate hoodoo folk magic into the practice of their religion. For more information about both traditions, consult such books as Jim Haskins's *Voodoo & Hoodoo* and Stephanie Rose Bird's *Sticks, Stones, Roots & Bones: Hoodoo, Mojo & Conjuring with Herbs*.

At first glance, it appears to be a rather sparse place; however, you'll find plenty of vampire accouterments like customizable fangs, sexy capes, enthralling chokers, old-world hats, and temporary bite tattoos. The proprietors, whose awesome German shepherd is often on-site, also stock candles, chalices, books, journals, perfume, soap, tarot cards, paintings, wine and wine-related paraphernalia, walking sticks, and Gothic jewelry—such as the curious poison ring that I often wear.

◀ MARIE LAVEAU'S HOUSE OF VOODOO

739 Bourbon St., 504/581-3751,
www.voodooneworleans.com
HOURS: Sun.-Thurs. 10 A.M.-11:30 P.M., Fri.-Sat.
10 A.M.-1:30 A.M.
`Map 1`

Amid the inebriated tourists on Bourbon Street lies one of my favorite shops in the city—a small, often crowded space filled with candles, incense, authentic masks, voodoo literature, spell kits, tarot cards, symbolic pendants and figurines, and locally crafted voodoo dolls. Opposite the register, you'll spy a cluttered,

hands-off voodoo altar, while in the rear room, you can experience private tarot-card readings. The folks behind Marie Laveau's also operate **Reverend Zombie's House of Voodoo** (504/486-6366) on St. Peter Street.

VOODOO AUTHENTICA

612 Dumaine St., 504/522-2111, www.voodooshop.com
HOURS: Daily 11 A.M.-7 P.M.
`Map 1`

Owned and operated by voodoo practitioners since 1996, Voodoo Authentica carries many of the same items that other French Quarter voodoo shops feature: incense, candles, potions, oils, gris-gris bags, ritual kits, handmade voodoo dolls, Haitian crafts, helpful books and DVDs, and unusual jewelry, such as necklaces made of alligator claws and teeth. Besides offering spiritual consultations, this unique cultural center presents **Voodoofest,** a free annual festival that occurs on Halloween and, for more than a dozen years, has celebrated the voodoo religion's influence on New Orleans traditions through educational presentations, book signings, and an ancestral healing ritual.

Shopping Centers and Malls

◀ FRENCH MARKET

Decatur St. and N. Peters St. btwn. St. Peter St. and
Barracks St., 504/522-2621, www.frenchmarket.org
HOURS: Vary depending on the business
COST: Free, though dining and shopping costs apply
`Map 1`

Not far from Jackson Square lies the French Market, a picturesque, multi-block collection of shops, eateries, and stalls that partially date to 1813. Besides **Café Du Monde** and other eateries, the market also houses retail shops that sell everything from toys, souvenirs, and candies to African oils, Latin American hammocks, and local artwork. One of the highlights here is the open-air pavilion at the eastern end. It features a small **farmers market** offering bottled hot sauce, Cajun spices, homemade pralines, fresh seafood and

produce, sandwiches, sno-balls, and other local vittles. There's also a daily **flea market,** which presents a wide array of jewelry, dresses, luggage, cookbooks, Asian figurines, African masks, homemade candles, and other souvenirs. Though it's rather crowded on the weekends, nothing here costs much.

LAKESIDE SHOPPING CENTER

3301 Veterans Memorial Blvd., Metairie,
504/835-8000, www.lakesideshopping.com
HOURS: Mon.-Sat. 10 A.M.-9 P.M., Sun. noon-6 P.M.
`Map 6`

If you're a fan of shopping malls, consider a trek to Metairie, which has one of the region's top shops. The Lakeside Shopping Center contains more than 120 stores and boutiques, among them Adler's, Mignon Faget, Banana

Republic, Guess, Jeantherapy, J. Crew, Eddie Bauer, Coach Leather, Victoria's Secret, Teavana, Pottery Barn, Restoration Hardware, Williams-Sonoma, Godiva, Brookstone, Dick's Sporting Goods, even an Apple Store. Featuring three parking garages and several parking lots, the mall is anchored by three major department stores: Dillard's, JCPenney, and Macy's. In addition, you'll find several dining choices on the premises, including Café Du Monde, Red Lobster, P. F. Chang's, and a food court.

OAKWOOD CENTER

197 Westbank Expwy., Gretna, 504/361-1550, www.oakwoodcenter.com

HOURS: Mon.-Sat. 10 A.M.-9 P.M., Sun. noon-6 P.M.

Map 6

While exploring the West Bank of the Mississippi River, you might just encounter this impressive shopping center, the largest in this part of the Greater New Orleans area. Anchored by Dillard's, Sears, and JCPenney, the spacious Oakwood Center features a food court, more than 100 specialty shops and

kiosks, and, of course, a Café Du Monde to satisfy your post-shopping beignet cravings. Familiar chain stores include Bath & Body Works, GNC, Old Navy, American Eagle Outfitters, Lady Foot Locker, Victoria's Secret, and GameStop.

RIVERWALK MARKETPLACE

500 Port of New Orleans Pl., 504/522-1555, www.riverwalkmarketplace.com

HOURS: Mon.-Sat. 10 A.M.-7 P.M., Sun. noon-6 P.M.

Map 3

Situated beside the Mississippi River, the Riverwalk Marketplace is, shop-wise, like many other midsize shopping malls, though it's fairly notable for its sweeping river views. This lengthy, serpentine building has more than 75 shops, some of which proffer local goods, souvenirs, and crafts, such as a Cajun ornament store, several mask emporiums, and a Brad Thompson art gallery. Admittedly, however, it's a less atmospheric locale for souvenir shopping than the Quarter's French Market. Chain shops include Gap, Ann Taylor Loft, Foot Locker, Nine West, Brookstone, and Rocky

FARMERS MARKETS

Farmers markets have been a part of life in New Orleans since the French and Spanish governments ruled the city in the 18th century, and they remain just as vibrant to this day. In fact, the recently renovated farmers market in the historic **French Market** (N. Peters St. and Ursulines Ave., www.frenchmarket.org, daily 9 A.M.-6 P.M.) is perhaps the most famous place in the city to procure gourmet edibles. Here, you'll find pralines and baked goods, fresh seafood and produce, Cajun spices and cooking kits, plus an array of freshly prepared foods, from gumbo and boudin to smoothies and sno-balls.

If you love browsing market-fresh food, you should also consider the **Crescent City Farmers Market** (www.crescentcityfarmersmarket.org), held three times a week at different locations around town and featuring a phenomenal

roster of vendors and chefs. Throughout the year, you'll spy pastries, Creole cream cheese, lentil balls, fudge, tamales, jams and honey, alligator sausage, Cornish hens, fresh-cut flowers, gourmet soups, and countless more delectables. Depending on the month, however, you might also see fresh shrimp, soft-shell crabs, kumquats, figs, watermelon, blueberries, asparagus, Creole tomatoes, okra, and other seasonal vittles. It's held in the Uptown neighborhood at 200 Broadway Street on Tuesday (9 A.M.-1 P.M.), in Mid-City at 3700 Orleans Avenue on Thursday (3-7 P.M.), and in the Arts District at 700 Magazine Street on Saturday (8 A.M.-noon). Note that vendors only accept cash and market tokens, a special currency that comes in $1 and $5 increments, never expires, and can be purchased in the Welcome Tent via Visa, MasterCard, and Discover Card.

Mountain Chocolate Factory. Here, you'll also find a small food court, several sit-down restaurants, and the Southern Food & Beverage Museum. Parking is available at the Hilton garage, inside the World Trade Center garage, and along Convention Center Boulevard; it costs just $5 for up to four hours of parking at any of these facilities if you spend more than $10 at any Riverwalk store and have your parking ticket validated.

THE SHOPS AT CANAL PLACE

333 Canal St., 504/522-9200,
www.theshopsatcanalplace.com
HOURS: Mon.-Sat. 10 A.M.-7 P.M., Sun. noon-6 P.M.
`Map 1`

Situated along the southwestern edge of the French Quarter, this massive building is the fanciest full-scale mall in the immediate downtown area, with branches of such acclaimed emporia as Saks Fifth Avenue, Coach, L'Occitane, Brooks Brothers, Ann Taylor, Banana Republic, and Anthropologie. Some of the other fine shops here include Jeantherapy, known for upscale denim; local jeweler Mignon Faget; and Wehmeiers, purveyor of alligator boots and ostrich handbags. There's also a small food court, a posh salon, a Westin hotel that features amazing river views, and a movie theater that serves gourmet meals along with independent films and blockbusters.

THE SHOPS AT JAX BREWERY

600 Decatur St., 504/566-7245,
www.jacksonbrewery.com
HOURS: Daily 10 A.M.-7 P.M.
`Map 1`

The former Jackson Brewery houses about 20 shops and eateries inside a dramatic 1891 structure that's just a crosswalk away from Jackson Square. Besides a small food court, you'll find a mix of chain stores like Chico's and Sunglass Hut International; touristy shops, such as the Cajun Clothing Company by Perlis (where you can pick up your very own crawfish-embroidered polo shirt); and unique spots like the JAX Art Gallery, which sells prints, posters, and postcards of local artists, and Street Scene Galleries, which offers hand-painted reproduction woodcarvings of vintage New Orleans tableaux. When you're done shopping, venture to the upper floors, where you can enjoy stunning views of the Mississippi River.

HOTELS

Given the Big Easy's reputation as a late-night party town, you probably won't be spending much time in your hotel room. Of course, that doesn't diminish the importance of choosing a hotel that's right for you. Luckily, there's a wide array of options in New Orleans—more than 200 in this relatively small city. With a little research, a bit of flexibility, and some advance planning, you're sure to find accommodations that suit your budget, style preference, and location needs.

New Orleans is a city that's at once classic and Bohemian, and it contains a fair share of unique accommodations. Historic hotels dot the French Quarter, like the literary Hotel Monteleone, the elegant Royal Sonesta, and the pampering Omni Royal Orleans, not to mention smaller, more affordable guesthouses. The nearby Faubourg Marigny nurtures several

funky hideaways and intimate mansions, such as the Elysian Fields Inn. Beyond high-end chain establishments, such as the pet-friendly Loews New Orleans, the CBD houses boutique-style options like the International House Hotel. The Garden District and Uptown areas feature elegant inns, such as the tropical Green House Inn and the traditional Terrell House, where my great-grandmother spent her childhood years. The Tremé and Mid-City areas encompass laid-back hostels and guesthouses, such as the 1896 O'Malley House, and even off-the-beaten-path places like Algiers and Lakeview offer a few small B&Bs, such as the Rose Manor Inn.

If you're more comfortable with chain hotels, you'll find plenty here, especially in the convention-catering Central Business District (CBD), in the suburbs of Metairie and New Orleans East,

HIGHLIGHTS

LOOK FOR ❰❰ TO FIND RECOMMENDED HOTELS.

❰❰ **Most Literary Landmark:** Distinctive for the enormous red neon sign on its roof, the handsome **Hotel Monteleone** has long been a favored address among American writers; former guests have included such luminaries as Eudora Welty, Truman Capote, William Faulkner, Sherwood Anderson, Ernest Hemingway, Tennessee Williams, and Anne Rice (page 219).

❰❰ **Best Hotel Service:** Situated amid the art galleries and antiques shops of Royal Street, the **Omni Royal Orleans** stands out not only for its stately historical architecture and contrastingly contemporary rooms but also for its outstanding, friendly, and knowledgeable service – it's ideal, in fact, if you're hoping to be pampered (page 222).

❰❰ **Best Spot on Bourbon Street:** While most visitors favor the **Royal Sonesta Hotel – New Orleans** for its hospitable staff, stylish decor, and on-site jazz club, it's also a suitable choice for those hoping to oversee the late-night revelry of Bourbon Street; from the balconies, you can even toss Mardi Gras beads to the eager throngs below (page 223).

❰❰ **Best Music Lover's Retreat:** A 10-minute walk from the French Quarter and just steps from the funky restaurants and music clubs along Frenchmen Street, the charming, friendly **Elysian Fields Inn** occupies an eye-catching 1860s house that features warmly furnished rooms and top-flight amenities (page 226).

❰❰ **Coolest Boutique Hotel:** Whimsically and creatively decorated, the 117-room, smoke-free **International House Hotel** draws a hip crowd to its artful confines, which include a swanky cocktail lounge, a see-and-be-seen restaurant, and a top-notch fitness center and spa (page 231).

❰❰ **Best Pad for Pets:** Upon first seeing its glossy lobby, you might not realize how pet-friendly the **Loews New Orleans Hotel** really is, but at this upscale spot in the CBD, pet lovers will find everything from food bowls and dog beds to scratching posts and pet-specific room service menus (page 233).

❰❰ **Most Offbeat Retreat:** A departure from the many traditional, antiques-filled B&Bs that you'll find in the Uptown area, **The Green House Inn** delights visitors with its funky, tropical decor, flower-named rooms, and modern amenities, including flat-screen TVs and a clothing-optional pool (page 238).

❰❰ **Best Bed-and-Breakfast:** Situated among the historic homes of the Lower Garden District, the **Terrell House Bed and Breakfast** provides luxurious accommodations in a grand, Italianate-style mansion built in the mid-1800s. Epitomizing Southern hospitality, the delicious breakfasts are especially memorable among former guests (page 241).

❰❰ **Best Hidden Gem:** Many tourists miss out on one of the best B&Bs in the city, the **1896 O'Malley House,** simply because it's a bit off the beaten path in the less-touristy Mid-City neighborhood, but this handsome inn is worth seeking out – if only for its delightful owners and beautiful furnishings (page 243).

❰❰ **Best Option for Lake Lovers:** If you'd prefer staying outside the main tourist areas, the elegant **Rose Manor Bed & Breakfast Inn** is an ideal choice, given that it lies a bit closer to Lake Pontchartrain than the Mississippi River (page 245).

Literary legends, from Ernest Hemingway to Anne Rice, have stayed at the French Quarter's Hotel Monteleone.

PRICE KEY

$ Under $125

$$ $125-250

$$$ Over $250

and near Kenner's Louis Armstrong New Orleans International Airport. Besides standard room amenities, these often spacious hotels typically offer swimming pools, business centers, meeting rooms, daily housekeeping, and off-street parking.

Where you choose to stay will greatly depend on whether you have a car. Fortunately, staying in the main neighborhoods of the French Quarter, the Faubourg Marigny, the CBD, the Garden District, and Mid-City will ensure convenient access to public transportation, namely the streetcar lines. Just be advised that some neighborhoods are safer than others and that not all hotels welcome pets and children. In addition, many places are largely, if not completely, smoke-free, and most of the privately owned inns have minimum stay requirements, particularly during the peak winter and spring seasons. At such times—especially during events like New Year's Eve, the Sugar Bowl, Mardi Gras, French Quarter Fest, and Jazz Fest—you can expect higher rates as well as the need for advance reservations. Even in the slower summer season, certain annual events—such as the Essence Music Festival and Southern Decadence—might necessitate a reservation.

CHOOSING A HOTEL

Given the sheer number of motels, hotels, inns, and cottages available in the Big Easy, choosing an accommodation can be a daunting task. Luckily, there are many websites and organizations willing to help. If you're looking for a bed-and-breakfast, consult the **Professional Innkeepers Association of New Orleans** (PIANO, www.bbnola.com) or the **Louisiana Bed and Breakfast Association** (LBBA, 225/769-7358, www.louisianabandb.com). You might also benefit from local reservation services

like **New Orleans Bed & Breakfast and French Quarter Accommodations** (504/524-9918 or 888/240-0070, www.neworleansbandb.com) and the **Inn the Quarter Reservation Service** (800/570-3085, www.innthequarter.com). For more specific accommodations, consider **Historic Hotels of America** (www.historichotels.org) and **Bluegreen Resorts** (www.bluegreenrentals.com).

Whether or not you decide to consult such organizations, it's important to keep a few pointers in mind when selecting your accommodations. If, for example, you're a business traveler in town for a convention, you'll likely want to stay in the centrally located CBD, which still offers easy access to the French Quarter; just bear in mind that many of the high-end chain hotels here charge exorbitant fees for parking and Internet access. If, on the other hand, you've come for pleasure, you'll probably want to book a room in the French Quarter, Faubourg Marigny, or Garden District. New Orleans is manageable enough in size that any of these neighborhoods, in addition to Mid-City, will guarantee easy access to major attractions, stellar restaurants, and seasonal events. So, how you choose your lodgings will ultimately depend on budget, availability, and occasion. If you're backpacking across America, you might crave the eccentric vibe of an inexpensive Mid-City hostel, while those visiting their children on Tulane's campus or hoping for a relaxing romantic weekend might prefer an intimate Uptown B&B.

Another consideration is whether or not you expect to get a full night's sleep. Visitors with late-night intentions will probably welcome a room on or near Bourbon Street, while privacy-seeking couples and antiques shoppers will prefer a quieter place, like many of the inns in the Lower Quarter or Marigny. Also keep in mind that the rates listed are based on double occupancy during high season, so if you want to save a little money, consider visiting during the summer or fall. In addition, you might want to take advantage of the special packages that many hotels and inns offer; depending on the deal, these can appeal to families, gourmands, romance-minded couples, and those in town for special events.

French Quarter
Map 1

ASTOR CROWNE PLAZA–FRENCH QUARTER ❸❸

739 Canal St., 504/962-0500 or 888/696-4806, www.astorneworleans.com

Close to the all-night action of Bourbon Street, the enormous Astor Crowne Plaza comprises more than 630 contemporary, well-illumined rooms and suites, all of which feature soothing color schemes, luxurious beds, flat-screen TVs, ergonomic chairs, and wireless Internet access. Concierge services and executive-level amenities, such as continental breakfasts, are also available, and all guests are welcome to use the fitness center, outdoor pool, and 24-hour business center. Be sure to have at least one meal at Dickie Brennan's Bourbon House, a well-regarded seafood restaurant on the ground level.

AUDUBON COTTAGES ❸❸❸

509 Dauphine St., 504/586-1516, www.auduboncottages.com

If money is no object, then consider a stay at this charming complex of historic cottages built in the late 18th century and operated by the nearby Dauphine Orleans Hotel. While some guests find the aging property more expensive than it should be, you're paying more for the seclusion rather than a ton of high-end amenities. The clean, comfortable one- and two-bedroom cottages have some nice features, such as shared or private courtyards, antique furnishings, plush bathrobes, complimentary wireless Internet, and private bathrooms, some of which have whirlpool tubs. Besides a daily continental breakfast, guests also have access to the pleasant on-site swimming pool plus the Dauphine's fitness center and secured valet parking. History buffs may especially relish the Audubon Cottages, named after the famous naturalist, who occupied Cottage 1 in 1820 while completing his *Birds of America* paintings.

BIENVILLE HOUSE HOTEL ❸❸❸

320 Decatur St., 504/529-2345 or 800/535-9603, www.bienvillehouse.com

Featuring hand-painted murals and wrought-iron balconies, this intimate, renovated hotel sits along Decatur, close to the river as well as several good bars and eateries with a more mellow ambience than those on Bourbon. (In fact, it's right across the street from one of my favorites, the Kerry Irish Pub.) By French Quarter standards, the 83 rooms here are large and airy with stylish furnishings, attractive bathrooms, and upscale amenities, such as luxurious robes, 300-thread-count linens, and designer toiletries. The best rooms have an inviting sun deck; there's also a heated saltwater pool with a surrounding courtyard. Other amenities include cable TV and wireless Internet access.

BISCUIT PALACE GUEST HOUSE ❸

730 Dumaine St., 504/525-9949, www.biscuitpalace.com

Inexpensive accommodations aren't easy to find in the French Quarter, so many budget-conscious travelers appreciate the Biscuit Palace, a classic Creole mansion on a quiet stretch of Dumaine, between Bourbon and Royal Streets—and only a few steps from the New Orleans Historic Voodoo Museum. Built in 1820 to house the family and law practice of Christian Roselius (who eventually became the dean of Tulane University's law school), this no-frills inn features four mini-suites, three full suites, and one rooftop apartment, all of which are individually decorated and equipped with private, though rather tiny, bathrooms. Curiously, most are named after key streets in the Vieux Carré, the city's oldest neighborhood. Though the staff is accommodating, be prepared for a funky, old-world building, in need of some renovations and safety updates.

BOURBON ORLEANS HOTEL ❸❸❸

717 Orleans St., 504/523-2222 or 866/513-9744, www.bourbonorleans.com

As the name indicates, the enormous Bourbon Orleans occupies most of a block at Bourbon and Orleans Streets, just behind the serene rear garden of the St. Louis Cathedral. It also lies within a heartbeat of Bourbon's all-night craziness, so if you hope to get any sleep, book a room facing one of the side streets. Even so, this historic, European-style hotel is one of the best properties in this part of the Quarter. The nonsmoking rooms and suites are large and elegant, with tall windows, luxurious beds, stylish bathrooms, and, in some cases, balconies. Amenities include ergonomically designed chairs, free wireless Internet access, cable TV, in-room spa services, a heated outdoor pool, a fitness center, valet parking, laundry and concierge services, and baggage storage. The on-site Creole restaurant, Roux on Orleans, serves breakfast and dinner; it also offers room service during those times.

BOURGOYNE GUEST HOUSE [$][$]

839 Bourbon St., 504/524-3621 or 504/525-3983, www.bourgoynehouse.com

Situated in the more residential part of the French Quarter, this intimate inn offers convenient access to Bourbon Street's late-night bars and dance clubs without sacrificing peace, quiet, and value. Like many structures in the French Quarter, this Creole mansion was built in the 1830s, decades after the two 18th-century conflagrations that destroyed much of the city's oldest neighborhood. Today, it features picturesque balconies, winding staircases, a plant-filled courtyard, and a handful of affordable accommodations, including a one-bedroom suite, a two-bedroom suite, and, in a separate wing, several cozy studio apartments. All options feature high ceilings, antique furnishings, private bathrooms, and equipped kitchens. Though you'll find more modern amenities elsewhere, you really can't beat the price for a Bourbon Street address.

CHATEAU BOURBON [$][$][$]

800 Iberville St., 504/586-0800 or 800/996-3426, www.chateaubourbonneworleans.com

Following a lengthy \$20 million renovation, this Wyndham-run hotel features spacious rooms and suites, with 12-foot ceilings, pillow-top mattresses, flat-screen TVs, luxurious bath products, wireless Internet access, and decor that exudes a simple elegance. Some rooms even offer balconies overlooking the picturesque courtyard or bustling Bourbon Street. Other on-site amenities include a business center, concierge services, in-room massages, and a refurbished swimming pool and fitness center. Be sure to sample a meal at Ralph Brennan's Red Fish Grill, a festive seafood restaurant near the corner of Bourbon and Bienville Streets.

CHATEAU LEMOYNE [$][$][$]

301 Dauphine St., 504/581-1303 or 888/465-4329, www.chateaulemoynefrenchquarter.com

The hospitable Chateau LeMoyne occupies four mid-19th-century townhouses on Dauphine, just a block from noisy Bourbon Street. Managed by Holiday Inn, the 171 nicely furnished rooms include period reproductions with the usual chain amenities, such as work desks, cable TV, and free high-speed Internet access. Some rooms are built in the classic Creole style, while others are richly architectural with cypress wood beams and exposed-brick walls. Other rooms include balcony access, and several allow in-room smoking. Facilities include a 24-hour business center, tree-shaded redbrick patios anchored by a heated pool, and the on-site Bienville Café.

THE CORNSTALK HOTEL [$][$]

915 Royal St., 504/523-1515 or 800/759-6112, www.cornstalkhotel.com

With its distinctive, cornstalk-inspired, cast-iron fence, this gorgeous, Victorian-style hotel is a frequent stop for camera-wielding tourists. Staying here is the real treat. Built in 1816 and fronted by lush gardens, including a tranquil fountain, the historic, yellow-hued Cornstalk offers 14 sumptuous guest rooms, all of which feature high ceilings, antique furnishings, private bathrooms (albeit rather small), and complimentary wireless Internet access. Besides the amicable staff, another advantage is the location, which offers guests an ideal spot for people-watching and easy access to art galleries, carriage tours, seafood restaurants, and late-night bars. No wonder it has lured such celebrities as Elvis Presley and Hillary Clinton and now serves as a popular spot for honeymoons and other romantic occasions.

DAUPHINE ORLEANS HOTEL ⬤⬤

415 Dauphine St., 504/586-1800 or 800/521-7111, www.dauphineorleans.com

Opened in 1969, this elegant yet simple hotel offers smoke-free tranquility and friendly hospitality only a block from boisterous Bourbon. Inside the magnificent main building, you'll find 111 comfortable guest rooms, all with modern furnishings. Besides the nearby Audubon Cottages, the Dauphine Orleans also manages well-appointed rooms and suites in the 14-unit Hermann House, which features whirlpool tubs, and the nine-unit Carriage House, with period antiques and courtyard views. Other in-room amenities include bathrobes, cable TV, free bottled water, complimentary wireless Internet access, and spa services. At the main property, guests can also take a dip in the saltwater pool, enjoy the renovated fitness room, relax in the palm-dotted courtyard, and have a drink in May Baily's Place, the hotel bar. Concierge services, secured valet parking ($32–50 daily), a free deluxe continental breakfast and afternoon tea, and complimentary newspapers are also available.

◖ HOTEL MONTELEONE ⬤⬤⬤

214 Royal St., 504/523-3341 or 866/338-4684, www.hotelmonteleone.com

Topped by a large red neon sign that seems to tower over the Quarter, the marvelous Hotel Monteleone is a favorite because of its rich history. This 1886 property hosted Tennessee Williams many times, as well as Eudora Welty, Sherwood Anderson, William Faulkner, Ernest Hemingway, Truman Capote, Richard Ford, and Anne Rice. You can sense the hotel's distinguished past simply by walking through the gorgeous marble lobby. This enormous hotel offers 600 luxurious rooms and 55 suites, equipped with in-room safes, refrigerators, flat-screen TVs, marble-and-granite

bathrooms, comfortable robes, and high-speed Internet access. Additionally, the sumptuous suites feature separate showers, Jacuzzi tubs, and, in some cases, wet bars and sofa beds. On-site amenities include the stylish Carousel Bar, a renovated restaurant, a full-service business center, the pampering Spa Aria, a modern fitness center, and a rooftop pool that's heated year-round. Its location on Royal Street is another huge bonus.

HÔTEL PROVINCIAL ⬤⬤

1024 Chartres St., 504/581-4995 or 800/535-7922, www.hotelprovincial.com

Essentially a complex of historic buildings that includes a former 1830s military hospital, the Hôtel Provincial has been owned by the Dupepe family since 1961. The cheery guest rooms are decorated with Southern antiques and reproduction French period furnishings; some feature balconies, views of the river, or access to sunny, private courtyards. Amenities include plush mattresses, flat-screen TVs, in-room climate control, wireless Internet access, a free continental breakfast, two swimming pools, an on-site bar, and secured valet parking ($24 daily). The staff here is efficient and friendly, and the property's superb restaurant, Stella!, is reason enough to stay at this upscale, family-run inn.

HOTEL ROYAL ⬤⬤

1006 Royal St., 504/524-3900 or 888/776-3901, www.frenchquarterhotelgroup.com/hotel-royal.html

Following a recent renovation, the Hotel Royal appeals to most guests seeking comfort and value. The location is hard to top, too. Situated along the quieter end of Royal, it still offers easy access to the art galleries and antiques shops on this world-famous street; as a plus, the popular CC's Community Coffee House sits on the opposite corner. Built in 1827, this Creole townhouse and the adjacent building now contain a variety of deluxe rooms, junior suites, and master king suites, most of which feature hardwood floors, high ceilings, marble bathrooms, feather beds, 300-thread-count linens,

© DANIEL MARTONE

the supposedly haunted Hôtel Provincial

ceiling fans, exposed brick walls, and flat-screen TVs. Some suites also have private balconies. However, some of the rooms are still pretty tiny, and noisy revelers can be heard through the walls. Don't let the mandatory amenity package ($6 daily)—which includes wireless Internet access, unlimited local and long-distance calls, and usage of the in-room safe—go to waste.

HÔTEL ST. MARIE [$][$]

827 Toulouse St., 504/561-8951 or 800/366-2743, www.hotelstmarie.com

Like many accommodations in the Quarter, the Hôtel St. Marie blends historical elegance with modern amenities. Situated just off Bourbon Street, this stunning hotel offers well-appointed, nonsmoking rooms and suites, all of which have tall ceilings, antique reproduction furnishings, cable TV, and free Internet access; some rooms even offer access to the wrought-iron balconies that overlook the bustling streets below. While here, you can also take advantage of the relaxing pool set amid a tropical courtyard, not to mention complimentary newspapers, 24-hour concierge services, and the on-site Vacherie bar and restaurant. Sister properties include the Place d'Armes and Prince Conti Hotels, and as with them, pets are unfortunately not allowed.

THE IBERVILLE SUITES [$][$]

910 Iberville St., 504/523-2400 or 866/229-4351, www.ibervillesuites.com

This lovely, pet-friendly hotel features clean, spacious suites, all of which have modern furnishings, separate sleeping and sitting areas, wet bars and refrigerators, Bath & Body Works toiletries, and wireless Internet access. It's ideal for families, business travelers, and small groups. Laundry service, pricey valet parking ($34 daily), 24-hour room service, and simple continental breakfasts are also available. Since the Iberville Suites is managed by the adjacent Ritz-Carlton, guests can enjoy some of its neighbor's amenities, such as the tranquil spa, state-of-the-art fitness center, acclaimed M bistro, and jazz lounge.

THE INN ON BOURBON $\$\$$

541 Bourbon St., 504/524-7611 or 800/535-7891,
www.innonbourbon.com

Occupying the site of the 19th-century French Opera House, the renovated Inn on Bourbon contains sumptuous nonsmoking rooms, many of which offer views of active Bourbon Street, quieter Toulouse, or the picturesque courtyard. Additional in-room amenities include impressively carved beds, comfortable work desks, refreshment centers, flat-screen TVs with premium cable, free newspapers and wireless Internet access, and, most welcome during the summer months, air-conditioning. Elsewhere in the hotel, you'll find a souvenir shop, a business center, a fitness room, an outdoor pool, and a cocktail bar. Valet parking, laundry services, and a free continental breakfast are also available, and the front desk is staffed 24 hours daily. The hotel sits directly on Bourbon Street, so depending on the room, early birds may find it hard to sleep.

© DANIEL MARTONE

The Le Richelieu hotel is situated on a relatively quiet stretch of Chartres.

LE RICHELIEU $\$\$$

1234 Chartres St., 504/529-2492 or 800/535-9653,
www.lerichelieuhotel.com

Le Richelieu books up quickly because it's been one of the Quarter's most popular midpriced hotels for many years. Contained within two historic buildings, the 69 guest rooms are clean and simple, but with a bit of character in the form of old-fashioned ceiling fans, reproduction antiques, varying color schemes, and, in some cases, pleasant views. There are also 17 roomy suites with large sitting areas. This smoke-free, European-style property lies along a quiet stretch of Chartres Street in the Lower Quarter, an easy walk from Bourbon Street, the French Market, and the Faubourg Marigny. An on-site café serves breakfast all day, and there's also a lounge, an unheated swimming pool, and 24-hour concierge services. In addition, the hotel offers satellite TV, air-conditioning, free wireless Internet access, laundry and babysitting services, and secured self-parking ($20 daily).

MAISON DUPUY HOTEL $\$\$\$$

1001 Toulouse St., 504/586-8000 or 800/535-9177,
www.maisondupuy.com

Privacy seekers will appreciate the hospitable Maison Dupuy, which sits at the corner of Toulouse and Burgundy Streets, a couple blocks away from the Bourbon madness. Opened in 1973 by the Dupuy brothers and encompassing five historic, ornately crafted townhouses, this enchanting boutique hotel is actually the last to have been built in the now-protected Quarter. Fashioned with French doors and wrought-iron balconies, the five-story hotel also features a spacious courtyard, with an impressive marble fountain, a roomy swimming pool, tasteful patio furniture, and plenty of tropical foliage. All of the tidy rooms and suites, including a stand-alone carriage house, boast modern yet elegant furnishings, pillow-top mattresses, luxurious bath products, personal safes, flat-screen TVs with premium cable, and complimentary wireless Internet access.

NINE-O-FIVE ROYAL HOTEL $$

905 Royal St., 504/523-0219, www.905royalhotel.com

Situated beside the oft-photographed Cornstalk Hotel, this aptly named inn makes it easy for wayward tourists to find their path home at night. Even better, all of the 10 Southern-style rooms and suites have their own private entrances, not to mention period furnishings, private bathrooms, equipped kitchenettes, basic cable TV, and central heat and air-conditioning. There's also a small patio, an inviting porch, and an upper balcony. Be advised, though, that the accommodations here are small, oddly laid out, and, in some cases, need an update—but it's hard to beat the price for this terrific location.

THE OLIVIER HOUSE HOTEL $$

828 Toulouse St., 504/525-8456 or 866/525-9748, www.olivierhousehotel.com

Quirky, offbeat, and offering one of the better rates in the French Quarter, this family-run hotel isn't far from the hubbub of Bourbon Street. Set within a towering 1839 Greek Revival–style townhouse and other nearby buildings, the rooms and suites here feature a mixture of antique and modern furnishings. Each space has a different layout, from small, single-bed rooms to two-bedroom suites with a living area, multiple bathrooms, a kitchenette, and courtyard access. Three specialty options include the Honeymoon Suite, with a four-poster bed, a working fireplace, floor-to-ceiling windows, and a stunning balcony; the Garden Suite, a split-level space with tropical decor; and Miss Anna's Creole Cottage, which my husband and I appreciate for its brick floors, convenient kitchen, and private courtyard. Other amenities include a swimming pool, off-street parking, and 24-hour concierge services, making this friendly, low-key property an excellent value. Unlike some places in the city, the Olivier House also welcomes children and pets.

[C] OMNI ROYAL ORLEANS $$$

621 St. Louis St., 504/529-5333 or 888/444-6664, www.omnihotels.com

With a prime spot in the Quarter—steps from dozens of great shops, galleries, and restaurants—and a wonderfully hospitable staff, this magnificent hotel obviously has a devoted following. The lavish, rambling property contains 346 smartly furnished rooms with 19th-century decor, marble bathrooms, executive writing desks, comfortable robes, individual climate control, and free wireless Internet access. Premier rooms and certain suites feature balconies, and just about all options afford an impressive view of the Quarter. On the roof, you'll find a state-of-the-art fitness center, a heated pool, and a year-round observation deck. Other on-site amenities include a beauty salon, a full-service barber shop, a 24-hour business center, concierge and babysitting services, the cozy Touché Bar, and the hallowed Rib Room restaurant, a retro favorite of carnivores. An airport shuttle ($20 one-way, $38 round-trip) and pricey valet parking ($34 daily) are also available.

PLACE D'ARMES HOTEL $$

625 St. Ann St., 504/524-4531 or 800/366-2743, www.placedarmes.com

Part of the Valentino French Quarter Hotels family (which also oversees the Prince Conti Hotel and Hôtel St. Marie), the Place d'Armes stands only a few steps from Jackson Square. It's also just a short walk from those heavenly beignets at Café Du Monde. This charming hotel consists of eight restored 18th- and 19th-century townhouses, containing a total of 84 snazzy, nonsmoking rooms and surrounding a delightful courtyard shaded by crape myrtle and magnolia trees and filled with lush plants and old-fashioned fountains. Some rooms have balconies, and all have exquisite furnishings, free high-speed Internet access, and standard appliances. Other amenities here include a daily continental breakfast, 24-hour concierge services, free newspapers, a lovely swimming pool, and wireless Internet access in the common areas.

PRINCE CONTI HOTEL $$

830 Conti St., 504/529-4172 or 800/366-2743, www.princecontihotel.com

Housed within a regal three-story structure built in the 19th century, this affordable hotel offers 76 basic guest rooms and suites, which vary greatly in features. For instance, some rooms don't have windows! Like its sister properties, the Hôtel St. Marie and the Place d'Armes Hotel, the Prince Conti provides free newspapers and wireless Internet access, plus 24-hour concierge services. Be advised, though, that smoking and pets aren't permitted here. In addition, given its location near Bourbon Street, this can be a particularly loud place to spend the night, so select your room carefully. Perhaps the best features of this hotel are the on-site Café Conti, which is open for breakfast, and the Bombay Club, a sophisticated restaurant, martini bar, and live music venue.

QUARTER HOUSE RESORT $$

129 Chartres St., 504/523-5906 or 800/736-5906, www.quarterhouse.com

Seemingly hidden from most travelers, the unusual Quarter House is actually a vacation ownership resort—surprisingly, the roomy condos are also available for short-term stays. Built in 1831 by James Gallier, the city's most renowned architect, this rambling property occupies half a city block at the upper end of Chartres Street, not far from well-regarded shops and restaurants. The one-bedroom, two-bedroom, and penthouse suites here all feature private bathrooms, fully equipped kitchens, and wireless Internet access. Other on-site amenities include a gym, a courtyard swimming pool, concierge services, laundry facilities, and limited parking.

THE RITZ-CARLTON NEW ORLEANS $$$

921 Canal St., 504/524-1331 or 800/241-3333, www.ritzcarlton.com

This is the perfect choice for the ultimate pampering vacation: The Ritz has a state-of-the-art day spa and fitness center; the Davenport Lounge, which presents live jazz and afternoon tea service; and M bistro, serving fresh, local cuisine. The well-trained staff tends to guests' every need, from valet parking to babysitting services to a free overnight shoeshine. Richly

furnished rooms feature 400-thread-count sheets, goose-down pillows, Italian marble baths, and wireless Internet access. For extra-special attention, consider staying at the hotel's club-level **Maison Orleans** at 904 Iberville Street.

◖ ROYAL SONESTA HOTEL–NEW ORLEANS $$$

300 Bourbon St., 504/586-0300 or 800/766-3782, www.sonesta.com/royalneworleans

Many out-of-towners choose the Royal Sonesta for its prime location on Bourbon Street, especially if they're lucky enough to snag a balcony room above the infamously rowdy street. Not only will you be able to oversee the late-night revelry from this vantage point, but you'll also be able to participate in the fun, as many partygoers will expect you to toss down a Mardi Gras–bead necklace or two. An even better enticement is the on-site jazz club, not to mention the hotel's hospitable staff, stylish decor, and pet-friendly policy. The 483 well-appointed

© LAURA MARTONE

the Desire Oyster Bar at Bourbon Street's Royal Sonesta Hotel–New Orleans

guest rooms and suites here feature standard amenities as well as flat-screen TVs, king-size pillows, and high-speed Internet access. Guests also appreciate the lush courtyards, outdoor swimming pool, fitness center, spa services, on-site lounge, and two eateries: PJ's Coffee (part of a local coffee-shop chain) and the Desire Oyster Bar.

SONIAT HOUSE HOTEL ⓢⓢⓢ
1133 Chartres St., 504/522-0570 or 800/544-8808, www.soniathouse.com

Directly across from the equally well-favored Le Richelieu, the refined Soniat House sits on a quiet part of Chartres, not far from the French Market and Faubourg Marigny. This intimate, luxurious hotel isn't cheap, but it isn't unreasonably priced either. Set within a trio of 1830s Creole townhouses built by one of New Orleans's most distinguished families, the 18 rooms and 12 suites include British, French, and Louisiana antiques, with fancy extras such as Frette Egyptian linens, goose-down pillows, and high-end toiletries. Relax in the elegant sitting room, or enjoy a breakfast of Southern biscuits, homemade strawberry preserves, and

café au lait at a table in the verdant courtyard. Secured parking ($25 daily), cable TV, wireless Internet access, and daily newspapers are also available. Just be advised that the hotel doesn't permit smoking, pets, or children under 10.

W NEW ORLEANS–FRENCH QUARTER ⓢⓢⓢ
316 Chartres St., 504/581-1200 or 888/625-5144, www.starwoodhotels.com/whotels

The W Hotel combines the alluring pizzazz and old-world charm of the French Quarter with the modern elegance and high-tech sophistication associated with this pet-friendly chain. The 98 rooms, which include two deluxe suites and four carriage houses, are decorated in cool earth tones with pillow-top mattresses, 350-thread-count linens, wireless high-speed Internet access ($15 daily), cable TV, DVD players, large work desks, Bliss bath products, and fully stocked minibars. When not exploring the city or unwinding in your room, sip cocktails in the W Living Room or take a dip in the courtyard pool. Meanwhile, the attentive and helpful staff will do just about anything to make your stay memorable.

Faubourg Marigny and Bywater   Map 2

BALCONY GUEST HOUSE ⓢ
2483 Royal St., 504/945-4425, www.balconyguesthouse.com

Situated above Schiro's Community Café—a corner grocery and popular hangout for artists, musicians, and other Bohemian types—this airy inn offers four guest rooms and one suite, all of which have hardwood floors, ceiling fans, simple furnishings, microwaves, mini-fridges, and private bathrooms. Two of the rooms also feature French doors and direct balcony access. Other amenities here include cable TV and air-conditioning, and the guesthouse lies only four blocks from Washington Square Park and the music clubs along Frenchmen Street. Just be prepared for tight bathrooms and the possibility of noisy revelers on the sidewalk below.

B & W COURTYARDS BED AND BREAKFAST ⓢⓢ
2425 Chartres St., 504/324-3396 or 800/585-5731, www.bandwcourtyards.com

To experience life in one of New Orleans's most charming and historic neighborhoods, consider a stay at this romantic B&B set inside three mid-19th-century Creole cottages with connecting courtyards. This peaceful hideaway is a favorite with guests seeking privacy—and consequently is not suitable for children. The four rooms and two suites are decorated with fine antiques and linens, all with private bathrooms, central heat and air-conditioning, cable TV, and free wireless Internet access; most rooms open onto one of the courtyards. In the rear patio, you can soak in a whirlpool tub under the stars. Other amenities include a

LEGAL AND ILLEGAL GUESTHOUSES

Some of the most charming rooms in the city are found in unlicensed, illegal B&Bs, guesthouses, or vacation rentals. Many of these "underground" establishments advertise heavily online, especially during major annual events, such as Mardi Gras and French Quarter Fest. Likely no harm will come to you simply for staying at one, and plenty of travelers certainly do it, so why even think twice before booking a room at such a property? Well, there are a few reasons.

Letting out rooms to tourists has long been a tradition in New Orleans, and its origins are harmless enough. Owners of the many grand, historic houses in the French Quarter and other visitor-friendly neighborhoods simply rented a room or two, or even several, as a way to earn a little extra income. Many travelers enjoyed staying at these informal accommodations, through which they could save some money, get to know the hosts, and live as though they were residents of New Orleans.

The problem is that the city of New Orleans requires all short-term rentals to be licensed, and yet it seems to make little effort to enforce this rule, despite growing pressure from community advocates like the French Quarter Citizens for the Preservation of Residential Quality. Consequently, the upstanding innkeepers around town who did go through the hassle of getting approval to open an inn, and then paid the various fees, are at a competitive disadvantage compared to those who run properties illegally.

As a consumer, the main risk you face by staying at an illegal B&B is that you have little or no recourse for remedying any disputes that arise with the owners, and you have no legal protection should you be injured. Illegal short-term rentals often fail to comply with fire and safety regulations; if they do so, it's on a voluntary basis, since nobody inspects them. They also rarely carry the proper commercial insurance that a licensed inn is required to have, which poses a liability risk to visitors.

Beyond protecting your own best interests, you're actually helping the city of New Orleans and its historic neighborhoods by choosing to patronize only licensed, legal B&Bs and guesthouses. Illegal vacation rentals don't contribute their share of taxes to the city – and worse, in a city with a high crime rate and a number of urban problems, they do little to foster community cooperation and neighborhood pride. Think of it this way: Every illegal vacation rental is a building that should, per zoning laws, be resident-occupied, and when neighborhoods such as the Upper French Quarter and Faubourg Marigny are filled with transient vacation rentals, neighborhood stability is lost. It's in the best interest of these parts of town to have as many buildings occupied by residents, or by legitimate inns where the owners live on premises or have regular on-site staff.

The easiest way to ensure that the B&B in which you're interested is licensed, legal, and adhering to proper standards is to choose one of the more than 50 properties that are members of **PIANO, the Professional Innkeepers Association of New Orleans** (www.bbnola. com), an organization that's been going strong since 2000. With so many excellent and reliable licensed inns in New Orleans, it's smartest to stick with PIANO members and avoid illegal guesthouses altogether.

small business center, unlimited local calls, and a continental breakfast.

THE BURGUNDY
BED AND BREAKFAST ⊙

2513 Burgundy St., 504/261-9477 or 504/942-1463, www.theburgundy.com

Nestled within the residential Faubourg Marigny, this whimsical, red-white-and-blue cottage epitomizes the 19th-century, Eastlake-style shotgun doubles prevalent throughout New Orleans. Boasting original hardwood floors, 12-foot ceilings, and louvered shutters, this lovingly restored inn houses four cozy guest rooms, each of which has distinctive decor, its own private bathroom, plus cable

TV and free wireless Internet access. Guests can utilize the communal kitchen, relax in the parlor, and enjoy the clothing-optional spa and sunbathing area. Smoking is allowed only on the back porch or in the courtyard.

BYWATER BED & BREAKFAST [$]

1026 Clouet St., 504/944-8438, www.bywaterbnb.com

A traditional, raspberry-and-white double shotgun, this quaint, arty cottage welcomes budget-conscious travelers with its four colorful guest rooms, all of which have high ceilings, large windows, ceiling fans, original fireplaces, and central heat and air-conditioning. Besides antique and contemporary furnishings, the entire house is filled with Louisiana art. Guests can relax in the front parlor, mingle on the rear porch and patio, and peruse the on-site collection of local books, regional music, and weekly magazines. A daily continental breakfast is included. The only drawbacks are the shared bathrooms and the location: While the Bywater is a funky neighborhood beloved by many locals, it's not as safe as the French Quarter and is not ideal for most tourists.

☾ ELYSIAN FIELDS INN [$][$]

930 Elysian Fields Ave., 504/948-9420 or 866/948-9420, www.elysianfieldsinn.com

This delightful B&B offers a lot for relatively reasonable rates. Built in the 1860s, the striking Greek Revival–style mansion contains eight tasteful, nonsmoking chambers with private Italian marble bathrooms, plus a large suite with a queen bed and a queen sleeper sofa. Rooms feature sleek and sophisticated Mission-style antiques, with polished mahogany floors, ceiling fans, and 10- to 14-foot ceilings. Amenities include central heat and air-conditioning, wireless Internet access, flat-screen TVs with VCR/DVD players, Aveda bath products, free secured parking, and a continental breakfast. Even better, the Elysian Fields Inn isn't far from the Quarter, and it's within easy walking distance of two popular gay bars, not to mention the hip eateries and nightclubs along Frenchmen Street.

ELYSIAN GUEST HOUSE [$][$]

1008 Elysian Fields Ave., 504/324-4311, www.elysianguesthouse.com

While this unassuming Creole bungalow attracts those seeking privacy, its location offers relatively easy access to the live music venues on Frenchmen and the shops, bars, and restaurants of the French Quarter. Just use caution when strolling through the Faubourg Marigny at night. As for the accommodations, you'll find three comfortable suites and two studios, each of which has a private bathroom, a separate outer entrance, convenient appliances, blackout curtains, and cable TV. In addition, all guests are welcome to use the sunny courtyards and shaded hot tub.

FRENCHMEN HOTEL [$][$]

417 Frenchmen St., 800/831-1781, www.frenchmenhotel.com

A sister property of the nearby Lamothe House Hotel, the Frenchmen is perhaps the ideal lodging option for those hoping to explore both the Marigny and the Quarter, as it's literally steps

© DANIEL MARTONE

the Faubourg Marigny's Frenchmen Hotel

from the border between these two distinctive neighborhoods. This hospitable, though somewhat aging, hotel offers cozy guest rooms and spacious suites, all individually decorated. Depending on the room, you may find canopy beds, decorative fireplaces, exposed brick walls, and private balconies. Additional amenities include a free continental breakfast, affordable on-site parking, and a romantic brick courtyard with lush plants, wrought-iron tables, and a small pool and Jacuzzi. You're also close to the popular clubs of Frenchmen Street, so music can be heard into the wee hours.

HOTEL DE LA MONNAIE $$

405 Esplanade Ave., 504/947-0009,
www.hoteldelamonnaie.com

Like other lodging options on the northeastern side of Esplanade Avenue, the Hotel de la Monnaie promises a terrific location for travelers hoping to explore the Faubourg Marigny, the French Quarter, and the Mississippi riverfront. It's also a good place for families and small groups of friends, since it only offers clean, affordable suites with one or two bedrooms, dining and living areas, private bathrooms, and kitchenettes. Built in 1984, the year that the World's Fair came to New Orleans, this spacious hotel blends traditional elements, such as balustrades, period furnishings, and outdoor courtyards, with modern amenities, such as cable TV, air-conditioning, and whirlpool tubs. Other on-site features include a fitness center, a wading pool, laundry facilities, free parking, and complimentary wireless Internet.

LA MAISON MARIGNY $$

1421 Bourbon St., 504/948-3638 or 800/570-2014,
www.lamaisonmarigny.com

La Maison Marigny blends the homey ambience of a small B&B with the creature comforts of a luxury hotel. This meticulously restored 1898 house includes three airy rooms and one suite, all of which have antique or reproduction beds, mahogany furnishings, hardwood floors, and 12-foot ceilings. Each room has a private bathroom, custom linens and 300-thread-count sheets, a flat-screen TV with cable access, plush bath towels, Bath & Body Works products, central heat and air-conditioning, and complimentary wireless Internet. Breakfast is served in a sunny, foliage-choked courtyard; other amenities include an extensive DVD collection and free local and long-distance calls. Children and pets are not permitted here, and smoking is only allowed in the courtyard.

LAMOTHE HOUSE HOTEL $$

621 Esplanade Ave., 800/367-5858,
www.lamothehouse.com

Run by the same folks who operate the Frenchmen Hotel and the Marigny Guest House, this 1830s townhouse is set along oak-lined Esplanade Avenue, the border between the Quarter and Marigny, ensuring an easy walk to clubs, restaurants, and shops in either neighborhood. At this cloistered inn, you may simply want to curl up in your gracious hand-carved canopy bed, or lie on a chaise-lounge in the lushly landscaped patio set around a small swimming pool and heated Jacuzzi. The 11 guest rooms and nine suites here contain original architectural elements and feature private bathrooms, air-conditioning, and cable TV. Other amenities include discounted off-street parking, wireless Internet access, 24-hour concierge services, and a free continental breakfast.

THE LANAUX MANSION
BED AND BREAKFAST $$

547 Esplanade Ave., 504/330-2826,
www.lanauxmansion.com

Conveniently situated on tree-lined Esplanade Avenue, the border between the French Quarter and Faubourg Marigny, the Lanaux Mansion lies within easy walking distance of laid-back eateries, famous jazz clubs, and the French Market. Built in 1879 by prominent attorney Charles Andrew Johnson and featured in the film *The Curious Case of Benjamin Button*, this exquisite Victorian hideaway offers four gracious lodging options: two spacious rooms in the former kitchen and servants' quarters, a suite in the main house, and a private cottage with its own patio. All possess sitting areas, private bathrooms, unique Victorian decor, antique furniture, hardwood floors, air-conditioning, and wireless Internet. Other possible amenities include kitchenettes, writing desks, and shared balcony access. Whichever you choose, you'll be able to relax in the enchanting garden, enjoy a daily continental breakfast in privacy, and consult the hospitable owner about the city's highlights.

LIONS INN BED & BREAKFAST 💲
2517 Chartres St., 504/945-2339 or 800/485-6846, www.lionsinn.com

Those seeking an authentic New Orleans ambience—and a bit more peace and quiet than most French Quarter hotels—will appreciate this accommodating B&B in the heart of the Faubourg Marigny. The two-story home contains 10 simply furnished, nonsmoking rooms, all of which feature wireless Internet access, cable TV, and air-conditioning. Other on-site amenities include a communal phone, a daily continental breakfast, a wine-and-cheese gathering each afternoon, and a fabulous pool and hot tub in a garden setting. Unfortunately, you'll have to rely on street parking, but once parked you're welcome to use the available bikes to tour the city. The Lions Inn also manages a few off-site properties, including a Marigny cottage and a French Quarter condo.

MAISON DE MACARTY 💲💲
3820 Burgundy St., 504/267-1564, www.maisonmacarty.com

The less-touristy Bywater, a Bohemian neighborhood east of the Marigny, boasts several one-of-a-kind inns, including this delightful B&B, which occupies a historic Victorian-style home built in the 1860s. Operated by friendly, knowledgeable hosts, the relatively peaceful Maison de Macarty offers six airy, comfortable rooms in the main house and two private cottages. All have unique furnishings and private bathrooms. While here, guests can savor an amazing gourmet breakfast, take a dip in the lovely pool, or relax in the shady courtyard. Perhaps the only drawback is that it's a bit of a

hike to the French Quarter and other tourist-friendly areas.

MAISON DUBOIS 💲💲
1419 Dauphine St., 866/948-1619, www.maisondubois.net

Located on the Marigny side of Esplanade Avenue, this elegant yet unpretentious B&B provides easy access to jazz clubs, funky eateries, and major French Quarter attractions. The five clean, comfortable suites can accommodate up to 16 guests, making the inn ideal for reunions and other small gatherings. All of the suites have antique furnishings, private bathrooms, ceiling fans, central air-conditioning, cable TV, and wireless Internet access. On-site amenities include a palm-shaded saltwater pool and hot tub, a well-appointed parlor and dining room, a free continental breakfast served daily in the kitchen or sun room, and complimentary newspapers, paperbacks, and VHS movies. In addition, the charming hosts will do their best to accommodate special requests.

MARIGNY MANOR HOUSE 💲💲
2125 N. Rampart St., 504/943-7826 or 877/247-7599, www.marignymanorhouse.com

Near the northern edge of this funky neighborhood, the Marigny Manor House sits along a quiet stretch that offers a wonderful sampling of vintage 19th-century residential architecture typical of New Orleans. Built in 1848, this lovingly restored Greek Revival–style house presents four color-themed, high-ceiling rooms neatly furnished with designer fabrics, antique furnishings, and, in some cases, crystal chandeliers, four-poster beds, and Oriental rugs over hardwood floors. One room has a balcony overlooking the brick fern-and-flower-bedecked courtyard. Amenities include private bathrooms, wireless Internet access, and delicious Southern breakfasts, and the offbeat bars and restaurants of Frenchmen Street are only a short walk away.

OLD HISTORIC CREOLE INN 💲
2471 Dauphine St., 504/941-0243, www.creoleinn.com

This charming inn lies just a few blocks

downriver from Washington Square Park and about eight blocks from the Quarter. A mix of single and two-bedroom suites, the inn features high ceilings, hardwood floors, antique beds, central heat and air-conditioning, and private bathrooms. Guests can relax on the outdoor patio, use the computer station in the parlor, and take advantage of amenities like free parking and free wireless Internet access. This friendly, easygoing guesthouse is indeed one of the better values within walking distance of the Quarter.

ROYAL STREET COURTYARD BED AND BREAKFAST $$

2438 Royal St., 504/943-6818 or 888/846-4004, www.royalstcourtyard.com

Situated in the Faubourg Marigny, just a few blocks east of Washington Square Park, this moderately priced B&B occupies a rambling 1850s Greek Revival–style home with a wrought-iron balcony and towering 14-foot ceilings. The five cozy guest rooms all have private bathrooms, ceiling fans, heat and air-conditioning, cable TV, and wireless Internet.

The tropical courtyard is punctuated with fishponds, blooming flower gardens, and a secluded hot tub. A free continental breakfast is served. Smoking, pets, and children are not allowed.

ROYAL STREET INN & BAR $$

1431 Royal St., 504/948-7499, www.royalstreetinn.com

If you're the adventurous sort who doesn't mind noisy places, then you'll likely love the Royal Street Inn, a funky guesthouse situated above a popular neighborhood bar. You'll find five unique, unpretentious suites here, from the cozy Marigny to the spacious Royal. All feature queen-size beds, couches, private bathrooms, cable TV, air-conditioning, and wireless Internet; three suites even offer balcony access. This so-called "bed and beverage" even divvies out drink tickets to its overnight guests in an attempt to entice you downstairs, where the boisterous R Bar has a pool table, a decent jukebox, and endless opportunities to mingle with eccentric locals and wide-eyed fellow travelers.

Central Business and Arts Districts   Map 3

COUNTRY INN & SUITES BY CARLSON– NEW ORLEANS FRENCH QUARTER $$

315 Magazine St., 504/324-5400 or 800/830-5222, www.countryinns.com

If you're looking for a clean, comfortable room at a relatively affordable price, consider the Country Inn & Suites, which promises quiet, smoke-free accommodations within easy walking distance of Harrah's New Orleans, the riverfront aquarium, and, of course, French Quarter diversions. Encompassing seven 19th-century buildings, this historic hotel combines old-world charm with modern amenities, such as in-room microwaves and refrigerators, an outdoor pool, a 24-hour fitness center, a lending library, laundry facilities, concierge services, and valet parking, plus free hot breakfasts and wireless Internet access.

DRURY INN & SUITES– NEW ORLEANS $$

820 Poydras St., 504/529-7800 or 800/378-7496, www.druryhotels.com

This Midwest-based chain offers one of the best values in the CBD. Occupying a handsome eight-story building, this 156-unit, pet-friendly hotel lies five blocks from both the French Quarter and the Superdome. The standard rooms and suites feature contemporary—if generic—furnishings, high ceilings, tall windows, cable TV, and microwaves. Many of the building's original details, such as the ornamental lobby staircase and Waterford crystal chandeliers, have been carefully preserved. Other amenities include a rooftop pool and hot tub, 24-hour fitness and business centers, off-site valet parking ($25 daily), a hot continental breakfast, evening refreshments, and free wireless Internet access.

HAMPTON INN & SUITES NEW ORLEANS– CONVENTION CENTER HOTEL $$

1201 Convention Center Blvd., 504/566-9990 or 800/292-0653, www.neworleanshamptoninns.com

This Hampton Inn differs a bit from the usual modern chain properties—it's set inside a five-story, redbrick, early-20th-century building where burlap sacks were once manufactured. Though completely renovated, the smoke-free, 288-unit hotel still contains original hardwood floors, exposed brick walls, tall windows, and high ceilings. The airy, spacious guest rooms, studios, and suites—some of which have kitchens—feature flat-screen TVs, curved shower rods, large work surfaces, and free wireless Internet access. An outdoor pool, business and fitness centers, a lobby bar, concierge services, and a free hot breakfast round out the amenities. Even better, the convention center, the National WWII Museum, Arts District, Riverwalk shops, and Harrah's New Orleans all lie within walking distance.

HARRAH'S NEW ORLEANS $$$

228 Poydras St., 504/533-6000 or 800/427-7247, www.harrahsneworleans.com

Situated directly across the street from the prominent Harrah's New Orleans casino, the 26-story hotel features 450 clean, spacious, ultra-comfortable rooms and suites with elegant furnishings, pillow-top mattresses and satin sheets, mini-fridges, original artwork, and high-definition, flat-screen TVs with cable. Premium bath products, lightweight robes, high-speed wireless Internet access ($11 daily), and an on-site parking garage are also available. In addition, guests appreciate the friendly staff, incredible river views, and proximity to excellent restaurants, including Besh Steak at the casino—which, besides an array of gaming options, also presents live concerts and comedy shows.

HILTON NEW ORLEANS/ ST. CHARLES AVENUE HOTEL $$$

333 St. Charles Ave., 504/524-8890 or 800/445-8667, www.hhneworleansstcharles.com

The 250-room, pet-friendly Hilton occupies an impressive 1920s building that once contained a Masonic temple and has since been completely renovated. The decor here is sophisticated and upscale, with fine linens, a full-size work desk, cable TV, Crabtree & Evelyn bath products, and colorful furnishings in each room. The 25 suites have whirlpool tubs and separate living areas, and there's also a five-bedroom Grand Suite on the premises. In addition, guests can utilize the indoor pool, a state-of-the-art fitness center, a convenient business center, concierge services, wireless Internet access ($13 daily), and valet parking. There's also a wedding chapel, a stunning terrace, and a well-regarded restaurant, Lüke, which is open daily.

HOMEWOOD SUITES NEW ORLEANS $$

901 Poydras St., 504/581-5599, www.homewoodsuitesneworleans.com

New Orleans has seen an influx of longer-stay hotels in recent years, among them this multistory building in the heart of the CBD. Here, you'll find both one-bedroom units and two-bedroom suites, all with full kitchens, a sleeper sofa, premium cable TV, and high-speed Internet access. A continental breakfast is included, and there's an evening cocktail reception Monday–Thursday. In addition, the Hilton-run Homewood Suites offers a heated indoor pool, a fitness room, a business center, and complimentary grocery service. It's especially popular spot for business travelers, though families or leisure visitors staying for several days can make good use of this hotel, which often offers reduced prices on slower weekends.

THE HOTEL MODERN NEW ORLEANS $$$

936 St. Charles Ave., 504/962-0900 or 800/684-9525, www.thehotelmodern.com

Prior to its recent renovation, the former Hotel Le Cirque garnered mixed reviews. Today, the colorfully lit, pet-friendly boutique hotel is celebrated for its eclectic style. The 135 contemporary rooms and suites feature antiques as well as modern furniture, plus minibars, large TVs, plush bathrobes and towels, and Bigelow bath products. Guests appreciate the multilingual staff, in-room spa and 24-hour concierge services, valet parking, and assistance with dry-cleaning, babysitting, and dog-walking needs. Additionally, newspapers, gym passes, an overnight shoeshine, and wireless Internet access are all included. Be sure to sample the French-Vietnamese cuisine at the on-site Tamarind by Dominique, and enjoy live burlesque at Bellocq, the hotel's sexy lounge. While the all-night traffic in nearby Lee Circle can be distracting, the hotel's proximity to the Ogden Museum of Southern Art is a definite plus.

HYATT REGENCY NEW ORLEANS $$

601 Loyola Ave., 504/561-1234 or 888/591-1234, www.neworleans.hyatt.com

Following a massive, post-Katrina renovation, the reopened Hyatt Regency is once again one of the CBD's premier convention hotels—particularly because of its nearly 1,200 stylish guest rooms and suites. In-room amenities include luxurious beds, refrigerators, wireless Internet access, and high-definition, flat-screen TVs with cable. Guests may also appreciate the multilingual staff, valet parking, laundry and concierge services, on-site restaurant and bar, 24-hour gym and outdoor pool, and 24-hour fresh market. In addition, the hotel features Borgne, chef John Besh's newest restaurant.

INTERCONTINENTAL NEW ORLEANS $$

444 St. Charles Ave., 504/525-5566 or 888/424-6835, www.ichotelsgroup.com

Not only does the pet-friendly InterContinental ensure a prime viewing spot for certain Mardi Gras parades, but it also offers relatively easy access to the aquarium, the casino, the Algiers ferry, the Superdome, various museums, and free concerts at lovely Lafayette Square. The modern, 14-story building houses 479 tasteful rooms and 31 varied suites, all of which feature cable TV, minibars, air-conditioning, full-length mirrors, and high-speed Internet access ($11 daily). The suites provide extras like whirlpool tubs and sofa beds. Other on-site amenities include a business center, a health club and outdoor pool, a 24-hour lounge, and concierge services.

◖ INTERNATIONAL HOUSE HOTEL $$$

221 Camp St., 504/553-9550 or 800/633-5770, www.ihhotel.com

This smoke-free hotel occupies a stunning 1906 Beaux-Arts building that once served as a bank and is now one of the coolest addresses in town. The 117 rooms, suites, and penthouses are decorated in stylish, muted tones with cable TV, stereo systems, free wireless Internet access, ceiling fans, down comforters, and Aveda bath products. A 24-hour concierge and pricey valet parking ($32–38 daily) are also available. There's no pool, but you can work out in the fitness center and relax in the top-notch spa afterward. Given the fashionable clientele

HOTELS

© DANIEL MARTONE

the Rambla restaurant at the CBD's International House Hotel

HOTELS

WELCOME, PETS!

©LAURA MARTONE

A little searching will reveal New Orleans' pet-friendly hotel rooms.

Although New Orleans is rife with animals – from stray cats in the Bywater to leashed dogs in the Garden District – there are surprisingly few hotels that allow pets. One that does, however, is the **Royal Sonesta Hotel – New Orleans** (300 Bourbon St.), which is located in the French Quarter and allows pets under 35 pounds for a nonrefundable fee of $75 per animal.

Even more impressive, however, are the **W New Orleans** (333 Poydras St.) and the **W New Orleans – French Quarter** (316 Chartres St.), both of which not only welcome pets but also provide pet tags, food and water bowls, comfy pet beds, clean-up bags, pet-in-room door signs, and information about local pet stores, veterinarians, groomers, dog-sitting and dog-walking services, and dog parks. From the Whatever/Whenever desk, you can also procure leashes, litter boxes, waste removal bags, first-aid kits, and toys, food, and treats for dogs as well as cats. Bear in mind, though, that both W Hotels only allow one pet (up to 40 pounds) per room and charge a daily fee of $25 per pet as well as a nonrefundable cleaning fee of $100.

Situated in the CBD, the **Loews New Orleans Hotel** (300 Poydras St.) is also incredibly pet-friendly, offering rooms specifically intended for pets, a "Loews Loves Pets" room service menu, and gifts such as pet tags,

pet bowls, and special treats upon check-in, plus detailed information about local dog-walking routes, veterinarians, pet shops, and groomers. Guests can also take advantage of items like dog and cat beds, assorted leashes and collars, rawhide bones, scratch poles and catnip, litter boxes and litter, and, yes, pooper-scoopers. Just be advised that Loews limits the number of pets to two per room and charges a one-time fee of $25 per stay.

Given the city's relatively small size, you'll also find that most pet-friendly hotels are conveniently close to pet-related establishments. While downtown, you can seek emergency medical services at the **French Quarter Vet** (922 Royal St., 504/322-7030, www.thefrenchquartervet.com), where I regularly take my own kitty. If you're a small dog owner, look for toys, costumes, and accessories at **Chi-wa-wa Ga-ga** (511 Dumaine St., 504/581-4242, www.chiwawagaga.com). You might also appreciate the dog-friendly **Cabrini Park** at Dauphine and Barracks Streets. If you're staying in the Uptown area, venture to **Petcetera New Orleans** (3205 Magazine St., 504/269-8711, www.petceteraneworleans.com), which provides a wide array of products for cats and dogs, plus pet portraits, grooming and spa services, and a gourmet bakery.

it courts, it's no surprise that the hotel's Loa Bar is a favorite spot for the well-heeled to rub elbows, as is the on-site restaurant, Rambla. Several times each year, the ornate lobby is reborn to celebrate a particular festival or holiday that's dear to New Orleanians, from All Saints' Day in early November to the voodoo-based St. John's Eve in late June.

JW MARRIOTT NEW ORLEANS $$

614 Canal St., 504/525-6500 or 888/364-1200, www.marriott.com

The CBD boasts several Marriott hotels, including this convenient option just a stroll across Canal Street from the French Quarter. True, frequent Marriott guests might be disconcerted by the snug rooms, but in general, this 30-story, smoke-free hotel has a lot going for it, including a fitness center, an outdoor saltwater pool, a full-service spa, a well-favored steakhouse, a jazz club, and a helpful staff. With its 487 contemporary rooms, nine suites, and 25 meeting rooms, it's an ideal spot for convention travelers. As with other Marriotts in the CBD, pets aren't allowed here, and prices are steep for high-speed Internet access ($15 daily) and valet parking ($35 daily).

LAFAYETTE HOTEL $$

600 St. Charles Ave., 504/524-4441 or 800/366-2743, www.lafayettehotelneworleans.com

Operated by the same local group behind the Quarter's Place d'Armes and Prince Conti Hotels, the stately Lafayette occupies a grand five-story 1916 building that served as a Navy barracks during World War II. Situated beside attractive Lafayette Square and directly on the St. Charles streetcar line, this well-loved, smoke-free boutique hotel features 44 luxurious rooms and suites, all of which are swathed in floor-to-ceiling drapes and designer fabrics. Expect to find mahogany furniture, British botanical prints, marble bathrooms, and French doors opening onto small wrought-iron balconies. In addition, the suites have wet bars, refrigerators, and, in some cases, four-poster beds. Besides cable TV, climate control, wireless Internet access, bathrobes, and bath

phones, guests have access to business and laundry services, plus the 24-hour front desk.

LE PAVILLON HOTEL $$$

833 Poydras St., 504/581-3111 or 800/535-9095, www.lepavillon.com

Constructed in 1907, this world-renowned hotel offers some of the most elegant rooms and suites in the CBD. Besides tall ceilings, mahogany armoires, handmade drapes, and other classic furnishings, you can expect terrycloth robes, designer bath products, minibars, a full-size desk, and wireless Internet access in every room. There are also seven exquisite suites; each has a unique theme, from art deco to presidential. While here, relax in the stunning lobby, burn a few calories in the fitness center, or take a dip in the heated rooftop pool, which affords incredible views of the city. Also on-site is the well-regarded Crystal Room, an opulent, cavernous restaurant serving classic New Orleans fare and French-inspired cuisine, from seafood gumbo to beef Burgundy.

(LOEWS NEW ORLEANS HOTEL $$$

300 Poydras St., 504/595-3300 or 866/211-6411, www.loewshotels.com

Part of the widespread Loews hotel chain, this towering downtown hot spot contains 285 spacious rooms and suites, many of which provide views of the French Quarter and the Mississippi River and all featuring 300-thread-count linens, all-natural bath products, luxurious robes, Keurig coffeemakers, ergonomic chairs, and wireless Internet access. Other draws here include the convenient business center, the on-site Café Adelaide and Swizzle Stick Bar, the full-service fitness center and indoor swimming pool, and the popular Balance Spa. Guests may also appreciate the babysitting and laundry services, complimentary shoeshine, valet parking ($34 daily), and live weekend entertainment in the lobby lounge. As a bonus, pets ($25 per stay) are not only welcome but pampered; besides providing pet-specific items like bowls, treats, beds, and collars, the staff will offer detailed information about area pet services, from veterinarians to groomers.

HOTELS

LOFT 523 $$

523 Gravier St., 504/200-6523, www.loft523.com

From your first look at the airy, minimalist lobby with its white walls and earthy tones, it's clear that Loft 523 deviates from the typically ornate style of many New Orleans properties. This pet-friendly place is sexy and swank, with the emphasis squarely on contemporary urban design. The 16 spacious, loft-inspired rooms and two penthouses feature low-slung, modern furnishings, king-size beds, luxurious linens, spa-like bathrooms, and plenty of high-tech gadgetry, including flat-screen TVs, cordless phones, and high-speed wireless Internet access. Each of the glass-and-limestone showers has double shower-heads and Aveda bath products. The high ceilings and tall windows of this former 1880s dry-goods warehouse help to create the artsy mood, and guests enjoy the chic ground-floor bar, 24-hour concierge services, and round-the-clock access to the fitness center at the International House.

OMNI ROYAL CRESCENT HOTEL $$$

535 Gravier St., 504/527-0006 or 888/444-6664, www.omnihotels.com

Intimate and nearly hidden away on a narrow CBD street, this classy hotel offers a low-key, boutique-style ambience. The 97 renovated, nonsmoking rooms and suites of this eight-story property are decorated in earthy tones with custom-made mattresses, imported bath amenities, plush robes, honor bars, and executive desks; some of the suites have whirlpool tubs, and many rooms boast floor-to-ceiling windows. The pet-friendly Omni Royal Crescent also features a rooftop sun deck and hot tub, a 24-hour fitness center, and a gourmet burger restaurant; in addition, guests can take advantage of cable TV, high-speed wireless Internet access, individual climate control, daily continental breakfasts, business and laundry services, and currency exchange.

QUALITY INN & SUITES DOWNTOWN $$

210 O'Keefe Ave., 504/525-6800 or 877/424-6423, www.qualityinn.com

Only a few blocks from Bourbon Street lies this retro-style building, with its hard-to-miss gray and blue outer panels. Though not as stylish or historic as other CBD hotels, this Quality Inn offers comfortable accommodations, a welcoming staff, and a terrific location—all at a much better price than other options in the area. Amenities include cable TV, air-conditioning, microwaves, mini-fridges, complimentary wireless Internet access, and a free continental breakfast. Guests can also take advantage of the on-site business center, fitness room, free weekday newspapers, and indoor parking ($17 daily). For some travelers, the only drawback is that pets aren't permitted.

RENAISSANCE NEW ORLEANS ARTS HOTEL $$

700 Tchoupitoulas St., 504/613-2330 or 800/431-8634, www.renaissancehotels.com

This upscale, smoke-free Marriott hotel occupies a five-story former warehouse dating from 1910. Its boutique-like ambience is distinctly urban—the 210 rooms and seven suites are modern, airy, and spacious with tall windows, luxurious bedding, air-conditioning, marble bathrooms, ergonomic office chairs, and Aveda bath products. Guests can also enjoy the heated rooftop pool, an on-site fitness center, and the in-house restaurant, La Côte Brasserie, a neighborhood favorite for its creative French Creole cuisine. Pricey amenities include high-speed Internet access ($13 daily) and valet parking ($35 daily). Unfortunately, pets aren't allowed.

RENAISSANCE NEW ORLEANS PERE MARQUETTE HOTEL $$

817 Common St., 504/525-1111 or 800/372-0482, www.renaissancehotels.com

Part of the Marriott chain, the smoke-free Renaissance rises 18 stories over the CBD, with 272 spacious, smartly furnished rooms and suites. Each room features the work of local photographers, and every floor commemorates a jazz luminary. Amenities include deluxe bedding, ergonomic office chairs, CD stereos, and cable TV. The huge bathrooms are done in sleek marble and equipped with hair dryers and lighted makeup mirrors. Like the

Renaissance Arts Hotel, this no-pet option offers an outdoor heated pool, a fitness center, high-speed Internet access ($13 daily), and valet parking ($33 daily). There's also a lobby bar, a Starbucks coffeehouse, and an on-site French restaurant, MiLa, which serves breakfast, lunch, and dinner.

THE ROOSEVELT NEW ORLEANS $$$

123 Baronne St., 504/648-1200 or 800/925-3673, www.therooseveltneworleans.com

Extensively renovated and now operated by the Waldorf Astoria hotel chain, the magnificent Roosevelt has been exuding old-world charm in the CBD since 1893. This historic, smoke-free landmark, which fringes the French Quarter along Canal Street, features 369 stunning guest rooms and 135 sumptuous suites with 300-thread-count sheets, down-filled comforters, luxurious bathrobes, flat-screen TVs, minibars, and Ferragamo bath products. This pet-friendly hotel also offers pricey extras like high-speed Internet access ($13 daily) and valet parking ($40–48 daily). The Sazerac Bar and Restaurant is another highlight of this property, and a Sunday Jazz Brunch is offered in the Blue Room. Teddy's Café, the well-regarded Domenica restaurant, a rooftop pool, a 24-hour fitness center, a gift shop, concierge services, and the Guerlain Spa round out the amenities.

W NEW ORLEANS $$$

333 Poydras St., 504/525-9444 or 877/946-8357, www.starwoodhotels.com/whotels

More contemporary and urbane in ambience than W's French Quarter property, this pet-friendly hotel occupies a 23-story downtown skyscraper, not far from the aquarium, Harrah's New Orleans, the shops of Riverwalk Marketplace, and the galleries of the Arts District. Rooms on the upper floors have exceptional river and city views. Bliss bath products, 350-thread-count sheets, and monochromatic color schemes complete the oh-so-cool look and feel of the W's varied rooms and suites. Other amenities include spa robes, minibars, DVD/CD players, high-speed Internet access ($15 daily), and in-room spa treatments. The hotel's sexy and sleek Zoë restaurant, ultra-cool Whiskey Blue lounge, on-site business center, 24-hour fitness center, and rooftop pool make this a favorite spot for young business execs.

THE WHITNEY WYNDHAM HOTEL $$

610 Poydras St., 504/581-4222 or 877/999-3223, www.wyndham.com

Set inside a vintage redbrick bank building near the bustling intersection of Poydras and St. Charles—an ideal locale for viewing Mardi Gras parades—this seven-story, non-smoking hotel offers one of the better values among downtown's upscale options. Because it's relatively small compared to other CBD hotels, the rooms and suites are also a bit small. Still, with earthy color schemes, plush linens, comfortable robes, ergonomic chairs and work desks, high-speed Internet access, central heat and air-conditioning, cable TV, and handsome marble bathrooms, the accommodations are completely inviting. The on-site restaurant, Lil' Dizzy's, is set inside the elegant former bank lobby; the menu features such local treats as jambalaya and fried chicken.

WINDSOR COURT HOTEL $$$

300 Gravier St., 504/523-6000 or 888/596-0955, www.windsorcourthotel.com

Established in 1984 and recently refurbished, this luxury, art-filled hotel has been ranked among the top hotels in the world. The large, nonsmoking rooms, most of them full suites, contain elegant furnishings and Italian-marble baths, giving them the look and feel of a posh English country home. Amenities include valet parking, complimentary wireless Internet access, 24-hour concierge services, in-room spa sessions, and authentic afternoon teas. Guests can also take advantage of the 24-hour business center, the pool and health club, a stylish boutique, the upscale Polo Club Lounge (ideal for business meetings), and the on-site Grill Room, one of the most lavish, formal restaurants in the city.

HOTELS

© DANIEL MARTONE

the entrance of the CBD's Windsor Court Hotel

Garden District and Uptown Map 4

AVENUE GARDEN HOTEL 🟢🟢
1509 St. Charles Ave., 504/521-8000 or
800/379-5322, www.avenuegardenhotel.com
Set within a restored 1897 building with gracious balconies and ample charm, this family-
owned inn lies within walking distance of the
CBD and is only a 10-minute streetcar ride
from the French Quarter. The well-appointed
rooms blend reproduction New Orleans–inspired antiques with such up-to-date amenities
as cable TV, free Internet access, and individual climate control. Accommodations are simple but comfortable—more than satisfactory
considering the price—and off-street parking
is conveniently available. The on-site concierge
can also arrange swamp adventures, haunted
history strolls, and other tours.

AVENUE INN BED AND BREAKFAST 🟢🟢
4125 St. Charles Ave., 504/269-2640 or
800/490-8542, www.avenueinnbb.com
One of the South's most well-favored B&Bs

sits along the St. Charles streetcar line, making it not only an intimate resting place but
also a convenient home base for exploring the
city's major attractions, from Audubon Zoo to
the National WWII Museum. Built in 1891 by
Thomas Sully—the same architect who fashioned the equally lovely Grand Victorian Bed
& Breakfast—this stunning Victorian mansion features 17 inviting, uniquely decorated
guest rooms and suites, all of which have tall
ceilings, hardwood floors, antique furnishings,
and private bathrooms. A complimentary continental breakfast is served daily in the elegant
dining room or on the sunny veranda. No wonder it's a favorite spot among repeat visitors to
New Orleans!

THE CHIMES BED & BREAKFAST 🟢🟢
1146 Constantinople St., 504/899-2621 or
504/453-2183, www.chimesneworleans.com
A longtime favorite in the Uptown area, this
delightful inn has just five lovingly furnished

rooms facing a lush courtyard. Each has a private bathroom, an elegant queen-size bed, fine linens, French doors, high ceilings, hardwood or slate floors, wireless Internet access, cable TV, and self-controlled heat and air-conditioning; two rooms have fireplaces, and two others have daybeds that can accommodate an additional guest. An expansive continental breakfast, a stocked refrigerator, laundry room access, and local restaurant guides are included. This is a great base for exploring Uptown, a wonderful neighborhood filled with winning shops, popular eateries, and must-see attractions.

CLARION HOTEL
GRAND BOUTIQUE 🛇🛇
2001 St. Charles Ave., 504/558-9966 or
877/424-6423, www.clarionhotel.com

This smoke-free, art deco–style hotel offers fair rates, a business center, valet parking, and a convenient location on St. Charles Avenue, just a few steps from the streetcar line. The clean, modern rooms boast large windows that let in plenty of light, and all have refrigerators and microwaves, cable TV, free wireless Internet access, air-conditioning, and bold, attractive furnishings; just bear in mind that, depending on your room, traffic noise can be an issue. Rates here include a continental breakfast, though the adjacent Copeland's Cheesecake Bistro also provides room service.

DIVE INN GUEST HOUSE 🛇
4417 Dryades St., 504/895-6555 or 888/788-3483,
www.thediveinn.com

Budget-conscious travelers with a Bohemian sensibility may appreciate the Dive Inn, a colorful, funky guesthouse a few blocks north of St. Charles Avenue. This place once served as an indoor scuba-diving school, and in keeping with the nautical theme you'll find eight uniquely furnished, nonsmoking rooms and suites with names like the Captain's Quarters, the Crow's Nest, and the Dolphin. Intended for open-minded, easygoing adults, this no-frills inn doesn't promise

off-street parking, in-room phones and TVs, or room service, and neither children nor pets are allowed here. You can, however, expect private bathrooms, air-conditioning, wireless Internet access, eccentric fellow guests, and a heated indoor pool and two hot tubs, all three of which are clothing-optional and open 24 hours daily.

FAIRCHILD HOUSE
BED & BREAKFAST 🛇
1518 Prytania St., 504/524-0154 or 800/256-8096,
www.fairchildhouse.com

Constructed in 1841, this Greek Revival–style home has served as an elegant B&B for more than two decades. All nine well-appointed rooms and suites feature hardwood floors, high ceilings, private bathrooms, and cable TV. In addition, guests can take advantage of free off-street parking and enjoy a complimentary continental breakfast in the lush courtyard. Situated in the Lower Garden District, the inn ensures convenient access to dog-friendly Coliseum Square, the St. Charles streetcar line, the CBD's well-regarded museums, and the antiques shops of Magazine Street.

GARDEN DISTRICT
BED & BREAKFAST 🛇
2418 Magazine St., 504/895-4302,
www.gardendistrictbedandbreakfast.com

Built in the late 1860s and allegedly serving as a brothel during the 1920s, this lovingly restored Victorian-style home now boasts four suites, all featuring hardwood floors, tall ceilings, queen-size beds, private bathrooms, microwaves, mini-fridges, and central heat and air-conditioning; each room promises either balcony or courtyard access. Cable TV and wireless Internet access are also available, and guests are welcome to use the formal dining and living rooms. From the B&B, you can tour the historic houses of the Garden District, explore the shops and eateries along Magazine Street, and hop aboard the St. Charles streetcar, which runs around the clock.

THE GRAND VICTORIAN BED & BREAKFAST $$

2727 St. Charles Ave., 504/895-1104 or 800/977-0008, www.gvbb.com

If you don't have a chance to visit the famed plantations along the Great River Road, you can at least get a sense of them by staying at this sumptuous inn, designed and built in 1893 by celebrated local architect Thomas Sully. The rooms in this fanciful, lovingly restored Victorian mansion are named for Louisiana plantation homes, such as Oak Alley and Destrehan, and all are filled with antique period furnishings. Whichever room you choose, expect an impressive antique bed and a comfortable feather mattress that you may not want to vacate in the morning. Tall windows in the parlor overlook the clanging St. Charles Avenue streetcar, and a continental breakfast is served in the sunny dining room. Other amenities include private bathrooms, whirlpool tubs, concierge services, cable TV, free parking, and wireless Internet access throughout the house.

© LAURA MARTONE

The Green House Inn, a vibrant lodging option on Magazine Street

☾ THE GREEN HOUSE INN $$

1212 Magazine St., 504/525-1333 or 800/966-1303, www.thegreenhouseinn.com

This unusual inn, set in the Lower Garden District, offers a pleasant change of pace from many of New Orleans's richly urbane B&Bs. Constructed in 1840, the Greek Revival–style townhouse has a tropical, whimsical vibe, from the palm tree–shaped, clothing-optional pool to the verdant landscaping. The flower-named, smoke-free rooms have private bathrooms and are well outfitted with the kind of amenities you'd expect at a much pricier hotel: king-size beds, deluxe sheets and towels, flat-screen TVs, mini-fridges, all-natural bath products, guest robes, free wireless Internet access, and individual climate control. Additionally, the pet-friendly Green House Inn offers gated off-street parking, an oversized hot tub near the pool, and easy access to area attractions, like Coliseum Square and the National WWII Museum.

HAMPTON INN NEW ORLEANS GARDEN DISTRICT HOTEL $$

3626 St. Charles Ave., 504/899-9990 or 800/292-0653, www.neworleanshamptoninns.com/garden-district

Unlike many chain hotels, this particular Hampton Inn successfully combines old-world grace with contemporary amenities. While the lovely lobby and peaceful courtyard exude a classic New Orleans vibe, the spacious guest rooms and suites are decidedly modern, with microwaves, flat-screen TVs, and curved shower rods. Freebies include parking, a hot breakfast, and wireless Internet access (though the speed can be a bit slow). Sofa beds and whirlpool tubs are available in some rooms, and guests can enjoy the small on-site swimming pool. Situated on the St. Charles streetcar line, this hotel is ideal for a variety of visitors, from business-minded travelers to the parents of Tulane and Loyola students.

HENRY HOWARD HOUSE INN $$

2041 Prytania St., 504/561-8550, www.henryhowardhouseinn.com

Built in 1850 by architect Henry Howard, this

stunning, impeccably restored mansion blends classic charm with modern conveniences. The 17 lavish rooms are uniquely decorated and are named after Mardi Gras krewes—from Bacchus to Endymion. Expect antique furnishings, luxurious linens and towels, private bathrooms, flat-screen TVs, temperature controls, and bold Mardi Gras–related paintings by local artist Will Smith. Other amenities include free long-distance calls, complimentary wireless Internet access, gourmet breakfasts, private balconies, and communal spaces like the parlor, media center, and appealing courtyards. Another bonus is its proximity to nearby shops and eateries, relaxing Coliseum Square, and, of course, the St. Charles streetcar line.

HUBBARD MANSION
BED & BREAKFAST $$

3535 St. Charles Ave., 504/897-3535,
www.hubbardmansion.com

Owned and operated by the Hubbard family, this handsome, Greek Revival–style home is actually a replica of a mansion in Natchez, Mississippi. One advantage, though, is that the B&B features the modern amenities of a new building, complete with thick walls, central air-conditioning, and wireless, high-speed Internet access. The five main suites overflow with authentic period antiques and reproductions, such as mahogany armoires, marble-topped dressers, and canopy beds with rich linens; in addition, you'll find a pair of two-bedroom apartments in the rear carriage house, ideal for longer stays. On-site parking and a continental breakfast are also available. Indeed, this is a perfect spot for a romantic nest, only a short trolley ride from the French Quarter.

MAGNOLIA MANSION $$$

2127 Prytania St., 504/412-9500,
www.magnoliamansion.com

One of the Garden District's fanciest lodging options is this stately, gleaming white mansion, designed in the mid-1850s by James H. Calrow, who also planned the Brevard-Clapp House, Anne Rice's former home. Completed in 1858 and formerly known as the Harris-Maginnis House, the Magnolia Mansion served as the headquarters for the American Red Cross from 1939 through 1954. Today, it strikes a dashing figure from the street, with elaborate Corinthian columns, a double-galleried veranda, moss-draped live oaks, and magnolias towering over the grounds. There are nine smoke-free, elaborately decorated rooms, which vary in price and theme—such as the elegant "Gone with the Wind" suite and the sexy "Vampire Lover's Lair." All have over-the-top furnishings, a private bathroom, cable TV, and wireless Internet access. Concierge services, an on-site library, and a continental breakfast are also available. Not surprisingly, honeymooners and others celebrating special occasions favor this property, especially since guests must be at least 21 years old.

MAISON PERRIER $$

4117 Perrier St., 504/897-1807 or 888/610-1807,
www.maisonperrier.com

Three blocks south of the St. Charles streetcar line, you'll encounter this whimsical yet elegant Victorian mansion. Built in 1892, this lovingly restored inn was the supposed site of a turn-of-the-20th-century gentlemen's club. In fact, the 16 spacious, distinctive rooms and suites are named after the ladies who might have entertained clients here, such as Jasmine, Claudette, and Desiree. Besides tall ceilings, antique furnishings, and private bathrooms, you can expect honor bars, blackout shades, plush robes, cable TV, central heat and air-conditioning, and wireless Internet access. Some rooms offer king-size beds, whirlpool tubs, and intimate balconies. Other amenities include a tranquil courtyard, inviting communal rooms, concierge services, free on-site parking, and complimentary Southern-style breakfasts, afternoon teas, and wine-and-cheese evenings.

MAISON ST. CHARLES HOTEL
& SUITES NEW ORLEANS $$

1319 St. Charles Ave., 504/522-0187,
www.maisonstcharles.com

While the stylish lobby might outshine some of the guest rooms at the Maison St. Charles,

HOTELS

its terrific location beside the St. Charles streetcar line—with convenient access to the CBD and French Quarter, not to mention other parts of Uptown—sets this collection of former antebellum homes apart from other midrange chain properties. Part of the Choice Hotels family, this historic place offers 113 rooms and 15 suites, all smoke-free. The rooms themselves, as well as the level of service, are fairly standard, but this is a dependable option with a pleasant swimming pool and hot tub, a coin-operated laundry, on-site gated parking ($17 daily), and free continental breakfasts and wireless Internet access. Its pet-friendly status has also been a plus for me and my husband in the past.

THE MCKENDRICK-BREAUX HOUSE [$][$]

1474 Magazine St., 504/586-1700 or 888/570-1700, www.mckendrick-breaux.com

Constructed in 1865 by plumber Daniel McKendrick and eventually restored by preservationist Eddie Breaux, this three-story, Greek Revival–style mansion lies on what was once part of the Sarpy Plantation. Today, it stands on the edge of Magazine Street's antique row, making it an ideal location for shoppers. Many rooms contain such architectural details as antique beds, claw-foot tubs, and galleries that overlook the lush courtyard. There are nine airy guest rooms, each named after one of the Greek muses. All have private bathrooms, high-thread-count linens, luxurious robes, local artwork, cable TV, and central heat and air-conditioning. Considering the amenities and first-rate staff, this is one of the best deals in the city; rates include an extensive continental breakfast and limited off-street parking.

PARK VIEW GUEST HOUSE [$][$]

7004 St. Charles Ave., 504/861-7564 or 888/533-0746, www.parkviewguesthouse.com

Literally situated beside Audubon Park, the aptly named Park View Guest House is ideal for travelers hoping to explore Audubon Zoo, the nearby campuses of Tulane and Loyola, and the rest of Uptown. The convenient St. Charles streetcar line is also just a stroll away. Erected in 1884—just in time for the World's Industrial and Cotton Centennial Exposition—this magnificent, recently restored inn lures guests with its smoke-free rooms, antique furnishings, luxurious beds, private bathrooms, complimentary breakfasts and afternoon refreshments, free wireless Internet access, and amicable staff. Relax on the inviting porch or, if you're lucky, on the upper balconies, which afford pleasant views of the oak-filled park.

THE PRYTANIA PARK HOTEL [$][$]

1525 Prytania St., 504/524-0427 or 800/862-1984, www.prytaniaparkhotel.com

With St. Charles Avenue just a block away, the Prytania is only a short streetcar ride from attractions in the CBD, including the Ogden Museum of Southern Art and the National WWII Museum. This charming hotel offers several wonderful features, such as verdant grounds, cheery courtyards, balcony access, and a family-friendly master suite, with a king-size bed on the lower level and two queen-size beds in an upper loft. Thirteen of the attractively furnished rooms have Victorian-style decor, while 49 rooms are contemporary in appearance. Rooms are set within four buildings, connected by landscaped walkways, and all have private bath areas. Amenities include ceiling fans, microwaves, cable TV, climate control, blackout drapes, and free wireless Internet access. You can also expect helpful, round-the-clock service at the front desk as well as a free continental breakfast, served daily on the patio.

THE QUEEN ANNE [$][$]

1625 Prytania St., 504/524-0427 or 800/862-1984, www.thequeenanne.com

Built in 1890 and operated by the same folks behind the charming Prytania Park Hotel, this stunning, carefully restored Victorian mansion contains a dozen elegantly furnished rooms, some of which boast 12-foot ceilings, hardwood floors, mahogany furniture, four-poster beds, and marble bathrooms. Other amenities include ceiling fans, microwaves, extra towels and bedding, cable TV, and free wireless

Internet access. There are no elevators here; be advised, too, that guests must be at least 25 years old. Like other inns in the Lower Garden District, the Queen Anne ensures easy access to historic homes, lovely parks, and the St. Charles streetcar line.

SOUTHERN COMFORT
BED & BREAKFAST ⬤⬤

1739 Marengo St., 504/895-3680 or 888/769-3868, www.southerncomfort-bnb.com

Only a couple of blocks north of the St. Charles streetcar line, this gorgeous B&B offers convenient access to the city's major attractions yet with all the ambience of an intimate hideaway. Built in 1910, this delightful cottage provides three unique guest rooms, each tastefully decorated and furnished with antique pieces as well as period reproductions. Every room features flat-screen TVs, honor bars, Sonoma bath products, ceiling fans, air-conditioning, and free wireless Internet access. Guests can take advantage of the full gourmet breakfasts, concierge services, DVD library, communal refrigerator, complimentary bikes, and day passes for a neighborhood gym. Depending on whether you've arrived by plane or car, you might also appreciate the personalized airport pickup or free parking.

ST. CHARLES GUEST HOUSE ⬤

1748 Prytania St., 504/523-6556, www.stcharlesguesthouse.com

Built in 1890, the St. Charles Guest House is a modest yet charming B&B that lies halfway between tranquil Coliseum Square and the bustling St. Charles Avenue streetcar line. Although the simply furnished rooms lack TVs or phones, wireless Internet access is available. While some guests complain about the small spaces and aging bathrooms, many of the free-spirited travelers who gravitate here appreciate the quaint, European vibe of this longstanding inn. It doesn't hurt that there's a secluded pool and courtyard, shaded by banana trees, and a free continental breakfast served daily in the sunny dining room. In addition, the friendly staff can offer advice and directions to shops, eateries, and attractions throughout the city.

SULLY MANSION
BED & BREAKFAST ⬤⬤

2631 Prytania St., 504/891-0457 or 800/364-2414, www.sullymansion.com

The breezy, wraparound porch isn't the only inviting aspect of this historic mansion. Built in 1890 by celebrated architect Thomas Sully—the same man who crafted the Avenue Inn and Grand Victorian B&Bs—this generally well-regarded inn offers eight airy, distinctive rooms and suites, each named after a famous New Orleans street. All chambers feature 14-foot ceilings, hardwood floors, graceful antiques, fine linens, private bathrooms, air-conditioning, cable TV, and wireless Internet access. Guests can also enjoy continental breakfasts on weekdays and gourmet dishes on the weekends.

◖ TERRELL HOUSE
BED AND BREAKFAST ⬤⬤

1441 Magazine St., 504/237-2076 or 866/261-9687, www.terrellhouse.com

Set amid the historic homes of Uptown's Lower Garden District, the hospitable Terrell House

the Garden District's Terrell House Bed and Breakfast

© LAURA MARTONE

HOTELS

has a special connection to my family— it's where my great-grandmother and her four siblings spent much of their childhood. Today, this magnificent, Italianate-style mansion, built in the mid-19th century, offers luxurious accommodations, plus delicious Southern-style breakfasts that are especially memorable among former guests. Only a block from restful Coliseum Square, this beloved B&B ensures convenient access to the shops and eateries along Magazine Street, plus the St. Charles streetcar line.

Tremé and Mid-City

Map 5

ASHTONS BED & BREAKFAST $$

2023 Esplanade Ave., 504/942-7048 or 800/725-4131, www.ashtonsbb.com

Unexpectedly, one of the city's most elegant inns sits not in the French Quarter or Garden District, but in a laid-back Mid-City neighborhood, far from touristy hot spots. Built in 1861, this Greek Revival–style, antebellum mansion features an inviting veranda, lush gardens, a shady rear yard, and, within the main house and patio wing, eight spacious, uniquely decorated, and impeccably furnished rooms. Aptly, each room is named after events, landmarks, or other iconic images unique to New Orleans, such as Mardi Gras and the *Creole Queen*. All have tall ceilings, private bathrooms, luxurious linens, and individual thermostats. Cable TV, wireless Internet access, secured parking, and a full gourmet breakfast are included.

DEGAS HOUSE $$$

2306 Esplanade Ave., 504/821-5009, www.degashouse.com

Relatively close to the New Orleans Museum of Art in City Park, the Degas House is both an inn *and* a museum. French Impressionist painter Edgar Degas lived in the house for about six months in 1872–1873 while visiting

Painter Edgar Degas once stayed in the historic Degas House on tree-lined Esplanade Avenue.

his maternal relatives, the Musson family; in fact, the artist painted several works while here. Built in 1852, the B&B contains six rooms and three suites that vary considerably in size and luxury. All have private bathrooms, soaring ceilings, and hardwood floors with well-chosen antiques; the two larger suites have both private balconies and whirlpool tubs. Other amenities include cable TV, wireless Internet access, secured parking, a guided house tour, and a Creole breakfast.

◖ 1896 O'MALLEY HOUSE ●●

120 S. Pierce St., 504/488-5896 or 866/226-1896, www.1896omalleyhouse.com

Not far from the busy intersection of Canal Street and North Carrollton Avenue, the O'Malley House is nevertheless one of the more hidden, less-touristy inns in the city. It is named for one of New Orleans's most prominent Irish citizens of the late 19th century, Dominick O'Malley—a newspaper publisher credited with exposing the corruption of local politicos. This gracious, Colonial Revival–style mansion features original cypress-wood mantels, pocket doors, and other artful details. The eight sumptuous suites are filled with exceptional antiques, handsome Oriental rugs, plush four-poster beds, and elegant tables. Most rooms have whirlpool tubs, and all have free wireless Internet access. Run by exceedingly hospitable hosts, the house lies within walking distance of several restaurants and just steps from the Canal streetcar line, which links City Park to the French Quarter. An especially bounteous continental breakfast is included.

FIVE CONTINENTS BED AND BREAKFAST ●●

1731 Esplanade Ave., 504/324-8594 or 800/997-4652, www.fivecontinentsbnb.com

Admittedly not in the best part of town, the Five Continents B&B is nevertheless one of New Orleans's more well-respected inns. The name derives from the fact that the former and current owners have all traveled to at least five continents. Housed within a two-story, Greek Revival–style home built in the late 1880s, the

inn features tall ceilings, crystal chandeliers, hardwood floors, and Oriental rugs. The four uniquely decorated two-room suites, which are situated in either the main house or the pet-friendly garden cottage, boast continent-specific artwork, antique furnishings, private bathrooms, ecofriendly toiletries, and luxurious linens. Other amenities include wireless Internet access and a gourmet breakfast that, depending on the day, might entail seasonal fruit, eggs Sardou, shrimp Benedict, crawfish hash, or other local delectables.

HH WHITNEY HOUSE ●●

1923 Esplanade Ave., 504/948-9448 or 877/944-9448, www.hhwhitneyhouse.com

Roughly eight blocks from the French Quarter, this handsome, Italianate-style home is adorned with ceiling medallions, elegant archways, antique Victorian furnishings, and numerous fireplaces. There are two suites and three well-appointed rooms, one of which is dedicated to Scarlett O'Hara. Besides standards like cable TV, wireless Internet access, air-conditioning, and private bathrooms, this smoke-free inn also offers private balconies, off-street parking, complimentary refreshments, and a full breakfast. Guests particularly relish the relaxing courtyard, swimming pool, and hot tub. Despite the inn's relative proximity to the Quarter, it's not advisable to walk through or alongside the Tremé at night.

INDIA HOUSE HOSTEL ●

124 S. Lopez St., 504/821-1904 or 504/324-4365, www.indiahousehostel.com

Given the Big Easy's Bohemian reputation, it's odd that the city doesn't boast more hostel options. Fortunately, budget-conscious travelers will find a lot to love about the India House. Just off Canal Street, this lively Mid-City hostel offers a fully equipped kitchen, a relaxing rear courtyard and swimming pool, spacious common areas with sofas and flat-screen TVs, dorms as well as private rooms, plus discounted tour tickets. Happily, the hostel has no curfew, and all facilities are available 24 hours daily.

Band nights, movie screenings, crawfish boils, barbecues, and other rowdy gatherings occur often, so it can definitely be a noisy place. On the bright side, though, you're sure to meet lots of kooky characters, and the streetcar line is just a short stroll away.

MONROSE ROW BED & BREAKFAST $$

1303 Gov. Nicholls St., 504/524-4950,
www.monroserow.com

The Greek Revival–style building that now houses the intimate Monrose Row Bed & Breakfast was originally constructed in 1839 for local baker Charles Monrose. Today, the carefully restored inn offers three individually decorated two-room suites with antique furnishings and private baths. Two of the rooms are situated in the slave quarters, overlooking the charming courtyard, while the third occupies the entire third floor of the main house. Amenities include ceiling fans, wireless Internet access, and a continental breakfast.

NEW ORLEANS GUEST HOUSE $

1118 Ursulines Ave., 504/566-1177 or 800/562-1177

With its lush, peaceful courtyard, the somewhat aging New Orleans Guest House serves as a popular, yet intimate, hideaway for travelers on a budget. The 14 guest rooms have high ceilings, antique furnishings, and, in many cases, vibrant color schemes. Although the privately owned inn lies within walking distance of the French Quarter, its dicey Tremé location means it's better to rely on taxis or bring your own car—which you can park in the small but secured on-site lot.

RATHBONE MANSIONS $$

1244 Esplanade Ave., 504/309-4479,
www.rathbonemansions.com

Rathbone consists of two lavish and expertly restored antebellum mansions, containing standard guest rooms as well as one- and two-bedroom suites. Some of the rooms have balconies, and all have high ceilings, well-chosen antiques, private bathrooms, flat-screen TVs, and air-conditioning. A continental breakfast is included, and free parking is available on a first-come, first-served basis. The saltwater pool and hot tub serve as a tranquil spot for whiling away an afternoon. These inns lie only a short drive south of City Park and within walking distance of the Quarter—though guests should exercise caution at night.

Greater New Orleans   Map 6

BELLEVILLE COTTAGE
BED AND BREAKFAST $

317 Belleville St., Algiers Point, 504/368-0117,
www.bellevillecottage.com

If you're looking for a truly intimate experience, consider this quaint, Arts and Crafts–style home in historic Algiers Point, only a short ferry ride from the French Quarter. Built in the 1920s and operated by a certified massage therapist, this tranquil place features just two accommodations: a garden room with private access to the backyard patio and a garden suite with a convenient kitchenette. Both options include private bathrooms, wireless Internet access, complimentary beverages, and breakfast vouchers to local restaurants.

COMFORT SUITES AIRPORT $$

2710 Idaho Ave., Kenner, 504/466-6066 or
866/267-3524,
www.comfortsuitesneworleansairport.com

In general, lodging options near the Louis Armstrong New Orleans International Airport constitute a variety of chain hotels, including this affordable, completely nonsmoking property just off the interstate. The 95 guest rooms are spacious, with mini-fridges, high-speed Internet access, and satellite TV. You'll also find an indoor/outdoor pool, a hot tub, and an exercise room. Free airport transportation, on-site parking, and a continental breakfast are included.

HOLIDAY INN NEW ORLEANS
WEST BANK TOWER 💲💲

275 Whitney Ave., Gretna, 504/366-8535 or
888/465-4329, www.holidayinn.com

For spectacular views of the Mississippi River
and the Crescent City's skyline, book a stay at
this 180-room Holiday Inn, a West Bank hotel
that, as the name indicates, features a tall, cy-
lindrical tower of well-appointed, nonsmoking
rooms and suites. Accommodations are spacious, with modern furnishings, flat-screen
TVs, and free wireless Internet access. Besides
free parking, guests can also take advantage
of the on-site fitness center, outdoor pool, 24-
hour lounge, and laundry facilities.

HOUSE OF THE RISING SUN
BED & BREAKFAST 💲

335 Pelican Ave., Algiers Point, 504/368-1123,
www.risingsunbnb.com

Erected in 1896 and named after the fictitious
brothel immortalized by the Animals' 1964 recording, this renovated hideaway features two
unique lodging options: the Asian-style "Red"
Allen room honoring the local jazz trumpeter
and the smaller "Memphis Minnie" room inspired by the Algiers-born blues singer. Both
options include private bathrooms, access to
relaxing porches, and a continental breakfast.
Guests can easily walk to the free ferry that
makes frequent trips across the Mississippi
River to downtown New Orleans.

🌙 ROSE MANOR
BED & BREAKFAST INN 💲

7214 Pontchartrain Blvd., 504/282-8200,
www.rosemanor.com

Nestled in the Lakeview neighborhood that was
so famously flooded by Hurricane Katrina, this
B&B is an ideal choice for those interested in exploring City Park, Lake Pontchartrain, and the
nearby town of Metairie. Offering 10 spacious,
uniquely decorated rooms and suites, the intimate Rose Manor epitomizes a medley of old and
new, with its old-fashioned dining room, antique
furnishings, private baths, central air-conditioning, and complimentary wireless Internet access.
The free, on-site parking is another big plus.

HOTELS

EXCURSIONS FROM NEW ORLEANS

Southern Louisiana—which encompasses the Northshore, the Great River Road, Baton Rouge, Cajun Country, and the waterlogged areas south of New Orleans—extends about 200 miles east to west along the I-10 corridor, and only about 75 miles north to south. While this region is fairly large, the most-visited areas are easily accessible from New Orleans, especially if you have your own vehicle. Most towns lie less than 45 minutes from the Big Easy, via either I-10 or the 24-mile-long Causeway bridge.

Separated from New Orleans by enormous Lake Pontchartrain, the Northshore comprises a string of middle-class and upscale suburbs, north of which lies a patchwork of rural, wooded towns extending about 40 miles to the Mississippi border. This is one of Louisiana's top areas for golfing, bird-watching, biking, canoeing, kayaking, and fishing. Hidden gems here include the Global Wildlife Center and Pontchartrain Vineyards.

In southern Louisiana, the Great River Road actually refers to a series of byways running along both sides of the Mississippi River, from New Orleans through the rural plantation country northwest of the city, then on to Baton Rouge and up to charming St. Francisville, the quintessential antebellum Southern town. This region is rife with plantation homes, from relatively modest raised cottages to enormous Greek Revival–style wedding cakes amid 200-year-old, moss-draped live oak trees.

As the city's state capital, Baton Rouge makes a great base for exploring the entire length of Louisiana's Great River Road, but

HIGHLIGHTS

LOOK FOR  TO FIND RECOMMENDED SIGHTS, ACTIVITIES, DINING, AND LODGING.

Best Place to Talk to the Animals: Don't mistake the **Global Wildlife Center,** which sits on the Tangipahoa-St. Tammany Parish line, for a mere zoo. About 3,000 wild animals, from zebras to kangaroos, roam freely amid the 900 rural acres, where visitors can view them via covered-wagon safaris (page 250).

Best Locale to Learn About the Sea: Although it began as a rather modest museum in the charming village of Madisonville, the **Lake Pontchartrain Basin Maritime Museum** has grown into one of the Northshore's best attractions, with excellent exhibits on the region's maritime history (page 251).

Best Place to Imbibe: Not only does **Pontchartrain Vineyards,** just north of Covington, produce the finest vintages in the state, but it also presents informative tours, popular concerts, and other enjoyable events on its bucolic grounds (page 251).

Best Spot for Boot-Stompin': A rollicking variety show, **The Abita Springs Opry** takes place at the Abita Springs Town Hall once a month in the spring and fall. At these down-home concerts, you'll hear wonderful country, gospel, bluegrass, and folk music in a quaint, small-town setting (page 253).

Most Fascinating Plantation: The engaging tours of **Laura: A Creole Plantation** distinguish this property from others along the Great River Road. During your visit, you'll learn not only about the four generations of women who presided over the plantation but also about the lives of the slaves who lived here (page 258).

Best Photo-Op: Few images in Louisiana are more recognizable than the stunning alley of live oak trees that brackets the Greek Revival-style home at **Oak Alley Plantation,** where visitors can tour the house and explore the beautifully landscaped grounds (page 259).

Coolest-Looking Government Building: Unlike any other state capitol in the country, the art deco-style **Louisiana State Capitol** soars 34 stories over the Baton Rouge skyline. You can view the scenery from an observation deck and also see exactly where notorious Governor Huey Long was assassinated (page 264).

Best Place to Understand Cajun History: Operated by the National Park Service, the modern **Acadian Cultural Center** tells the Cajun story with state-of-the-art exhibits and an excellent movie on the Acadian banishment from Canada— all of which provide a sense of southwestern Louisiana's rich and moving history (page 267).

Best Pseudo-Island: Technically a salt dome rather than an actual island, **Avery Island** is owned by the McIlhenny family and is the site of two seminal attractions: the McIlhenny Tabasco Company and the Jungle Gardens and Bird City (page 269).

Best Living History Museum: Cajun Louisiana's answer to Colonial Williamsburg, the fascinating **Vermilionville** outdoor museum recounts the Cajun experience through historic buildings and reproductions, music-and-dance presentations, crafts demonstrations, and regional cuisine (page 270).

© LAURA MARTONE

Birds congregate in the Jungle Gardens on Avery Island.

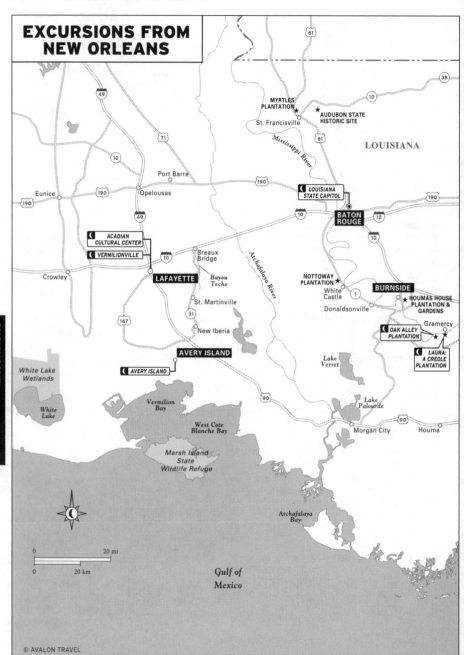

EXCURSIONS FROM NEW ORLEANS

EXCURSIONS

© AVALON TRAVEL

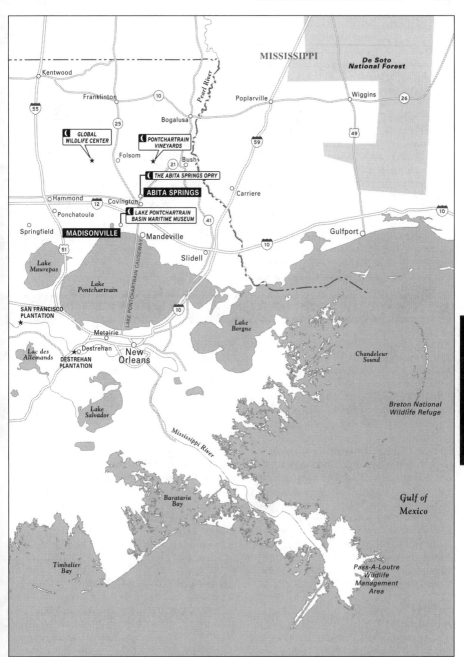

it also has a number of worthwhile attractions in its own right, plus a wide range of affordable restaurants and chain hotels. Beyond Baton Rouge, Louisiana's Cajun Country is the most visited and perhaps the most intriguing part of the state. Although several inland and coastal towns compose this lively region, its geographical and cultural center is the city of Lafayette, an ideal place to begin your explorations, as it has several excellent museums that interpret and introduce the heritage of the Cajun people.

PLANNING YOUR TIME

As with New Orleans, spring and fall are the most popular seasons for visiting southern Louisiana. If you only have a little time to spare, head to the **Northshore.** Though you could spend an entire weekend exploring the parks, communities, and other diversions north of Lake Pontchartrain, you can easily hit the highlights, such as the Global Wildlife Center, in less than a day.

From the Big Easy, you can also spend an entire day—if not a long weekend—touring the plantations along the **Great River Road,** from Destrehan to St. Francisville, about two hours from New Orleans. Of course, a day trip to **Baton Rouge** is more than feasible, especially if you focus on key attractions like the State Capitol building and the USS *Kidd.*

Cajun Country, which extends from Houma to Lafayette and beyond, is a more complicated endeavor. To get the most out of this region, plan at least two days. Most visitors head first to Lafayette, which lies about 2.5 hours northwest of New Orleans via I-10. As an alternative, you can take U.S. 90 to Lafayette through the towns of Morgan City and New Iberia—a route that'll require about three hours.

The Northshore

Mainly divided into St. Tammany and Tangipahoa Parishes, the Northshore might be less famous than New Orleans, but while its most prominent communities—Slidell, Mandeville, Covington, Ponchatoula, and Hammond—all contain their share of gated communities and strip shopping malls, they're also a treasure trove of nature preserves, tranquil forests, and funky historical districts. Diversions here include touring a brewery, shopping for antiques, and visiting curious museums. The architecture, topography, and even climate are distinct from the rest of southern Louisiana, bearing a closer resemblance to the charming vintage towns of Mississippi, Alabama, and Georgia. Like New Orleans, the Northshore took a hard hit from Hurricane Katrina in August 2005, but in the years since, most of its attractions, restaurants, and hotels have reopened.

SIGHTS
Abita Brewery

The Abita Brewing Company opened in 1986, taking full advantage of Abita Springs' famed water. Today, the Abita Brewery (166 Barbee Rd. off LA-36, Abita Springs, 985/893-3143, www.abita.com) offers free tours and tastings at 2 P.M. on Wednesday, Thursday, and Friday and at 11 A.M., noon, 1 P.M., and 2 P.M. on Saturday. These tours are fun and low-key, offering the opportunity to learn about the brewing process from friendly staff members who usually take the time to chat with visitors. Abita produces several kinds of beer, including seasonal varieties as well as standard ones that vary from the dark and rich Turbo Dog to the pleasantly fruity Purple Haze (my personal favorite) to the light and bubbly Abita Amber. Just be advised that all visitors to the brewery must wear closed-toe shoes and be at least 21 years of age.

◖ Global Wildlife Center

Though less visited than other attractions in southern Louisiana, the remarkable Global Wildlife Center (26389 LA-40, Folsom, 985/796-3585, www.globalwildlife.com, tours vary daily, $17 adult, $15 senior, $11 child

2–11, free under 2) is well worth venturing off the beaten path. Once you're within the 900-acre grounds, it's hard to imagine that you're still in Louisiana. Giraffes, zebras, antelope, llamas, camels, and three dozen other species of mostly African wildlife (nearly 3,000 animals all together) roam freely across the property. Visitors board covered wagons, which are pulled across the grounds by tractors, in tours that last about 90 minutes.

The safari guides simply go where the animals are, and in many cases, you're allowed to come extremely close to the wildlife—an excellent opportunity for photographers. Reservations are not required (except for groups), but visitors should call for the schedule of guided tours, which changes weekly. The center has a huge gift shop, selling all manner of wildlife toys, prints, books, and stuffed animals (the proceeds benefit the care of the animals), and there's a small concession stand. You can also buy cups, buckets, sacks, or bins of feed to tempt some of the tamer animals—which kids especially enjoy.

Kliebert's Turtle and Alligator Farm

Southwest of Hammond, accessible via I-55, lies Kliebert's Turtle and Alligator Farm (41083 W. Yellow Water Rd., Hammond, 985/345-3617 or 800/854-9164, www.kliebertgatortours.com, tours daily noon–sunset Mar.–Oct., $12 adult, $7 child 4–12, free under 4), one of the few alligator farms in southern Louisiana open to the public. Louisiana limits the hunting of American alligators in the wild, so these farms raise and harvest the animals, helping to protect the wild species. All farms, including Kliebert's (pronounced KLEE-BAIRS), are required to return to the wild a significant percentage of the alligators born in captivity. Here, you can get a firsthand look at more than 300 gators and 47,000 turtles; there's also a gift shop that offers alligator heads, turtle shells, and handcrafted novelties. Just be sure to call ahead and confirm the hours, which often depend on the weather.

(Lake Pontchartrain Basin Maritime Museum

On the banks of the Tchefuncte River, you'll encounter the Lake Pontchartrain Basin Maritime Museum (133 Mabel Dr., Madisonville, 985/845-9200, www.lpbmm.org, Tues.–Sat. 10 A.M.–4 P.M., Sun. noon–4 P.M., $5 adult, $3 senior and child, free under 6), which contains several excellent exhibits documenting the region's seafaring heritage, including the canals of New Orleans and the lighthouses of Louisiana. Especially worth a look is the Port Century exhibit, which chronicles how steamboats played a vital role in the growth of the region. The museum also offers boat-building classes, in which you actually learn to construct an authentic Cajun-style pirogue, a lake skiff, or other craft common to Louisiana's waters. The museum also hosts a wide range of lectures, classes, and events, including the annual Wooden Boat Festival, which it partially sponsors.

(Pontchartrain Vineyards

In the rural, northern end of St. Tammany Parish lies the beautiful Pontchartrain Vineyards (81250 Old Military Rd., Bush, 985/892-9742, www.pontchartrainvineyards.com, tours and tastings Wed.–Sun. noon–4 P.M.), set amid the horse farms of Bush and western Folsom. Begun in 1996, this award-winning winery is the only serious one in the state, and its food-friendly wines are served at some of the area's major restaurants. Depending on when you go, you might end up participating in the harvest or catching one of the many concerts held there during the spring, summer, and fall, including the Jazz'n the Vines series, which features jazz performances ($10 adult, free under 18) every two or three weeks. The inexpensive tastings are held in a French Provincial–style brick building, which overlooks the gentle hillside planted with grapes. The tours are short but informative and personable.

RESTAURANTS

While many people consider New Orleans to be the region's hub of exceptional cuisine, the Northshore actually boasts its own wealth

Soft-shell crab can be found on menus throughout southern Louisiana.

of culinary options, including the well-favored **Dakota** (629 N. U.S. 190, Covington, 985/892-3712, www.thedakotarestaurant.com Tues.–Thurs. 11:30 A.M.–1 P.M. and 5:30–9 P.M., Fri. 11:30 A.M.–1 P.M. and 5:30–10 P.M., Sat. 5:30–10 P.M., $15–39). Here, the contemporary American cooking is anything but ordinary. Signature dishes include the jumbo lump crabmeat and French Brie soup, crispy soft-shell crab with lemon-parmesan risotto, and pan-sautéed tilapia with artichokes and wilted spinach.

Famed chef John Besh now oversees **(** **La Provence** (25020 U.S. 190, Lacombe, 985/626-7662, www.laprovencerestaurant.com, Wed.–Sat. 5–9 P.M., Sun. 11 A.M.–9 P.M., $26–44), a welcoming temple of gastronomy. With its rustic facade, red-tiled roof, and authentic furnishings, this place really does look as though it's been airlifted to the Northshore from the south of France. The constantly evolving menu might feature sweet potato ravioli, quail gumbo, or seared venison loin.

For a more casual meal, head to the **Abita Brew Pub** (72011 Holly St., Abita Springs, 985/892-5837, www.abitabrewpub.com, Tues.–Thurs. 11 A.M.–9 P.M., Fri.–Sat. 11 A.M.–10 P.M., Sun. 11 A.M.–9 P.M., $9–23), an off-shoot of the famous Abita Brewery. The pub serves tasty comfort food that complements, and even incorporates, the locally crafted beers; crab claws are served with a rosemary, barbecue, and Abita Amber dipping sauce. Other good bets include pecan-crusted catfish, muffulettas, crawfish cakes, and barbecued ribs marinated in Abita's Purple Haze. The pub also features scenic views of the Tammany Trace biking path, which plenty of patrons use to reach this down-home hangout. With several outdoor tables and a sports-bar atmosphere, it's no wonder that the crowd tends toward the young and hip.

NIGHTLIFE

Though it might seem more sedate than New Orleans, the Northshore actually has a handful of popular bars and music clubs, including the **Columbia Street Tap Room and Grill** (434 N. Columbia St., Covington, 985/898-0899, www.columbiastreettaproom. com, Mon. 11 A.M.–10 P.M., Tues.–Thurs. 11 A.M.–midnight, Fri. 11 A.M.–1:30 A.M., Sat. noon–1:30 A.M.), a cool, smoke-free corner bar that presents first-rate rock, folk, funk, soul, and blues bands Thursday–Saturday. For a more down-home ambience, head to **Ruby's Roadhouse** (840 Lamarque St., Mandeville, 985/626-9748, www.rubysroadhouse.com, Mon.–Fri. 10 A.M.–2 A.M., Sat.–Sun. 9 A.M.–2 A.M.), which presents everything from rock to Cajun.

ARTS AND EVENTS

Southeastern Louisiana University is home to the beautifully restored 850-seat **Columbia Theatre for the Performing Arts** (220 E. Thomas St., Hammond, 985/543-4371, www.columbiatheatre.org), an elegant 1928 building that now serves as the city's premier performing arts center. Events here include pop and classical concerts, plays, musicals, and dance performances.

Usually occurring in mid-April, the **Ponchatoula Strawberry Festival** (Memorial Park, 6th St. and Willow St., Ponchatoula, 800/917-7045, www.lastrawberryfestival.com) has lured oodles of visitors to Hammond for more than four decades. Considered one of the nation's largest three-day festivals, it features a wide array of family-friendly diversions, including live concerts, strawberry-eating contests, sack races, and, of course, a parade. You'll also find a slew of food booths offering strawberry lemonade, strawberry beignets, and chocolate-covered strawberries.

Boating enthusiasts should not miss the **Wooden Boat Festival** (985/845-9200, www.woodenboatfest.org) in mid-October. Hundreds of beautiful, mostly handcrafted wooden boats sail, motor, or row along Madisonville's Tchefuncte River. Beyond the boats themselves, you'll be treated to live concerts, parades, a variety of food and crafts, a boatbuilding contest, and a model boat–building workshop for kids.

◖ The Abita Springs Opry

As a kid, I would often venture across Lake Pontchartrain with my mother to witness the Northshore's most acclaimed musical event: the Piney Woods Opry, now known as the Abita Springs Opry (985/892-0711, www.abitaopry.org). Essentially a series of six concerts, the Opry is held on every third Saturday March–May and September–November at the Abita Springs Town Hall (22161 Level St., Abita Springs). Tickets cost $18 per concert, and the two-hour shows begin at 7 P.M. Founded to preserve and celebrate Louisiana's "roots" music, the Opry features rollicking country, bluegrass, Southern gospel, Cajun, zydeco, and other traditional folk music. Given the intimate seating, homemade vittles on sale, and small-town ambience, the Opry truly feels like a welcome return to a simpler time.

RECREATION

Enjoying the great outdoors is the key draw for many visitors to St. Tammany and Tangipahoa Parishes, which are noted for swamps and wildlife preserves, several popular state parks, an exceptional bike trail, a few fine golf courses, and excellent fishing and boating opportunities.

Biking

St. Tammany Parish has one of the best biking resources in the South, the **Tammany Trace** (985/867-9490, www.tammanytrace.org), a 28-mile rails-to-trails bikeway that runs from Slidell west to Mandeville and then north to Abita Springs before curving west again into downtown Covington. The paved path also services joggers, strollers, inline skaters, wheelchair users, and horseback riders. This was the first rails-to-trails conversion in Louisiana; Tammany Trace follows the path of the old Illinois Central Railroad, winding beneath boughs of pine, oak, and magnolia trees, across 31 bridges, and through some of the state's verdant wetlands. The trail cuts right through or near all of the downtown retail and dining districts in the area.

Fishing and Boating

In addition to several charter-fishing operations,

anglers will find plenty of great freshwater fishing in the muddy bayous of St. Tammany Parish, especially in lush 99-acre **Fairview-Riverside State Park** (119 Fairview Dr., Madisonville, 985/845-3318 or 888/677-3247, www.crt.state.la.us/parks, Sun.–Thurs. 7 A.M.–9 P.M., Fri.–Sat. 7 A.M.–10 P.M., $1 pp). Shaded by dozens of massive live oak trees, the park includes campsites for tent and RV camping, a playground, picnic tables, comfort stations, and terrific fishing and crabbing opportunities along the Tchefuncte River. You can also put in a boat at the Madisonville public boat launch; besides fishing, waterskiing and tubing are quite popular on the Tchefuncte. Here, you're likely to encounter bass, white perch, bluegill, and bream, while down where the river joins Lake Pontchartrain, you can catch channel catfish, redfish, and speckled trout.

Golf

St. Tammany Parish has some of the best golf courses in the whole state, including the **Oak Harbor Golf Club** (201 Oak Harbor Blvd., Slidell, 985/646-0110, www.oakharborgolf.com), one of the best semi-private golf courses in the South. Originally opened in 1992 and extensively renovated in 2006 following Hurricane Katrina's destruction, the 18-hole championship course also offers private lessons, a nine-acre practice facility, and a well-appointed clubhouse.

Parks

At 2,800 acres, **Fontainebleau State Park** (62883 LA-1089, Mandeville, 985/624-4443 or 888/677-3668, www.crt.state.la.us/parks, Sun.–Thurs. 7 A.M.–9 P.M., Fri.–Sat. 7 A.M.–10 P.M., $1 pp) is the region's largest recreation area, with camping facilities, a sandy beach, and direct access to Lake Pontchartrain. It's a great park for bird-watchers and hikers. Trails meander through the pine-shaded forest, passing through an ancient grove of live oaks and the crumbling brick ruins of an 1829 sugar mill opened by Mandeville's founder, Bernard de Marigny de Mandeville. The Tammany Trace trail also runs through the

park, drawing bikers, hikers, and inline skaters. Visitors can often observe turkeys, woodpeckers, and hundreds of other bird species, all of which are listed in the park's official bird-watching guide.

In Tangipahoa Parish, **Tickfaw State Park** (27225 Patterson Rd., Springfield, 225/294-5020 or 888/981-2020, www.crt.state.la.us/parks, Sun.–Thurs. 7 A.M.–9 P.M., Fri.–Sat. 7 A.M.–10 P.M., $1 pp) lies in the middle of what seems like nowhere, about 15 miles west of Ponchatoula. This 1,200-acre park sits astride the Tickfaw River and features camping facilities, a water playground, and a mile of boardwalks through the lush wetlands, encompassing four different ecosystems: cypress/tupelo swamp, bottomland hardwood forest, mixed pine/hardwood forest, and the river itself. You might see herons and egrets swoop into the swamp to grab a crawfish snack. Other wildlife includes turtles, snakes, wild turkeys, opossums, and wildfowl; on rare occasions, you might spot a coyote, deer, fox, or beaver. Rent a canoe for the best chance to see wildlife, and be sure to stop by the **nature center** (daily 9 A.M.–4:30 P.M.), which contains excellent exhibits on the park's flora and fauna.

HOTELS

The Northshore features a decent selection of modern chain hotels just off the interstate in Slidell and Covington, plus a slew of enchanting inns, from Mandeville to Tickfaw. Just steps from Covington's historical district, the **Camellia House** (426 E. Rutland St., Covington, 985/893-2442, www.camelliahouse.net, $95–185) offers gorgeously furnished suites with air-conditioning, cable TV, plush linens, and private entrances. The lovely, early-20th-century house is filled with stylish antiques, and guests can enjoy the home's wide veranda, courtyard garden, swimming pool, and hot tub, plus complimentary bikes. As a bonus, hosts Linda and Don Chambless know a great deal about the area.

Another unique option is the **Michabelle Inn** (1106 S. Holly St., Hammond, 985/419-0550, www.michabelle.com, $85–125), a wonderfully decadent B&B on the south side of Hammond's historic downtown. This imposing white Greek Revival mansion adroitly blends classic French style with Old South charm. The four well-appointed rooms and four luxurious suites are rife with late-Victorian antiques, Oriental rugs, and gilt-framed paintings. In addition to relaxing amid the lush grounds, guests might also relish the excellent on-site restaurant and relatively new spa and fitness center.

For more seclusion, opt for **(Little River Bluffs** (11082 Garden Ln., Folsom, 985/796-5257, www.littleriverbluffs.com, $150–300), which anchors a 50-acre wooded property on the artesian-fed Little Tchefuncte River. This is a naturalist's dream, offering the chance to kayak on the river, hike through the woods, and sunbathe on a sugary-white sandbar. Great blue herons, egrets, otters, and other wildlife inhabit this lush woodland, which feels light-years away from New Orleans. There are four accommodations here: the luxurious, light-filled Lodge House, which overlooks the river; the A-frame River Chalet, which sits on a forested bend in the river; the shaded Meadow Cabin, tucked near a stocked pond and a wildflower meadow; and the Tree House, perched high amid the pines and magnolias. All of these cabins are romantic, relaxing, and equipped with screened porches, complete kitchens, and other modern conveniences. Note that there's a two-night minimum.

PRACTICALITIES
Information

For more information about Slidell, Covington, Mandeville, Abita Springs, and other communities in St. Tammany Parish, contact the **St. Tammany Parish Tourist & Convention Commission** (68099 LA-59, Mandeville, 985/892-0520 or 800/634-9443, www.louisiananorthshore.com). The **Tangipahoa Parish Convention & Visitors Bureau** (13143 Wardline Rd., Hammond, 985/542-7520 or 800/542-7520, www.tangi-cvb.org) is a helpful resource if you plan to visit Hammond, Ponchatoula, and other communities in Tangipahoa Parish.

Although most people in this region rely on New Orleans's *Times-Picayune* (www.nola.com), Hammond also has a daily newspaper, *The Daily Star* (www.hammondstar.com). Nondaily papers on the Northshore include the *St. Tammany News Banner* (www.thesttammanynews.com), the *Slidell Sentry* (www.thesttammanynews.com), and *The Ponchatoula Times* (www.ponchatoula.com/ptimes).

Getting There and Around

The Northshore lies at the junction of four interstates: I-10, I-12, I-59, and I-55. This makes driving here from New Orleans or Baton Rouge easy and direct. From New Orleans, you can come via I-10, a 40-minute route that deposits you in Slidell; the Lake Pontchartrain Causeway (www.thecauseway.us), a 45-minute drive that places you in Mandeville; or I-55, which skirts the western edge of Lake Pontchartrain, toward Hammond. Note that there's no toll for crossing the Causeway from south to north, but you will be charged a toll of $3–15 for crossing north to south. Driving here is your best bet; you really need a car to explore this region. Just be advised that rush-hour traffic jams are common along all of these routes, so figure an extra 20–30 minutes depending on when you make these drives.

Unfortunately, traffic can be rather slow throughout the region, especially U.S. 190 in Slidell and LA-59 between Mandeville and Abita Springs. As a plus, some of the highways are quite scenic. For speed, I-12 can be a lifesaver, and it's usually free from major traffic jams. I-12 runs east to west across St. Tammany and Tangipahoa Parishes, connecting the junction of I-59 and I-10 in Slidell with Mandeville and Covington before continuing to Tangipahoa Parish, which sits at the crossroads of I-12 and I-55.

Great River Road

A leisurely drive along the Great River Road, which snakes along both banks of the Mississippi River, reveals some of the most striking contrasts between past and present that you'll find anywhere in the country. Less than 30 minutes after leaving New Orleans, you can find yourself standing on a plantation with fields of sugarcane and more acreage than the French Quarter. But the Great River Road, even in the sparsely populated areas, is not exactly quaint. Along considerable stretches, you'll also see oil refineries, chemical plants, and other fortresses of mining and manufacturing, sometimes within a stone's throw of old plantations. Another reminder that the days of paddle-wheel riverboats and quiet agrarian living have long since passed is the high grassy levee that runs virtually uninterrupted along

PLANTATION TOURS

Official bus tours of the plantations along the Mississippi River between New Orleans and St. Francisville provide a convenient way to see one or more plantations if you're visiting New Orleans for only a short time. Many of these companies also offer money-saving combination packages that include swamp tours, city tours, and the like.

Via small, air-conditioned buses, the **Cajun Encounters Tour Co.** (504/834-1770 or 866/928-6877, www.cajunencounters.com) leads guided excursions (daily 8:30 A.M.–2:30 P.M. and noon–5:45 P.M., $79 adult, $59 child under 12) of the scenic Great River Road, which feature walking tours of two of the region's most notable structures: the Laura Plantation and the Oak Alley Plantation.

For a guided excursion of the national historic landmarks along the Great River Road, consider **Celebration Tours** (504/587-7115 or 888/587-7115, www.celebrationtoursllc. com), which offers a plantation tour (daily 8:30 A.M.–2 P.M., $85 pp) that, depending on your group's selections, may stop at the Destrehan Plantation, Laura Plantation, Oak Alley Plantation, or Houmas House.

One of the best general tour companies in New Orleans, the ubiquitous **Gray Line Tours** (504/569-1401 or 800/233-2628, www.graylineneworleans.com) provides an assortment of excursions, including a cemetery tour, a walking cocktail tour, and a boat ride through Barataria Preserve. Gray Line also features tours of Laura: A Creole Plantation (Mar.–June daily 9 A.M.–1:30 P.M., July-Oct. Mon., Wed., Fri.-Sat. 9 A.M.–1:30 P.M., $58 adult, $26 child) and the Oak Alley Plantation (Mar.–Oct. daily 9 a.m.–1:30 p.m., $58 adult, $26 child).

Through the **Louisiana Tour Company** (504/689-3599 or 888/307-9267, www. louisianaswamp.com), you can take a guided plantation tour of Oak Alley (daily 8:30 A.M.–2 P.M., $55 adult, $35 child 4-12, child under 4 free), Laura: A Creole Plantation (daily 8:30 A.M.–2 P.M., $55 adult, $35 child 4-12, child under 4 free), and, if you have time, both plantations (daily 10:30 A.M.–6 P.M., $80 adult, $60 child 4-12, child under 4 free).

Since 1979, the family-operated **Tours by Isabelle** (504/398-0365 or 877/665-8687, www.toursbyisabelle.com) has been providing personalized trips throughout the region, including tours of the city, area plantations, and nearby swamps. If you're curious about the Great River Road, you can choose from four options, including the Oak Alley and Laura Plantation Tour (daily 8:30 A.M.–2 P.M. and 12:30–6 P.M., $86 pp), which entails guided tours of the two featured properties as well as narrated glimpses of the Whitney, St. Joseph, and Evergreen Plantations, and the East Bank Plantation Tour (daily 8 A.M.–5 P.M., $125 pp), which provides guided tours of the Destrehan Plantation, San Francisco Plantation, and Houmas House.

© LAURA MARTONE

the Destrehan Plantation on the Great River Road

the Mississippi River. In most places, a path runs along the top, where you can jog, walk, or ride a bike. It's often so peaceful that it's hard to believe the Mississippi River was the main thoroughfare between New Orleans and Baton Rouge well into the 19th century. The eventual construction of I-10 diverted traffic from many of the towns along the Great River Road, resulting in what you see today: a rural, Depression-era byway, pockmarked with refineries and factories, fringed by massive levees, and peppered with lovely plantation homes.

SIGHTS
Audubon State Historic Site

Good hiking trails wind through the magnolia and poplar trees at the 100-acre Audubon State Historic Site (11788 LA-965, St. Francisville, 225/635-3739 or 888/677-2838, www.crt. state.la.us/parks, daily 9 A.M.–5 P.M., $4 pp, free over 62 and under 13). The on-site 1806 **Oakley House,** a distinctive West Indies–style colonial home, is where famed wildlife painter John James Audubon lived briefly in 1821;

records indicate that he worked on at least 32 of his bird paintings while living in this house. Other facilities include a picnic shelter and several outbuildings from the original plantation. Guided tours of the house are given throughout the day.

Destrehan Plantation

One of the oldest house-museums on the Great River Road, and also one of the nearest to New Orleans, Destrehan Plantation (13034 Great River Rd., Destrehan, 985/764-9315 or 877/453-2095, www.destrehanplantation.org, tours daily 9 A.M.–4 P.M., $18 adult, $7 children 6–16) was built in 1787, although the sweeping Greek Revival mansion you see today, with its eight front columns and double galleries, is the result of a major renovation and expansion in the 1830s. Robin de Logny originally commissioned the construction of the house, hiring a freed mulatto named Charles (whose last name isn't known) to build it; this process took three years, and de Logny died just two years after inhabiting it. The estate then passed into the hands of de Logny's son-in-law. Eventually, Jean Noel Destrehan, a French aristocrat, bought the house and added the twin wings on either side of the facade in 1810. He and his brother-in-law, Etienne de Boré (the first mayor of New Orleans), earned fame for perfecting a means of granulating sugar, thus helping to turn southern Louisiana into one of the top sugarcane-farming regions in North America. De Boré owned a plantation several miles downriver, in what is now the Audubon Park section of New Orleans. Details still visible in this rambling structure include hand-hewn cypress timbers and the distinctive hipped roof typical of West Indies architecture. The house is less than 25 miles west of New Orleans and a mere 10-minute drive from the Louis Armstrong New Orleans International Airport, making it popular with visitors who don't have time to explore the entire River Road but would still like to see a grand Louisiana plantation before heading home.

Houmas House Plantation and Gardens

Once the setting of the Bette Davis film *Hush...Hush, Sweet Charlotte* (1964), the stunning Houmas House Plantation and Gardens (40136 LA-942, Darrow, 225/473-9380, www.houmashouse.com, Mon.–Tues., 9 A.M.–5 P.M., Wed.–Sun. 9 A.M.–8 P.M., tours $20 pp for mansion and gardens, $10 pp for gardens and grounds) encompasses a dramatic 1840 Greek Revival mansion, situated on an extensive property of oak-shaded grounds. At the plantation's peak, it encompassed 300,000 acres, much of which were devoted to sugarcane crops. An Irishman named John Burnside bought it for the princely sum of $1 million in 1857 and promptly declared his immunity during the Civil War, on the grounds that he was a British subject. Union forces honored the declaration and left Burnside and his house alone during their march up the Mississippi River from New Orleans to Baton Rouge.

By the end of the century, a new owner, Colonel William Porcher Miles, increased sugarcane production to 20 million pounds

per year, more than any other operation in the state. Houmas House fell gradually upon hard times during the early 20th century, but in 1940, the house and remaining grounds were bought by Dr. George B. Crozat, who set about restoring the place. Hollywood came calling in the early 1960s, and a new owner took over in 2003, furthering the restoration efforts and helping to turn this into one of the most appealing plantation museums in the region. Houmas House employs excellent guides who offer detailed tours of the plantation house, which is filled with antiques and artwork and decorated much as it might have looked during its prime in the mid-19th century. On Wednesday through Sunday, it's possible to take one of these tours in the early evening, which is unusual for a Louisiana plantations. Even if you don't tour the house, though, it's worth checking out the dramatic grounds and beautifully kept gardens.

◖ Laura: A Creole Plantation

You can embark on one of the most unusual plantation-tour experiences in the country at Laura: A Creole Plantation (2247 LA-18, Vacherie, 225/265-7690 or 888/799-7690, www.lauraplantation.com, tours daily 10 A.M.–4 P.M., $18 adult, $5 child 6–17, free under 6), which differs from most of the others along River Road in a couple of ways. First, it has a fascinating legacy, as its slave cabins were where the folktales known as *Br'er Rabbit* were recorded in the late 1870s. A young man named Alcée Fortier, who lived near Laura, took a great interest in the stories recounted by former slaves living on the plantation, and he set about writing down the tales exactly as he heard them here. Fortier went on to become a professor at Tulane University, where he published the collection of stories under the title *Louisiana Folktales*. His friend Joel Chandler Harris then published the considerably more famous *Tales of Uncle Remus,* based on his interviews with slaves in the Carolinas and Georgia. The stories came to be known as the *Br'er Rabbit* tales because one of the two main characters in Fortier's and Harris's collections was Lapin (French for "rabbit").

But maybe the most interesting thing about a visit to Laura is that tour guides base their one-hour talk on the memoirs—which total about 5,000 pages—of the four generations of women who oversaw the compound's inner workings; it's a condensation of the fascinating lives of the Creole women who ran the plantation, along with intimate and telling details about their children and extended family, and their slaves. The memoirs were compiled in the 1930s by Laura Locoul Gore, who grew up on the plantation and represents the final generation of women at Laura. The tour of Laura offers a provocative and colorful look into the high and low points of Creole life in the early 19th century. At most of the other plantations in this area, tours might discuss the original owners, the architecture of the house, and its basic history, but they're often based on general second- and third-hand information, and they rarely discuss the lives of the slaves and the day-to-day, firsthand observations of the plantation's occupants.

Another difference at Laura is the plantation house itself, which is not one of the typical glowing white Greek Revival mansions found in this region, but rather a relatively modest, infinitely colorful, raised Creole house that has been, intentionally, only partly restored in order to give guests a more realistic sense of what the house looked and felt like when it was occupied by Laura and her ancestors. The house suffered a major fire in 2004, but staff still managed to give tours the very next day, and restoration work continued unabated. As good as this museum is, the quality of your tour varies from guide to guide, as is true at all plantations, but most of the interpreters here do a very nice job.

Myrtles Plantation

One of the more colorful attractions in St. Francisville is the Myrtles Plantation (7747 U.S. 61, St. Francisville, 225/635-6277 or 800/809-0565, www.myrtlesplantation.com, daily 9 A.M.–5 P.M., adult $8, children under 12 $4), which bills itself as being among the most haunted houses in the United States. Apart from this considerable lure, the 1796 house is notable for its hand-painted stained glass and crystal chandeliers. Little expense seems to have been spared in its construction. Engaging historical tours touch on the house and its grounds, but the considerably more colorful Mystery tours (Fri.–Sat., reservations required) are the real draw. The home also operates as a bed-and-breakfast and there is an on-site restaurant.

Nottoway Plantation

The 64-room Nottoway Plantation (31025 LA-1, White Castle, 225/545-2730 or 866/527-6884, www.nottoway.com, daily 9 A.M.–4 P.M., tours adults $20, children 6–12 $6) is an immense Greek Revival mansion, with an interior of about 53,000 square feet. John H. Randolph built this "white castle" in 1859, where it served as the centerpiece of his sugarcane plantation. An on-site museum details the history of the Randolphs, up to and including the Civil War. Nottoway also functions as a small hotel and has a popular restaurant. Nottoway lies about 12 miles upriver from Donaldsonville, on the same side of the river.

◖ Oak Alley Plantation

One of the best photo ops in the South, Oak Alley Plantation (3645 LA-18, Vacherie, 225/265-2151 or 800/442-5539, www.oakalley-plantation.com, daily 9:30 A.M.–5 P.M. Mar.–Oct., Mon.–Fri. 9 A.M.–4:30 P.M., Sat.–Sun. 9 A.M.–5 P.M. Nov.–Feb., $18 adult, $7.50 youth 13–18, $4.50 child 6–12) features an incredible alley of 28 live oak trees, planted in two rows bordering the front walk. Dating from about 300 years ago, these trees have been here much longer than the present mansion, which, though beautiful, certainly wouldn't stand out as it does today without the graceful, arching trees framing it. An early French settler, clearly with some aristocratic aspirations, planted the oaks in the early 1700s to lead from the river down a path to his rather modest house. More than 100 years later, the property's owner, Jacques Telesphore

ANGOLA: THE LOUISIANA STATE PENITENTIARY

About 22 miles northwest of the beauty and gentility of St. Francisville lies perhaps the most notorious prison (at least historically) in the United States. Officially known as the Louisiana State Penitentiary, Angola has also been dubbed the "Alcatraz of the South," among many less flattering things. These days, Angola has been reformed, and its notoriety has died down, but it's still the largest maximum-security prison in the country – definitely not a place you'd want to spend time in involuntarily.

The 18,000-acre prison sits in a bend of the Mississippi River, surrounded on three sides by water and by the gently rising Tunica Hills on the other; it's just a few miles south of the Mississippi border. Much of Angola is farmland, and inmates are required to work the fields five days a week, eight hours a day. Corn and soybeans are the main products grown here, but there are many other crops, plus a herd of cattle numbering about 1,500.

Angola's legacy is a grim one. The prison was run privately when it was founded in 1844, then occupied by Union troops during the Civil War, and then run privately again by a Confederate general named Samuel James from 1869 until 1900. Brutality was rampant in those years – it's reported that the average lifespan of inmates at Angola was just five years.

The state took over Angola in 1901, but medical treatment and living conditions remained poor for many years. Music played a vital role for many Angola inmates, the most famous being the blues pioneer Leadbelly, who served time here for brandishing a knife during a fight. Leadbelly's blues music was so well received that it caught the attention of record makers, who recorded his hit "Good Night, Irene" here while the promising talent served his time. Leadbelly was soon freed from prison, and in the late 1930s, he developed a tremendous musical reputation in New York City and, later, Paris.

Amazingly, for about 50 years, Angola operated with no paid guards. Instead, it was staffed with so-called "trusty guards," favored inmates who were furnished with weapons and were notorious for ignoring or perpetuating prison violence. In the 1960s and early '70s, stabbings, beatings, and deadly fights were commonplace, occurring once a day on average.

Angola began its most dramatic period of reform in 1973, when it eliminated the "trusty guard" system and began changing many of its policies. It finally obtained accreditation from the American Correctional Association (ACA) in 1993. Perhaps Angola's most recent claim to fame, however, is the 1978 incarceration of Elmo Patrick Sonnier, whose presence on Death Row inspired Sister Helen Prejean's best-selling book *Dead Man Walking*. The book was eventually adapted for the big screen as the Oscar-winning 1995 film of the same name, starring Sean Penn and Susan Sarandon. Of course, Angola has also appeared in such films as *Out of Sight* and *Monster's Ball*.

In an effort to clean up its image, Angola has created the engaging and surprisingly forthcoming **Angola Museum** (225/655-2592, www.angolamuseum.org, Mon.-Sat. 8 A.M.-4:30 P.M., donation suggested), which examines the facility's history as well as its onetime reputation as the "bloodiest prison in America." To reach the museum, follow U.S. 61 from St. Francisville and veer northwest on Highway 66.

One of the best times to plan a visit is October, when from 2 to 5 P.M. on each Sunday, the prison hosts the **Angola Rodeo** (225/655-2030, www.angolarodeo.com), which was begun in 1965 and is the longest-running prison rodeo in the country. The event, which is indeed no amateur show, features professional judges and takes place in a 7,500-seat stadium. In the late 1990s, an arts-and-crafts show was added, which typically occurs from 9 A.M. to 5 P.M. on each day of the rodeo and includes a variety of wares and decorative items produced by inmates. This, like the rodeo itself, has become a phenomenally popular event. Tickets to the rodeo cost $15 per person, the proceeds of which help to cover expenses and benefit a fund that provides education and recreational supplies for the inmates.

Roman, used his considerable sugarcane fortune to construct the present Oak Alley mansion. The entire property now comprises about 25 acres; much of the original plantation, which had encompassed more than 1,000 acres, is now undeveloped forest, but about 600 acres is still leased to sugarcane farmers.

As you approach the property, you'll pass the rather modest front gate that marks the beginning of the alley of oaks; you can't enter the property here, as the actual driveway for automobiles lies a short distance farther down the road. But you can park your car along the dirt driveway leading up and over the Mississippi River levee and walk up to the gate to snap a picture and admire the trees and the house in the distance. If you walk up the short dirt drive to the top of the levee, you can glimpse a very nice view of the river—there's often a tanker or freighter chugging along, contributing to that peculiar contrast between modern industry and 19th-century plantation living that characterizes the whole region. Once you drive onto the grounds, you buy your tickets at a booth and proceed to the Big House, as the mansion is called, for a guided tour. The tours themselves are fairly straightforward and not overly exciting, unless you happen to get an especially colorful guide, but after the tour, you can spend as much time as you'd like exploring the grounds and relaxing amid the oaks, crape myrtles, and azaleas, or admiring the peacocks and friendly bobtail cats wandering about the property.

San Francisco Plantation

The opulent San Francisco Plantation (2646 LA-44, Garyville, 985/535-2341 or 888/509-1756, www.sanfranciscoplantation.org, daily 9:30 A.M.–4:40 P.M. Apr.–Oct., daily 9 A.M.–4 P.M. Nov.–Mar., $15 adult, $10 student, free under 7) sits on the east bank of the Mississippi River, about 23 miles upriver from Destrehan. The house was constructed by Edmond Bozonier Marmillion in 1855, shortly before he died; in the 1970s, it was authentically restored to its original, antebellum appearance. The exquisite hand-painted ceilings

are an important detail, as are the fine antiques and extensive faux marbling.

RESTAURANTS

If you know where to look, you're likely to find several worthy eateries along the Great River Road, between New Orleans and St. Francisville. One such place is the **⟨ Grapevine Café and Gallery** (211 Railroad Ave., Donaldsonville, 225/473-8463, www.grapevinecafeandgallery.com, Tues.–Thurs. 11 A.M.–2 P.M. and 5–9 P.M., Fri. 11 A.M.–2 P.M. and 5–9:30 P.M., Sat. 11 A.M.–9 P.M., Sun. 11 A.M.–2 P.M., $8–28), a delightful restaurant housed within a 1920s art deco–style building in Donaldsonville's historical district. Award-winning Cajun and Creole cuisine is served in a cozy dining room filled with local artwork. Crawfish pie is a specialty here. If you have room for dessert, consider the white-chocolate bread pudding or lemon ice-box pie.

For a more casual option, head to **The Cabin** (Hwy. 22 and Hwy. 44, Burnside, 225/473-3007, www.thecabinrestaurant.com, Mon. 11 A.M.–3 P.M., Tues.–Thurs. 11 A.M.–9 P.M., Fri.–Sat. 11 A.M.–10 P.M., Sun. 11 A.M.–6 P.M., $10–20), which is as much a museum of the area's Cajun culture as it is a restaurant. The walls of this former slave cabin (circa 1850), with its original cypress roof, are papered with old newspapers, a traditional insulation in the 19th century. The rustic dining room is packed with interesting memorabilia, including vintage farming tools, old paintings, and furniture. Dining is also available in an inviting courtyard out back. This is a terrific place to try classic Louisiana dishes, from crawfish pies to jambalaya. Another casual choice in the region is the **Magnolia Café** (5689 Commerce St., St. Francisville, 225/635-6528, Sun.–Wed. 10 A.M.–4 P.M., Thurs. 10 A.M.–9 P.M., Fri. 10 A.M.–10 P.M., Sat. 10 A.M.–9 P.M., $6–24), which serves a nice mix of salads, sandwiches, pizzas, Mexican fare, and specialties like an eggplant pirogue, fried eggplant with seafood stuffing. Seafood enchiladas, French dip po-boys, and burgers are popular items here, and there's live music on Friday nights.

FESTIVALS AND EVENTS

Aside from its tourist following, this area is strung with villages and towns with low populations, so large gatherings and festivals are few and far between. One event is the **Audubon Pilgrimage** (225/635-6330, www.audubonpilgrimage.info), a mid-March festival in St. Francisville. Since 1972, the event has celebrated the life of painter John James Audubon by welcoming visitors to various historic gardens and homes where docents in authentic 1820s-period costumes offer guided tours. Some of the plantations also have annual events, such as the Destrehan Plantation's annual **spring and fall festivals** (www.destrehanplantation.org), which feature live music, regional foods, and a wide assortment of local arts, crafts, and antiques. You can often tour the historic mansion and witness living-history demonstrations, such as blacksmithing.

Christmas is one of the best times to explore the Great River Road, particularly during the **Festival of the Bonfires** (Lutcher Recreation Park, Lutcher, www.festivalofthebonfires.org, mid-Dec.), a three-day event of local food and crafts, carnival rides, live entertainment, and bonfire lightings. Ultimately, it's a precursor to the **Christmas Eve Bonfires,** when many riverside towns light bonfires of their own. Some claim that this longtime Louisiana tradition was begun as a way to welcome the Cajun version of Santa Claus, PaPa Noel, while others suggest that the fires were lit to help riverbound travelers make their way to midnight Mass.

HOTELS

Lodging options vary along the Great River Road, ranging from modern hotels in Gonzales to quaint inns in St. Francisville. You can even stay on the premises of some of the plantations, including the **◖ Nottoway Plantation** (31025 LA-1, White Castle, 225/545-2730 or 866/527-6884, www.nottoway.com, $160-190), the largest plantation house remaining in the South. This renovated gem encompasses 40 rooms and two honeymoon suites, spread throughout the main house and various cottages. Amenities include private bathrooms,

high-speed Internet access, and cable TV. Overnight guests can enjoy a guided tour of the house, explore the oak-shaded grounds, and have a meal in the Mansion Restaurant, which serves Creole-inspired cuisine. This gorgeous property also features an outdoor pool, tennis courts, and a game and fitness center.

For the chance to stay in what many believe to be the most haunted house in Louisiana, book a room at **◖ The Myrtles Plantation** (7747 U.S. 61, St. Francisville, 225/635-6277 or 800/809-0565, www.myrtlesplantation.com, $115-250), one of the most popular touring plantations in the St. Francisville area. Situated on 70 lush acres, the ornately furnished 1796 French Mediterranean–style main house contains six handsome, expansive rooms and suites, including the luxurious General David Bradford Suite, which has two adjoining verandas and a huge four-poster bed. There are also six options in outbuildings near the main house: the old caretaker's cottage, which has its own porch; the four garden rooms, each with an antique Chippendale claw-foot tub; and the two-bedroom Coco House. The Myrtles Plantation also has a fine full-service restaurant, the Carriage House.

If you want an even more intimate experience, consider the **Cabahanosse Bed & Breakfast** (602 Railroad Ave., Donaldsonville, 225/474-5050, www.cabahanosse.com, $160), a handsome 1890s inn in downtown Donaldsonville. Here, you'll find four sumptuously outfitted suites with high ceilings, separate sitting rooms, and wide-plank pine floors that date to the house's original construction. Each suite is uniquely decorated; the room with mallard duck decor has a relaxing balcony. All of these spacious suites are ideal for a romantic retreat; at night, you'll even find brandy and chocolates at your bedside.

PRACTICALITIES
Information

If you're curious about Destrehan and Luling, contact the **St. Charles Parish Tourist Information Center** (13825 River Rd., Luling, 985/783-5145, www.stcharlesgov.

net). For information on Gramercy, Lutcher, Vacherie, and Convent, consult **St. James Parish Tourism** (5800 LA-44, Convent, www.stjamesla.com). The **Ascension Parish Tourism Commission** (6967 LA-22, Sorrento, 225/675-6550 or 888/775-7990, www.ascensiontourism.com) handles tourism in the towns of Gonzales, Sorrento, Darrow, and Donaldsonville. Check in with the **Iberville Parish Tourist Commission** (17525 LA-77, Grosse Tete, 225/687-5198, www.ibervilleparish.com) for information on White Castle and Plaquemine.

Information about New Roads and St. Francisville can be obtained from the **Pointe Coupee Parish Office of Tourism** (727 Hospital Rd., Ste. B, New Roads, 225/638-3998, www.pctourism.org) and **West Feliciana Parish Tourist Commission** (800/789-4221, www.stfrancisville.us), respectively. Jackson's tourism is handled by the **East Feliciana Tourist Commission** (225/634-7155, www.felicianatourism.org). There's also information about the entire River Road region available online (www.neworleansplantationcountry.com) or by phone (866/204-7782).

Getting There and Around

This part of the state has little or no public transportation, but it does have a very good network of roads, so plan to visit the area via car. If you're staying in New Orleans, check with your hotel concierge or bed-and-breakfast for information on companies that offer half- or full-day tours out to some of the plantations.

To reach the lower towns along the Great River Road from New Orleans, follow I-10 west to I-310, and exit onto LA-48, which puts you right by Destrehan. From here, you can follow LA-48 northwest along the east bank of the Mississippi River, or you can cross the I-310 bridge and follow LA-18 along the west bank. Keep in mind that River Road is not just one road—it's a combination of numbered highways that run alongside both banks of the river. So, while traveling, it's best to have a map with you and to stick with the roads that hug the river, not just to a particular route number.

Along the west bank, LA-18 is River Road for many miles, as far as Donaldsonville. North of that, the river's west bank is traced by LA-405 and LA-988 up to Port Allen, opposite Baton Rouge. Along the east bank from Destrehan, the river is traced by LA-48, then Spillway Road across the Bonnet Carré Spillway (which can be closed because of high water and flooding, in which case traffic is detoured along the interior to U.S. 61), and then along LA-628, LA-44, LA-942, LA-75, LA-141, LA-75 again, LA-991, and LA-327 clear to Baton Rouge. Several bridges and ferries connect roads on either bank of the river between New Orleans and Baton Rouge, making it very easy to get back and forth.

The highlights of River Road are mostly in St. James and Ascension Parishes, about midway between New Orleans and Baton Rouge. If you're planning to spend most of your time in this area, near Donaldsonville and Vacherie, it's quickest to drive up I-10 for 50 miles to Sorrento, and then follow LA-22 and LA-70 over the Sunshine Bridge to LA-18, which leads to Donaldsonville to the north and Vacherie to the south. To reach St. Francisville, it's roughly a 30-mile drive up U.S. 61 from Baton Rouge. As with the rest of the Great River Road, a car is your best way to get around.

EXCURSIONS

Baton Rouge

Ever since Hurricane Katrina, when many evacuees of New Orleans (including some of my own relatives) relocated to Baton Rouge, the city has witnessed a remarkable population surge, as evidenced by the enhanced number of new restaurants, shops, and hotels—not to mention the increased traffic. Even without Katrina's effects, however, Baton Rouge seems more like a typical new Southern city than New Orleans does. Sprawling in virtually every direction with charming residential neighborhoods, Baton Rouge feels clean and prosperous, but perhaps lacking a distinct identity of its own. At once the state capital and home to Louisiana State University, Baton Rouge is the sort of town where government and education provide its personality more than the streets, buildings, and topography. Nevertheless, you'll find several of Louisiana's most engaging attractions here.

SIGHTS
◖ Louisiana State Capitol
The Louisiana State Capitol (State Capitol Dr.

and N. 3rd St., Baton Rouge, 225/342-7317, www.crt.state.la.us, daily 8 A.M.–4:30 P.M., free) was completed in March 1932. A nifty 34-story art deco wonder, it took 14 months to build with a resulting price tag of about $5 million (not exactly chump change in those days). It is, at 450 feet, the tallest U.S. capitol building. One of the highlights of a visit here is touring the 27 acres of spectacularly landscaped gardens. In addition, you can look around the grand entrance and Memorial Hall; peek inside the chambers (when the state legislature is not in session); ride the elevator to the 27th-floor observation deck, which affords spectacular views of the city; and see exactly where the flamboyant governor Huey P. Long was assassinated.

LSU Rural Life Museum
Only a short drive southeast of downtown, the LSU Rural Life Museum (4560 Essen Ln., Baton Rouge, 225/765-2437, http://rurallife. lsu.edu, daily 8:30 A.M.–5 P.M., $7 adult, $6

© DANIEL MARTONE

the Old Louisiana State Capitol in Baton Rouge

senior and child 5–11, free under 5) is a living-history museum situated on the 450-acre **Burden Research Plantation.** Dedicated to preserving and interpreting the lifestyles and cultures of preindustrial Louisiana, the museum comprises numerous buildings and exhibits, which show different aspects of early Louisiana living. The plantation quarters constitute a complex of authentically furnished 19th-century structures, including a kitchen, a gristmill, a sugarcane house, a schoolhouse, a blacksmith shop, and slave cabins. Inside a large barn, you can examine tools and vehicles spanning more than 300 years. Here, you'll also spy several historic houses that reveal Louisiana's rich tradition of folk architecture, from a country church to an Acadian house to a shotgun home. You can also tour the extensive Windrush Gardens, a 25-acre plot of semiformal gardens abundant with winding paths, ponds, and flora typically found in 19th-century plantation gardens.

Old Louisiana State Capitol

Once the seat of the state government, the Old State Capitol (100 North Blvd., Baton Rouge, 225/342-0500 or 800/488-2968, www.louisianaoldstatecapitol.org, Tues.–Sat. 9 A.M.–4 P.M., free) was constructed between 1847 and 1852; it's one of the state's few prominent examples of large-scale Gothic architecture. Inside, you'll find a vast and wonderfully presented collection of interactive and multimedia exhibits on a wide variety of topics, including the history of Baton Rouge and the legacy of controversial governor Huey P. Long. There's also a governors' portrait gallery, plus rotating exhibits. It's the sort of museum that's enjoyable for kids as well as adults, and the breadth of documents, artifacts, collectibles, and curios displayed here is impressive.

USS *Kidd* and Veterans Memorial Museum

The USS *Kidd* (305 S. River Rd., Baton Rouge, 225/342-1942, www.usskidd.com, daily 9 A.M.–5 P.M., $8 adult, $7 senior, $5 child 5–12, free under 5) is the only ship of its kind that's still in its wartime camouflage paint. This World War II–era Fletcher-class destroyer was awarded 12 battle stars for serving during World War II and the Korean War; it was struck by a Japanese kamikaze plane during the World War II Battle of Okinawa—an attack that killed 38 members of the *Kidd's* crew. It has been carefully restored and can now be toured, along with the nearby Veterans Memorial Museum, which features a nuclear-powered submarine, the pilothouse of the steamboat *Louisiana,* a World War II–era fighter plane and a Vietnam-era bomber, a Korean War monument, the gundeck of the USS *Constitution,* and the South's largest model ship collection.

RESTAURANTS

Where there are politicians, there are almost always good restaurants, and Baton Rouge confirms this rule with its wide variety of well-favored eateries. It's also a student town, which means you can find several decent, relatively affordable joints around LSU's campus. Perhaps the most stylish restaurant in Baton Rouge is ◖ **Juban's** (3739 Perkins Rd., Baton Rouge, 225/346-8422, www.jubans.com, Mon. 5:30–10 P.M., Tues.–Fri. 11 A.M.–10 P.M., Sat. 5:30–10 P.M., Sun. 10:30 A.M.–3 P.M., $10–60). Juban's has been serving innovative Louisiana-influenced fare since the early 1980s, when owner-chef John Mariani's temple of fine cuisine was named one of America's "Best New Restaurants" in the pages of *Esquire.* The restaurant is known for such signature dishes as Louisiana crawfish pasta with shiitake mushrooms and white truffle Madeira cream, seafood-stuffed soft-shell crab topped with Creolaise sauce, and a pork rib chop with honey-bourbon glaze.

For local flavors that won't blow your budget, head to **Jasmines on the Bayou** (6010 Jones Creek Rd., Baton Rouge, 225/753-3668, www.jasminesonthebayou.com, Mon.–Thurs. 10:30 A.M.–8:30 P.M., Fri. 10:30 A.M.–9:30 P.M., Sat. 11 A.M.–9:30 P.M., $11–17), one of my favorite eateries in Baton Rouge. Essentially a Cajun seafood restaurant,

Jasmines offers such tasty regional fare as corn and crab bisque, grilled shrimp rémoulade, pasta jambalaya, and fried catfish. Be sure to start with an order of rocket shrimp, which are lightly battered and tossed in a spicy chili aioli sauce.

NIGHTLIFE

Between bars, music clubs, and casinos, Baton Rouge provides a decent share of nightlife options. The low-key **Phil Brady's Bar & Grill** (4848 Government St., Baton Rouge, 225/927-3786, Mon.–Fri. 11 A.M.–2 A.M., Sat. 5 P.M.–2 A.M.) is a fun place to drink with pals, play a round of pool, or enjoy some live music, particularly the well-attended Thursday night blues jams. College students and other music fans have been packing into the cutting-edge **Cadillac Cafe** (5454 Bluebonnet Blvd., Baton Rouge, 225/296-0288, www.cadillaccafe.net, Mon. 4–11 P.M., Tues.–Fri. 4 P.M.–2 A.M., Sat. 7 P.M.–2 A.M.) since 1989 for hard-driving rock and blues; karaoke and DJ dance parties are also big draws here.

The city's favorite gay and lesbian dance club is **Splash Nightclub** (2183 Highland Rd., Baton Rouge, 225/242-9491, www.splashbr.com, Thurs.–Sat. 9 P.M.–2 A.M.), situated in a slightly dodgy neighborhood near LSU's campus. Featuring multiple rooms and several bars, Splash presents a variety of music, from country to techno, plus one of Baton Rouge's best drag shows. If you're in more of a gambling mood, then head to the **Belle of Baton Rouge Casino** (103 France St., Baton Rouge, 225/242-2600 or 800/676-4847, www.belleofbatonrouge.com, daily 24 hours), which is housed inside a three-deck riverboat that's docked permanently on the Mississippi River.

ARTS AND EVENTS

For a bit of culture, head to the **Baton Rouge Little Theater** (7155 Florida Blvd., Baton Rouge, 225/924-6496, www.brlt.org), which has been presenting live theater since the late 1940s. Each season's lineup typically includes several well-known plays and musicals, such as *A Streetcar Named Desire* and *Hairspray*.

Another cultural option is the **Varsity Theatre** (3353 Highland Rd., Baton Rouge, 225/383-7018, www.varsitytheatre.com), a legendary concert venue that features salsa, alternative rock, and everything in between.

From balloon festivals to Fourth of July fireworks displays, Baton Rouge presents a slew of crowd-pleasing events throughout the year. One of the most popular is the **Baton Rouge Blues Festival** (www.batonrougebluesfestival.org), a free, one-day event that usually takes place in mid-April in the city's Town Square. Founded in 1980, it's one of America's oldest blues festivals, featuring a lineup of well-respected blues guitarists, pianists, and bands. In late October, literary fans will appreciate the **Louisiana Book Festival** (www.louisianabookfestival.org), another free, one-day event that typically occurs at various locations in downtown Baton Rouge, such as the Louisiana State Capitol and the State Library of Louisiana. Activities include readings, workshops, and a book discussion group.

HOTELS

While the Baton Rouge area has its share of quaint inns and B&Bs, most of the city's lodging options comprise major chain hotels and motels, primarily set just off I-12 and I-10, on the southeast side of town. Perhaps Baton Rouge's most impressive property is the **Hilton Baton Rouge Capitol Center** (201 Lafayette St., Baton Rouge, 225/344-5866 or 877/862-9800, www.hiltoncapitolcenter.com, $159–209), which opened in 2006 in the historic buildings that once housed the Heidelberg and Capitol House Hotels. Developers spent about $70 million creating this elegant property with 290 smartly furnished rooms, a full-service spa and fitness center, a pool deck overlooking the Mississippi River, and a lavish restaurant, Kingfish. Other amenities include free wireless Internet access, complimentary newspapers, and 24-hour room service.

PRACTICALITIES
Information

For more information about the state's capital city, consult the **Baton Rouge Area**

Convention and Visitors Bureau (359 3rd St., Baton Rouge, 225/383-1825 or 800/527-6843, www.visitbatonrouge.com). In addition, the city's daily newspaper, *The Advocate* (www.theadvocate.com), offers a plethora of helpful tidbits, including details about local sports and entertainment.

Getting There and Around

Unfortunately, there aren't too many back ways to drive from New Orleans to Baton Rouge. You could take the commercially robust Airline Highway (U.S. 61), which has numerous traffic lights and little character, or slip along the Great River Road, a time-consuming route that only makes sense if you allow yourself an overnight stop and explore some of the plantations en route. Most visitors opt for the speedier if less interesting I-10, a straight 80-mile shot that, without traffic, usually takes less than 90 minutes. Although you can also reach Baton Rouge directly via the **Baton Rouge Metropolitan Airport** (9430 Jackie Cochran Dr., Baton Rouge, 225/355-0333, www.flybtr.com), it's easiest to explore the area by car. Even in Baton Rouge, which has a semi-compact downtown, many attractions, restaurants, and hotels lie beyond this pedestrian-friendly area, making a car handy and public transportation impractical.

Cajun Country

Cajun Country, also known as Acadiana, extends from just southwest of New Orleans, around the town of Houma, to the Texas border, out near the city of Lake Charles. It's in this down-home, hospitable region that you'll discover the rich and distinctive heritage of the Cajun people, who were expelled from Canada in the mid-1700s before eventually relocating to this terrain of swampland, rivers, and fertile prairies. Beyond Lafayette, however, and the region's other urban anchor, Lake Charles, Cajun Country is largely a collection of small to midsize towns, many of them rural and quite historic in character. Wetlands communities like New Iberia, St. Martinville, and Breaux Bridge are great for dining on Cajun food (such as crawfish pie and blackened redfish), exploring historic sites, and venturing into the swamps on guided boat excursions. Prairie towns such as Eunice and Opelousas are best known for their Cajun and zydeco musical heritage. Of course, in this region, you'll also find rustic bed-and-breakfasts, quaint house-museums, and relatively affordable antiques shops and art galleries.

SIGHTS
◖ Acadian Cultural Center

The National Park Service's superb Acadian Cultural Center (501 Fisher Rd., Lafayette, 337/232-0789, www.nps.gov/jela, daily 8 A.M.–5 P.M., free) offers an excellent overview of Cajun history and culture. Housed within a contemporary building designed to resemble a Cajun cottage, the museum space contains well-labeled, often large-scale exhibits, artifacts, and photos. You can easily spend an hour in here absorbing the lore of Cajun music, family life, cooking, language, and fishing, and exploring the serpentine route that Acadians journeyed from Nova Scotia to southern Louisiana. Through such exhibits as well as varied films, you'll have a gut-wrenching but inspirational look at the plight of Cajuns and their astounding resolve, balanced with their love of celebration and tradition that has kept them a distinct cultural group to this day. Check for interpretive programs, videos, and performances scheduled regularly throughout the year.

When in New Orleans, be sure to drop in on the headquarters of the Jean Lafitte National Historical Park and Preserve in the French Quarter. Here, you'll find information on all of the park's six sites throughout southern Louisiana, including the Prairie Acadian Cultural Center in Eunice and the Wetlands Acadian Cultural Center in Thibodaux.

EXCURSIONS

SWAMP TOURS

Guided excursions into the swamps around New Orleans can be an ideal way to explore such vast, ravishingly beautiful areas. The top destinations for swamp tours are Slidell, Houma, and towns along the Atchafalaya Basin east and south of Lafayette, but you can also find operators south of Baton Rouge and throughout metro New Orleans. The best times to go are spring and fall.

Situated on the West Bank, near Barataria Preserve, **Airboat Adventures** (504/689-2005 or 888/467-9267, www.airboatadventures.com) leads guided two-hour excursions (daily 9:45 A.M., noon, and 2 P.M., $30-65 pp) into a private, 20,000-acre swamp. Via high-speed airboats of varying sizes, you'll have the chance to observe swamp creatures amid vibrant wildflowers and haunting cypress trees.

A favorite near Houma is **A Cajun Man's Swamp Cruise** (985/868-4625, www.cajunman.com, times vary, $25 adult, $15 child under 13), an entertaining tour conducted by Captain Ron "Black" Guidry, a former U.S. Army Green Beret and Louisiana State Trooper. Guidry, who's fluent in French and English, plays guitar and accordion and sings Cajun ditties while maneuvering his covered boat through the cypress swamps of southeastern Louisiana.

In the heart of Cajun Country, **Champagne's Cajun Swamp Tours** (1209 Rookery Rd., Breaux Bridge, 337/230-4068, www.louisianaswamptours.net, times vary, $20 adult, $10 child under 13) takes passengers out in a relatively quiet, 20-foot aluminum crawfish skiff. The narrated, two-hour tour leaves from the banks of Lake Martin and passes through a dramatic flooded cypress and tupelo forest, as well as one of the state's largest nesting areas of wading birds.

One of the most respected operators in the state, **Honey Island Swamp Tours** (41490 Crawford Landing Rd., Slidell, 985/641-1769, www.honeyislandswamp.com, times vary, $23 adult, $15 children) can handle nearly 150 guests per trip, using up to seven boats. These two-hour tours pass through Honey Island Swamp, a lush overflow river swamp and the second-largest swamp in Louisiana.

For a more intimate experience, try **The Last Wilderness** (225/659-2499 or 225/692-4114, www.lastwildernesstours.com, times vary, $30 adult, $25 child under 10), which uses a small, six-person Cajun fishing boat for two-hour tours of the Atchafalaya Basin. Guide Dean Wilson takes passengers well off the beaten path, even by swamp standards, and into tight, shallow bodies of water that larger vessels can't reach.

A highly recommended company, **McGee's Landing** (1337 Henderson Levee Rd., Henderson, 337/228-2384, www.mcgeeslanding.com) operates narrated tours through the Atchafalaya Basin (daily 10 A.M., 1 P.M., and 3 P.M., $20 adult, $18 senior, $15 child under 12), featuring live entertainment and a homestyle café.

To experience the relatively untouched Honey Island Swamp, you can hitch a ride with **Pearl River Eco-Tours** (985/649-4200 or 866/597-9267, www.pearlriverecotours.com, times vary, $23 adult, $15 child), led by Coast Guard-certified guides who are all native to the area and experts on the swamp ecosystem.

Situated in Kraemer, **Torres Cajun Swamp Tours** (985/633-7739, www.torresswamptours.net, times vary, $15 adult, $10 student, $8 child under 12) operates tours in the scenic Bayou Boeuf area. Led by Coast Guard-certified guides, these educational 1.5-hour tours provide guests with the opportunity to observe and photograph a wide array of native inhabitants.

© LAURA MARTONE

a swamp tour in the Atchafalaya Basin

The Acadian Cultural Center is a short drive southeast of downtown Lafayette, just off U.S. 90 by Lafayette Regional Airport.

◖ Avery Island

Perhaps the most visited section of New Iberia, the community of Avery Island is home to a pair of seminal Cajun Country attractions, Jungle Gardens and the Tabasco Factory. Avery Island is not, in fact, an island—it is not surrounded by water. Rather it is a salt dome, which rises rather gently above the surrounding wetlands and has been a source of commercial salt since the 1860s. The earliest salt works on the island were short-lived but important for Confederate troops during the Civil War. It was in 1862 that a significant cache of rock salt was discovered here—the first such deposit in all of North America. Union troops, upon securing the area, immediately destroyed the salt mines, which were not reopened until 1880.

MCILHENNY TABASCO COMPANY

Though Avery Island continues to be a source of commercial salt, its actual claim to fame is another savory condiment, Tabasco Sauce, which Edward McIlhenny first bottled on Avery Island in 1868. The regular tour of the McIlhenny Tabasco Company (337/365-8173 or 800/634-9599, www.tabasco.com, daily 9 A.M.–4 P.M., free) is actually pretty underwhelming, beginning with a shamelessly promotional video expounding on the virtues of Tabasco Sauce. You're then given a small souvenir bottle of the vaunted condiment before proceeding along a wall of windows through which you can observe the inner workings of the factory, where a jumble of machines and conveyor belts bottles, caps, and labels the sauces. At the end of your tour, you'll walk through a small museum of Tabasco memorabilia, after which you can wander across the parking lot to the old-fashioned Country Store. It's all good, clean fun, and the experience is especially nice for kids who might be getting a little tired of touring historic house-museums.

JUNGLE GARDENS AND BIRD CITY

Slightly less famous on Avery Island is the McIlhenny family's 170-acre Jungle Gardens and Bird City (daily 9 A.M.–5 P.M., $8 adult, $5 under 13). A narrow four-mile country lane winds through this garden complex, which you can tour in less than an hour by car or in the course of a few hours if you decide to hoof it. (You can also park in several spots along the drive.) Thousands of subtropical plants and trees, including massive moss-draped live oaks, grow throughout these wild gardens, which are home to deer, turtles, nutria, raccoons, black bears, and alligators. The gardens also include the most complete collection of camellias in the world and a Buddhist temple containing a statue that dates to the 12th century. Although the gardens are open year-round, they're less thrilling in winter (Nov.–Feb.), when much of the plant life is dormant and the alligators hibernate.

No matter when you visit, you should take a few minutes to observe Bird City, a massive nesting ground for graceful great white egrets. Long stilted platforms rise out of a large marshy pond, and the egrets build nests here. The egrets are most prolific from December through July, when you may see hundreds of these creatures squawking, gathering branches, mating and courting, flying overhead, and putting on a spectacular show. A three-story observation deck sits opposite the nesting platforms, close enough to snap some wonderful pictures. You can reach Bird City by parking at the designated spot, as indicated on the souvenir trail map.

PRACTICALITIES

To reach Avery Island, follow LA-329 about six miles southwest from U.S. 90 in New Iberia. You'll come to a small guardhouse where you'll have to pay a nominal toll of $1, the money going toward the maintenance of the community roads. From here, proceed to the driveways for the Tabasco factory and, beyond that, Jungle Gardens.

Shadows-on-the-Teche

To experience one of the true must-see museums of Acadiana, head to Shadows-on-the-Teche

(317 E. Main St., New Iberia, 337/369-6446 or 877/200-4924, www.shadowsontheteche. org, Mon.–Sat. 9 A.M.–4:30 P.M., $10 adult, $8 senior, $6.50 student 6–17), a dignified white-columned brick house built by sugarcane farmer David Weeks in 1834. Unfortunately, Weeks died of an unknown malady during a trip to New Haven before ever living in the house. His wife, Mary Weeks, ran the house and oversaw the plantation for years afterward. The house is much smaller than some of the leviathan plantation houses along the Great River Road, and that's one reason it makes for a better tour—you aren't treated to an endless march through rooms and outbuildings. But the best things about Shadows is that the National Trust for Historic Preservation, which owns the house, also has a collection of about 17,000 documents relevant to the lives of the plantation's inhabitants and its day-to-day inner workings. Guides at Shadows draw on these records to help paint a vivid picture of life here, and often the most fascinating bits of information to modern visitors revolve around seeming minutiae, such as inventories of the house pantry, rather than the grandest or fanciest antiques. Some of the volunteer guides who give house tours are descendants of David and Mary Weeks. In addition to having a well-documented history, Shadows-on-the-Teche is one of the better-furnished plantation homes around. Other details inside the Classical Revival house include a lavish Italian marble floor in the formal dining room and the wide galleries at the exterior facade.

The home's last private owner, David Weeks Hall, worked hard to find a way to have the house saved as a museum; as fate would have it, he died in 1958 exactly one day after the National Trust for Historic Preservation agreed to take the house. Hall was something of a renaissance man and a well-known figure among the assorted literati who passed through New Iberia during the first half of the 20th century. You can still see the autographs of many of his distinguished guests on a door in his ground-floor studio—among the signatures are those of Elia Kazan, Walt Disney, Cecil B. DeMille,

and Henry Miller. Across the street from the plantation in a former bank building, a visitors center presents a brief film on the Weeks family and plantation's history, and rotating exhibits offer further insights into the property.

Center Street in New Iberia is so named because it was the center of the vast Weeks plantation, which once extended many miles south from this building, clear out to Weeks Island (a.k.a. Grand Cote), the actual sugarcane-farming operation that so enriched the Weeks family. One of the many interesting details that comes out during the tour is that the Weeks family actually had to pay dearly for processed sugar. Sugarcane was harvested here in southwestern Louisiana but refined in factories on the East Coast, so Louisiana families had to buy it back at a considerable cost in its refined form (ironic when you consider that unrefined "sugar in the raw" today now commands high prices in supermarkets and gourmet-food shops). Like many others in Louisiana, the plantation was occupied by Union troops during the Civil War. Soldiers camped on the grounds, and officers lived on the ground floor. It was an uneasy time for the Weeks family, and the matron of the family, Mary Weeks, died in the house during the Union occupation. The house's verdant grounds sweep right back to the muddy Bayou Teche, and you can stroll through the beautiful, somewhat formal gardens, which feature about 25 varieties of trees.

◖ Vermilionville

Within view of the Acadian Cultural Center, Vermilionville (300 Fisher Rd., Lafayette, 337/233-4077, www.bayouvermilion.org, Tues.–Sun. 10 A.M.–4 P.M., $10 adult, $8 senior, $6 student 6–18, free under 6) is another must-see for understanding Cajun culture. This 23-acre, living-history compound comprises five restored historic houses, 12 reproduction period buildings, and exhibits about the indigenous people, the area's wetlands, and Cajun and zydeco music (which is performed live here regularly). You can attend cooking demonstrations, eat in the casual

© DANIEL MARTONE

Cajun music demonstrations in an old schoolhouse at Vermilionville

La Cuisine de Maman restaurant, and walk along a nature trail identifying Louisiana plant life. Vermilionville is, rather oddly, set near the airport and several modern warehouses, but once you enter the re-created village, it feels quite authentic; there's even a lazy bayou running through the property. The buildings here include a chapel and *presbytère*, where a clergyman would have lived; an Acadian barn where volunteers engage in boat-building and net- and trap-making; a nostalgic schoolhouse; and several residences, the oldest dating from 1790. Every element of Vermilionville sheds light onto the culture of the area's original Cajuns, from homestyle cooking to live music-and-dance programs. As a bonus, the guides here are knowledgeable and enthusiastic.

RESTAURANTS

Not surprisingly, Acadiana is widely celebrated for its Cajun cuisine, and like most Cajun restaurants in New Orleans, those in Lafayette, New Iberia, Opelousas, and other Cajun towns feature staples like gumbo, jambalaya, red beans and rice, fresh seafood, and bread pudding with rum sauce. One ideal option is **Prejean's** (3480 NE Evangeline Trwy.,

Lafayette, 337/896-3247, www.prejeans.com, daily 7 A.M.–9:30 P.M., $9–25), which is as popular for its live Cajun music as for its delicious cuisine. The rambling dining room is presided over by a friendly and efficient staff; of the big Cajun dance hall–dining rooms in the region, Prejean's serves the best, most inventive Cajun and Creole food, including such specialties as catfish Catahoula (stuffed with shrimp, crawfish, and crab and served with a decadent crawfish and tasso cream sauce). While you're savoring dinner, you can also enjoy live music; once your food settles, you can even venture onto the dance floor. Lunch is also served, and the breakfasts at Prejean's are legendary.

For a more casual option, head to **Boudreau & Thibodeau's Cajun Cookin'** (5602 W. Main St., Houma, 985/872-4711, www.bntcajuncookin.com, Sun.–Thurs. 10 A.M.–10 P.M., Fri.–Sat. 10 A.M.–11 P.M., $5–24), which serves some of the tastiest home-style local fare in the area, from seafood gumbo to po-boys to redfish courtbouillon. You won't go home hungry after a platter of country-fried steak, soft-shell crab, or fried seafood. As the name indicates, the place is silly and festive, with goofy Cajun jokes printed on both the walls and the menu.

BAYOU TECHE

Bayou Teche, a 125-mile-long waterway in southern Louisiana, runs through the Cajun towns of Breaux Bridge, St. Martinville, and New Iberia. Its name, *teche*, is an old Attakapas Indian term for "snake." Native American legends offer different origins for the name, including one that suggests that a snake actually created the river: Chitimacha warriors destroyed a massive venomous serpent many miles in length, and as the beast died from its wounds, it writhed and deepened a twisting track in the mud that became the riverbed of Bayou Teche.

The Teche begins just east of Opelousas in the town of Port Barre, where it flows from Bayou Courtableau. Roughly paralleling I-49, it meanders through the towns of Arnaudville and Cecilia before cutting beneath I-10 and entering Breaux Bridge. It's along this stretch, from Arnaudville to Breaux Bridge, that the banks of the river are shaded by tall oak trees, dramatically draped with moss. A couple of miles downstream from St. Martinville, the Teche passes through the Keystone Locks and Control Structure, constructed by the U.S. Army Corps of Engineers to increase the bayou's water level, making it navigable for boats heading upstream to Port Barre.

You can drive alongside much of the Teche via several state highways, especially from New Iberia south through Jeanerette and Franklin. It eventually passes through yet another flood-control structure before finally emptying into the Lower Atchafalaya River.

Of course, Cajun food isn't the only option in Acadiana. You'll also find creative, contemporary cuisine at places like **C The French Press** (214 E. Vermilion St., Lafayette, 337/233-9449, www.thefrenchpresslafayette.com, Tues.–Thurs. 7 A.M.–2 P.M., Fri. 7 A.M.–2 P.M. and 5:30–9 P.M., Sat. 9 A.M.–2 P.M. and 5:30–9 P.M., Sun. 9 A.M.–2 P.M., $6–39), one of my favorite restaurants in southern Louisiana. With high ceilings, weathered walls, and tall windows, this well-lit eatery is ideal for both casual lunches and romantic dinners. The constantly evolving menu features classic dishes such as grits and grillades, plus innovative options like smoked duck breast with sweet potato spaetzle, roasted brussels sprouts, and dried cranberry glacé. The wine, beer, and cocktail lists are worth considering, too.

NIGHTLIFE

In this part of the world, it's the restaurant that *doesn't* have live music that's the exception. You can catch Cajun and zydeco bands at a number of places all through the area, but Lafayette and the neighboring towns seem to support any kind of music that you can tap your toes to. Popular **Blue Moon Saloon & Guesthouse** (215 E. Convent St., Lafayette, 337/234-2422 or 877/766-2583, www.bluemoonpresents.com, show times vary) has a large, outdoor deck where musicians of all types perform Wednesday–Sunday to an eclectic crowd of all ages. The place, which also offers affordable overnight accommodations, is usually packed with locals and visitors alike.

The Cajun Prairie also boasts its share of swamp pop, zydeco, and other live music; in fact, it's one of the country's premier live-music regions. **Slim's Y-Ki-Ki** (8410 LA-182, Opelousas, 337/942-6242, www.slimsykiki.com) has been one of the area's favorite zydeco dance halls since shortly after World War II; it's open mostly on weekend evenings and brings in some of the top bands in Louisiana. The big, low-slung building is sparse on decor (except for a few palm trees painted on the walls), but there's a huge, wide-open dance floor where enthusiasts cut loose to the music—and you're welcome to dance yourself. This is one of the best places in the region to hear zydeco.

ARTS AND LEISURE

Lafayette is home to the stately **Heymann Performing Arts Center** (1373 S. College Rd., Lafayette, 337/291-5555 or 337/291-5540, www.heymann-center.com, show times vary), which hosts a variety of entertainment, including pop concerts, dance troupes, theater, opera, and recitals. Another good option for cultural events is the famous **Liberty Theater** (S. 2nd St. and Park Ave., Eunice, 337/457-7389, www. eunice-la.com), an old movie house and vaudeville theater built in 1924. Back in the day, such illustrious performers as Tex Ritter, Fatty Arbuckle, Roy Rogers, and Jimmy Clanton performed here. After falling into a state of neglect, it was restored in 1986 when local citizens banded together to revive it. Today, it's the site of *Rendezvous des Cajuns* (Sat. 6 P.M., $5), a two-hour live radio and TV variety show with Cajun and zydeco music, along with storytelling, jokes, recipes, and other tidbits of Cajun lore. This legendary show is a memorable way to become acquainted with the region and its rich musical history. Tickets are available at the theater beginning at 4 P.M. on the day of the performance.

Outside New Orleans, no part of the state enjoys a good festival more than Acadiana. Scores of engaging events are held in towns throughout the region, virtually year-round. Besides staging the second-largest Mardi Gras celebration in the state, Lafayette hosts the annual **Festival International de Louisiane** (Lafayette, 337/232-8086, www.festivalinternational.com), a massive five-day party in late April that showcases all kinds of local and French music, French-language plays, and other Francophone fun, plus oodles of regional food.

In early May, fans of mudbugs gather at the **Breaux Bridge Crawfish Festival** (Breaux Bridge, 337/332-6655, www.bbcrawfest. com) to sample tasty treats and listen to live Cajun and zydeco music; it's one of the most popular events in the region. Fun-lovers also favor the family-oriented **Cajun Heartland State Fair** (Cajundome, 444 Cajundome Blvd., Lafayette, 337/265-2100, www.cajundome.com), a lively, 11-day indoor celebration that features carnival rides, regional cuisine, and live entertainment; it usually takes place in late May and early June. Over Labor Day weekend, music lovers flock to the **Southwest Louisiana Zydeco Music Festival** (Opelousas, 337/942-2392, www. zydeco.org), which has, for three decades, presented great concerts, varied foods, and lots of arts and crafts in Opelousas.

In mid-October, just as the hot weather generally begins to break, Lafayette holds its rollicking **Festivals Acadiens et Créoles** (Lafayette, www.festivalsacadiens.com), a chance for visitors to learn about Cajun culture through its rich musical traditions. Here, you can learn the Cajun waltz or two-step, and how accordions and fiddles figure into the sounds of Cajun song and dance. Outside Mardi Gras, this is one of the region's most popular, well-attended festivals, comprising several smaller events, including the Festival de Musique, the Bayou Food Festival, the Louisiana Craft Fair, and Louisiana Folk Roots. Events are held at lovely Girard Park near the University of Louisiana at Lafayette.

The 6,000-acre **Lake Fausse Pointe State Park** (5400 Levee Rd., St. Martinville, 337/229-4764 or 888/677-7200, www.crt. state.la.us/parks, Sun.–Thurs. 6 A.M.–9 P.M., Fri.–Sat. 6 A.M.–10 P.M., $1 pp, free over 62 and under 4) sits on the eastern side of Lake Fausse, fringing the Atchafalaya Swamp; it may take a little effort to get here, but the scenic drive through beautiful wetlands is well worth it. Although Lake Fausse is popular for boating and fishing, it's generally a tranquil place that is a favorite haunt of wildlife photographers and bird-watchers. Facilities include a boat launch, a boat dock with rentals, picnic pavilions, a camp store, a conference center, an RV camping area, campsites, hiking trails, and 18 overnight camping cabins with screened-in porches, air-conditioning, and piers over the water.

SHOPS

Stores selling Cajun-related music, books, gifts, arts and crafts, and gourmet treats are easy to find throughout Acadiana. New Iberia is one of the region's best towns for shopping, as it's home to a handful of pleasant boutiques that deal in antiques. Be sure to check out **Books**

EXCURSIONS

THE ATCHAFALAYA BASIN

The Atchafalaya (pronounced UH-cha-fuh-lye-uh) is the main distributary of the Mississippi River and an active, living delta through which flows the 135-mile-long Atchafalaya River. At about 15 miles in width, the basin is the largest overflow swamp in the United States and covers roughly 850,000 acres, about a third of the total landmass of Louisiana.

A swamp is any low ground overrun with water but punctuated by trees; marshes are similar but have few or no trees. This swamp began forming around A.D. 900, when the Mississippi River started to change its course, which had previously favored a westerly shift once it reached southern Louisiana. For many centuries, the river then flowed through the present-day Bayou Lafourche, which passes through the city of Houma and eventually empties into the Gulf.

Annual flooding forced heavy waters into the low-lying and dense forest on either side of the Mississippi River. Eventually, natural levees formed and contained the water permanently. In recent centuries, the Mississippi River has shifted still farther back toward the southeastern section of the state.

Historically, this swamp cultivated some of the richest and most fertile soil in the South, not to mention prolific fishing grounds, making it the perfect place for the exiled Acadian refugees who arrived in the mid- to late 18th century and established roots all through the basin. The geography of the swamp effectively cut the early Cajun settlements off from the rest of the state, helping them to preserve their distinct heritage and language. They remain a remarkably close-knit society to this day.

The Atchafalaya Basin's appearance and character both changed dramatically throughout the 20th century. Discoveries in the 1920s of vast oil and natural-gas reserves brought prosperity to the region, as well as large numbers of newcomers. Major floods, most notably in 1927, have, at different times, forced small communities within the basin to abandon their homes and settle on higher land, and in 1973, the federal government constructed an 18-mile-long bridge through the swamp,

extending I-10 from New Orleans and Baton Rouge to Lafayette. The work of the U.S. Army Corps of Engineers, which involved erecting massive floodgates at the intersection of the Mississippi and Atchafalaya Rivers, is what prevented the Mississippi from seeking a permanent shortcut through the swamp to the Gulf.

The construction of these flood-control systems and levees, as well as oil pipelines and other man-made structures, has not only forever altered the swamp but has also, at times, threatened its well-being. The largest bottomland hardwood forest in the country, the Atchafalaya is still home to fertile, productive fish and wildlife habitats. More than 50,000 egrets, ibises, and herons nest in the region, with about 300 additional bird species, such as bald eagles, wood ducks, cranes, and ospreys, represented. The basin also claims roughly 65 reptile species, including turtles and alligators, and 90 types of fish; other inhabitants include deer, bobcats, bears, nutrias, raccoons, possums, and coyotes.

© LAURA MARTONE

cypress trees in the Atchafalaya Basin

along the Teche (106 E. Main St., New Iberia, 337/367-7621 or 877/754-0849, www.booksalongtheteche.com, Mon.–Fri. 9:30 A.M.–5:30 P.M., Sat. 9:30 A.M.–5 P.M.), a small but first-rate independent bookstore that offers both new and used books. It specializes in regional books and music, with signed copies of all the books written by James Lee Burke, author of the popular Dave Robicheaux detective novels and longtime resident of New Iberia.

For local treats, head to **Champagne's Breaux Bridge Bakery** (105 S. Poydras St., Breaux Bridge, 337/332-1117, www.champagnesbakery.com, Mon.–Fri. 7 A.M.–5:30 P.M., Sat. 7 A.M.–1 P.M.), which has been a snacking institution in Breaux Bridge since 1888. The wonderful cakes, breads, bite-size cookies, and other baked goods make a wonderful picnic before an outing or a dessert en route to your hotel.

In downtown Lafayette, art lovers should stop by the **Sans Souci Fine Crafts Gallery** (219 E. Vermilion St., Lafayette, 337/266-7999, www.louisianacrafts.org, Tues.–Fri. 11 A.M.–5 P.M., Sat. 10 A.M.–4 P.M.), featuring the traditional and contemporary works of members of the Louisiana Crafts Guild. Housed within a 19th-century structure that has served as a pecan buyer's store, an overnight inn, a post office, and a bookstore, this well-regarded gallery features textiles, jewelry, pottery, glass, wood, and other types of decorative items.

HOTELS

Louisiana's Cajun Country boasts a wide selection of chain hotels, historic inns, and intimate cabins. If you're more comfortable with familiar names, then consider the **Hilton Lafayette** (1521 W. Pinhook Rd., Lafayette, 337/235-6111 or 800/445-8667, www.hilton.com, $119–159), perhaps the region's fanciest chain property. Situated on the banks of Bayou Vermilion, the Hilton houses 335 warmly furnished rooms and suites with French Provincial–inspired furnishings. The 15-floor, pet-friendly hotel offers scenic views of the countryside and proximity to the airport and downtown. Other amenities include a 24-hour business center, a fitness center, an outdoor pool and sundeck, high-speed Internet access, concierge services, a full-service restaurant, and a hotel bar that's popular with locals.

With rates lower than most of the cookie-cutter motels around the area, **Bayou Cabins** (100 W. Mills Ave., Breaux Bridge, 337/332-6158, www.bayoucabins.com, $60–135) is a fun and funky alternative. There are 13 cozy cabins right by Bayou Teche, close to downtown Breaux Bridge. The cabins are rustic but endearingly furnished: one has old newspaper for wallpaper, another contains a pencil-post, queen-size bed, some have screened porches, and one is decked in 1950s-style furnishings. All cabins have cable TV and wireless Internet access. There's also a home-style café right on the premises, serving pork boudin, cracklings, and beignets. A full breakfast is included.

If you'd prefer to stay in the Cajun wetlands, head to one of St. Martinville's architectural gems, the **Bienvenue House** (421 N. Main St., St. Martinville, 337/394-9100, www.bienvenuehouse.com, $100–120), which was built around 1830 and now contains four lovely rooms with a mix of formal and country-inspired antiques. Breakfasts here are a lavish affair, and many of the town's restaurants and shops are within a short stroll. To the south, ◖ **The Gouguenheim** (101 W. Main St., New Iberia, 337/364-3949, www.gouguenheim.com, $225–325) is an impressive, elegant 1894 building originally constructed as the Washington Ballroom, where it hosted many wedding receptions and important social functions. In 2001, it was beautifully restored by its current owners and converted into a B&B. There's a large veranda that wraps around the second floor, and four large guest apartments: a one-bedroom, a two-bedroom, and two with three bedrooms. Hardwood floors, detailed woodwork, exposed brick, and posh furnishings give this the feel of a small luxury hotel; some units have spiral staircases leading up to sleeping lofts. Amenities include cable TV, designer kitchens with granite counters and stainless-steel appliances, and private balconies overlooking downtown New Iberia's historic district.

Closer to New Orleans, you'll find the

Grand Bayou Noir Bed & Breakfast (1143 Bayou Black Dr., Houma, 985/873-5849, www.grandbayounoir.com, $120–160), which sits on four acres studded with gracious oak and fruit trees, fronting the peaceful Bayou Black. The three guest rooms in this imposing 1930s Colonial Revival house have queen-size beds, private baths, and elegant antiques, plus cable TV and air-conditioning; one suite has a private balcony, hot tub, and sitting area. While here, you can relax on the large screened porch or the varied swings, rocking chairs, and hammocks that pepper the grounds, all of which make this B&B truly ideal for a quiet retreat or a romantic getaway.

PRACTICALITIES
Information
For more information about Louisiana's Cajun Country, consult the **Lafayette Convention and Visitors Commission** (LCVC, 1400 NW Evangeline Trwy., Lafayette, 337/232-3737 or 800/346-1958, www.lafayettetravel.com), which serves as an umbrella tourism organization for most of the Acadiana towns between Opelousas and Morgan City, and between Jennings and Henderson. Most of the nearby parishes also have tourism organizations, such as the **Iberia Parish Convention and Visitors Bureau** (2513 LA-14, New Iberia, 337/365-1540 or 888/942-3742, www.iberiatravel.com), the **St. Martin Parish Tourism Commission** (St. Martinville, 337/298-3556 or 888/565-5939, www.cajuncountry.org), and the **St. Landry Parish Tourism Commission** (978 Kennerson Rd., Opelousas, 337/442-1597 or 877/948-8004, www.cajuntravel.com). For more detailed information about the Cajun wetlands, contact the **Cajun Coast Visitors and Convention Bureau** (112 Main St., Patterson, 985/395-4905 or 800/256-2931, www.cajuncoast.com) or the **Houma Area Convention and Visitors Bureau** (114 Tourist Dr., Gray, 985/868-2732 or 800/688-2732, www.houmatravel.com).

The Times (www.timesofacadiana.com) provides Lafayette and its environs with tons of listings and entertainment coverage. Another great freebie is *The Independent Weekly* (www.theind.com), which is strong on arts, dining, and entertainment. Houma's free *Gumbo Entertainment Guide* (www.tri-parishtimes.com/gumbo) is a monthly paper filled with event and nightlife listings and other lively goings-on.

Getting There and Around
Roughly shaped like a scythe, Acadiana follows U.S. 90 west to southeast, from Lake Charles to Houma. The long, rectangular handle of the scythe extends from Lake Charles to Lafayette along both U.S. 90 and the parallel U.S. 190 corridor, from Kinder to Eunice to Opelousas. This part of Acadiana is considered the Cajun prairie, where early settlers earned their livelihood by farming. The curving blade of the scythe extends southeast along the U.S. 90 corridor from Lafayette down through New Iberia, Morgan City, and Houma. This region is considered the Cajun wetlands, where the settlers derived their livelihood chiefly from fishing and trapping. From Houma, it's just a 60-mile drive via U.S. 90 to New Orleans.

In order to maximize your flexibility, the entire region is best explored by car. The **Lafayette Transit System** (LTS, 337/291-8570, www.ridelts.com) does provide bus service around Lafayette, but since many of the area's main attractions are in outlying towns not served by LTS, this is an impractical option.

From New Orleans, there are two main routes to Lafayette and its environs. You can either take the straight, easy 135-mile shot across I-10 through Baton Rouge, which takes a little more than two hours, or opt for the more circuitous 153-mile route via U.S. 90, which requires a little less than three hours. I-10, which leads from Lafayette to Lake Charles, is a wide interstate highway with a 70-mph speed limit, as is I-49, which leads north from Lafayette to Opelousas. While U.S. 190 is a much slower route, especially where it passes through the downtown areas of Eunice, Basile, and several other towns in the region, it definitely offers a more scenic view of Cajun Country.

BACKGROUND

The Setting

GEOGRAPHY

Louisiana, especially the southern end of the state, is—in geological terms—brand spanking new. It's largely made up of sediment deposited by the Mississippi River or left in the wake of the continuously shifting Gulf of Mexico shoreline. It's tied with Florida for having the second-lowest mean elevation of any state (about 100 feet). Its highest point, "Mount" Driskill up north near Grambling and Minden, is only 535 feet in elevation. New Orleans itself lies eight feet below sea level, a point made abundantly clear during the flooding aftermath of Hurricane Katrina. The city rises to perhaps 300 feet in a few slightly elevated areas north of Lake Pontchartrain.

Rivers

The Mississippi River plays a vital role in the appearance, development, and economy of New Orleans. The river forms the border between Mississippi and Louisiana, cutting directly through Baton Rouge and New Orleans before emptying into the Gulf of Mexico. At its end, the mighty river and its many tributaries form a fan-shaped delta. The Mississippi River is the definitive drain for about 40 percent of the United States.

The Mississippi River Delta, which extends

across the southern Louisiana shoreline, took about 6,000 years to form. Its largest tributary, the Atchafalaya River, flows into the western end of the delta, southeast of Lafayette. The Atchafalaya's delta will eventually fill in much of northern Atchafalaya Bay, and will come to resemble the fully formed Mississippi River Delta.

Louisiana's jagged shoreline comprises 3 million wetland acres, roughly 40 percent of the entire nation's marsh ecosystem. Unlike the considerably more stable Gulf shorelines, Louisiana's coast is continuously shifting, the result of the evolving play between the Gulf currents and the flow of the Mississippi and other tributaries.

Bayous

Of course, rivers aren't the only major waterways found in southern Louisiana. Bayous are also an important part of the regional culture. The word "bayou" derives from the Choctaw term for a river, *bayuk*. These sluggish bodies

marsh plants fringing a bayou in southeastern Louisiana

© LAURA MARTONE

of water are large enough here that they'd be called rivers elsewhere in the country. Some of the larger bayous include Teche (which flows through the Cajun Country through St. Martinville and Breaux Bridge), Vermilion (which flows through Lafayette), LaFourche (which runs through Houma), and Boeuf (which passes near Opelousas in St. Landry Parish).

Lakes and Lagoons

In the southern part of the state, many "lakes" are really salt- or brackish-water lagoons that were once bays or inlets of the Gulf but were eventually sealed off by the formation of barrier beaches or delta ridges. The largest and most famous of these is Lake Pontchartrain, which is traversed by one of the longest bridges in the world, the 24-mile Lake Pontchartrain Causeway. Other examples include Barataria Bay, south of New Orleans; Lake Maurepas, west of Lake Pontchartrain and connected to it by Bayou Manchac; and Lake Salvador, just southwest of New Orleans and fringed by Jean Lafitte National Historical Park and Preserve.

CLIMATE

Southern Louisiana is jokingly called the northernmost coast of Central America, and not just because of its banana-republic politics—it also has a climate that's more similar to Costa Rica's than to that of most of the United States. It is considered a semihumid, subtropical zone, and it almost never receives snow; in New Orleans, when the temperature occasionally dips to freezing on the coldest winter evenings, locals bundle up as though they're about to run the Iditarod. The average rainfall is about 58 inches per year, but some of the southern parishes average closer to 65 inches of rain annually. It's rainy all year, with the highest totals in the summer and the lowest in October, but there are no bone-dry months here.

With a low atmospheric ceiling and high humidity, nighttime-to-daytime low and high temperatures don't usually span a great range. The mean temperature for the year is about 68°F, but New Orleans usually feels warmer;

MUDDY WATERS

Contrary to popular belief, the muddiness of the Mississippi River, and many of the other rivers and bayous in the state, is not a sign of pollution. The rivers become muddy because the fast-moving current is constantly transporting natural and easily eroded bottom sediments. Of course, this doesn't mean that the muddy Mississippi – the lifeblood of the Crescent City – is free from pollution. In fact, according to studies recently submitted to the Environmental Protection Agency (EPA), the Mississippi is one of the most contaminated rivers in the country, mainly due to cancer-causing toxic discharges from industrial facilities. Other Louisiana-based waterways, such as the Red, Pearl, and Calcasieu Rivers, are also suffering from chemical contamination.

Another potentially dangerous thing about the state's rivers is that many of them flow at a higher elevation than the floodplains that surround them. The sediment brought downriver and deposited in Louisiana has built up the riverbanks, forming natural levees. When the river runs high (as it did in the spring of 2011), as much as one-third of the state – including all of metropolitan New Orleans – would be one massive pool of water were it not for the intricate system of man-made levees and spillways constructed all along the river and its tributaries.

---

there's less breeze and the concrete roads and buildings tend to absorb and retain heat. Average high temperatures in New Orleans in summer are about 91°F, with nighttime lows averaging a still very hot 74°F. In winter (December, January, and February), highs average a pleasant 65°F, with lows a manageable 46°F. Winter is a wonderful time to visit, but summer can be simply unbearable on the most humid days—even with air-conditioning. The touristy French Quarter, which can be littered with garbage along Bourbon and outside bars on weekend mornings, can feel and smell positively foul on a summer day. Spring and fall are fairly genial times to visit. Temperatures can easily reach into the 90s during warm spells, but more typically average in the upper 70s in September and October and in April and May.

New Orleans itself averages about 110 days a year with completely sunny skies, and about the same number of days with rain. Otherwise, it's partly sunny or partly cloudy, depending on whether you're an optimist or a pessimist.

Hurricane Season

The weather has been a hot topic in southern Louisiana for as long as people have lived here—long before Hurricanes Katrina and Rita barreled through the state in 2005. Hurricane season begins in June each year and lasts through November. Hurricanes have always been a threat to the Louisiana shoreline, and given the increasing numbers and magnitude of these storms in recent years, one suspects Louisiana will have plenty of brushes with violent storms in the future.

History

EARLY CIVILIZATION

In northeastern Louisiana, not too far from the city of Monroe, archaeologists have identified a series of ancient ceremonial mounds that some in the scientific community believe are the earliest physical evidence of human settlement on the entire continent. More recent but still prehistoric mounds dot the landscape of the state, especially in the northern and eastern regions. These mounds were a fixture in the early Native American farming communities that proliferated in these parts for the 2–3 millennia before European settlement.

Louisiana's Hopewell indigenous tribes thrived in the Gulf South from about 200 B.C. until nearly A.D. 900, with Mississippian tribes succeeding them in the 1500s. Native Americans of the 1600s and 1700s, when Europeans first began exploring the region, comprised three distinct branches, each with its own culture and language: Caddoan, Muskogean, and Tunican. It was this last branch, which included the Chitimacha, Attakapa, and other tribes, that mostly inhabited what is now southern Louisiana, with Muskogean and Caddoan Indians living in the central and northwestern parts of the state, respectively.

The effect of French and then Spanish settlement on indigenous people living in Louisiana was, as it was wherever Europeans explored the New World, devastating. Many tribes were annihilated by disease, others squarely routed out, enslaved, or massacred by settlers. Still, some Native Americans managed to hang on and thrive in Louisiana, many of their members intermarrying with African Americans. Today, there are Chitimacha, Houma, Tunica-Biloxi, Coushatta, and Choctaw settlements in the state. Many geographical names in Louisiana have indigenous origins, among them Bogalusa (which means "black water"), Opelousas ("black leg"), and Ponchatoula ("hanging hair").

Most people think of the French explorer René-Robert Cavelier, Sieur de La Salle, as the earliest European settler in the region, and he was the first to establish a permanent stronghold in the name of his own country, in 1682. But 140 years earlier, Spaniards led by explorer Hernando de Soto first visited what is now Louisiana. They didn't stay, but they did leave behind diseases that proved fatal to many of the indigenous people they encountered.

La Salle entered Louisiana down the Mississippi River from the north and claimed for France all the land drained by not only this massive river but also its vast network of tributaries. This parcel covered about 830,000 square miles and ran from the Gulf of Mexico to Canada, and from the Rocky Mountains to Mississippi. He first termed the region Louisiana (well, technically, Louisiane, which is its name in French) after France's reigning monarch of that period, Louis XIV.

THE FOUNDING OF NEW ORLEANS

Louisiana's period of French rule was barely more than three generations—France would cede the territory to the Spanish in 1762 before occupying it again for a short period preceding the Louisiana Purchase. Neither the first nor second period of French rule proved to be profitable for France, and from a colonial perspective, one could say that the entire episode was a failure. On the flip side, the French occupation planted the seeds for the emergence of New Orleans as one of young America's most fascinating cities.

New Orleans was not the first settlement in Louisiana by the French, although explorer Pierre Le Moyne, Sieur d'Iberville, did establish a toehold near the city on March 3, 1699, which was coincidentally Mardi Gras. That same year, the French built a permanent fort about 90 miles east in Biloxi (now Mississippi) and, three years later, another 60 miles east in Mobile (now Alabama). The first permanent French settlement to go up in what is now Louisiana, in 1714, was Natchitoches, a still-charming small city in northwestern Louisiana, about 300 miles northwest of New Orleans. By the late 1710s, however, France had already failed to invest substantially in its new settlement, and unable to fund a full-fledged colony, the monarchy transferred control of Louisiana to Antoine Crozat, a French financier of considerable acclaim.

Crozat was able to make little headway with Louisiana, and just five years later, control of Louisiana was shifted to Compagnie d'Occident, led by a wealthy Scotsman named John Law. It became quickly apparent to Law and other authorities, however, that the southern Mississippi was vulnerable to plays for control by the two key competing European powers in colonial America, Great Britain and Spain. To protect their interests, the French built a new fort in 1718 along the lower Mississippi, christening the settlement La Nouvelle-Orléans, after Philippe, Duc d'Orléans. A handful of settlements were added along the Mississippi River to the north, and in 1722, France named young New Orleans the territorial capital of Louisiana.

The beginnings of Nouvelle Orléans were almost pathetically modest. The site, at a sharp bend of the Mississippi River more than five feet *below* sea level, was little more than bug- and alligator-infested swampland, which the city's earliest residents shored up with landfill and dams. Part of the settlement covered one of the few bumps of higher ground along the river's banks. The site was chosen in part because a bayou (now known as Bayou St. John) connected the Mississippi River at this point to Lake Pontchartrain, which itself emptied into the Gulf. For eons, the area's Native Americans had used the bayou as a shortcut for getting from the river to the Gulf without having to paddle all the way south, nearly another 100 miles, to where the Mississippi entered the Gulf.

Today's French Quarter, also known as the Vieux Carré (literally, Old Square), for the first several decades encompassed all of New Orleans. It was anchored by the Place d'Armes,

which would later be renamed Jackson Square. The river's course in relation to the city has changed slightly since the city's founding; in the early days, Jackson Square faced the river-front directly, whereas today a significant strip of land and levee acts as a barrier between it and the river.

Law can be credited with making the earliest effort to attract European settlers to Louisiana. His first successful campaign brought not Frenchmen but Germans to the new territory. Law would convince Germans to move to Louisiana as indentured workers, meaning they were bound to work for an established period, and once their service commitment was complete, they were granted freedom. Law's Occidental Company used all the usual trickery and false advertising common throughout Europe in those days to attract immigrants and investors: It promised vast riches, huge mining reserves, and easy agricultural opportunities, virtually none of which was accurate.

During Law's first few years of controlling Louisiana, his company managed to convince about 7,000 mostly German and French residents to migrate to Louisiana. A significant percentage of these migrants died from disease or starvation, as the colonial authorities were in no position at all to feed, clothe, and house the arrivals. In all likelihood, if you stayed in Louisiana during these early days, you did so only because you hadn't the means to return to Europe. Word of the false promise of Louisiana spread quickly back to France, but authorities allowed Law and his company to administer the territory until 1731, when the French monarchy finally stepped in to resume control.

Law was responsible for first importing West African slaves to Louisiana. His Compagnie d'Occident also owned the French Compagnie du Senegal, which controlled all French slave trade. During roughly a 10-year period, about 3,000 slaves, mostly Senegalese, were taken from their homeland to Louisiana. Slaves worked on the handful of early plantations and also on the countless smaller subsistence farms that developed around southern Louisiana, most engaged in the production and export of indigo and tobacco.

Back in control of the colony from 1731 through 1762, France failed utterly to turn Louisiana into a profitable venture. Furthermore, its strategic importance diminished sharply as England developed an upper hand during the French and Indian War, which had begun in 1754, toward controlling Canada. In 1762, France hatched a diplomatic scheme to help impel Spain to join it and rout the British: It secretly handed over the Louisiana Territory to Spain in the Treaty of Fontainebleau. In fact, the territory stayed in the family, as France's King Louis XV simply transferred the land to his own cousin, Spain's King Charles III.

The move ended badly for both France and Spain. France lost the war with Britain in 1763 and lost control of Canada. And Spain ended up with a lemon. One might argue that France really didn't lose a colony so much as rid itself of what had become an enormous and depressing financial burden. Furthermore, as part of the peace treaty between the joint powers of Spain and France with their victor, Great Britain was awarded all of Louisiana east of the Mississippi River, which became known as West Florida. Spain kept a much larger tract, which included all of Louisiana west of the river, along with a critical little area along the lower Mississippi River called Île d'Orléans, which included the city of New Orleans. France was free of any part of Louisiana.

SPANISH RULE

The actual physical transfer of Louisiana, and especially New Orleans, to Spain was an unmitigated disaster fraught with rebellion, virtual martial law, and ugly acts of violence. It didn't help that the residents of New Orleans had no idea that they had become subjects of Spain until 1766, when the first Spanish governor, Antonio de Ulloa, arrived that March and, like a wicked stepmother, immediately instituted a strict rule upon the city's inhabitants.

© DANIEL MARTONE

Lafitte's Blacksmith Shop Bar is one of only a few structures that survived the great fires of the 18th century.

Almost as immediately, there were insurgencies, and in 1768, the situation became particularly dire when locals actually drove Ulloa and his cronies clear out of town. Spain hired a tyrannical military man, General Alejandro O'Reilly, to beat down the rebellion, which he did, quite successfully, in August 1769. He managed to get Spain in firm control of New Orleans, a rule that would last until the United States orchestrated the Louisiana Purchase in 1803, for although France technically owned Louisiana at that time, Spaniards continued to govern the city's day-to-day affairs right through to the end.

The Spanish, like the French, made every possible effort to boost the colony's population, sending plenty of Spaniards to Louisiana throughout their period of rule. From a cultural standpoint, Louisiana remained squarely French, as the colonists from France far outnumbered any newcomers. The only reason the appearance of the French Quarter today more closely resembles Spanish colonial than French colonial architecture is that two huge fires burned much of the city during the Spanish occupation, and many of the new buildings that went up were constructed by Spanish authorities. The first fire hit the Quarter in 1788, apparently started by candles at a religious observation; about 850 buildings burned, and about 200 of those were again lost in a smaller fire in 1794. It's Spain's influence that resulted in the wrought-iron balconies, shaded courtyards, and other features that typify French Quarter architecture.

Ironically, the majority of the newcomers to Louisiana during the Spanish period were actually French, or French-speaking, refugees. The most famous were the Acadians, who had been cruelly expelled from the Maritime Provinces of Canada after the British victory. The French immigrants living in Acadian Canada were typically rounded up and forced onto ships— some were sent back to France, and others were reluctantly taken in by certain British colonies in what is now the United States. Many died in passage or of poverty that they encountered where they landed. Spain, looking to boost the population of the Louisiana colony, enthusiastically welcomed the Acadians, who arrived in two major waves, the first in 1764 and an even larger one in 1785. Most of them settled in the marshes and swamplands of south-central and southwestern Louisiana. In Louisiana, the name Acadian gradually morphed into Cajun, as we all know it today, and Lafayette, Louisiana, became the hub of Cajun settlements.

A lesser-known group of refugees that also came to New Orleans and Louisiana in great numbers from 1791 through 1803 were white French settlers and some free people of color from the French colony of Saint-Domingue (now Haiti), who fled the island during the violent revolution of the 1790s.

Louisiana's makeup changed a bit during the American Revolution, as Spain worked in concert with the American colonists to undermine their rivals, the British. They sent supplies and munitions to the colonists, and in 1779, after formally declaring war on Britain, their Louisiana militia captured all of the British settlements of West Florida. This included all of the Gulf Coast region between the Mississippi River and the Perdido River, which today forms the east-west state border between Alabama and Florida. Per the terms of the Treaty of Paris in 1783, Spain's assistance was, at the war's conclusion, rewarded with a chunk of land that included all of both East Florida (today's Florida) and West Florida (which today includes Alabama, Mississippi, and the nine Louisiana parishes east and north of the Mississippi River, now sometimes referred to as the Florida parishes).

With the young United States now in control of all the land east of the Mississippi River (except for East and West Florida), New Orleans and the entire Louisiana Territory grew dramatically in strategic importance. New Orleans became the seaport serving America's interior, as important rivers throughout Ohio, Kentucky, and Tennessee all fed into the Mississippi.

In yet another secret treaty, however, Spain in 1800 decided to transfer all of the

Louisiana Territory, including New Orleans, back to France. The actual residents of New Orleans never even knew they were residents of a French colony for the three years they were back under the country's rule, as in 1803, the United States bought Louisiana from France for a mere $15 million. Even by the standards of that day, $15 million was a paltry sum for such an enormous parcel of land—approximately one-third of the land that now makes up the present-day continental United States. Because Spain still possessed East and West Florida, the nine Louisiana parishes east and north of the Mississippi River remained in Spanish hands until 1810, when the American residents of West Florida declared their independence and asked to be annexed by the United States.

LIFE IN THE 19TH CENTURY

Upon buying Louisiana from France, the United States immediately split the territory in two at the 33rd parallel, which today forms the northern border of Louisiana. All land south of that point became known as the Territory of Orleans, and, confusingly, all land to the north became known as the Territory of Louisiana.

William C. C. Claiborne was named governor of the Orleans territory, which he ruled from the territorial capital, New Orleans. He endured a difficult period, attempting to introduce the American democratic political system to a people entirely unused to self-determined government. In 1790, about 10,000 new refugees from Saint-Domingue moved into New Orleans, doubling the population but adding further chaos to the city. In many respects, it's this final wave of French-speaking people from Haiti—white colonists of French descent and free people of color (*gens de couleur libres*)—that ultimately established the French-Caribbean character that exists to this day in New Orleans.

For a time, New Orleans deviated from rural Louisiana in its relative tolerance of racial diversity. The *gens de couleur libres* were, in many cases, well educated and quite able to forge good livings as builders, designers,

the Andrew Jackson statue in Jackson Square

artisans, and chefs. These early Creole immigrants were in a large way responsible for the intricate and fanciful Creole cottages and other buildings still found throughout the city and southern Louisiana, and these same immigrants helped to develop New Orleans's inimitable Creole cuisine, which blended the traditions of France, Spain, the Caribbean, Africa, and even the American frontier and Native Americans.

Intermingling was considerable in this early New Orleans society, as wealthy Europeans and Creoles commonly had mistresses, some who were *gens de couleur libres,* quadroons (one-fourth black), octoroons (one-eighth black), or some other mix of Anglo, Latin, African, and Native American descent. It's largely for this reason that the term Creole, when applied to people, is rather confusing. The name was first applied to upper-crust French settlers born in Louisiana but descended from mostly wealthy European families, as the very word derives from the Spanish *criollo,* a term that described people born in the colonies rather than born in Europe or, for that matter, Africa. These days, just about any New Orleanian or Louisianian who can claim some direct combination of French, Spanish, Caribbean, and African blood can justly consider him- or herself a Creole, the exception being the descendants of the original French-Canadian refugees from Acadia, known as Cajuns.

The United States accepted the Territory of Orleans as the state of Louisiana on April 30, 1812. It thereby became the 18th state of the union, preceded only by Vermont, Kentucky, Tennessee, and Ohio after the original 13 states. The political system, with Claiborne as governor and New Orleans the capital, continued largely as it had from the time of the Louisiana Purchase.

America wasted no time in exploiting its new purchase, as thousands of entrepreneurial-minded settlers flocked to the busy port city during the first decade after the Louisiana Purchase. They were not welcomed in the French Quarter at all, and in fact, the original Creoles would have nothing to do with

American settlers for many decades. Some of these upstarts immediately began amassing great riches in shipping and trade enterprises, building lavish homes in the American Quarter, which is now the Central Business District (CBD). Canal Street divided the two enclaves, and the median down this street came to be considered New Orleans's "neutral ground." Today, the city's residents refer to any street median as neutral ground.

By the early 1800s, a century's worth of immigrants from all walks of life had contributed to one of the most racially, culturally, and economically diverse populations in the nation. Freed prisoners from France, Haitian refugees, slaves, European indentured servants, American frontiersmen, Spanish Canary Islanders, nuns, military men, and others now formed New Orleans's population and that of many of the communities upriver.

The War of 1812

Britain and the United States had remained hostile to one another since the Revolution, and shortly after Louisiana became a state, the two nations entered into the War of 1812, which would last three years. By 1814, New Orleans figured heavily in the campaign, as the faltering British decided to go after several key ports along the Gulf Coast and the Mississippi River in an effort to cut off the supply-and-trade system serving the interior United States. New Orleans, defended by Major General Andrew Jackson, was attacked by the British on January 8, 1815—several days after British and American leaders had signed a peace treaty ending the War of 1812. Still, many believe that the British would not have formally ratified the treaty had they been able to pull off that final battle. Andrew Jackson's victory in the Battle of New Orleans helped to propel his political career, and in 1828, he was elected the seventh president of the United States.

The year 1812 was significant in New Orleans for another reason—it received the first steamboat, aptly called the *New Orleans,* ever to navigate the Mississippi River system; the boat steamed all the way from Pittsburgh via the Ohio River. Steamboats would greatly alter the nature of commerce in New Orleans, as, up until 1812, trade had been conducted by small vessels propelled chiefly by the river current, meaning that they could not return upstream once they arrived in New Orleans. In many cases, the boats were simply scrapped once they arrived.

Robert Livingston and inventor Robert Fulton were given a monopoly on the steamboat business for the first few years, but the two abandoned their stronghold in the face of outraged legal challenges, and the number of steamboats arriving and departing New Orleans grew rapidly; by the mid-1840s, more than 1,000 different steamboats were calling on New Orleans each year. Steamboats left New Orleans for the Midwest and the East Coast carrying tobacco, cotton, sugarcane, and many other goods. New Orleans also became a major trade port with the Caribbean Islands, from which it imported fruit, tobacco, rum, and—illegally, after their importation was banned in 1808—slaves.

The Civil War Era

Louisiana's population stood at about 150,000 by 1820, having increased greatly since statehood with the arrival of settlers from other parts of the United States, who moved here to pursue new land and to farm. The population grew to 350,000 by 1840, and to 700,000 by 1860, the start of the Civil War. During this period, the state became a U.S. superpower owing to its phenomenal agricultural growth, chiefly in cotton and sugarcane. Both small farms and massive plantations grew these crops, using largely slave labor. Cotton was grown just about everywhere in the state, but somewhat less in the swampy southern regions, where sugarcane thrived in the warmer and wetter climate. In fact, sugarcane was always a more lucrative crop than cotton. The state also became a major rice grower—the crop was first planted in the southern and Mississippi River areas to feed slaves, but it proved profitable and was developed into a valuable commercial crop by the end of the 19th century.

With the outlying areas seeing huge growth in agriculture, the region's key port and gateway, New Orleans, grew dramatically. By 1820, it had already become the largest city in the South, with a population of about 27,500, surpassing Charleston. After New York City, it was America's leading immigrant port of entry from 1830 until the Civil War, as immigrants headed to the interior Ohio and Mississippi River valleys by way of the city. By the 1850s, New Orleans had grown to become the fourth-largest city in the United States and a leading cultural hub. Visitors from other parts of the country were struck by the city's distinctly Spanish architecture and Parisian ambience— it was a city of high fashion, opera and theater, lavish dining, and sophisticated parties. Already by this time, the city was beginning to celebrate Mardi Gras with parties and simple parades.

The hot and humid summers proved to be breeding grounds for yellow fever and other subtropical maladies, and although many residents died from the disease during these years, the city's population still grew to a staggering 170,000 by 1860.

The dynamic changed in the middle of the 19th century with the construction of railroads and canals, which made it possible for Midwestern states to move their products to the eastern United States more quickly and cheaply than by way of New Orleans and the Gulf. The city continued to prosper as a shipper of cotton and sugarcane. Louisiana relied heavily on slave labor to ensure the profitability of its agricultural markets, and New Orleans prospered hugely in this ignominious trade. Had the Midwestern states remained as dependent on New Orleans for trade as they were in the early part of the century, it's quite possible the state would not have sided with the South in favor of secession during the Civil War, but by 1860, Louisiana's interests were completely in step with the rest of the South's.

As the state capital, New Orleans enjoyed significant economic and political advantages that alienated it from the rest of Louisiana. After years of debate about this issue, the legislature finally resolved, in 1849, to move the capital to Baton Rouge, about 60 miles up-river, where it has remained to this day the state political seat, excepting a 20-year period during and after the Civil War.

When South Carolina seceded from the Union in December 1860 after the election of Republican Abraham Lincoln, who sought to curb the spread of slavery, it set off a flurry of similar withdrawals among other southern states, with Louisiana seceding on January 26, 1861, the sixth to do so. It then joined in the effort toward war in becoming a member of the Confederate States of America.

Although much of the fighting took place in the coastal and mid-Atlantic states, New Orleans and Louisiana were vulnerable to Union attack for exactly the same reason they were attacked by the British during the War of 1812. If the Union army could capture and control the Mississippi River, it could cut off supply lines between the Confederacy and any states west of the river, and it could enjoy a continuous supply line to the interior Midwest. Anticipating just such an attack, the Confederates built fortifications along the river south of New Orleans.

In April 1862, Captain David G. Farragut led a flotilla of Union Navy ships to the mouth of the Mississippi, where it proceeded north toward New Orleans. He made it with little trouble, shelling and ultimately disabling the Confederate fortification and sailing rather easily to capture the South's largest city. Immediately, New Orleans was named the Union capital of all the territory held by the Federal army in Louisiana, which soon included Baton Rouge, taken by Farragut's troops shortly afterward. The Confederate state government moved west about 60 miles to Opelousas and then scrambled nearly another 200 miles northwest to Shreveport, where it remained until the war's end.

A corrupt northern fat cat, Union Major General Benjamin F. Butler, assumed control of New Orleans and Union-occupied Louisiana, running things a bit like the Spanish had—he was hated by all, including more than a few Union troops, and eventually was removed from office. By the war's end, the state itself stood politically divided, with the Mississippi River valley (including New Orleans and Baton Rouge) in Union control and the western and northern regions still under Confederate control.

THE RECONSTRUCTION PERIOD

The period immediately after the Civil War, known as Reconstruction, was a grim one, and its policies, which attempted to create an integrated society of whites and free blacks, actually backfired, although it's much easier to criticize these measures with more than 145 years of hindsight.

President Lincoln signed the Proclamation of Amnesty and Reconstruction into law in December 1863, and so, even before the war had ended, a civil government was established in those parts of Louisiana held by Union troops. When the war ended, this civil government assumed control of the state. Early on, it seemed as though little had changed for blacks, even though slavery had been formally abolished by this civil government. A number of the former Confederate leaders of prewar Louisiana held office in this new civil government, which immediately passed the infamous Black Codes. These edicts placed enormous restrictions on the rights and freedoms of the state's African Americans, who were also denied the right to vote.

These conditions led to an extreme see-saw of power between the Republican and (largely ex-Confederate) Democratic sides of the government, which would bitterly divide Louisianians and precipitate tragic violence for the rest of the 19th century and well into the 20th. Blacks struck back against the government in New Orleans, first by rioting violently in 1866 until finally the federal government stepped in to impose order. These same issues, revolts, and riots flared up in other Southern states, and Congress responded by drafting the Reconstruction Acts in 1867 and 1868, which President Andrew Johnson vetoed, but which

DEAL OF THE CENTURY

By 1876, the divide between Republican and Democratic voters had narrowed, not only in Louisiana but all over the country. The U.S. presidential election at the time – with Republican Rutherford B. Hayes pitted against Democrat Samuel J. Tilden – was so controversial and hotly disputed that it makes the Bush-Gore debacle of 2000 look relatively mild.

In three states – Louisiana, South Carolina, and Florida – both parties claimed victory in the state gubernatorial elections and, thus, the electoral votes due either Hayes or Tilden. To win the presidency, Hayes needed the electoral votes of all three states.

Consequently, the lawmakers struck a rather sleazy but sly compromise. If the Democrats from all three states agreed to hand over the electoral votes to make Hayes the president, the Republicans would cede the three gubernatorial elections to the Dems. As a result, Louisiana elected Governor Francis R. T. Nicholls (incidentally, a Republican would not occupy the governor's office again until 1980). This deal effectively ended Reconstruction in Louisiana; although Hayes was a Republican, he withdrew federal troops from New Orleans in appreciation of those much-needed electoral votes.

constitution in March 1868, which wholly deferred to the sentiments of Congress: Adult males of all races were granted the right to vote—excepting fully declared ex-Confederates, who actually had their voting rights revoked—and blacks were assured full civil rights. Interestingly, when the new constitution was presented to Louisiana citizens, voters approved it overwhelmingly. The majority of those who registered to vote that year were, in fact, black; whites, discouraged and disgusted by the process, largely stayed away from the polls.

Pro-Union white Southerners (called "scalawags" by their detractors), opportunity-seeking whites from the North (called "carpetbaggers" and hated even more by their detractors), and former slaves held the clear majority of political seats in Louisiana (and many other Southern states) during the eight years of Reconstruction. Among these Republican officeholders were Louisiana's first elected black governor, P. B. S. Pinchback; the first black U.S. senator, Blanche K. Bruce; as well as black members of the U.S. Congress and black holders of just about every state political post.

In the meantime, the most ardent opponents of Reconstruction, including quite a few prominent ex-Confederate leaders, went to extreme lengths to sabotage, tear down, and otherwise render ineffective the state's Republican leadership. From this effort came the development of such antiblack groups as the Ku Klux Klan (in northern Louisiana), the Knights of the White Camellia (in southern Louisiana), and the especially terror-driven White League. These and other groups, sometimes systematically and sometimes randomly, intimidated, beat, and often lynched blacks and more than a few white sympathizers. The White League took credit for the assassination of several Republican-elected officials. About 3,500 members of the White League actually attempted to overthrow the state government during what came to be known as the Battle of Liberty Place in New Orleans in 1874. During a fierce riot, they took over the city hall, statehouse, and state arsenal until federal troops arrived to restore order.

passed with a two-thirds' majority nonetheless. And so, formally, began the period of Reconstruction in the American South.

Reconstruction dictated that the 10 ex-Confederate states that had been returned to the Union would lose their rights to self-govern, and the federal military would instead step in to govern until these states rewrote their constitutions with laws and language that Congress deemed acceptable. In effect, Louisiana was no longer a state until it submitted to the wishes of the federal government. The federally controlled state government then drafted a new

For the next four years, the troops remained in New Orleans, overseeing the city's—and the state's—order.

During the course of Reconstruction, the voting situation in Louisiana grew increasingly volatile, as whites intimidated or threatened blacks to keep them from voting and rallied voter support among anti-Republican whites. More and more officials and congressmen sympathetic to the South gained office, and they in turn pardoned and restored voting rights to many of the ex-Confederates.

White Democrats were swift in removing from blacks any rights they had gained during Reconstruction, and then some. In 1898, the state constitution was rewritten. Without expressly denying suffrage to blacks, it required poll taxes, literacy, and property ownership in order to vote, which disqualified most of the state's black voters.

While Reconstruction had a profoundly negative effect on the plight of blacks, a few strides were made during the 19th century. Many blacks ended up returning to work at a subsistence level on the farms where they once had been slaves, but some headway was made in education and social relief. The federal government established the Freedmen's Bureau, which helped to fund public schools for blacks throughout the South and issued other forms of assistance and economic relief.

The economy of the rural South faltered greatly after the Civil War, and various depressions, labor problems, and episodes of social unrest conspired to put many large and small farm owners out of business. For much of the 19th century, a large proportion of southern farms were run by sharecroppers, whereby the owners of the land—many of them northerners who had bought failed farms—gave tenants equipment and materials to farm the land and live on a fairly basic level. The workers were also entitled to a small cut of the crop yield. Farm production in Louisiana began to increase under this system, but it was still far lower than before the Civil War, and even with bounteous crops, many farmers could not make ends meet.

New Orleans, whose economy had been devastated by the war, gradually staged an economic comeback during the course of the next half century. The renewed growth in cotton and sugarcane trafficking helped to jumpstart the city's shipping and trade economy, and the mouth of the Mississippi River was deepened and made accessible to much larger ships, many of which sailed from ports much farther away than in earlier times. Railroads were built across much of Louisiana, and in 1914, the opening of the Panama Canal brought new trade to New Orleans by way of Latin America. The city's population stood at 290,000 by 1900, with the state population up to about 1.4 million.

THE 20TH CENTURY

Louisiana's economy began to diversify throughout the early 20th century, much more so than in most other agrarian southern states. Significant sources of oil were discovered in the northwestern part of the state, and natural gas sources were developed all over Louisiana. In 1938, huge oil deposits were discovered off the coast, and a massive oil-drilling industry grew up in southern Louisiana, especially in the towns southeast of Lafayette and southwest of Houma. Salt and sulfur mining also grew into a big contributor to the economy, chiefly in the southern belt extending from Lake Charles to southeast of Lafayette.

The farming economy continued to suffer through the early 1900s, however, and a severe recession took hold throughout the 1920s. The growing anguish and desperation among rural farmers helped to promote the ascendancy of one of the most notorious and controversial political figures in American history, Huey P. Long, a colorful, no-nonsense straight talker whose fervently populist manner played well with poor farmers and laborers. Long declared war on big corporations, especially Standard Oil, and took up the cause of small businesses and the common people. His actions early in his political career squarely favored those he claimed to want to help. Long was elected governor in 1928 and then U.S. senator in 1930, although he kept the governor's seat until 1932, when a handpicked successor took office. Still, he pretty much called the shots in state politics right up until his death. Long was assassinated in 1935 by Dr. Carl Weiss, the son-in-law of one of his political archenemies.

Long was instrumental in developing state public assistance and public works programs across Louisiana during the Great Depression, but he was also infamous for his nepotism and corruption, routinely buying off colleagues and tampering with the political process. The "Kingfish" ran the state like a fiefdom, and he actually ended up preventing federal funds from reaching the state during his last few years in office as a U.S. senator. Long may have died in 1935, but his brother, Earl K. Long, succeeded him as governor, as did his son, Russell Long. Until the early 1960s, anti- and pro-Long factions continued to dominate Democratic party politics and therefore, because Democrats controlled just about everything in Louisiana, state politics.

World War II boosted the Louisiana economy with its need for mineral and oil resources. It was during this period that Louisiana developed the massive refineries and chemical plants still found along much of the Mississippi River and all through the lower third of the state (especially Lake Charles and Baton Rouge), and it was also during the 1940s that the state's population demographic changed so that more Louisianians lived in cities than in rural areas.

At the same time, many rural citizens, especially blacks fed up with the state's segregation and racial mistreatment, left the South to seek factory jobs in Chicago, Oakland, and other northern and western cities. Other Louisianians moved to southeastern Texas, where jobs at refineries, factories, and shipyards in Beaumont, Orange, and Port Arthur abounded.

CONTEMPORARY TIMES

During the second half of the 20th century, New Orleans steadily blossomed into one of the nation's—and the world's—most popular

Many fishing camps were destroyed by Hurricane Katrina.

© LAURA MARTONE

vacation destinations. Mardi Gras evolved, especially during the 1960s, from a largely regional celebration into an international festival, and Jazz Fest became similarly popular. The economy came increasingly to depend on tourists, and then, throughout the 1970s and 1980s, convention business. Though Hurricane Katrina dampened both tourism and convention business for a while, the city has worked hard to regain its stature as a leading leisure and business destination.

Hurricane Katrina and Recovery

On August 29, 2005, Hurricane Katrina's storm surge caused the breach of 53 levees in New Orleans, flooding 80 percent of the city and resulting in the deaths of more than 1,500 people.

The French Quarter, CBD, Garden District, and Uptown were largely spared the worst flooding and, with significant exceptions, rebounded fairly quickly. Within two months of New Orleans's horrifying brush with the storm, most restaurants, hotels, and shops had reopened, and many residents had returned. In 2006, New Orleans enjoyed well-attended and lively Mardi Gras and Jazz Fest celebrations.

A year after Katrina, parts of the city that experienced extensive damage, such as Mid-City and City Park, had come back significantly. However, the population of New Orleans stood at about half that prior to the hurricane. Crowds, both in terms of residents and visitors, hadn't returned anywhere near pre-Katrina numbers.

The hardest-hit neighborhoods were residential areas north and east of the French Quarter and CBD, where the destruction affected residents of all income brackets, ages, races, and creeds. Visitors saw little of these neighborhoods in the past, and weren't keenly affected by their demise. Although some of these neighborhoods have been slow to recover—with blocks that are still lined with empty, decimated homes and businesses—some, such as Lakeview, are thriving once again. Arguably, nothing in the past 50 years has had more impact on the city than Hurricane Katrina, but though parts of New Orleans will take years to rebuild, the city as a whole is as vibrant as ever. While many residents vacated New Orleans never to return, an entirely new crop of residents (including many young, Bohemian types) has helped to inject some much-needed vitality back into one of the country's unique cities.

Government and Economy

GOVERNMENT

New Orleans is a predominantly Democratic, politically left-of-center city, and is generally quite progressive on social issues. Louisiana, however, tends to be more conservative regarding social issues, and the proportion of Democrats to Republicans is closer statewide.

ECONOMY

New Orleans has several important industries going for it. Even before Katrina, the city had experienced quite a few booms and busts since World War II. Today, it is the largest port in the United States, and it's second in the world only to Rotterdam in its value of foreign commerce and waterborne commerce. The state continues to rely heavily on the seafood industry as well as natural resources like salt, agricultural products, sulfur, petroleum, and natural gas, and many of the ships transporting these goods leave by way of New Orleans.

The intense trade presence has spawned an important commercial byproduct: banking. The CBD remains one of the nation's leading centers of finance, with dozens of commercial banks. During the strongest oil years of the early 1970s through the early 1980s, the city's banks and other industries raked in plenty of money financing offshore oil production. Although Katrina's devastation and BP's Gulf oil spill have put a damper on the industry's growth, oil and natural gas industries remain vital to both the city and state economies.

THE NAPOLEONIC CODE

Established in 1804 by Napoleon Bonaparte as the *code civil des Français* (French civil code), the Napoleonic Code transformed the French legal system from the confusing collection of feudal laws, aristocratic privileges, and local customs that had existed prior to the French Revolution (1789-1799) into one easy-to-understand legal code. In essence, it permitted religious freedom, allowed divorce on a more liberal basis, forbade secret laws and privileges based on birth, encouraged judges to interpret the law rather than rely on precedent, and indicated that government jobs should be granted to the most qualified candidates. The Napoleonic Code was the first modern legal code to be adopted with a Pan-European scope, ultimately influencing the law systems of many other European nations, including Italy, Spain, Portugal, Belgium, and the Netherlands.

Interestingly, the Napoleonic Code has also influenced countries and territories in Latin America and North America, from Chile to Quebec. In Louisiana, for instance, the legal system is partially based on Roman law, Spanish civil codes, and the Napoleonic Code, rather than English common law (as is the case in all other U.S. states). Louisiana's legal education, bar exam, and standards of legal practice are, therefore, significantly different from those of other states. Although it's misleading to attribute such differences exclusively to the Napoleonic Code – which was, after all, established in France in 1804, a year following the Louisiana Purchase – many New Orleanians still claim otherwise.

The truth, however, is more complicated, for New Orleans's culture and government have been shaped by a variety of sources. Just consider the fact that Creole cottages stand alongside Spanish-style buildings in the so-called French Quarter, and stranger still, Louisiana is the only state in the Union to divide its land by parishes, not counties – just one of many vestiges of the 18th-century French rule.

Agriculture

Sugar is a particularly important crop in Louisiana's history. Based chiefly in Acadiana, Louisiana's sugarcane industry extends across 23 parishes and encompasses about 420,000 acres of farmland. The earliest Louisianians engaged in this industry were Jesuit priests who planted crops along what is now Baronne Street in New Orleans's CBD. This was in 1751, nearly a half century before the city's earliest mayor, a sugar planter named Etienne de Boré, developed the first method of granulating sugar commercially at his plantation, which stood where Audubon Park is today. Many of the plantations along River Road and throughout Cajun Country were sugarcane plantations. Striking plantation homes—from relatively modest cottages to enormous Greek Revival–style mansions—dot this area and are popular day trips for visitors.

The industry has suffered setbacks in the form of floods, occasional disease epidemics, and some prolonged deep-winter freezes, but it has for the most part been a steady crop for Louisiana for the past 200 years.

Tourism

Although tourism has been an important source of revenue for New Orleans for centuries, its prominence has grown dramatically during the past 50 years. Pre-Katrina, nearly 100,000 Louisianians worked in the state's tourism industry, and travelers spent more than $5 billion during their visits to the state each year. A glamorous byproduct of tourism is the local film industry, which is still going strong since Katrina.

Beyond local attractions, including the restaurant and nightlife scenes, tourists also venture here for the region's wealth of outdoor diversions. The state's mild winters are ideal for outdoor activities, and New Orleans provides excellent opportunities for hiking, biking, camping, boating, fishing, bird-watching, and golfing. In addition, swamp tours, which constitute a profitable business, offer a popular way to explore the bayous of Greater New Orleans.

People and Culture

The strongest influence on New Orleans may arguably be French, but no one nationality represents a decisive majority here. The city's distinctive cuisine and music, the pervasive infatuation with things carnal and pleasurable, the Gothic literary traditions, and the long-standing practice of voodoo-tinged Catholicism are legacies contributed not only by the French and Spanish settlers, but by the vast numbers of Acadian refugees ("Cajuns"), slaves brought from West Africa, American frontier settlers and traders, German farmers, Irish and Italian laborers, Slavs, Creole refugees from Haiti, and Vietnamese. These people haven't just left their mark on a particular neighborhood during a specific period; they've migrated to New Orleans in significant enough numbers to have a pervasive and lasting influence. The cultural gumbo has resulted in some rather odd traditions that last to this day. Many street and neighborhood names are pronounced differently in New Orleans than anywhere else in the world, from Conti (KON-tie) and Cadiz (KAY-diz) Streets to the Michoud (MEE-shoh) neighborhood. Sometimes, French and Spanish names are pronounced roughly as the French and Spanish would pronounce them; sometimes, they're pronounced as virtually nobody else on the planet would say them.

Given the ethnic diversity of southern Louisiana, it's no surprise that residents tend to practice a variety of religions, or none at all. New Orleans was founded by Catholics, as evidenced by historic landmarks like the St. Louis Cathedral, and influenced by cultural traditions such as Mardi Gras. Nevertheless, you'll spot a wide array of religious institutions here,

The St. Louis Cathedral looms above Jackson Square.

© LAURA MARTONE

from Touro Synagogue to the First Unitarian Universalist Church of New Orleans.

The cuisine unique to New Orleans also borrows widely from myriad cultures. Ingredients and dishes like filé (a powder of dried sassafras leaves popularized by the Choctaw), jambalaya (a rice casserole very similar to Spanish paella), okra (a podlike vegetable introduced by African slaves), and crawfish (a small freshwater crustacean that's prevalent in local waters) are as common in New Orleans's restaurants as hamburgers and apple pie.

The Arts

While New Orleans is known for its fine art galleries and historical architecture, and has inspired countless writers, artists, and filmmakers over the decades, its biggest artistic claim to fame is indeed its music. This city is one of the world's most dynamic live-music scenes. Jazz was invented here, a conglomeration of mostly African-American traditions that has rural counterparts elsewhere in southern Louisiana in the form of zydeco and Cajun music. There are only a few large-scale venues for formal concerts; in fact, many big-name musicians favor comparatively smaller stages when in town. New Orleanians are loyal, knowledgeable, and excited about music, and performers appreciate the enthusiasm, relishing the chance to play a club that's small enough to encourage a close connection between the musicians and the fans. It takes almost no planning and very little effort to find a place to catch a jamming live show in New Orleans, even on a Monday

or Tuesday night. Just check the listings in the *Gambit* or *The Times-Picayune,* or simply stroll through the French Quarter or Faubourg Marigny. Dozens of clubs bellow music from their doors every night of the week, and many of these places rarely charge a cover, although they will typically have a one- or two-drink minimum.

JAZZ AND BLUES

Jazz wasn't invented in one definitive instant—it evolved over perhaps 20 or 30 years during the early part of the 20th century and in several parts of New Orleans's African American community. The state has produced several jazz luminaries, among them Jelly Roll Morton, Doc Souchon, Sidney Bechet, King Oliver, and crooner Harry Connick Jr.

Jazz music typically uses both individual and collective improvisation, syncopation, and distinctive vocal effects, and it has its origins in

old-time jazz musicians on Royal Street

© DANIEL MARTONE

European, African, and Caribbean traditional music. Commonly, you'll hear blues vocalizing sung to jazz instrumental accompaniment. Many people trace jazz to a popular cornet player named Buddy Bolden, who performed regularly in New Orleans from the mid-1890s until about 1910. Through the 1910s and '20s, ragtime-style jazz and other music forms, with a spontaneous, upbeat tempo, began to attract a following, albeit an underground one, in New Orleans.

This thoroughly modern and iconoclastic style of music was not, initially, well received by the mainstream. In fact, hard as it is to believe now, it was shunned by organizers of Mardi Gras parades for years. During the early years, many people considered this musical style to be scandalous and impudent—they criticized it at least as harshly as early critics of rock-and-roll denounced that music. Jazz was seen as a crude bastardization of more acceptable musical styles. In 1901, the American Federation of Music spoke of efforts to "suppress and discourage the playing and publishing of such musical trash as ragtime"; the *Musical Courier* in 1899 referred to a "wave of vulgar, filthy, and suggestive music which has inundated the land." But through time, jazz would win the hearts of even the harshest naysayers, and today, there's really no style of music for which the city is better regarded.

Blues music has its origins upriver a bit from New Orleans, about 300 miles north in the fruitful delta farming regions of northwestern Mississippi, especially the towns near Clarkdale. It's said that blues derives from the field hollers of cane and cotton workers in these parts. Eventually, the soulful vocals were joined with guitars, drums, and horns to become the modern form of blues celebrated today all through the South and especially in Louisiana. Huddie "Leadbelly" Ledbetter, who wrote such classics as "Good Night, Irene" and "Midnight Special," grew up in Shreveport, in the northwestern corner of the state, and is often credited as the father of blues music.

Blues, along with New Orleans jazz, melded together in the 1950s to influence a new genre:

rhythm and blues, or R&B. It is a distinctly commercial genre that was begun with the express intent of getting airplay on the radio and acclaim for its stars through record sales, and to that end, it has always incorporated the catchiest and most accessible elements of the genres from which it borrows.

All around the state—though especially in Baton Rouge and New Orleans—clubs present live blues performers, and this often sorrowful, sometimes joyous, style of music also influences much of the jazz, rock, country-western, and gospel music heard elsewhere in the state.

CAJUN AND ZYDECO

Cajun and zydeco are terms often confused with one another or used to describe the same music, but they have distinct origins and subtle but important differences. Both have their origins in southwestern Louisiana's Cajun Country, and they have each enjoyed a huge surge in worldwide popularity since the 1980s. They're also sometimes credited with being the progenitors of modern country-and-western music, which is a relatively new phenomenon when compared with Cajun and zydeco.

Cajun music derives, as one would guess, from the French culture of Cajun settlers who came to southwestern Louisiana primarily during the 18th and early 19th centuries—it's nearly always sung in French—but this upbeat, danceable musical form also has German, Anglo American, and African influences. Originally, Cajun tunes revolved around fiddles, but the influence of German settlers led to the use of push-button accordions during the late 1800s, and now, both these instruments are the keystones of any good Cajun band. Nowadays, Cajun bands typically include a bass and drums. A *tit fer* is another instrument common to the genre— this iron triangle struck with a spike is used to add rhythm.

When live Cajun is performed, you'll generally see folks dancing either waltzes or two-steps. Like many of the country tunes that have been inspired by it, Cajun music often tells the tale of something tragic or unhappy, such as failed romances, early deaths, or other hardships common to life among the Acadian immigrants of early southern Louisiana.

But many songs are funny and self-effacing, playing on an often unfortunate circumstance for laughs. Many of today's Cajun tunes have their origins in the Acadian folk music of Canada and also in the traditional fiddling tunes of France. It is truly folk music, and the early traditions were never written down but passed along from generation to generation, just as many old Cajun tales were. The earliest recordings of Cajun music date to the late 1920s. Top venues for Cajun tunes today include Prejean's Restaurant in Lafayette and Mulate's in New Orleans.

One of the most famous and distinguished Cajun-Western bands was the Hackberry Ramblers, whose albums were nominated for Grammies. Back in 1933, fiddler Luderin Darbone and accordionist Edwin Duhon formed the band, mixing the toe-tapping sounds of traditional Cajun music with western swing and folky hillbilly influences. They used to power the electric sound system at local dance halls by hooking up to Darbone's Model-T Ford. They released their first album with RCA Bluebird in 1935, and they continued to perform and record for decades. In the early 1980s, a renewed interest in Cajun music was born, and the Ramblers, based in Lake Charles, enjoyed a popular resurgence. The music now tends toward a faster-paced, rollicking honky-tonk vibe. In 2003, the Ramblers were filmed performing at Eunice's weekly Rendezvous des Cajuns on NBC's *Today* show to celebrate the band's 70th anniversary. Leading the performance were fiddler Darbone and accordionist Duhon, at the time still both going strong at ages 90 and 92 respectively. Sadly, both have since passed away, though their music lives on.

While Cajun is a predominantly Anglo musical form, its cousin zydeco has its roots with the African American sharecroppers and farmers of the same region. The two musical styles clearly influenced each other, with zydeco evolving from a tradition called "La La," a

term for an early style of music played among African Americans in homes and at some clubs that used only an accordion and a washboard for instruments. Zydeco is much more closely linked to blues and R&B music. It's a younger musical genre than Cajun; it uses either an accordion or push-button piano and also incorporates a *frottoir* (literally "rub board," or washboard), as opposed to the *tit fer* (triangle) used in Cajun music.

Many of the Creole African Americans in southern Louisiana came from the Caribbean, which also helped to shape this musical style. In Afro-Caribbean culture, there's a syncopated style of a cappella music called *juré* that is sometimes cited as zydeco's true predecessor.

In the middle of the 20th century, zydeco came to be influenced by the burgeoning R&B and blues music of the South, and it continues to evolve and change as zydeco musicians borrow from rock, jazz, soul, and even rap and hip-hop. Clifton Chenier, of Opelousas, is often considered the father of modern zydeco—he toured throughout the United States and Europe in the 1960s, helping to spread the popularity of this inimitable style.

The name zydeco is said to derive from the French phrase, *les haricots sont pas salés,* meaning "the snapbeans are not salty." The first two words, *les haricots,* are pronounced lay-ZAH-ree-coh, which has been shortened through the years to zydeco, pronounced ZAHy-di-koh. The phrase in question referred to a period of such financial hardship that one could not afford to so much as season basic foods—and so, as with Cajun music, zydeco often touches on themes of struggling to persevere and make do during difficult times.

Both zydeco and Cajun music are best appreciated live, ideally someplace where you can get out on the dance floor and cut loose, or at the very least—if you're shy—tap your toes a bit. Both forms go hand-and-hand with eating, and you'll find that many of the best Cajun and soul restaurants of southern Louisiana, especially near Lafayette, have live zydeco and Cajun music many nights of the week. The little town of Eunice, about 45 miles northwest of

Lafayette, is one of the best places to catch live performances—here the Liberty Center for the Performing Arts hosts live Cajun and zydeco music on Saturday evenings.

ROCK AND SOUL

Rock music was a natural outgrowth of blues, gospel, and country-western traditions, and some say it was born in New Orleans, where, in the late 1940s, a singer named Roy Brown sang a tune called "Good Rockin' Tonight," the first song that used "rock" as a term for this faster-paced, danceable variation on the blues. A book by music historian Robert Palmer called *Memphis Rock and New Orleans Roll* traces the development of rock music to these two cities along the Mississippi.

New Orleans's jazz traditions contributed the sassy roll to rock music, while Memphis contributed the harder-edged blues born in the Mississippi Delta towns south of the city. The area between the two cities was rich with Pentecostal gospel sounds, which also influenced the development, ironically, of that devil music, rock-and-roll. New Orleans's brand of rock music is especially influenced by piano playing, keyboards, and even accordions, which suggests a link between rock and zydeco.

Maybe the most famous Louisiana rock legend is Fats Domino, who emerged from the New Orleans club scene and made famous the song "Walkin' to New Orleans." Local session musicians have long attracted the attention of big-city record producers, who sent stars such as Little Richard to the Big Easy to make albums. Other rock, pop, and soul greats from the New Orleans area include Allen Toussaint, Percy Mayfield, the Dixie Cups, Ernie K-Doe, Irma Thomas, the Neville Brothers, Professor Longhair, Frankie Ford, Lee Dorsey, and Dr. John, many of whom recorded at the Cosimo Matassa music studio. More recently, New Orleans's music scene spawned the alternative pop-rock band Better Than Ezra, as well as the gangsta sounds of Master P and his empire of rappers, including his young son, Lil' Romeo (born in 1989).

Rock has been shaken up a bit with Louisiana influences, such as country and bluegrass, to form rockabilly music, made famous by the likes of Jimmy Clanton, Joe Clay, Floyd Kramer, Jerry Lee Lewis, Jim Reeves, Farron Young, Slim Whitman, and Hank Williams Sr. The term bandied about today for Cajun- and zydeco-tinged rock music is "swamp pop," and you'll hear it in the more current clubs all throughout Cajun Country.

COUNTRY AND BLUEGRASS

Country music, and its close cousin bluegrass (or perhaps child is a better term, since this style was born out of old-time country music traditions), share certain similarities with Cajun and even zydeco, but their routes are distinctly Anglo American (specifically Scots-Irish) rather than French, German, or African American. Many of the first Anglo settlers in Louisiana, who began arriving in the early 1800s, hailed from Kentucky and neighboring states and brought with them traditions of fiddling and ballad-singing.

Early barn dances and jamborees gave country music a widespread following, and the *Louisiana Hayride,* broadcast out of Shreveport's Municipal Auditorium on KWKH, popularized the genre in the 1940s and '50s, introducing Americans to Hank Williams, Johnny Horton, Johnny Cash, and Elvis Presley. The rocking honky-tonk style of country music, though not unique to Louisiana, thrives throughout the state. Western swing, which bands like the Hackberry Ramblers once performed, mixes country music with Cajun, blues, jazz, and other genres in a distinctly Louisiana way.

Northern Louisiana has especially strong country and bluegrass traditions, but you can find live performances at venues in New Orleans, as well as in the Florida Parishes. Jerry Lee Lewis was born in Ferriday, and in Abita Springs, *The Abita Springs Opry* is an annual, six-concert series of bluegrass, country, and other "roots" music. Former governor Jimmie Davis was one of the state's earliest country recording stars; his most famous song was "You Are My Sunshine," which became the official state song of Louisiana in 1977. Current country stars with Louisiana roots include Sammy Kershaw, Tim McGraw, and Michael Rhodes.

GOSPEL

Gospel has deep roots in Louisiana, although it tends to be more often performed in the northern half of the state. Black gospel music, which has been celebrated in the state for many years, has its origins with the African slaves who first sang biblical songs and hymns known as "spirituals." Generally, these songs, which are performed in churches today, are performed a cappella, but other gospel music is accompanied by instruments and often has jazz, bluegrass, soul, and blues overtones. You can find performances not only at churches but at festivals and conventions. Some of the bigger music clubs in New Orleans, notably the House of Blues, feature gospel choirs from time to time.

CLASSICAL AND OPERA

Classical music and opera have been little influenced by Louisiana's other more homegrown musical forms, but they've been appreciated in this region since the late 18th century, when the first opera ever performed in the United States made its debut in New Orleans. An early American classical composer, Louis Moreau Gottschalk, was born in New Orleans, and he incorporated African and Caribbean themes in his music. Classical concerts are held in just about every city in the state, and the Louisiana Sinfonietta, based in Baton Rouge and led by acclaimed composer Dino Constantinides, is especially well regarded. Notable Louisianians who have earned acclaim in this genre include Shirley Verrett, a New Orleans–born opera singer who passed away in 2010, and Van Cliburn, a virtuoso pianist from Shreveport.

ESSENTIALS

Getting There

New Orleans's airport is well served by most major airlines and has direct flights to many of the nation's largest cities. It's conveniently located in a nearby suburb, usually not terribly expensive, and pleasant to fly into and out of, so if you're coming for a short period or from a long distance, flying here makes plenty of sense. The city also has direct Amtrak train service and Greyhound bus service from many big cities, but these modes of transport are often quite time-consuming and, especially in the case of trains, not always less expensive than flying. Some travelers arrive here via cruise ship and many come by car—the major east–west I-10 runs directly through New Orleans, less than a half mile from the French Quarter.

BY AIR

Louis Armstrong New Orleans International Airport (900 Airline Dr., Kenner, 504/303-7500, www.flymsy.com), 15 miles west of downtown New Orleans via I-10, is a massive facility that accommodates the entire Gulf South with service on several airlines. Despite the decreased capacity immediately following Hurricane Katrina, it's easy to find direct flights from most major U.S. cities: Dallas, Houston, Atlanta, Orlando, Miami, Charlotte, Newark, New York,

© JEFF ANDING

Chicago, Minneapolis, Denver, Las Vegas, Reno, and San Francisco.

Commercial air service is also available to Baton Rouge, Lafayette, and Lake Charles. Generally, it's more expensive to fly to one of the smaller regional airports than to New Orleans, especially when factoring in the cost of driving. Situated roughly eight miles north of downtown Baton Rouge via I-110, **Baton Rouge Metropolitan Airport** (9430 Jackie Cochran Dr., 225/355-0333, www.flybtr.com) is served by American Airlines, Continental Airlines, Delta Air Lines, and US Airways, with frequent direct flights to and from Atlanta, Dallas, Houston, and Memphis. **Lafayette Regional Airport** (200 Terminal Dr., 337/266-4400, www.lftairport.com) is three miles southeast of downtown Lafayette via U.S. 90. It is served by American Eagle, the Delta Connection, and Continental Express, with direct flights to and from Atlanta, Dallas, Houston, and Memphis. **Lake Charles Regional Airport** (500 Airport Blvd., 337/477-6051, www.flylakecharles.com) is nine miles south of downtown Lake Charles via LA-385. You can take direct flights to and from Houston, courtesy of Continental Airlines, and Dallas, courtesy of American Airlines. If you choose to fly into one of these three regional airports, you'll have to rent a car to reach New Orleans; Avis, Budget, Hertz, National, and Enterprise serve all three locales.

Airport Transportation

Depending on traffic, the 15-mile trip from the airport to the French Quarter can take 25–35 minutes by car. A **taxi** from the airport to the Central Business District (CBD) usually costs $33 for one or two passengers and $14 per person for three or more passengers. Pickup occurs on the airport's lower level, just outside the baggage claim area. Just be advised that extra baggage might require an additional charge; the good news, though, is that credit cards are typically accepted.

If you'd prefer to travel in style, consider **Airport Limousine** (504/305-2450 or 866/739-5466, www.airportlimousineneworleans.com), the airport's official limo service, which has handy kiosks in the baggage claim area. The number of passengers will determine the type of vehicle selected: sedans for up to three passengers, SUVs for up to five, and limos for six or more. For one-way trips to the French Quarter and CBD, rates start at $58 for one or two passengers; a nominal fuel charge is generally applied to all rides.

To save a little money, opt for the **Airport Shuttle** (504/522-3500 or 866/596-2699, www.airportshuttleneworleans.com, $20 adult one-way, $38 adult round-trip, children under 6 free), which offers shared-ride service to hotels in the French Quarter, the CBD, and Uptown as well as the Ernest N. Morial Convention Center (www.mccno.com). From the upper level of the airport, you can also hop aboard the **E-2 Airport Bus** (504/818-1077 or 504/364-3450, www.jeffersontransit.org, $2 pp). On weekdays, the bus takes about 35 minutes to reach the CBD; on weekends, it only travels to Mid-City and you'll have to rely on an RTA bus route to reach destinations in Uptown or downtown New Orleans.

If you're headed north of New Orleans, there are two helpful services at the airport. The **Northshore Airport Express** (985/386-3861, www.nsairportexpress.com) offers shuttle service to and from Slidell, Covington, Hammond, and other communities on the Northshore; advance reservations are required. The **Tiger Airport Shuttle** (225/333-8167, www.tigerairportshuttle.com) provides transportation to and from Baton Rouge. Though fares vary for both, it's often more economical to share such lengthy rides with other passengers.

BY TRAIN

Amtrak (800/872-7245, www.amtrak.com) operates three rail routes across southern Louisiana, all of which include stops at the New Orleans Amtrak Station (1001 Loyola Ave., daily 5 A.M.–10 P.M.). Amtrak offers a number of promotions and special rail passes (which allow you to overnight in U.S. cities served by Amtrak), making this a practical way to visit several places on one pass. The USA Rail Passes are available in three travel durations: 15 days/8 rail segments ($429 adult, $214.50 child 2–15), 30 days/12 rail segments ($649 adult, $324.50 child 2–15), and 45 days/18 rail segments ($829 adult, $414.50 child 2–15). All passes allow you to hop between routes during your trip. Just be advised that, even with a pass, you'll still need to reserve a ticket for each train you plan to board. There are rental car agencies at Amtrak stations in most big cities.

These rail routes serve New Orleans:

- City of New Orleans runs daily from Chicago to New Orleans, with major stops in Memphis, Jackson, and Hammond (19 hours).
- Crescent runs daily between New York City and New Orleans, with major stops in Philadelphia, Baltimore, Washington D.C., Charlotte, Atlanta, Birmingham, and Slidell (30 hours).
- Sunset Limited, an east–west train, runs from Los Angeles to New Orleans three times weekly, with major stops in Tucson, El Paso, San Antonio, Houston, Lake Charles, and Lafayette (48 hours).

BY BUS

Greyhound (800/231-2222, www.greyhound.com) is the definitive bus provider for New Orleans, with frequent and flexible service throughout the country. Buses depart daily from the New Orleans Greyhound Station (1001 Loyola Ave., 504/525-6075, daily 5:15–10:30 A.M., 11:30 A.M.–1 P.M., 2:30–9:30 P.M.) with multiple stops throughout Louisiana to many neighboring states. Travel times can be significantly longer than by train (although not always), but fares are generally much cheaper.

If you're planning a lengthy trip, consider Greyhound's **Discovery Pass,** which you can buy in increments of 7–60 days, allowing unlimited stopovers throughout the duration of the pass. Different types and prices of passes are available to U.S., Canadian, and international travelers. As with Amtrak's USA Rail Passes, a ticket is required for each bus trip taken with the Discovery Pass.

BY CAR

The New Orleans metro area is about 20 miles from west to east and 10 miles from north to south. The I-10 runs directly through New Orleans and provides the closest access to the French Quarter. West of the Quarter, the I-10 connects with the Pontchartrain Expressway (U.S. 90) in the CBD. The Pontchartrain Expressway splits west through Uptown; south alongside the Garden District, crossing the Mississippi River; and north to Mid-City and I-610. Though traffic can be difficult in this city, you can usually get from one end of New Orleans to the other in about 30–40 minutes.

If you plan to stay in New Orleans the entire time you're visiting this region, then you won't need a car. If, however, you're planning one or two days outside the city, rent a car downtown for a short term. A car may also be handier than public transportation for exploring Uptown and Mid-City. Consult the **Louisiana Department of Transportation & Development** (225/379-1100, www.dotd.state.la.us) for maps, publications, and extensive information about public transportation, highway safety, traveler resources, road conditions, and upcoming projects.

Car Rental

Just about all the major car-rental agencies are represented at Louis Armstrong New Orleans International Airport (900 Airline Dr., Kenner, 504/303-7500, www.flymsy.com): **Advantage** (800/777-5500, www.advantage.com), **Alamo** (800/462-5266, www.alamo.com), **Avis** (800/331-1212, www.avis.com), **Budget** (800/527-0700, www.budget.com), **Dollar** (800/800-4000, www.dollar.com), **Enterprise** (800/736-8222, www.enterprise.com), **Hertz** (800/654-3131, www.hertz.com), **National** (800/227-7368, www.nationalcar.com), and **Thrifty** (800/847-4389, www.thrifty.com). In New Orleans, rates for car rentals typically start at $30 daily for economy cars but can easily rise at busy times, such as during Mardi Gras or when conventions are in town. Weekly rates begin at $180 for an economy car and $200 for a midsize car. While most car-rental agencies will only rent to properly licensed drivers who are at least 25 years old, some will rent to customers between the ages of 21 and 24, as long as they have a valid credit card and driver's license and are willing to pay a daily surcharge of $27.

Getting Around

New Orleanians rarely refer to compass directions when discussing how to navigate the city. The city is bound on one side by the highly irregular Mississippi River, which forms the western, southern, or eastern border; main roads tend to run parallel or perpendicular to the river. Since the river's direction changes, this means that New Orleans's street grid also changes its axis in different places. As a result, most residents employ the terms "lakeside" (meaning north toward Lake Pontchartrain) and "riverside" (meaning south toward the Mississippi) when referring to streets perpendicular to the river. The terms "upriver" or "uptown" refer to westerly directions; the terms "downriver" or "downtown" are used for easterly directions. For example, Canal Street, which tourists generally consider a north–south thoroughfare, actually runs in a southeasterly direction toward the river. If you're still confused, be sure to have a city map with you at all times, as this is one place where it is absolutely indispensable—whether you're walking, driving, taking public transportation, or even using cabs. New Orleans is very much a collection of neighborhoods, and residents refer to neighborhood names almost as much as specific streets.

PUBLIC TRANSPORTATION

New Orleans is served by an extensive network of buses and streetcars, operated by the **New Orleans Regional Transit Authority** (RTA, 504/248-3900, www.norta.com). The standard fare is $1.25 per person ($0.40 seniors, children under 3 free) plus $0.25 per transfer; express buses cost $1.50 per person. You must pay with exact change by depositing coins or inserting $1 bills into the fare box at the front of the bus or streetcar. Food, beverages,

smoking, and stereos are not permitted on buses and streetcars.

The handy **Jazzy Pass,** a magnetized card presented upon boarding the bus or streetcar, allows unlimited rides during the active period; it's available in 1-day ($3), 3-day ($9), or 31-day ($55) increments. The 1-day pass can be purchased on the bus or streetcar, though only cash is accepted. Other passes are available from various hotels, banks, and retailers, such as Walgreens.

Bus

Although Hurricane Katrina initially affected many bus routes, service is now operational to the French Quarter, the Faubourg Marigny, the CBD, Uptown, Mid-City, and other parts of Greater New Orleans. All RTA buses can accommodate people with disabilities. The one-way fare is $1.25 (plus $0.25 per transfer) and passengers must pay with either exact change (coins or $1 bills) or the Jazzy Pass.

Tourists often utilize the **Magazine line** (11), which runs from Canal Street in the CBD through the Garden District and Uptown, along a six-mile stretch of galleries, shops, and restaurants, before ending at Audubon Park. Another important route is the **Jackson-Esplanade line** (91), which runs from Rousseau Street in the Garden District, through the CBD, along the north edge of the French Quarter, up Esplanade Avenue, and past City Park, ending at the Greenwood Cemetery. For a complete map of all bus lines, plus individual maps and schedules, visit the RTA website (www.norta.com).

Streetcar

The RTA also operates New Orleans's iconic

streetcars. The one-way fare is $1.25 per person (plus $0.25 per transfer), and passengers must pay with either exact change (coins or $1 bills) or the Jazzy Pass.

The famous **St. Charles streetcar** line, which operates 24 hours daily, runs along St. Charles and South Carrollton Avenues, from Canal Street to Claiborne Avenue; a one-way trip lasts about 45 minutes. Given their historic status, the St. Charles streetcars are exempt from ADA (the Americans with Disabilities Act) compliance, so unfortunately passengers with disabilities may have trouble boarding them. The St. Charles line has been in operation since 1835, when it began as the main railroad line connecting the city of New Orleans with the resort community of Carrollton, now part of the city; the olive-green cars date to the 1920s, when they were built by the Perley Thomas Company. Today, the line is a wonderful, scenic, and atmospheric way to travel between the CBD and Uptown.

The **Canal Street streetcar** line extends from Canal Street to Mid-City before splitting into two branches. The "Cemeteries" branch (daily 5 A.M.–3 A.M.) runs from the foot of Canal Street, not far from the ferry terminal for Algiers Point, all the way up to the historic cemeteries along City Park Avenue. The "City Park/Museum" branch (daily 7 A.M.–2 A.M.) takes North Carrollton Avenue to Esplanade Avenue, right beside City Park and the New Orleans Museum of Art. A one-way trip along either branch lasts about 30 minutes.

The **Riverfront streetcar** line (daily 7 A.M.–10:30 P.M.) uses newer streetcars and runs a short but scenic 1.8-mile route along the Mississippi River, from the French Quarter to the CBD. These modern red streetcars were built by New Orleans metal- and woodworkers; a one-way ride lasts about 15 minutes. For maps and schedules of all three streetcar lines, visit the RTA website (www.norta.com).

Ferry

The **Algiers/Canal Street ferry** (504/250-9110, www.friendsoftheferry.org, daily 6 A.M.–12:15 A.M.) provides ferry service across the Mississippi River, from the foot of Canal Street in the CBD to Algiers Point. Though free for pedestrians, the five-minute service costs $1 per car on the Algiers side; the boat departs every 30 minutes on either shore. The **Gretna/Canal Street ferry** (Mon.–Thurs. 6:30 A.M.–5:30 P.M., Fri. 6:30 A.M.–11:30 P.M., Sat. 12:30–11:30 P.M., Sun. 10:30 A.M.–5:30 P.M.) offers hourly service between the foot of Canal Street and the West Bank community of Gretna; the trip usually lasts 15–20 minutes and costs $1 per car on the Gretna side, but is free for pedestrians. Contact the **Crescent City Connection Police** (504/376-8180) for up-to-the-minute information regarding breakdowns.

TAXIS AND PEDICABS

Taxis are *highly* recommended over public transportation at night, especially when traveling solo. This is the sort of city where it's easy to lose track of time, particularly if you're bar-hopping, so it's always a smart idea to have the name and number of at least a couple of cab companies with you at all times. Taxi rates within the city typically start at $3.50 per ride, plus $2 per mile thereafter; there's also a charge of $1 for each additional passenger. You will often find taxis waiting at major intersections near Bourbon Street and other nighttime hot spots in the Quarter. Be sure to use taxis operated by licensed and established cab companies, such as **Checker Yellow Cabs** (504/943-2411), **New Orleans Carriage Cab** (504/207-7777, www.neworleanscarriagecab.com), **United Cabs** (504/522-9771 or 504/524-9606, www.unitedcabs.com), and **White Fleet Cab and Elk's Elite Taxi** (504/822-3800). Taxi rates are often higher during peak times, such as Mardi Gras and Jazz Fest; expect to pay $5 per person or the meter rate, whichever is greater.

As an alternative to taxis, hop aboard one of the relatively new pedicabs often seen trolling the streets of the French Quarter. Operated by knowledgeable guides and equipped with safety belts, headlights, and flashing taillights, these ecofriendly, person-powered vehicles can accommodate up to three or four passengers, making them ideal for getting you and a couple friends back to your home or hotel after a long night of partying in the Quarter. Currently, there are two pedicab companies in the city: **Bike Taxi Unlimited** (504/891-3441, www.neworleansbiketaxi.com), which serves the French Quarter, the Faubourg Marigny, the CBD, the Arts District, and Uptown; and **NOLA Pedicabs** (504/274-1300, www.nolapedicabs.com), which mainly serves the Quarter, the CBD, and the Arts District. Standard fares are $5 per passenger for the first six blocks, after which each passenger will be charged $1 per city block. During special events, such as Mardi Gras, expect to pay $50 per half hour and $100 hourly.

DRIVING

When driving in New Orleans, be forewarned that many streets are one-way and riddled with potholes, street parking is scarce, and garage and hotel parking is expensive. On the other hand, the main neighborhoods are easily walkable, taxis are easy to find, and public transportation is decent, especially from the French Quarter to Uptown and Mid-City, so having a car isn't necessary. Given the city's compact size many travelers rely on motorcycles and bikes, which are often much easier to park on the street. If you do bring or rent a car to explore the Greater New Orleans area, note that most city roads have speed limits of 25–35 mph; two-lane state and U.S. highways generally have speed limits of 55 mph along narrow rural stretches and 70 mph in wider spots. Roads in rural areas are sometimes very heavily patrolled by police. They are also highly unsafe to speed on—they're bumpy and narrow, with virtually no shoulders. As in other parts of the country, it's illegal to drive without a seatbelt or while intoxicated.

Parking

Given New Orleans's high crime rate, parking here is a gamble—if parking on the street or in an unattended lot, keep as few of your belongings in your car as possible. For a bit more security, you can pay $15–50 nightly to park

Parking lots are ubiquitous throughout downtown New Orleans.

© DANIEL MARTONE

your car at a hotel or commercial lot. Relying on hourly rates can be considerably more expensive, though many downtown businesses and stores offer free or discounted parking with minimum purchase and validated parking tickets. Even with secured parking areas, refrain from leaving valuables in plain sight.

Even beyond security concerns, finding street parking in the French Quarter, the CBD, and other tourist areas can be extremely difficult. The Quarter is especially tough because most blocks are restricted for residents with permits. In such cases, you can usually park for no more than two hours during the restricted time period. Many hotel properties in the Quarter have no dedicated parking facilities. You'll find parking meters throughout the French Quarter and CBD—both the old-fashioned, coin-operated meters as well as new-fangled ones that accept dollar bills and credit cards and offer a printed receipt to place on your dashboard. The meters are typically enforced Monday–Saturday 8 A.M.–6 P.M.; while they're not usually enforced on Sundays or holidays, always read the meters before parking. If you're staying beyond the downtown area, it might be better to park in the Uptown or Mid-City neighborhoods and use public transportation to visit the French Quarter and CBD.

If you do decide to park on the street, be sure to read the parking signs carefully; the rules can differ from neighborhood to neighborhood, and some violations can be extremely costly—from $20 for an expired meter to $200 for parking on a French Quarter sidewalk. In general, avoid parking:

- over 18 inches from the curb
- at bagged or broken meters
- across a driveway or fire lane
- on sidewalks or neutral grounds
- on a narrow street without allowing 10 feet of unobstructed roadway
- on the street for more than 24 consecutive hours
- in handicapped spaces
- in loading, service, bus, and taxi zones
- within 15 feet of fire hydrants
- within 20 feet of corners and crosswalks
- within 50 feet of railroad crossings
- during rush hours (Mon.–Fri. 7–9 A.M. and 4–6 P.M.) on major streets
- on street-cleaning days (usually Tues. and Thurs. 8 A.M.–noon)
- on a parade route within two hours of a parade

Additionally, avoid parking vehicles longer than 22 feet overnight in the CBD and having three or more unpaid parking violations. If your car is towed away, contact the **Claiborne Auto Pound** (504/565-7450 or 504/565-7451). For general questions about parking in New Orleans, consult the city's **Parking Division** (504/658-8200).

Conduct and Customs

SOUTHERN ETIQUETTE

New Orleans has always been a big city with small-town sensibilities, and many New Orleanians adhere to the same temperament and traditions of other Southern states; you'll often hear "please," "thank you," "you're welcome," "yes, ma'am," and "no, sir" while visiting New Orleans. It's also common for restaurant staff to call patrons "sweetie" or "darling." Residents appreciate qualities like modesty, courtesy, chivalry, patience, and friendliness, and while having a good time is encouraged in the Big Easy, being loud, uncouth, and disrespectful is rarely tolerated in most places. Although some old-fashioned manners have gone by the wayside in modern-day New Orleans, others are still common: always open doors for others, smile at and make eye contact with strangers, use proper table manners, apologize when you're at fault, and

A NATIVE'S GUIDE TO NEW ORLEANS

New Orleanians have their own special way of saying things, including local street names, neighborhoods, and suburbs. In many cases, there are two or more commonly accepted (though often hotly debated) ways to pronounce the same word, especially considering one's accent. If you hope to sound like a local, though, here's a guide to the more puzzling pronunciations.

STREETS AND NEIGHBORHOODS
- Burgundy (street): bur-GUN-dee
- Cadiz (street): KAY-diz
- Calliope (street): KALE-ee-ope
- Carondelet (street): kare-OHN-deh-LET
- Chalmette (suburb): SHALL-mett
- Chartres (street): CHAR-ters
- Clio (street): KLYE-o
- Conti (street): KON-tie
- Decatur (street): de-KAY-dur
- Iberville (street): IBB-bur-ville
- Loyola (street/school): lye-O-luh
- Marigny (street/neighborhood): MAH-rah-nee
- Melpomene (street): MEL-po-MEEN
- Metairie (suburb): MED-uh-ree
- Michoud (street/neighborhood): MEE-shoh
- Milan (street): MYE-lan
- Pontchartrain (street/lake): PON-chuh-train
- Prytania (street/theater): prih-TAN-ya
- Socrates (street): SO-krates
- Tchoupitoulas (street): chop-ah-TOO-lehs
- Terpsichore (street): TERP-sih-kore
- Toulouse (street): tuh-LOOS
- Tulane (street/school): TOO-lane
- Vieux Carré (neighborhood): VOO kah-RAY

GREATER NEW ORLEANS
New Orleans (noo OHR-lins or noo OHR-lee-ahns) isn't the only place in Louisiana (le-WEE-zee-ann-ah or LOO-zee-ann-ah) with some oddly sounding locales. If you're planning to explore other parts of the state,

it might help to be able to pronounce where you're going.

Towns and Parishes
- Amite: AYE-meet
- Basile: bah-ZEEL
- Baton Rouge: BAT-ten ROOZH
- Bossier City: BOH-zher SIT-ee
- Breaux Bridge: BROH bridge
- Calcasieu: KAL-kuh-shoo
- Carencro: KARE-en-krow
- Cloutierville: KLOO-chee-vill
- Erath: EEH-rath
- Grand Coteau: GRAND kuh-TOE
- Houma: HOAM-uh
- Iowa: EEH-o-way
- Jeanerette: JENN-urh-ette
- Lafayette: LAFF-ee-ette
- Lafourche: la-FOOSH
- Mamou: MAH-moo
- Monroe: MUN-roe
- Natchitoches: NACK-ih-tish
- Opelousas: AH-puh-loo-suss
- Plaquemines: PLACK-ih-mens
- Ponchatoula: PON-chuh-tool-uh
- Port Barre: PORT BAR-eeh
- Shreveport: SHREEV-port
- Tangipahoa: TAN-jah-puh-ho
- Thibodaux: TIB-uh-doe
- Vacherie: VASH-er-ee

Parks and Waterways
- Atchafalaya (river/swamp): UH-cha-fuh-lye-uh
- Bayou Teche (bayou): BYE-oo TESH
- Bogue Chitto (river): boe-guh CHEE-tuh
- Bonnet Carré (spillway): BON-ee KARE-ee
- Borgne (lake): BORN
- Fontainebleau (park): FOWN-ten-bloo
- Manchac (bayou): MAN-shack
- Maurepas (lake): MOOR-uh-paw
- Ouchita (river): WAW-shuh-taw
- Sabine (river): suh-BEAN
- Tchefuncte (river): chuh-FUNK-tuh

say "excuse me" when having to walk in front of someone.

By the same token, it's easy to misinterpret the friendliness that you'll surely encounter. When walking through the French Quarter, many a tourist has been stopped by a seemingly friendly local with a scam up his or her sleeve. One such scam entails what seems like a harmless wager: A man might approach you and say, "I bet I can guess where you got those shoes," and if you choose to accept his challenge, he'll inevitably win with a simple reply, "On your feet." So, as in any major U.S. city, it pays to be both courteous and cautious.

Because of the mass exodus following Hurricane Katrina, a lot of the locals weren't necessarily born here. Plenty of local transplants escaped colder climates in New England and the Midwest, giving them a sense of appreciation for the benefits of living in a laid-back, amicable town like New Orleans. Because of the region's multiethnic history and reliance on tourism, foreigners and tourists are generally welcome here. Overall, the residents are helpful, hospitable, and gregarious, so while in New Orleans, do as the natives do. Be kind and considerate, ask for help when you need it, thank others for their time, and, as a courtesy, seek permission before taking a photo.

LANGUAGE

Many visitors often wonder how to pronounce "New Orleans." Though it's sometimes heard as "N'AW-luhns" in movies and TV commercials, native New Orleanians definitely don't pronounce it this way. The more conventional incorrect pronunciation is "NOO or-LEENS." Say it this way, and you'll be marked as an outsider (probably a Northerner), but at least, you won't be accused of being disrespectful. Locals pronounce the city's name in a handful of relatively similar ways, the simplest and most common being "noo OHR-lins." You don't have to say it with a big, silly drawl or with delicious emphasis, as if you're a damsel in a Tennessee Williams play. Just say it quickly and casually, though you might hear some locals, especially those with aristocratic tendencies, pronounce it "noo OHR-lee-ahns."

As for the name of the state, that is a bit more straightforward. Here, you have two options: "LOO-zee-ann-ah" or "le-WEE-zee-ann-ah." Both pronunciations are common and considered acceptable.

Pronouncing the rest of the rivers, lakes, towns, and streets of New Orleans and Louisiana can be extremely tricky for outsiders. "Correct" pronunciation isn't really the point here. After all, according to your French teacher, Chartres Street, in New Orleans's French Quarter, would be pronounced "SHART," but the correct local pronunciation is "CHAR-ters" or "CHART-uz."

If you'd rather not sound like an outsider, do your best to learn the major place-name pronunciations. Granted, locals won't generally torment you for mispronouncing words, especially since, depending on one's regional accent, there are often two or more commonly accepted (though hotly debated) ways to pronounce the same word. However, if you try to sound like a local—even with a Yankee or international accent—you may be taken more seriously by the Louisianian you're addressing.

While the pronunciation keys listed in this guide are approximate and imperfect—owing to the many regional nuances among locals, who sometimes have grown up on the same block but still favor one pronunciation over another—they will surely assist you in your travels. Just be advised that syllables set in capital letters are stressed (as in "CHAR-ters"). If a common street or place-name isn't listed, assume that it's generally pronounced as it is elsewhere in the United States. For example, St. Louis Street in the French Quarter is said here as the Missouri city is—"saynt LOO-iss"—and not the way that the French would pronounce it.

BUSINESS HOURS

New Orleans and Louisiana fall within the central standard time (CST) zone. The region observes central daylight time (CDT), which means that you'll have to adjust your watches and alarm clocks accordingly when visiting during the second weekend of March and the first weekend of November. Standard business hours for banks tend to be Monday–Friday 9 A.M.–4 P.M., with limited hours on Saturday. Post offices are typically open Monday–Friday 8:30 A.M.–4:30 P.M., though some have longer hours and are open on Saturday. Art galleries and antiques shops are often open daily 10 A.M.–6 P.M.; souvenir shops, especially in the French Quarter, usually have much longer hours.

Smaller attractions are frequently staffed by volunteers and tend to have limited hours; call ahead to ensure that the place will be open or to set up an appointment to visit. Popular attractions are typically open 9 A.M.–5 P.M. 5–7 days each week; some attractions close on Sunday, Monday, and major holidays. In many cases, hours are reduced on Sunday and may fluctuate during the summer months. Given New Orleans's laid-back vibe, posted hours and other policies aren't always observed, especially in the case of small or privately owned businesses.

Some restaurants are open 24 hours daily, while others only serve food until midnight. In the French Quarter, many bars stay open 24 hours daily; you may see folks with plastic "to go" cups wandering around, especially during Mardi Gras. Elsewhere in the city, bars more commonly close between 2 and 4 A.M.

COSTS AND TIPPING

As a town that relies heavily on tourism, New Orleans has its share of pricey hotels, restaurants, boutiques, and parking lots. Luckily, though, it's easy to find deals here. Staying outside the Quarter and CBD can often save you quite a bit of money, especially since public transportation is very inexpensive. There are also plenty of affordable eateries, vintage shops, and close-to-free attractions throughout the city; at many attractions, children, college students, senior citizens, military personnel, and holders of AAA cards will receive substantial discounts. However, most retail items and services cost more than their listed price due to sales taxes. The state sales tax is 4 percent, while the sales tax for Orleans Parish is 5

percent; this means that in New Orleans, most goods and services will incur a rather high sales tax of 9 percent. In Metairie, Kenner, and other cities in Jefferson Parish, goods and services will incur an 8.75 percent sales tax. The hotel tax in New Orleans is a whopping 13 percent.

Given the city's reliance on tourism, tipping is critical here. Although the amount of a gratuity depends on the level of service received, there are general tipping guidelines. Restaurant servers should receive 15–20 percent of the entire bill, while pizza delivery drivers should receive at least 10 percent. Taxi and limousine drivers should receive at least 15 percent of the entire fare, while valets, porters, and skycaps should expect around $2 per vehicle or piece of luggage. The housekeeping staff of your inn or hotel also deserves a tip; a generally accepted amount is $2 per night.

Tour guides, fishing guides, and other excursion operators should be tipped as well. No matter how much such experiences cost, the gratuity is never included in the quoted price. How much you choose to tip is entirely up to you. While the exact amount of a tip will depend on the cost, length, and nature of the trip in question—not to mention your satisfaction—it's generally accepted to tip 10–20 percent of the overall cost. If a guide or operator makes an exceptional effort, then it's highly recommended to increase the size of the tip accordingly.

PUBLIC RESTROOMS

Most travelers to New Orleans spend a lot of time outside their hotel rooms, so it's helpful to know where public restrooms are located, especially if you're traveling with children. In the French Quarter, you'll find public restrooms at the Shops at Canal Place, the Shops at Jax Brewery, and the French Market. Plenty of bars and restaurants also have reliable facilities, which you're welcome to use as long as you're willing to purchase something, even an inexpensive drink. Given that several establishments are open 24 hours daily, there's no excuse for public urination, which, though a sadly frequent occurrence in New Orleans, can result in being ticketed or getting arrested.

SMOKING

All restaurants in New Orleans are nonsmoking, and though at least 50 percent of all hotel and motel rooms must be designated nonsmoking, plenty of lodging options are completely smoke-free. There are no smoking restrictions in bars and clubs. In fact, nonsmokers may be surprised by the smoky nature of many taverns, lounges, and live music venues in New Orleans. While some places don't allow smoking, such as Tipitina's and the Snug Harbor Jazz Bistro, plenty of joints can still get disconcertingly cloudy. If it's an issue for you, call any questionable establishments before your next visit.

Tips for Travelers

FOREIGN TRAVELERS

While international travelers are required to show a valid passport upon entering the United States, most citizens from Canada and the 36 countries that are part of the **Visa Waiver Program (VWP)**—including France, Italy, Germany, Spain, Australia, New Zealand, Japan, and the United Kingdom—are allowed to travel to New Orleans and its environs without a visa. However, they still need to apply to the **Electronic System for Travel Authorization (ESTA).** All other temporary international travelers are required to secure a nonimmigrant visa before entering Louisiana. For more information, consult the **U.S. Department of State's Bureau of Consular Affairs** (202/663-1225, www.travel.state.gov).

Upon entering Louisiana, international travelers must declare any dollar amount over $10,000 as well as the value of any articles that will remain in the country, including gifts. A duty will be assessed for all imported goods, though visitors are usually granted a $100 exemption. Illegal drugs, Cuban cigars, obscene items, toxic substances, and prescription drugs (without a prescription) are generally prohibited. In order to protect American agriculture, customs officials will also confiscate certain produce, plants, seeds, nuts, meat, and other potentially dangerous biological products. For more information, consult the **U.S. Customs and Border Protection** (703/526-4200, www.cbp.gov).

While the embassies for most countries are located in Washington, D.C., some nations have consular offices and honorary consuls in New Orleans. Though you should research such matters before leaving your home country, you can also contact the **World Trade Center of New Orleans** (WTCNO, 365 Canal St., Ste. 1120, 504/529-1601, www.wtcno.org) for assistance.

OPPORTUNITIES FOR STUDY AND EMPLOYMENT

With several colleges and plenty of businesses in southeastern Louisiana, there's an array of educational and work-related opportunities for residents and travelers. If you're interested in a long-term stay, research the schools and companies that interest you, consider details like transportation and accommodations, and, for foreign travelers, look into U.S. visa and permit policies *before* making travel or relocation plans.

It's also helpful to be realistic about living in New Orleans. Real estate prices, including rental rates, are a bit higher than they used to be, and the crime rate hasn't much improved, though the French Quarter seems to be much safer due to an increased police presence. Unless you're transferred here by your company or interested in working in the tourism industry, you might find it challenging to find a job, though the standard of living is lower here than in several other U.S. cities.

For educational opportunities, one short-term possibility is **Cook New Orleans** (www. cookneworleans.com), a five-day, adults-only series of cooking classes and tours offered in May, July, and November. For more information about education, business, and other

LOUISIANA TAX-FREE SHOPPING

If visiting from another country, you're entitled to a refund of the state sales tax and, in certain cases, the local sales tax on goods bought in Louisiana. This policy, first among the 50 states, was introduced as a way to help promote visitation by foreign travelers, and depending on how much shopping you do, you really can save a bit of money.

The refund is available to visitors who have a valid foreign passport *and* an airline or other international round-trip ticket of up to 90 days' duration. Canadians are the one exception to the passport rule; they may provide proof of residency by showing a driver's license or birth certificate. If you are a resident of any other country, you must supply a passport. Resident aliens, foreign students, U.S. citizens living in other countries, and citizens with dual citizenship in the United States and another country are not eligible. The refund does not apply to services, hotel charges, car rentals, food and beverages, or personal goods bought for use while in Louisiana, and only purchases made at participating shops qualify.

To take advantage of this program, ask for a refund voucher at the shop where you make your purchase – any participating merchant will be able to provide you with this, once you show your passport (or other ID, if Canadian). It's important to remember that you will not be given the refund at the time of purchase – this happens at the **Louisiana Tax Free Shopping Refund Center** (504/467-0723, www.louisianataxfree.com, Mon.-Fri. 8:30 A.M.-4:30 P.M., Sat.-Sun. 9 A.M.-1 P.M.) at the Louis Armstrong New Orleans International Airport, or at two other locations: the **Downtown Refund Center** (Riverwalk Marketplace, 1 Poydras St., 2nd Fl., 504/568-3605, daily 9:30 A.M.-4:30 P.M.) and **Macy's Refund Center** (Lakeside Shopping Center, 3301 Veterans Memorial Blvd., 3rd Fl., Metairie, 504/484-4665, Mon.-Sat. 10 A.M.-5 P.M., Sun. 11 A.M.-6 P.M.). At the actual shop, you'll pay the full price, including tax, for your purchase, and you'll be issued a voucher in the amount of the refund that you're due. You must present the voucher and all original receipts for every purchase to qualify for the refund.

Refunds under $500 are issued in cash; refunds over $500 are issued by check and mailed to your home. You can also mail in your vouchers and receipts to receive a refund. In this case, you must mail the original vouchers and sales receipts, copies of your travel ticket and passport, and a statement explaining two things – why you didn't redeem the vouchers at any of the refund centers and where the merchandise is currently located – to the Louisiana Tax Free Shopping Refund Center (P.O. Box 20125, New Orleans, LA 70141).

aspects of living in New Orleans, consult www.makeneworleanshome.com.

VOLUNTEER VACATIONS

Sometimes, being a tourist isn't enough. If you want to explore southeastern Louisiana *and* lend a helping hand, then perhaps "voluntourism" is right up your alley. National and state parks can especially use some extra assistance, and working in such diverse environments can be a truly rewarding experience. Hurricane Katrina left behind a great need for volunteers. Even today, organizations like the **New Orleans Area Habitat for Humanity** (504/861-2077 or 504/861-4121, www.habitat-nola.org) and the **Preservation Resource Center of New Orleans** (504/581-7032, www.prcno.org) welcome the assistance of dedicated volunteers. Both have been instrumental in helping to restore the city's most damaged historic areas since Hurricane Katrina.

TRAVELING WITH CHILDREN

Although New Orleans tends to be geared more toward adults than children, there are nevertheless some outstanding attractions for kids, such as the Audubon Aquarium of the Americas, the Audubon Insectarium, Blaine

Children adore the exhibits at the Audubon Aquarium of the Americas.

Kern's Mardi Gras World, the Audubon Zoo, Storyland at City Park, and the Louisiana Children's Museum, right in the CBD. Many of the excursions offered throughout the city, such as swamp tours, riverboat rides, and haunted strolls, are a big hit with kids, especially teenagers. For more ideas, consult www. neworleanskids.com, which offers a slew of tips regarding family-friendly hotels, restaurants, attractions, and activities.

If you do decide to travel here with children, remember to supervise them at all times—both to keep them safe from harm and to minimize the possibility of disturbing others. While plenty of inns and hotels welcome children—such as the Quarter's Ritz-Carlton New Orleans and the CBD's Loews New Orleans Hotel, both of which offer babysitting services—some lodging options, such as Uptown's Magnolia Mansion, are adults-only establishments.

WOMEN TRAVELERS

While it's admirable for an independent woman to explore the world on her own or in the company of other female travelers, it's important to take precautions, especially in a potentially dangerous place like New Orleans. Although much of the French Quarter is relatively safe, there are still too many things that can go wrong—even in a crowd—and other neighborhoods, such as the Tremé and Bywater, can be downright perilous for women.

If you venture out alone, tell someone back home about your intended travel plans, stick to daytime driving, and stay close to busy attractions and streets. Try to stow your money, credit cards, and identification close to your person, as big purses make easy targets. If you feel that someone is stalking you, find a public place (such as a store or late-night restaurant), and don't hesitate to alert the police. Keep the doors to your hotel room and vehicle locked at all times.

Before heading out on your trip, invest in a canister of pepper spray as well as a cell phone, which can be useful in an emergency (however, cellular reception is limited in the more remote areas of southeastern Louisiana).

SENIOR TRAVELERS

Although the wild nightlife scene around the French Quarter can be off-putting to some, New Orleans is overall quite appealing to senior travelers, particularly those who appreciate historical architecture and one-of-a-kind attractions, such as the National WWII Museum. For those who'd prefer a quieter place to sleep, the good news is that the Quarter isn't the only neighborhood that offers unique hotels. For a more relaxed local experience, consider staying in the Garden District or farther Uptown, especially at one of the hotels and inns along St. Charles Avenue.

Even better, seniors often qualify for age-related discounts at restaurants, attractions, and other establishments throughout New Orleans. The **American Association of Retired Persons** (AARP, 888/687-2277, www.aarp.org) offers members a myriad of travel discounts as well as a newsletter that often touches on travel issues. **Road Scholar** (800/454-5768, www.roadscholar.org) also organizes a wide variety of educationally oriented tours and vacations that are geared toward seniors; some even highlight the distinct cultures of New Orleans and Lafayette.

In general, New Orleans and southeastern Louisiana are exceptionally helpful places, so senior travelers should have little trouble finding assistance here. For help with directions, there are several visitors centers and tourism bureaus throughout the region, not to mention plenty of locals able to point you in the right direction.

GAY AND LESBIAN TRAVELERS

New Orleans is a bastion of gay-friendliness, with gay newspapers, numerous gay and lesbian organizations and gay-owned businesses, and several gay-dominated bars and nightclubs, many of which rub right up against the more mainstream nightlife district in the French Quarter. Locals tend to be rather blasé about the sight of two women or two men walking hand in hand in the Big Easy, especially in the Quarter, the Faubourg Marigny, and Uptown, which tend to have the highest lesbian and gay populations. Some tourists, however, come from less tolerant places, and sadly, drunken disagreements occasionally occur along Bourbon Street, where the city's straight and gay nightclub rows collide.

Three annual events—Mardi Gras in the late winter, the Southern Decadence celebration over Labor Day weekend, and Halloween in the fall—draw the greatest numbers of gay and lesbian visitors to New Orleans, but the city is always popular with gay and lesbian travelers. Many inns and B&Bs, especially in the Faubourg Marigny, are gay-owned, and places like Uptown's Green House Inn offer such attractive features as clothing-optional pools.

For more information about gay and lesbian activities, consult the free bimonthly **Ambush Mag** (www.ambushmag.com). The same publication also has a website just for gay goings-on during Mardi Gras (www.gaymardigras.com). Another helpful website is www.gayneworleans.com.

TRAVELERS WITH DISABILITIES

Within new hotels, some large restaurants, and most major attractions, you can expect to find wheelchair-accessible restrooms, entrance ramps, and other helpful fixtures; even RTA buses are wheelchair-accessible. But New Orleans has many hole-in-the-wall cafés, tiny B&Bs, historic house-museums with narrow staircases or uneven thresholds, and other buildings that are not easily accessible to people using wheelchairs. Unfortunately, the city's historic streetcars are also not wheelchair-accessible. If you're traveling with a guide animal, be sure to contact every hotel or restaurant in question to confirm access and accommodation. A useful resource is the **Society for Accessible Travel & Hospitality** (212/447-7284, www.sath.org).

TRAVELING WITH PETS

Although pets aren't allowed within many of New Orleans's hotels, restaurants, and stores, several places do welcome them, including state park campgrounds and some downtown hotels. In locations where dogs, cats, and other pets are allowed, it's crucial to understand and follow any relevant rules. Typically, guests will be asked to keep any pets on a leash at all times, walk animals in designated areas, control their behavior so as not to disturb or endanger others, and always pick up their droppings. Barking or aggressive dogs are usually forbidden everywhere. When in doubt, call ahead to verify the pet policies of a particular hotel, park, attraction, or establishment.

Health and Safety

HOSPITALS

Despite the best-laid plans, trouble can occur at any time. Before hitting the road or boarding a bus, plane, boat, or train, it's critical to pack a well-stocked first-aid kit and prepare yourself for a potential accident or illness. Although you can utilize free services like **MD Travel Health** (www.mdtravelhealth.com) to learn about infectious diseases and illness prevention in the United States, it's good to know that if you experience an illness or injury while traveling through southeastern Louisiana, you'll find several well-regarded hospitals and clinics in New Orleans and its environs.

Some of these helpful places include the **Tulane Medical Center** (1415 Tulane Ave., 504/988-5263, www.tulanehealthcare.com), the closest general hospital to the French Quarter and the CBD; the **Interim LSU Public Hospital** (2021 Perdido St., 504/903-3000, www.mclno.org), the active part of a major medical center still in progress; and the **Ochsner Baptist Medical Center** (2700 Napoleon Ave., 504/899-9311, www.ochsner.org), an Uptown hospital with a 24-hour emergency room. If you're in need of emergency dental care, consider the **Louisiana Dental Center** (4232 St. Claude Ave., 504/947-2958, www.ladentalcenter.com, Mon.–Thurs. 7:30 A.M.–4 P.M., Fri. 7:30 A.M.–3 P.M., Sat. 9 A.M.–3 P.M.), which offers several locations in southeastern Louisiana, from Metairie to Gonzales. Most medical and dental facilities will require insurance or a partial payment before admitting patients for treatment or dispensing medication.

PHARMACIES

If you need to fill a prescription or pick up over-the-counter medication, you'll be able to do so at various drugstores throughout New Orleans and southeastern Louisiana. Some pharmacies include **Walgreens** (619 Decatur St., 504/525-7263 or 800/925-4733, www.walgreens.com, daily 8 A.M.–10 P.M.) in the French Quarter, **CVS/pharmacy** (4901 Prytania St., 504/891-6307 or 800/746-7287, www.cvs.com, daily 24 hours) in the Uptown area, and **Rite Aid Pharmacy** (760 Harrison Ave., 504/483-2383 or 800/748-3243, www.riteaid.com, Mon.–Sat. 7 A.M.–9 P.M., Sun. 8 A.M.–8 P.M.) in Lakeview. In all cases, the in-house pharmacy has shorter hours than the rest of the store, so be sure to call ahead.

EMERGENCY SERVICES

All of Louisiana is tied into the **911** emergency system. Dial 911 free from any telephone (including pay phones) to reach an operator who can quickly dispatch local police, fire, or ambulance services. While this service also works from cell phones, you may find it difficult to make calls from rural areas or offshore waters, where reliable cellular service isn't always guaranteed. For nonemergencies, contact the **Louisiana State Police** (504/471-2775, www.lsp.org) or the **New Orleans Police Department** (www.nola.gov/government/nopd)—including the First District (501 N. Rampart St., 504/658-6010) in the Tremé, the Second District (4317 Magazine St., 504/658-6020) in Uptown, the Fifth District (4015 Burgundy St., 504/658-6050) in the Bywater, and the Eighth District (334 Royal St., 504/658-6080) in the French Quarter. In the event of a hurricane or other natural disaster, contact the **New Orleans Office of Homeland Security and Emergency Preparedness**

HURRICANE CHECKLIST

Since Hurricane Katrina, some out-of-town-ers have become apprehensive about visiting southern Louisiana during the Atlantic hurricane season, which usually runs June–November. The truth is, however, that hurricanes are infrequent in this region, and many of the most popular events, such as Southern Decadence, occur during this half of the year. Nevertheless, it's always a good idea to be prepared for the worst. So, if you do plan to visit New Orleans during hurricane season – whether for a quick getaway or an extended stay – keep apprised of weather updates and be prepared to evacuate if necessary.

In addition, residents and seasonal visitors alike should stock up on certain essentials in advance, as you'll surely face long lines and depleted supplies once a storm threatens. Listed here are some suggested items, which will come in handy whether you're forced to stay through the storm or you find yourself stuck in an evacuation route. Of course, this isn't an exhaustive list, so be sure to set aside other items as well, such as cell phones, identification cards, house keys, photo albums, important papers, pet supplies, asthma inhalers, and other necessities.

FOOD SUPPLIES

In general, you should have a two-week supply of nonperishable foods, especially low-salt and low-fat items that will minimize your thirst. Necessary goods, some of which must be purchased just before the storm, include:

- bread and cereals
- canned fruit and vegetables
- dried fruit
- dry and canned pet food if necessary
- ice and drinking water (1 gallon per person daily)
- powdered, canned, or other nonrefrigerated beverages (coffee, fruit juice, milk, etc.)
- prepared foods (canned soups, corned beef hash, tuna, etc.)
- raw vegetables
- snacks (crackers, cookies, nuts, etc.)
- snack spreads (peanut butter, fruit preserves, etc.)
- sugar, salt, and pepper

KITCHEN SUPPLIES

The following items will be especially handy if you have to evacuate to a strange place, such as an ill-equipped motel:

- bottle opener and manual can opener
- camp stove and canned cooking fuel
- ice chest or cooler
- paper plates and napkins
- plastic cups and utensils
- pocketknife
- waterproof matches

HARDWARE

Most of these items will only be necessary if you live in New Orleans year-round or stay here for extended periods of time:

- canvas tarps
- hammer and nails
- plastic sheeting to cover furniture
- power screwdriver
- rope and duct tape

(504/658-8700) for instructions and evacuation assistance.

CRIME AND HARASSMENT

New Orleans has a reputation for crime—partially deserved, partially exaggerated. While crime is prevalent in sketchy neighborhoods, such as the Tremé and Bywater, a lot of crime is also centered in or near tourist areas, and muggings or carjackings, while infrequent, do occur. To minimize any threat to your safety and your belongings, follow these common-sense precautions:

- Never leave valuables in plain view on a car seat; secure them in the trunk, where they're less tempting to thieves.
- In case of an accident on the highway, do

- screwdrivers and screws
- sheets of exterior plywood to board up windows
- shovel and pickax
- sturdy working gloves

MEDICAL NEEDS AND TOILETRIES

Given that drugstores will be mobbed just before a storm and closed for days afterward, it's always advisable to collect the following items ahead of time, along with a two-week supply of prescription drugs:

- aspirin
- bandages, sterile rolls, and adhesive tape
- child and pet medication if necessary
- cotton-tipped swabs
- deodorant
- diarrhea and constipation medication
- disinfectant and antiseptic
- emergency toilet (small, lidded garbage can with disinfectant, deodorizer, and plastic bags as liners)
- feminine hygiene products
- first-aid kit and first-aid handbook
- insect bite lotion
- insect repellent sprays and candles
- Medic Alert tags
- over-the-counter cold and allergy medicine
- plastic bags and jugs to store extra ice and water
- soap and shampoo
- sunscreen
- tweezers, needles, and a sewing kit
- water filter and purification tablets

BABY NEEDS

Obviously, these items will only apply to people with children:

- baby cold and pain medication
- baby formula and food
- baby wipes
- diaper-rash ointment or petroleum jelly
- disposable diapers
- medicine dropper

HURRICANE KIT

Typically, it's a good idea to assemble this kit as soon as possible and store it in a cool, dry place. Be sure, too, to refresh the stock when necessary. Important items include:

- area maps
- auto supplies and gas can
- battery-operated clocks and lanterns
- battery-operated radio or television
- copies of insurance policies
- emergency and nonemergency phone numbers
- extra bulbs and batteries
- hand-crank flashlights
- operational fire extinguishers
- paper towels
- plastic garbage bags
- rabbit ears–style television antenna
- rain gear and extra clothes
- scissors
- swamp boots
- toilet paper

not abandon your vehicle, as this might also invite thieves.

- Don't display money, valuables, or jewelry conspicuously.
- Keep your money, credit cards, identification, and other important items hidden on your person; purses and backpacks are much easier to steal.

- Leave all but the most necessary items at home or at your hotel.
- Store laptop computers, cameras, jewelry, or any other expensive or irreplaceable item in the hotel safe.
- Secure your bike whenever it's left unattended.
- Lock your hotel and car doors at all times.

- Pay attention to your surroundings and walk along well-lit, well-traveled streets.
- Avoid dark and mostly residential areas.
- Never go into cemeteries after dark.
- Travel in groups of at least two whenever possible.
- Take cabs to parts of town with which you're unfamiliar.
- If you're traveling via RV, do not boondock alone in an isolated place; try to stay in an RV park, a campground, or, at the very least, a well-lit parking lot.

The most frequent targets of crime in New Orleans are inebriated tourists, and these, unfortunately, are easy to find in the French Quarter late at night. The simplest way to keep safe is to avoid drinking yourself into a stupor. If anticipating a night of revelry, keep the name and address of your hotel written down someplace safe—but never write your hotel room number down somewhere that a thief or pickpocket could get it. Also be sure to carry the name and number of at least one or two cab companies, and keep your cell phone handy.

If you require assistance while in downtown New Orleans, contact **SafeWalk** (504/415-1730, daily 10 A.M.–10 P.M.), a free service provided in the CBD and Arts District. With at least 20 minutes' advance notice, Public Safety Rangers will escort residents and visitors to their cars or other areas within the designated zone. If you do find yourself in trouble, whether in the CBD or another area of New Orleans, don't hesitate to find a phone and dial **911.** Just remember that the time it takes police and emergency vehicles to reach you will depend upon your location.

If you witness a crime of any kind while in New Orleans, contact the **Greater New Orleans Crimestoppers** (504/822-1111, www.crimestoppersgno.org) to offer an anonymous tip. Likewise, you can consult the **Orleans Parish Sheriff's Office** (504/822-8000 or 504/826-7045, www.opcso.org).

HEATSTROKE

Hot, sunny days are common in southeastern Louisiana, and it's crucial to prepare for them. Although sunscreen will help to prevent sunburn, you must apply it frequently and liberally. Prolonged sun exposure, high temperatures, and little water consumption can also cause dehydration, which can lead to heat exhaustion—a harmful condition whereby your internal cooling system begins to shut down. Symptoms may include clammy skin, weakness, vomiting, and abnormal body temperature. In such instances, you must lie down in the shade, remove restrictive clothing, and drink some water.

If you do not treat heat exhaustion promptly, your condition can worsen quickly, leading to heatstroke (or sunstroke), a dangerous condition whereby your internal body temperature starts to rise to a potentially fatal level. Symptoms can include dizziness, vomiting, diarrhea, abnormal breathing and blood pressure, cessation of sweating, headache, and confusion. If any of these occur, you must be taken to a hospital as soon as possible. In the meantime, your companions should move you into the shade; remove your clothing; lower your body temperature with cool water, damp sheets, or fans; and try to give you some water to drink, if you're able.

HURRICANE PREPARATION

One of the biggest concerns for travelers to southeastern Louisiana is, of course, the possibility of facing a hurricane. Generally, the Atlantic hurricane season runs from June through November, though hurricanes have certainly occurred beyond this time frame. The best advice is to stock up on extra water, flashlights, batteries, and other supplies during the season, develop a possible exit strategy, and keep apprised of the weather at all times. Although most radio and TV stations provide weather updates, the **National Weather Service** (62300 Airport Rd., Slidell, 504/522-7330 or 985/649-0357, www.srh.noaa.gov) is also a good source of information for tropical storms and hurricanes.

INSURANCE

Although you might be the sort of traveler who likes to live dangerously, insurance is highly recommended while traveling in southeastern Louisiana. Whether you're a U.S. citizen driving your own car or an international traveler in a rented RV, you should invest in medical, travel, and automotive insurance before embarking upon your trip in order to protect yourself as well as your assets. Research your insurance options and choose the policies that best suit your needs and budget. For travel insurance (which should include medical coverage), consider a company like **Travel Guard** (800/826-4919, www.travelguard.com).

WATER SAFETY

Given New Orleans's location at the southern end of the Mississippi River, it's not surprising that some people would question the safety of its water supply. In general, the tap water here is relatively safe. It's tested daily by the **Sewerage & Water Board of New Orleans** (www.swbno.org) for microbial, organic, chemical, and metallic contaminants. If

you're still concerned, however, you can always purchase bottled water or a filtration system.

While visiting New Orleans, you might venture into the countryside, bayous, and lakes beyond the city. If so, you'll encounter a lot of brackish water, which you should never drink, due to the high probability of dehydration. In various places, you may also find fresh water, and while the water may look inviting, don't take a chance. Many of Louisiana's inland bodies of water may be tainted with *Giardia lamblia,* a nasty little parasite that is most commonly transmitted through mammal feces. The resulting illness, **giardiasis,** can result in severe stomach cramps, vomiting, and diarrhea. While Halizone tablets, bleach, and other chemical purifiers may be effective against such organisms, your best bet is to use an adequate water filter (which filters down to 0.4 micron or less) or boil the water for at least five minutes.

WILDLIFE ENCOUNTERS

With its humid, subtropical climate and prevalence of marshes, southeastern Louisiana is home to a wide array of insects, from

© LAURA MARTONE

Unfortunately, the bustling Mississippi is one of the most polluted rivers in the country.

harmless dragonflies to more bothersome critters. Perhaps the biggest concern is **mosquitoes,** whose stings can cause itchy red welts or worse. Mosquitoes are typically more prevalent June–September, when the humidity is at its worst. To protect against these relentless creatures, use a combination of defenses, including light-colored clothing, long-sleeved shirts, long pants, closed shoes, scent-free deodorant, and insect repellents containing DEET. Avoid grassy areas and shady places and instead seek open, breezy locales (especially out on the water) and avoid peak hours for mosquito activity, namely sunrise and sunset. Try to open and close your car doors quickly and keep your car windows rolled up, as there's little worse than being stuck in a vehicle with a roving, bloodthirsty mosquito.

If you are stung you should be fine, unless you have an unforeseen allergy or the mosquito is a carrier for a disease like the West Nile virus. Beyond cleaning the affected area and treating it with calamine lotion, hydrocortisone cream, or aloe vera gel, all you can do is take some anti-inflammatory or antihistamine medication for the pain and swelling and wait for the skin to heal.

Insects aren't the only perils in the wild. While hiking amid southeastern Louisiana's forests, marshes, and beaches, be careful where you step; it's easier than you think to trip on a root or other obstruction. Refrain from digesting any tempting berries, flowers, and plants without first consulting local residents or expert field guides.

Since much of southeastern Louisiana comprises undeveloped marshes and forests, not to mention surrounding waters, you're bound to encounter wild animals. While many of these, such as lizards and shorebirds, are fairly harmless, more dangerous creatures, such as alligators, live here, too. To avoid perilous encounters with such animals, don't venture into places like Barataria Preserve or the Atchafalaya Basin by yourself, and try to observe all wildlife from a distance. Although it should go without saying, never taunt, disturb, or feed any of the wildlife.

Information and Services

MAPS AND TOURIST INFORMATION

For general information about traveling in southeastern Louisiana, your best source is the state-run **Louisiana Office of Tourism** (800/994-8626, www.louisianatravel.com), which offers a tour guidebook, interactive maps, travel tips, and oodles of information about the state's accommodations, restaurants, attractions, events, live entertainment, and outdoor activities, plus live operators willing to assist with your tourism needs. Visitors to the Big Easy should also consult the **New Orleans Convention & Visitors Bureau** (2020 St. Charles Ave., 504/566-5011 or 800/672-6124, www.neworleanscvb.com, Mon.–Fri. 8:30 A.M.–5 P.M.) or the **New Orleans Tourism Marketing Corporation** (2020 St. Charles Ave., 504/524-4784, www.neworleansonline.com), both of which provide a slew of information about the city's myriad lodging, dining, and activity options. The **New Orleans Welcome Center** (529 St. Ann St., 504/568-5661, www.crt.state.la.us, daily 9 A.M.–5 P.M.) also provides maps and brochures and arranges tours. For information about the Greater New Orleans area, consult the **Jefferson Convention & Visitors Bureau** (1221 Elmwood Park Blvd., Ste. 411, 504/731-7083 or 877/572-7474, www.experiencejefferson.com). The Northshore, Tangipahoa Parish, Baton Rouge, Houma, Lafayette, and Lake Charles all have helpful CVBs as well.

In a state known for its tourism industry, you'll find no shortage of helpful maps, including those produced by **AAA** (800/564-6222, www.aaa.com), which offers both a *Louisiana/Mississippi* state map ($4.95 nonmember, free for members) as well as a *New Orleans* map ($4.95 nonmember, free for members) that features smaller maps of the city's

© DANIEL MARTONE

one of several helpful visitor centers in the French Quarter

airport and streetcar system. **Rand McNally** (800/333-0136, www.randmcnally.com) also publishes several helpful maps, including an easy-to-fold *Louisiana* map ($7.95), a folded *New Orleans, Hammond, Ponchatoula, Slidell* map ($5.99), a folded *Baton Rouge, Shreveport, Bossier City* map ($5.99), a laminated *Streetwise New Orleans* map ($6.95), and a comprehensive *New Orleans Street Guide* ($19.95). If exploring the backcountry, you may also want to order an official topographical (topo) map produced by the **U.S. Geological Survey** (888/275-8747, www.usgs.gov).

MONEY

Bank debit cards and major credit cards (like Visa and MasterCard) are accepted throughout southeastern Louisiana, especially in major cities like New Orleans and Baton Rouge. Automated teller machines (ATMs) have become more prevalent throughout the region and are available everywhere from gas stations and souvenir stores to funky dive bars and late-night eateries. Most banks—such as **Chase**

(800/935-9935, www.chase.com), **Regions** (800/734-4667, www.regions.com), **Iberia Bank** (800/682-3231, www.iberiabank.com), **First NBC Bank** (866/441-5552, www.firstnbcbank.com), **First Bank and Trust** (888/287-9621, www.fbtonline.com), and **Bank of Louisiana** (800/288-9811, www.bankoflouisiana.com)—provide access to ATMs inside and/or outside their branches. (Just be prepared to pay $2–3 per ATM transaction if the machine isn't operated by your bank.) You can also find a bank open during regular business hours (Mon.–Fri. 9 A.M.–4 P.M.) and sometimes on the weekend.

Many bars, eateries, stores, and tour operators will accept only cash or travelers checks, so you should never rely exclusively on plastic. Foreign currency can be exchanged at the **Whitney Bank** branch (900 Airline Dr., Kenner, 504/838-6491 or 800/844-4450, www.whitneybank.com, Mon.–Fri. 8:30 A.M.–4 P.M.) in the ticket lobby of the Louis Armstrong New Orleans International Airport; cash advances and travelers checks are also available here. For up-to-date exchange rates, consult www.xe.com.

COMMUNICATIONS AND MEDIA
Phones

Public pay phones can be found throughout southeastern Louisiana—at airports, gas stations, stores, bars, restaurants, hotels, even near certain corners in the French Quarter. To place a call, listen for a dial tone, deposit the necessary coins, and dial the desired number (including 1 and the area code, if you're making a long-distance call). For local and regional calls, the area code for New Orleans is 504, while much of the surrounding area, including towns on the Northshore and parts of Cajun Country, uses the area code 985. Baton Rouge and Lafayette, meanwhile, utilize 225 and 337, respectively. In the case of an emergency, you can dial **911** at no charge. For international calls, it's best to use a prepaid phone card, often available for purchase in gas stations or convenience stores. To figure out the correct international calling code, visit www. countrycodes.com.

A cell phone is a necessary tool for travelers—it can make it easier to get roadside assistance, call an establishment for directions, and seek help in an emergency situation. However, cellular reception may be unreliable when traveling in rural areas or offshore waters. Although Verizon and T-Mobile offer 4G cellular coverage, it's not always accessible in the French Quarter. Check with your provider to determine coverage and reception within the New Orleans area.

Many hotels charge a $0.50–1.50 surcharge for local calls, toll-free calls, or just about any other kind of call placed from their phones, and long-distance rates can be outrageous. Some inns, however, offer free local and long-distance calls; the Henry Howard House Inn and La Maison Marigny are two such places.

Internet and Mail Services

Most of New Orleans's hotels, not to mention other establishments, offer wireless Internet access. Internet cafés make it easy to stay in touch, as do places like the **French Quarter Postal Emporium** (1000 Bourbon St., 504/525-6651, www.frenchquarterpostal.com, Mon.–Fri. 9 A.M.–6 P.M., Sat. 10 A.M.–3 P.M.), which offers Internet access as well as mailing, shipping, faxing, and copying services, plus postcards, greeting cards, kooky gifts, and shipping supplies.

A post office is never terribly far away, especially via car, so it's easy to purchase stamps, receive mail (via General Delivery for temporary visitors), and send letters and packages. To locate a post office in New Orleans or its environs, consult the **U.S. Postal Service** (800/275-8777, www.usps.com). The main branch is in the CBD (701 Loyola Ave., 504/589-1706, Mon.–Fri. 7 A.M.–7 P.M., Sat. 8 A.M.–5 P.M.), though other branches include Lakeside Shopping Center (3301 17th St., Metairie, 504/828-6058) and the Uptown Station (2000 Louisiana Ave., 504/891-0350, Mon.–Fri. 8 A.M.–4:30 P.M., Sat. 8 A.M.–noon).

Newspapers and Periodicals

The major newspaper for New Orleans is *The Times-Picayune* (www.nola.com), which provides up-to-date information about restaurants, sporting events, and live entertainment. For nightlife and live music listings, pick up a copy of the monthly *OffBeat Magazine* (www.offbeat.com); the website includes a monthly electronic newsletter, for which you can sign up online, and a free iPhone app keeps club listings in your pocket. An excellent resource for arts, dining, shopping, clubbing, and similar diversions in metro New Orleans is the decidedly left-of-center *Gambit* alternative newsweekly (www.bestofneworleans.com). The monthly *Where Y'at* magazine (www.whereyat.com) also offers information about the city's dining and nightlife scenes.

New Orleans Magazine (www.myneworleans.com) is a useful, well-produced monthly, with excellent dining, shopping, arts, and events coverage. Its glossy offshoot, *Louisiana Life* (www.myneworleans.com/Louisiana-Life), comes out six times yearly and has a wide variety of features on what to see and do across the state, with a focus on food, history, art, and music. Two other offshoots are the quarterly *New Orleans Homes & Lifestyles* (www.myneworleans.com/New-Orleans-Homes-Lifestyles) and the monthly *St. Charles Avenue* (www.myneworleans.com/St-Charles-Avenue), both glossy lifestyle magazines. Other helpful publications include *The Louisiana Weekly* (www.louisianaweekly.com) and *Louisiana Cookin'* (www.louisianacookin.com).

Radio and Television

Local radio and TV stations can be useful sources of information for everything from upcoming concerts and festivals to weather updates during hurricane season. For excellent local music, tune your radio to **WWOZ** (90.7 FM, www.wwoz.org), which typically plays jazz, blues, and R&B, plus healthy doses of swing, Cajun and zydeco, country and bluegrass, and gospel. Other popular radio stations in the Big Easy include **WWNO** (89.9 FM, www.wwno.org), which is broadcast from the University of New Orleans and offers classical music, cultural programming, and NPR news; **WTUL** (91.5 FM, www.wtulneworleans.com), Tulane University's progressive radio station; and **WRNO** (99.5 FM, www.wrno.com), which offers an all-news format featuring the likes of Rush Limbaugh, Glenn Beck, and other conservative personalities. The city's four main TV stations include **WWL-TV** (www.wwltv.com), the CBS affiliate; **WDSU** (www.wdsu.com), the NBC affiliate; **WGNO** (www.abc26.com), the ABC affiliate; and **FOX8** (www.fox8live.com).

PUBLIC LIBRARIES

Despite Hurricane Katrina, which destroyed a majority of the public libraries throughout the city, including those in Lakeview and New Orleans East, the **New Orleans Public Library** (NOPL, www.nutrias.org) has been working steadily to rebuild these precious facilities. Many are open to the public, including the **Main Library** (219 Loyola Ave., 504/596-2560, Mon.–Thurs. 10 A.M.–6 P.M., Fri.–Sat. 10 A.M.–5 P.M.), located in the CBD and offering an extensive collection of books, maps, periodicals, and other materials that relate to New Orleans. Other popular branches include Uptown's stunning **Milton H. Latter Memorial Library** (5120 St. Charles Ave., 504/596-2625, hours vary daily) and the **Mid-City Branch** (3700 Orleans Ave., 504/596-2654, Mon.–Thurs. 10 A.M.–7 P.M., Sat. 10 A.M.–5 P.M.).

PLACES OF WORSHIP

Founded by French Catholics, New Orleans has a rich Catholic tradition as evidenced by the prevalence of Catholic churches, cemeteries, and schools; a passion for annual events and holy days like Mardi Gras and All Saints' Day; and even in the name of the city's NFL team, the New Orleans Saints. New Orleans is also home to the **Ursuline Academy** (2635 State St., 504/861-9150, www.ursulineneworleans.org), originally founded in 1727 by Ursuline nuns from France and now the oldest Catholic school in the United States. While tourists may be familiar with the city's more notable Catholic churches—the **St. Louis Cathedral** (615 Père Antoine Alley, 504/525-9585, www.stlouiscathedral.org) in the French Quarter, **St. Patrick's Church** (724 Camp St., 504/525-4413, www.oldstpatricks.org) in the CBD, and the **Our Lady of Guadalupe Church** (411 N. Rampart St., 504/525-1551, www.judeshrine.com) in the Tremé—plenty of others abound in New Orleans. For specific information about the various Catholic parishes as well as Mass times, consult the **Archdiocese of New Orleans** (www.arch-no.org).

Naturally, other religions have also made their home in New Orleans, and their houses of worship can be found throughout the city and its environs. Followers of the Jewish faith revere the magnificent **Touro Synagogue** (4238 St. Charles Ave., 504/895-4843, www.tourosynagogue.com) in the Uptown area. Another notable church is the **Holy Trinity Greek Orthodox Cathedral** (1200 Robert E. Lee Blvd., 504/282-0259, www.holytrinitycathedral.org), site of the first Greek Orthodox church in the Americas and home to a popular Greek festival. Baptists, Episcopalians, Presbyterians, Methodists, Lutherans, and Unitarian Universalists will all find places of worship here. For a list of possibilities, consult www.neworleanschurches.com; note that, as with many third-party websites, some of the information may be outdated.

If you find yourself outside New Orleans, rest assured that surrounding cities have their share of places of worship, too. In the state capital, you'll encounter a truly stunning, relatively new **Church of Jesus Christ of Latter-Day Saints** (10339 Highland Rd., Baton Rouge, 225/769-1197, www.lds.org) as well as the tranquil **Tam Bao Temple** (975 Monterrey Blvd., Baton Rouge, 225/248-8263, www.batonrougebuddha.com), where Buddhists and others congregate for weekly meditation practices.

LAUNDRY SERVICES

If you end up staying longer in New Orleans than you intended—or just have a sudden

Locals and tourists bring their laundry to the Quarter's Suds Dem Duds on Bourbon Street.

Garden District's Maison St. Charles Hotel & Suites New Orleans—offer laundry services or coin-operated laundry facilities. There are also numerous coin laundries throughout the city, including **Suds Dem Duds** (1101 Bourbon St., 504/309-9871, Mon.–Sat. 9 A.M.–6 P.M.), conveniently located in the French Quarter and offering self-serve washers and dryers as well as other services, such as dry-cleaning delivery. Curiously, you'll also find self-serve laundry facilities in some late-night bars, such as **Igor's Buddha Belly Burger Bar** (4437 Magazine St., 504/891-6105, daily 11 A.M.–3 A.M.).

WEIGHTS AND MEASURES

In New Orleans, most standard electrical outlets operate at 120 volts. So, if you're coming from Europe, Asia, or a country that operates at 220–240 volts, bring an adapter in order to use your hair dryer, laptop, or other small appliance. Outlets here vary between two-pronged and three-pronged and may also need an adapter—easily purchased in any decent hardware or building supply store. There are several branches of the Home Depot in southern Louisiana, including one in Mid-City (500 N. Carrollton Ave., 504/482-1985, Mon.–Sat. 7 A.M.–9 P.M., Sun. 8 A.M.–7 P.M.).

need for clean clothes—you'll find a variety of helpful options. Many of the city's hotels—such as the French Quarter's Bourbon Orleans Hotel, the Marigny's Hotel de la Monnaie, the CBD's Hyatt Regency New Orleans, and the

RESOURCES

Glossary

The following regional terms and phrases will help you navigate New Orleans and its environs—and perhaps better understand the area's unique people, culture, cuisine, and ecology.

andouille (an-DOO-ee) a spicy, smoked pork sausage prepared with garlic and Cajun seasonings and used in dishes like red beans and rice, gumbo, and jambalaya

bananas Foster a rich dessert consisting of bananas, brown sugar, and rum over vanilla ice cream, invented at Brennan's in the French Quarter

bayou (BAHY-oo) a sluggish body of water within a marsh, prevalent throughout southern Louisiana

beignet (ben-YAY) a squarish, fried pastry made from doughnut batter and sprinkled with powdered sugar

blackened a Cajun preparation that involves coating fish or meat with a spicy seasoning blend and flash-frying it in a hot, cast-iron pan

bobo a small injury, similar to a "boo boo"

boil a quintessential, often seasonal Cajun seafood dish in which shrimp, crabs, or crawfish are boiled in a spicy broth

boudin (boo-DAN) a hot, spicy pork sausage typically mixed with onions, herbs, cayenne pepper, and cooked rice

brackish water a mixture of freshwater and saltwater

brake tag an annual vehicle inspection sticker

bread pudding a traditional dessert made with soaked French bread and often served with rum sauce

buggy a shopping cart

café au lait (KAFF-ay oh LAY) a hot drink made equally of coffee (usually coffee with chicory) and steamed milk

Cajun referring to the French Acadians that relocated from Canada to southern Louisiana

cher (SHA) a French term of endearment

cochon de lait (koh-SHON duh LAY) a French term that literally means "pig in milk" and regionally refers to a Cajun pig roast

Coke a term used to describe any soda; also known as a "soft drink"

courtbouillon (KOO-boo-YAWN) a Cajun-style, tomato-based bouillabaisse, or seafood stew, the most popular version being redfish courtbouillon

Creole referring to the descendants of French, Spanish, and Caribbean slaves and natives

Crescent City a nickname for New Orleans, referring to how the Mississippi River curves around the city

Crescent City Connection the twin bridges that span the Mississippi River and connect the East Bank of New Orleans with the West Bank; also known as the GNO Bridge

dirty rice pan-fried rice cooked with onions, green peppers, celery, stock, and giblets

doubloon an aluminum or plastic coin stamped with the insignia and theme of a Mardi Gras krewe

dressed an expression used when ordering a sandwich, meant to indicate that everything (e.g., lettuce, tomato, and mayonnaise) be included

epiphyte a plant, such as an orchid, moss, or fern, that grows on the branches, trunks, and leaves of trees and derives its water and nutrients from the air

étouffée (ay-too-FAY) a dark roux of seasoned vegetables, usually poured over rice and served with shrimp or crawfish

fais do-do (FAY doh-doh) a Cajun dance party

filé (FEE-lay) ground sassafras leaves used to season gumbo and other dishes

fixin' to a Southern expression used when one is preparing to do something

gallery a second-floor balcony that covers the sidewalk, especially common in the French Quarter

grillades (gree-YAHDZ) a dish of diced meat marinated in vinegar to produce a rich gravy, usually served with grits

gris-gris (GREE-gree) a voodoo good-luck charm

grits ground corn kernels, typically boiled and served with a Southern-style breakfast

gumbo a thick filé soup made from a roux, served with rice, and filled with ingredients like chicken, andouille, okra, shrimp, and crab meat

hoodoo the ancient West African practice of "folk magic," which, in New Orleans, incorporates European and Native American influences and involves the use of herbs, incense, candles, talismans, and Biblical psalms

hurricane a multi-use term referring to a destructive tropical storm and a popular drink made of rum and fruit punch

hush puppy a crunchy, cornmeal fritter popular in the South and typically served with fried seafood

jambalaya (juhm-buh-LAHY-uh) a Cajun or Creole rice dish containing chicken, sausage, seafood, celery, onions, tomatoes, and spices

j'eat an expression used in place of "Have you eaten yet?"

king cake an iced coffee cake, often shaped like an extra-large doughnut, containing a small plastic baby and served during the Mardi Gras season

krewe a private organization that usually operates a parade during the Mardi Gras season

lagniappe (LAN-yap) a French expression meant to indicate a bonus

laissez les bons temps rouler (lay-ZAY lay BAWN tawn ROO-lay) a French expression meaning "let the good times roll"

Lundi Gras (LUN-dee grah) the day before Mardi Gras; also known as Fat Monday

macque choux (MOCK SHOE) a popular side dish of sautéed corn, tomatoes, bell peppers, onions, and various spices

make dodo to sleep

make groceries to buy groceries

Mardi Gras (MAHR-dee grah) traditionally, the last day to celebrate before the Catholic season of Lent begins; also known as Fat Tuesday

mirliton (MER-li-tawn) a pear-shaped squash (also called chayote) commonly stuffed with seasoned meat or seafood

mosquito hawk a colloquial term for a dragonfly

mudbug a slang expression for crawfish, the freshwater shellfish that other states refer to as "crayfish"

muffuletta (muff-uh-LET-uh) a round, oversized sandwich made from Italian bread, ham, salami, mortadella, provolone, and olive salad; also spelled "muffaletta"

neutral ground the grassy part between the paved areas of a boulevard; also known as a median

nutria a large, beaver-like rodent commonly seen in the canals and swamps of southern Louisiana, often considered a nuisance due to its destructive tendencies

parade a Mardi Gras procession of colorful floats and marching bands, during which spectators vie for tossed beads and doubloons

parish the official term for a county in Louisiana

picayune (pick-uh-YOON) a historical Spanish coin worth a little over six cents, which inspired the name of the city's newspaper, *The Times-Picayune*

pirogue (PEE-rohg) a small, flat-bottomed canoe

po-boy the quintessential New Orleans sandwich, made on French bread, with fillings like roast beef or fried shrimp

praline (prah-LEEN or PRAY-leen) a sweet confection made from pecans, cream, butter, and carmelized brown sugar

red beans and rice a traditional New Orleans

dish consisting of kidney beans and a spicy gravy, often served with ham hocks, tasso, or andouille

rémoulade (rey-moo-LAHD) a spicy, mustard-based sauce, typically served with boiled shrimp

roux (ROO) a slowly cooked mixture of butter (or water) and flour used to thicken gumbo, sauces, and soups

Sazerac a popular cocktail made with bitters, Pernod, sugar, lemon oil, and rye whiskey or bourbon

shotgun a one-level architectural style whereby all rooms are positioned consecutively, interconnected by doors in lieu of a hallway

slave quarters smaller houses situated behind large plantation homes, common in the French Quarter

sno-ball a cup of shaved ice served with flavored syrups; usually called a snowcone in other states

Spanish moss a specific epiphyte that resembles a grayish, lacy cluster and typically hangs from oak trees

tasso smoked beef or pork sausage, specially seasoned and often used in regional stews and pastas

Twinspan the two bridges that cross Lake Pontchartrain, from New Orleans to the Northshore

Vieux Carré (VOO kah-RAY) a reference to the French Quarter, meaning "old square" in French

voodoo an ancient West African religious faith that, in New Orleans, blends African, Haitian, Native American, European, and Catholic traditions; also known as the "dancing religion"

wetland a lowland area saturated by surface or ground water, with vegetation adapted to such conditions, prevalent throughout southern Louisiana

where y'at? an expression used in place of "Where are you?"

y'all a commonly used contraction for "you all"

y'at a native New Orleanian, especially one who speaks with the Brooklyn-style accent commonly heard in areas like Chalmette

zydeco (ZAHY-di-koh) a blues-influenced, Cajun-style type of dance music popular in southern Louisiana and typically featuring the sounds of guitars, violins, and accordions

Suggested Reading

More books have been written about New Orleans and its environs than can possibly be included here. Still, while not an exhaustive list of titles, the following books may shed some light on the singular geography, history, culture, and offerings of southern Louisiana—and further enhance your experience in the region. Peruse them before your trip, and bring a few along for the ride.

CUISINE

Besh, John. *My New Orleans: The Cookbook.* Kansas City, MO: Andrews McMeel Publishing, LLC, 2009. Written by the celebrated chef-owner of August, Lüke, and several other New Orleans–area restaurants, this collection contains roughly 200 of Besh's favorite local recipes and stories about his hometown.

Fitzmorris, Tom. *Tom Fitzmorris's Hungry Town: A Culinary History of New Orleans, the City Where Food Is Almost Everything.* New York: Stewart, Tabori & Chang, 2010. Penned by a native New Orleanian, this fascinating history of the New Orleans dining scene, before and after Hurricane Katrina, also includes key recipes related to the text.

Fitzmorris, Tom. *Tom Fitzmorris's New Orleans Food: More than 250 of the City's Best Recipes to Cook at Home.* New York: Stewart, Tabori & Chang, 2010. A thorough food lover's companion written and recently revised by one of the city's top food experts.

Guste Jr., Roy F. *The 100 Greatest New Orleans Creole Recipes.* Gretna, LA: Pelican

Publishing Company, Inc., 1994. Guste may not be a household name like Emeril or Prudhomme, but his collection is uncompromisingly authentic and filled with flavor.

Lagasse, Emeril, and Marcelle Bienvenu. *Louisiana Real & Rustic*. New York: William Morrow & Company, Inc., 2009. Compiled by the city's most boisterous celebrity chef, this collection features 150 classic Louisiana recipes, from gumbo to jambalaya to meat pies.

Prudhomme, Paul. *Chef Paul Prudhomme's Louisiana Kitchen*. New York: William Morrow & Company, Inc., 1984. A compendium of classic recipes by the New Orleans master of Cajun cooking.

Roahen, Sara. *Gumbo Tales: Finding My Place at the New Orleans Table*. New York: W. W. Norton & Company, Inc., 2008. A passionate culinary tour of the Crescent City's signature dishes, from seafood gumbo to sno-balls.

FICTION AND PROSE

Burke, James Lee. *The Tin Roof Blowdown*. New York: Simon & Schuster, 2007. Set in the wake of Hurricane Katrina, this gripping mystery is one of nearly 20 novels in a popular crime series featuring Dave Robicheaux, a homicide detective living in southern Louisiana. Other titles include *Black Cherry Blues* (1989), *Purple Cane Road* (2000), and *The Glass Rainbow* (2010).

Cable, George Washington. *Old Creole Days: A Story of Creole Life*. Gretna, LA: Pelican Publishing Company, Inc., 1991. In this reprint of his 1879 story collection, Victorian novelist and essayist Cable, who wrote many popular books about the city, captures life in old Creole New Orleans during the 19th century.

Chopin, Kate. *The Awakening and Selected Short Stories*. New York: Simon & Schuster, 2004. One of the great literary classics of the South, Chopin's 1899 novella, which focuses on a woman who flouts New Orleans Creole society by leaving her husband and children, caused a huge scandal when it was first published. Though the circumstances may seem tame today, this remains an emotionally powerful work.

Clark, Joshua, ed. *French Quarter Fiction*. New York: Fall River Press, 2010. Originally published in 2003, this riveting anthology explores "America's oldest Bohemia" through the contemporary eyes of local writers like John Biguenet, Andrei Codrescu, and Chris Rose.

Long, Judy, ed. *Literary New Orleans*. Athens, GA: Hill Street Press, 1999. A delightful anthology of fiction, poetry, memoirs, and essays by some of the city's most notable authors, including James Lee Burke, William Faulkner, and Tennessee Williams.

Percy, Walker. *The Moviegoer*. New York: Vintage Books, 1998. Percy, who died in 1990, was one of Louisiana's most talented writers, and this existential story about a New Orleans stockbroker, originally published in 1961, is one of his finest.

Rice, Anne. *Interview with the Vampire*. New York: Alfred A. Knopf, Inc., 1976. Perhaps the Garden District's most famous former resident, Anne Rice has set several vampire and witchcraft tales throughout the New Orleans area, including the first of her acclaimed *Vampire Chronicles* series. Other novels in the series include *The Vampire Lestat* (1985), *The Queen of the Damned* (1988), *The Tale of the Body Thief* (1992), *Memnoch the Devil* (1995), *The Vampire Armand* (1998), *Merrick* (2000), *Blood and Gold* (2001), *Blackwood Farm* (2002), and *Blood Canticle* (2003).

Rice, Christopher. *A Density of Souls*. New York: Hyperion, 2000. The uneven debut novel of Anne Rice's son depicts the lives of four high-school students grappling with coming-of-age issues and sexual identity in contemporary New Orleans.

Saxon, Lyle, and Robert Tallant. *Gumbo Ya-Ya: Folk Tales of Louisiana.* Gretna, LA: Pelican Publishing Company, Inc., 1987. This reprint, originally sponsored by the Works Progress Administration (WPA) in 1945, offers an enthralling look at the state's legends and practices.

Smith, Julie. *New Orleans Mourning.* New York: Ivy Books, 1990. An award-winning entry in the series of popular mystery books revolving around policeman Skip Langdon. Other engrossing books in the collection include *Crescent City Kill* (1998) and *Mean Woman Blues* (2003).

Toole, John Kennedy. *A Confederacy of Dunces.* Baton Rouge: Louisiana State University Press, 1980. A critically acclaimed tragicomic novel published more than a decade after the suicide of its young author, this peculiar tale hosts a bizarre yet entertaining cast of New Orleans characters.

Walker, Rob. *Letters from New Orleans.* New Orleans: Garrett County Press, 2005. Released shortly before Hurricane Katrina struck New Orleans, this is a collection of humorous, scary, and improbable tales about the Crescent City, related by a writer who moved to the city in 2000.

Warren, Robert Penn. *All the King's Men.* Orlando: Harcourt Brace & Company, 1990. A thinly veiled fictional look at the life of Huey Long, Warren's Pulitzer Prize–winning work, which was originally published in 1946, goes beyond mere political rehashing to become a gripping and compelling study of one of 20th-century America's most controversial figures.

Williams, Tennessee. *A Streetcar Named Desire.* New York: New Directions Publishing Corporation, 2004. Originally published in 1947, this is the seminal Williams play set in New Orleans. Less famous but more directly about life in the French Quarter is *Vieux Carré,* which was inspired by journals that Williams kept while living in New Orleans.

HISTORY AND GEOGRAPHY

Asbury, Herbert. *The French Quarter: An Informal History of the New Orleans Underworld.* New York: Thunder's Mouth Press, 2003. In an unconventional look at the city's seedy side, Asbury's colorful account, originally published in 1936, surveys the city's infamous red-light districts, illegal gaming, and other not-so-legitimate activities.

Benfey, Christopher. *Degas in New Orleans: Encounters in the Creole World of Kate Chopin and George Washington Cable.* Los Angeles: University of California Press, 1997. Benfey uses Degas' brief visit to New Orleans in the early 1870s to examine the city and its Creole society during the late 19th century.

Brinkley, Douglas. *The Great Deluge: Hurricane Katrina, New Orleans, and the Mississippi Gulf Coast.* New York: William Morrow & Company, Inc., 2006. This is one of the most comprehensive and insightful accounts of Hurricane Katrina, written by a noted historian and Tulane professor who experienced the storm's devastating aftermath firsthand.

Campanella, Richard. *Time and Place in New Orleans: Past Geographies in the Present Day.* Gretna, LA: Pelican Publishing Company, Inc., 2002. Filled with historical and contemporary maps and photos that trace the city's evolution, this eye-opening book explores the unlikely establishment of New Orleans in the middle of a malaria-ridden swamp.

Chase, John Churchill. *Frenchmen, Desire, Good Children...and Other Streets of New Orleans!* Gretna, LA: Pelican Publishing Company, Inc., 2001. Originally published in 1949, this humorous book reveals the origin of the Big Easy's fascinating, often hard-to-pronounce street names.

Cowan, Walter G., John C. Chase, Charles L. Dufour, O. K. LeBlanc, and John Wilds. *New Orleans Yesterday and Today: A Guide to the City.* Baton Rouge: Louisiana State University

Press, 2001. A wonderful collection of historical essays that trace the city's history by offering concise glimpses into areas such as food, music, and race. Several of the same authors penned a broader history on the state, *Louisiana Yesterday and Today: A Historical Guide to the State,* which was published in 1996 by Louisiana State University Press.

Horne, Jed. *Breach of Faith: Hurricane Katrina and the Near Death of a Great American City.* New York: Random House, Inc., 2006. A riveting account of the storm by the metro editor of *The Times-Picayune.*

Johnson, Walter. *Soul by Soul: Life Inside the Antebellum Slave Market.* Cambridge, MA: Harvard University Press, 1999. Using narratives, court records, bills of sale, and other documents to trace the harrowing legacy of slavery, this book offers a gripping and raw account of North America's largest and most notorious slave market, which was centered in New Orleans.

Piazza, Tom. *Why New Orleans Matters.* New York: HarperCollins Publishers, 2005. This heartfelt, firsthand celebration of the Big Easy after Hurricane Katrina makes a case for why it's so important that the city rebuild and flourish.

Remini, Robert V. *The Battle of New Orleans: Andrew Jackson and America's First Military Victory.* New York: Viking Penguin, 1999. Remini examines the great battle that secured a young America's victory against the British during the War of 1812.

Rose, Al. *Storyville, New Orleans: Being an Authentic, Illustrated Account of the Notorious Red Light District.* Alabama: University of Alabama Press, 1978. An informative history of Storyville, the only officially sanctioned and legal red-light district in the country.

Sublette, Ned. *The World That Made New Orleans: From Spanish Silver to Congo Square.*

Chicago: Lawrence Hill Books, 2008. A well-researched study of the Crescent City's economic and cultural roots prior to the 20th century.

Sullivan, Lester. *New Orleans Then and Now.* San Diego: Thunder Bay Press, 2003. This collection contrasts vintage black-and-white photos of city landmarks and streets with contemporary shots of the same scenes, offering a wonderful look at how the city has changed and, more importantly, how in so many places it hasn't.

van Heerden, Ivor, and Mike Bryan. *The Storm: What Went Wrong and Why During Hurricane Katrina—The Inside Story from One Louisiana Scientist.* New York: Viking Penguin, 2006. The title here pretty much says it all: As deputy director of the Louisiana State University Hurricane Center, van Heerden gives a very good sense of how Katrina was as much—if not more—a human-made catastrophe as a natural one.

Williams, T. Harry. *Huey Long.* New York: Vintage Books, 1981. Originally published in 1969, this gripping biography explores the infamous "Kingfish," the man who shaped Louisiana politics for many years after his death.

MUSIC AND CULTURE

Armstrong, Louis. *Satchmo: My Life in New Orleans.* Cambridge, MA: Da Capo Press, Inc., 1986. Originally published in 1954, this is the definitive autobiography by the definitive New Orleans jazz icon.

Berry, Jason, Jonathan Foose, and Tad Jones. *Up from the Cradle of Jazz: New Orleans Music Since World War II.* Lafayette: University of Louisiana at Lafayette Press, 2009. A terrific survey tracing the history of music in the Big Easy, from the 1940s to the post-Katrina era.

Bird, Stephanie Rose. *Sticks, Stones, Roots & Bones: Hoodoo, Mojo & Conjuring with Herbs.* St. Paul, MN: Llewellyn Publications, 2004. A practical history of hoodoo.

Florence, Robert. *New Orleans Cemeteries: Life in the Cities of the Dead.* New Orleans: Batture Press, Inc., 1997. An insider's history and tour of the city's famous aboveground cemeteries.

Gessler, Diana Hollingsworth. *Very New Orleans: A Celebration of History, Culture, and Cajun Country Charm.* Chapel Hill, NC: Algonquin Books of Chapel Hill, 2006. Filled with the author's detailed sketches and watercolors, this charming book celebrates all that makes southern Louisiana unique, from Jackson Square and the Garden District to Creole cuisine and Cajun music.

Haskins, Jim. *Voodoo & Hoodoo.* Chelsea, MI: Scarborough House, 1990. The history of voodoo and hoodoo.

Huber, Leonard V. *Mardi Gras: A Pictorial History of Carnival in New Orleans.* Gretna, LA: Pelican Publishing Company, Inc., 2003. A decent overview of the city's most famous celebration, originally published in 1977.

Lomax, Alan. *Mister Jelly Roll: The Fortunes of Jelly Roll Morton, New Orleans Creole and "Inventor of Jazz."* Los Angeles: University of California Press, 2001. Originally published in 1950, this fascinating examination of a New Orleans jazz luminary also explores the development of the city's music scene.

Ondaatje, Michael. *Coming Through Slaughter.* New York: Vintage Books, 1996. Penned by the author of *The English Patient* and originally published in 1976, this colorful tale illustrates the life of Buddy Bolden, one of the earliest New Orleans jazz greats.

Sexton, Richard, and Randolph Delehanty. *New Orleans: Elegance and Decadence.* San Francisco: Chronicle Books LLC, 1993. A handsome photo essay that distills the essence of New Orleans's architecture, art, landscape, and culture.

Tallant, Robert. *Voodoo in New Orleans.* Gretna, LA: Pelican Publishing Company, Inc., 2003. Written by the author of *The Voodoo Queen* and originally published in 1946, this classic compendium covers one of New Orleans's most fascinating topics.

RECREATION AND TRAVEL

Douglas, Lake, and Jeannette Hardy. *Gardens of New Orleans: Exquisite Excess.* San Francisco: Chronicle Books LLC, 2001. A companion photo book to *New Orleans: Elegance and Decadence,* this sumptuous tome, filled with photographs by Richard Sexton, takes readers into the many secret and sensuous gardens of the Big Easy.

The Federal Writers' Project of the Works Progress Administration. *New Orleans City Guide.* New Orleans: Garrett County Press, 2009. Originally compiled in 1938 by the Works Progress Administration (WPA), this dense, fascinating work is one of the best treatments of the city ever written.

Fry, Macon, and Julie Posner. *Cajun Country Guide.* Gretna, LA: Pelican Publishing Company, Inc., 1999. Originally published in 1992, this in-depth tour guide of Cajun Country offers extensive anecdotes and histories on just about every town in the region, large or small.

Sternberg, Mary Ann. *Along the River Road: Past and Present on Louisiana's Historic Byway.* Baton Rouge: Louisiana State University Press, 2001. This revised and expanded edition provides an amazingly thorough history and description, mile by mile, of the towns and plantation homes strung along the Great River Road.

Suggested Viewing

Not surprisingly, the lush landscape, antebellum plantation homes, and well-preserved historic districts of southern Louisiana have long been favored by filmmakers and television producers. In fact, hundreds of movies and shows have taken advantage of this unique culture and atmosphere, including classic, Oscar-winning films like *Jezebel* (1938) and *A Streetcar Named Desire* (1951), both of which were partially filmed in southern Louisiana. More recent productions have included HBO's much-acclaimed series *Treme,* which authentically chronicles the lives of various Big Easy residents and musicians in the wake of Hurricane Katrina. Before your trip, take the time to view some of the following selections and experience how others have been inspired by this one-of-a-kind region.

All the King's Men (2006). Written and directed by Steven Zaillian, starring Sean Penn, Jude Law, Kate Winslet, and Anthony Hopkins. Based on Robert Penn Warren's classic novel, this drama showcases the life of populist Willie Stark, a character loosely based on Louisiana's infamous Governor Huey Long.

Angel Heart (1987). Written and directed by Alan Parker, starring Mickey Rourke, Robert De Niro, and Lisa Bonet. In this sultry thriller, which was based on a novel by William Hjortsberg and partially shot in New Orleans, New York–based gumshoe Harry Angel follows a voodoo trail to the Big Easy in search of a missing singer.

The Big Easy (1986). Written by Daniel Petrie Jr., directed by Jim McBride, and starring Dennis Quaid, Ellen Barkin, and Ned Beatty. Set in New Orleans, this film focuses on a local homicide detective facing three concurrent dilemmas: bribery charges, a series of gang killings, and a sexy lawyer from the District Attorney's police corruption task force.

Cat People (1982). Written by Alan Ormsby, directed by Paul Schrader, and starring Nastassja Kinski, Malcolm McDowell, and John Heard. Featuring New Orleans landmarks like the Audubon Zoo and the Gallier House, this erotic remake of the 1942 horror classic follows two unusual siblings, whose sexual urges transform them into deadly black leopards.

The Curious Case of Benjamin Button (2008). Written by Eric Roth, directed by David Fincher, and starring Brad Pitt, Cate Blanchett, and Taraji P. Henson. Based on a short story by F. Scott Fitzgerald and filmed throughout southern Louisiana, this Oscar-winning drama tells the fantastical story of a man who ages backwards.

Dead Man Walking (1995). Written and directed by Tim Robbins, starring Susan Sarandon and Sean Penn. Based on a biographical account by Sister Helen Prejean and partially filmed at the Angola state prison, this Oscar-winning drama follows the story of a nun who, while comforting a convicted killer on death row, comes to empathize with both the killer and his victims' families.

Déjà Vu (2006). Written by Bill Marsilii and Terry Rossio, directed by Tony Scott, and starring Denzel Washington, Paula Patton, Val Kilmer, and Jim Caviezel. In post-Katrina New Orleans, an ATF agent travels back in time to prevent a ferry explosion on the Mississippi River and, in the process, save a woman from being murdered.

Easy Rider (1969). Written by Peter Fonda, Dennis Hopper, and Terry Southern, directed by Dennis Hopper, and starring Peter Fonda, Dennis Hopper, and Jack Nicholson. During their soul-searching ride from Los Angeles to New Orleans, two counterculture bikers face small-town bigotry, meet fellow nonconformists, and experience a drug-enhanced Mardi Gras amid the city's aboveground cemeteries.

Eve's Bayou (1997). Written and directed by Kasi Lemmons, starring Samuel L. Jackson, Lynn Whitfield, and Jurnee Smollett. Filmed amid the marshes north of Lake Pontchartrain, this atmospheric saga follows the ill-fated Batiste family, torn apart by adultery, obsession, and murder in 1962 Louisiana.

Hatchet (2006). Written and directed by Adam Green, starring Joel David Moore, Deon Richmond, Tamara Feldman, and Kane Hodder. In this entertaining horror comedy, several tourists embark on a haunted swamp tour in the outskirts of New Orleans, only to be stranded in the wilderness with a mythical madman.

Heaven's Prisoners (1996). Written by Harley Peyton and Scott Frank, directed by Phil Joanou, and starring Alec Baldwin, Kelly Lynch, Mary Stuart Masterson, and Eric Roberts. In this adaptation of a James Lee Burke novel, ex-detective Dave Robicheaux and his wife, Annie, rescue a young girl from a plane crash in the outskirts of New Orleans—an act that forever changes their lives.

Hotel (1967). Written by Wendell Mayes, directed by Richard Quine, and starring Rod Taylor, Catherine Spaak, and Karl Malden. Based on a novel by Arthur Hailey, this drama chronicles the round-the-clock activities of a large New Orleans hotel.

Interview with the Vampire: The Vampire Chronicles (1994). Written by Anne Rice, directed by Neil Jordan, and starring Tom Cruise, Brad Pitt, Antonio Banderas, Kirsten Dunst, and Christian Slater. In this award-winning adaptation of Anne Rice's acclaimed novel, a brooding vampire records his epic life story, beginning with his life-altering encounter with the flamboyant vampire Lestat in 18th-century New Orleans.

In the Electric Mist (2009). Written by Jerzy Kromolowski and Mary Olson-Kromolowski, directed by Bertrand Tavernier, and starring Tommy Lee Jones, Mary Steenburgen, Peter Sarsgaard, and John Goodman. In this recent adaptation of a 1993 James Lee Burke novel, New Iberia detective Dave Robicheaux has visions of dead Confederate soldiers while investigating corrupt businessmen, local prostitute murders, and a 1965 lynching.

JFK (1991). Written by Oliver Stone and Zachary Sklar, directed by Oliver Stone, and starring Kevin Costner, Gary Oldman, Jack Lemmon, and Sissy Spacek. In this Oscar-winning film, based on real-life events as well as historical interpretations by Jim Garrison and Jim Marrs, a New Orleans district attorney tries to uncover the truth behind the Kennedy assassination.

King Creole (1958). Written by Herbert Baker and Michael V. Gazzo, directed by Michael Curtiz, and starring Elvis Presley, Carolyn Jones, and Walter Matthau. Inspired by a Harold Robbins novel, this musical crime drama tells the story of Danny Fisher, a cash-strapped young man who becomes a New Orleans nightclub singer after flunking graduation.

Live and Let Die (1973). Written by Tom Mankiewicz, directed by Guy Hamilton, and starring Roger Moore, Yaphet Kotto, and Jane Seymour. Featuring a jazz funeral in the French Quarter and a speedboat chase in Slidell, this James Bond adventure pits Ian Fleming's 007 against a heroin magnate and his psychic tarot card reader.

Pretty Baby (1978). Written by Polly Platt, directed by Louis Malle, and starring Brooke Shields, Susan Sarandon, and Keith Carradine. A young girl grows up in a house of prostitution in the Storyville section of 1917 New Orleans.

Runaway Jury (2003). Written by Brian Koppelman, David Levien, Rick Cleveland, and Matthew Chapman; directed by Gary Fleder; and starring John Cusack, Rachel Weisz, Gene Hackman, and Dustin Hoffman. Based on a John Grisham novel and featuring iconic New Orleans settings like Café Du Monde and St. Charles Avenue, this riveting thriller pits a mysterious juror and his girlfriend against a man who manipulates court trials involving gun manufacturers.

The Skeleton Key (2005). Written by Ehren Kruger, directed by Iain Softley, and starring Kate Hudson, Gena Rowlands, Peter Sarsgaard, John Hurt, and Joy Bryant. When a young hospice nurse takes a position at a creepy plantation home outside New Orleans, she becomes ensnared in a mystery involving hoodoo folk magic and the property's dark past.

Internet Resources

The following websites will provide valuable information before, during, and after your trip to New Orleans.

CUISINE AND TRAVEL
About.com New Orleans
www.neworleans.about.com
Beyond information about citywide events, activities, museums, shops, bars, restaurants, and entertainment venues, this website also offers details about hurricanes, local media, specific neighborhoods, street names, and the city's vibrant history.

Baton Rouge Area Convention & Visitors Bureau
www.visitbatonrouge.com
Visitors will find a wealth of information about the events, tours, shops, attractions, restaurants, accommodations, recreational opportunities, and nightlife options in Louisiana's capital city.

Cajun Coast Visitors & Convention Bureau
www.cajuncoast.com
Through this website, visitors to St. Mary Parish can learn about swamp tours, Cajun restaurants, day trips, and other diversions in the coastal area west of New Orleans.

Citysearch
www.neworleans.citysearch.com
This well-known website contains listings and limited editorial information on bars, restaurants, hotels, events, movie showings, and other diversions in the New Orleans area. Just be advised that outdated information routinely appears here.

Experience New Orleans!
www.experienceneworleans.com
This portal offers a ton of useful information for visitors to New Orleans, from local lingo to free coupons to hotel availability.

FrenchQuarter.com
www.frenchquarter.com
Visitors to the French Quarter will find a cornucopia of helpful resources, including maps, hotel reservations, event listings, historical information, and details about sightseeing, shopping, dining, and nightlife.

Gambit
www.bestofneworleans.com
The official website of this free alternative weekly contains plenty of information about the city's bars, restaurants, shops, film screenings, music and arts scenes, and current events.

GayNewOrleans.com
www.gayneworleans.com

Here, gay and lesbian travelers will find advice about tours, attractions, bars, restaurants, and accommodations, plus gay-friendly organizations and events, such as PFLAG and Southern Decadence.

Houma Area Convention
& Visitors Bureau
www.houmatravel.com

Through this website, travelers to the self-described "heart of America's wetland" can search for information about swamp tours, fishing camps, Cajun cuisine, and other activities in and around Houma.

Jefferson Convention & Visitors Bureau
www.experiencejefferson.com

Travelers to Jefferson Parish can learn more about the accommodations, attractions, and activities available in areas like Kenner, Metairie, Grand Isle, and Barataria Preserve.

Lafayette Convention
& Visitors Commission
www.lafayettetravel.com

This comprehensive website features a wealth of information for visitors to Cajun Country, including dining and lodging options, event and attraction listings, shopping and nightlife suggestions, and Cajun recipes.

Lake Charles/Southwest Louisiana
Convention & Visitors Bureau
www.visitlakecharles.org

Here, travelers headed west of New Orleans will find a trove of details about regional events, attractions, restaurants, accommodations, entertainment options, and other diversions.

Louisiana Tourism Coastal Coalition
www.visitlouisianacoast.com

Visitors to this website will find up-to-date news, event reminders, and extensive information about accommodations and outdoor activities related to the areas along Louisiana's southern coast.

LouisianaTravel.com
www.louisianatravel.com

The state's official online travel source provides a variety of links related to events, attractions, hotels, restaurants, entertainment options, and other activities throughout Louisiana.

MyNewOrleans.com
www.myneworleans.com

The official website of Renaissance Publishing, which produces the monthly *New Orleans Magazine,* provides excellent dining, shopping, arts, and events coverage.

NewOrleans.com
www.neworleans.com

Travelers can use this website to make hotel reservations, research tours and attractions, and learn more about the city's festivals, sporting events, restaurants, and nightlife scene.

New Orleans Convention
& Visitors Bureau
www.neworleanscvb.com

This comprehensive website offers a ton of resources for travelers to the Big Easy, including maps, current temperatures, and information about the city's music, dining, shopping, lodging, nightlife, tours, festivals, attractions, and outdoor recreation.

The New Orleans Menu
www.nomenu.com

This comprehensive website, operated by local food expert Tom Fitzmorris, gives details on the city's famous food scene, including recipes and restaurant listings.

NewOrleansRestaurants.com
www.neworleansrestaurants.com
In addition to featuring a New Orleans restaurant guide, this food-focused website invites gourmands to peruse local recipes, learn key culinary terms, and make dining reservations.

New Orleans Tourism
Marketing Corporation
www.neworleansonline.com
The official tourism website of New Orleans provides comprehensive information about area accommodations, attractions, and activities, plus maps, itineraries, coupons, and a neighborhood guide.

St. James Parish
www.stjamesla.com
Travelers can search here for activities and events in St. James Parish, situated between New Orleans and Baton Rouge.

St. Landry Parish
Tourist Commission
www.cajuntravel.com
Visitors can use this website to learn more about the tours, festivals, attractions, accommodations, and other diversions in the region between Lafayette and Baton Rouge.

St. Tammany Parish Tourist
& Convention Commission
www.louisiananorthshore.com
The official website of Louisiana's Northshore features plenty of shopping, dining, and activity suggestions for travelers to Slidell, Covington, and Abita Springs.

Tangipahoa Parish Convention
& Visitors Bureau
www.tangi-cvb.org
Visitors will find plenty of useful dining, shopping, lodging, and activity information about Hammond, Ponchatoula, Kentwood, and other communities in Tangipahoa Parish.

The Times-Picayune
www.nola.com
Produced by the state's most widely read newspaper, this website ranks among the most informative online resources related to New Orleans.

GENERAL INFORMATION
Amtrak
www.amtrak.com
The official website for America's national rail service provides routes and schedules for train trips throughout Louisiana, with stops in Lafayette, Hammond, and New Orleans.

City of New Orleans
www.nola.gov
The city's official website allows you to pay for parking tickets, check for up-to-date emergency information, and learn about area attractions, shopping locations, sporting events, and transportation facilities.

Country Codes
www.countrycodes.com
If you decide to make any international phone calls while visiting southern Louisiana, you'll need this handy website, an easy-to-use directory of country calling codes.

Greyhound
www.greyhound.com
As this website indicates, the nation's leading bus line makes a number of stops in Louisiana, including Lafayette, Baton Rouge, and New Orleans.

Louisiana Department of
Transportation & Development
www.dotd.louisiana.gov
This website provides extensive information about area bridges and ferries, road conditions, and upcoming construction projects, plus useful state, parish, and tourist maps.

MakeNewOrleansHome.com
www.makeneworleanshome.com
New residents will find helpful resources here, including information about neighborhoods, businesses, education, entertainment, health services, transportation, retirement, permits and licenses, and other aspects of city living.

MDtravelhealth.com
www.mdtravelhealth.com
Updated daily, this medical website is an excellent resource for travelers. You'll find information about specific destinations, available clinics, infectious diseases, and illness prevention.

OnlineConversion.com
www.onlineconversion.com
This website will enable you to make any U.S.-metric conversion, from temperatures to distances to clothing sizes.

State of Louisiana
www.louisiana.gov
The official state website comes in handy when you're looking for detailed information about regional demographics, state and local politics, the state library system, various state departments, and fishing licenses.

U.S. Department of State's Bureau of Consular Affairs
www.travel.state.gov
U.S. citizens can use this website to travel safely, via cruise or flight, to other countries, while international travelers will find guidelines for flying into and out of southern Louisiana.

HISTORY AND CULTURE
Gateway! New Orleans
www.gatewayno.com
Visitors to this website will find detailed information about the city's history, cuisine, music, and culture.

The Gumbo Pages
www.gumbopages.com
This no-frills website offers travelers plenty of information about the Big Easy's history, music, and culture, including local lingo.

LSU Press
www.lsupress.org
Since 1935, the official press of Louisiana State University has been publishing books about Louisiana history, culture, music, and architecture, most of which you can find through this website.

MardiGrasDay.com
www.mardigrasday.com
Curiosity seekers can learn all about the Big Easy's most famous holiday, from related lingo to the history of king cakes. Just be aware that the website contains some outdated information regarding annual festivities.

PARKS AND RECREATION
Louisiana Department of Culture, Recreation & Tourism
www.crt.state.la.us
This state government–run website provides information regarding state museums, cultural districts, historical preservation, the Audubon Golf Trail, and the state park system, including details about pets, trails, and wireless Internet access.

Louisiana Department of Wildlife & Fisheries
www.wlf.louisiana.gov
Among Louisiana's top Internet resources for outdoor enthusiasts, this website provides information and policies pertaining to boating, fishing, and hunting.

Louisiana Golf Association
www.lgagolf.org
Here, golfers can learn about the state's many public golf courses, including those in the New Orleans area.

Louisiana Sportsman
www.louisianasportsman.com

The official website of this monthly magazine offers anglers, hunters, and other outdoor enthusiasts a ton of links to relevant businesses, news, reports, forums, columns, and classified ads.

National Park Service
www.nps.gov

The National Park Service provides detailed maps, brochures, and contact information for each of its nearly 400 parks, monuments, recreation areas, trails, and other natural and cultural sites, including Louisiana's Jean Lafitte National Historical Park and Preserve.

The Nature Conservancy
www.nature.org

Hikers might want to visit this website, which contains information about the Conservancy's Louisiana refuges and preserves.

Orleans Audubon Society
www.jjaudubon.net

Bird-watchers will appreciate this website, which offers specifics on the Audubon Society's New Orleans–area chapter.

U.S. Coast Guard's Boating Safety Division
www.uscgboating.org

Use this comprehensive resource center to prevent accidents and fatalities while boating in southern Louisiana.

U.S. Fish & Wildlife Service
www.fws.gov

Here, you can find useful information about the state's most threatened species, like the Louisiana black bear, as well as wildlife refuges near New Orleans, such as the Delta National Wildlife Refuge.

Index

Restaurants Index

Nightlife Index

Shops Index

Hotels Index

Acknowledgments

I grew up in New Orleans and spent much of my adulthood there, so I find it difficult to thank each and every person who's helped me, often unknowingly, to write this book. Naturally, there are several people to whom I'm particularly grateful. First, I offer a special thanks to the tourism officials—such as Jeff Anding and Jennifer Lotz in New Orleans, Kelly Gustafson in Houma, and Renee Kientz on the Northshore—who provided information as well as photographs for this edition. Thanks, too, to the ultra-patient editors at Avalon Travel who offered invaluable assistance during the rather lengthy preparation of *Moon New Orleans;* in particular, I definitely couldn't have finished this guide without the support of Sabrina Young, Darren Alessi, and Albert Angulo. Thanks also to Grace Fujimoto, who initially gave me the chance to write about my favorite U.S. city, and Andrew Collins, who wrote the first two editions of this book.

In addition, I'd like to thank my friends and family, all of whom have supported me during each of my frenzied writing projects. Most of all, I'm grateful to my beloved kitty, Ruby Azazel, who encouraged me to take breaks whenever possible, and to my husband, Daniel, who even provided many of the images in this guide.

Moreover, I thank the city of New Orleans—for despite tragic events like Hurricane Katrina and the much-publicized Gulf oil spill, this continues to be one of the most vibrant, resilient, and extraordinary cities I've ever encountered. Lastly, I thank you, the reader. May your next trip to the Big Easy be thrilling, memorable, and, above all, safe!

www.moon.com

DESTINATIONS | ACTIVITIES | BLOGS | MAPS | BOOKS

MOON.COM is ready to help plan your next trip! Filled with fresh trip ideas and strategies, author interviews, informative travel blogs, a detailed map library, and descriptions of all the Moon guidebooks, Moon.com is all you need to get out and explore the world—or even places in your own backyard. While at Moon.com, sign up for our monthly e-newsletter for updates on new releases, travel tips, and expert advice from our on-the-go Moon authors. As always, when you travel with Moon, expect an experience that is uncommon and truly unique.

KEEP UP WITH MOON ON FACEBOOK AND TWITTER
JOIN THE MOON PHOTO GROUP ON FLICKR